CW00926692

HISTORY OF THE ROYAL REGIMENT OF ARTILLERY

THE FAR EAST THEATRE 1939 - 1946

His Majesty's King George VI
Colonel-in-Chief of the Royal Regiment of Artillery

HISTORY OF THE ROYAL REGIMENT OF ARTILLERY

THE FAR EAST THEATRE 1939 - 1946

GENERAL SIR MARTIN FARNDALE KCB

This Book is Dedicated to

All Members of The Royal Regiment of Artillery
and their Bretheren from the Dominions and Empire

Who Gave their Lives, or Who Suffered Privation, in the Course of

Their Duties in the Far East Theatre

December 1941 to November 1946

'When You Go Home,
Tell Them of Us, And Say,
For Your Tomorrow,
We Gave Our To-Day.'

First English Edition 2000 published in the UK by Brassey's
This revised edition 2002

A member of the Chrysalis Group plc

Brassey's, 9 Blenheim Court, Brewery Road, London N7 9NT

Martin Farndale has asserted his moral right to be identified as the author of this work.

Library of Congress Cataloging in Publication Data
available

British Library Cataloguing in Publication Data
A catalogue record for this book is available from the British Library

ISBN 1 85753 331 3

Typeset by SX Composing DTP, Rayleigh, Essex
Printed by Just Colour Graphic, Spain

CONTENTS

LIST OF ILLUSTRATIONS

Unless otherwise stated photographs were provided by the Imperial War Museum (IWM). The author is very grateful for the assistance of the Director General and Trustees of that museum.

Frontispiece, His Majesty King George VI, Colonel-in-Chief 1936 - 51, Captain General Royal Artillery 1951 - 52. Denis Fildes, 1951. Reproduced by Gracious Permission of Her majesty The Queen.

LIST OF MAPS AND DIAGRAMS

Note: Many maps are based in part on those in *The War Against Japan*, spot heights are in feet and North is at the top of the map.

LIST OF REFERENCES AND SUGGESTIONS FOR FURTHER READING

Note: RAI refers to the Royal Artillery Institution; RAHT refers to the Royal Artillery Historical Trust; RAHS refers to the Royal Artillery Historical Society.

The Army List.
The Indian Army List.
The Royal Regiment of Artillery (Blue) List.
War Diaries (detailed in the text).
Anon, 'The murder of the crew of the SS Behar', *Gun Post*, the Journal of the Maritime Royal Artillery Old Comrades Association, No. 20, Sept 1966.
Anon, 'The Story of the March of 115th Field Regiment with 19th Indian (Dagger) Division' Typescript copy held by the RAHT.
Anon, 'The Dagger Division's Private Air OP.' Typescript held by the RAHT.
Anon, 'Diary of 135th (Herts Yeomanry) Field Regiment RA (TA) During the Campaign in Malaya and Singapore, January - February 1942. Typescript held by the RAHT (covers the period 13th January to 11th February 1942).

Divisions:
2nd British, *see* Beale.
5th Indian *see* Brett-James.
7th Indian *see* Roberts.
17th Indian, *see* Black Cat Division.
81st (WA), Artillery in, A paper held by the RAHT and *see* Hamilton *and* Clarke.
82nd (WA), Farewell Broadcasts on departure from Rangoon. MSS held by RAHT *and see* Brooks, J, and Davidson.

Regiments (additional to War Diary accounts):
8th Medium *see* Roy.
9th Coast *see* Changi Fire Command.
16th Field *see* Uniacke *and see* Hammond.

24th Indian Mountain, extracts from history of, MSS held by the RAHT *and see* Kenyon.
27th Field (at Akyab), *see* Guild
99th (Buckinghamshire Yeomanry) Field *see* White.
114th (Sussex) Field *see* Crooks.
115th Field *see* Anon, 'The Story of the March of 115th Field Regiment . . .'
122nd (West Riding) Field *see* Ackroyd.
129th (Lowland) Field, extracts from monthly letters to MGRA
see Younger, typescript copy held by the RAHT, *and see* Thomson, WH.
135th (Hertfordshire Yeomanry) Field *see* Anon Hertfordshire Yeomanry.
136th (1st West Lancashire) Field, extracts from Monthly Newsletters to the MGRA India. Typescript copy held by the RAHT *and see* Robertson.
139th (4th London) Field *see* Harding.
145th (Berkshire Yeomanry) Field, MSS account held by the RAHT *and see* Skrine.
155th (Lanarkshire Yeomanry) Field *see* Sewell.

Batteries
414th Battery RHA. Typescript held by the RAHT.
1st Australian Mountain Battery, *see* Allen, Jack and Cutts, Chis.
2nd (Minden) Battery. Papers held by the RAHT.
3rd Indian LAA Battery, *see* MacFetridge.
19th (Niagara) Medium Battery, *see* Dunne, Major T.
12th (Poonch) Indian Mountain Battery, *see* Howard, AB.
25th Indian Mountain Battery, *see* Pugh.
50th(Meiktila) Battery, *see* Preston.
79th LAA Battery, *see* Paley, Tony.
101st (WA) Mortar Battery *see* Clarke, Michael.
503rd Field Battery (139th Jungle Field Regt), *see* Harding.

Ackroyd, Ernest, *A Freedom Dearly Bought*, (122nd (West Riding) Field Regiment). Privately published by Ernest Ackroyd, Bradford, 1995.
Adamson, Lieutenant Arthur, 'An Artillery AOP in Burma.' MSS held by the RAHT.
Allan, Jack and Cutts, Chis, [Eds] *As It Seemed to Us* [1st Australian Mountain Battery, 1942 - 1945] Aebis Publishing, Brisbane, 1994.
Allen Louis, Burma, *The Longest War 1941 - 45*, JM Dent & Sons Ltd, London, 1984.
Alexander, Stephen, *Sweet Kwai Run Softly*, Merroitt's Press, 1995.
AOP, 656 AOP Squadron, RAF, notes held by the RAHT.
Armstrong, Geoffrey, *The Sparks Fly Upward*, Gooday Publishers, East Wittering, West Sussex, 1991.
Bailey, Reginald, W, 'Personal Experiences in the 7th Div 'Admin Box' 4th - 24th February 1944, C Flight 656 AOP Squadron RAF.' MSS held by the RAHT.
Baker, Alfred TJ, 'What Price Bushido.' (RA POW at Rabaul). MSS held by the RAHT.
Barber, Laurie, 'Jitra, The Forgotten Battle', *Journal of the Society for Army Historical Research*, Vol LXXV No. 304, London, Winter 1997.
Bidwell, Shelford, 'The guns of Singapore, the myths and the facts', *Battle* Magazine, No. 8, 1971.
Bidwell, Shelford, *Gunners at War*, Arms & Armour Press, London, 1970.
Bidwell, Shelford, *The Chindit War, The Campaign in Burma, 1944*, Hodder and Stoughton, London, 1979.
Bidwell, Shelford, '*Wingate and the Official Historians: An Alternative View*', Journal of Contemporary History (SAGE, London and Beverly Hills), Vol 15 (1980).

Bidwell, Shelford and Graham, Dominic, *Fire-Power, British Army Weapons and Theories of War*, 1904 - 1945, George Allen & Unwin, London 1982.
'Black Cat Division', pamphlet history of 17th Indian Division. Printed in New Delhi. Distributed in UK by Gale & Polden Ltd. Aldershot. nd.
Boatner, Mark M, *Biographical Dictionary of World War II*, Presidio Press, Novato, California, 1996.
Bond, Brian, *British Military Policy between the Two World Wars*, Clarendon Press, Oxford, 1980.
Boys, Captain Rex, 'Prelude to Action and its Outcome' an extract from the Memoirs of Captain Rex Boys RA, Officer Commanding 'C' Flight. 656 AOP Squadron. Typescript held by the RAHT.
Brett-James, Anthony, *Ball of Fire*, Gale & Polden, Aldershot, 1951.(5th Indian Division at War).
Bridgman, Leonard (Ed), *Jane's Fighting Aircraft of World War II*, Studio Editions, Random House, London, 1989.
Brooks, J, Jnr, War Correspondent for the *Chicago Independent*, article of February 1945 (82nd West African Division, Arakan). Typescript copy held by the RAHT.
Brown, Major Peter, 'Report on Artillery Operations in Burma.' MSS held by the RAHT.
Bryant, Arthur, *The Turn of the Tide*, Collins, London 1957.
Bryant, Arthur, *Triumph in the West*, Collins, London, 1959.
Burne, Rev CJS, An account, written for his parents, of events following the crossing of the Irrawaddy. Manuscript held by the RAHT.
Bury, RJ, Lieutenant Colonel, 'The Evolution of Army Air Support' *Proceedings of the Royal Artillery Historical Society*, Woolwich, Jan 1995.
Cardew, Lt Col HGStG, 'Faber Fire Command', typescript of a diary written in captivity, PRO WO 172/180.
Carew, Tim, *The Fall of Hong Kong*, Anthony Blond, London, 1960.
Chamberlain, Peter and Gander, Terry, *Infantry, Mountain and Airborne Guns*, World War 2 Fact Files, Macdonald and Jane's, London, 1975.
Chamberlain, Peter and Gander, Terry, *Mortars and Rockets*, World War 2 Fact Files, Macdonald and Jane's, London, 1975.
Chamberlain, Peter and Gander, Terry, *Light and Medium Field Artillery*, World War 2 Fact Files, Macdonald and Jane's, London,1975.
Chamberlain, Peter and Gander, Terry, *Heavy Artillery*, World War 2 Fact Files, Macdonald and Jane's, London, 1975.
Chamberlain, Peter and Gander, Terry, *Anti-Aircraft Guns*, World War 2 Fact Files, Macdonald and Jane's, London, 1975.
'Changi Fire Command, Report on Landwards Firing and Demolitions 5 February to 12 February 1942'. Typescript probably written by or for Lt Col CP Heath, CO 9th Coast Regiment. PRO WO 172/176.
Channer, Captain R De R, 'FOO, Imphal, June 1944.' *Gunner*, August 1994.
Chaplin, Colonel JB, *Action in Burma 1942-1945*,. privately published, London, 1984.
Chippington, George, *Singapore, The Inexcusable Betrayal*, Self Publishing Association Ltd 1993.
Churchill, Winston, *The Gathering Storm*, Cassel & Co Ltd, London, 1952.
Clarke, Michael S, *Kaladan Mortars*, Woodfield Publishing, Sussex. 1994. (101st (WA) Mortar Bty, 41st (WA) Mortar Regt, 81st West African Division).
Collier, Basil, *The War in the Far East 1941-45, a Military History*, William Heinemann Ltd, London, 1969.
Colvin, John, *Not Ordinary Men*, The Battle of Kohima Re-assessed, Leo Cooper, London, 1994.
Crooks, Captain Stanley, '114 [Field Regiment] War History', Chapter Four - French Indo-

China, from 114 (Sussex) Field Regiment's "Newsletter" No. 34, October 1990. Typescript held by the RAHT.

Davidson, Brigadier, 'Report on Operations 82nd West African Division', MSS held by RAHT

Dexter, David, *The New Guinea Offensives*, being Series 1 (Army) Vol VI of *Australia in the War of 1939 - 1945*, Australian War Memorial, Canberra, 1961.

Dimitriadi, Michael, Letters held by the RAHT.

Dixon-Nuttall, Colonel JF, letter to the Editor, *Gunner*, No. 329, April 1998.

Dover, Major Victor, *Sky Generals*, Cassel & Company, London, 1981.

'Dracular,' Operation orders for, MSS held by RAHT.

Duncan, WE ed, *The Royal Artillery Commemoration Book 1939 - 1945*,
G Bell and Sons Ltd, London, 1950.

Dunne, Major T ff, 'Battery History of 19th (Niagara) Medium Battery Royal Artillery [6th Medium Regiment], The Arakan Campaign - 1943/1944', copy of a typescript held by the RAHT.

Dutch East Indies, A Synopsis of Artillery Units. Typescript held by the RAHT.

Ellis John, *The Sharp End of War*, David & Charles, Newton Abbot, 1980.

Elphick, Peter, *Singapore: The Pregnable Fortress*, Coronet Books, Hodder and Stoughton, London 1995.

Emmet, Major Maitland, *The Arakan Campaign of the Twenty-Fifth Indian Division*, Kuala Lumpur, nd [1946]. A paperbacked printed narrative of the division's history from its raising in 1942.

Farndale, General Sir Martin, *History of the Royal Regiment of Artillery, The Years of Defeat, 1939-41*, Brassey's (UK) Ltd, London, 1996.

Farrar-Hockley, General Sir Anthony, *The Army in the Air, The History of the Army Air Corps*, Alan Sutton Publishing, Stroud, Gloucs/Army Air Corps, 1994.

Fernyhough, Colonel HE, 'East African Artillery', *Journal of the Royal Artillery*, Vol LXXV, 1948.

Fraser, David, *Alanbrooke*, Collins, London, 1982

Given, Mr EF, letter to Colonel W Stanford (qv) (303rd (EA) Field/Light Regiment EAA).

Gordon, GT. 'Outflanking Attack', a personal narrative and eye-witness account of the march made by 4th Infantry Brigade to outflank the Japanese positions at Kohima, 23 April to 7 May 1944, culminating in the brigade's attack on GPT Ridge. Typescript held by RAHT. (Mr Gordon was then a Lance Corporal, Royal Corps of Signals, serving with 99th Field Regiment).

Graeme, Ian, 'Singapore 1939 - 1942' *Journal of the Royal Artillery*, Vol CIII No 1, 1976. (3rd HAA Regt).

Graham, Brig CAL, *The History of Mountain Artillery*, Gale & Polden, Aldershot, 1957.

Grant, Ian Lyall, *Burma The Turning Point*, The Zampi Press, Chichester 1993. (The seven battles of the Tiddim Road).

Grant, Peter, *A Highlander Goes to War*, Pentland Press Ltd 1995.

Guild, Lieutenant Colonel SA, 'Going Waterborne from Airborne' ('E' Troop, 27th Field Regiment at Akyab aboard Z Craft), a typescript held by the RAHT.

Hammond, Lieutenant Colonel BAT. 'The Guns at Kohima' Parts 1 and 2. *Gunner* Magazine No 281 April 1994 and No 282 May 1994.

Hammond, Lieutenant Colonel BAT, 'Reflections on a War Diary, 2nd British Infantry Division, 1942-44', (16th Field Regt). Typescript held by the RAHT. Summary at Annex U of this book.

Hamilton, JAL, Account of 81(WA) Division in 1944. MSS at RAHT.

Harding, Bill. 'A Troop Called Fox.' ('F' Troop, 503 Battery, 139 Jungle Field Regt, 7th Indian Division) Copy of a typescript, held by the RAHT.

Haywood, Col A and Clarke, Brig FAS, *The History of the Royal West African Frontier Force*, Gale and Polden Ltd, Aldershot, 1964.

Hepper, Lieut Colonel JM, 'A Light Regiment in the Imphal Campaign.' *Journal of the Royal Artillery*, Vol LXXIV No 4 January 1947.
Hogg, IV and Thurston, LF, *British Artillery Weapons and Ammunition, 1914 - 1918*, Ian Allan, London, 1972.
Hogg, Ian V, *British and American Artillery of World War 2*, Arms and Armour Press, London, 1978.
Holloway, Captain AF, Extract of memoirs of service in 34th Battery, 16th Field Regiment, 25th March 1944 to 23rd June 1944, copy of a manuscript held by the RAHT.
Horner, David M, *The Gunners. A History of Australian Artillery*, Allen and Unwin Pty Ltd, St Leonards, NSW, 1995.
Howard, Major AB, 'Screw Guns in Action, 1940-45. 12 (Poonch) Indian Mountain Battery.', *Journal of the Royal Artillery*, Vol LXXIII, 1946.
Howard, John Hunter, 'Kohima to Mandalay', Unpublished account held by the RAHT.
Howard, Michael, *British Intelligence in the Second World War*, Volume Five, *Strategic Deception*, HMSO, London, 1990.
Hughes, Major General BP, *Honour Titles of the Royal Artillery*, 2nd Ed RAI, Woolwich, 1988.
Hughes, Major General BP, [Ed] *History of the Royal Regiment of Artillery, Between the Wars, 1919-39*, Brassey's (UK) Ltd, London, 1992.
Indian Armed Forces in World War 2, 1939-45. Government of India, HMSO, Calcutta, 1948.
Johnson, Brigadier GD, 'The Battle of Hong Kong', *After the Battle*, No 46, Battle of Britain Prints International Ltd, London, 1984.
Keegan, John (Ed), *Churchill's Generals*, Weidenfeld and Nicolson, London, 1991.
Kempton, Chris, *A Register of the Titles of the Units of the H.E.I.C &Indian Armies 1666 - 1947*, British Empire and Commonwealth Museum Research Paper No 1, British Empire and Commonwealth Museum, Bristol, 1997.
Kelly, Brigadier TED, 'The Occupation of Sumatra, October 1945 - March 1946'. Typescript held by the RAHT.
Kelly, Brigadier TED, 'Heaquarters Medan Area, Commander's General Report, October 1945' (The first month of the occupation of Sumatra written by the CRA, 26th Indian Division). Typescript held by the RAHT.
Kenyon, John, 'Diary of Events with 24th Mountain Regiment in the Arakan.' MSS held by RAHT.
Kirby, Major General S Woodburn et al, *The War Against Japan*, five volumes, HMSO, London 1957-1969.
Kirby, Major General S Woodburn, *Singapore, The Chain of Disaster* Cassel & Company Ltd, London, 1971.
Latham, Brigadier HB, 'Notes on the Maritime Regiments RA, 1941 - 46', MSS held by the RAHT.
Law, Major DD, 'Report on 25-pr at DC's Bungalow, Kohima.' MSS at RAHT.
Leach, Lieutenant Colonel LR, 'India January 1942 to May 1945', typescript autobiography held by RAHT. (the author was BMRA 7 Indian Div and also served with 25 Mtn Regt)
Legh, Lieutenant Colonel RFD, '33 Ind Corps Arty supporting the crossing of the Irrawaddy by 2 and 20 Ind Divs', typescript held by the RAHT.
Lewendon, Brigadier RJ, 'Gunners in Java', *Journal of the Royal Artillery*, Vol CVIII Mar 1981.
Lewendon, Brigadier RJ, 'Personal Reminiscences of the Arakan Feb 1944. *Journal of the Royal Artillery*, Vol CXV, Mar 1989.
Lewendon, Brigadier RJ [Ed], *7th Indian Field Regiment Royal Indian Artillery, A Narrative 1943 - 47*, Privately printed, RAHT, 1996.
Lindsay, Oliver, *At the Going Down of the Sun*, Hamish Hamilton Ltd, London, 1981.

Litchfield, Norman EH, *The Territorial Artillery 1908 - 1988*, The Sherwood Press (Nottingham) Ltd, Nottingham, 1992.

Long, Gavin, *Australia in the War of 1934 - 1945*, Series 1 (Army), Vols I (1952) and II (1953), Australian War Memorial, Canberra.

Love, Brigadier RHAD, 'Maritime Royal Artillery', in Duncan *qv*.

Lucas-Phillips, CE, *Springboard to Victory*, Heinemann, London, 1966.

Maltby, Major General CM, Despatch, 'Operations in Hong Kong from 8th to 25th December 1941', Supplement to *The London Gazette*, 27th January 1948.

Maurice-Jones, Colonel KW, *The History of Coast Artillery*, RAI, Woolwich, 1951.

MacLeod, Brigadier T and Ryan, Major CL, 'Diary compiled in a POW Camp in Hong Kong.' MSS held by RAHT.

Mackenzie, Compton, *Eastern Epic*, Chatto & Windus, London, 1951.

MacFetridge, Lieutenant Colonel CHT and Warren JP, *Tales of the Mountain Gunners*. Wm Blackwood, Edinburgh 1973.

MacFetridge, Lieutenant Colonel CHT, 'The Light Anti-Aircraft Battery in the Withdrawal from Burma, January-May 1942.' *Journal of the Royal Artillery*, Vol CIX No 1, Mar 1982.

MacFetridge, Lieutenant Colonel CHT, 'Indian Mountain Regiments and Batteries, Locations and Movements 1939 - 46', *Journal of the Royal Artillery*, Vol CXIV, No 1, 1987.

Masters, John, *The Road Past Mandalay*, Michael Joseph Ltd, London, 1961.

Maslen-Jones, EW, *Fire By Order*, Pen and Sword Books, Leo Cooper, London and Pen and Sword Books, Barnsley, 1997 (656 AOP Squadron).

McCaig, Lieutenant Colonel R, Series of Articles in *Journal of the Royal Artillery*. 'The Second World War - The Far East' Vol CXXI September 1994, Vol CXXII March, September 1995. Vol CXXIII March, September 1996 Vol CXXIV Autumn 1997. Also an exchange of letters with the author about Burma operations, held by the RAHT.

McMath, Frank, 'The Jungle Lay Beneath'. Typescript held by the RAHT. (656 Air OP Squadron).

Manchester Regiment, 2nd Battalion the, Narrative (MG Battalion). Fleur de Lys Publishing, Manchester 1995.

Maurice-Jones, Colonel KW, *The History of Coast Artillery in the British Army*, Royal Artillery Institution, London, 1959.

Mawer, HBV, 'Through Chaos.' (Anti-tank troop commander and prisoner of war in Singapore and Siam). Typescript held by the RAHT.

Mead, Peter, *Gunners at War*, Ian Allan Ltd, London 1982.

Mead, Peter, *The Eye in the Air, History of Air Observation and Reconnaissance for the Army 1785 - 1945*, HMSO, London, 1983.

Mead, Peter, '*Orde Wingate and the Official Historians*', Journal of Contemporary History, Vol 14, 1979 (SAGE, London and Beverly Hills).

Mondey, David, *The Hamlyn Concise Guide to British Aircraft of World War II*, Chancellor Press, London 1994.

Mondey, David, *The Concise Guide to American Aircraft of World War II*, Chancellor Press, London 1996.

Moyes-Bartlett, Lieutenant Colonel H, *The King's African Rifles*, Gale and Polden Ltd, Aldershot, 1956.

Mydin, Iskander, 'Laying the Ghost to Rest. The Guns of Singapore.' *Journal of the Royal Artillery*, Vol CXIX, Sep 1989.

'Notes From Theatres of War' No 19, Burma 1943/44, War Office, London, May 1945.

Nicholls, Captain SR, 'Field Gunners in the 1944 Chindit Campaign.' *Journal of the Royal Artillery*, Vol CXVI Mar 1989. ('S' and 'T' Troops 160 Field Regiment)

Nicholls, Captain SR, 'An Account of the Role of Field Gunners in the 1944 Chindit Campaign in Burma'. Typescript held by the RAHT.
('U' ('Blackpool') and 'R' ('Broadway') Troops, 160th Field Regiment).
Nicholson, Brigadier RAG, '115th Field Regiment', MSS held by the RAHT.
Nicholson, Brigadier RAG, 'Indin April 6th, 1943. A Gunner Battle', *Journal of the Royal Artillery*, Vol LXXVI No 1 1949.
Nicholson, Brigadier RAG, 'Sugar 5. Arakan 1943', *Journal of the Royal Artillery*, Vol LXXVI, No 1, 1949.
Noble, Ted, 'Burning City - 50 Years Ago', *Gunner*, February 1992.

Obituaries:
Bates, Major General Sir John, *The Times*, 1st February 1992.
Christison General Sir Philip, *The Times*, 23rd December 1993.
Cole, Colonel RB, *Daily Telegraph*, 25th September 1991.
Graeme Major General Ian, *The Times*, 27th May 1993.
Hill, Brigadier RHM, *Daily Telegraph*, 18th October 1991.
Jarrett, Colonel Jimmy, *Daily Telegraph*, 15th December 1992.
McNeill, Major General JM, *The Times*, 15th June 1996.
Pugh, Major General LHO, *Daily Telegraph*, 17th March 1981.
Wade, Major General Ashton, *The Times*, 31st January 1996

Osbourn, HJL, 'Experiences of a Wartime Gunner Officer in Malaya and as a POW on the Burma Railway', *Proceedings of the Royal Artillery Historical Society*, Woolwich, March 1997.
Pakenham-Walsh, Major General RP, *History of the Corps of Royal Engineers*, Vol IX, 1938 - 1948, The Institution of Royal Engineers, Chatham, 1958.
Paley, Tony *The Sparrows*, The Self Publishing Association, Hanley Swan, Worcs., in association with Tony Paley, 1991 (79th LAA Battery)
Palit, Major General DK [Ed] *History of the Regiment of Artillery, Indian Army*, Director of Artillery, Army HQ, New Delhi and Leo Cooper Ltd, London, 1972.
Parvin GR, *Yasumai*, Digit Books, Brown, Watson Ltd, London [nd]. (118th Field Regiment).
Parham, Major General HJ and Belfield, EMG, *Unarmed into Battle*, Warren & Son Ltd, The Wykeham Press, Winchester, 1956.
Payne, Captain DK, '33rd Anti-Tank Regiment 1945'. MSS held by the RAHT.
Pemberton, Brigadier AL, *The Development of Artillery Tactics & Equipment*, War Office, London, 1950.
Percival, Lieutenant General AE, *The War in Malaya*, Eyre & Spottiswoode, London, 1949.
Postan, MM, Hay, D, and Scott, JD, *Design and Development of Weapons*, HMSO and Longmans Green & Co, London, 1964.
Powell, Major RD, 'The Battle for Able.', *Journal of the Royal Artillery*, Vol CXXII No 2, Sep 1995.
Preston, Major IO'D, '50th (Meiktila) Field Battery', *Gunner*, October 1968.
Probert, Air Commodore Henry, *The Forgotten Air Force 1941-45*, Brassey's (UK) Ltd, London, 1995.
Pugh, Lieutenant Colonel LHO, 'Ukhrul', *Journal of the Royal Artillery*, Vol LXXIII, 1946.
Pugh, Lieutenant Colonel LHO, 'Ukhrul Operations', typescript copy of a personal account by the CO of 25th Indian Mountain Regiment, held by the RAHT. (The original was submitted by Lieutenant Colonel Pugh to HQRA 7th Indian Division).
Pugh, Lieutenant Colonel LHO, 'Soerabaja', *Journal of the Royal Artillery* 1948.

Rhodes James, Richard, *Chindit*, John Murray, London, 1980.

Roberts, Brigadier MR, *Golden Arrow, The Story of 7th Indian Division in the Second World War 1939-1945*, Gale & Polden Ltd, Aldershot, 1952.

Robertson, Major GW, 'Gunners in the Far East' in *Dekho*, the Journal of the Burma Star Association, Winter 1990.

Robertson, Major GW, *The Rose and the Arrow*, 136 Field Regiment RA Old Comrades Association [1986].

Robertson, Major GW, 'Notes on Jungle Field Regiments in Burma.' MS held by the RAHT.

Robertson, Major GW, 'Notes on Anti-Tank Regiments in Burma in 1945.' held by the RAHT.

Robertson, Major GW, 'Notes on 7.2-inch howitzers in Burma in 1945.' held by the RAHT.

Rollo, Maj Denis, research material for a proposed book about the guns and gunners of Singapore.

Rollo, Major Denis, *The Guns and Gunners of Hong Kong*, The Gunners' Roll of Hong Kong, Hong Kong, 1991.

Rollo, Major Denis, Analysis of RA Strengths in World War II as at 30th September 1939, 1940, 1941, 1942, 1943, 1944 and 1945.

Rooney, David, *Wingate and the Chindits, Redressing the Balance*, Arms and Armour Press, London 1994.

Routledge, Brigadier NW, *History of the Royal Regiment of Artillery, Anti-Aircraft Artillery 1914-55*, Brasseys (UK) Ltd, London, 1994.

Roy, Captain AD, Some Notes on 8th Medium Regiment RA in the battles around the Imphal Plain, 1944. (Captain Andrew Roy was adjutant of the regiment at the time). Typescript held by the RAHT.

Royal Artillery Commemoration Book 1939-1945 see Duncan, WE.

Sawyer, Major HV, 'The Anti-Aircraft Branch of the Indian Artillery 1940-45.' Typescript and letters held by the RAHT.

Sawyer, Lieutenant Colonel EL, 'Prisoner of War in Changi', *Journal of the Royal Artillery*, Vol CXXIV No 1 March 1997. (4th Mountain Battery)

Sawyer, Lieutenant Colonel EL, 'Prisoner of War in Changi: A Memoir', *Journal of the United Service Institution of India*, Vol CXXV, No 522, October-December 1995.

Schaefli, Robin, *Emergency Sahib: Of Queen's, Sikhs and Dagger Division*, RJ Leach & Co, London, 1992. (Machine Gun Battalion, 11th Sikh Regiment).

Sewell, Captain ERA, '155 (Lanarkshire Yeomanry) Field Regiment Royal Artillery, Malaya 8 Dec 41 - 15 Feb 42'. Prepared in Changi POW camp, Summer 1942, copied by Lieutenant PR Coope, and the copy passed to Major ERA Sewell in 1948. Typescript held by the RAHT.

Skey, Lieutenant Colonel SE, 'The Last Days of Singapore', in Duncan *op cit*.

Skrine, WH, *The White Horse, A History of the Berkshire Yeomanry*, Vol II, 1921-1946. Typescript (145th Field Regiment) held by the RAHT.

Smurthwaite, David, [Ed], *The Forgotten War, The British Army in the Far East 1941-1945*, National Army Museum, London, 1992

Slim Field Marshal Sir William, *Defeat into Victory*, Jarold and Sons, Norwich,1956.

Stanford, Lieutenant Colonel W, correspondence, held by the RAHT

Stephens, Wilson, 'The Bonds of War', *The Field*, 1995.

Thomson, WH, 'Experiences of a Gunner in Burma 1942 - 1945' A typescript account by an officer of 129th (Lowland) Field Regiment held by the RAHT.

Thompson, Julian, *The Imperial War Museum Book of War Behind Enemy Lines*, Sidgwick & Jackson in association with the Imperial War Museum, London 1998.

Tsuji, Colonel Masanobu, Singapore *The Japanese Version*, Constable and Company Ltd, London, 1962.

Tucker, KW, 'Gunners in Burma in World War 2.' Notes held by the RAHC.
Turnbull, Patrick, *The Battle of the Box*, Ian Allen, London, 1979.
Uniacke, Lieutenant Colonel RJ. 'Diary' 16th Field Regiment RA June 1942 - November 1945.' Copy of a typescript held by the RAHT.
Watt, Donald Cameron, *How War Came*, Mandarin Paperbacks, London 1991.
Wavell, General Sir Archibald, *Despatch by the Supreme Commander of the ABDA Area to the Combined Chiefs of Staff* (August 1942), HMSO, London, 1948.
White, Lieutenant Colonel OG, *Straight On For Tokyo*, Gale and Polden, Aldershot, 1948. (2nd Battalion the Dorset Regiment).
White, Steve [Ed], *Strike Home. The Royal Bucks. Yeomanry 1794 - 1967*, Published by Steve White, 1992. Printed account of the services of 99th (RBY) Field Regiment RA, held by the RAHT.
White, Steve [Ed], *More Wartime Memories of the men who served with the 99th (RBY) Field Regiment RA*. A supplement to *Strike Home*, Published by Steve White, 1993, held by the RAHT.
Wigmore, Lionel, *The Japanese Thrust*, Australian War Memorial, Canberra, 1957. (Vol III, Series 1 (Army) of *Australia in the War of 1939-1945*).
Wilberforce, Brigadier WHH, '5 (Bombay) Mountain Battery . . . The 1st Burma Campaign 1941/42', MSS notes held by the RAHT.
Woodcock, Howard, letters to the author held by the RAHT. (16th Field Regiment).
Younger, Lieutenant Colonel Charles, Reports to MGRA India November 1942-February 1945 then to BRA ALFSEA from March to August 1945 on events in 129 (Lowland) Field Regiment, Typescript held by the RAHT.

CHRONOLOGY OF THE WAR IN THE FAR EAST

All dates are local

1940

Sep 27th Tripartite Pact signed by Japan, Germany and Italy.
Oct 18th Britain re-opens Burma Road.

1941

April 13th Japanese - Soviet non-aggression pact signed.
July 26th USA freezes all Japanese assets.
Oct 16th General Tojo becomes Prime Minister of Japan.
Nov 26th USA demands Japanese withdrawal from China.
Pearl Harbour Strike Force sails.
Nov 27th Japan rejects US demand.
Nov 30th Japanese decide to attack Pearl Harbour.
Dec 7th Japanese attack Pearl Harbour.
Dec 8th Japanese bomb Singapore.
Japanese attack Hong Kong.
Japanese attack Malaya. Land at Kota Bharu.
Dec 10th Prince of Wales and Repulse sunk.
Dec 12th 11th Indian Division withdraws from Jitra and Alor Star.
Dec 15th Japanese enter Burma in Kra Isthmus.
Dec 16th Penang evacuated.
Dec 18th Japanese cross to Hong Kong Island.
Dec 22nd Japanese land in Philippines.
Arcadia Conference.
Dec 25th Hong Kong surrenders.
Dec 28th General Wavell takes command in Burma.

1942

Jan 7th Japanese capture Sarawak.
Battle of Slim River.
Jan 14th Wavell sets up HQ ABDA at Batavia.

Jan 15th Japanese invade Burma.
Jan 19th Japanese capture British Borneo.
Jan 21st General Stilwell appointed Chief of Staff to Chiang Kai-shek.
Jan 22nd 18th British Division reaches Singapore.
Jan 25th Japanese invade New Guinea.
Jan 30th Moulmein falls.
Jan 31st British evacuate Malaya.
Feb 9th Japanese land in Singapore.
Feb 11th Japanese cross the Salween.
Feb 14th Japanese land in Sumatra.
Feb 15th Singapore surrenders.
Feb 20th Japanese land in Timor.
Feb 23rd Sittang River bridge blown.
Mar 5th General Alexander takes command in Rangoon.
Mar 8th Japanese enter Rangoon.
Mar 12th Andaman Islands evacuated.
Mar 19th General Slim takes command of Burma Corps.
Mar 22nd Japanese make air attacks on Darwin.
Apr 5th Japanese make air attacks on Colombo.
Apr 18th First US air attack on Japan.
Apr 30th Burma Corps withdraws over Irrawaddy.
May 1st Japanese capture Monywa and Mandalay.
May 5th British invade Madagascar.
May 7th Battle of the Coral Sea.
May 20th British evacuate Burma.
Jun 4th - 6th Battle of Midway.
Aug 7th US forces land on Guadalcanal.
Dec 17th First Arakan Campaign begins.

1943
Jan 7th First Battle of Donbaik.
Feb 1st Second Battle of Donbaik.
Feb 13th First Chindit campaign starts by crossing the Chindwin.
Mar 18th Third Battle of Donbaik.
Mar 19th Chindits cross the Irrawaddy.
Apr 15th Slim assumes command in the Arakan.
Apr 29th All Chindits back in Burma.
May 14th Japanese capture Maungdaw.
Sep 4th Australians attack Lae.
Oct 6th Mountbatten assumes command of SEAC.

1944
Feb 5th Second Chindit Campaign begins.
Feb 6th Japanese launch operation HA GO in the Arakan.
Feb 7th Battle of the 'Admin Box' begins.
Mar 5th 77th and 111th Chindit Brigades fly in.
Mar 7th Japanese attack Fort White and 17th Indian Division
Mar 11th Buthiedaung re-captured.

Mar 14th Japanese attack 20th Indian Division at Tamu.
Mar 24th Major General Wingate killed in an air crash.
Apr 3rd Battle of Kohima begins.
Jun 15th First B-29 bomber raid on Japan.
Jun 22nd Kohima - Imphal Road re-opened.
Jul 30th New Guinea secured.
Aug 3rd Stilwell captures Myitkyina.
Oct 20th US forces land on Leyte.
Dec 3rd British attack in Burma begins.

1945

Jan 4th Akyab occupied without opposition.
Jan 14th 19th Indian Division crosses Irrawaddy.
Feb 19th US forces land on Iwojima.
Feb 22nd 17th Indian Division begins race for Meiktila.
Feb 24th 2nd British Division crosses the Irrawaddy.
Mar 3rd US forces capture Manila.
Mar 20th Mandalay falls.
Mar 30th Advance to Rangoon begins from Meiktila.
Apr 1st US forces land on Okinawa.
Apr 29th 14th Army reaches Pegu.
May 1st Landings south of Rangoon.
May 6th Rangoon falls.
Aug 6th Atomic bomb dropped on Hiroshima.
Aug 9th Atomic bomb dropped on Nagasaki.
Aug 14th Japan surrenders.
Sep 9th British forces land in Malaya.
Sep 12th Japanese surrender formally in Singapore.
Sep 29th British forces move to Java.

INTRODUCTION

Many were the warnings between the wars of 1914-18 and 1939-45 that all was not well, but the signals were ignored and predictions that another war would not occur were made with awful frequency. The confusion over what to do in the Far East was but one example and in the end little was done until it was too late. The need to be seen to be ready in peacetime was ignored, thus the German, Italian and Japanese governments were not afraid to try policies which might lead to war on the assumption that they would win it. By 1937, politicians realised that they had predicted wrongly and that war in Europe was clearly coming, but by then it was too late. The Nation did its best to gear itself once again for war, but there was not enough time. The Army that went to war did not lack in gallantry, but it had been expanded too quickly and regiments had been diluted as they split to form second and third line units. Then there was not enough time to train before they were committed to combat. Tactical and technical training was fair but operational training at formation level was not understood.

The Japanese watched the ease with which the British and French Armies were defeated in Norway, France, Greece and Crete and monitored the apparent success of the air battles in the West. They saw also the paucity of defences and force levels in the Far East. Whereas these were not the reason for war in South East Asia and the Pacific, they encouraged rather than deterred it. British policy from 1939 to 1941 was not to antagonise Japan. By June 1940 Britain was already fighting Germany and Italy alone and the last thing she wanted was a war against Japan as well. Her defences in Hong Kong, Singapore and Burma were still incomplete, and India, Australia and New Zealand were also at war although heavily committed to the Middle East.

The Gunners in the Far East had taken second place to their comrades in Europe who were themselves still not properly equipped for a modern war. The guns in Hong Kong were for the most part obsolete and there were too few of them. The great controversy of how to defend Singapore still raged at the outbreak of hostilities. Should it be by naval and air forces or should it be by land forces or should it be a combination and if so what should that be? Where was the threat? Was it by sea from the south or by land from the north? It was reckoned to be the former until, too late, it was recognised as the latter. The installations of the great coast batteries facing south cause controversy to this day even though most of them engaged the enemy, often with unsuitable ammunition and poor to non-existent observation. In Burma there were hardly any Gunners at all when the first attacks came. The build up, however, was remarkably quick and efficient when it did get under way. Nothing could be done about Hong Kong, which was regarded as indefensible, where, alongside the infantry, the Gunners fought hard and with great gallantry against impossible odds but leaving the survivors to spend the rest of the war in the appalling conditions of Japanese captivity.

During the battles of Malaya the Gunners played a significant part, but in many cases they were not used properly and in any case their training was not up to the speed of Japanese operations. Nevertheless on many occasions they did more than they have been given credit for as this book will tell. Their battles in Malaya led to those in Singapore and to the same captivity that befell their comrades in Hong Kong. There was fighting also in Java and Sumatra, mainly, where the British were concerned, by anti-aircraft Gunners sent there to guard RAF airfields set up there as the Japanese closed on Singapore. Again it was captivity that followed their action.

Much the same was to happen when the Japanese launched their attack on Burma. They were too powerful and too well trained and time and again got inside the British decision-making cycle, outflanking them and causing them to pull back. Army/Air co-operation was not good enough, nor was all arms training within the Army. Eventually by the end of 1942 the British were forced back into India.

But by then the tide was turning. The USSR and the United States were in the war, the Empire was girding its loins, industry was turning out the new weapons which were much superior to the old. Training was tempered by experience, concepts were making more sense, all arms training improved beyond bounds, the Army had its own small air force and Army/Air co-operation began to improve. By early 1944 the Japanese met their first defeats in Arakan, they had already suffered many reverses at sea and now there were further ones in the Pacific and later in the year they reached as far as they were ever to get in Assam and soon earlier Allied defeat was turned into victory.

Throughout all this the Royal Regiment played a fundamental part. By 1944 it formed over 30% of the Army. The Gunners of Australia, New Zealand, India, Ceylon and Africa had expanded beyond recognition and were playing their full part in the great battles raging across the theatre. This book aims to tell the story of the Gunners of the United Kingdom in the Far East and much of that of their comrades of the Empire who had rallied to the same cause. The facts of what they achieved are gathered together but so big is the story that every incident cannot be recorded. Nevertheless most regiments are mentioned and the exploits of as many as possible are told. The technique, as in the other books of this series, has been to extract the outline story from the official histories and then to create the Gunner story from the War Diaries, relevant books, documents, interviews and letters, which are listed for reference. For sure some things have been omitted which should have been included and indeed some of the information presented may not be quite right. It is therefore important that those Gunners 'who were there' comment on the book so that future editions can be made more accurate.

I am indebted to many for help and advice. To Brigadier Ken Timbers, Historical Secretary of the Royal Artillery Institution and to his wife Bridget for sorting out War Diaries and many other documents, to Brigadier Peter Painter, Secretary of the Royal Artillery Institution for constant advice, to those at the Royal United Services Institute and Imperial War Museum, National Army Museum and Ministry of Defence Libraries for all their help and advice too. I am also most grateful to Janet McCallum for once again drawing the maps and to Major Denis Rollo not only for advice on many points but in particular for all his work on orders of battle. I am grateful to Michael Dimitriadi of 1st Royal Scots who fought through many of the battles for keeping me straight on the Donbaik battles of the first Arakan campaign and many others who have also contributed. But I must in particular thank Major GW (Robbie) Robertson for all his months of basic research through countless documents and for his pages of magnificent notes which made my task so very much easier. This was the more effective because he served with 136th Field Regiment in the Burma campaign and has himself written an excellent book about it. Without his help this book would never have been ready so soon nor would it have been so complete. I am also indebted to Colonel GR Armstrong, who commanded 136th Field Regiment, and to

Lieutenant Colonel R McCaig, who served as Brigade Major RA of 7th Indian Division. Brigadier RJ Lewendon, who served with 7th Indian Field Regiment, has also very kindly assisted with the chapters on the Arakan and subsequent actions and on the record of events in Sumatra. Frank Cole, who served with 42nd Mortar Regiment WAA in 82nd West African Division in Burma has also been very helpful as has Howard Woodcock who served with 16th Field Regiment from 1941 to 1945. Lieutenant Colonel W. Stanford and John Watson-Baker have both contributed information about the East Africa Artillery for which I am very grateful. Finally as always the brunt of the work fell to Philip Annis who had read all the drafts, edited all the material and put it all together, then tragically died. I owe a very great deal for all his dedicated work on this and previous books and in a sense this volume is his epitaph. Finally my thanks to our publishers, Brassey's.

This is a book about the Gunners' war in the Far East from 1941 to 1946 and I am most conscious of not doing full justice to the other arms and services who also fought with the greatest gallantry in these same battles. This is especially so for the infantry who bore the brunt of the close quarter fighting in the jungle, to the engineers who overcame almost insuperable odds, frequently under fire, to all the logistic services whose task was vital and who never failed, again in near impossible conditions. I have also not done justice to the Royal Air Force, the Royal Navy and the United States Army Air Force whose roles in the Far East were fundamental to success and whose bravery and skill are acknowledged by all who served there. The same is true of the Gunners of Australia and New Zealand. However, their stories are told elsewhere while up to now that of the British, Indian, Burmese, Chinese, Malay and African Gunners has not been. There is much new material in this book which to date has lain hidden because it belongs to regiments long since disbanded. There is little doubt that the Gunners played a greater part in these battles than they have hitherto been given credit for. This was certainly so in the defence of Hong Kong and in the retreat through Malaya and Burma in 1942.

Once again this book is a memorial; it is dedicated to the Gunners of the Empire who fought with such courage and devotion during the Second World War in the Far East and who died for their countries and their regiments or suffered untold hardship as prisoners of war or as a result of wounds and, sometimes, of memories. It is to record forever what they did so that freedom might be restored and, also, to ensure that they never were in fact a Forgotten Army.

Many readers will now know that the author of this book, General Sir Martin Farndale, died on 10th May 2000.

The work that he did on the series of histories of the Royal Regiment of Artillery was of inestimable value. Besides writing this Volume VI he had also written Volume I, The Western Front 1914-18, Volume II, The Forgotten Fronts and the Home Base 1914-18, and Volume V, The Years of Defeat 1939-41.

Only two weeks before his death he gave the new Editor the text and Annexes of Volume VII, The Mediterranean and Middle East June 1942 to 1945.

There is no doubt that this important series of histories would never have been written or published had it not been for the dedicated work of General Farndale. The Regiment owes him a great debt of gratitude.

This early second, revised, edition has been published since General Farndale's death, and takes account of many of the suggestions and amendments that have been made by readers of the first edition.

CHAPTER 1

THE PRELUDE TO WAR IN THE FAR EAST and THE NORTH WEST FRONTIER OF INDIA

1921 - 1941

(Maps 1 and 2)

At the end of the First World War there was much debate in London about British Defence policy in the Far East. The situation was examined by the Committee of Imperial Defence in 1921 and this concluded that Hong Kong could never be made secure as a naval base. It went on to recommend that Singapore was best situated as a base for the control of sea communications in the Indian Ocean and the South Pacific. A conference in Washington in November 1921 laid down the permissible size of the British, American and Japanese fleets and the zones in which they were free to operate. Further treaties defined the scope and status of the various British, American, French and Japanese possessions in the area. It was hoped that this would prevent Japanese expansion in the Pacific, but American-Japanese relations were poor, mainly concerning the former's immigration policies. Thus, when Britain abrogated her treaty with Japan in order not to antagonise America and on the grounds that this treaty was, in any case, redundant in the light of the new treaties, the effect on Japan was profound. She took it as a sign that she was being isolated. At this time the Japanese had a relatively liberal government pursuing a policy of peace. For this reason the British thought that their action would be understandable to them. After all it had also been agreed that neither Britain nor America would construct naval bases nearer to Japan than Singapore and Hawaii.

In 1922 Britain was considering two sites on Singapore Island for a new naval base, one at the existing civil harbour on the south side at Keppel Harbour and one on the northern side in the Johore Strait. The Admiralty recommended the latter and this was approved by the Cabinet in 1923. Then the project was abandoned by the short lived Labour government in 1924 only to be resurrected again on the return of the Conservatives later that year. A committee headed by Lord Curzon confirmed the Johore site and recommended an airfield to go with it at Seletar. This committee concluded that the threat to Singapore was not from the north, overland from Malaya, but from the south by sea. It also stated that aircraft could do the job of fixed gun defences which would not, therefore, be needed. This caused a ten year argument among the Chiefs of Staff and this in turn imposed further delay. It was not until 1926 that the Committee of Imperial Defence ordered at least some work to start on some gun defences. The idea was to provide some close, some medium range and three long range 15-inch guns and a study was set in hand to see if aircraft really could make it unnecessary to provide more.

Lieutenant General Sir Webb Gillman went to Singapore to recommend a plan for its defence. When he arrived there was further delay caused by local arguments over land rights. Nevertheless, in 1928, he reported a three phase plan and the Chiefs of Staff ordered it to be completed to Phase 1 by 1933, but that further work should be postponed. They reiterated that the threat was from the sea and not from the land to the north. This decision was coupled with the British Government's continuing assumption that there would be no major war for ten years.

The second Labour government, in 1929, pursued a policy of disarmament; it ordered fleet reductions and a slowing of the work on the Singapore defences leading both Australia and New Zealand to express concern. Meanwhile the expansionists were flexing their muscles in Japan and in 1931 fighting broke out between Chinese and Japanese forces in Mukden and the latter occupied Manchuria. China appealed to the League of Nations and was supported by America, but the Japanese refused to leave and created the puppet state of Manchukuo. Rioting broke out in Shanghai, Japanese naval forces were rushed there and further fighting ensued. Then in 1932 a Japanese division landed just north of Shanghai. Although this was withdrawn in May that year, the writing was on the wall.

The Chiefs of Staff recommended that 'It would be the height of folly to perpetuate our defenceless state in the Far East'. The Cabinet agreed but would not authorise work to re-start in Singapore. Stanley Baldwin chaired a committee to study coast defences throughout the world. The Air Ministry pressed for an aircraft solution rather than guns for the defence of Singapore on the grounds of mobility and range. The Army and the Royal Navy thought otherwise because, they said, an overseas base must be able to protect itself against surprise attack round the clock until reinforcements can arrive or when aircraft were engaged elsewhere or when they could not fly because of enemy action or the weather. Baldwin compromised and recommended both, that is guns and aircraft, and at last authorised work to begin in Singapore in 1933.

In March 1933 the League of Nations condemned Japan as an aggressor in Manchuria. Accordingly Japan withdrew from the League, crossed the Great Wall and advanced south into China. Later that year Germany also left the League and in October the Chiefs of Staff stressed the need for rapid re-armament. In 1934 Germany repudiated the Versailles Treaty and openly began to re-arm. With Germany a clear potential aggressor and Japan on the march, Britain reluctantly decided that she must also re-arm.

Only the first stage of the Singapore defences was due for completion by 1936 or 1937 at the earliest. In 1935 authority was given to build more gun emplacements and two airfields. Singapore, it was said, must be able to hold for 90 days until the arrival of the fleet. Then in 1936 Japan walked out of a conference in London which refused to allow her a fleet of the size she wanted. She immediately expanded her intensive ship building programme.

Meanwhile in Malaya three new airfields were authorised, at Kota Bharu, Kuantan and Kahang, by the Air Ministry. But the Army was not consulted; as a result they were built in areas almost impossible to defend. Attention was by then beginning to concentrate on the defence of the Malayan Peninsula because it was now recognised as relevant to the defence of Singapore. In 1937 Major General WGS Dobbie, GOC Malaya, reported that sea-borne landings on the east coast were possible even in the monsoon period of October to March. Then in 1938 he warned that, in many places, the jungle was not impassable to infantry. As a result General Dobbie was authorised to begin constructing defences in Johore.

In 1938 Italy aligned herself with Germany and it was recognised that this would threaten communications with the Far East. When Hitler re-occupied the Rhineland in 1936 and when Britain and France took no action, an expansionist government, subservient to the Army, seized power in Japan. This Government also aligned itself with Germany and again began flexing its muscles against China. In 1937 the effect of a war with Germany, Italy and Japan at the same time was debated by the Chiefs of Staff. They concluded that a fleet at least equal to that of Germany must remain in Home Waters; that the French could neutralise the Italian fleet in the Mediterranean and that a strong Far East fleet must be sent to protect Singapore. They also concluded that Hong Kong was an important, though not vital, outpost but, if attacked, it must be defended for as long as possible. Then on 7th July 1937 war broke out between Japan and China and in December British and American gun boats were shelled by the Japanese in the Yangtze River. In May 1938 the Japanese landed at Amoy, some 300 miles north of Hong Kong. In October they cut off the colony by landing at Bias Bay and marching into Canton.

The Godesberg and Munich meetings between Chamberlain and Hitler took place in 1938 and early in 1939 it was decided that a fleet would have to be sent to the Far East. But because of the threat from Germany and Italy it could consist of only two capital ships. In March 1939 Hitler invaded Czechoslovakia and in April Mussolini invaded Albania. Then in August it was decided to reinforce the garrison of Singapore with land and air forces. War was declared on Germany in September 1939 and on Italy in June 1940. 12th Indian Infantry Brigade Group from 4th Indian Division, then in India under Brigadier ACM Paris, was first to go to Singapore. This brigade included 122nd Field Regiment, consisting of 278th and 280th Batteries, which had mobilised in 1939 and sailed from England on 11th January 1941 for India. Meanwhile 2nd Argyll and Sutherland Highlanders, 5/2nd Punjab, 5/14 Punjab, which moved on to Penang, and 4/19th Hyderabad Regiments arrived in Singapore from India. In addition 22nd Mountain Regiment, consisting of 4th (Hazara), 7th (Bengal), 10th (Abbottabad) and 21st Batteries, under Lieutenant Colonel GL Hughes was also sent from India. Until these units arrived the only forces in Singapore were seven British, Indian and Malay battalions and five regiments of the Royal Artillery and Hong Kong-Singapore Royal Artillery deployed around the island under two headquarters known as Fire Commands. Their duty was to co-ordinate defensive coastal and anti-aircraft fire in the event of attack. The regiments at that time were:

Malaya and Singapore

Faber Fire Command

7th Coast Regiment RA, (11th & 31st British & 5th & 7th HK-S RA Batteries). Lieut Col HD St G Cardew.

Changi Fire Command

9th Coast Regiment RA, (7th, 22nd & 32nd Batteries). Lieut Col CP Heath.

Anti-Aircraft Defence Command

1st HAA Regiment HK-S RA, (6th, 9th & 10th Batteries). Lieut Col AE Tawney

2nd HAA Regiment HK-S RA, (11th, 12th & 13th Batteries). Lieut Col HW Allpress & later R McL More.

3rd HAA Regiment RA (11th, 29th & 30th Batteries). Lieut Col FE Hugonin.

Penang

11th Coast Regiment (8th Coast and 20th HAA Batteries HK-S RA).

The defence of the Malay States was in the hands of local State forces until the arrival of 12th Indian Infantry Brigade Group, 22nd Indian Mountain Regiment and six RAF squadrons consisting of some 58 aircraft.

Hong Kong

In Hong Kong the coast defences had been modernised, there were four destroyers and some coastal craft but no aircraft other than a small communication flight. The land forces consisted of two Indian infantry battalions and the following Gunners:

8th Coast Regiment RA (12th, 30th and 36th Batteries). Lieut Col S Shaw.

12th Coast Regiment RA (20th and 26th Batteries). Lieut Col RJL Penfold.

5th HAA Regiment RA (7th RA and 17th & 18th Batteries HK-S RA). Lieut Col FD Field.
1st Hong Kong Regiment, HK-S RA (1st & 2nd Mountain Batteries each with 4 x 3.7-inch howitzers and 3rd, 4th & 25th Medium Batteries each with 4 x 6-inch 26 cwt howitzers Lieut Col JC Yale.
1st, 2nd, 3rd, 4th Batteries (Coast) and 5th (AA) Battery, the artillery of the HKVDC.
956th Defence Battery (1 x 6-inch gun, 2 x 4.7-inch guns, 6 x 18-pdrs and 4 x 2-pdrs).

Burma

In Burma the defence forces were very small as no threat was envisaged from the east. There was a small local force of infantry and Gunners known as Burma Auxiliary Force (BAF). The Gunner garrison at the outbreak of war was:

2nd (Derajat) Mountain Battery IA at Maymyo (4 x 3.7-inch howitzers).
5th Field Battery BAF (6 x 18-pounders).
Rangoon Coast Battery BAF (2 x 6-inch guns).

In addition there was a considerable British garrison in India, essentially to defend the North West Frontier where trouble, mainly with the supporters of the Fakir of Ipi had been continuous since the 1920s. These actions are told in another volume in this series, *Between the Wars 1919-39*. The artillery involved was mainly the mountain batteries which, on 1st August 1939, became part of the Indian Army and ceased to belong to the Royal Artillery. On 1st September 1939 the distribution of the Mountain Artillery was as follows (the word 'Indian' was not added until October 1942):

20th Mountain Regiment (22nd, 23rd, 24th and 25th Batteries) at Quetta
21st Mountain Regiment (1st Royal (Kohat) FF, 6th (Jacobs), 9th (Murree) and 14th (Rajputana) Batteries) at Kohat
22nd Mountain Regiment (4th (Hazara) FF, 7th (Bengal), 10th (Abbottabad) and 21st Batteries) in Malaya
23rd Mountain Regiment (3rd (Peshawar) FF, 8th (Lahore), 12th (Poonch) and 17th (Nowshera) Batteries) at Abbottabad
24th Mountain Regiment (11th (Dehra Dun), 16th (Zhob), 18th (Sohan) and 20th Batteries) at Peshawar
25th Mountain Regiment (5th (Bombay), 13th (Dardoni), 15th (Jhelum) and 19th (Maymyo) Batteries) in Waziristan

2nd (Derajat) Battery FF was stationed in Maymyo and there was an independent section in Chitral. During the early part of the Second World War there were several disturbances on the North West Frontier, but not on a large scale. They did nevertheless tie down considerable forces to the area throughout the war. There were some outrages in the Bannu area in the latter part of 1939 for which gangs based on the Ahmedzai salient were responsible. After a British officer and two Indian other ranks were killed some three miles from Bannu, it was decided to eliminate these gangs. In February 1940 the 3rd and the Kohat Indian Infantry Brigades with 21st Mountain Regiment attacked northwards from Bannu itself. 5th (Bombay) Mountain Battery had temporarily replaced 1st Royal (Kohat) Mountain Battery, so it and 6th (Jacob's) went with 3rd Indian Infantry Brigade and 9th (Murree) and 14th (Rajputana) Batteries went with the Kohat Indian Infantry Brigade. 1st Battery moved with a small column from Damdil but replaced 5th Battery on 24th March. Meanwhile 3rd (Peshawar) Battery carried out some operations further north but returned to Abbottabad in May.

3rd Indian Infantry Brigade met stiff opposition and The Kohat Infantry Brigade suffered much from sniping. However it got through to Gumatti with the help of the guns by 22nd February. Prisoners were taken, about 100 casualties were inflicted and villages were burnt which sufficed to break the back of the opposition. All efforts then went into road building until the force withdrew in May. In all the Gunners had fired some 2000 rounds. Patrolling continued throughout the area and the Indian Air Force played an ever increasing part in these operations. When 25th Indian Mountain Regiment left for Burma in 1943, its place in Waziristan was taken by 26th Indian Mountain Regiment, made up of 18th, 20th, 27th Batteries and 1st Jammu and Kashmir State Battery (later 30 Mountain Battery), when it returned from the Middle East in March/April 1942.

By September 1939 the Japanese controlled most of the Chinese coast and were advancing south westwards towards Indo-China. In order to avoid war with Japan, Britain decided to withdraw her gunboats from the Yangtze River in October 1939. However the three British battalions in Shanghai and Tientsin were left in place. The GOC Malaya, Major General LV Bond, expressed concern over the nature of the Malayan defences. Both he and Air Marshal JT Babington, AOC Far East, stated strongly that the security of Singapore depended on a successful defence of Malaya. But the Foreign Office said that since Japan had been at war for three years she would never take on the might of the British Empire! As a result it was decided not to increase force levels in the Far East. Accordingly General Bond sent an assessment of the Malayan defences to the War Office on 13th April 1940. He pointed out that the effect of the Chiefs of Staff stating that the colony must now hold for 180 days before relief could reach it meant that the strengths of the garrison, and of the defences themselves, were far too small. He stressed that the Japanese could land anywhere in Malaya at any time of the year and that they could assemble a force to do so in southern China. Furthermore they would soon be in a position to move through Siam and then right up to the Malayan border without hindrance. This meant in turn that Malaya must be defended from its northern border southwards and this was quite beyond the capabilities of the volunteer forces alone. He said that he needed at least three divisions immediately and two more if the Japanese moved into Siam. If these could not be provided then he needed much more air power to hold the enemy at bay while the Army concentrated on the defence of Singapore, Penang and certain key areas in Malaya. The only reply he got was authority to order a limited conscription in Malaya and improve the training of his volunteer forces!

Meanwhile the RAF continued to go its own way by building airfields in northern Malaya, again without reference to the Army which concentrated on the defences of Singapore, and the gulf between the services widened. General Bond considered that with the forces he had, or was likely to get, he could only defend the naval base at Singapore. This left him only one battalion and the volunteers to defend the airfields in Malaya. Air Marshal Babington said his priorities were the airfields at Alor Star, Kota Bharu and Kuantan. At this stage the Governor became concerned and passed the problem to the Chiefs of Staff, saying that the only solution was more reinforcements. This request however came at the time that the Army was being evacuated from Dunkirk with the loss of nearly all its equipment and when the invasion of the UK seemed imminent. At the same time the defeat of France meant the loss of the French fleet to contain the Italians in the Mediterranean. This in turn meant no large fleet for the Far East and thus the need to defend Singapore without naval reinforcements when the whole concept of defence was built up around naval and air power. The Chiefs of Staff said nothing must be done to provoke war with Japan and that all remaining British troops were to be withdrawn from China forthwith. They reiterated their previous view that Hong Kong was not a vital interest, that it could not be expected to hold for long and that requests to reinforce it must be resisted. This philosophy was supported by Winston Churchill, the new Prime Minister.

We must now turn to the state of affairs in India. In 1939, in line with the recommendations of the Chatfield Commission's report, India had just begun to modernise her Army but little was done for the Air Force. Then in late summer 1939 4th Indian Division comprised of 5th and 11th Indian Infantry Brigades was sent to Egypt, its third brigade, the 12th, had already gone to Singapore. After Dunkirk, India offered to raise one armoured and five infantry divisions. Accordingly in 1940 she set about raising 31st Armoured and 6th, 7th, 8th, 9th and 10th Infantry Divisions. This was done by milking existing units to form the nuclei of the new ones. But there was a real difficulty in providing artillery. There were only enough resources to provide one field regiment per division to start with. There were even greater problems in providing equipment. In 1935 the Indian Regiment of Artillery had been created. The title changed in November 1940 to The Regiment of Indian Artillery. Its one unit was 'A' Field Regiment of four 4-gun horsed batteries stationed at Bangalore, one battery each of Punjabi-Mussulmans, Ranghars, Rajputs and Madrassis. It was not part of the Royal Artillery and had adopted its own badge exactly like that of the Royal Artillery but with a star in place of the crown, and the words 'India' and, a new motto, 'Izzat o Iqbal' included. A start had been made. By 1940, 5th Indian Division, consisting of two brigades, was sent to the Sudan, Headquarters 11th Indian Division was sent to Malaya and plans were set in motion to raise 14th, 17th, 19th, 20th and 34th Infantry Divisions.

The pressures grew and the demand for reinforcements everywhere became so great that formations had to be sent overseas long before they were ready to go. The 6th and 8th Indian Infantry Brigades went to Malaya to form 11th Indian Infantry Division in October and November 1940. 9th Indian Infantry Division, 15th and 22nd Indian Infantry Brigades, followed in March and April 1941. 6th, 8th and 10th Indian Infantry Divisions were sent to Iraq in the Spring and Summer of 1941 and two more brigades, 13th and 16th went to Burma at the same time. None was fully trained or equipped, such is the price of rapid expansion in time of war.

Efforts were also made to expand the air force in India but little could be done at the height of the Battle of Britain. In February, Nos. 27 and 60 Squadrons RAF, with Blenheims and Hawker Harts, were sent to Singapore and Burma respectively. With the declaration of war by Italy in June 1940 it became vital to develop India's industrial output to equip the armies of the Empire east of Suez and this was done with considerable success. Indeed, Britain owes much to the way in which India and her industries rallied to the cause at that critical time in the history of the Empire.

During the 'phoney war' in Europe, Japan played a waiting game as her armies advanced ever deeper into China. It was the collapse of France in June 1940 that was to have such major repercussions throughout the Far East. Seeing the ease with which France, Holland and Belgium were overrun, Japan was confident that the defeat of Britain would soon follow. A second cabinet was formed in Japan under Prince Konoye, with Yosuke Matsuoka as Foreign Minister and General Hideki Tojo as Army Minister. The new Government resolved to defeat China and force concessions for oil and raw materials from the Netherlands East Indies. Pressure was put on Britain to close the Burma road and to stop supplying China. Then on 23rd September the Japanese Army moved into the northern provinces of Indo-China; the French did not resist, having been ordered not to by the government in Vichy. The die was cast.

The situation was critical. Britain and the Empire faced the might of Germany and Italy alone and the Chiefs of Staff recommended some sort of settlement with Japan unless the Americans would offer support, but this was not forthcoming. Accordingly the British reluctantly agreed to close the Burma Road for three months in order not to provoke Japan. In August 1940 they ordered the remaining British garrisons to withdraw from China. Then the Japanese signed the Tripartite Pact with Germany and Italy. The aim of this was to face America with a threat from both flanks and to prevent her going to the aid of Britain but it had the opposite effect. American-British-Dutch talks were held in Singapore, and America increased her aid to Britain. Meanwhile the Dutch negotiated a limited supply of oil to Japan. By this time however, the *Luftwaffe* had lost the Battle of Britain and Singapore had been reinforced by the 11th Indian Infantry Division commanded by Major General DM Murray-Lyon; it had no artillery. Britain then told the Americans that they could use Singapore and reopened the Burma road to resume aid to China.

The Commanders-in-Chief in Singapore re-appreciated their requirements in October 1940, saying that they would need 31 more air force squadrons totalling some 556 aircraft, 26 battalions, 176 heavy and 100 light anti-aircraft guns and 186 searchlights together with three flotillas of motor torpedo boats. Their concept of operations was to destroy any attack, while it was still at sea or as it landed, using naval and air power, then to use the Army for the close defence of the naval and air bases. After a conference in Singapore it was decided to approach Australia, India and New Zealand to seek help. But still there was no co-ordinated defence plan as the three Services went their own way. Accordingly, the Chiefs of Staff, with Churchill's support, appointed Air Marshal Sir Robert Brooke-Popham as Commander-in-Chief of a new Far East Command. His job was to co-ordinate a defence strategy for the Far East; his aim was to avoid war with Japan and plan to defend the area with air power until the fleet could arrive. This did not work because the new Commander-in-Chief had no authority to co-ordinate his defence plans with the civil authorities in Hong Kong or Burma. Nevertheless some co-ordination with the forces of the Netherlands East Indies was achieved.

Brooke-Popham's appreciation was that, if he was to prevent war, he had to convince the Japanese that an attack would fail. He stressed the importance of Anglo-American solidarity. He also said that, if the Japanese moved into Siam, he should be allowed to move a force into the Kra Isthmus and that meanwhile every effort should be made to aid Chiang Kai-shek in China. The Chiefs of Staff accepted that reinforcements were necessary but that they could not make available more than 336 aircraft until the end of 1941. They agreed to 26 infantry battalions and said that another division would arrive by June 1941. They agreed also to find the anti-aircraft guns and searchlights. But Churchill was not happy with what he saw as a dispersion of resources around the world.

Meanwhile an Anglo-Dutch-Australian defence plan was drawn up to define the method of command in the event of war. It stated that the most likely threat was from Siam and Indo-China. In February 1941 the 8th Australian Infantry Division arrived in Singapore, under the command of Major General HG Bennett, but it consisted only of 22nd Australian Infantry Brigade which had with it 2/10th Field Regiment RAA armed with two batteries of 18-pounders and two of 4.5-inch howitzers. In March, 9th Indian Division, under Major General AE Barstow and consisting of 15th and 22nd Indian Infantry Brigades, arrived in Singapore without any artillery. At the end of April 1941 Lieutenant General AE Percival became GOC Malaya and Lieutenant General Sir Lewis Heath, who had led 5th Indian Infantry Division to victory at Keren in Eritrea, arrived to command the new 3rd Indian Corps, designed to defend Malaya north of Johore and Malacca, with 9th and 11th Indian Divisions.

Politically the situation was very complex. The Japanese were concerned about their lack of war materials and about their northern front with the Soviet Union. They tried to woo that country before risking war with Britain and the United States and in April they succeeded in signing a non-aggression pact with her. Then they made an agreement with Siam and Indo-China to mediate over the fighting that had broken out on their frontiers. These measures set the stage for future operations in Malaya and the Netherlands East Indies in order to secure raw materials there when the time was ripe. At a conference held in Singapore between the British, Americans and Dutch an attempt was made to define responsibilities in the event of war but it was inconclusive. Then in May talks started in Washington between the Americans and the Japanese to find a peaceful solution to the crisis rapidly building up in the Far East. These broke down without result on 17th June 1941 and then, on the 22nd, Germany invaded the Soviet Union. This gave real protection to Japan's northern front and enabled her to press on south regardless of the danger of war with Britain, America, the Netherlands, Australia and New Zealand. Accordingly preparations were set in hand to prepare for war and mobilisation was ordered.

The Japanese next threatened French Indo-China and America decided that if they invaded she would stop all trade with Japan and enforce an embargo. Thus when the Japanese occupied Saigon and Camranh Bay at the end of July, the Americans broke off all trade contact with them. Japan was isolated and realised that her war supplies would not last long. There was much argument about what to do next. The Imperial Navy said that Japan must either negotiate or go to war, to do neither would mean total collapse within two years. Japan decided on war which would be caused by provocation.

On 8th August the Japanese offered an ultimatum which gave them great advantages, though saying that if their conditions were agreed they would not move south of Indo-China. The next day Churchill and Roosevelt met off Newfoundland. Together they decided to warn Japan that any further advance could lead to war. Churchill publicly reinforced this on his return but agreed to leave any subsequent negotiation to the Americans. By September all attempts to solve the problem came to nothing. The Japanese High Command told its government that time was of the essence, oil was running out, the Americans and the British were daily increasing their strength and the monsoon season would soon make landings in Malaya and the Philippines hazardous. They had reached the point of no return.

Meanwhile Britain was working out how best to send a fleet to the Far East and General Percival was working out plans for the defence of northern Malaya. His demands far exceeded anything requested so far and included the need for five divisions with a full complement of artillery, including 212 heavy and 124 light anti-aircraft guns. This was backed by Brooke-Popham as Commander-in-Chief. He also wished to move into southern Siam, at Singora, as soon as the Japanese made a move. But the Chiefs of Staff were unable to agree or to provide what was wanted. After a visit to the Far East in September 1941, Mr Duff Cooper, sent to Singapore by the War Cabinet, proposed the establishment of a Commissioner General who would establish a Council of War should it become necessary. It was at this stage that the Chiefs of Staff decided to replace Brooke-Popham with someone with war experience and they suggested Lieutenant General Sir Henry Pownall, a Gunner, who had been Chief of Staff to Gort in France. But the appointment was delayed when the Japanese attacked and it was then decided not to alter the existing command arrangements. By the end of September, 27th Australian and 28th Indian Infantry Brigades had arrived in Singapore, the former with 2/15th Field Regiment RAA equipped with 3-inch mortars. New 25-pounders were, however issued in November. 2/4th Anti-Tank Regiment RAA also arrived at this time with 12 x 2-pounders and 24 x 75mm guns.

Back in London, on 26th October General Sir Alan Brooke, Commander-in-Chief Home Forces, was summoned to Chequers by the Prime Minister, Winston Churchill. After dinner that night Churchill invited 'Brookie' to become CIGS in place of Dill. That night Brooke wrote in his diary 'I got into bed with my brain in a whirl trying to fathom the magnitude of the task I am about to take on . . . many many thoughts kept galloping through my head and by 4 am I was still tossing about without sleep.' Then, on 16th November, the day he took over, he wrote 'I had never hoped or aspired to reach these dizzy heights and now that I am stepping up onto the plateau land of my military career the landscape looks cold, bleak and lonely with a ghastly responsibility hanging as a black thundercloud over me . . .'

On 11th November 1941, 5th Field Regiment, consisting of 63/81st and 73rd Batteries, under Lieutenant Colonel EWF Jephson, arrived in Singapore from Rawalpindi with 16 x 4.5-inch howitzers and on 7th December 88th Field Regiment, 351st and 352nd Batteries, under

Lieutenant Colonel SC D'Aubuz, arrived from the UK and joined 9th Indian Division. On the same day 80th Anti-Tank Regiment arrived with 2nd (Minden), 215th, 272nd and 273rd Batteries under Lieutenant Colonel WES Napier and went to 11th Indian Division.

By this time Major General CM Maltby, a Canadian by birth, had arrived in Hong Kong to take command. Negotiations between America and Japan were floundering. There was much debate in Japan. Konoye resigned as Prime Minister on 6th September 1941 to be replaced two days later by General Tojo. The new cabinet decided to make final preparations for war and the decision as to whether and where to attack would be made on 25th November. The armed forces of Japan were told to be ready for war by 1st December. An ultimatum, which they knew would be unacceptable, was prepared to be presented to America on 25th November. In London Churchill persuaded the Admiralty to send the battlecruiser HMS *Repulse* and the battleship HMS *Prince of Wales* to the Far East. There were no escorts available so they sailed alone. On 26th November, as predicted, America told Japan that her ultimatum was not acceptable. On 2nd December all Japanese armed forces were told that war would begin on 8th December 1941.

To be sure of survival the Japanese deduced that they must seize Malaya, Java and Sumatra to secure the vital oil, tin, rubber and other raw materials that they must have to win the war. This meant war with Britain and the Netherlands could not be avoided and probably with America too. Japan reckoned that it must be a short war, since her industrial base could not support a long one. She also recognised that the main attacks must be over before the monsoon and she could not ignore totally her border with Russia despite the neutrality pact signed in the Spring. The attack plan was finalised by September and it envisaged five simultaneous operations:

- A surprise attack on Pearl Harbour to destroy the American Pacific Fleet.
- A move into Siam to secure a base for operations in Malaya and Burma.
- Landings in northern Malaya with a view to capturing Singapore.
- Air attacks on Luzon and attacks on Guam and Wake Islands to sever American communications with the Philippines in general.
- The capture of Hong Kong.

There was then to be a second phase which would:

- Secure the Bismarck Archipelago.
- Capture the whole of Malaya and Singapore.
- Occupy the airfields in southern Burma from Siam.

These operations were to be completed within a total of five months, that is by June 1942. The Japanese *15th Army* composed of *33rd* and *55th Divisions* would attack Siam and Burma; *25th Army* consisting of *5th, 18th and 56th Divisions* supported by *3rd Air Division* would attack Malaya while a reinforced *38th Division* would capture Hong Kong. So the battle lines were drawn and nothing could now stop what was to become one of the most fierce, cruel and bloody wars in modern history.

By December 1941 the Gunner order of battle in Hong Kong, Singapore, Malaya and later in Java and Sumatra was as set out at Annex A. The regiments were by no means fully trained, nor were Territorials who had been put together quickly and none was trained or equipped for jungle operations. From a gunnery point of view the jungle was certainly uninviting; almost no observation, difficult gun positions and difficult movement. Thus the role of artillery was limited. When they attacked, the Japanese relied on relatively small infantry guns, mortars and tanks for firepower and were always looking to conduct outflanking movements. The British field artillery, though at times highly effective in Malaya, was seldom able to make full use of its capabilities; the roads and tracks simply would not enable it to deploy and bring fire to bear in time against a fast moving enemy with air superiority. What is more, as in other theatres, commanders did not fully understand the importance of firepower and frequently the guns were not used as well as they could have been.

The field Gunners had the 25-pounder in increasing numbers but there were still many 18-pounders in action. The two medium batteries in Hong Kong had 6-inch guns while the mountain batteries had the 3.7-inch howitzer. The anti-aircraft Gunners in Hong Kong had a mixture of 12 x 3-inch semi-mobile and 4 x 3.7-inch mobile guns in four batteries. There was no radar. In addition there were 6 x 40mm Bofors guns and some machine guns. In Malaya/Singapore there were 54 x 3.7-inch, 22 x 3-inch, 4 x 4.5-inch and 77 x 40mm Bofors anti-aircraft guns but these batteries also lacked experience and were still busy organising themselves and engaged in basic training when the first attacks came.

The coast Gunners in December 1941 had 5 x 15-inch; 6 x 9.2-inch; 18 x 6-inch and 4 x 6-pounders organised into seven batteries in Singapore and 4 x 6-inch guns in one battery in Penang. In Hong Kong there were 6 x 9.2-inch; 10 x 6-inch and 4 x 4.7-inch guns organised into five batteries. The batteries in Singapore were deployed primarily to meet an attack from the sea and their primary arcs of fire therefore faced south, but most could traverse towards the mainland and had tasks facing north. Most of the ammunition, however, was armour piercing designed to deal with warships and although there was HE ammunition the scale was quite small. In Hong Kong the coast guns were also deployed against a sea attack, but again some had a degree of capability against an attack from China. In both places morale was good. Nearly everyone believed in the defences of Singapore and Hong Kong. For some reason no one really believed that they would be attacked.

Japan had been studying the problem of attacking Pearl Harbour since January 1941, but the plan was not approved until 5th November that year. It was based on the assumption that the American Pacific Fleet would be in harbour on the day of the attack, hence a Sunday was chosen. A strike fleet of carriers would approach as close as possible and then the actual attack would be carried out by aircraft. A northern approach was selected to ensure surprise. The *Combined Fleet Strike Force* consisted of six carriers escorted by two battleships and two cruisers and there were eight tankers. Five submarines moved ahead to give early warning. The fleet reached the take off point some 200 miles north of Hawaii at 0600 hours 7th December 1941 without having been detected. By 0715 hours some 360 aircraft had been launched consisting of torpedo, dive and high level bombers with fighter escorts and were racing towards that unsuspecting island base just getting up to a sunny Sunday off duty.

At Pearl Harbour all was quiet, there was a general radar scan every morning from 0400 to 0700 hours and all aircraft were at four hours notice to fly. There were no air defence batteries manned but the eight battleships, eight cruisers and 29 destroyers in the harbour mounted some 780 anti-aircraft guns between them although only one in four was manned. The raiders were detected by a mobile Army radar at 0700 hours at a range of 132 miles but were thought to be friendly and no action was taken. The first bombs fell at 0755 hours and surprise was complete. There was hardly any opposition, by 0945 hours it was all over. In less than two hours all eight battleships had been sunk or put out of action, together with three cruisers, three destroyers and a number of other vessels. 188 aircraft were destroyed on the ground, 2,403 men were killed and 1,178 were wounded. The Japanese lost 29 aircraft. It was a catastrophe for the Americans. Fortunately, however, the two American carriers were at sea and were neither found nor hit and this would cost the Japanese dear at Midway some six months later when they were defeated by these same ships.

At the same time as the attack on Pearl Harbour, attacks were launched on Hong Kong, Malaya and the Philippines. At 0930 hours (local) waves of Japanese bombers struck at the airfields of northern Luzon while a landing was carried out on Batan Island. More air attacks followed on Manila airfield at 1300 hours and these caught more American aircraft by surprise, doing terrible destruction. The main invasion began on 10th December with a landing at Lingayen Bay and Lamon Bay. Two divisions were ashore by 24th December and by then Mindanao had fallen and the Japanese were moving on towards the Netherlands East Indies.

Meanwhile, by 10th December, Guam, the Marshall Islands, Makin Island and the rest of the Gilberts including Tarawa were all taken. Then Wake Island was attacked on the 23rd and it was here that the Japanese faced a setback for a time. By 23rd January 1942 the Bismarck Islands had fallen and all was set for an attack on New Guinea. The Japanese had achieved more than their wildest hopes. Not only had they closed the ring in the east but they had done so with the greatest ease. Everywhere they had been victorious, nothing could stand in their way, they seemed invincible. The Americans were reeling, but at least they were in the war and nothing would be the same from then on. Once they pulled themselves together and set about the war with characteristic vigour and determination the tide would turn, but that seemed far away in January 1942. So the war in the Far East had started and we must turn next to the battles already raging in Hong Kong and Malaya and examine the part played in them by the Gunners of the Empire.

CHAPTER 2

THE LOSS OF HONG KONG

DECEMBER 1941

(Maps 3, 4 and 5)

The island of Hong Kong has an area of 29 square miles and is steep and rocky. Victoria Harbour lies on its northern shore facing Kowloon, beyond which lay the Leased Territories. It is 17 miles from the harbour north to the Chinese border. The Leased Territories, later known as the New Territories, cover some 400 square miles. They too are steep and rocky but with large valleys and flat areas which, in 1941, were covered in bamboo, pine and scrub. A single railway connected Kowloon to Canton and there were several roads. The population at that time was some 1.75 million, almost all Chinese. The winter months of December and January are relatively cool and dry. Water supply was a problem.

The defence plan was based on the principle of denying the use of the harbour to the Japanese if they attacked. Thus the idea was to fight a delaying action through the Leased Territories and then to hold a ring of high ground to deny enemy observation of the harbour basin. In mid 1941 the GOC British Troops in China, Major General AE Grasett, had only two British and two Indian battalions and he reckoned he must leave one on the island which left only three to span the breadth of the Leased Territories. There was not enough artillery to provide adequate firepower, let alone to cover obstacles and demolitions which reduced their value to a considerable degree. He also estimated that, in the worst case, all battalions might have to be withdrawn to the island after 48 hours, that during this period the harbour would have to be destroyed and the redeployment for the defence of the island completed.

For coast defence there were 29 guns, 8 x 9.2-inch, 15 x 6-inch, (including three on Stonecutters Island) 2 x 4.7-inch and 4 x 4-inch. These were manned by men of the 8th and 12th Coast Regiments RA, a mixture of British, Hong Kong-Singapore RA (HK-SRA) and Hong Kong Volunteer Defence Corps (HKVDC) troops. All possible landing places on the island were mined, wired and covered by beach lights, machine guns and 18-pounders. The idea was to defeat the landings on the beaches and prevent an enemy build-up. The island was divided into four defence sectors to ensure rapid reaction to a landing anywhere. Apart from a few target-towing Vildebeeste torpedo bombers and Walrus amphibians there were no combat aircraft in the colony. What is more there was an acute shortage of anti-aircraft artillery. Little was done to protect civilians from air attack but several thousand European and Indian women and children were evacuated, mostly to Manila and Australia, between June and November 1941.

In December 1941 8th Coast Regiment consisted of 12th, 30th and 36th Coast Batteries and had its Regimental Headquarters in Stanley Barracks. 12th Battery was at Stanley Fort, with 3 x 9.2-inch 35 degree guns and 30th at Bokhara Fort, with 2 x 9.2-inch 15 degree guns. These guns fired 380 pound shells. Their task was the seaward defence of the colony. 36th Battery was at Collinson, with 2 x 6-inch, and Chung Hum Kok Fort with another 2 x 6-inch guns, firing 100 pound shells. 12th Coast Regiment had 24th Battery RA at Mount Davis with 3 x 9.2-inch guns and 26th Battery HK-S RA on Stonecutters Island with 3 x 6-inch, and 2 x 60-pounders. There were another 3 x 6-inch guns at Jubilee and 965th Defence Battery RA at Belcher's Point, at the west end of Victoria, had 2 x 4.7-inch guns. Their task was to cover the sea approach to Lye U Mun and East Lamma Channel. All had secondary tasks to engage any enemy on the mainland as best they could.

Major General CM Maltby took over command in July 1941 and on 10th September Sir Mark Young arrived as the new Governor and Commander-in-Chief. The garrison at that time consisted of:

CRA: Brigadier Tom MacLeod

Regiment	Batteries	Commanders
8th Coast RA		Lt Col S Shaw
	12th Coast RA	Maj WM Stevenson
	30th Coast RA	Maj CR Templer
	36th Coast RA	Maj WNJ Pitt
12th Coast RA		Lt Col RJL Penfold
	24th Coast RA	Maj EWS Anderson
	26th Coast* (Stonecutters)	Maj AOG Mills
	(Jubilee Fort) HK-S RA	Maj WH Beaman
	965th Defence HK-S RA	Maj BTC Forrester
5th Anti-Aircraft RA		Lt Col FD Field
	7th HAA RA	Maj WACH Morgan
	17th HAA HK-S RA	Maj AR Colquhoun
	18th LAA HK-S RA	Maj C Rochfort-Boyd
	5th AA HKVDC	
1st Hong Kong HK-S RA		Lt Col JC Yale
	1st Mountain	Maj EWFdeV Hunt
	2nd Mountain	Maj JP Crowe
	3rd Medium	Maj HL Duncan
	4th Medium	Maj GES Proes
	25th Medium	Maj WT Temple

*20th Coast Battery RA was ordered, on 8th December 1941, to change its designation to 26th Coast Battery HK-S RA. In view of the date this change may not have occurred.

The infantry element of the garrison consisted of:
2nd Battalion The Royal Scots.
1st Battalion The Middlesex Regiment.
5th Battalion 7th Rajput Regiment
2nd Battalion 14th Punjab Regiment.

The Hong Kong Volunteer Defence Corps (HKVDC) consisted of light armour, artillery, engineer, signals, infantry, service, medical and pay units, a total of some 94 officers and 1,566 other ranks. Of these there were, by December 1941, 18 Gunner officers and 384 Gunners who became very closely associated with the Royal Regiment and were to behave with great distinction in the defence of the colony. They were organised as follows:

HKVDC	Officers	Other Ranks	Place & Armament
Artillery HQ	3	2	
1st Battery	3	65	D'Aguilar, 2 x 4-inch
2nd Battery	3	83	Bluff Head, 2 x 6-inch
3rd Battery	3	75	Aberdeen, 2 x 4-inch
4th Battery	3	94	Pak Sha Wan, 3 x 6-inch
5th AA Battery*	3	65	Saiwan

* Attached to 5th AA Regiment RA

The infantry battalions were under strength and not yet at the peak of training or fitness. The Hong Kong-Singapore Royal Artillery was a regular unit, a part of the Royal Artillery, manned from India, by arrangement with the Indian Army, for the defence of Hong Kong and Singapore. Officers and some NCOs were British and there were some Indian Viceroy's Commissioned Officers. Each mountain battery had one troop of 4 x 3.7-inch pack howitzers and one troop of 4 x 4.5-inch howitzers of First World War vintage. The medium batteries each had 4 x 6-inch howitzers which had also seen service in that war. Thus there were 8 x 3.7-inch pack howitzers, 8 x 4.5-inch howitzers and 12 x 6-inch howitzers. In total only 28 guns which had any mobile capability at all.

The idea of recruiting Hong Kong Chinese to serve as Gunners came to fruition in 1937 when 23 men were enrolled for training on Stonecutters Island under Major Brown, Lieutenant JH Monro, Sergeant Makel and Bombardier Silk. It proved to be a great success and training was extended in 1938 when Mr Cheung Yan-lun was appointed interpreter in the rank of sergeant. At the end of 1940 the force was about 150 strong and was located at Stanley. Its task was to supplement the manpower of 8th Coast Regiment. Another 150 were soon recruited and trained more specifically to help man the AA guns of 5th AA Regiment RA. The last batch were still under training at Stonecutters Island under, by then, Captain Monro when the Japanese attacked. By this time many were NCOs and Henry Chan was Battery Sergeant Major. Anti-aircraft equipments in the hands of 5th AA Regiment RA consisted of 12 x 3-inch semi-mobile, 4 x 3.7-inch and 6 x 40mm AA guns together with a varying number of light machine guns.

When General Grasett returned to England, on being relieved by General Maltby, he stopped off in Ottawa where he told the Chief of the Canadian General Staff that the addition of two or more battalions would make Hong Kong strong enough to withstand a Japanese attack for a prolonged period (Kirby). In November 1941, therefore, two more battalions arrived from Canada, the Royal Rifles of Canada and the Winnipeg Grenadiers, under the command of Brigadier John K Lawson. Unfortunately, neither of these new battalions was trained, having had only garrison experience, nor had they any transport. With their arrival, however, Maltby was able to alter his defence plan by putting three battalions on the island and three on the mainland where he also put part of his mobile artillery. Thus a meaningful plan to defend the island could be made while the mainland battle was being fought, but there was a desperate shortage of guns.

There was no question of defending the frontier itself as it was too long and too far away for such a limited garrison. A defensive line was therefore chosen to run from Gindrinkers Bay in the west, then on to the north of Golden Hill and Smuggler's Ridge, to Tide Cove and thence along the southern edge of the cove and southwards through the hills to Port Shelter (Map 3). This line was some 11 miles long and needed much work to make it effective as a defensive position. Since it was only three miles north of Kowloon it was to be held until a decision was made to withdraw to the island. There was no depth for a second fall-back position. The Gindrinkers Line was also overlooked from Tai Mo Shan and Needle Hill to the north of it.

The garrison of Hong Kong was divided into two brigades. First, the Mainland Brigade under

Brigadier Cedric Wallis consisting of 2nd Royal Scots, 2/14th Punjab and 5/7th Rajputs with 2nd Mountain Battery (4 x 4.5-inch and 4 x 3.7-inch howitzers), one troop 1st Mountain Battery (4 x 3.7-inch howitzers) and 25th Medium Battery (4 x 6-inch guns). One troop of mountain guns was allotted to each battalion and the mediums were superimposed across the whole front. In addition there were three static 6-inch howitzers and two 60-pounders, of the movable armament, on Stonecutters Island which could fire on some mainland targets. Thus for the size of front and strength of the likely threat, together with a total lack of air support, there was precious little firepower. The Island Brigade, under Brigadier JK Lawson, consisted of the Royal Rifles of Canada, the Winnipeg Grenadiers and the 1st Middlesex. They had one troop of 1st Mountain Battery (4 x 4.5-inch howitzers), 3rd and 4th Medium Batteries (8 x 6-inch guns) and 965th Battery of 18-pounders as beach defence guns. The total strength of the whole Hong Kong garrison was 12,000 men.

Work on the defences began in earnest in November with the arrival of the Canadians. A covering force of one company, a platoon of armoured cars of the HKVDC and the Punjab's carriers, was put forward to Fan Ling. The remainder prepared defences on the Gindrinkers main defence line. It would have taken two divisions to defend the line properly, so all that could be expected was to hold until the harbour had been destroyed and evacuation to the island completed. There was also a great shortage of transport for the rough hilly country where movement was slow anyway. The Royal Navy was to destroy the harbour facilities and then ferry the army across to the island. By mid November the garrison began to get reports of Japanese troops massing across the frontier. This was in fact the *18th, 38th, 51st and 104th Divisions*, forming Japanese *23rd Army,* and the artillery of three divisions (Maltby).

In December many non-combatants were evacuated to Singapore, lights were extinguished at night and vulnerable points were put under guard. But even on 6th December General Maltby did not think an attack was imminent. Nevertheless preparations were stepped up and by 0700 hours on 7th December all artillery reported ready for action while 26 merchant ships sailed for Singapore. Although life went on as usual, even though all militia men were told to report for duty, the population knew only too well that an attack was likely and there was much apprehension. By midnight all forces were at battle stations.

Early on 8th December General Maltby's intelligence staff intercepted a Japanese message warning all Japanese nationals that war was imminent. At 0500 hours a report was received from Singapore that Japanese landings had occurred in Malaya, then at dawn came the first reports that the Japanese were closing up to the Sham Chun River and approaching the frontier. By 0730 hours all bridges were blown by the engineers of the Hong Kong Volunteer Defence Corps. Then at 0800 hours on 8th December 1941, diving out of the sky came a wave of 12 Japanese bombers with 36 fighter escorts which swooped down on Kai Tak airfield and bombed and shot up all they saw. All five military and eight civil aircraft were destroyed, some bombs fell on Shamshuipo Barracks but there were few casualties. Meanwhile the Japanese Army crossed the Sham Chun River and advanced into the colony in two columns. The guns at Stonecutters and Mount Davis registered zones on the mainland and OPs took up their positions. By 1000 hours the 6-inch guns of 30th Coast Battery at Bokhara near Stanley were engaging an enemy destroyer. Later that day they were shelling Japanese infantry advancing down the Tai Po - Sha Tin road. It had been a very sudden change from peace to war.

The Japanese West Group, commanded by Major General Ito, consisted of the *228th Infantry Regiment*, under Colonel Doi, the *230th Infantry Regiment*, under Colonel Shoji, and three mountain artillery battalions. *229th Infantry Regiment*, under Colonel Tanaka formed the East Group. All were from *38th Division* commanded by Lieutenant General T Sano. At Shui Tau the West Group turned south east towards Chuen Lung while the East Group advanced on Tai Po. Here they were stopped by a successful ambush mounted by 'C' Company of 2/14th Punjab Regiment. Once under way again the Japanese did not hurry but worked their way forward led by local guides along tracks across the hills, always covered by their artillery which engaged anything which might hold them up. The British covering force, including the HKVDC armoured cars, fell back taking up a position on Grassy Hill at last light on the 8th. Dawn on 9th December saw the covering force back on Needle Hill with the Punjabis on Monastery Ridge to the east. The destruction of the harbour installations was ordered to begin. All day the enemy was held everywhere but the main attacks were yet to come. At 1120 hours 1st Hong Kong Regiment reported to Brigadier Tom MacLeod at HQRA that an enemy OP on Grassy Hill had been destroyed. 2nd Mountain Battery reported engaging an enemy working party and a light gun at Lo Wai. More targets were engaged at 1437 and 1740 hours. Seldom in the next three days were the guns of these mountain Gunners silent. No call for fire went unanswered, and by all accounts they were splendid. The 60-pounders on Stonecutters Island were by then within range and opened up effectively, controlled from an OP on Shing Mun with 'A' Company, 2nd Royal Scots. At last light Brigadier Cedric Wallis withdrew the covering force who had done their work admirably and had inflicted many casualties on the advancing enemy.

As darkness fell on 9th December there came reports that the enemy, in the shape of *229th Regiment*, was across Tide Cove approaching Buffalo Hill away to the right flank and closing on the Rajputs. Then at 2200 hours *228th Regiment* carried out a surprise attack on the vital Shing Mun Redoubt, immediately south of the Shing Mun (Jubilee) Reservoir, which guarded the approach to Smuggler's Ridge (Map 4). This was defended by a platoon of the Royal Scots and was also the location of an OP of 2nd Mountain Battery manned by Second Lieutenant WJ Willcocks. He immediately called for fire onto the Shing Mun River but the enemy closed onto the OP itself and were soon throwing grenades into it. The fight lasted for two hours but eventually the little force was overrun, two Indian Gunners were killed as the enemy broke in and the remainder were captured although they later escaped. The guns then brought down fire onto the redoubt and in front of the Royal Scots and the Rajputs. This fire was reported as very effective causing many Japanese casualties. Later the 9.2- and 6-inch batteries put down concentrations on the approaches to the reservoir. Wallis wanted the Royal Scots to counter-attack at dawn but their reserve company was only at half strength due to malaria and they felt they could not do so. When Maltby heard that the Shing Mun Redoubt had fallen he knew that he had few hopes of retaining his hold on the Gindrinkers Line.

Then at 0745 hours the Japanese mounted an attack, after a heavy bombardment, on the Rajputs' detached company on Smuggler's Ridge, south east of the redoubt, but were beaten off after an hour of tough close-quarter fighting. Wallis, mindful of his lack of reserves, withdrew the Royal Scots to new positions south west of Golden Hill, thus considerably shortening his line. 10th December was a day of considerable artillery activity by both sides. At mid-day a concentration was put down on Shing Mun Redoubt using the guns on Stonecutters Island with considerable effect. These guns were in turn engaged and attacked from the air suffering some damage and casualties. Though the Japanese shelled the Gindrinkers Line their infantry made no attempt to close. But, with the loss of the redoubt, Maltby, knowing that he would not be able to hold a major attack, set in hand plans to evacuate his forces from the mainland. During that night Hong Kong Island was shelled for the first time in Albany, Kennedy and Bowen Roads. A battery of Japanese 5.9-inch howitzers shelled the two 60-pounders on Stonecutters Island and also the battery on Mount Davis whose 9.2-inch guns were engaging enemy moving along Castle Peak road. The gunboat HMS *Cicala* joined in with her 6-inch guns and shelled Japanese working parties attempting to clear demolitions left by the British. She came under heavy fire and had to go into dock to effect repairs.

At 0800 hours in the morning of 11th December, a well co-ordinated and concentrated artillery and infantry attack fell onto the Royal Scots who were forced back to positions just north of Lai Chi Kok. The situation was then very serious. The guns of 2nd Mountain Battery, under Major James Crowe, were firing at very short range and all round defensive positions were adopted by the battery. Then at 1125 hours they were ordered to withdraw. The 4.5-inch troop was engaging targets at 600 yards. Next came orders to move with all speed to Hong Kong Island and all save one section of 2nd Mountain Battery reached the island successfully. That section tried to get through Beacon Hill railway tunnel but found it blocked, had to retrace its steps and was shelled as it emerged, losing one gun. An improvised flash spotting and gun locating line had been created to back up the Gindrinkers Line but it was lost when the withdrawal was ordered.

Meanwhile the Japanese were pressing on but could not dislodge two companies of the Royal Scots on the reverse slopes of Golden Hill even after some fierce hand-to-hand fighting. The guns on Stonecutters Island were themselves under artillery and air attack but kept up direct fire onto the Japanese attacking the Royal Scots just north of Lai Chi Kok. Then at 1500 hours came the order to evacuate Stonecutters Island. The guns were destroyed and all movable stores were back at the Naval Dockyard Kowloon by 0130 hours on 12th December. The Gunners had suffered several casualties from 40 direct hits but had done all they could to assist the battle on the mainland. In addition all Japanese attempts to land on Lamma Island were broken up by the fire of the guns at Aberdeen and Mount Davis Lower Battery. An attempt to land on Ap Lei Chau, where 3rd Battery HKVDC was located, was beaten off by machine gun fire. Then a fleet of about 100 junks was seen off Lamma Island and it too was broken up by the guns.

During that fateful afternoon much of the dockyard and the power station were destroyed, all remaining merchant ships were scuttled while evacuation across to the island went on all night. The situation in Kowloon was chaotic. The Royal Scots got away at 1930 hours and the rest of the brigade and the Punjabis followed. By this time over on the right flank the Sikhs and Punjabi Mussulmans of 1st Mountain Battery had moved back under cover of the fire from the guns on the island to Mau Lau Tong (Map 4) and were ready in action by 0400 hours 12th December. Then the Rajputs fought their way back to the gun line of 1st Mountain Battery. By 1500 hours the Japanese closed up but were beaten off by the guns on the island and those of 1st Battery whose OP was on Black Hill. During these operations the battery fired over 400 rounds from four guns. Throughout 12th December the enemy kept up heavy pressure on the Mau Lau Tong Line but with the greatest gallantry all attacks were beaten off. At 1800 hours orders were received to move to the island and this was done during the night. Unfortunately the lighters for the battery's mules and horses failed to arrive and these had to be left behind; nevertheless all guns, men and most of the ammunition were taken off. The loss of the mules was to severely restrict the battery's mobility in the subsequent fight for the island. The crossing was covered by the fire of the Bofors guns of 18th LAA Battery from the island. The men who got back were hungry, tired and thirsty but inspired by their ability to halt the enemy in hard fighting.

The enemy did not interfere with this part of the action and were without doubt surprised because it soon became clear that, at the very moment of the British withdrawal, they were planning a set piece attack. By the time it was launched the British had gone. Although they saw what had happened they were not flexible enough to call it off and their attack fell on vacated positions. The evacuation of Kowloon had been a near run thing. The rearguard was commanded by the indefatigable Lieutenant Nigel Forsythe of the 2/14th Punjab. He organised everyone including many Gunners into a final perimeter and defeated attack after attack. Finally Forsythe was the last man to board the last boat. He stood defiantly firing his Tommy gun as the boat pulled away from the jetty with the Japanese rushing forward to prevent its departure.

Although the withdrawal had been a success, the defence of the mainland had lasted only five days. However the harbour was of no more use as such and the Japanese had suffered severely while British casualties overall had not been heavy.

At 0945 hours on 13th December a launch, bearing a white flag, crossed to the island. It carried a staff officer bearing a letter from General Takaishi Sakai, commanding the Japanese *23rd (South China) Army*. This demanded that the defenders surrender with the threat of severe aerial and artillery bombardment if they did not do so. The Governor refused the summons. The Japanese artillery attack began and fire was directed at the town and the coastal batteries on the north shore of the island throughout the 13th and continued on the 14th. The Mount Davis Battery, with its 3 x 9.2-inch guns manned by 24th Coast Battery, was set ablaze and serious fires were started in the city, then the water mains were damaged beyond repair. One gun at Mount Davis was destroyed by a direct hit. 30th Coast Battery, at Stanley, engaged Japanese forces on the mainland landing one 9.2-inch shell in the middle of a battalion forming up and doing great execution. There was little naval activity on the part of the attackers, a few destroyers were seen on occasion, but Sergeant CBJ Stewart, of 30th Battery, refers to '. . . the action against a Japanese cruiser the HIJMS *Myoko* which we hit'. There was also a fifth column style attack on one of the anti-aircraft gun positions which failed. Then Belcher's Battery was ordered to sink all vessels lying against the Kowloon wharves, six were sunk and many more damaged and at 1330 hours the Waterfall Bay AA gun brought down an enemy seaplane.

The Japanese carried out a reconnaissance in force during the night 12/13th December but this was beaten off (Map 5). On the 13th December, 4th Battery HKVDC at Pak Sha Wan was heavily bombarded.

Hong Kong Island was divided into two brigade commands, East and West. East under Brigadier Wallis had 5/7th Rajput on the north shore from Pak Sha Wan to Causeway Bay. The Royal Rifles of Canada manned the seaward defences from D'Aguilar Peak northwards through Obelisk Hill then south to Stone Hill and Stanley Village. They had a reserve company covering the Lye U Mun Gap. Two companies of the Hong Kong Volunteers were also in reserve. There was one medium battery of 4 x 6-inch howitzers, one mountain troop with 4 x 4.5-inch howitzers and a second mountain troop with 3 x 3.7-inch howitzers in this brigade area. The main task of the guns was to cover the north east corner of the island where the main attack was expected and to destroy it on the beaches. The beach defences on each side of the isthmus at Stanley and Tai Tam Bay were strengthened by 2 x 18-pounders Mark I, which had been used as saluting guns, drawn from Ordnance that day. In West Brigade, Brigadier Lawson had 2/14th Punjab on the north shore from Causeway to Belcher's Point. The Winnipeg Grenadiers were on the south west coast with one company in reserve at Wong Nei Chong Gap. 1st Middlesex occupied the defences on Leighton Hill and the Fortress reserve was the 2nd Royal Scots near Wanchai Gap together with four companies of the Hong Kong Volunteers near The Peak. The remaining anti-aircraft guns were located at Wong Nei Chong Gap, Wanchai Gap and Aberdeen.

By this time the five batteries of the HKVDC were deployed, as part of 8th Coast Regiment, to cover possible landing places on the island as follows:

1st Battery	Cape D'Aguilar, 2 x 4-inch
2nd Battery	Bluff Head, Stanley, 2 x 6-inch
3rd Battery	Aberdeen Island at Ap Lei Chau, 2 x 4-inch
4th Battery	Pak Sha Wan, 3 x 6-inch
5th AA Battery	Saiwan Hill, Lye Mun

But the bombardment of Belcher's Battery began to have effect. The OP was put out of action by a direct hit wounding Second Lieutenant EH Field, the fort commander, mortally wounding Master Gunner Cooper and killing one and wounding two Indian Gunners. When this happened the remainder of the battery joined the local infantry with small arms. A counter-battery organisation was set up under Major GES Proes, but the rest of the army were not well trained on reporting enemy batteries and it was not very effective. The AA Battery at Mount Davis was badly hit, reducing it to firing only over open sights, and had nine men killed and six wounded. 4th Battery at Pak Sha Wan, under Captain Kenneth Barnett, and the Sai Wan battery were also hit, the former at about 1100 hours having its OP knocked out and both guns reduced to open sight firing after its instruments were hit, but under Master Gunner Cousins, its two remaining 6-inch guns were engaging enemy shipping in Kowloon harbour to great effect. The British guns were fighting back and many hits were recorded on enemy batteries on Stonecutters Island, Kowloon and Ma Lau Tong.

Meanwhile 1st Battery HKVDC under Captain FG Rees was at Cape D'Aguilar and 2nd Battery, with its 2 x 6-inch and 3 x 9.2-inch guns under Captain DJS Crozier, were engaging whenever they could. 3rd Battery under Captain CWL Cole was in constant action from its positions on Ap Lei Chau island. 5th AA Battery still sat on Sai Wan Hill near Lye Mun. Throughout 14th December all batteries were engaged in the fierce artillery duel which developed. 1st Battery engaged an enemy cruiser and forced it back out of range. Then the 4.7-inch guns at Belcher's Point were hit and put out of action. 4th Battery was again attacked by enemy guns but somehow remained in action with its two 6-inch guns, what was left of it was now part of the front line and its commander, Ken Barnett, was wounded but carried on.

At dawn on 15th December the Japanese began a systematic artillery, air and mortar attack which grew in intensity over the next four days, some of the fire was directed by fifth columnists on the island. At 0815 hours the Pinewood AA gun site was engaged by direct fire. One gun was destroyed and the predictor and height finder damaged. One man was killed and one wounded. At 1925 hours lookout men gave the alarm, the searchlights illuminated the water of the Lye U Mun Gap and three rubber boats carrying about 100 men were seen trying to cross. All units opened fire, the 6-inch battery firing 58 rounds. The landing was beaten off and no enemy landed. Ken Barnett's 4th Battery HKVDC was particularly complimented for its part in this action. The bombardment continued on the 16th with all guns firing continuously and many landing craft were engaged and set on fire. The Mount Davis Battery was hit and the plotting room put out of action. At 0925 the AA Section at Wong Nei Chong shot down an enemy aircraft and the Brick Hill section destroyed another at 1028 hours which crashed on Lamma Island. But the Saiwan AA Battery was badly hit that evening and had to be reinforced by men of 20th Coast Battery. After dark a Bofors gun at North Point, a 2-pounder near the Hong Kong Club and an 18-pounder were deployed right forward to cover the beaches. That day six 12-pounder naval guns and a 3.7-inch howitzer on a Mark 1 carriage had been drawn from the Royal Naval Dockyard. The latter went to 1st Mountain Battery and the former to 965th Defence Battery for deployment along the south shore thereby relieving 18-pounders and 2-pounders for the north shore. By this time the defenders were suffering from almost paralysing weariness, incessant shelling and lack of sleep.

Victoria was attacked by air at 0930 hours on 17th December. This was followed by heavy artillery attacks across the island. Then two motor boats carrying a white flag crossed the harbour with another demand to surrender issued by Lieutenant General Takaishi Sakai and Vice-Admiral Masaichi Niimi. The party was led by Colonel Tada and consisted of Lieutenant Mizuno and Mr Ottisu Dak, a diplomat. They were allowed ashore and were met by Major Charles Boxer who took their request to the Governor. This was again flatly turned down. Later in the day the Japanese could be seen assembling boats and barges in Kowloon and enemy air and artillery attacks increased in intensity. Much damage was done to the defences. The British guns were doing all they could to engage enemy wherever they were located. They had some notable successes against troops of *229th Regiment* moving down the Devil's Peak peninsula. In the early hours of 18th December Lieutenant JSM Winter of 1st Hong Kong Regiment tried to sink three freighters lying in Kowloon Bay with a 60-pounder which had to be run into an open position on the northern waterfront. One ship was hit but after some 30 rounds the enemy fire was so great that the gun had to be pulled back. The Japanese artillery attacks went on, Causeway Bay, North Point and Sau Ki Wan taking the brunt. Saiwan was both bombed and shelled. All day saw intense fifth column activity in the OP and battery areas and signals were being made from the island to identify targets to the enemy. At 2125 hours 4th Battery at Pak Sha Wan engaged launches around Devil's Peak village and several hits were achieved. By this time it was clear that the assault across the channel was imminent.

The attack came on the night of 18/19th December starting at 2030 hours; it was made by all three regiments of *38th Division* between Pak Sha Wan and North Point. *230th Regiment* on the right was directed at Victoria, *228th Regiment* in the centre against Mount Butler and then on to Repulse Bay and Colonel Tanaka's *229th Regiment* on the left against Mount Parker and then on to Stanley. Each regiment attacked with two battalions up and one in reserve and all landings were covered by very heavy enemy artillery attacks which caused many fires and a huge pall of smoke hung along the beaches providing excellent cover for the invaders. This was improved when the searchlight at North Point was put out of action. Nevertheless as the Japanese emerged from their boats onto the beaches the Rajputs and their mortars did much execution and the Gunners concentrated all available fire mainly on Tai Koo Dockyard and the Sugar Refinery, but it was not enough against an attack of this size. By midnight all six enemy battalions were ashore and pressing on inland. By 2255 hours they had reached Saiwan Fort and had overrun a 3.7-inch howitzer under Captain EA Bompass on the way. This officer rallied some Canadians and attempted to put in a counter-attack on the redoubt to recapture it and his gun, but it failed.

Captain Ken Barnett, commanding 4th Battery HKVDC, suspecting what the Japanese would do to Chinese in British uniform, told his men to disperse. One of them, Maximo Cheng, walked to Chunking and joined the Chinese Army there; an astonishing achievement.

It was at Saiwan Fort that the appalling massacre of 5th AA Battery HKVDC occurred. The Japanese surrounded it and demanded its surrender. Its commander had no option as he and his 29 remaining men were hopelessly outnumbered by several hundred Japanese. The enemy commander banged on the door of the fort and demanded that the garrison come out one by one. The Japanese infantry stood in a circle around the door with fixed bayonets grinning in anticipation. As each man came out he was bayoneted and thrown into a ditch. But Gunner Chan Yan Kwong was bayoneted across the stomach and Bombardier Martin Tso Hiu Chi in the thigh. Both men pretended to be dead. They survived the war and it was their evidence that helped sentence Colonel Tanaka to a long term of imprisonment in 1946.

4th Battery had opened fire at 2130 hours and was then attacked by Japanese infantry but for some reason the attack was not pressed. Lieutenant HT Buxton of 2nd Battery took a party of men from Pak Sha Wan to see what was happening at Lye Mun Barracks. Here they were challenged in English by a Japanese patrol and, as they advanced, all were killed by machine gun fire, save one who lived to tell the tragic tale.

Lieutenant General Sano, commanding *38th Division,* landed at 0100 hours and took direct command of operations. *3rd Battalion, 229th Regiment* had landed at Aldrich Bay and attacked Mount Parker while the *2nd Battalion* attacked Saiwan Hill and Lye Mun. *228th Regiment* moved onto Mount Butler after landing at Braemar Point while *230th Regiment*, under Colonel Shoji, crossed from Kowloon and landed at North Point coming under heavy machine gun and artillery fire from Causeway Bay. They eventually got ashore, assembled south of the Reservoir and advanced onto Jardines Lookout and Wong Nei Chong Gap. The Rajputs took the brunt of this operation and fought back magnificently, losing almost all their officers. 'D' Company under Captain Bob Newton faced Colonel Doi's men of *228th Regiment* and fought like tigers until all ammunition was expended. They then fought hand to hand with bayonets; only two men survived as no quarter was given. After the surrender, Bob Newton was found lying dead facing the enemy with an empty revolver in his hand and six dead Japanese around him.

When the enemy captured Saiwan Hill Brigadier Wallis ordered an immediate counter-attack using a company of the Royal Rifles of Canada and the two 6-inch guns still in action at Pak Sha Wan. It went in with great gallantry at 0130 hours but failed at the walls of the fort on the top of the hill. At about 0200 hours the order to retire to Mount Parker was given and the two 6-inch guns at Saiwan were put out of action by removal of breech blocks and dial sights.

Throughout that long night of bitter fighting a gallant band of older volunteers under a veteran, Colonel Owen Hughes, and known as the 'Hughesiliers' held out against all odds at the Power Station on the water front. They fought until overrun, by which time almost all had been killed, but they had held a superior enemy for many hours and were a constant thorn in the side of *228th Regiment*.

The loss of the Saiwan position was followed by the loss of the Lye Mun peninsula and the Lye U Mun Gap. Brigadier Wallis ordered the Royal Rifles to occupy Mount Parker but as they approached they found the Japanese already there. By dawn on 19th December the mobile artillery left on the island was deployed as follows:

6-inch howitzers:

two at Austin
two at Gough
two at Parker
two on Caroline Hill
two at Stanley Gap

4.5-inch howitzers:

two at Mount Kellett
two at Sanatorium
two at Tai Tam Hill
two at Red Hill

3.7-inch howitzers:

three at Stanley Gap
two at Gauge Basin
one at Tai Tam Fork

When Brigadier Lawson, commanding West Brigade, heard of the landings he ordered the Winnipeg Grenadiers to occupy Mount Butler, Jardine's Lookout and the Filter Beds. This they did but they were driven off the first two by first light on 19th December, though they retained the Filter Beds. He then ordered another company of the battalion to attack Jardine's Lookout and go on to Mount Butler. Meanwhile General Maltby ordered reinforcements to Wong Nei Chong Gap. Shortly before dawn the section of AA guns at this gap reported being attacked from the north, then there was silence and nothing more was heard of them. This battery was captured at about 0800 hours. The enemy then worked his way eastwards towards Gauge Basin, capturing the 6-inch and 3.7-inch howitzer positions at Stanley Gap and the 4.5-inch section at Tai Tam Hill. Early in the morning Second Lieutenant JA Trapman RA, at Wanchai Gap, spoke on the telephone to Major GES Proes RA at Wong Nei Chong. Major Proes said that he was wounded. Trapman also spoke to Captain JH Fox, Adjutant of 1st Hong Kong Regiment, who was shooting the battery from a forward OP. Then all communications with Wong Nei Chong were cut. Nothing was heard again of Majors WT Temple and GES Proes or Captain Fox and it is presumed that they were killed in these actions. Lieutenant BE Platts was also killed at the same time manning his OP near Jardine's Lookout. These Gunner officers had done much to keep some kind of cohesion in the battle so far and had paid the supreme sacrifice, manning their positions to the end.

By last light on 19th December the Japanese *229th Regiment* was across the Lye U Mun Gap and firmly on Mount Parker. *228th Regiment* was secure on Mount Butler and Jardine's Lookout. East Brigade, therefore, held a line running from Tai Tam Gap, Wong Nei Chong Gap to Causeway Bay. The Royal Rifles of Canada were in Tai Tam Gap with two companies of 1st Middlesex, two companies of the Hong Kong Volunteers and 2nd Mountain Battery by then at Tai Tam Hill. Lawson had a company of the Winnipeg Grenadiers and the men of 7th HAA Battery in Wong Nei Chong Gap, a platoon of Grenadiers at the Filter Beds, a company of Punjabis at the Mound and then his line stretched from Caroline Hill to the sea where were the survivors of the Rajputs and some of the Middlesex. Maltby next ordered Wallis to recapture Mounts Parker and Butler but Wallis said his force was so mixed up that he would be better to assemble them north of Stanley and then make a properly organised attack. Maltby agreed. At this time Brigadier Tom MacLeod, the CRA, was desperately trying to re-establish some co-ordinated artillery structure. He ordered Lieutenant Trapman to establish a headquarters for West Brigade's artillery at Wanchai Gap and for Major HL Duncan to come over from East Group's artillery to take command. This was completed by 2330 hours that night.

By 1000 hours that day the enemy had forced East Brigade back to Stanley and this meant that 30th and 36th Batteries at Collinson, Bokhara and Chung Hum Kok had to be destroyed and evacuated. The men went immediately to act as infantry in the defence of Stanley. At the same time the West Bay AA Section was ordered to Stanley. A 2-pounder at Tai Koo Dockyard was lost and the detachment escaped to Stanley. At the same time came orders to evacuate the Mount Parker, Gauge Basin, Tai Tam Fork and Red Hill Batteries to Stanley. Only one 3.7-inch howitzer from Tai Tam Fork reached Stanley because there was no transport. All the rest were put out of action by the detachments or by enemy action. At 1100 hours Captain Bompass and Second Lieutenant JSB Eddison engaged enemy in the vicinity of Gauge Basin over open sights until they were driven back by small arms fire at close range. One gun was destroyed and some parts of the second and two lorry loads of ammunition were got away. Captains Bompass and Feilden and Second Lieutenant Eddison displayed great bravery in evacuating wounded under heavy fire. At 1200 hours attempts were made to engage Wong Nei Chong Police Post but the crest problem prevented it.

By last light the situation at Wong Nei Chong was very confused. The British somehow clung on to Post Bridge and Ridge House. The former was held by a party of 1st Hong Kong Regiment under Major James Crowe and included Captains AG Atkinson, AS Avery, WH Hoyland, Lieutenant JSM Winter and 29 British and Indian Gunners. During the afternoon a party of 100 men from 1st Mountain Battery and 3rd Medium Battery, under Major Ted Hunt and Captain Feilden were ordered to clear some road blocks and then to assist in the attack on Wong Nei Chong Police Post. They arrived at 1925 hours and made several attempts to seize the Post but failed. Captain Feilden was killed and Lieutenant Colonel JLC Yale of the 1st Hong Kong Regiment was wounded and never seen again. Meanwhile Post Bridge held, but at a heavy cost, until the little garrison of Gunners were forced out by intense mortar fire at 2330 hours. Captain Avery died of wounds there and Major Crowe and Captain Atkinson were wounded. The party trekked across country and arrived at West Admin Pool at 0600 hours on the 20th December.

We must next return to the fortunes of West Brigade under Brigadier Lawson. At dawn on 19th December a company of Winnipeg Grenadiers advanced on Jardine's Lookout. With great gallantry they crossed the crest at the point of the bayonet and pressed on to Mount Butler where they held for several hours. Then, with all officers killed, the depleted company found itself surrounded. It was here that Company Sergeant Major JR Osborn was to win the Victoria Cross for extreme gallantry in action. Osborn lifted his men onto Mount Butler by sheer force of personality and leadership. He clubbed two Japanese to death with his rifle, wrested a sword from the hands of a Japanese officer and killed him with it. He then threw back grenades as they came in and fought with his fists while shouting encouragement to his men. They were soon down to 12 and then to six when a grenade fell among them. CSM Osborn could not reach it in time so he fell on it, dying as it exploded. By his magnificent gallantry he had willed his men to hold Mount Butler for eight hours and had given vital time to the defence to prepare for the next attack. The Japanese spared the lives of the five survivors out of sheer respect for their gallantry and all five survived the war. This small group of Canadians held the *228th Regiment* in spite of artillery and machine gun fire until nightfall. The remnants then slipped away and *228th Regiment* swept on and fought the action with the men of 7th HAA Battery previously recounted.

After this the *228th Regiment* linked up with the *230th* at Wong Nei Chong Gap and together they pushed on to Mount Nicholson. At 0730 hours a company of the Royal Scots got to within 100 yards of the gap and hung on all day. Then disaster struck; at 1000 hours West Brigade Headquarters came under attack and Brigadier Lawson was killed in its defence. He was last seen going out to face the enemy, a revolver in each hand. He died with the greatest gallantry fighting to the end, taking eight Japanese with him. Colonel Henry Rose of the HKVDC assumed command of the brigade. At 1330 hours Maltby decided on a general counter-attack from Victoria at 1500 hours, under the fire of the eight remaining field guns, directed at Mount Nicholson.

By a supreme effort the attack started on time but, at the Police Station just north of the Wong Nei Chong Gap, it met a withering fire and could go no further. To the north a Punjabi company was held at the Mound as were the Rajputs and the Middlesex on Leighton Hill. Although the objectives were not reached this attack stopped the enemy advance, but there were now no more reserves, very little artillery and all ranks were dead tired.

On the other flank, East Brigade's attack got under way at 0800 the next morning, 20th December. It first advanced along the main road to Repulse Bay and the Royal Rifles got onto the west end of Violet Hill. Then, using the remaining three mountain guns and one 18-pounder, they drove the enemy out of the grounds of the Repulse Bay Hotel, so relieving the women and children and two 3.7-inch howitzers which were there. The 18-pounder under Second Lieutenant EG Phillips played a major part in these operations engaging the enemy over open sights, destroying four mortars and causing him many casualties. The Canadians, however, could get no further because of intense fire coming from the Japanese positions on Stanley Mound and Point 362. Heavy rain fell at last light and Brigadier Wallis realised that there was real danger of this force being cut off. Accordingly he left one company at the hotel and withdrew the rest to the Stone Hill - Stanley Mound area. It was at this time that 12th Coast Battery, near Stanley Fort, which had been engaging targets with great effect, became part of the front line and engaged a Japanese headquarters over open sights blasting it to pieces. The battery had already fired 850 9.2-inch rounds.

Attempts were made to relieve Repulse Bay Hotel from the west but it was not possible. A further attack attempted to clear the Wong Nei Chong Gap but it also failed. Severe fighting went on all day at The Mound and the Japanese could make no progress. But as 20th December drew to a close the strain on the men was very great. They had had almost no rest since the fighting started, the weather had broken and they were disorganised having formed themselves into *ad hoc* groups. In spite of all this morale remained remarkably high. On the 21st, East Brigade attempted an attack on Tai Tam Gap and got as far as the bridge and Notting Hills. But Wallis could see that his men were at the end of their tether, almost all officers had been killed, and they were under severe artillery and mortar fire. He therefore reluctantly withdrew them, but this action did hold the Japanese for another day. The only artillery at Stanley by then were two 3.7-inch howitzers with an OP in the officers' mess. The ammunition situation was serious. Throughout the day fighting continued at Mount Cameron, Mount Nicholson and Repulse Bay. The Bluff Head and Stanley coast batteries engaged many enemy positions as the day wore on.

At 1030 hours on 21st December the gallant Captain Bompass led a fighting patrol to Red Hill to clear an enemy post which had been holding up operations at Tai Tam Fork and to withdraw a 4.5-inch howitzer which was also there. It went in with great vigour but Bompass, who had fought so hard both as Gunner and infantryman, was killed along with all other officers. Sadly the operation failed and the little force had to withdraw.

One of the great problems at this time was ammunition supply to the guns. Most was stored at Lye Mun Magazine but when this fell to the enemy the only supply came from the Little Hong Kong Magazine. Thus every night a party had to go, often through the enemy lines, to retrieve the vital ammunition. Outstanding in this respect was BQMS CE Barman of 25th Medium Battery. Night after night he led ammunition parties with great gallantry and devotion to duty, almost always successfully and then spent all the next day distributing the precious rounds to the guns. At all times his example was an inspiration to his men. In 1946 he was presented with the Military Medal by His Majesty The King in person, in Hong Kong, after his release as a prisoner of war.

It was then that Maltby ordered Major CR Templer to organise another attack on Wong Nei Chong from the Repulse Bay area. Templer gathered together an assortment of Canadians, Hong Kong Volunteers and Gunners and set off in a mixed bag of vehicles. He got to the final bend before the gap and was held up by heavy fire. Here he held until last light before withdrawing to the hotel. The fighting around Repulse Bay over these two days had been particularly vicious. It had given the Japanese a severe shock and had cost them dear, as many of their subsequent reports testify. At this stage West Brigade tried again but suffered heavily on Mount Nicholson. Then, during the afternoon and after more fierce fighting, the Punjabis and the Royal Scots were forced off the Mound. Yet, despite great pressure from their commanders, the Japanese could not advance further that day. The remaining British, Canadian, Indian and Hong Kong soldiers were fighting with the greatest tenacity despite their desperate fatigue, disorientation and severe casualties. By this time the force around the Mound consisted of several hundred Gunners fighting as infantry. But fatigue was very great, ammunition was running out fast, all reserves had been committed, some more than once, and casualties were heavy.

At the Repulse Bay area, Maltby was deeply concerned about the safety of the women and children cut off in the Repulse Bay Hotel. It is said that he called Major Templer on the telephone and said, 'Bob, there's a hell of a mess at the hotel, go and clear it up!' Taking another small force of Canadians, Hong Kong Volunteers and Gunners, Templer got into the hotel. Here he went through it like a dose of salts, organising it for defence. He transformed the muddle he found, never slept and tirelessly personally led the fighting patrols each day. His energy, courage and devotion to duty inspired everyone. He was looked after by his indefatigable Bombardier Harry Guy who, on the evening of 21st December came up to him and said, 'Sir, there are Japs in the West Wing!' 'The devil there are', said Templer, 'Come on, let's chuck them out.' They went and bowled hand grenades down the carpeted corridors and did so; 'An exhilarating experience.' said Templer after the war.

By the evening of 22nd December the hotel was surrounded again and ammunition was fast running out. Templer said, 'I then had to give the worst conceivable order, to go and leave the women and children.' This he did. 'The awful shame I felt,' said Templer but it had to be done. He got his force back to Stanley to fight on. The women and children became prisoners, surrender was in fact the only way to save their lives.

At this stage Brigadier Wallis was trying to organise a defensive position around Stone Hill and Stanley Mound. This was attacked with vigour but it held. At dawn on 22nd December the Japanese held Brick Hill, Point 143, Mount Nicholson, the Mound and the eastern end of Causeway Bay. They were faced by the weary men of West Brigade. The small group of Winnipeg Grenadiers surrounded at Wong Nei Chong Gap still fought fiercely but in the end were forced to surrender later in the day when all ammunition ran out. Maltby paid special tribute to them and the Japanese report of this action states, 'The enemy fire from these positions was so heavy that not only was the advance checked, but our troops were thrown into confusion'. (Kirby). Only 37 Canadians were left, all of them wounded. Throughout the 22nd the Japanese made no move but their aircraft and mortars were very active and eliminated many pockets of British resistance.

Also on 22nd December orders were received from London to destroy all oil installations. Accordingly that morning the Gunners destroyed the Texaco Oil Depot and the Tai Koo and Kowloon Naval oil tanks. The one at Lai Chi Kok was left because it was close to a hospital. Later on Major JP Crowe returned to duty from hospital and assumed command of RA West Group. At 1027 hours a Bofors gun on the cricket ground was shelled and forced to withdraw to the grounds of Government House, later that night it moved to the Victoria Recreation Club.

Over in the east many targets were engaged by an 18-pounder of 965th Defence Battery over open sights from a position on the main road just north of Stanley View. It then came under heavy fire and its ammunition truck was hit and the towing vehicle broke down. With great gallantry and with the aid of some infantry, this gun was man-handled back up the road to Stanley View. Later it had to be abandoned when it was destroyed. Meanwhile two 18-pounders shelled the Tai Tam Road area while the 3.7s engaged the enemy on Red Hill, Twins and Stanley Mound with direct fire. Ammunition was by then very scarce but some 40 rounds came in that night by boat.

In West Brigade at 2200 hours the defenders around Mount Cameron heard the unmistakable noise and shouting of a fresh Japanese attack, this time with fresh troops. The weary men of West Brigade again rose to the occasion but the enemy came on with great ferocity and the remnants of the brigade were forced back to Magazine Gap. Major James Crowe established a mobile artillery headquarters at Wanchai Gap and did all he could to co-ordinate fire from his few remaining guns. A withdrawal from Bennett's Hill to Aberdeen could not then be avoided. Then for some reason the Japanese halted and did not follow up. But throughout the day fighting went on along Hennessy, Perceval and Blue Pool Roads. Crowe's problems were very great. He had almost no officers left to direct fire in highly complex situations, he had great difficulty maintaining communications, there were major crest clearance problems and he had no reliable information on the location of the enemy or his own troops. But that night, miraculously, the ammunition convoy from Little Hong Kong arrived yet again with five loads; a great improvement. Throughout 23rd December fighting raged on, in and around Victoria, on the western slopes of Mount Cameron and Little Hong Kong. It was on this day that the Japanese were forced to bring up the last reserve battalion of *38th Division* in order to clear Victoria on the 24th. It had been much more difficult than they had expected.

Meanwhile, at Stanley, the Royal Rifles of Canada attacked and drove the enemy off Stone Hill and Stanley Mound but they could not withstand the terrific Japanese artillery attacks which followed and they were driven back into Stanley Village. Again the Japanese did not follow up, but they kept up an incessant artillery bombardment. The British guns did what they could. 2nd Battery HKVDC, at Bluff Head, engaged the enemy on Stanley Mound while Stanley Battery took on Tai Tam Gap. The men of 30th and 36th Coast Batteries were in the line as infantry. They occupied positions from the pumping station to Stanley itself and were constantly in action with small arms until the surrender. They had 14 killed and 26 wounded.

By this time the Royal Rifles were exhausted. They had fought non-stop for five days and nights; for a part-trained battalion they had been magnificent. Wallis decided to pull them right back to rest and to replace them with a mixed group of Middlesex and Hong Kong Volunteers. A new enemy attack came in at noon but again it was held this time by the Winnipeg Grenadiers and again the Japanese artillery kept up its pounding of the weary defenders. A shell hit the water tank and water had to be severely rationed. The Royal Scots were down to 175 men, artillery and mortar attacks were incessant and there were continuous low level air attacks.

The situation in West Brigade was most serious. On Leighton Hill the Middlesex Regiment, the famous 'Die Hards' were shelled and attacked on all sides. The Rajputs fought furiously on Mount Parrish and across on the north west corner of the Race Course. Again the Japanese could not follow up and they postponed their final attack to 25th December. On the 24th the section of guns on Mount Kellett had to pull back to Peak School and great difficulty was experienced in maintaining communications with the one remaining OP at Upper Levels. At 1300 hours a party of 50 Gunners of 12th Coast Regiment went to reinforce the Middlesex in the firing line. Lieutenant AE Clayton was in command but was killed leading them forward on Canal Road at about 1930 hours. That evening another Bofors gun went to assist the infantry at Graingegower Cricket Club and was most effective. In the evening an OP was established in the top flats of the Hong Kong & Shanghai Bank building to get observation over North Point and Happy Valley. It had a direct link to Fortress and RA West Headquarters. During the night of 24/25th December the enemy renewed his attacks on the gallant Middlesex and Gunners on Leighton Hill. The defenders had been joined by more Volunteers and Prison Warders but after savage fighting they were all overrun. They had done their best to the very end and stood their ground, going down fighting as hard as ever.

At Stanley the end was in sight. A defensive line was established with a platoon of Middlesex and 1st Battery HKVDC between Ma Kok and the Tun Tau Wan roads and with Lieutenant HS Jones's section at the entrance to St Stephen's College, near Barton's Bungalow. All communications were severed at noon. In the afternoon Bluff Head Battery which had taken such a heavy toll of the Japanese, was itself the target of a massive artillery attack. No 2 gun ammunition recess was blown away and the gun put out of action.

During the night the enemy launched vicious attacks against this little force with machine guns, grenades and the bayonet. 1st Battery's defence of Barton's Bungalow must go down as one of British artillery's finest hours. They beat off attack after attack. The Japanese brought up flame throwers and mortars but still the battery held although badly depleted in numbers. It became a fight to the finish and no quarter was given as the Japanese rushed in regardless of casualties and bayoneted everyone they found alive or dead. In the end they wiped out this gallant band of 30 Hong Kong Gunners but at an awful cost. Their own dead were piled along the ridge around the bungalow and were counted in hundreds. The men of the 1st Battery HKVDC had, like their comrades in the Middlesex, died hard. Lieutenant HS Jones RA, Lieutenant KE Muir RA and 33 men were killed and Captain FG Rees RA and three men were wounded. These figures alone are testimony of the ferocity of the fighting. It was probably during this action on 24th December that Lance Bombardier John Bullen, of 1st Hong Kong Regiment HK-S RA, 'displayed great courage and outstanding leadership at a difficult time. In the absence of officers or senior N.C.Os, he inspired his comrades to prolong their resistance to a Japanese attack and finally lost his life whilst enabling some of the survivors to withdraw from an untenable position.' (from the citation for a posthumous mention in dispatches based on eye witness accounts received by the War Office in 1954 and recorded in *Gunner* magazine in 1955).

During the night a 2-pounder of 965th Battery engaged an enemy machine gun using the light of a searchlight. The light was quickly put out of action and in the darkness the gun was overrun. Another 2-pounder near Stanley Police Station disabled three enemy tanks coming along South

Bay Road. In trying to hold its position this gun was also overrun in the darkness. A third 2-pounder got back to Stanley Fort and many of the men from the two guns that were lost also found their way back. Four 18-pounders were trapped by close range machine gun fire and could not be got out. This left only the two 3.7s in Stanley. At 1445 hours came reports that Brick Hill AA section was surrounded and under heavy attack. This gallant section held all night but was overrun at 0730 hours on 25th December; Captain HB Bartram was killed engaging the enemy at point blank range with a Tommy gun. The only survivors were Lieutenant GH Fairclough who was wounded and took refuge in a cave for three days and was captured only after hostilities had ceased, and one British Gunner who swam to Aberdeen with a few Indian Gunners. For the rest of the night the Japanese kept up a merciless artillery attack right across the front.

It was a tragic Christmas Day that dawned in Hong Kong in 1941. In Victoria the day broke with more heavy shelling and mortar fire in Happy Valley, Gloucester Road and Wanchai. Yet another Bofors gun had crept forward in the night to assist the gallant Middlesex at Wanchai. Early that day Major CM Manners, a retired Gunner, and Mr AHL Shields, both of whom had been captured, were ordered by the Japanese to tell the British of the futility of further resistance while the Japanese promised a cease fire until noon. In fact they continued to shell and dive bomb Gloucester and Hennessy Roads, Mount Kellett, Austin and The Peak all morning. Maltby would have none of it and was busy planning another counter-attack. During the afternoon, however, his worst fears were confirmed; the situation was indeed grim. Most positions had been lost. He had only eight guns left and their ammunition was low. After much thought and with a heavy heart, at 1515 hours he was forced to advise the Governor that further resistance was not possible. After discussion with his Defence Council and his other commanders, Sir Mark Young was forced to agree and with much regret he ordered Maltby to arrange a cease fire.

Sporadic fighting went on at Stanley until, at about 2000 hours, a party from Fortress Headquarters was allowed through by the Japanese to inform the garrison that an unconditional surrender had been agreed. The Gunners then set about the destruction of their remaining guns which were no longer fit for action. They were ordered to wait by Brigadier Wallis until he had received written confirmation of the surrender. That evening at the Peninsular Hotel the Governor and Commander-in-Chief Hong Kong, Sir Mark Young, formally surrendered the Crown Colony of Hong Kong to Lieutenant General Takaishi Sakai, commanding Japanese *23rd Army*.

At the time of surrender there were nine guns still in action in the Colony; two 6-inch howitzers at Austin, two 6-inch howitzers at Gough, two 4.5-inch howitzers at Peak School and two at Sanatorium, one of which was out of action, and the two damaged 3.7-inch howitzers at Stanley. Many others were in place but were damaged either by enemy action or because they had been disabled.

Next followed unspeakable horror as Japanese soldiers shot and bayoneted prisoners and wounded alike. In the British Military Hospital they systematically bayoneted each wounded man in his bed and one surgeon as he was in the middle of an operation. They then took the nurses away in an orgy of rape before killing them. In Happy Valley Hospital, the converted Jockey Club, there was a giant artilleryman called 'Geordie' remembered by those who survived as some 6' 5" tall. As the Japanese entered the hospital wards and started bayoneting his comrades, he rose in a fury, his face covered in bandages from shrapnel wounds, and rushed at a Japanese officer who drew his sword and took a swipe at Geordie's head but Geordie ducked with remarkable agility. 'Do tha' agen,' he said, 'An' I'll break your ******* neck'. He did but Geordie was too quick for him and grabbed his wrist and the sword clattered to the floor. Five or six Japanese soldiers rushed forward and clubbed and bayoneted the gallant Gunner who held the officer round the neck and did not let go until a sharp crack showed that he had carried out his threat. Geordie then sank to the floor and died in a pool of his own blood. No one remembers his name now, but we must never forget such courage.

News of the loss of Hong Kong after only 18 days of fighting came as a shock to London. The Japanese attack had been well-planned, based on good intelligence built up over a period of years. It was carried out by well-trained, battle hardened and brutal troops. They did not outnumber the British in infantry but they had far more guns and they had complete control of the air. Their commanders were well trained at the operational level and their formations had also trained at that level. The British were not well-trained in all arms tactics; rather they were a collection of units hastily cobbled together on an *ad hoc* basis. Furthermore there was nothing like enough firepower for a garrison of this size. Additionally, there was a total lack of air power and virtually no sea capability, so reasons for the failure are not hard to find.

During the battle the loss of the Shing Mun Redoubt on the mainland was a serious blow but, in retrospect, not really as serious as it appeared at the time. It caused an early withdrawal, before the island defences were ready. The Japanese had little trouble establishing themselves ashore on Hong Kong Island. They then avoided any centre of resistance and encircled wherever they could. This enabled them to split the defence very early on and was helped by the very early withdrawal of East Brigade, which in turn ensured that contact was lost with West Brigade. In addition, there was no really strong force at Wong Nei Chong Gap and this enabled the Japanese to become established there without too much difficulty. Finally the British were simply not well enough trained to mount rapid counter attacks, so vital against an enemy struggling ashore. Nor did Gunner or Infantryman understand how to concentrate the fire of the few guns there were and these in turn tended to fight their own individual battles, albeit with great gallantry. As it was the counter-attacks that were mounted were composed of scratch troops and were too weak to be effective.

All this said there, was no shortage of gallantry and good leadership at unit level. British, Canadians, Indians and Hong Kong Volunteers of all cap badges fought with great ferocity and taught the Japanese many a lesson. The Gunners were a great credit to their Regiment. They fought their guns as hard as they could in some of the worst ground for artillery anywhere, frequently over open sights and at point blank range. They lost nearly all their officers leading from the front and in the end the majority turned to help their hard pressed comrades of the infantry as one by one their guns were lost or knocked out. Major Bob Templer was to receive a well earned DSO. He mentions the gallantry of Sergeant Stewart of his battery who in turn singles out Bombardier Stone and Gunner Blackwell. There was Major Ted Hunt, a distinguished Horse Gunner, who fought his mountain battery with great skill on the mainland and then got them all back to resist to the bitter end. When he heard of the surrender he went off towards the enemy with a Tommy gun under each arm and was never seen again; his name like so many others is on the walls of the Saiwan Military Cemetery. Also there lies a British Lance Bombardier and a Gunner next to Sikhs and Punjabi Mussalmans of the Hong Kong-Singapore Royal Artillery. In 1973 Brigadier CR Templer, who in 1941 had commanded 30th Coast Battery, and had done so much to save those in the Repulse Bay Hotel, erected a Memorial in St Barbara's Church at Stanley Barracks to the fallen of 8th Coast Regiment.

Also there are the names of the Hong Kong Chinese Gunners of 965th Defence Battery who fought alongside the men of 8th Coast Regiment with such great gallantry in Collinson, Pak Sha Wan and Chung Hom Kok and the men of 1st and 5th Batteries HKVDC who fought and died at Barton's Bungalow and Saiwan Fort. The memorials include the one to Gunner J Flanders who was killed in the church itself and to 27 more who were to die in captivity and a further 103 officers and men of 8th and 12th Coast Regiments who died when a ship taking them to Japan was sunk by a US submarine. All in all 74 officers and 814 men of the Royal Regiment were killed or captured in the defence of Hong Kong. The location, movement and fate of the guns of Hong Kong is given at Annex B.

The British lost in all some 4,500 battle casualties in Hong Kong and, if the number taken prisoner is included, the total loss was nearly 12,000; the Japanese recorded the loss of about 2,700 but there are reasons for thinking this an underestimate. Churchill wrote, in the third volume of *The Second Word War*, 'Under their resolute Governor, Sir Mark Young, the colony had fought a good fight. They had won indeed the "lasting honour" which is their due'. The Chiefs of Staff had demanded that they resist as long as possible, which they did but had not then been able to give them the means to do so for more than a very limited period. They had done all they could to obey that order. Many who were captured were yet to suffer great hardship as prisoners of the Japanese and many died in captivity and the great majority continued to show heroism and resilience. The small band of Gunners did not have enough guns to have a real impact on the battle but they did their best in appalling conditions and lent their hands to many tasks other than their own, with considerable effect. They can be very proud of what they achieved.

CHAPTER 3

THE BATTLE FOR MALAYA

DECEMBER 1941 - JANUARY 1942

(Maps 6, 7, 8, 9 and 10)

The Malay Peninsula is some 400 miles from north to south and varies from 60 to 200 miles in width. In 1941 it was covered by primary and secondary jungle, rubber plantations and other cultivated land. The coastal areas were, in many places, covered by mangrove swamps but there were many large open beaches and river estuaries. Where cultivation had been abandoned, secondary jungle was very thick and virtually impassable although this did not apply to the large tracts of primary jungle and the plantations. Rainfall is heavy, especially in the two monsoon periods of June to September and November to March; it was this latter, the north east monsoon, that concerns us here. Besides heavy rain the temperature is high and the humidity very high. There was a single track railway from Singapore to Bangkok running along the west side of the country and another which followed the centre of the peninsula turning east to Kota Bharu before joining the western line inside Siam. The road system was extensive. The bulk of the population were Malays and Chinese in about equal numbers and there were many Indians. There was also a small but significant number of Japanese citizens, some of them servicemen *incognito*, who set up an intelligence organisation of great value to the invader. Many Malays and Chinese made themselves available for military service when the war started. There were about 18,000 Europeans, mostly British, engaged in Government service, rubber planting, mining and commerce. Some efforts had been made to organise civil labour for defence tasks but little had been achieved when the attack came.

In the armed forces at the time of the Japanese attack there were only 158 aircraft in RAF, RAAF and RNZAF hands and also some from the Royal Netherlands East Indies Army Air Corps. Most were obsolete; this against a stated requirement of 566. Army forces consisted of three divisions, the 8th Australian and the 9th and 11th Indian. Each division had only two brigades. In addition there were two Fortress Brigades in Singapore, a battalion in Penang and another in Sarawak. There were also some locally enlisted units, Chinese and Malay. The total strength was about 88,600 of which some 19,600 were British, 15,700 Australian, 37,000 Indian and 16,800 locally enlisted. Of all these only 4,612 were Gunners.

By 1st December 1941 the Gunners in Malaya and Singapore were:

9th Indian Division

GOC: Major General AE Barstow.

CRA: Brigadier EW Goodman*.

5th Field Regiment (63/81st & 73rd Btys). Lt Col EWF Jephson.

88th Field Regiment (351st & 352nd Btys). Lt Col SC D'Aubuz.

*Brigadier Goodman acted as senior Artillery officer in the whole theatre and later became BRA Malaya.

11th Indian Division

GOC: Major General DM Murray-Lyon (Maj Gen ACM Paris from 24th December 1941).

CRA: Brigadier AE Rusher.

137th Field Regiment (349th, 350th & 501st Btys). Lt Col GD Holme.
155th Field Regiment (B and C Btys**). Lt Col A Murdoch.
22nd Mountain Regiment (4th, 7th, 10th & 21st Btys). Lt Col GL Hughes.
80th Anti-Tank Regiment (2nd, 215th, 272nd & 273rd Btys)***. Lt Col WES Napier.

** A Bty was left in India and later served in Burma.
*** This regiment was formed at Hitchin on 20th July 1941. 2nd Battery came from 13th Anti-Tank Regiment, 215th Battery from 54th (Queen's Own Royal Glasgow Yeomanry) Anti-Tank Regiment, 272nd Battery from 68th (Duke of Wellington's) Anti-Tank Regiment, and 273 Battery from 69th Anti-Tank Regiment.

8th Australian Division

GOC: Major General HG Bennett

CRA: Brigadier CA Callaghan (Lt Col CA McEachern from 8th February 1942)

2/10th Field Regiment (20th, 29th & 30th Btys). Lt Col AW Walsh.
2/15th Field Regiment (19th, 60th & 65th Btys). Lt Col JW Wright.
2/4th Anti-Tank Regiment (13th,14th,15th & 16th Btys). Lt Col CA McEachern.

12th Indian Brigade

122nd Field Regiment (278th & 280th Btys). Lt Col G St JA Dyson.

Anti-Aircraft Artillery

1st HAA Regiment HK-S RA (6th, 9th, & 10th Btys). Lt Col AE Tawney.
2nd HAA Regiment HK-S RA (11th, 12th & 13th Btys). Lt Col HW Allpress.
3rd HAA Regiment RA (11th, 29th and 30th Btys). Lt Col FE Hugonin.
3rd LAA Regiment HK-S RA (14 & 16 Btys). Lt Col DV Hill.
5th Searchlight Regiment RA (13, 14, SSVC, 315 & 316 Btys). Lt Col RAO Clarke.
1st Indian HAA Regiment (2, 3 and 4 HAA Btys and 1 and 5 LAA Btys). Lt Col JR Williamson

Coast Artillery

7th Coast Regiment (11th & 31st RA & 5th & 7th HK-S RA Btys). Lt Col HD St G Cardew.
9th Coast Regiment (7th, 22nd & 32nd Btys). Lt Col CP Heath
Detachment HK-S RA (2 x 6-inch guns) Sarawak.
Detachment HK-S RA (1 x 6-inch gun) Christmas Island.

Singapore Royal Artillery Volunteers

Individuals posted to several units.

Federated Malay States Volunteer Force

Light Battery (4 x 3.7-inch howitzers)

To meet the requirements of the Middle East, Iraq and Malaya, the Indian Army had, by 1941, quadrupled itself. This resulted in milking units of trained officers, non-commissioned officers and men to form new ones and their replacement by inexperienced war-commissioned officers, non-commissioned officers and men. Inevitably this had a serious effect on unit standards and efficiency. The British units in India had been on garrison duty for many years and also had to send reinforcements to other units in India, the Middle East and even to the UK when the war started. Accordingly their efficiency was also reduced. Commanders and staffs were not trained above unit level and had little idea of how to conduct war at the operational level. Nor were new arrivals trained in the arts of jungle warfare or battlecraft in light mobile operations in Far East conditions of terrain and climate. Furthermore Headquarters Far East Command consistently played down the fighting qualities of the Japanese. All this was then compounded by the piecemeal arrival of regiments and the cobbling together of units and sub-units which had never met before, let alone trained together. Thus cohesion and all arms training at brigade and divisional level hardly existed. Finally, the lack of organised civil labour and the refusal of London to authorise its use meant that the servicemen, who should have been training to rectify these deficiencies, were themselves employed on the construction of defences.

The Japanese, on the other hand, had been specially trained for the invasion of Malaya. Their tactics were based on surprise, using roads for speed and encircling movements to overcome defensive positions and to get inside the defenders' decision-making cycle. They planned to use tanks in the lead followed by infantry, covered by as much artillery as they could deploy well forward, and at all times to have air superiority. Against such tactics the British had no answer. It would have required professional soldiers of many years hard training to be able to meet such attacks. But Britain had run down her defences when she could see no threat, so that right up to 1939 there were never enough troops to do more than meet emergency tasks and to police the Empire. Co-ordinated training at formation level was seldom carried out. In addition the British were short of tanks, anti-tank guns and anti-aircraft guns. The one bright spot was that 8th Australian Division did manage a considerable amount of all arms training at the higher level and by the outbreak of the fighting was in a good state of training, though under strength.

General Percival ordered Lieutenant General Sir Lewis Heath to defend northern Malaya and gave him 9th and 11th Indian Divisions and 28th Indian Infantry Brigade with which to do so, thus constituting 3rd Indian Corps. He ordered 8th Australian Division to prepare to defend Johore and Singapore, with 1st and 2nd Malay Infantry Brigades in Singapore and 12th Indian Infantry Brigade in reserve. In the north, General Heath had his hands tied because he had to defend the airfields which had been so badly sited for defence and which forced him to spread his meagre forces. Thus 8th Indian Infantry Brigade was sent to Kota Bharu and 22nd Indian Infantry Brigade to Kuantan. Similarly on the west coast he was forced to deploy 6th Indian Infantry Brigade to Kedah and 15th Indian Infantry Brigade to cover Alor Star airfield on ground unsuitable for defence and easily outflanked by enemy landings further south. To offset this he put 28th Infantry Brigade right back at Ipoh to give depth and effective reserves. Finally, Percival ordered beach defences to be built on Singapore island and at Mersing, Kuantan and Kota Bharu on the eastern side of the peninsula, and defensive positions to be prepared at Jitra and Kroh in the north.

On 3rd December HM Ships *Prince of Wales* and *Repulse* , which had arrived in the theatre with escorts but no aircraft carrier to provide protective air cover, docked in Singapore .

In July 1941 the Japanese occupied southern Indo-China so that they were then poised to attack Siam and/or Malaya. In August came reports that they were building airfields and assembling landing craft, yet still the Foreign Office did not believe that they intended to attack. But by November the signs were more ominous and all troops were brought to a higher state of alert. At this time there was a plan, Operation MATADOR, designed to allow British troops to move into Siam and seize Singora to forestall an invasion, but only if the Japanese invaded that country first. To be effective, obviously, MATADOR had to be ordered in time. Thus on 29th

November when the men of the 3rd Indian Corps were put on 36 hours notice to carry out MATADOR they could do nothing but stand and wait for the order to move. Intelligence was then received from America that the Japanese had plans to attack without warning on 1st December to provoke Britain into invading Siam as the first aggressive act. The Chiefs of Staff told the Governor that he could order MATADOR when invasion was imminent without further reference to them.

Meanwhile the Japanese Government had detailed Lieutenant General Tomoyuki Yamashita to prepare to attack Malaya and Singapore with his *25th Army* consisting of *5th, 18th, 56th* and *The Imperial Guards Divisions* (Map 6). In the event *56th Division* did not fight in Malaya but went to Burma. *5th Division* was to be the spearhead with landings at Singora and Patani while *56th Infantry Regiment of 18th Division* was to land at Kota Bharu. *11th and 41st Infantry Regiments* were to advance on Alor Star while *42nd Regiment* was to attack Kroh from Patani. *5th Division* was to capture the airfields of Kedah and then to seize Kuala Lumpur. Meanwhile *56th Regiment* was to capture the airfields of Kota Bahru and then to advance to Kuantan. While all this was happening, *15th Army* with the *Imperial Guards Division* under command was to enter Bangkok and then advance south west and capture Victoria Point and so cut off Malaya from Siam and Burma. When this was complete, the *Imperial Guards* were then to revert to *25th Army*, follow *5th Division* and concentrate around Ipoh by 23rd December. *18th Division* was to send *124th Regiment* to invade Borneo and then to stand by to invade Singapore or Sumatra.

The first waves of *5th Division* embarked at Samah on Hainan Island on 4th December and sailed at 0150 hours on the 5th. The attack convoys assembled in the Gulf of Siam on 7th December as a deception that they were going to attack Siam. The operation was covered by the *3rd Air Division* of the Japanese Army operating from airfields in southern Indo-China, with possible additional support from the Japanese Navy's *11th Air Fleet*. Their first targets were to be the airfields at Kota Bharu, Alor Star and Patani. At noon on 6th December a lone Hudson aircraft, of the RAAF, spotted the convoys heading for the Gulf of Siam. The British thus knew that the Japanese were on the move but where to; was it Bangkok, Singora, Malaya or all three? Knowing that negotiations to stop war breaking out were going on in Washington, Air Chief Marshal Sir Robert Brooke-Popham, Commander-in-Chief Far East, decided that he still did not know enough to order MATADOR so he kept all troops at immediate readiness. No further contact with the convoys was made until late on 7th December. Then the Siamese Government said that on no account did it want the British to enter its territory. Nevertheless General Heath was ordered to stand by to execute MATADOR at 0800 hours 8th December.

But it was not to be. At 0025 hours (local) on 8th December reports from 8th Indian Infantry Brigade at Kota Bharu said that it was under fire and that Japanese transports were disembarking troops. Brigadier BW Key, commanding the brigade, reported the first landings at 0100 hours. Wing Commander Noble, RAAF, at Kota Bharu airfield immediately ordered all available aircraft to attack the invaders. The first shot of the Malayan campaign was fired by an 18-pounder saluting gun purloined by the 3/17th Dogras for beach defence. This gun claimed to have sunk one landing craft, then the remainder in the initial wave were hit by either guns or aircraft. 21st Mountain Battery was also in action and in range of the landing beach. It also claimed sinking several landing craft but the Japanese kept coming ashore despite their casualties. While attention was focused on Kota Bharu, the Japanese moved into Singora and Patani at 0220 hours to secure the Kra Isthmus. 272nd Anti-Tank Battery, under Major McD Slater, in action near Kota Bharu, suffered casualties and loss of vehicles from enemy bombing The Japanese landed against almost no opposition. Then at 0330 hours came warnings that large numbers of unidentified aircraft were approaching Singapore and all defences were put on alert. The first air attacks against the British of the war in the Far East fell on Singapore at dawn just before the attacks on Hong Kong;

all available guns opened fire but without success. Much damage was done and 200 civilian casualties were testimony that war had started with a vengeance.

22nd Mountain Regiment, less 21st Battery, under Lieutenant Colonel GL Hughes, was with 11th Indian Division on the Siamese frontier. 4th Battery, Major EL Sawyer, was deployed astride the Alor Star - Singora road with 1/14th Punjab in 15th Indian Infantry Brigade. 7th Battery, Major JWP Scott, and 10th Battery, Major DGC Cowie, were further south in the Jitra defences with 6th Indian Infantry Brigade, less the Sikh section of 7th Battery at Padang Besar on the frontier with a detachment of the 2/16th Punjab. A single gun of 10th Battery was standing by to advance with the spearhead of two companies of 1/8th Punjab. Graham states that 'The division had been keyed up for an offensive but 'political restrictions' prevented the order for this being given until it was too late. The change to the defensive certainly had a depressing effect on the troops'. 21st Battery, Major JB Sopper, was on the airfield at Kota Bharu

At 0630 hours the C-in-C Far East and the naval C-in-C China, Vice Admiral Sir Geoffrey Layton, issued an Order of the Day putting everyone on full alert. At 0730 hours came fresh air attacks on all northern airfields, catching many British aircraft on the ground. On receiving the news of the landings at Singora and Patani, Brooke-Popham, who had already decided to delay MATADOR, ordered 3rd Indian Corps to occupy the Jitra position and send a delaying column into Siam and another to the Ledge, a position on the Patani road inside Siam. Thus 11th Indian Division was to fight where it was at Jitra but, because it had been at such short notice to move on Operation MATADOR for so long, it had had no time to prepare positions. The division was given 28th Indian Infantry Brigade at Ipoh as it moved forward to Alor Star to face the advancing Japanese. It arrived there at 0900 hours 9th December but ten vital hours had been lost waiting and this was to prove disastrous. Another part of the plan was to advance into Siam at Betong with 'Krohcol' a force consisting of the 3/16th Punjab, the 5/14th Punjab, 10th Mountain Battery and 273rd Anti-Tank Battery. They set off on the morning of 10th December and soon made contact with the Japanese who were advancing with tanks in the lead. Severe fighting broke out and two companies of 3/16th Punjab were lost, although one returned next day. The 5/14th Punjab and 10th Mountain Battery arrived at Kroh and were ordered to take up a defensive position nine miles north of Betong. The Japanese had by then captured the Ledge position 30 miles inside Siam, which was essential to the security of 11th Division.

During the afternoon of 11th December 3/16th Punjab repelled many attacks but casualties began to mount and the battalion was ordered to withdraw at 0900 hours on the 12th, which they did under heavy artillery fire. The 5/14th Punjab and 10th Mountain Battery advanced to extricate the 3/16th and in a sharp action on 13th December they practically exterminated two companies of Japanese. The 3/16th passed through the 5/14th Punjab north of Betong and prepared a new position at Baling three miles west of Kroh. It was here that 10th Mountain Battery engaged the enemy at 1000 yards, all guns loaded with shrapnel, and stopped them. Meanwhile a small mechanised force consisting of two companies and the carriers of 1/8th Punjab, a section of 273rd Anti-tank Battery and two sections of 17th Field Company, Sappers and Miners, advanced into Siam from northern Kedah to harass the Japanese advance from Singora. It then withdrew, destroying bridges behind it and passed through a position held by 1/14th Punjab, 4th Mountain Battery, a section of 2nd Anti-Tank Battery and 23rd Field Company, Sappers and Miners, some three miles north of Jitra. A covering position in front of Jitra was held by two companies of 2/16th Punjab, 7th Mountain Battery, a section of 273rd Anti-Tank Battery and 3rd Field Company, Bengal Sappers and Miners, at Padang Besar.

At Kota Bharu (Map 7) the Japanese were still coming ashore but with great difficulty in the wind, rain, swell and ferocious defence by the 3/17th Dogras and the four 3.7-inch howitzers of 21st Mountain Battery, under Major JB Sopper, in action on the edge of the airfield near Sabak.

The battery had two OPs on the beach. At dawn Lieutenant CJK Toombs manning one OP was surrounded but he carried on engaging the enemy because his line was still intact. Jemadar Gurmukh Singh in the other OP beat off an enemy infantry attack and then ran across to an infantry mortar position and directed its fire himself. His communications to the guns were cut but eventually he got his entire party back through enemy lines. By this time 73rd Battery of 5th Field Regiment was also hotly engaged.

However, in spite of a gallant counter-attack by the Dogras, further air attacks and the fire of the guns, the Japanese kept up the pressure. Soon the airfield had to be evacuated. Lieutenant Elliott, the OP officer of 73rd Field Battery, got out in a Malay boat crossing a creek 200 yards wide under fire from Japanese infantry. Before leaving, 73rd Field Battery fired at point blank range to destroy fuel tanks on the airfield. During 9th December 8th Indian Infantry Brigade withdrew to Mulong and on the 10th to Chondong, where it again destroyed airfield facilities, but not the runways. It did the same later on at Gong Kedah.

Meanwhile the enemy continued his remorseless air attacks on all airfields in northern Malaya, catching more British aircraft on the ground because they had no warning systems. Much gallantry was shown by the pilots at this time and Squadron Leader ASK Scarf RAF, based at Butterworth, won a posthumous Victoria Cross. There were very few anti-aircraft guns and those that there were did what they could but with little effect since they had no early warning radar. Within 24 hours the RAF had lost half of its 110 aircraft. Thus, having relied mainly on airpower for the defence of Malaya, the Commanders-in-Chief were in trouble. 9th HAA Battery of 1st HAA Regiment HK-S RA had 4 x 3-inch guns at Alor Star and four more at Kota Bharu. 13th HAA Battery of 2nd HAA Regiment HK-S RA had 8 x 3.7-inch guns at Sungei Patani and two 3-inch at Gong Kedah. 16th LAA Battery of 3rd LAA Regiment HK-S RA was split between the brigades of 3rd Indian Corps.

Next came reports of landings at Kuantan and the beaches were engaged by 22nd Indian Infantry Brigade under Brigadier GWA Painter. There were many calls for fire but there was only one section of two 3.7-inch howitzers of 21st Mountain Battery available. However the landing turned out to be a false alarm. Although there was evidence of boats approaching nothing could be found next day. It was at this time that Admiral Sir Tom Philips took HM Ships *Prince of Wales* and *Repulse* to sea, with a small escort of four destroyers, to attack the invasion fleets. By the evening of 9th December, when off Kota Bharu, he realised that he had been spotted and that the enemy could easily reach him with aircraft. He therefore decided to return to Singapore but, just as he was doing so, he received the report of landings at Kuantan, which later turned out to be false, and altered course to deal with them. This honourable decision was to prove fatal.

At 0230 hours on 10th December the *22nd Air Flotilla* at Saigon was preparing to attack Singapore when it was informed of the location of the British heavy ships. Bombs were quickly exchanged for torpedoes and 85 aircraft took off just before dawn. At 0800 hours the two ships had arrived off Kuantan to find nothing and accordingly altered course to the east. At 1020 hours enemy aircraft were sighted and the first attacks were made at 1100 hours. The battlecruiser *Repulse* was hit but not seriously at 1113 hours, then at 1144 hours the battleship *Prince of Wales* was hit by two torpedoes stopping both port propeller shafts, knocking out her steering gear and giving the ship a 13 degree list. At 1210 hours she was hit by three more torpedoes, and *Repulse* by four more and she too listed violently. Captain WG Tennant RN who, with General Alexander, had been the last man to leave the Dunkirk beaches in June 1940, ordered the ship to be abandoned and two minutes later *Repulse* heeled over and sank. 42 officers and 754 men were picked up by the destroyers *Vampire,* of the Royal Australian Navy, and *Electra*. By now, with her quarter deck awash, *Prince of Wales* was also finished and at 1320 hours she also heeled over and sank, taking Admiral Philips with her. In her case some 90 officers and 1195 ratings were picked up. The loss of these great ships cast a gloom over the western world. How could it have happened? It had a profound effect on the faith of all ranks in Malaya and Singapore. They then knew that the seas around them were firmly in enemy hands. After the dreadful loss suffered by the American Pacific Fleet at Pearl Harbour, this action led to a belief in the invincibility of the Japanese forces and the myth that they were superior on land, at sea and in the air.

In northern Malaya the destruction of the RAF went on. Airfields were abandoned and, by the evening of 9th December, there were only some ten aircraft serviceable and these were withdrawn to Singapore. On 9th December 9th HAA Battery at Kota Bharu was in action when the RAF decided to evacuate. 13th HAA Battery at Sungei Patani shot down two enemy aircraft but again the RAF ordered evacuation and two static 3.7-inch guns were lost; both batteries went to Butterworth. At this stage 14th LAA Battery was ordered north from Singapore. Meanwhile the Japanese *5th Division* continued its attacks towards Kroh and Alor Star and met 11th Division at Jitra while trying to cut off all British forces in Perak by attacking Kroh.

At Jitra (Map 8) 15th Indian Infantry Brigade, under Brigadier KA Garrett, had 2nd/9th Jat Regiment on the right and 1st Leicestershire Regiment on the left. To the left of them was 6th Indian Infantry Brigade with 2nd East Surreys and 2nd/16th Punjab. To cover them all was 155th Field Regiment (The Lanarkshire Yeomanry) less one battery, 22nd Mountain Regiment less 21st Battery and 80th Anti-Tank Regiment less one battery. A small force of two companies of the 1st/8th Punjab and a section of 273rd Anti-Tank Battery went forward to harass the enemy as they approached Sadeo. It was here that they first met Japanese tanks. Lieutenant May in command of the anti-tank guns held his fire and knocked out the first one with his first shot, so blocking the road. The infantry with anti-tank rifles got two more. The Japanese were quick off the mark and started an outflanking movement. Nevertheless the little force got out blowing bridges behind it.

11th Indian Division was by then holding forward to protect the airfields which had already been abandoned. Brigadier KA Garrett, commanding 15th Indian Infantry Brigade, put 2/1st Gurkhas forward at Asun with 4th Mountain Battery and a section of 2nd (Minden) Anti-Tank Battery. The 1/14th Punjab were further forward at Changlun. Meanwhile 2/16th Punjab were ordered to recapture the Ledge with 10th Mountain Battery. It failed to turn up, so the Punjabis were left without artillery support. Then, when 5/14th Punjab arrived from Penang, it was ordered to a position some nine miles north of Betong with 10th Mountain Battery which had now arrived. The 3/16th fought like tigers but were eventually overrun at Changlun with the section of 2nd Anti-Tank Battery which was limbered up ready to move when Japanese tanks suddenly appeared. The remnants had to escape through the jungle, falling back on 1/14th Punjab.

The Jitra position lay astride the main road into Siam. Brigadier WO Lay's 6th Indian Infantry Brigade, on the left, was responsible for ten miles of paddy and swamp with 2/16th Punjab on the left and 2nd East Surreys on the right linking up with 1st Leicesters which was the left forward battalion of 15th Indian Infantry Brigade with 2/9th Jats to their right. Then disaster struck. The bridge at Manggoi was prematurely blown, cutting off two companies of 2/16th, 7th Mountain Battery and seven anti-tank guns of 2nd Anti-Tank Battery. The guns and vehicles had to be abandoned and this was a severe blow. It is the sort of thing that happens in war when units have not trained together properly. Gallant efforts were made to recover the guns but all failed. 7th Mountain Battery was given two 18-pounders to replace its lost guns. By this time Major General DM Murray-Lyon's 11th Indian Division had used up two of its reserve battalions and the last one was sitting way back at Alor Star guarding an empty airfield. Thus the GOC had no more reserves to hand with which to affect his battle. The news of the loss of the guns and vehicles arrived at the same time that the positions at Changlun and Asun were reported overrun.

By this time Brigadier Garrett was missing, so Brigadier WStJ Carpendale took command of 15th Indian Infantry Brigade. The men were tired and morale was slipping when, during the night of 11th December, the Japanese closed on 2/9th Jats and the Leicesters. As enemy tanks reached the demolition in front of the Leicesters they were engaged by a section of 273rd Anti-Tank Battery which knocked out four, blocking the road.

The story of 155th Field Regiment at Jitra is told by Captain ERA Sewell who was a troop commander in the regiment at the time. He describes how the regiment came into action in Jitra village in pouring rain and thick mud on 8th December. On the morning of the 11th targets were registered by each troop and these were the first rounds fired by the regiment in the field and were noticeably erratic. 'F' Troop's first round appeared to be a dud since it was fired 'capped'. 'D' Troop's first, owing to a line error, fell perilously close to 'C' Troop's OP. Later, when Japanese aircraft came overhead dropping leaflets, 'D' Troop claimed a hit with a machine gun. The locals were rounded up and sent to Alor Star since there was much evidence of fifth column activity and sniping.

Contact came at last light when Lieutenant France in 'C' Troop's OP saw an enemy tank coming down the main road. He engaged with 'B' Battery and the tank sheered off. Early on 12th December a shell from 'E' Troop hit a tree and exploded killing Bombardier Hall and wounding Lance Bombardier Carson and Gunner Spooner. The same day a barrage was put down in front of the Leicesters, who said it was very effective and stopped the enemy closing up on them. Also on 12th December a battery of 137th Field Regiment and another from 22nd Mountain Regiment came under command. Then 'C' Troop OP was rushed by Japanese infantry. It was with the Leicesters and Captain Forster, who had relieved Lieutenant France, and his OP Assistant were both killed, although his signaller got away under machine gun fire. The Japanese then worked round the flank cutting off the Jats and this caused the gun troops to leap-frog back. Second Lieutenant the Honourable Edward Douglas-Home was hit in the chest by a bullet at 'F' Troop OP as he was establishing it on the Sungei Bata. Second Lieutenant Robinson established another 'F' Troop OP. By this time 'C' Battery Command Post was under machine gun fire and Major Philip Gold, the Battery Commander, ordered it to move to Alor Star. During the move two guns were lost from 'F' Troop. By 2200 hours 12th December the regiment was in action on Alor Star airfield.

Major General Murray-Lyon wanted to withdraw to the better position at Gurun and was supported by Lieutenant General Heath but Lieutenant General Percival and the War Council would have none of it. So the battle went on. At dawn on 12th December the Japanese attacked with fury between the Leicesters and 2/9th Jats. 1/8th Punjab was ordered to counter-attack, which it did under cover of fire from 155th Field Regiment. As the attacking troops moved through the Jats they were mistaken for the enemy and met with a withering fire. The confusion between the various troops on the British side was a constant problem because most had never seen a Japanese soldier and undoubtedly the quite wide range of Indian soldiers were sometimes mistaken for enemy. With great gallantry the battalion pressed on but in the end failed. At noon the Japanese attacked 'D' Company of the Jats but were beaten off by the fire of the 155th Field Regiment. Then ammunition began to run out just as the Japanese massed for another attack. The Jats fought hard but slowly the numbers of these splendid men were being wasted away. The pressure was very great and Murray-Lyon realised that he must get behind the Kedah River if he was to survive at all. Finally he was given permission but his men were dead tired and were now asked to break contact and withdraw as the enemy closed, a most difficult and dangerous operation of war. After Jitra, 7th Mountain Battery went to Bukit Mertajam where it collected four 3.7-inch howitzers from the Perak Volunteers who were rearmed with 4.5-inch howitzers.

Jitra was a disaster for the defenders of Malaya. Two Japanese battalions and a company of tanks had defeated a division of seven battalions and forced it out of its defensive positions in some 36 hours and inflicted serious losses. Two guns and much equipment had been lost and almost more serious was that morale had deteriorated considerably. With no reserves to stabilise the situation the cohesion of the division was at stake. All this had happened because the division had been kept standing by at short notice to advance into Siam instead of preparing defences and because the British Government would not authorise the employment of civil labour to do the construction work. When the soldiers should have been training or resting they were digging, against the clock, as the Japanese closed on them. On top of all this had been the rapid expansion of the army in crisis. This had removed many experienced officers and NCOs, and regiments were composed of men who hardly knew each other and were in no way welded together as a fighting team. Thus when the Japanese attacked with tanks and highly trained infantry units they met partially trained men whose officers had no experience, even in training together, who had no air cover and very few anti-tank guns, men who were already off balance and very tired; the result was inevitable and proved decisive.

Meanwhile the battle was getting far more serious around Kroh. 'A' Company of the 2nd Argyll and Sutherland Highlanders, of 12th Indian Infantry Brigade, was sent to Grik while the rest of the battalion went to Baling. 5/2nd Punjab was sent to Merbau Pulas. The aim of these moves was to protect the right flank of 11th Indian Division as it was trying to sort itself out at Alor Star which it had more or less done by 13th December. The Japanese closed during the day and were held. During the night of 13/14th December Murray-Lyon withdrew again, this time to the Gurun position some 20 miles further south. 155th Field Regiment was in action with OPs deployed by last light on 13th December at Gurun, the guns being directed north to cover the withdrawal of 28th Infantry Brigade. The move was carried out by desperately weary men in very heavy rain. On arrival, sick with lack of sleep, the men set to dig in yet again because none of the planned defences, which should have been prepared by civil labour, had been built. 6th Indian Infantry Brigade was to the left of the road and 28th Indian Infantry Brigade moved in on the right with a much depleted 15th Indian Infantry Brigade, by then only some 600 strong, in reserve. 88th Field Regiment covered the position together with three anti-tank batteries of 80th Anti-Tank Regiment but fields of fire were extremely limited. By this time 80th Regiment had lost 13 anti-tank guns. For a while the remains of 2nd and 273rd Anti-Tank Batteries were amalgamated but a few days later 2nd Battery was sent to Ipoh to refit.

The last of the troops had hardly reached Gurun when the first Japanese approached with, as usual, tanks in the lead. The anti-tank Gunners engaged and destroyed the lead tanks, causing the rest to withdraw but not for long. 'C' Battery of 155th Regiment reported infantry withdrawing through their guns saying that the enemy was only a few hundred yards away. (Sewell). During the afternoon Heath, the victor of Keren in Eritrea, visited Murray-Lyon at his headquarters some four miles to the south of Gurun. The latter stressed the urgent need to pull well back and to prepare properly co-ordinated defences. Heath agreed but Percival would not hear of it and ordered 3rd Indian Corps to continue to hold far enough north to cover Penang until further orders from him. Back at Gurun the Japanese continued their relentless attacks.

At 0130 hours 14th December they again came straight down the main road under heavy fire and penetrated right through 6th Indian Infantry Brigade's position destroying its Headquarters in doing so. Quick action by Brigadier Carpendale using his own 28th Indian Infantry Brigade alongside 15th Indian Infantry Brigade managed to hold onto Gurun itself. Major Philip Gold arrived on 'C' Battery's gun position and ordered Left Section to slew round and prepare to engage Gurun itself. By then Indian troops were pulling back in some disorder. At this point the position was dive bombed and Gunner Edgar was killed. (Sewell). By 15th December the situation was critical and Murray-Lyon ordered a withdrawal over the Muda River some seven

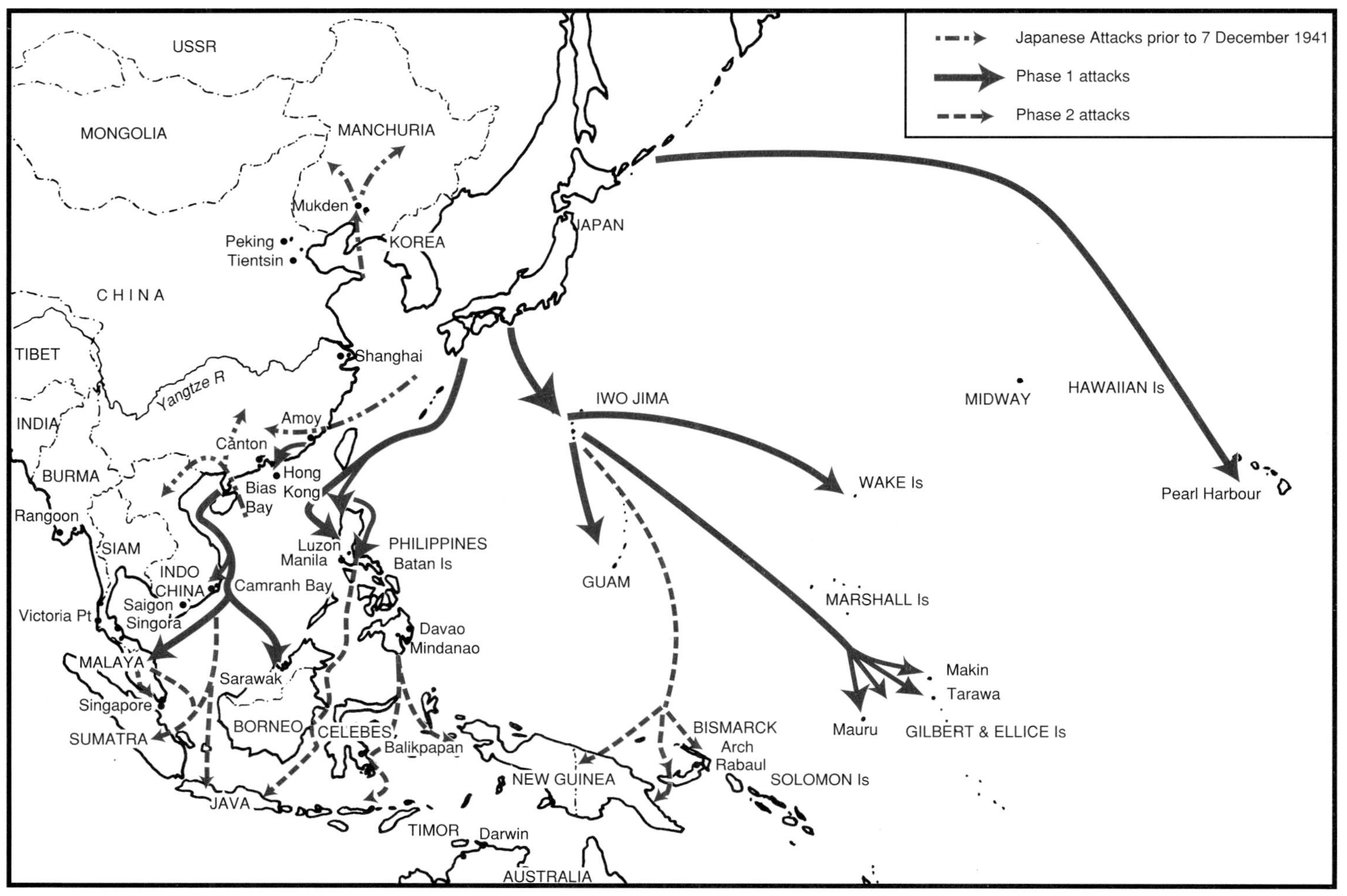
Japanese Attacks prior to 7 December 1941
Phase 1 attacks
Phase 2 attacks
USSR
MONGOLIA
MANCHURIA
Mukden
Peking
Tientsin
KOREA
JAPAN
CHINA
TIBET
Shanghai
Yangtze R
INDIA
Amoy
Canton
Hong
Kong
Bias
Bay
BURMA
Rangoon
SIAM
INDO
CHINA
Camranh Bay
Saigon
Singora
Victoria Pt
MALAYA
Singapore
SUMATRA
Sarawak
BORNEO
CELEBES
Balikpapan
JAVA
TIMOR
Darwin
AUSTRALIA
Luzon
Manila
PHILIPPINES
Batan Is
Davao
Mindanao
NEW GUINEA
BISMARCK
Arch
Rabaul
SOLOMON Is
IWO JIMA
GUAM
WAKE Is
MARSHALL Is
Makin
Tarawa
Mauru
GILBERT & ELLICE Is
MIDWAY
HAWAIIAN Is
Pearl Harbour

Map 1 The Far East, Japanese plans

Map 2 The North West Frontier of India, 1941

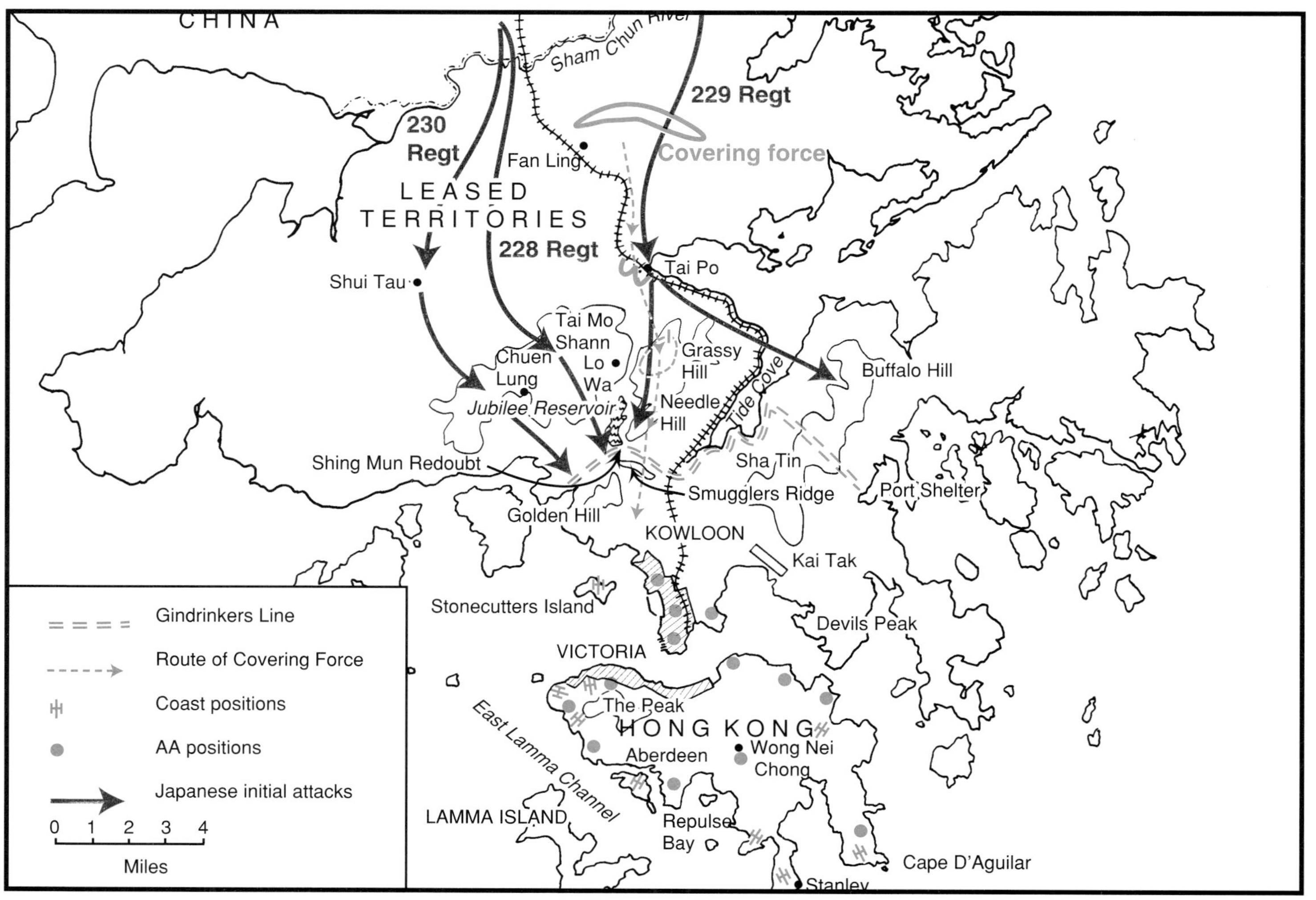

Map 3 Hong Kong and the Leased Territories 1941

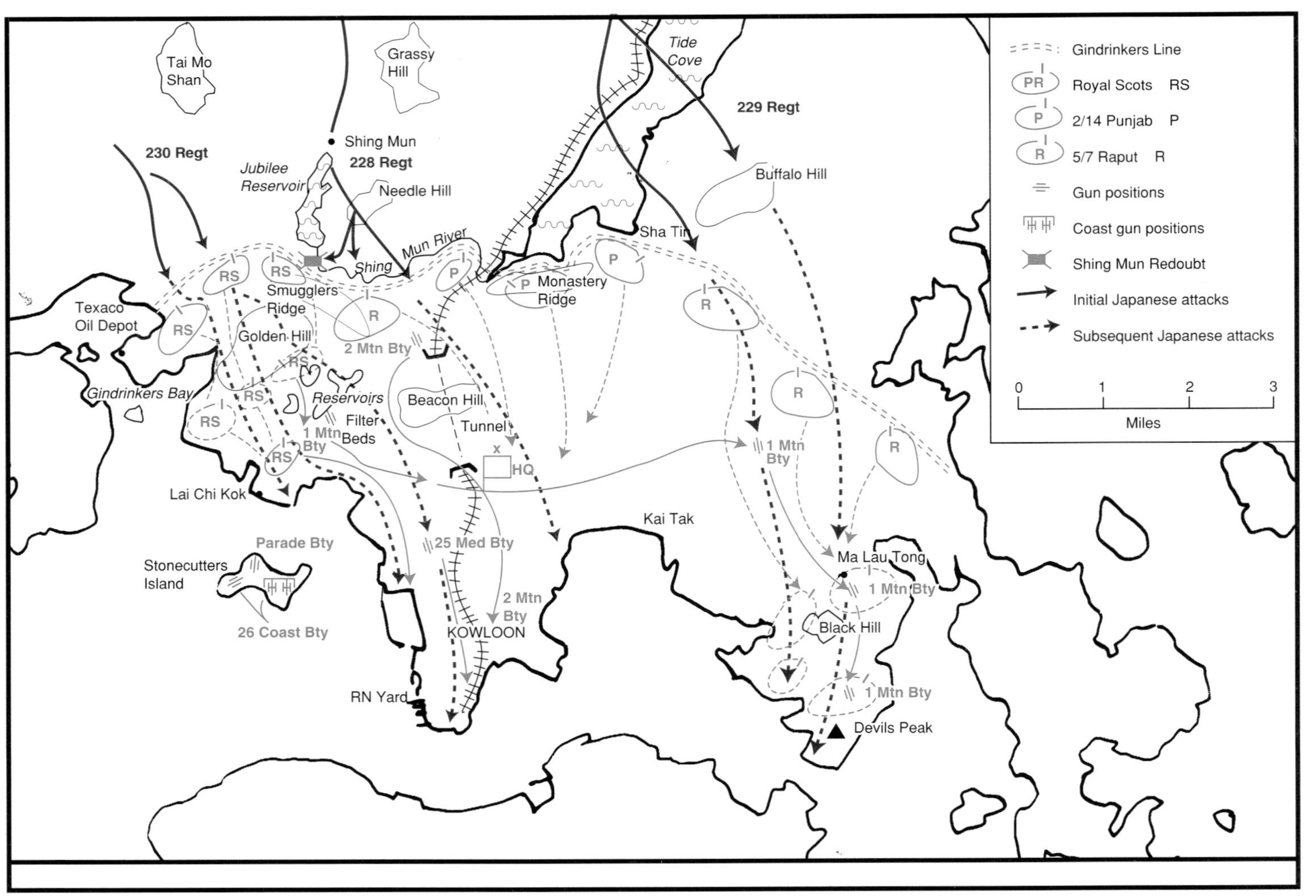

Map 4 The battle for the Leased Territories

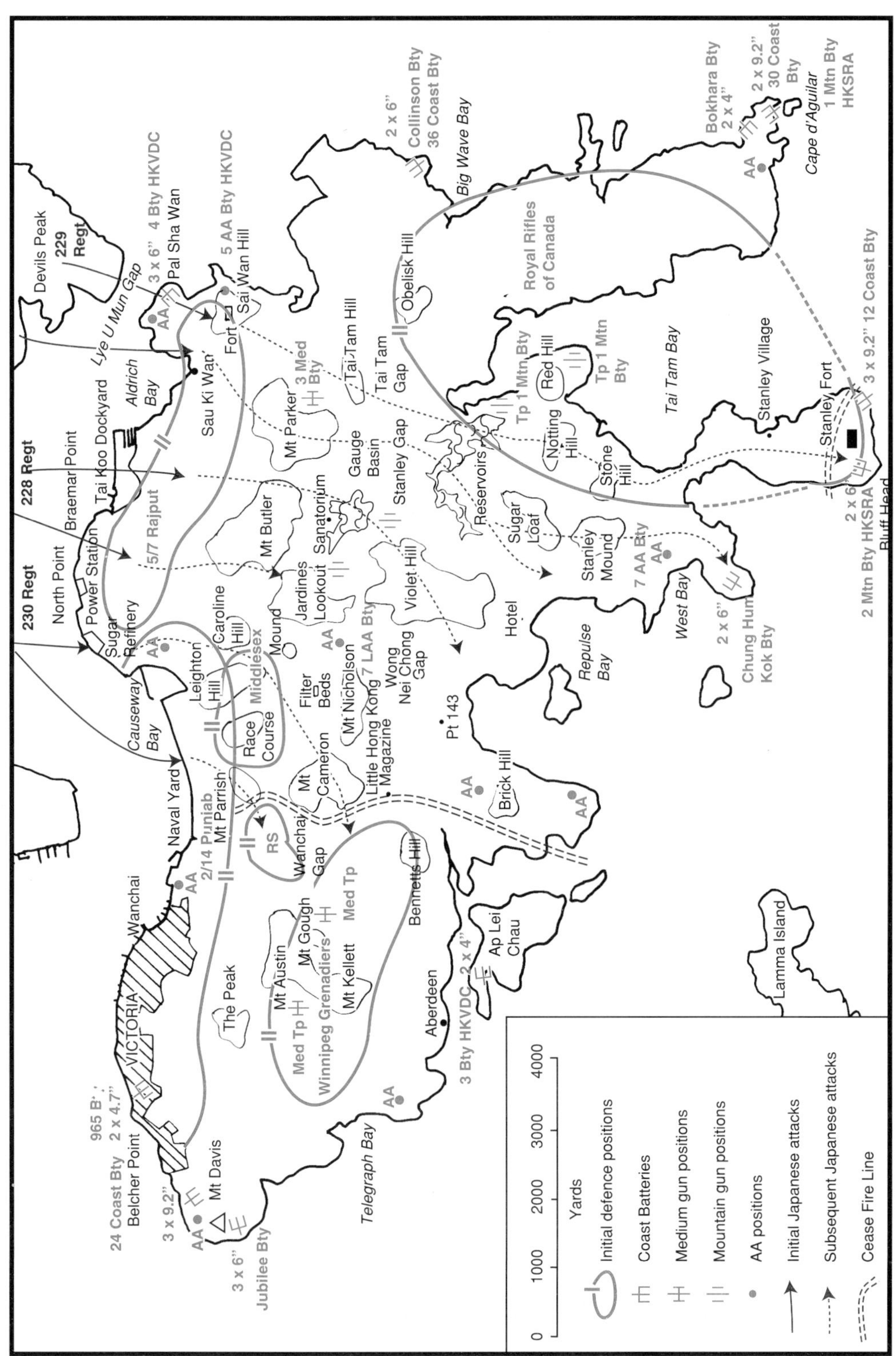

Map 5 The defence of Hong Kong Island

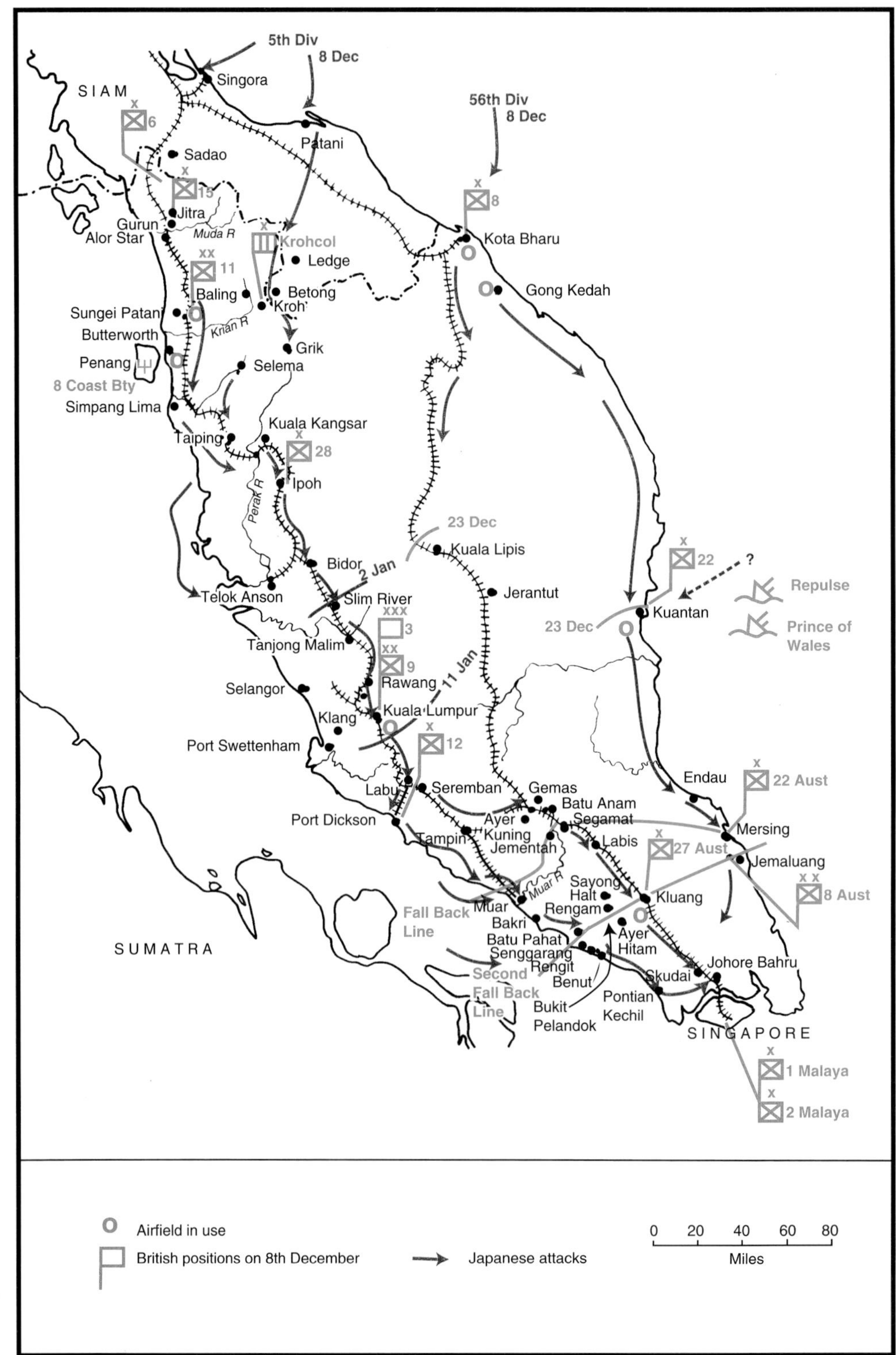
5th Div
8 Dec
Singora
SIAM
6
Patani
56th Div
8 Dec
Sadao
15
8
Jitra
Gurun
Alor Star
Muda R
Krohcol
Kota Bharu
Ledge
11
Gong Kedah
Baling
Betong
Kroh
Sungei Patani
Butterworth
Krian R
Grik
Penang
Selema
8 Coast Bty
Simpang Lima
Kuala Kangsar
Taiping
28
Ipoh
Perak R
23 Dec
Kuala Lipis
Bidor
2 Jan
22
Repulse
Jerantut
Telok Anson
Slim River
Kuantan
Prince of Wales
23 Dec
3
Tanjong Malim
9
11 Jan
Rawang
Selangor
Kuala Lumpur
Klang
12
Port Swettenham
Endau
22 Aust
Labu
Seremban
Gemas
Batu Anam
Port Dickson
Segamat
Mersing
Ayer Kuning
Tampin
Jementah
Labis
27 Aust
Jemaluang
Sayong Halt
8 Aust
Muar R
Muar
Rengam
Kluang
Fall Back Line
Bakri
Ayer Hitam
Batu Pahat
Senggarang
Rengit
Johore Bahru
SUMATRA
Second Fall Back Line
Benut
Skudai
Bukit Pelandok
Pontian Kechil
SINGAPORE
1 Malaya
2 Malaya
Airfield in use
British positions on 8th December
Japanese attacks
0 20 40 60 80
Miles

Map 6 Malaya

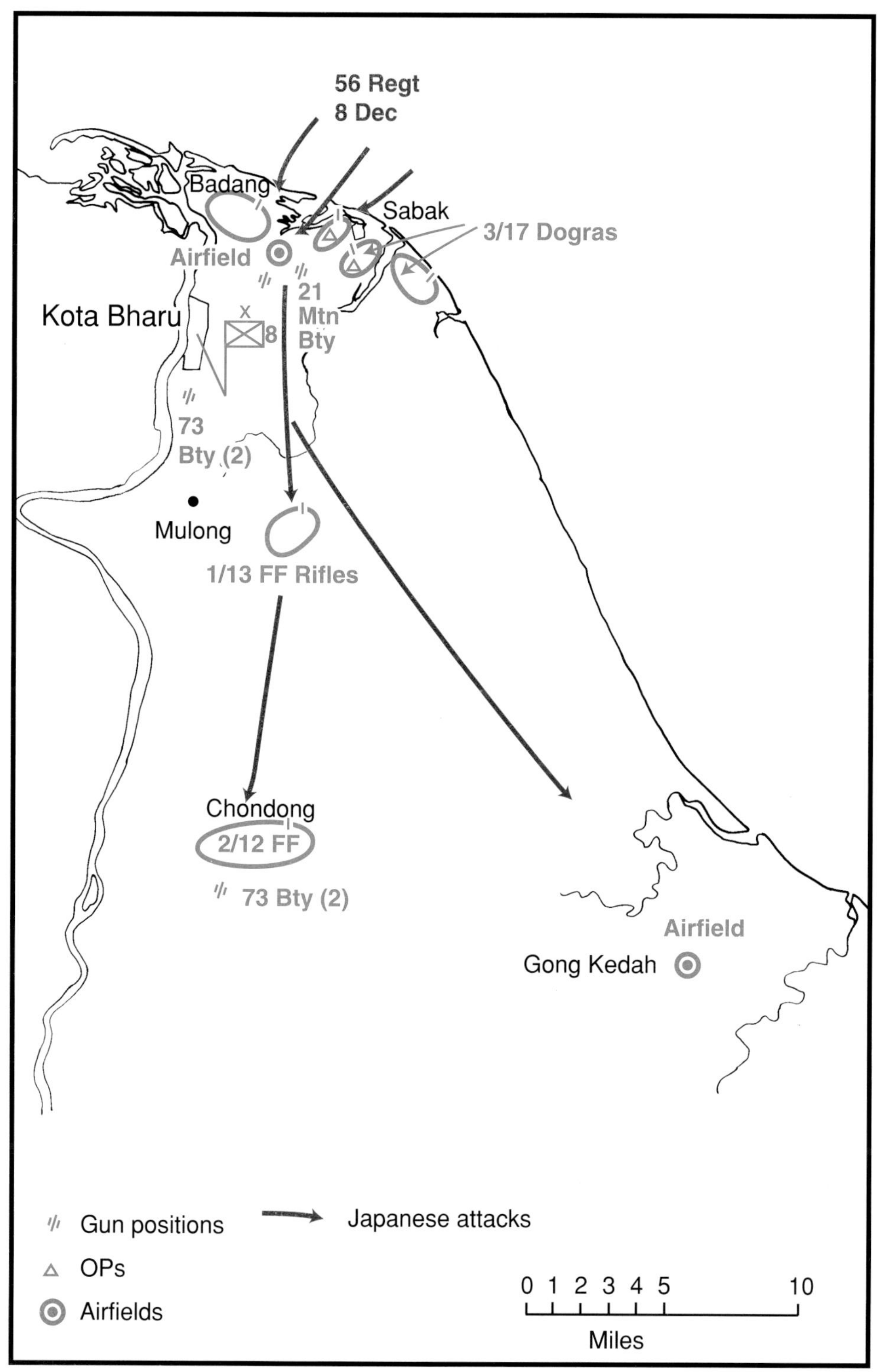

Map 7 The action at Kota Bharu

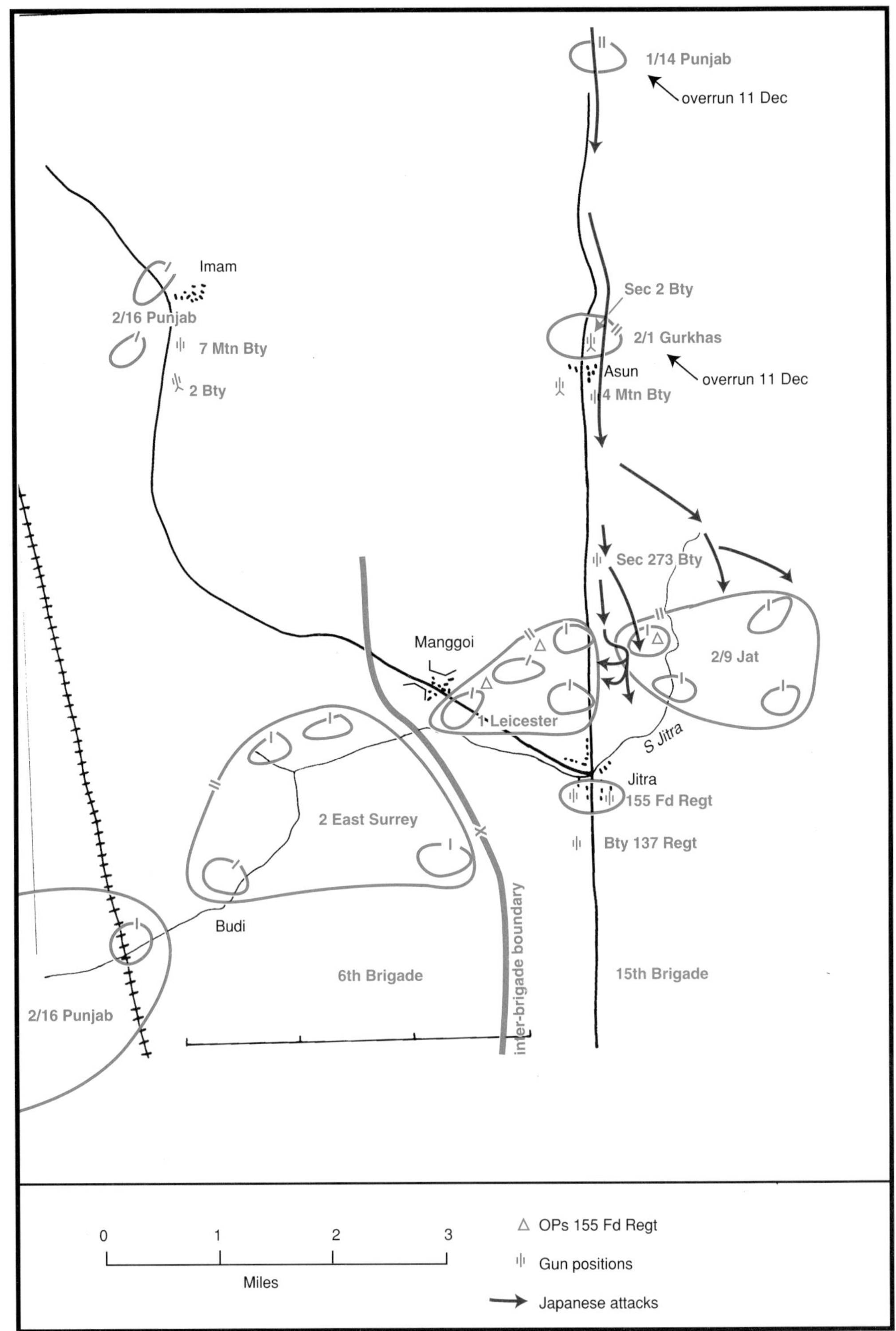

Map 8 The action at Jitra 11/12 December 1941

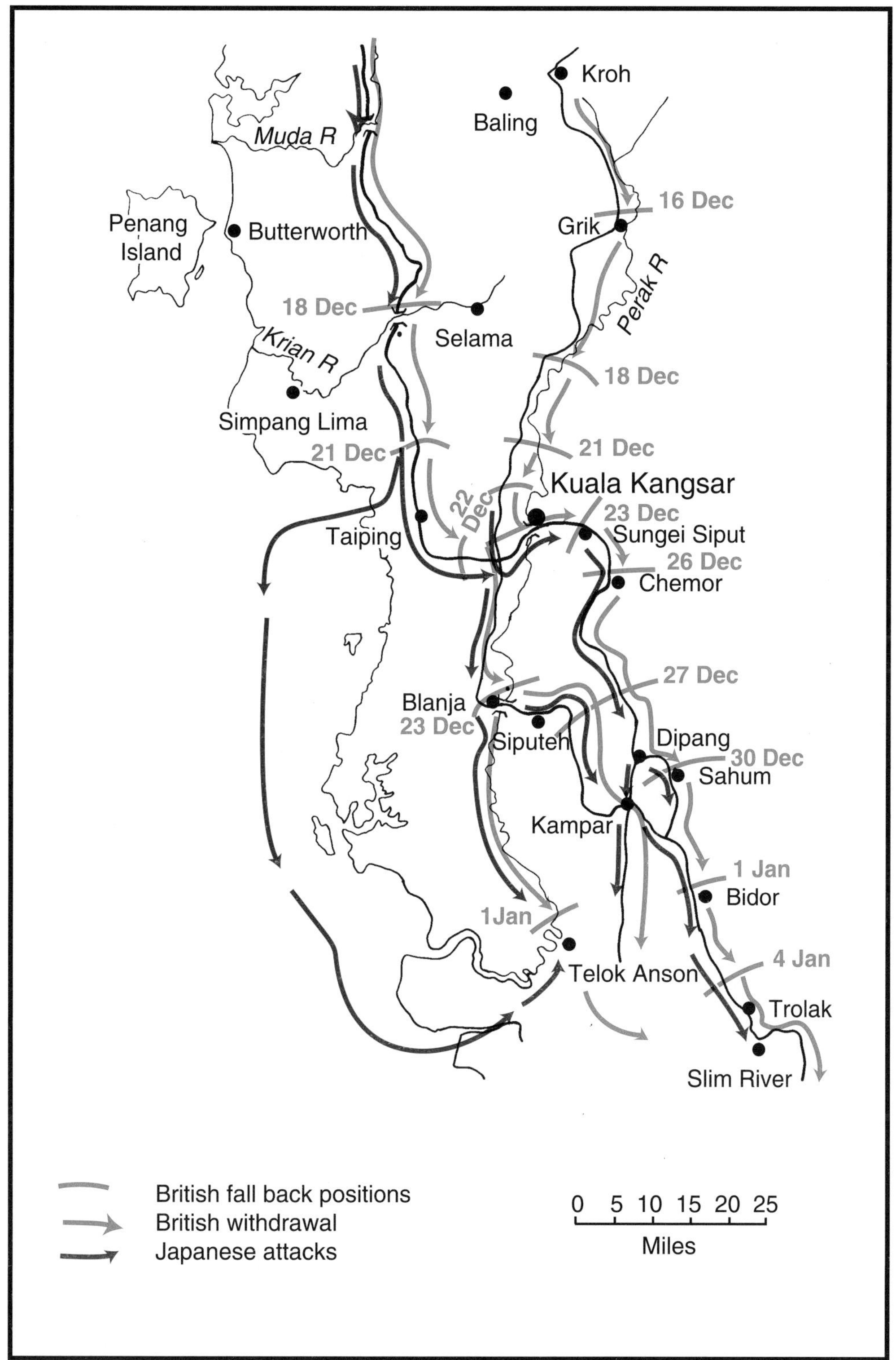

Map 9 The Japanese advance through Perak, December 1941

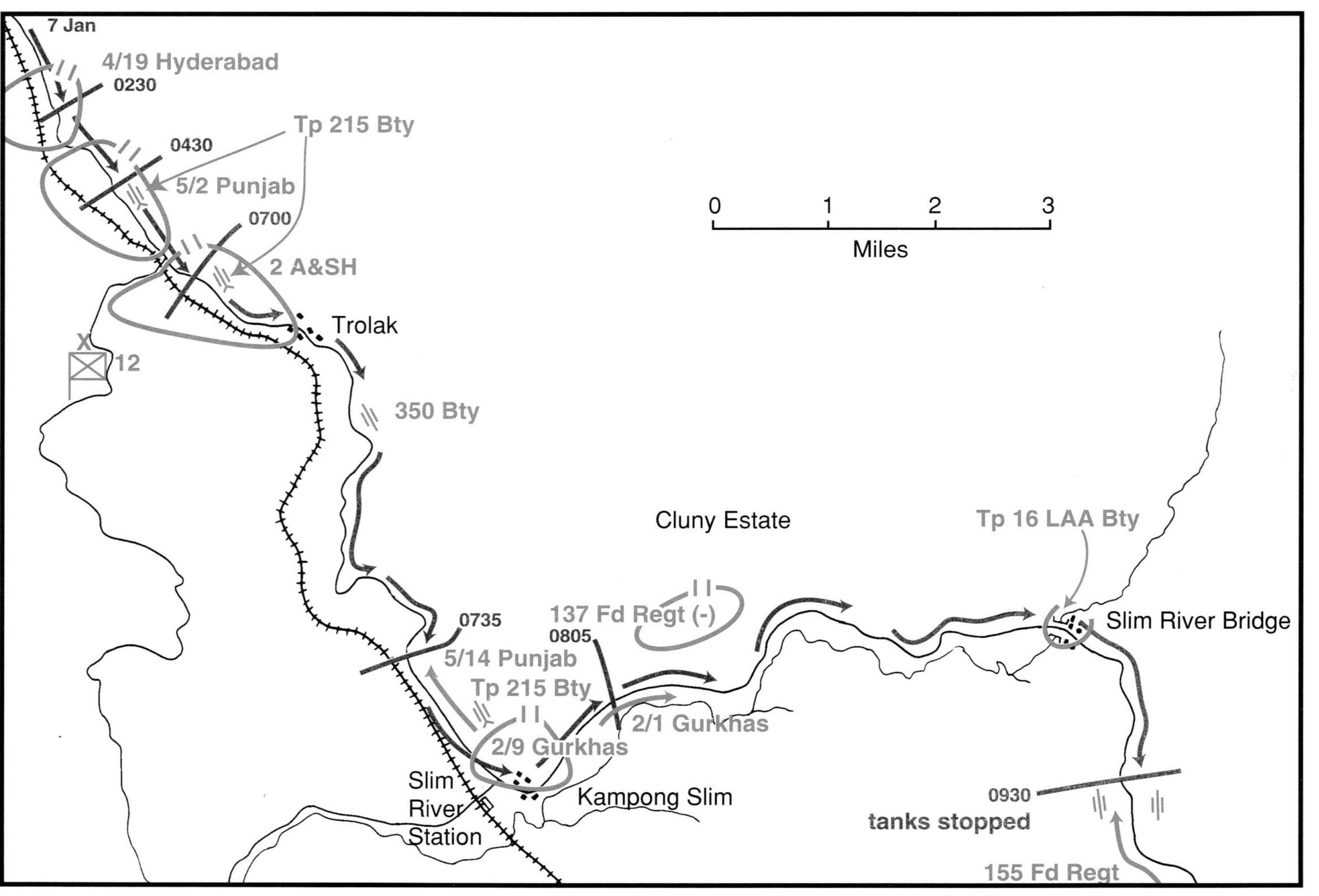

Map 10 The action at Slim River. 7th January 1942

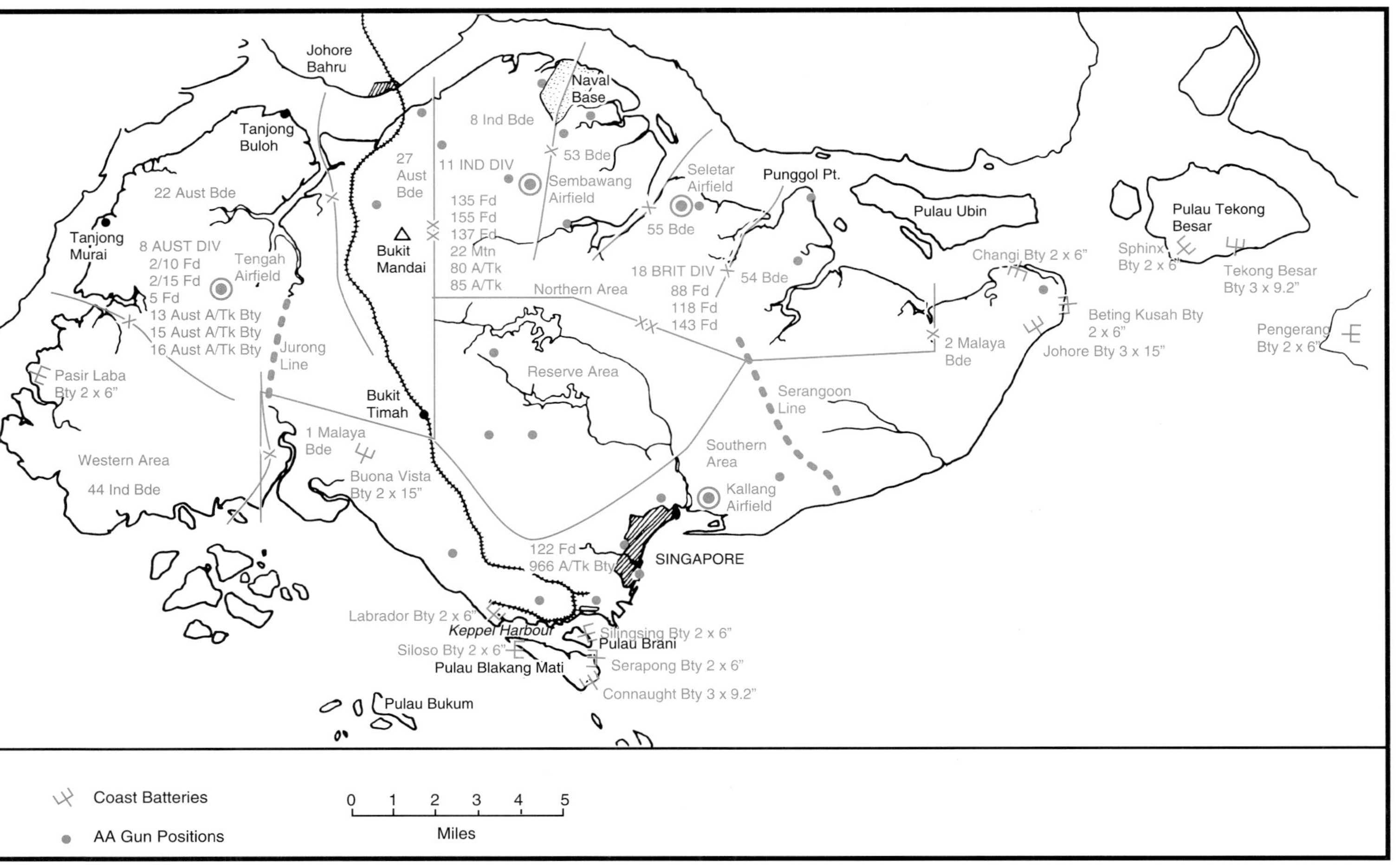

Map 11 Singapore Island Artillery Defences, February 1942

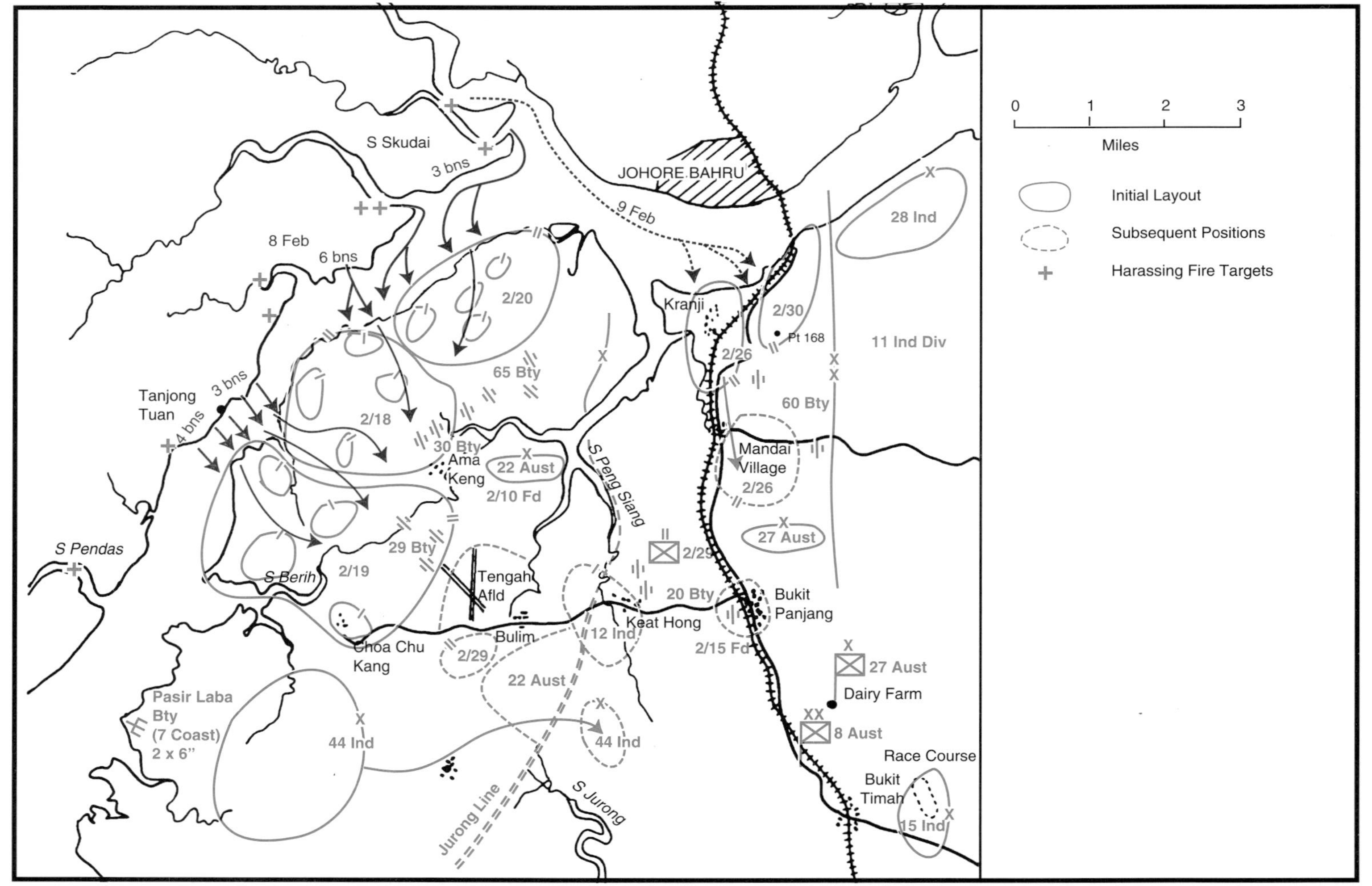

S Skudai
3 bns
JOHORE BAHRU
9 Feb
8 Feb
6 bns
2/20
28 Ind
Kranji
2/30
Pt 168
11 Ind Div
2/26
65 Bty
60 Bty
Tanjong Tuan
3 bns
4 bns
2/18
30 Bty
Ama Keng
22 Aust
2/10 Fd
S Peng Siang
Mandai Village
2/26
27 Aust
S Pendas
29 Bty
2/19
S Berih
Tengah Afld
2/29
20 Bty
Bukit Panjang
Keat Hong
12 Ind
Bulim
Choa Chu Kang
2/29
2/15 Fd
27 Aust
22 Aust
Dairy Farm
Pasir Laba Bty (7 Coast) 2 x 6"
44 Ind
44 Ind
8 Aust
Race Course
Bukit Timah
15 Ind
Jurong Line
S Jurong
0
1
2
3
Miles
Initial Layout
Subsequent Positions
Harassing Fire Targets

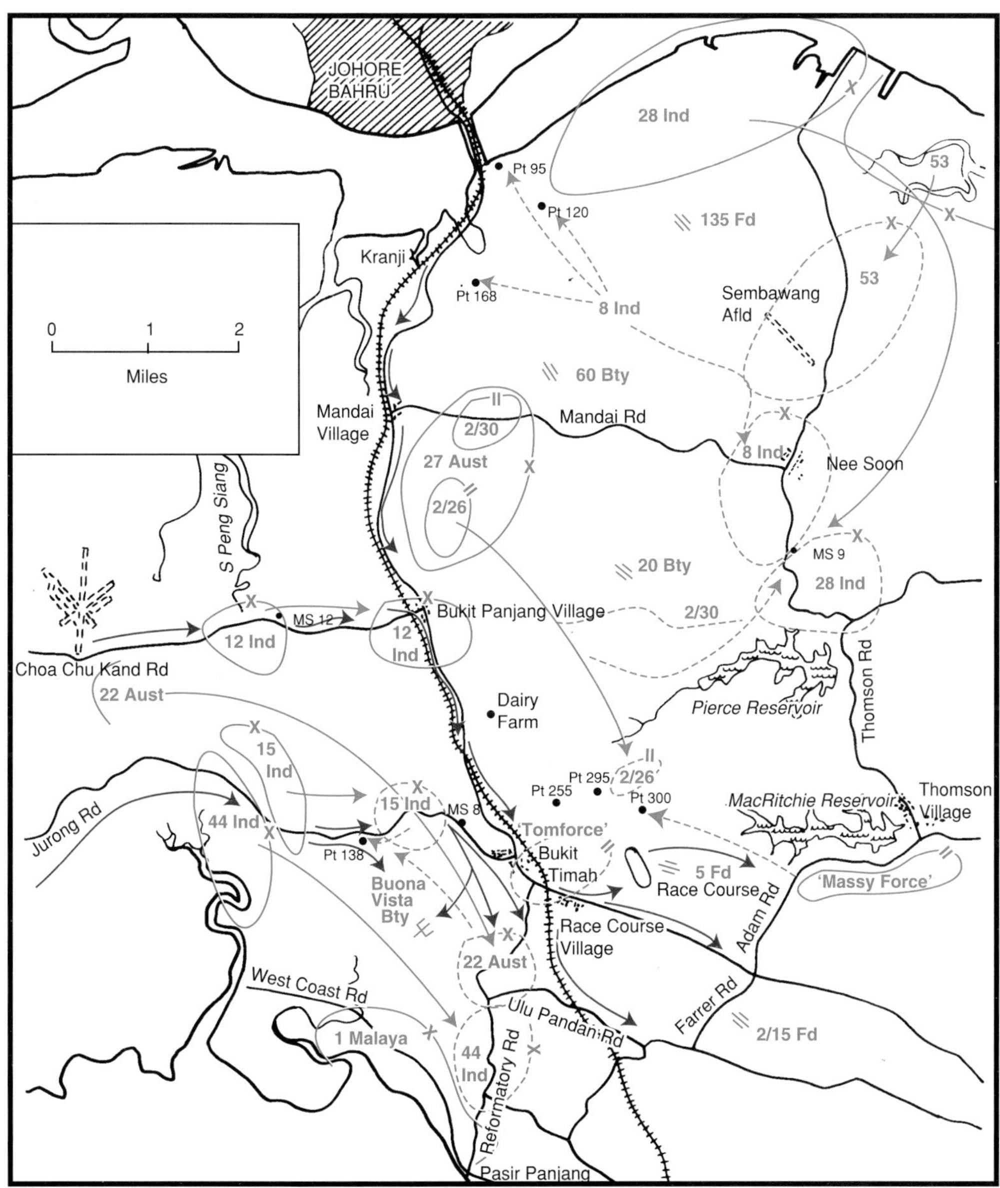

Map 13 Operations on Singapore Island, 10 - 11 February 1942

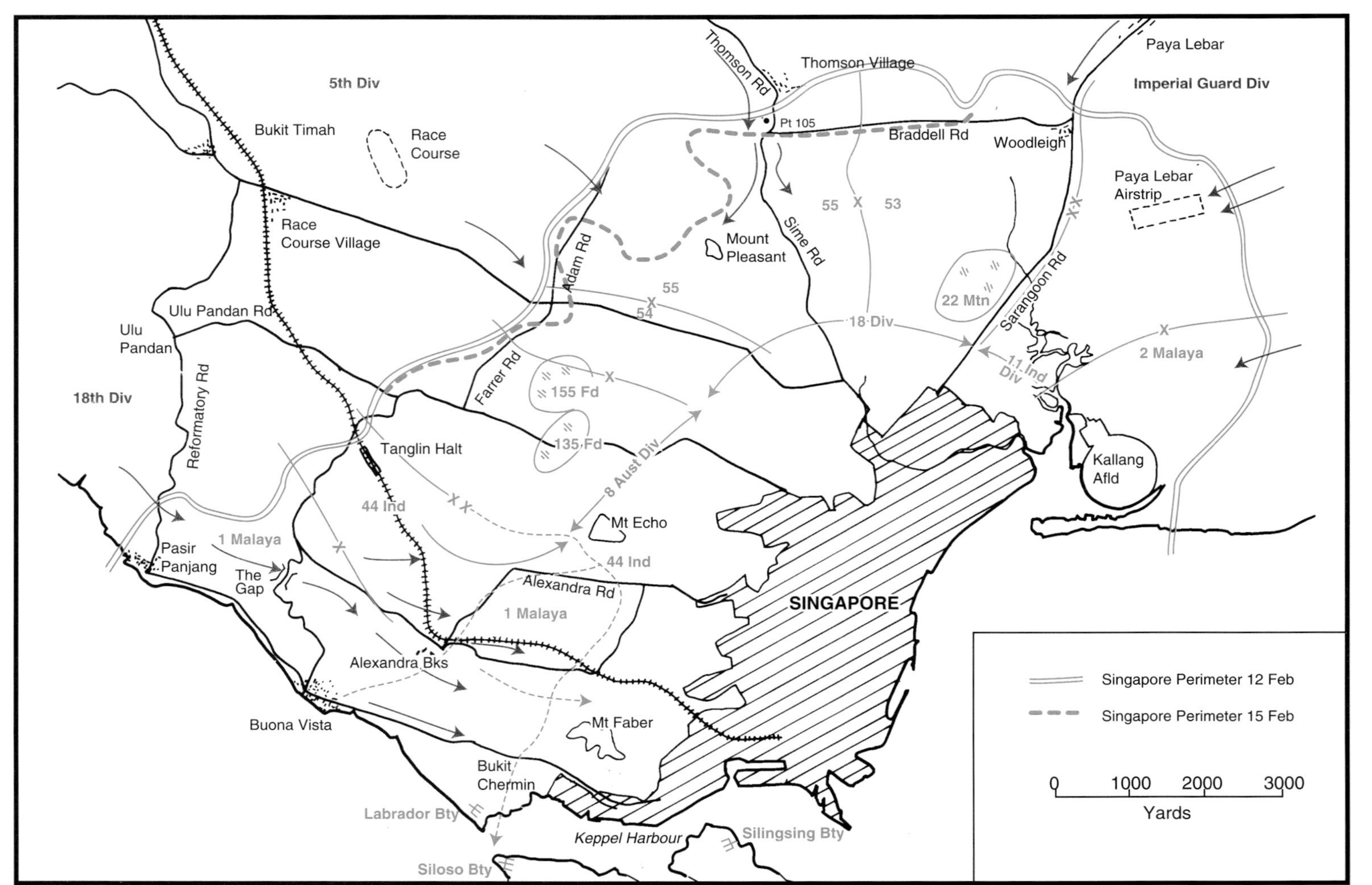

Paya Lebar
Imperial Guard Div
Thomson Rd
Thomson Village
5th Div
Bukit Timah
Race Course
Pt 105
Braddell Rd
Woodleigh
Paya Lebar Airstrip
Race Course Village
55
X
53
Mount Pleasant
Sime Rd
Adam Rd
22 Mtn
Sarangoon Rd
X-X
Ulu Pandan Rd
55
54
18 Div
2 Malaya
Ulu Pandan
11 Ind Div
18th Div
Reformatory Rd
Farrer Rd
155 Fd
135 Fd
Tanglin Halt
8 Aust Div
Kallang Afld
44 Ind
Mt Echo
1 Malaya
Pasir Panjang
44 Ind
The Gap
Alexandra Rd
SINGAPORE
1 Malaya
Alexandra Bks
Buona Vista
Mt Faber
Bukit Chermin
Labrador Bty
Keppel Harbour
Silingsing Bty
Siloso Bty
Singapore Perimeter 12 Feb
Singapore Perimeter 15 Feb
0
1000
2000
3000
Yards

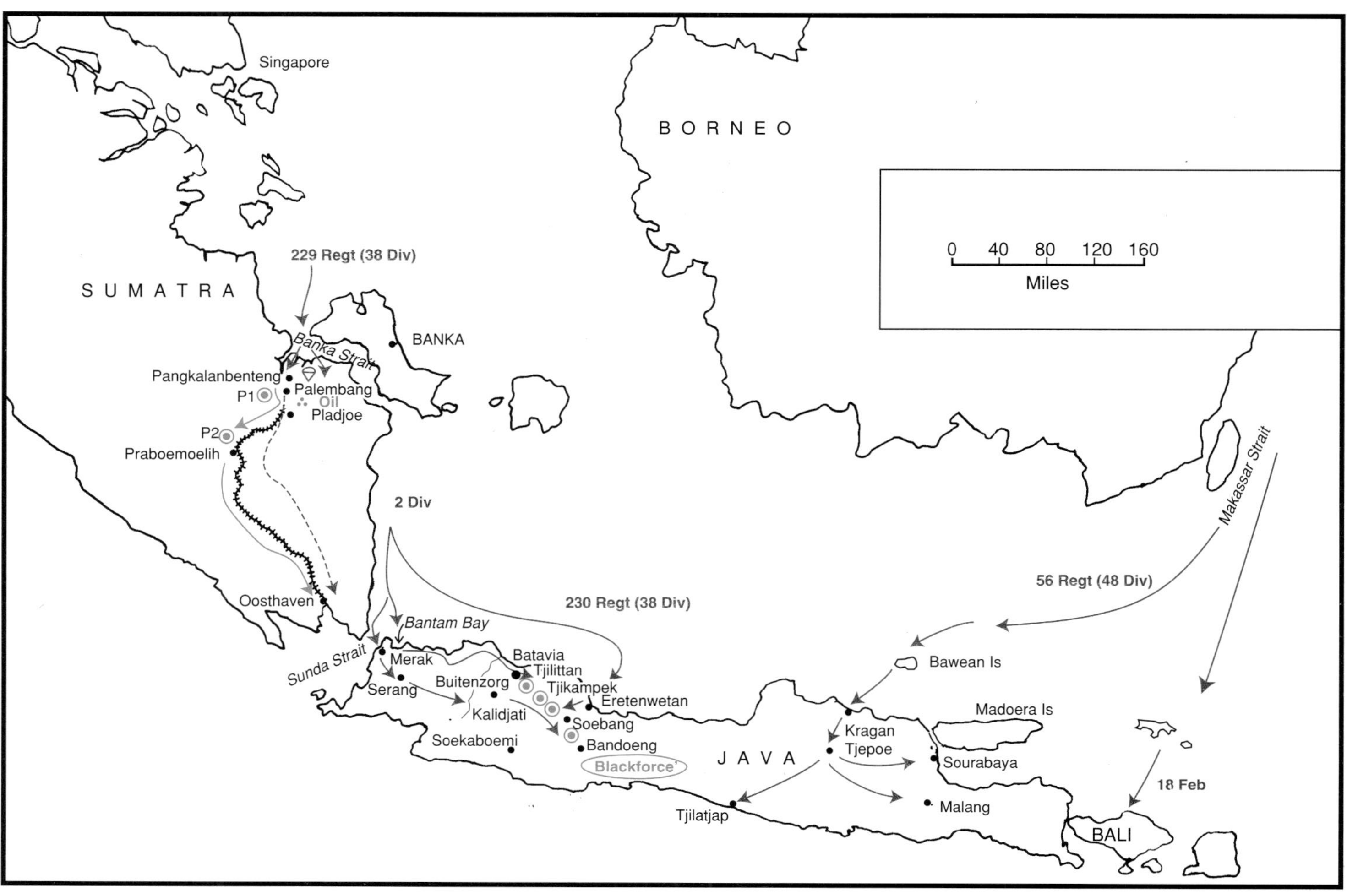

Map 15 Battles for Sumatra and Java, 14th February to 8th March 1942

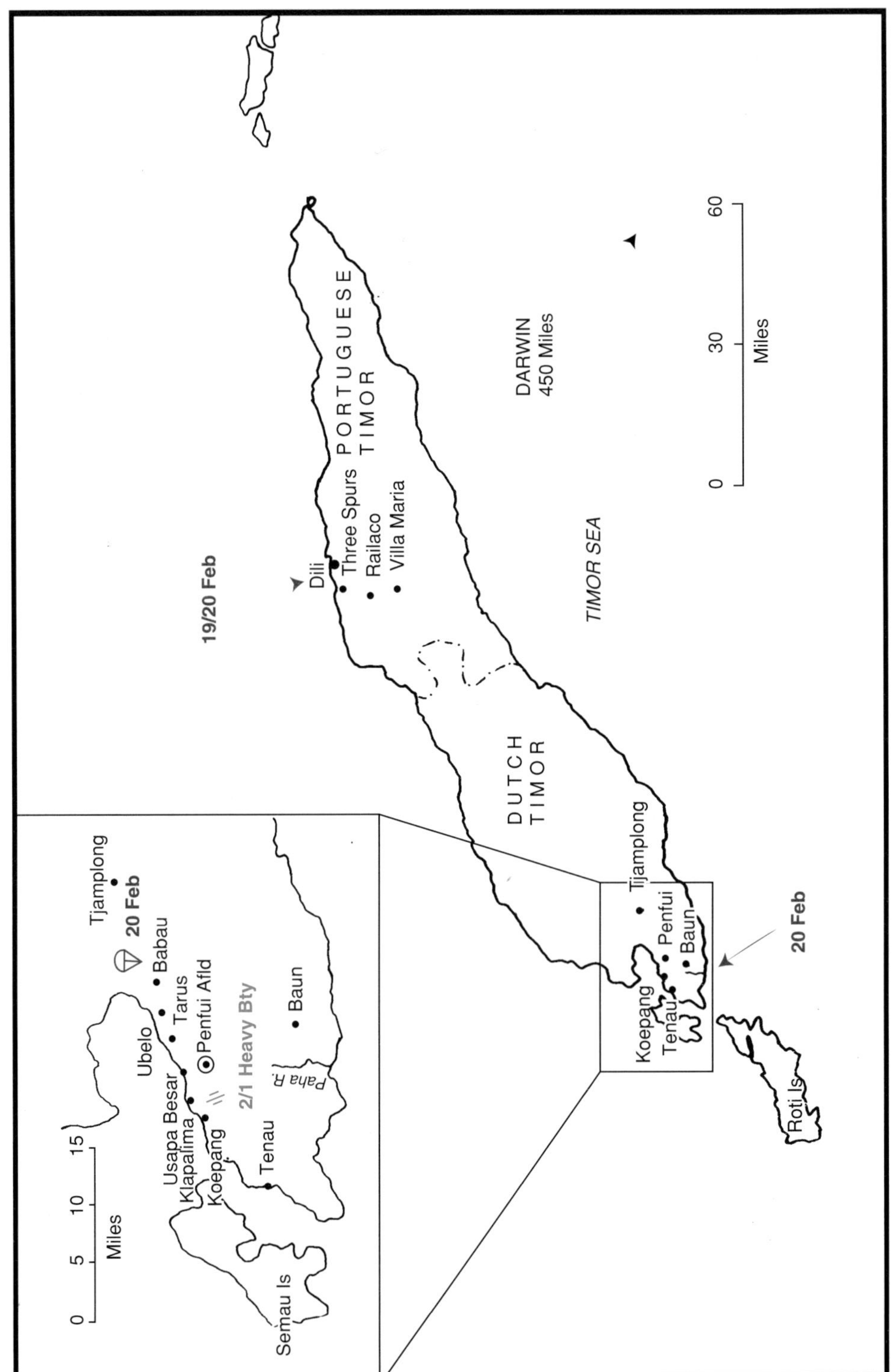

PORTUGUESE TIMOR
DUTCH TIMOR
19/20 Feb
Dili
Three Spurs
Railaco
Villa Maria
TIMOR SEA
DARWIN
450 Miles
0
30
60
Miles
Tjamplong
Penfui
Baun
Koepang
Tenau
20 Feb
Roti Is
Tjamplong
20 Feb
Babau
Tarus
Penfui Afld
Ubelo
Usapa Besar
Klapalima
Koepang
2/1 Heavy Bty
Baun
Paha R.
Tenau
Semau Is
0
5
10
15
Miles

Map 16 Timor

miles to the south. As the infantry pulled out the enemy was held in check almost entirely by the guns of 155th Field Regiment causing him many casualties. The division managed to get south of the Muda River by dawn on the 16th, but neither 6th nor 15th Brigades were fit for action. It was at Gurun that 'B' Battery of 155th Regiment was ordered back to Ipoh to collect 25-pounders to replace their 4.5 inch howitzers. As the battery prepared to withdraw, Japanese pressure increased and it came into action by the Police Barracks in Taiping before it was able to continue to Ipoh. By then 'B' Battery had 25-pounders and 'C' Battery had 4.5-inch howitzers.

The anti-aircraft Gunners were doing their best to conform to the withdrawal. 9th HAA and 14th LAA Batteries concentrated at Ipoh while 13th HAA Battery relieved 11th British HAA Battery at Kuala Lumpur. The guns were under constant attack by Japanese aircraft. 9th Battery then moved south to Kuala Lumpur and 14th to Port Swettenham. Then came massed attacks on Kuala Lumpur when the guns shot down seven attacking aircraft including some Junkers Ju 87s. Penang was bombed on 11th and 12th December. There were no anti-aircraft guns or aircraft to defend the island and much damage was done. It was decided to evacuate all European women and children to the mainland and then on 17th December came orders to evacuate the island by sea. In the rush to do so the radio station and most of the ships in the harbour were left intact and these were both to be of great value to the Japanese. At Penang 8th Coast Battery HK-S RA was manning two 6-inch batteries at Batu Maung and two more at Cornwallis. The guns of the former were destroyed by exploding gelignite in the chambers and those of Cornwallis, in full view of the enemy on the mainland, were put out of action by burring the breech screws which were then broken with sledge hammers and jammed home. The searchlights and engines were smashed and the ammunition, 1,500 rounds, blown up by delayed action charges. The men of the battery reached Singapore safely on 18th December.

Eight days after the start of the attack on Malaya, the Japanese attacked Borneo, which was defended by the 2/15th Punjab, a single 6-inch gun of the HK-S RA, the local Volunteer Corps, Coastal Marine Service, the police and the Sarawak Rangers. Lieutenant Colonel CM Lane, the Punjab battalion commander, was in charge and had orders to destroy the oilfields at Miri where the Japanese landed on 15th December. On the 23rd they appeared off Kuching and landed there on 24th December. An 18-pounder and a mortar sank four landing craft before being surrounded and the detachments killed. The 2/15th Punjab withdrew into Dutch Borneo and remained active against the enemy until 9th March when they were ordered to surrender. They had put up a gallant resistance in impossible conditions.

On the Malayan west coast 11th Indian Division was ordered behind the Krian River to avoid being outflanked on the Muda (Map 9). 6th and 15th Indian Infantry Brigades were ordered back to Taiping to refit and rest while 28th Indian Infantry Brigade with 88th Field Regiment and two anti-tank batteries was told to take up positions at Simpang Lima. 3/16th Punjab with 10th Mountain Battery were to cover the right flank at Selama while 12th Indian Infantry Brigade was to withdraw through them to Taiping to refit. On the coast, a special force based on 137th Field Regiment, joined by a section of 22nd Mountain Regiment, a troop of 2nd Battery of 80th Anti-Tank Regiment, a company of the Leicesters, a squadron of 3rd Cavalry and an armoured train, all under Lieutenant Colonel GD Holme, the commanding officer of 137th Field Regiment, was to hold the south bank of the Muda River for as long as possible after destroying all bridges over it. By dawn on 18th December all British forces were south of the Krian River. Then a new threat developed southwards from Grik towards Kuala Kangsar and Heath ordered 12th Indian Infantry Brigade forward to meet it.

Percival's problem was that he knew sea convoys were approaching with reinforcements and that these would arrive early in January. He also knew that they would be attacked from the air as they approached Singapore unless he could hold the Japanese far to the north. Against this was his need to conserve his forces as much as he could for the defence of Singapore. He therefore decided to withdraw 3rd Indian Corps to new positions south of the Perak River, while 9th Indian Division would protect Kuantan airfield and meet any threat from the east. 11th Indian Division was reorganised to consist of a combined 6th and 15th Indian Infantry Brigade, to be known as 15th Indian Infantry Brigade, and 12th Indian Infantry Brigade. At this point the Commanders-in-Chief signalled London saying that the situation was grave and that they needed more aircraft, another infantry division of at least two brigades, three light and two heavy anti-aircraft regiments, an anti-tank regiment, 50 light tanks and more ammunition. Then 28th Indian Infantry Brigade was forced back under pressure towards Taiping while 12th Indian Infantry Brigade sent the 2nd Argyll and Sutherland Highlanders and one field battery to reinforce Grik. Unhappily they met the enemy before they got there and were forced to withdraw.

By 22nd December Murray-Lyon decided that it was time to get everyone back behind the Perak River. He therefore ordered 12th Indian Infantry Brigade to Sungei Siput and 28th Indian Infantry Brigade to Blanja and Siputeh. By the 23rd all bridges were blown. Then, because he feared an attack from Grik, Heath ordered 11th Indian Division back to Sungei Siput and in doing so allowed the Japanese to cross the Perak River unopposed.

It was on 23rd December that Lieutenant General Sir Henry Pownall, a Gunner who had been Chief of Staff to General Gort in France, arrived to assume command of the Far East from Brooke-Popham. It was decided, however, not to interrupt command now that the fighting had started. On the following day Brigadier ACM Paris relieved Murray-Lyon in command of 11th Indian Division and plans were made for the division to occupy new positions around Kampar.

By 26th December the very tired 12th Indian Infantry Brigade was defending Chemor with 137th Field Regiment when the Japanese attacked in force and fierce fighting broke out. General Paris was forced to pull back again that night, but his hope of getting some vital respite for his men was dashed as the Japanese pressed on relentlessly and more desperate fighting occurred. By then the men were so weary that they could hardly stay awake, let alone fight. Fortunately Sergeant Anderson's troop of 2nd Anti-Tank Battery stood firm a mile north of Dipang and would not be moved despite the enemy action. It destroyed the lead enemy tank as it approached and this blocked the road. It then destroyed several other vehicles and this action rallied the infantry, but it was at a cost. The battery lost one gun to a direct hit and had four men killed. The rest of 12th Indian Infantry Brigade passed through this gallant band of Gunners and made for Bidor and a rest at last. The bridge at Dipang was blown by some brave Sappers of 3rd Field Company, Sappers and Miners, right in the face of the enemy. At dawn on 30th December Captain McKenzie, FOO of 'B' Battery of the Lanarkshire Yeomanry, saw four Japanese staff cars approach the demolished bridge. He had its co-ordinates and ordered his battery to prepare. As the occupants alighted from their cars he ordered 'Eight Rounds Gunfire', and that was the end of them all.

'Meanwhile 272nd Anti-Tank Battery was deployed along 22 miles of coast at Port Swettenham. Apart from regular air attacks and the sinking of two junks, both unfortunately Chinese, not much happened. Then on 15th January the Japanese landed to the north of Port Swettenham and the battery was ordered to pull back to Labu and then on to Tampin.' (Podmore).

General Heath was determined to hold the Kampar position and began to build it up. He put 15th Indian Infantry Brigade with 88th Field Regiment and 273rd Anti-Tank Battery astride the road in Kampar itself and 7th Mountain Battery east of the road with the British Battalion (The 2nd East Surreys and the 1st Leicesters combined). 28th Indian Infantry Brigade, a Gurkha formation, was to go astride the road at Sahum with 155th Field Regiment and one troop of 215th Anti-Tank Battery, while 12th Indian Infantry Brigade with 137th Field Regiment and

215th Anti-Tank Battery less two troops was astride the road at Bidor with the added task of covering the approach from Telok Anson.

155th Field Regiment had OPs with 2/9th Gurkhas, 'C' Troop was deployed in front overlooking Dipang bridge, 'E' Troop had a good view of Sungei Siput tin mines. 'F' and 'D' Troops were on a spur on the right. Much digging and camouflage was carried out, ammunition was dumped and everyone had some rest. Morale improved and the food was excellent. 'B' Battery opened fire on the night of 28/29th December and Captain Mackenzie, besides destroying the group of enemy officers described earlier, knocked out a field gun with a direct hit. BSM Roadnight conducted several successful shoots against enemy infantry from 'F' Troop OP. Captain Sewell records that 'The fire from the guns at this time was considerably more intense than ever before and was not without its effect on the equipment. The 25 prs gave trouble with their packings and the 4.5 hows. had leaking cylinders - the former on account of their newness, the latter on account of their great age.'

The enemy attacked on New Year's Eve and the guns were in action continuously but the Japanese came on in strength. Their main attack began at 0700 hours 1st January 1942 after an intensive bombardment but was held everywhere. Great was the pressure on 2/9th Gurkhas and the guns of the 155th Field Regiment, but the tenacity of the infantry and deadly accuracy of the Scottish Gunners held them back. Ferocious attacks fell on the Leicesters yet all day they held even when a part of the *Imperial Guards* was committed. It was during this action that, 'early in the morning of 2nd January 1942 Troop Sergeant Major Harold Hugill was FOO with the Leicesters at Kampar. A party of enemy got into the position but Hugill from a forward trench continued to engage them and alone defeated them just as they looked likely to succeed. His OP line was cut so he traced it back to his main OP and met a party of enemy in one of our machine gun posts. Hugill took charge of some infantry and led a bayonet charge which destroyed them. He then reported to battalion headquarters. It was mainly due to the skill and tenacity of this Warrant Officer that a heavy attack was beaten off.' (From his citation for the Distinguished Conduct Medal). It was also at Kampar that Gunner Harold Walker was awarded the Military Medal for gallantry in action. 'On arriving at a forward post with rations he came under machine gun fire at 40 yards range. He then stalked the enemy and found six men in a post. He killed two and dispersed the rest and then held the post until relieved.' (From his citation). The next day the pressure increased and forward positions were lost but a splendid counter-attack by a company of the Jat/Punjab battalion saved the day. This was led by Captain Graham of 1/8th Punjab who lost both legs in doing so and then died as he was told that the attack had been successful.

The Gunners of 88th Field Regiment had been in continuous action for three days and nights and had fired off all their dumped ammunition. That evening an attack began up the Perak River towards Telok Anson and as the Japanese closed, they were severely dealt with by the guns of 137th Field Regiment and later by the 2nd Argylls and the 5/2nd Punjab. Nevertheless this threat meant that 11th Indian Division, whose lines of communication were now very vulnerable, was forced to withdraw to new positions at Slim River. Accordingly, by last light on 4th January, 28th Indian Infantry Brigade was at Slim River, 12th Indian Infantry Brigade was at Trolak and 15th Indian Infantry Brigade at Bidor. In 155th Field Regiment, 'C' Battery moved first and 'B' Battery remained behind to act as rearguard for 2/9th Gurkhas. It then moved to Bidor while RHQ and 'C' Battery moved to a harbour six or seven miles south of Tapah to cover the British battalion.

There was no air support at all now and the enemy had freedom of the skies and were constantly attacking forward troops and supply lines. Lack of air reconnaissance was most serious and meant that the flow of information about the enemy was always poor. It was on 3rd January that 45th Indian Infantry Brigade, of 17th Indian Division, arrived in Singapore from India. The Far East urgently needed reinforcements to meet the might of Japan, but nothing of significance was available. The Royal Navy had no ships and the RAF no aircraft to spare. Auchinleck had just relieved Tobruk and was told to hold on the border of Tripolitania and to provide reinforcements for the Far East. Thus Major General MB Beckwith Smith's 18th Division, consisting of 53rd, 54th and 55th Infantry Brigades, 82nd Anti-Tank Regiment without its guns, 85th Anti-Tank Regiment (48 x 2-pounders), 6th HAA Regiment (16 x 3.7-inch guns) and 35th LAA Regiment (24 x 40mm Bofors) were diverted to Singapore. Then four Hurricane squadrons and 7th Armoured Brigade were sent from North Africa. 21st LAA and 77th HAA Regiments were also sent but were diverted to Java to protect the airfields there when the RAF withdrew from Singapore. But none of these reinforcements was trained or ready for combat in Malayan conditions and in any case would still take 10 to 14 days to arrive. Apart from the North Africa units the remainder had been told that they were going to the Middle East and would be given time to train when they got there. Thus they were not tactically loaded on ships and came ashore in Singapore in dribs and drabs.

On 4th January General Sir Archibald Wavell was appointed Supreme Commander of a new American, British, Dutch and Australian Command based in Java known as ABDA, with General Pownall as his Chief of Staff. The command had a huge span and an immense range of problems but did not have the resources to meet them. It did not last long but it was the first unified command in the war and provided a pattern of guidance for the future.

Towards the east (Map 6) Brigadier Key had successfully withdrawn 8th Indian Infantry Brigade to Kuala Lipis. Then on 23rd December the Japanese *56th Infantry Regiment* had made contact with 22nd Indian Infantry Brigade just north of Kuantan. On the 30th, *56th Regiment* was followed up by the *55th Regiment*. 22nd Indian Infantry Brigade was told to defend Kuantan with its three battalions and 5th Field Regiment less one battery but plus a battery of 88th Field Regiment. Some guns were deployed west of the Kuantan River close to the main road, others some nine miles from the coast. Heath was adamant that 22nd Indian Infantry Brigade should not be wasted protecting an airfield that was of no further use and ordered it back south of the Kuantan River, but before it could move the Japanese attacked. On the morning of 27th December five Japanese lorries approaching Kampong Balok came under fire from 5th Field Regiment, two were destroyed and the rest withdrew. Then attacks continued and the guns did much to help the infantry as they all re-deployed on the west bank of the river, especially 2/18th Royal Garhwal Rifles. On 28th December the enemy attacked Kuantan airfield where 21st Mountain Battery under Captain R Coleman was hotly engaged. 22nd Indian Infantry Brigade was told on 1st January to deny the airfield to the enemy for five days to prevent them using it to attack the approaching reinforcement convoys. But on 3rd January it was forced to leave or be overrun. The withdrawal was covered by 21st Mountain Battery which eventually got out and was ordered to Kuala Lumpur to rejoin 22nd Mountain Regiment in 11th Indian Division. Such was the gallantry in breaking contact at Kuantan that a Victoria Cross was awarded to Lieutenant Colonel Arthur Cumming, commanding 2nd/12th Frontier Force Regiment, as the force pulled out to take up new positions at Jerantut.

On the west coast General Heath was told to hold Kuala Lumpur for as long as possible but he recognised a threat from sea landings at Selangor. Accordingly he established a force consisting of the 3rd Cavalry, 3/17th Dogras and 73rd Field Battery, under Brigadier HRG Moir, to protect the flank of 11th Indian Division. He planned to hold at Slim River and Tanjong Malim (Map 6). The guns of 73rd Field Battery broke up attacks by the Japanese on 2nd and 3rd January but the size of the attacks caused Heath to reinforce Moir's force with three more battalions, 88th Field Regiment and 272nd Anti-Tank Battery. 15th Indian Infantry Brigade moved to Rawang and this stabilised the sea flank at least for a while. Meanwhile General Paris, by then in command of 11th Indian Division, was preparing his position at Slim River (Map 10). He put a reinforced 12th Indian Infantry Brigade forward at Trolak with 137th Field Regiment and one troop of 215th Anti-Tank Battery. He then put 28th Indian Infantry Brigade with 155th Field Regiment and another troop of 215th Anti-Tank Battery at Slim River Station and at Slim River Bridge. 80th Anti-Tank Regiment less the forward troops was in divisional reserve. The jungle in the Trolak area was extremely thick and was thought to be tank proof. Gun positions were hard to find and only one battery of 137th Field Regiment, 350th, was deployed in action; the rest were on wheels in the Cluny Rubber Estate between Kampong Slim and Slim River Bridge. All ranks were still dead tired. They had withdrawn 176 miles in three weeks and had managed only three days rest.

The battle of Slim River began on the afternoon of 5th January 1942. It was to have a major effect on the outcome of the Malayan campaign. The first attacks came in against the 4/19th Hyderabad Regiment, of 12th Brigade, and were held. There was not much activity on the 6th until just after midnight in bright moonlight when the Japanese, in their usual style, attacked straight down the main road with tanks leading and infantry close behind with heavy artillery and mortar support. They overran one company and forced the rest of the Hyderabads to retire. They hit the 5/2nd Punjab at 0430 hours, the fighting became confused and communication to the guns was broken. As a result 350th Battery of 137th Field Regiment, the only battery in action, continued to shell the area beyond the Hyderabads, which was no longer relevant. By 0530 hours the enemy had reached the rear company position. The noise was terrible, roaring engines, screaming Japanese, tracer fire and two anti-tank guns firing at point blank range and scoring hits before retiring. Next in line were the 2nd Argylls which, at 0700 hours, was hit by Japanese tanks and artillery which were working well together. Lieutenant Howard manned the last remaining 2-pounder of 215th Anti-Tank Battery in action alongside the Argylls. He loaded and fired six rounds before the gun was overrun by tanks although he managed to escape through the jungle. The fighting was furious and casualties were heavy on both sides. Next day only four officers and 90 men of the Argylls remained; they had fought magnificently.

By now all communications had gone and commanders had no idea what was happening. They were thus astonished when Japanese tanks hit 5/14th Punjab just north of Slim River Station at 0735 hours just as another troop of 215th Anti-Tank Battery was establishing another blocking position on the main road. The lead company of 5/14th Punjab was scattered and the second was left with only 20 men, all of whom were wounded. The two leading anti-tank guns were overrun and, as BSM White tried to bring a third into action, the tanks were on top of him before he could do so. There was then nothing to stop the Japanese and they swept through an unsuspecting 2/9th Gurkha Rifles and overran 2/1st Gurkhas. Next they surprised the other two batteries of 137th Field Regiment in harbour on the Cluny Estate, raking them with fire as they raced past. By 0840 hours they were at Slim River Bridge where a troop of 16th LAA Battery stood. Their commander, warned of the enemy approach, ordered 'Sights Near' and held his fire until the range was 100 yards. But when he opened fire the little 40mm shells bounced off the tanks and his exposed detachments soon took heavy casualties. It had been a brave attempt.

At this time 155th Field Regiment was in a hide at Behrang six miles south of Slim Bridge when at 0800 hours it received orders to deploy against tank attack. Lieutenant Colonel Murdoch and three officers, Captain Mackenzie, Lieutenant Hinton, the Gun Position Officer of 'C' Troop and Lieutenant Ronaldson with a 4.5-inch howitzer of 'E' Troop and BSM Billings moved forward. The party went ahead on motor cycles to find positions and to open an advanced

Headquarters when about one mile north of Slim village they met the Japanese tanks head on at 0845 hours. Colonel Murdoch, who had achieved so much in this campaign, was killed, two of the officers were captured but Captain Mackenzie took cover and saw the Japanese soldiers leap out of their tanks and start slaughtering the LAA Gunners. It was here that BSM Billings was killed.

155th Field Regiment was still advancing with its guns at 400 yard intervals. The lead gun was the 4.5-inch howitzer of 'E' Troop which was following the commanding officer's party which had bumped into the enemy. The gun came round a corner and met Lieutenant Eustace who said that enemy tanks were just ahead. Lieutenant Ronaldson, running back, ordered the 4.5 into action where it was. At this point Captain CG Brown, the Adjutant, arrived and took charge. As the first tank clanked round the bend in the road, Sergeant Keen, the Number 1 on the 4.5-inch howitzer, waited holding the lanyard and then fired at a range of 125 yards. The first round hit the lead tank but did not stop it, but a second caused it to burst into flames. Then a second tank arrived. Four more rounds were fired when Sergeant Keen was told to limber up. By this time Captain Brown lay wounded by the road as he controlled the operation. Two Japanese soldiers leapt from a tank and ran towards him but he and Lance Bombardier Mair dispatched them with their pistols. As the gun tractor pulled away it was hit but did not stop. The gallant Sergeant Keen was himself cut down by automatic fire as he ran after it. His body was picked up and he was later buried in 'C' Battery wagon lines. He had behaved with the greatest calmness and gallantry. So had Captain Brown, who was later awarded a Military Cross for his gallantry in this action.

As there were no infantry available, 'C' Battery sent patrols forward under BSM Roadnight who engaged the Japanese tank crews and suffered one man wounded. An anti-tank troop moved up and came into action with them and this little force stopped all further penetration south that night. The cost had been high; the commanding officer, Lieutenant Colonel A Murdoch, BSM Billings, Sergeant Keen and Signaller Warner killed and Captain CG Brown and Gunner Warwick wounded with Bombardier Edel missing. The fate of Colonel Murdoch will never be known. He was last seen riding pillion on a motor cycle on his way to report to his brigade commander. He was a most gallant man and was sadly missed by all ranks. Once again these splendid Scottish Gunners had saved the day. Major Philip Gold assumed command and Captain Stewart became adjutant.

Meanwhile Major J Wilson, commanding 'B' Battery 155th Field Regiment, was trying to collect the disorganised remnants of 12th and 15th Indian Infantry Brigades who were pushing down the railway towards Tanjong Malim. 'C' Battery covered them with two guns near the North Road - Behrang junction while 'B' Battery came into action covering Tanjong Malim itself. Here Captain Mackenzie established an OP.

350th Field Battery of 137th Field Regiment also withdrew to new positions at Tanjong Malim and was joined by an anti-tank troop and an infantry battalion. But there was little left of the regiment after Slim River and it was broken up save for 350th Battery, which became part of 155th Field Regiment. The action at Slim River had been a major disaster and resulted in the loss of central Malaya. After Slim River 11th Indian Division ceased to exist as an effective formation for some time. One cause of the defeat was the failure to use artillery correctly, especially anti-tank guns. When a regiment was available only one troop was used. The field regiments were not given any priority and were told to sit back in hides when their concentrated fire would surely have stopped the enemy advancing nose to tail down narrow roads. To make matters even worse, communications failed so that British commanders were always behind events.

Percival next ordered the newly arrived 45th Indian Infantry Brigade forward to come under the command of 3rd Indian Corps to help deny the airfields at Kuala Lumpur to the enemy while a new defensive line was formed from Mersing through Segamat to Muar. 9th HAA Battery had been ordered from Ipoh to Kuala Lumpur and one troop of 14th LAA Battery went to Port Swettenham. On 21st December Kuala Lumpur had been heavily bombed, a Junkers 87 and three other bombers were destroyed by the guns. On 23rd December 11th HAA Battery shot down another and on 27th two more. The guns were becoming much more effective with practice. 3rd Indian Corps was next ordered to move south to defend western Johore while 8th Australian Division held the eastern sector. Meanwhile the remains of 11th Indian Division moved south; 15th Indian Infantry Brigade under Brigadier RG Moir had been defending the left flank in the Selangor area. On 4th January an enemy landing was stopped by the fire of the 18-pounders of the FMSV Battery. On 7th January, 7th and 10th Mountain Batteries were in action covering the withdrawal from Kuala Lumpur through the Seremban Pass at Labu. It was here that Major Scott ran into an enemy ambush and was killed instantly. He was much mourned by 7th Battery and was buried on the gun position. Captain Standish took command. Then on the 8th the guns of 22nd Mountain Regiment sank another four boats, breaking up another landing near Selangor. Many enemy did get ashore, however, and overran headquarters 1/14th Punjab, killing the commanding officer. Further south 3rd Cavalry and the Gunners of the FMSV were again heavily involved at Klang. Then the order to withdraw from Kuala Lumpur had to be given and 28th Indian Infantry Brigade fell back through Seremban and Port Dickson to Tampin. Three days later the weary troops passed through the 8th Australian Division at Gemas and Batu Anam in northern Johore. 12th Indian Infantry Brigade went to Singapore and 28th Indian Infantry Brigade to Pontian Kechil on the coast of south west Johore ostensibly to rest.

On 8th January Wavell arrived to see the situation for himself and noted the weary state of the men. He said that Johore must be held until reinforcements could arrive. He also ordered defences to be prepared along the north shore of Singapore Island. Fortunately the Japanese used their air power badly otherwise, said Wavell, '. . . there would have been complete disaster'. Nevertheless they had increased their air attacks on Singapore. The raids came in at over 20,000 feet which was outside the range of the 3-inch and 40mm guns. Only the 3.7s could engage and there were only 40 of them and that was nothing like enough. The few fighters did their best and somehow the combined effort of both enabled the reinforcements to land without too many casualties. First came 53rd Infantry Brigade, of 18th British Division and then 6th HAA and 35th LAA Regiments together with 85th Anti-Tank Regiment plus some 51 Hurricanes in crates. On 12th January the Japanese had established their *5th Divisional Headquarters* in Kuala Lumpur. The net was closing.

The anti-aircraft Gunners also fell back. 11th HAA Battery had an adventurous drive of 100 miles to reach Batu Pahat where it deployed to defend the airfield and harbour. Here it was joined by a section of 3-inch guns of 9th HAA Battery which had endured four days of persistent attack and had shot down at least one enemy aircraft. At Ayer Hitam 18 Bofors guns of 9th and 16th LAA Batteries and 89th and 144th LAA Batteries of 35th LAA Regiment were sent north from Singapore to help.

By this time the Japanese were planning their next phase, a three-pronged attack, to capture the Netherlands East Indies (Map 1). Western Force: *229th Infantry Regiment* assembled in Camranh Bay, in French Indo China, and was ordered to invade southern Sumatra and *2nd Division*, together with *230th Infantry Regiment*, was to invade western Java. Central Force; *48th Division,* based on Jolo Island and *56th Regiment Group*, based on Davao, in the Philippines, was to occupy the oilfields of Tarakan, Balikpapan and Bandjermasin in eastern Dutch Borneo and then move on to invade eastern Java. Eastern Force, *Sasebo Combined Special Landing Force* and *228th*

Infantry Regiment, also operating from Davao, would capture Celebes, Amboina and Timor. This great southward movement, commanded by Vice Admiral Nobutake Kondo's *2nd Fleet* and supported by *21st* and *23rd Air Flotillas*, began on 7th January 1942. At Tarakan the Dutch managed to destroy the oilfields but Menado near the northern tip of Celebes was captured by 11th January. With the spreading of the Far East war, General Wavell set up his new Headquarters ABDA at Lembang some ten miles north of Bandoeng in Java with General Pownall, his Chief of Staff. It took full command of the ABDA area on 15th January. Lieutenant General H ter Poorten, of the Netherlands, was to control operations with Major General ISO Playfair as his Chief of Staff. By this time the Army Commanders in the Far East were:

Burma: Lieutenant General TJ Hutton, (British).
Malaya: Lieutenant General AE Percival, (British).
Philippines: Lieutenant General D MacArthur, (American).
Darwin Sub-Area: Major General DJV Blake, (Australian).

Air Marshal Sir Richard Pierce commanded the Air Forces, with Major General LH Brereton USAAF as deputy commander. Admiral TC Hart USN commanded all naval forces in the area with Rear Admiral AFE Palliser, RN, as his deputy. It was a brave attempt at a multi-national command structure but there was much to do to make it work with the enemy pressing on relentlessly. Wavell again visited Singapore on 15th January to find that the Japanese had indeed pressed on and were in contact with the Australians and the Indians in northern Johore. He warned the Chiefs of Staff that the forthcoming battle for Singapore would be a close run thing. By the 24th the Japanese were off Balikpapan and a threat was developing towards Burma; both of these diverted much needed resources. On 25th Wavell flew to meet Hutton in Rangoon and found him confident.

In Malaya, General Yamashita, at *25th Army*, decided to rest his *5th Division* at Seremban after the capture of Kuala Lumpur on 11th January. The advance was to be continued by the *Imperial Guards Division* in the west and the *55th Infantry Regiment* in the east. The latter was to advance towards Endau and Mersing. General Bennett decided to defend the line Batu Anam - Muar (Map 6). He placed 27th Australian Infantry Brigade astride the main trunk road at Gemas. Behind them lay 9th Indian Division which had 8th Indian Infantry Brigade, also on the trunk road at Batu Anam. 22nd Indian Infantry Brigade was deployed between Segamet and Jementah and 45th Indian Infantry Brigade was stretched out along the Sungei Muar guarding against sea-borne landings. Deployed in this area were 2/10th and 2/15th Australian and 5th and 88th British Field Regiments together with 2/4th Australian Anti-Tank Regiment.

On the morning of 15th January, after a heavy bombardment, the Japanese closed up on the trunk road and fell into a carefully laid Australian ambush near Gemas which caused them many casualties, mainly from the guns of 30th Field Battery of 2/15th Field Regiment. But they kept up the pressure with an outflanking movement through Ayer Kuning. At the same time the *Imperial Guards* advanced down the coast towards Muar and attacked the new and wholly inexperienced 45th Indian Infantry Brigade and also 65th Battery of 2/15th Field Regiment RAA. Muar was attacked and for a while it was held mainly by a single Australian 25-pounder and two 2-pounders, of 2/4th Anti Tank Regiment, both firing over open sights. Soon only Lance Sergeant KI Harrison and Gunner J Bull of one the 2-pounders were still fit for action, but three tanks had been knocked out and the Japanese had withdrawn. Nevertheless it was not long before they were over the river and the whole left flank was exposed. Then came more landings at Batu Pahat. Bennett rushed the 2/29th and 2/19th Battalions to reinforce the left at Bakri. Later that day 11th Indian Division was ordered to Yong Peng with the newly arrived 53rd

Infantry Brigade of 18th British Division. By this time the enemy had closed on Mersing on the east coast.

'Near Yong Peng 155th Field Regiment had a splendid 'OP, one of the best in Malaya, [it] had an excellent view over open ground towards Parit Sulong on the right, and over rubber to Batu Pahat and the coast on the left and in the centre' (Sewell). The 6th Battalion, the Royal Norfolk Regiment, of 53rd British Infantry Brigade which had just arrived in Malaya, was deployed in depth with 'A' Company around the guns. From the OP, enemy landings at Batu Pahat could be seen but were out of range. It was here that 6th Norfolks had its first battle experience when it was bombed. Then on the morning of 19th January came reports of enemy advancing from Batu Pahat. At 1100 hours they attacked 'C' Company of the Norfolks, driving it back. 'F' Troop engaged the enemy over open sights while 'D' Company and the carriers gave ground slowly. It was the battalion's first battle and it was nervous and inexperienced and as 'A' and 'B' Companies passed through the guns they said, 'give 'em Hell.' BSM Roadnight took a small party of Gunners forward to give local protection to the guns and dealt with an enemy party with grenades.

The remnant of 45th Indian Infantry Brigade was gathering itself together having suffered severely and lost its commander killed in action. It was then assisted by two Australian battalions, 2/19th and 2/29th, who fought magnificently to the east of Muar; the commanding officer of the former, Lieutenant Colonel CGW Anderson, was awarded the Victoria Cross. 15th Indian Infantry Brigade moved up towards Batu Pahat with 53rd British Infantry Brigade in the Bukit Pelandok defile. 45th Indian Infantry Brigade was to withdraw to Yong Peng and then force its way to Labis, but the Japanese cut the road behind it at Bukit Pelandok and it was unable to move. In spite of gallant work by 'C' Battery of 155th Field Regiment firing point blank, the Japanese pressed on. BSM Roadnight led six Gunners in a bayonet charge against a Japanese platoon and routed it, buying much needed time. 3/16th Punjab tried again but they suffered terribly and their commanding officer, Lieutenant Colonel HD Moorehead, was mortally wounded. Captain Sewell of 115th Field Regiment had retaken his OP and engaged the enemy with a mortar which he and his assistant, Bombardier Shone, had never fired before. Sewell was badly wounded by a grenade. He was later to receive a Military Cross and Shone a Military Medal for this action.

They had all fought like tigers and the enemy was held. At 1730 hours the guns of 155th Field Regiment got out just in time. By 22nd January 'C' Battery was in Johore Bahru. The remains of 45th Indian Infantry Brigade tried to get out in small groups through the jungle but few succeeded. By 21st January 22nd Indian Infantry Brigade was around Labis, 8th Indian Infantry Brigade further south and 27th Australian Infantry Brigade, which had arrived in Yong Peng after a nightmare march through enemy lines, was to learn that the wounded they left behind under the protection of the Red Cross had been butchered by the Japanese. In 1950 General Nishimura of the *Imperial Guards* was found guilty of this atrocity and went to the gallows. It was on 19th January that 2/19th Australian Battalion was attacked by tanks at Parit Sulong. One 25-pounder of 2/15th Field Regiment under Lieutenant JF Ross RAA and Sergeant B Tate engaged the enemy at 50 yards range. When they had knocked out two and all their ammunition was expended, Lieutenant Ross crawled along a ditch and disabled the third with a grenade in its tracks. (Horner).

Percival next issued orders to hold a line from Jemaluang in East Kluang to Ayer Hitam and on to Batu Pahat. But the pressure at this latter place built up to such an extent that withdrawal became inevitable. Radio again broke down and Brigadier BS Challen, commanding 15th Indian Infantry Brigade at Benut, had no contact with Headquarters 11th Indian Division. General Key visited him on the 27th and ordered a special force, which would be commanded by Major CFW

Banham, commanding 336th Battery of 135th Field Regiment (The Hertfordshire Yeomanry), to break through to Senggarang and Rengit. This force, 'Bancol', met the enemy 150 yards north of the latter place and the new young conscripts they had with them were massacred. Out of 112 men all but 18 were killed. The first gun of the leading battery came into action and engaged over open sights but all its detachment were killed. Lieutenant Mackwood ordered it out of action and got it back to Rengit, Lieutenant Stebbing was killed. The second gun was saved by Bombardier Thompson. His driver was killed and two sergeants mortally wounded so he assumed command, unlimbered the gun, climbed into the driver's seat, turned the unwieldy tractor in the narrow road under fire, loaded the quad with wounded Gunners and infantry, hooked in his gun and crouching low drove back to safety, a most gallant action.

At Batu Pahat the guns of 9th LAA and 11th HAA Batteries fought a hard ground action alongside the stricken 45th Indian Infantry Brigade. 11th HAA Battery got out just in time but 9th had to destroy its guns and the men had to take to the jungle. 65th Field Battery RAA was forced to destroy its guns but 98 of its men managed to get back to Allied lines. Meanwhile at Senggarang, the gallant Major Banham had raced right through the Japanese position and linked up with Brigadier Challen, who decided to destroy all equipment and attempt to break out through the jungle leaving his wounded behind. They left at last light 26th January. This time the wounded were not butchered. Meanwhile Brigadier CLB Duke, commanding 53rd British Infantry Brigade, and Lieutenant Colonel PJD Toosey, commanding 135th Field Regiment, went forward to Rengit to see what had happened but had to withdraw rapidly.

During the night 21/22nd January 1942 the Japanese attacked 'C' Troop of 155th Field Regiment just south of Ayer Hitam but did not close when the infantry protecting the guns engaged them. Then at 0900 hours on 22nd 'D' Troop was attacked and the guns under Lieutenant Ffolkes engaged over open sights and several men engaged with small arms. Captain Anderson engaged the attacking Japanese from a flank with 'C' Troop. Major J Wilson, Battery Commander 'B' Battery, arrived in a carrier but was instantly killed by a sniper. The Japanese then charged and overran the position at the point of the bayonet. Captain Mackenzie took command and ordered 'C' Troop and the one surviving gun of 'D' Troop into action in a new position nearer to Batu Pahat. The Gunners had fought to the end.

Plans were by then being made to withdraw the whole force to Singapore Island should it become necessary. Wavell visited Singapore again on 20th January to find that little had been done to improve the defences of the north of the island, despite his previous orders. He reported to the Chiefs of Staff that he was planning to make maximum use of the fortress guns against land attack from the north, prepare obstacles on the approaches to the island from Johore, divert forces from the south to the north of the island, destroy all boats which could help the enemy and establish mobile reserves to counter-attack any landings. Churchill replied by cable on the 20th, 'I want to make it absolutely clear that I expect every inch of ground to be defended, every scrap of material or defences to be blown to pieces to prevent capture by the enemy, and no question of surrender to be entertained until after protracted fighting among the ruins of Singapore city.'

Percival ordered plans to be drawn up to defend the island in three sectors; the Western Sector was to be held by 8th Australian Division, the Northern, where he expected the landings to come, by 18th British Division and the Southern by 11th Indian Division. The pressure in south Malaya continued. *5th Division* had joined in and had reached Labis and the *Imperial Guards* had by-passed Batu Pahat to the south. Percival decided to fall back on Ayer Hitam, leaving the remains of 15th Indian Infantry Brigade at Batu Pahat. The RAF, RAAF, RNZAF and the Dutch did what they could but were down to some 70 old bombers and 20 fighters. Many were being lost on the ground as they refuelled and Percival agreed that they should move to Sumatra as Japanese bombing increased considerably. By this time 44th Indian Infantry Brigade, 54th and 55th British Infantry Brigades and the balance of 18th British Division had arrived but none was trained or ready for combat.

By the morning of 24th January 3rd Indian Corps was deployed as follows:

East Force. 22nd Australian Brigade, less a battalion, but with one British and two Indian battalions and some Malay troops, was in contact at Mersing.

West Force. 9th Indian Division, 8th and 22nd Indian Infantry Brigades, with 5th and 88th Field Regiments at Kluang and 27th Australian Infantry Brigade with 2/15th Field Regiment and one battery of 155th Field Regiment at Ayer Hitam.

West Coast Force. 15th Indian Infantry Brigade at Batu Pahat, 28th Indian Infantry Brigade at Pontian Kechil and 53rd British Infantry Brigade with 135th Field Regiment and another battery of 155th Field Regiment at Benut.

'On 25th January 272nd Anti-Tank Battery was at Kluang. Here Lieutenant Moser and his troop were in action. It retired to Johore on the 27th before moving into Singapore. One troop under Lieutenant JDP Hoyle acted as rearguard to the Argyll and Sutherland Highlanders who were the last troops to cross the Causeway before it was destroyed.' (Podmore).

As the battle for Batu Pahat raged on, and plans to link 15th Indian with 53rd British Infantry Brigades together failed at Senggarang, orders were given to pull right out of the area, but the fighting became even more ferocious. Eventually the two brigades broke out as best they could, some men by sea and some through the jungle. At 1600 hours on 26th January two guns of 'D' Troop, one given by 'C' Troop, of 'B' Battery, 155th Field Regiment, were taken up close to blast out of the way some enemy machine guns which were preventing the break out. This failed as most shells burst in the trees. It was here that Gunner Holdsworth won the Military Medal for gallantry in action. At 1800 hours orders were given to destroy all guns and equipment and to make for the coast. The march through the swamp was hard going, the men were dead tired and covered in mud and slime. After many adventures the men of 'B' Battery were taken off by the Royal Navy, not one being lost since the Battery Commander, Major Wilson, had been killed at Ayer Hitam. The rest of the splendid 155th Field Regiment which had done so much to bring some order and cohesion to the fighting in Malaya, crossed the Causeway into Singapore during the night of 27th January 1942.

On the east coast 22nd Australian Infantry Brigade was ordered to withdraw from Mersing, which it did covered by 2/16th Australian Infantry Battalion and two field batteries. They formed a defensive box at Jemaluang and sprang a most successful ambush on the advancing Japanese. The fighting was again vicious, with the Japanese coming off the worse. It was on the afternoon of 26th January that Heath ordered the withdrawal of 3rd Indian Corps to Singapore. East Force moved first and reached Johore Bahru on the 30th. After their bloody nose at Jemaluang, the Japanese did not follow up. On the coastal road 11th Indian Division withdrew to Skudai while 28th Indian Infantry Brigade held Pontian Kechil until midnight on 29th January. Again the Japanese did not follow up.

In the centre, however, they did follow up closely. 27th Australian Infantry Brigade was some three miles south of Ayer Hitam on the main road, 8th Indian Infantry Brigade was at Sungei Sayong Halt and 22nd Indian Infantry Brigade at Rengam. For the withdrawal, 9th Indian Division was to follow the line of the railway because there was no road. It sent its guns and vehicles along some planters' tracks and made the best time it could on foot. 22nd Indian Infantry Brigade was to deny a position at Milestone 437 until midnight 28th January. 8th Indian Infantry Brigade was to hold Senenak until midnight on the 30th and then 22nd Indian Infantry Brigade was to deny Kulai until midnight on 31st January. The enemy closed up on the night of the 27th and a fighting withdrawal began. Then by mistake the railway bridge was blown, destroying the only link between the two brigades, and a dangerous gap opened up between them. The Japanese were quick to exploit this and confusion reigned. Major General AE Barstow, GOC 9th Indian Division, was killed as he tried to sort it out.

Meanwhile the Australians were withdrawing down the main road as 22nd Indian Infantry Brigade struggled through the jungle and suffered terribly. In the end the remaining 350 survivors were forced to surrender and 22nd Indian Infantry Brigade was no more. Percival reported to Wavell that the situation was again critical and that he was falling back on Singapore with all speed. Wavell agreed. Special instructions were given to protect the vital Causeway which carried the only road and rail link available. 6th and 11th HAA Batteries HK-S RA and 4th Indian HAA Battery together with 16th HAA Battery HK-S RA and 89th and 144th LAA Batteries were deployed around it with a total of 60 guns, some to the north in Johore. 22nd Australian Infantry Brigade plus artillery formed an outer ring of defence. The Argylls, now only 250 strong, formed a close protection force. Although the Japanese kept up a relentless ground pressure, for some reason they did not attack the Causeway from the air, thus by 0530 hours the whole of 3rd Indian Corps was across and on the island, followed by the anti-aircraft guns and finally the Argylls marching to the skirl of the pipes. The causeway was then blown up and the battle for Malaya was over.

In his diary Alanbrooke wrote on 30th January 1941 'Today is one of the blackest days of the war, news bad on all sides. Benghazi has been lost again and Singapore is in a bad way. The defence is retiring to the island tonight. I doubt whether the island can hold out very long,'

As is so often the case with the British Army, the regiments and units fought well. There was much individual heroism and men died in gallant defiance to the last or advanced in local counter-attack with great ferocity. Many times the Japanese reported the toughness of the fighting and many times they held back when they knew the consequences of attacking prepared positions. But it was above unit level that the problems arose. Units were cobbled together in brigades and commanders lacked experience at the operational level, co-ordination failed frequently, as will always be the case if training at this level is faulty. More than anywhere else the disaster in Malaya was caused by failure to keep the armed forces up to date and to make timely decisions once the die was cast. The result was the loss of many fine men and their units as they struggled to rectify these deficiencies in the face of the enemy.

The men of the Royal Regiment and their Australian, Indian and Malayan comrades did all they could. It was not good country for artillery but where the guns could be used they had dramatic effect, and they were fought with the greatest gallantry. Many times the Gunners fought as infantry. Once some Gunners suddenly found themselves with small arms alone at a cross roads and decided that survival in the jungle was better than being bayoneted by Japanese infantry, so they disappeared, but it was an isolated case. The gunnery problems were very great, platforms were never ideal, observation was almost always poor, communications unreliable and sometimes non-existent and roads and tracks poor and easy to ambush. Gun positions were always under threat of direct attack. But almost always there was a Gunner commander ready at each level of command to do his utmost to provide the vital firepower when it was needed. The anti-aircraft

Gunners had real problems and there were far too few of them; frequently they engaged over open sights in the ground role to beat off direct attack. Sadly it was their lot to protect airfields badly located for defence and which were in any case hurriedly evacuated as the enemy closed. They all did their duty in the service of the guns fighting against jungle, sickness, fatigue and a skilful, merciless enemy who had total air superiority; in doing so they added another chapter to the story of the Regiment. But it was not over yet, they next faced another great test, this time joined by the men of the Coast Artillery in the defence of the fortress and naval base of Singapore.

CHAPTER 4

THE LOSS OF SINGAPORE

JANUARY - FEBRUARY 1942

(Maps 11, 12, 13 and 14)

The Gunners who fought the battle for Singapore and in Malaya are listed separately at Annex A. They were weary men who for the most part had been fighting non-stop through Malaya or who had recently arrived and were doing what they could to prepare to defend the island against both ground and air attack. The coast batteries were hard at work trying, where necessary, to make it possible for their guns to open arcs towards Johore by demolishing structures which would prevent this. It was not possible in some cases as concrete structures had been erected to afford protection against air attack. The batteries' primary role was, after all, coast defence and they could do nothing about the higher ground which could not be cleared by flat-trajectory high-velocity guns. So far the coast Gunners had not opened fire. No Japanese warship had come within range of their positions but they had suffered from air attack.

Great efforts were made to turn the huge 15-inch guns at Buona Vista so that they could hit Johore but without success (Map 11). The three 9.2-inch guns at Connaught and the 6-inch guns at Pasir Laba could certainly engage to the north west. Efforts were made to ensure that the batteries at Labrador, Serapong and Changi could traverse towards the north and were able to engage land targets should the enemy get ashore on the island. Land service high explosive ammunition, however, was in very short supply, as only a small proportion was scaled for the 6-inch and the 9.2-inch guns and none for the 15-inch. There were, however, plenty of armour piercing projectiles. Many of the batteries were very vulnerable to attack from the north, especially those in Changi Fire Command at Pengerang, with its 2 x 6-inch, and Tekong Island, with its 3 x 9.2-inch and 2 x 6-inch, so all were given infantry protection and all Gunners were warned to be prepared to fight as infantry. It is therefore true that the guns were sited to face a sea-borne attack from the south and east but it is quite untrue to assert that none could be fired onto land targets. Some successful efforts were made to rectify the situation where guns were unable to bear. In several cases, as will be shown, they were used to good effect when fighting on the island began. Lieutenant Colonel HDStG Cardew RA, commanding 7th Coast Regiment and Changi Fire Command, produced a detailed account of the battle written in pencil while he was in Changi gaol. Part of this is reproduced at Annex C. He shows how the 6-inch guns at Pasir Laba and the 15-inch at Buona Vista were almost in the front line once the Japanese were ashore and were, therefore, severely restricted. Buona Vista Battery was unable to bear on the attackers and was ordered to be demolished on 11th February. Demolitions were partly successful. Other coast guns primarily of Faber Fire Command, engaged targets on the mainland and on the island most effectively as this narrative will recount.

The air defence plan for the island was made by Brigadier AWG Wildey, Commander AA Defences Singapore, at his Headquarters at Fort Canning. Once again the main task was to protect the airfields, the naval base, the harbour and the city. Allowing for losses in the battle for

Malaya it would seem that Brigadier Wildey had some 70 heavy and 65 light anti-aircraft guns available for the defence of the island. These were in 12 heavy and six light batteries. However many of the heavy guns were the old 3-inch which were frequently outranged. There were air attacks on 21 days in January. Tengah airfield was put out of action on 21st January and shortly afterwards so were Seletar and Sembawang. A total of 41 enemy aircraft was shot down in this period and on one occasion 10th HAA Battery of 1st HAA Regiment HK-S RA shot down the three leading aircraft of an attack formation with the opening rounds from their 4.5-inch AA guns. The anti-aircraft artillery which fought at Singapore is also listed at Annex A and the layout is marked on Map 11.

Major Ian Graeme, who was commanding 29th HAA Battery of 3rd HAA Regiment RA, writes, 'Our 3-inch guns were replaced by the new 3.7-inch mobile guns and I was lucky enough to have, in 29th HAA Battery, eight mobile guns and four static guns. This meant that I had a permanent gun site at Mandai just south of the Johore Causeway with the static guns and the opportunity to move the mobile guns around. We were given a secondary role of moving up country with the mobile guns in a field role in support of the infantry'. (Graeme). Major Graeme was posted to the staff of Sir Robert Brooke-Popham in Singapore, working for General Pownall and moved to Java and eventually to Ceylon.

At the end of December 1941 the Chiefs of Staff decided to re-direct Convoy WS14 from its destination in the Middle East to Singapore. On board was 77th HAA Regiment from South Wales consisting of 239th, 240th and 241st HAA Batteries, 21st LAA Regiment with 48th and 69th LAA Batteries from Cheshire and 79th LAA Battery from Walton on Thames and 48th LAA Regiment consisting of 49th, 95th, and 242nd LAA Batteries. The convoy arrived in Singapore on 13th January 1942 but most of the equipment had gone to the Middle East. The regiments were, however, re-equipped from the Singapore stockpile. While this was going, on what remained of the RAF, RAAF, RNZAF and the Netherlands East Indies Airforce was ordered to re-deploy to Sumatra and Java to escape the air attacks. Convoy WS14, which was still in harbour, was again diverted, this time to Batavia (Djakarta). It also took 6th HAA Regiment less 3rd HAA Battery which remained in Singapore, 78th LAA Battery and two troops of 89th LAA Battery from 35th LAA Regiment in Singapore, 21st and 48th LAA and 77th HAA Regiments which had just arrived. They all left Singapore on 30th January 1942.

The field and anti-tank artillery was grouped with divisions as it arrived from the battles of Malaya or as reinforcements. In Western Area was 8th Australian Division with 2/10th Australian Field Regiment, by then equipped with 24 x 25-pounders and 6 x 4.5-inch howitzers, and 2/15th Australian Field Regiment, with 16 x 25-pounders, 4 x 18-pounders and 10 x 4.5-inch howitzers, 5th Field Regiment RA, in 44th Indian Infantry Brigade now part of 8th Division, and 2/4th Australian Anti-Tank Regiment, 13th, 15th and 16th Anti-Tank Batteries, with 30 x 2-pounders and 13 x 75mm guns. In Northern Area was 11th Indian Division, incorporating what remained of 9th Indian Division, with 135th and 155th Field Regiments and 350th Battery, formerly of 137th Field Regiment. There also was 22nd Mountain Regiment in action west of the Seletar River. Its 4th Mountain Battery had 2 x 6-inch howitzers and its 7th, 10th and 21st Batteries each had 6 x 3.7-inch howitzers. 21st Mountain Battery was sent to defend the naval base. In Northern Area also was 18th British Division HQ and two brigades which had arrived in Singapore only on 29th January 1942 with 88th, 118th and 148th Field Regiments.

155th Field Regiment had 'C' Battery in action with its 4.5-inch howitzers about a mile south of Sembawang airfield on the Nee Soon road. RHQ was a mile north east at Chong Peng alongside the headquarters of 53rd British Infantry Brigade. All were dug in, wired and OPs established in the naval base in readiness for a long siege. By 1st February 'B' Battery, 155th Field

Regiment had recovered from its battle at Batu Pahat, had drawn new 25-pounders and moved into action about a mile east of Chong Peng where Major GM Campbell, of 135th Field Regiment, arrived to assume command. The guns first opened fire on 4th February, BSM Roadnight sinking five enemy barges loaded with infantry. It was here that Roadnight was awarded his well deserved DCM for so many gallant and courageous acts during the long withdrawal through Malaya.

Enemy air attacks began in earnest and on 5th February the *Empress of Asia* was attacked as she approached Singapore loaded with reinforcements. Lieutenant Colonel James Dean RA was OC Troops and by his cool action, when the ship caught fire from air attacks, evacuated troops into boats with the loss of only 20. He was then driven from the bridge which was on fire and went on deck where he continued to control operations. He joined in firing the ship's guns until the order to abandon ship was given. He was the last man to leave as the ship sank. (Taken from the citation for his DSO which joined his MBE and DCM).

At dawn on 8th February 1942 enemy air attacks increased in ferocity against Singapore, especially in the area of 22nd Australian Infantry Brigade in whose area were 2/15th Field Regiment and 15th Anti-Tank Battery RAA (Map 12). Enemy artillery also engaged targets everywhere. Further east, 135th Field Regiment was badly hit but its guns and those of 22nd Mountain Regiment replied as best they could, controlled from an OP on Bukit Mandai manned by Lieutenant Skene. 135th Field Regiment was galvanised into action by its commanding officer, Lieutenant Colonel PJD Toosey, who was later awarded a DSO for his splendid leadership during the battle and was to become famous as the commander of the prisoners on the Burma railway (and role model for the part played by Sir Alec Guinness in the film of the *Bridge on the River Kwai* which, unfortunately, gives a completely false portrayal of the officer concerned). The bombing and shelling went on all day. There was a lull at sunset and then the Japanese guns opened with renewed fury and almost all telephone lines were cut. The CRA of 8th Australian Division, Brigadier Callaghan, was taken to hospital suffering from malaria and Lieutenant Colonel McEachern took his place. At 0130 hours 9th February the Japanese artillery switched to the attack of all forward defences, headquarters and communications and did great damage. They were employing all the artillery of *5th* and *18th Divisions*.

Neither HQ Malaya Command nor HQ Western Area thought that this was more than the start of several days of bombardment and so gave no orders for retaliation onto likely forming up areas. Thus, when a mass of landing craft raced across the mere 300 yards of water between the mainland and the north west coast of the island between Tanjong Buloh and Tanjong Murai, surprise was complete. What is more, only those on the beaches knew what was happening and they were unable to tell anyone else because most of the cables had been cut by shell fire. By the morning of 9th February, 2/10th Field Regiment was employing six motor cyclists to pass fire orders to its guns (Horner). The crossings were supported by intense artillery and mortar fire concentrated on the landing beaches.

Orders had been given not to expose any lights of 5th Searchlight Regiment, to illuminate the attackers, without specific instructions to do so. Desperate calls for defensive fire never reached the batteries until SOS light signals were put up by the infantry. Based on these the guns fired pre-recorded tasks which may or may not have been relevant. In any case the amount of artillery to cover the front of 2/18th and 2/19th Battalions was inadequate. Only 29th, 30th and 65th Australian Field Batteries were in range. Infantry machine guns did much execution but soon ran out of ammunition. Seven 2-pounders of 2/4th Anti-Tank Regiment RAA had been placed on the beaches to deal with landings but they were neutralised by enemy fire and impossible to get out. Thus in spite of suffering heavy casualties the Japanese, by sheer weight of numbers, soon gained footholds all along the front. Once ashore they pressed on quickly between the widely separated

Australian positions so that soon the defenders, who fought most valiantly, found themselves attacked on all sides. Enemy parties, clearly well briefed, had raced on towards Ama Keng to cut the position in two.

It was not until 0300 hours on 9th February that Brigadier HB Taylor, the commander of 22nd Australian Infantry Brigade, was able to give a meaningful report to HQ Western Area and in doing so he stressed the need for a counter-attack at dawn as he had no reserves strong enough to carry out such a move. Accordingly Major General HG Bennett, GOC 8th Australian Division, placed 2/29th Battalion under the command of 22nd Australian Infantry Brigade. At the same time he ordered the battalion forward to Tengah airfield. He ordered 2/10th Field Regiment to engage the mainland at Sungei Skudai and asked Malaya Command for maximum air attacks at first light. Next, at 0445 hours, he also placed 2/4th Machine Gun Battalion and his Special Reserve Battalion under the command of Brigadier Taylor, ordering it forward to Tengah airfield as well.

During the night of 8/9th February the two 6-inch guns of Pasir Laba Battery, Captain JR Asher RA, manned by men of 7th Coast Battery HK-S RA '. . . had calls from 44 Indian Inf Bde and AIF for night harassing fire onto all likely embarkation places between Sungei Pendas and Tanjong Tuan on the southern Johore coast. . . . OC Pasir Laba immediately answered these calls with the only gun (No. 1) which could bear. The overhead cover on this gun was cut away to permit the maximum traverse for fire. The gun fired 40 rds up to 0430 hrs . . . At 0630 hrs the BC telephoned FC to report dive bombing of Pasir Laba . . . [At about 0715 hrs] shells began to land on the fort. Between 0715 and 0815 hrs the OP was hit twice, both gun emplacements were also hit several times and the overhead cover on No. 2 gun was in a very demolished state and, according to Captain Asher, No. 1 gun could not be fired except in the gravest emergency. At about 0745 the BC asked FC for permission to prepare for demolition as a message had been received that 44 Indian Inf Bde were withdrawing. HQ FD gave permission.' Captain Asher gave orders to prepare for demolition. He was killed while attempting to drag his BSM, Boon, and other wounded men to safety, assisted by Bombardier FR Cherrington. Lieutenant ES Senior and two more men were wounded. A demolition party arrived from Siloso Battery at 1230 hours but it experienced difficulty in finding the charges prepared by Asher and Senior. The Fire Command then sent a team from Labrador Battery, under Lieutenant CH Finch, which arrived at about 1830 hours and, after any items of use had been collected, the battery was destroyed with the assistance of a detachment of Royal Engineers. The men and the Malay company then withdrew marching down the Jurong road. (From the recollected 'War Diary' of Faber Fire Command). Asher, Senior and Cherrington were all 'Mentioned in dispatches in recognition of gallant and distinguished services in Malaya in 1942' (*London Gazette* 1 August 1946).

Also at Pasir Laba, Lieutenant Henderson was in command of a section of two 18-pounders engaged in beach defence. 'On 9th February his section was evacuated but he remained behind, under heavy and continuous fire, to destroy his guns. Subsequently he made his way back through enemy lines and took command of a section of 2-pounder anti-tank guns which he handled most successfully again under severe shelling and machine gun fire. Throughout he displayed courage, resourcefulness, initiative and had a most stimulating effect on all under his command. (From the citation for his Military Cross).

Meanwhile Johore Battery, in the east of the island, with three 15-inch guns, and Connaught Battery, on Blakang Mati island in the south, with three 9.2-inch, kept up attacks on the enemy but they too were under constant air attack. Observation was almost impossible, communications most uncertain and by then only armour piercing ammunition was available, so the damage done could not have been great except at the point of impact.

At dawn all available aircraft on the island, ten Hurricanes and four Swordfish, attacked some

80 enemy aircraft and with great gallantry, and despite overwhelming odds, destroyed several of them. At 0830 hours Percival ordered his only reserve, 12th Indian Infantry Brigade, to move at once to Keat Hong and to come under the command of Western Area. Meanwhile the commander of 22nd Australian Infantry Brigade had ordered all forward troops to make their way back to predetermined positions. This they found extremely difficult to do and it disorganised the whole area. Companies became hopelessly mixed up; some assembled north of Ama Keng, some at Choa Chu Kang and others right back at Bukit Timah. Meanwhile the guns did their best in the confusion. By dawn on 9th February 2/15th Field Regiment had fired 4,800 rounds; "there was practically no cessation of firing", At one stage regimental headquarters handled fire orders of some 70 guns in three field regiments, [5th, 2/10th and 2/15th] "calling for tasks of 100 rounds gunfire on targets in the Bukit Timah Racecourse and High School areas - 7,200 shells in each case." (Horner, quoting the history of 2/15th Field Regiment).

Fierce fighting broke out with the remnants of 2/18th Battalion near Ama Keng and by 0930 hours it was forced back to Tengah airfield. The remains of 2/20th Battalion ended up near 22nd Australian Infantry Brigade, with its headquarters at Bulim, while survivors of 2/19th Battalion were surrounded and had to cut their way out in small parties reaching Tengah by 1000 hours. By this time 22nd Australian Infantry Brigade was no longer a cohesive fighting formation. There had been considerable delay in collecting the reserve, 2/29th Battalion, consequently it did not arrive at Tengah until 0600 hours on 9th February. By this time Brigadier Taylor was desperately trying to organise a defensive line along the northern edge of the airfield and link 2/29th Battalion to the remains of the 2/19th Battalion at Choa Chu Kang. Behind this line he set to work to organise what was left of his brigade. When the Special Reserve Battalion arrived at 0745 hours he placed it in reserve. Then at 0930 hours Bennett ordered 2/29th Battalion to re-capture Ama Keng and Sungei Berih. All guns of 2/10th and 2/15th Australian Field Regiments were to attack at Zero Hour, ordered for 1300 hours.

The enemy, however, had not been idle and had worked his way round the Australian right flank to such an extent that Bennett was forced to cancel the counter-attack. Then at 1015 hours Brigadier Paris arrived with 12th Indian Infantry Brigade and was ordered by Bennett to move forward onto the Australian right flank and protect 22nd Australian Infantry Brigade. He reached Keat Hong at noon and by 1330 hours had taken up defensive positions on the Choa Chu Kang road at milestone 12 at the northern end of what had been the Jurong Line. This was a pre-planned and partially prepared position and easily the best to the west of the city. Meanwhile 2/15th Australian Field Regiment, which had lost eight guns during the night, moved back to Bukit Panjang village from where it could cover the former Jurong Line; some order was beginning to be achieved. All this was completed by 1500 hours without interference on the ground by the enemy, though air attacks continued remorselessly. These movements did, however, uncover the right flank of Brigadier GC Ballentine's 44th Indian Infantry Brigade, so Brigadier Taylor sent a liaison officer to inform him of his intentions. Bennett, who regained contact with Taylor during the afternoon, was not happy with these moves, since he was still looking for offensive action and not withdrawals.

That afternoon Percival ordered 27th Australian Infantry Brigade, Brigadier DS Maxwell, together with 2/10th Field Regiment and 13th Anti-Tank Battery, to stay covering the causeway, 44th Indian Infantry Brigade to occupy the southern end of the Jurong Line at milestone 12 on the Jurong Road and 15th Indian Infantry Brigade, Brigadier KA Garrett, to become Command Reserve at the Racecourse on the Bukit Timah Road. All this was good sensible stuff and cohesion improved.

44th Indian Infantry Brigade, which had 5th Field Regiment RA and 16th Anti-Tank Battery RAA, had not yet been in action although it had been shelled. By 2200 hours on 9th February, it was in its new position. Thus by last light it did look as if these four brigades could stabilise the situation. *5th* and *18th Japanese Divisions* were firmly established on the island having captured all their Phase 1 objectives and were building up with tanks and artillery. It was at this stage that Percival made a great mistake. He issued in writing his plans to fall back to a new line running from Pasir Pajang, through Bukit Timah, Point 581 to Nee Soon, if necessary (Map 13). On receipt of this, Western Area issued a normal operation order allotting brigades to their positions on this line. That night Percival also agreed to the withdrawal of all remaining aircraft to Sumatra. Withdrawal was in everybody's mind.

We must next look at the new action about to start in the Causeway Sector (Map 13). Brigadier Maxwell, commanding 27th Australian Infantry Brigade, had his headquarters at Dairy Farm, six miles south of the causeway. The removal of his 2/29th Battalion from its position south of Mandai village to act as reserve for Brigadier Taylor on 9th February had exposed his left flank. He therefore requested permission to withdraw his 2/26th Battalion from Kranji so that he could face west. Bennett refused but agreed that he could place two companies to cover the right bank of the Sungei Peng Siang. Maxwell did this and gave orders to withdraw if necessary.

Once again at 1800 hours Japanese artillery attacks began against 27th Australian Infantry Brigade's positions. These intensified and at 2030 hours *4th Imperial Guards Regiment*, leading the *Imperial Guards Division*, began its assault by landing craft. 27th Australian Infantry Brigade front was covered by the fire of only two batteries of 2/10th Australian Field Regiment, 20th and 60th. When the attack came, however, 20th Battery was on the move, so only 60th was available. The Australians fought hard, the infantry machine guns and the fire of 60th Field Battery caused many enemy casualties. The infantry held on to their positions at Kranji. Permission was given to withdraw to Mandai village and 2/10th Australian Field Regiment was pulled right back to the racecourse at Bukit Timah. Thus the enemy were left to consolidate on the exposed left flank of 11th Indian Division. The divisional commander, Major General BW Key, ordered 8th Indian Infantry Brigade to counter-attack and re-capture Point 168 and get into a position to cover Woodlands Road using the guns of 135th Field Regiment.

Bennett was still most concerned about his western front and ordered 15th Indian Infantry Brigade into the Jurong Line at Milestone 12. It was at this point that Brigadier Taylor received his copy of Bennett's repeat of Percival's order to pull back to the emergency line. He assumed that this should be obeyed as soon as possible. Accordingly he ordered 22nd Australian Infantry Brigade to withdraw and instructed 2/15th Australian Field Regiment to move right back to places from which it could cover the brigade's new positions along Reformatory Road. This in turn caused Brigadier Paris, who was out of touch with Western Area Headquarters, to move 12th Indian Infantry Brigade back to Bukit Panjang village. Thus by early afternoon 10th February, with no pressure from the enemy, the northern half of the Jurong Line had been abandoned. Meanwhile at 1030 hours Brigadier Ballantine, of 44th Indian Infantry Brigade, received his copy of the offending order and immediately told his battalion commanders to pull back to Pasir Panjang if forced to do so. He then heard, wrongly, that 15th Indian Infantry Brigade had already pulled back and, without checking, ordered his brigade to do likewise. This in turn caused 1st Malaya and 15th Indian Infantry Brigades to withdraw to conform. Thus by last light the best defensive position available on the west of the island had been abandoned with no pressure from the enemy and all brigades were once again dispersed. This was a disaster. While all these moves were taking place the Japanese *5th Division,* supported by tanks, was in occupation of Tengah airfield waiting to follow up *18th Division* which began its advance along the Jurong road as the sun set on 10th February.

Wavell paid what was to be his last visit to the stricken island on 10th February. Percival said that the key to the defence was by then Bukit Timah. Accordingly he ordered 18th British

Division to form an *ad hoc* force and occupy it. This was to be commanded by Lieutenant Colonel LC Thomas and was known as 'Tomforce'. It consisted of 18th Battalion the Reconnaissance Corps, 4th Norfolks, 1/5th Sherwood Foresters, one battery 85th Anti-Tank Regiment and one battery 5th Field Regiment. Percival next ordered 27th Australian Infantry Brigade to re-capture Mandai village and to take 'Tomforce' under command. It was only then that Percival heard that the Jurong Line had been given up. At this Wavell, who was still there, said that an immediate counter-attack must be made to re-capture it. This order was given to 11th Indian Division, with 27th Australian Infantry Brigade under its command.

While all this was happening, 8th Indian Infantry Brigade, under Brigadier WA Trott, had taken Point 95 and Point 120 but had failed to take its objective, Point 168. This attack went in under the most effective fire of Toosey's 135th Field Regiment which bombarded the enemy in this sector with some 7,000 rounds in 24 hours, much to Wavell's delight. When the brigade was ordered to retake Point 95, which overlooked the Causeway, 135th was ordered to support it. '. . . it was arranged that the Regt should fire a concentration on Hill 95 of 10 minutes intense from zero hour (1700 hrs) . . . The Regt concentration was duly fired, and the attacking force then walked on to the hill entirely unopposed and established themselves there. . . That evening the C.O. was rung up by H.Q.R.A., received congratulations on the result of the concentration, and was also given a message from General Wavell direct to the Regt, asking him to thank all ranks for their efforts.' ('Diary' of 135th (Herts Yeomanry) Field Regiment).

Then, 27th Australian Infantry Brigade, because it did not receive the order putting it under command of 11th Indian Division, failed to move against Mandai. Even worse, it received its copy of Percival's offending order and told its battalions that, if they could not hold, they were to withdraw down the pipeline to the racecourse. These orders reached 2/26th Battalion but failed to get through to 2/30th. Maxwell had meanwhile moved his headquarters back to Holland Road where he received the order to come under command of 11th Indian Division and to attack Mandai village, which area he had just left! The best he could do was to order 2/30th Battalion which was still in the area to remain and put itself under the command of 11th Indian Division. Trott, of 8th Indian Infantry Brigade, on hearing of this, decided to conform by attacking Point 120 at dawn on 11th February.

On the western front General Bennett was desperately trying to organise the attack to recover the Jurong Line, using 12th and 15th Indian and 22nd Australian Infantry Brigades with 44th Indian Infantry Brigade in reserve. He ordered an artillery attack by 5th and 2/15th Field Regiments to cover the operation. But, as these orders were being put together and unknown to Bennett, all the brigades in question were on their way back to Percival's emergency line on their own initiative. It did, however, so happen that when they received their orders for the attack, they were not far from the start line envisaged for it. 5th Field Regiment was in a good position near Racecourse Village but 2/15th Field Regiment had by then moved back to Farrer Road and was out of range. Nothing could be done until after dark but, as the sun set, the regiment moved forward to new positions near Bukit Timah to get into range for the attack. As it advanced, however, it met tanks of the *18th Division* and spent all night avoiding them only to end up at dawn, exhausted, back at Farrer Road.

Meanwhile the three brigades did the best they could to be ready to attack at dawn and by midnight they all reported that they could do so; it was a splendid effort. But the enemy were also attacking and by midnight were pressing westwards down the Choa Chu Kang road and some tanks broke through at Bukit Panjang village and turned south towards Bukit Timah. It was these tanks that met 2/15th Australian Field Regiment. Bukit Timah was soon in flames and this caused 2/29th Battalion to pull back to the racecourse. The enemy then stopped and sent out fighting patrols towards the 15-inch gun position at Buona Vista Battery and nearly overran Headquarters Western Area in doing so.

The advancing Japanese caused the Gunners of the Buona Vista Battery of 31st Coast Battery, to begin to destroy their guns. The Battery Commander, Major PSF Jackson, sent Lieutenant Simpson, his Gun Position Officer, to contact 1st Malaya Infantry Brigade, made up of 2nd Loyals and 1st Malay Regiment, and obtain information. Meanwhile both guns were reporting automatic fire all around them. 'At about 0430 hrs on 11 Feb the FC [(Faber) Fire Command] gave full authority to BC Buona Vista Bty to deny his guns to the enemy as soon as he . . . considered it essential to do so . . . At about 0600 hrs the BC gave the orders to carry out demolitions . . . 250 lbs of gelignite were used on each gun. The Bofors gun, engine rooms, W/T Station and Fire Control Instruments were all destroyed. The Magazines were not destroyed. . . . It appears that no officer was sent to examine the results of the demolitions on the guns before the final withdrawal took place.' (Cardew) There was much fighting in the tunnels around the guns and several Gunners were captured. The remainder managed to withdraw along the railway line. 'At about 1600 hrs on 11 Feb orders were received . . . that 31 Coast Bty was to be reorganised as an infantry coy . . . At 1400 hrs on 12 Feb orders were received from Comd 1 Malay Inf Bde for the bty to move out at 1600 hrs and come under orders of OC 2 Loyals.' (Cardew). It should be noted that in fact these demolitions were not entirely successful, since one gun was found undamaged when the Japanese surrendered in 1945.

While this was in progress 15th Indian and 22nd Australian Infantry Brigades had started their counter-attack and had recaptured Point 138 by 0230 hours 11th February but then they met the full force of the Japanese *18th Division* attacking astride the Jurong Road. They were hopelessly outnumbered and their only hope was to try to break clean back to their Reformatory Road positions by moving across country. Brigadier JB Coates of 15th Indian Infantry Brigade, hearing firing behind him, cancelled his attack but the order never reached the 2/9th Jats who continued and were never seen again, being wiped out in a bitter fight to the end. Then brigade headquarters was attacked and Brigadier Coates had to withdraw to 22nd Australian Brigade's position with only 400 survivors out of the original 1500 men of his brigade. Not knowing of the disaster suffered by 15th Indian Infantry Brigade, Bennett ordered 'Tomforce' to re-take Bukit Timah and then Bukit Panjang village which it attempted to do. 4th Norfolks captured Point 255 and Point 275 but were driven off. On the left the 1/5th Sherwood Foresters got as far as Milestone 8 on the Jurong Road but were then forced back. This was hardly surprising because both attacks hit the Japanese *18th* and *5th Divisions*. 'Tomforce' then came under ferocious enemy aerial and artillery attack. 'On 11th February 272nd Anti-Tank Battery was ordered back to defend Headquarters 3rd Indian Corps but was severely engaged and the gallant Lieutenant Moser was killed and five of his men wounded.' (Podmore).

It was at noon on 11th February that the great 9.2-inch guns of Connaught Battery, manned by men of 11th Coast Battery, commanded by Major JWH Hipkin, on Blakang Mati island (Map 11) opened fire on Japanese attacking in the Jurong and Bukit Timah area. Soon they were joined by the 6-inch guns of Siloso Battery, commanded by Major RG Ray, the Gunners of which came from 7th Coast Battery HK-S RA, which engaged Jurong and Ulu Padang. Both batteries kept up a constant fire all afternoon and, after dark, the 9.2s engaged Tengah airfield. By dawn on 12th February these two guns alone had expended 200 rounds, each weighing 290 lbs. All through 12th February the guns of Blakang Mati continued to fire; Pulau Bukam, Bukit Timah and Tengah were hit time and time again. Many of the shells were high explosive which did massive damage, others were solid shot which did a lot less. Tsuji Masanobu in his book about the Japanese in Singapore describes the terror these great shells caused as they tore into the ground making huge craters. Shelford Bidwell describes how the survivors of the 1st Malay Regiment 'testified to the encouragement they gained from the roar of the 9.2s of Connaught Battery and the sound of the shells passing overhead like express trains.' The noise was certainly deafening and was reported on by many. The Gunners at these batteries became exhausted, the magazine lifts broke down through excessive use and the great shells had to be brought up by hand and winch. It was a magnificent effort to keep the guns in action.

By then a serious gap appeared west of MacRitchie Reservoir. With Bukit Timah in enemy hands and the left flank of 11th Indian Division exposed, there was an even more serious threat of enemy infiltration. Accordingly General Heath ordered the formation of another *ad hoc* force this time under Brigadier TH Massy-Beresford, to be known as 'Massy-Force', to block the enemy advance through Thompson village from the north. It consisted of 1st Cambridgeshires, 4th Suffolks and 5/11th Sikhs, 342nd Field Battery, a detachment of 3rd Cavalry and 18 obsolescent light tanks from 100th Light Tank Squadron, of 11th Indian Division, which had recently arrived. Meanwhile in that formation the situation was going from bad to worse. The division still had an order to attack Bukit Panjang village from the north east and it tried to do so at 1030 hours on 11th February. An effort was made to get 2/10th Australian Field Regiment to provide firepower but communications had failed and it was not possible. Also the two battalions which were to attack were still in close contact with a superior enemy. In the end the attack was called off and the remnants of both battalions were told to rendezvous at Milestone 9 on Thompson Road. By then 8th Indian Infantry Brigade was becoming isolated on the Mandai Road while 53rd British Infantry Brigade was facing south at Sembawang airfield. 8th Indian Infantry Brigade withdrew to Nee Soon to conform, while 28th Indian Infantry Brigade was at Pierce Reservoir in reserve.

General Percival, with General Heath's agreement, ordered 'Massy-Force' to capture Point 300 and to link up with 'Tomforce' which was in touch with 22nd Australian Infantry Brigade further south along the Ulu Pandan Road. It must be noted that by this time reference to a brigade was often to no more than a few hundred assorted men who had survived, reinforced by untrained reinforcements or logistic troops pressed into service. All positions were attacked all afternoon on 11th February but they held. The Japanese records admit heavy casualties. South of 22nd Australian Infantry Brigade was 44th Indian Infantry Brigade along Reformatory Road, with 1st Malaya Infantry Brigade at Pasir Panjang. During the afternoon, 5th and 2/15th Field Regiments sorted themselves out after the confusion of the previous day and began to affect the battle with their fire. That evening General Yamashita dropped a message by air calling for the surrender of the Fortress. Percival had no means of replying but informed Wavell that he would refuse. That same evening the *Empire Star*, HMS *Durban* and two destroyers left Singapore with most of the shore-based naval personnel, the remainder of the RAF ground staff, many technicians and civilians. They were heavily attacked and suffered casualties but managed to reach Batavia.

On the morning of 12th February the Japanese attacked 'Massy-Force' and by 0830 hours they had reached Racecourse Village. Here they were brought to a halt by the dogged resistance of a troop of 45th Anti-Tank Battery. But by noon 'Massy-Force' was forced back to the line of the Adam Road - Farrer Road. Their move back was covered by the fire of Connaught and Siloso Coast Batteries and was successfully completed. Pressure was by then mounting against 8th Indian Infantry Brigade at Nee Soon. 1/8th Punjab had been reformed but consisted almost entirely of untrained soldiers and soon began to disintegrate so that 2/9th Gurkhas and 499th Field Battery of 135th Field Regiment had to be moved from 28th Indian Infantry Brigade to fill the gap thus created. At this moment the danger of an enemy breakthrough along the Bukit Timah Road and into the city had become very real.

Accordingly Percival decided that the time had come to withdraw into a tight perimeter around the town itself during the night 12/13th February (Map 14). The line, from east to west, was to run from Lallang airfield, to the east of Paya Lebar airstrip, to Woodleigh crossroads, Thompson Village, Adam Road, Farrer Road, Tanglin Halt and thence via The Gap to Buona Vista Village, after withdrawal from Pasir Panjang. At noon on 12th February, 11th and 18th Divisions began to withdraw to positions along this line. As 53rd British Infantry Brigade began to move back south of Nee Soon they were attacked by enemy tanks but these were repulsed by the fire of 273rd Anti-Tank Battery and the guns of 499th Field Battery. Three tanks were destroyed and the brigade reached its new positions intact. 8th and 28th Indian Infantry Brigades were in turn withdrawn safely. By last light on 12th February 155th Field Regiment reported itself in action in Newton Road, Singapore.

The anti-aircraft defences were disintegrating. The loss of the Bukit Timah depots resulted in a total loss of 40mm Bofors ammunition so that the guns soon had only what they carried. Many had been overrun but the few that were left made for the city and fought on. Many of their actions had been over open sights in their own defence. One troop of 1st Indian HAA Regiment fought on with small arms amid flames, smoke and exploding mortar bombs, its troop commander earning an immediate Military Cross. One troop of Bofors guns fought back street by street doing much execution to the advancing Japanese until it ran out of ammunition. But the situation was deteriorating fast. On 14th February Sergeant LH Fowler was in action on the Serangoon road where his gun was in a very exposed position and was being bombed and machine gunned by low flying aircraft. He remained at his post and shot down two enemy aircraft with two successive rounds. He was later awarded a Military Medal for bravery in action (information taken from his citation).

By the morning of 13th February some coast guns were still in action but it is not always possible to identify the sub-units manning them. In most cases a mixture of 7 Coast Regiment RA and officers and men from HK-S RA sub units were involved (Map 11):

Battery	**Manned by**	**Armament**
Labrador	7 Coast Bty HK-S RA	2 x 6-inch Mk VII
Batu Berlayer	31 Coast Bty RA	2 x 12-pounders
Pulau Hantu	31 Coast Bty RA	1 x 18-pounder
Connaught	11 Coast Bty RA	3 x 9.2-inch
Siloso	7 Coast Bty HK-S RA	2 x 6-inch
Serapong	7 Coast Regt RA	2 x 6-inch
Siloso Point	7 Coast Regt RA	1 x 12-pounder
Berhala Reping	7 Coast Regt RA	2 x 6-pounder
Silingsing	5 Coast Bty HK-S RA, 35 Fortress Coy RE	2 x 6-inch
Tanjong Tereh		1 x 12-pounder

During 13th February Blakang Mati, Pulau Brani and Batu Berlayer were heavily shelled and bombed but Connaught, Serapong, Siloso and Labrador Batteries continued to engage the enemy attacks. At about 1500 hours the enemy decided to silence Labrador Battery with a violent artillery concentration. Both guns were knocked out and many men of 7th Coast Regiment who manned them were killed and wounded. Captain G Kinloch, Battery Commander Labrador Battery and the Faber Fire Command War Diary state, '13th February. The bombing of the AA positions on Keppel Golf Course continued in the morning. At 1300 hrs FC ordered the engagement of a land target . . . an enemy infantry bn . . . approaching Pasir Panjang. No direct observation was possible and the shoot was carried out by 1/25,000 map. Silent registration of this area had been carried out and recorded at the Battery. At 1400 hrs hostile shelling of the fort commenced, presumably by way of retaliation, by an enemy battery of 5.9-inch guns located somewhere in the vicinity of the Jurong Road.' (Cardew). There was extensive damage to accommodation and searchlights and three IORs were killed and six wounded. As a result the

Indian ORs left the fort and took shelter. The battery commander ordered them back and enough came, under Jemadar Lal Khan, to man one gun. The battery engaged another target on West Coast Road and again enemy guns replied. This caused all Indians to leave. They were utterly demoralised by the heavy shelling and almost continuous bombing, the great majority of them being raw recruits. By this time the enemy were in Alexandra Road and demolition was ordered to be carried out at 1830 hours. The maximum right traverse was 310 degrees, just permitting the battery to hit Pasir Panjang. All demolitions were successful and the magazine was blown up. Captain Kinloch, Lieutenant Francis Hayhurst and 26 men were formed into an infantry platoon and were placed under the command of 1st Malaya Infantry Brigade occupying positions along Pender Road, Horse Road and Keppel Harbour.

At 1200 hours on 11th February the 6-inch guns of 'Siloso and Labrador Forts engaged an enemy concentration at the west end of West Coast Road at the request of HQ 1 Malay Inf Bde. . . . At 1630 hrs Siloso and central barrack block was heavily bombed . . . and 2Lt Carver was killed. . . [on 12th February] Siloso and Labrador engaged further land targets on the West Coast Road. On instructions from HQ FD [Fixed Defences] Siloso Battery was called upon to destroy remaining oil tanks and drums of oil which had not been destroyed in the original denial of oil storage on Pulau Bukam. About 40 rds were expended on this task with fairly successful results. . . . At 2100 hrs Siloso and Labrador Forts engaged a sea target . . . The target was quickly set on fire and sunk. . . . the shoot . . . [afforded practice] for the HK-S RA personnel and stimulated morale which had been badly shaken by continuous air raids . . . [on 13th February] At 1100 hrs Siloso and Labrador engaged further land targets . . . at request of 1 Malay Inf Bde. At about 2115 hrs a large "koli" was observed approaching the western entrance contrary to orders. Two rounds were fired and it was sunk. Subsequently it turned out that the occupants were stragglers of the AIF, one of whom reached the shore wounded and was sent to hospital. . . [on 14th February] At 0415 hrs orders were given for Siloso to prepare for demolitions and at 0500 hrs the guns were blown up. . . The Magazine was blown up. . . [on 15th and 16th February] There was also much looting of the barrack area and RA Mess. . . . The looters were mainly Asiatics from Pulau Brani but some British stragglers from odd units including HK-S RA participated. '(Cardew).

At Fort Connaught, with its three 9.2-inch guns, 11th Coast Battery RA, under Major JWM Hipkin and Second Lieutenant SE Armitage, was bombed and suffered damage and casualties. 'No sea targets appeared during the whole course of the operations and all firing was directed onto land targets.' (Cardew). On 11th February the battery reported that it engaged targets on Jurong and Ulu Pandan villages and 36 rounds were fired. During the night 11/12th February the battery engaged Tengah Airfield at 0130, 0330 and 0630 hours and 63 rounds were fired. On the 12th it engaged the Japanese on Jurong Road and at Bukit Timah on the orders of the Counter-Bombardment Officer (CBO) 3rd Indian Corps and 60 rounds were fired. Further targets were engaged during the night 12/13th February including enemy tanks reported at Bukit Timah. By dawn on 14th February, with enemy on Alexandra Road, the guns badly worn, magazine lifts out of action and men exhausted, the guns were destroyed at 0715 hours.

During this period Changi, Johore, Tekong and Sphinx Batteries engaged targets north of Punggol Point as far as Johore Bahru, resulting in Johore Fort and Selarang Barracks being bombed. On 11th February Tekong and Sphinx Batteries engaged targets on Pulau Ubin.

Thus the coast batteries of Singapore, organised as they were into two Fire Commands, Changi and Faber, did the best they could to engage enemy coming from the north and north east. Their ammunition expenditure was:

Guns	Changi FC	Faber FC
15-inch	194	Nil
9.2-inch firing HE	75	75
9.2-inch firing AP	200	217
6-inch firing HE	600	240
6-inch firing CPBC	50	54
Totals	1119	586

A grand total of 1705 rounds.

Throughout 12th February the Japanese *18th Division* attacked 22nd Australian Infantry Brigade, now commanded by Brigadier AL Varley. This formation fought very hard, frequently at bayonet point, and its line held until dark when it also pulled back to a position in the new line. To its south 1st Malaya and 44th Indian Infantry Brigades also pulled back to conform. Thus by first light on 13th February the 28 mile front covering Singapore was complete. 2nd Malaya Infantry Brigade was to the east, then came the remains of the gallant 11th Indian Division as far as Woodleigh, where 18th British Division had its 53rd, 55th and 54th Infantry Brigades in line respectively. 55th Infantry Brigade had absorbed 'Massy-Force' and 54th had absorbed 'Tomforce'. With 53rd Infantry Brigade was 22nd Mountain Regiment in action north of the Serangoon Road but with a total of only 750 rounds for all guns. Then came 8th Australian Division which had fought so very well in Malaya. It held as far as Tanglin Halt where it joined with 44th Indian Infantry Brigade which had in turn 1st Malaya Infantry Brigade to their south as far as the sea at Pasir Panjang. Although it was to be a fight to the finish, all was not well. 'Some of the troops forming the garrison had begun to lose confidence in their leaders, and their morale, already low, had started to crack.' (Kirby). Reports were reaching Percival at Malaya Command of armed gangs of deserters roaming the town and looting, a sure sign that morale was low. Some began to seize small boats and tried to get away and many had to be forcibly stopped. Others tried to reach Java and Sumatra by forcing their way on board ships destined for those islands. These men were deserters from administrative units or others who had only recently arrived as reinforcements and were untrained as well as ill-disciplined.

By 13th February 155th Field Regiment was in action at Farrer Park. Guns were very close together and were mixed with those of other regiments, all firing in different directions as they responded to calls for fire. A fire fight broke out between some Punjabis and Manchesters each convinced, in the dark, that the other was Japanese. Then a section of 135th Field Regiment fired some rounds over open sights narrowly missing 'B' Battery's command post. There was continuous enemy shelling during the night of 13/14th February causing many casualties. An ammunition truck was hit and exploded and Captain Eustace, who had done so well at Slim River, was hit by splinters and died on his way to hospital. There were many more casualties that night as the Gunners did what they could amidst growing confusion.

Two months of continuous retreat, destruction of the naval base, the lack of air and naval support, the evacuation of so many and the myth of the invincibility of the Japanese had undoubtedly sapped morale and the will to fight of many. Most units had by this time lost many of their officers, NCOs and trained men either in battle or to create new units and most had been reinforced by new, unknown and untrained men who lacked the team spirit, military experience and ability to conduct operations. Nevertheless most of the combat units fought with great bravery and gallantry and against great odds. For example, the 1st Malay Infantry Brigade at Pasir Panjang, and the 22nd Australian Infantry Brigade throughout. The Gunners fought hard and several times their fire saved the day. The men of the Hong Kong-Singapore Royal Artillery stood bravely to their guns bringing great credit to the Royal Regiment of Artillery. So did the Gunners of Australia. In the whole Malaya and Singapore campaign they lost 41 all ranks killed, 49 missing and 112 wounded, a total of 202 casualties. Something like 500 Australian Gunners died in Japanese captivity and David Horner writes 'In terms of intense combat, battle casualties and suffering in captivity, no gunners in the history of Australian artillery faced a more severe trial than those who served in Malaya and Singapore.' (Horner).

Islands are very hard to defend. The defender has to be everywhere and the attacker, who by definition has the initiative, can concentrate and then chose a point where he can arrive in overwhelming superiority. Also it is easy for him to deceive the defender as to where he will attack. If he is not destroyed as he approaches the beaches and if he gets a foothold and is not immediately destroyed by counter-attack and is able to build up his artillery, then the defender is in real trouble. And this is exactly what happened at Singapore in February 1942. It is true that attempts were made to counter-attack but this was always too late and too weak. In any case mounting counter-attacks is a complex phase of battle and the forces of the Empire in Singapore were just not up to it. What is more they did not have enough artillery or air power for any chance of success and in any case all arms battle procedures at formation level hardly existed. The flow of information was slow and ponderous and often inaccurate, hence wrong deductions were frequently made. Perhaps the main error was not to appreciate the severity of the enemy attacks early enough and not to send the 18th British Division as a whole to Bukit Timah to become a really powerful reserve capable of counter-attacking and driving the enemy into the sea as they landed. Another was the premature withdrawal of 27th Australian Infantry Brigade from Kranji, thus allowing a second landing to build up unopposed but, perhaps above all, the issue of confusing orders about a withdrawal which was made too soon. These are the sorts of things that will always go wrong in war if training, particularly formation training, in peacetime is inadequate.

By 13th February the Naval Base had been destroyed and the administrative situation on the island was causing deep concern. Refugees were flooding through the new perimeter of the city which was only three miles in radius from the water front. Soon there were over a million people in this tiny area. Enemy bombing and shelling could hardly fail to hit something and cause great damage and casualties with a further adverse effect on morale. The main water pipes and pumps were hit so that the water supply soon became precarious. The loss of the Bukit Timah Depots caused concern, putting food, ammunition and petrol in very short supply.

Percival held a conference at 1400 hours on 13th February to see if it would be possible to conduct a counter-attack of some kind. But Generals Heath and Bennett both said that fatigue, morale and state of training made success most unlikely. The situation was indeed serious. It was decided that a final fleet of small ships should leave that night and again there was some indiscipline as weary and terrified men struggled to get on board. Even so these were relatively isolated incidents. The only enemy attacks on 13th February were against 1st Malaya Infantry Brigade at Pasir Panjang. These splendid soldiers fought all day against fearful odds and held the line well supported by such guns of the nearby coast batteries, manned by the men of the Royal Artillery and Hong Kong-Singapore Royal Artillery, as still existed. By last light the enemy had captured The Gap which forced the 1st Malaya and the 44th Indian Infantry Brigades to withdraw to a new line between Mount Echo and Buona Vista Village.

After dark on 13th February Lieutenant Colonel Philip Gold and nine men of 155th Field Regiment including BSM Roadnight, who had just been told of his award of the DCM, were told to try to escape with an official evacuation party. They found a junk and rowed out of the harbour with the blazing city behind them. They were swamped, bombed and machine gunned but somehow reached Ringat in Sumatra in nine days. They then took a bus to Padang where they were taken on board HMAS *Hobart* and 19 days later they were in Colombo. (Ted Noble).

It was on 13th February that, after his guns had been destroyed, Lieutenant Lionel Andrew took command of his troop to act as infantry. In spite of heavy fire and air attacks he held his ground, so allowing other troops on his flanks to withdraw. Finally when closely attacked by enemy infantry on three sides he remained alone to allow his own men to withdraw, displaying conspicuous courage and bravery. (From his citation for the Military Cross)

On the same day Lieutenant Colonel PJD Toosey, Commanding Officer of 135th Field Regiment, was summoned to 11th Indian Division Headquarters to be told that he had been selected for evacuation so that his experience could be used elsewhere. He refused to leave his regiment, quoting *Artillery Training* Volume III which says quite clearly that in any withdrawal the Commanding Officer leaves last. This was accepted and one of his battery commanders was nominated to depart in his place. Had he gone, of course, he would have escaped three years as a prisoner, much of it on the terrible Burma Railway.

Early on 14th February came the news of the expected failure of the water supply system. Percival ordered the Royal Engineers to do what they could but he was forced to warn the Governor, Sir Shenton Thomas, that the future of the garrison was extremely serious. At 0830 hours new and ferocious attacks came in against 1st Malaya Infantry Brigade yet again. The enemy gunfire was particularly savage and there were heavy casualties. Soon the fighting was hand to hand with the Malay and British troops giving as good as they got but gradually, yard by yard, they were forced back to Bukit Chermin. The Australian Gunners to the north were out of ammunition and unable to help. Next came attacks down Thomson Road and the Japanese captured Point 105, causing a gap between the 53rd and 55th British Infantry Brigades. Yet another attack developed down Sime Road in the afternoon and enemy tanks reached Mount Pleasant. At the same time attacks were reported in the eastern sector at Paya Lebar but these were stopped. The line had held by last light but only just. After dark the enemy made no move all night. It was strange how often this happened with the Japanese. It was perhaps easy to forget that they too were suffering very seriously and had their hands full in keeping up the pressure.

On the morning of 14th February while acting as FOO with 118th Field Regiment, 'Captain Robert Johnson rallied a group of infantrymen whose officers had been killed. Communications to his battery had failed so he ran to and from Regimental Headquarters under small arms fire with fire orders which were then relayed to the guns. The fire that came down as a result of his bravery prevented further withdrawal and so destroyed the enemy that some ground was actually gained.' (From the citation for his Military Cross).

On the morning of 15th February the Director General of Civil Defence, Brigadier Ivan Simson, reported a severe deterioration in the water supply and Percival called a conference to discuss the situation. At the conference it was revealed that stocks of food, artillery ammunition and petrol would last for only two days at the most although there was plenty of small arms ammunition. Percival said that in his opinion he had only two options. The first was to counter-attack at once and regain the reservoirs and food depots at Bukit Timah, the second was to capitulate. When the commanders, all of whom were present, said that a counter-attack was impracticable, Percival decided to surrender. At 1130 hours a flag of truce was sent to the Japanese lines proposing the end of hostilities. But the fighting did not stop instantly. 'At 1300 hours that day a troop of 272nd Anti-Tank Battery under Lieutenant Fosbery went to the aid of the hard-pressed Malay battalion. Fosbery was killed and Lance Sergeant Tuck was later awarded the Military Medal for his bravery in action that day.' (Podmore).

The men of the regiments could hardly believe that it was all over. They had fought like demons. GR Parvin of 118th Field Regiment, which had done so well on Bukit Timah Road, writes in his book, *Yasumai*, 'The drivers lay dead in twin ragged heaps between the wheels, there had been no time to bury them, no time to rest, no time to sleep, and barely time to eat in those last days. Like automatons we had humped the ammunition, loaded fired, loaded fired, loaded fired until the gun was hot and black with carbon, until the breech was so sticky with burnt cordite that it had to be hammered open after each round. . .', then later when ordered to destroy the guns, 'We loaded the stained and dust covered gun for the last time. One shell in the breech in the proper manner and the second down the barrel from the muzzle end. A long piece of signal cable and a sharp tug. The dear old gun jumped violently, flashing arcs of glowing sparks from its muzzle. The whole two inch thick steel barrel split and peeled back like the skin of a monstrous banana. With Bren guns and rifles we completed the terrible task, pouring bullets into all her vulnerable parts in a frenzy of destruction. All the items we had cherished for years we smashed in a few seconds. We then stared in horror at what we had done to our old gun . . .'

Many were still doing their best to escape. One such was John Crawley, also of 118th Field Regiment, and for which the Commanding Officer, Lieutenant Colonel CE 'Peanut' Mackellar was to receive a Mention in Dispatches. Crawley managed to find 60 NCOs and men willing to try to escape. He secured a junk and with almost no nautical knowledge the party reached Sumatra. Later they sailed for Ceylon, only to be captured when some 300 miles to the south of the island. Later Crawley became Adjutant of a POW Camp in Siam displaying great courage and resource in combating the Japanese for which he was severely beaten. After the war he stayed on in Bangkok to assist with the evacuation of prisoners.

Lieutenant Colonel Mackeller, who had already fought at Gallipoli and been taken prisoner by the Turks at Kut in the First World War, was captured at Singapore and somehow survived the 'Death Railway' with his second-in-command, Major Sir Watkin Williams-Wynn. Mackeller insisted on keeping up standards in POW Camps and spent many months in solitary confinement. He died aged 94 in 1991. Brigadier Arthur Rusher, CRA 11th Indian Division was also a tower of strength to all Gunners in Changi, in Shirakawa Camp, Taiwan and again in Manchuria.

But it was still not quite over. On the morning of 15th February 4th Suffolks, of 54th British Infantry Brigade, were holding positions on Mount Pleasant Road with 'D' Troop, 215th Anti-Tank Battery of 80th Anti-Tank Regiment, which was commanded by Sergeant Harry Salter. As the enemy closed, Salter manhandled a 2-pounder under sniping and machine gun fire, ordering his detachment to use their small arms. Alone he then fired six rounds into a house containing the enemy and destroyed their attack. Later more enemy assembled in another house and began causing casualties to the Suffolks who were desperately weary and disorganised. Again Sergeant Salter wheeled his 2-pounder under fire to within 40 yards of the house and, under point blank machine gun fire, he engaged it until it burst into flames and the enemy fled to be shot down by the Suffolks. Sergeant Salter's action saved the situation on Mount Pleasant Road and he was awarded the Distinguished Conduct Medal.

By the time the surrender was ordered, 53rd British Infantry Brigade had been forced back behind Braddell Road and 1st Malaya Infantry Brigade was at Mount Faber so losing the Alexandra Depot and Military Hospital. The Japanese entered the hospital, killed many of the staff in cold blood and then shot all walking wounded in bloody massacre, a dreadful omen for the future. Shelling continued everywhere, even while negotiations were in progress. It was not until 1715 hours that Percival met Yamashita at the Ford Factory at Bukit Timah to discuss terms. Yamashita would accept only unconditional surrender and at 1810 hours Percival was forced to sign. The terms being that:

a) The British Army shall cease hostilities at 8.30 p.m.

b) The British Army shall disarm themselves in the positions they occupy on the cease fire by 9.30 p.m., with the exception of 1000 men who will be allowed to carry arms in order to maintain peace and order in Singapore until further notice.

'We are paying very heavily', Brooke wrote in his diary, 'for failing to face the insurance premium essential for the security of an Empire. This has usually been the cause for the loss of Empires in the past.'

So it was over. 155th Field Regiment reports destroying its guns at 1730 hours. The campaign had lasted 70 days, 30 less than the Japanese had allowed themselves in their original plan. They had prepared carefully and had excellent intelligence about the ground and their enemy and they exploited them to the full. The British, Australian, Indian and Malayan forces varied greatly but only relatively few were properly trained. Many of the individual regiments fought bravely but this is never enough. It is vital that all arms learn to fight together effectively and the experience to do this takes years to achieve. As a result the Japanese were almost always able to get inside the British decision-making cycle. This enabled them to split the defences even though it could be seen what their intentions were. There was never enough time to react, let alone take the initiative. British reaction was too slow because they had not been given the time to train. General Percival has taken much of the blame and some of his actions can certainly be criticised with hindsight. However, given the faulty strategic situation he inherited, the poor standard of all-arms and inter-service training, the lack of proper air support and communications varying from the poor to the non-existent, the result was almost inevitable whatever he did. It takes years to train a modern army for combat and rapid expansion, almost always ordered too late, simply dilutes what is already there.

There had been much gallantry in the defence of the guns. The coast Gunners fought very well. It was not their fault that some of the great coast guns were facing an expected threat from the south, indeed it is to their eternal credit that they worked so hard, hacking away at concrete, to turn so many of them round to face the threat from the north so effectively. But there were errors and things did go wrong. Sadly some of the less experienced Indian Gunners did leave their posts and not all returned when the real fighting started. Some guns were destroyed on false, unverified reports that the enemy were close. A suspect but friendly boat was sunk and there was failure in at least one case to verify the destruction of the guns. Finally there must have been a major manufacturing fault in the construction of the 9.2-inch ammunition lifts to cause them to break down after firing only some 200 rounds. But, remembering that the coast Gunners were fighting a battle for which they were not equipped, trained or prepared in any way, in the great confusion that occurred it is perhaps surprising that the errors were not greater. As we have seen their firing did have important effects wherever they were able to apply it.

The field Gunners in Singapore were too few and too spread but they fought hard and held the enemy several times so allowing the infantry to re-deploy to fight again. Little could be done, however, to concentrate fire effectively. Similarly the anti-tank Gunners did what they could, often operating on their own without orders, meeting the enemy where they could as they worked out where to go next. Last but far from least, the anti-aircraft Gunners. Again too few to be able to protect an island the size of Singapore. but they did manage to keep the enemy bombers high and cause their bombing to be inaccurate for a while. There was, however, no way that they were going to be able to prevent them from bombing on their own. They then fought their guns to the end in the ground role until their ammunition gave out. Throughout, all Gunners were short of ammunition which caused many engagements to be reduced or even stopped altogether with a dire effect on operations. So at the fall of Singapore the following artillery Regiments went into captivity:

ROYAL ARTILLERY

5th Field Regiment
88th Field Regiment
118th Field Regiment

122nd Field Regiment
135th Field Regiment
137th Field Regiment
148th Field Regiment
155th Field Regiment
80th Anti-Tank Regiment
85th Anti-Tank Regiment
125th Anti-Tank Regiment
3rd HAA Regiment
35th LAA Regiment
5th Searchlight Regiment
7th Coast Regiment
9th Coast Regiment
11th Coast Regiment
12th Coast Regiment

HONG KONG-SINGAPORE ROYAL ARTILLERY
1st HAA Regiment
2nd HAA Regiment
3rd LAA Regiment

ROYAL AUSTRALIAN ARTILLERY
2/10th Field Regiment
2/15th Field Regiment
2/4th Anti-Tank Regiment

REGIMENT OF INDIAN ARTILLERY
1st AA Regiment
22nd Mountain Regiment

The British, Australian, Indian and HK-S RA Gunners lost 3,571 all ranks killed in action or who died in captivity as a result of the campaigns in Hong Kong and Singapore. In addition 11,691 were missing or prisoners in the Malaya - Singapore Campaign. All in all 85,000 men went into captivity at the surrender, many more if all the civilians are included. The story of the privations in the prison camps is one of horror unparalleled, but also of splendid courage, endurance, stoicism, gallantry and pride. The Gunners of 18th British Division led by their CRA, Brigadier HC Servaes, led the march of the prisoners of war into Changi Prison Camp where they were ordered to concentrate. 'As, led by our CRA, we marched down a main street of Singapore, strewn with burnt-out vehicles, wreckage and corpses, we were cheered by our infantry, waiting beside the road to join in behind us - they knew their Gunners had not let them down.' (Lieut Col SE Skey, then BMRA, 18th Division in Duncan). Lieutenant Colonel GL Hughes took the salute as the men of the four mountain batteries of 22nd Mountain Regiment marched into Farrer Park and captivity. (Graham)

Then came the long years in prison. Denis Russell-Roberts, himself a prisoner, wrote afterwards, 'Those of us who were privileged to observe both officers and men of the Lanarkshire Yeomanry during those years of captivity in Changi are able to testify to the value of a County Association in that important relationship between officers and men. This Yeomanry regiment set an example of behaviour as prisoners of war which simply could not be rivalled. (Their outstanding part in the campaign, especially at Slim River, is another story). They were like one great big family in which everyone took care of everyone. When small parties or even individual soldiers of the regiment were taken away by the Japs and transferred to remote camps, somehow or other an officer of the regiment would be sure to find his way. No soldier of that regiment was ever allowed to feel forgotten. They seemed to possess a spirit which said 'we came through this as a regiment and not as individuals.' It was one of those things which sticks in the memory, which some of us talk about even today.' (Russell-Roberts).

At the beginning of May 1942, 135th Field Regiment prisoners were moved from Changi to Bukit Timah Camp which was commanded by Brigadier WL Duke, commander 53rd British Infantry Brigade. Lieutenant Colonel Toosey became Camp Second-in-Command until June when Duke was removed to Japan. Toosey then became Camp Commandant and began his astonishing period of selfless duty looking after all prisoners in Singapore, Siam and on the Burma railway. He went on looking after their interests long after the war. His story is told in the book, *The Man Behind the Bridge*, by Peter N Davies. Because his action brings the greatest credit to the Regiment and epitomises the gallantry of all members of the Regiment who suffered as prisoners of war in the Far East, a synopsis of what he did is at Annex D.

Prison was to last for three years and six months, for deliverance was not to come until 19th August 1945. By then many had paid the supreme sacrifice, dying of wounds, starvation, illness or brutality. Perhaps the heroism of those dark years is best told by their commander, General Percival, who was with them. 'Finally let me pay tribute to the British soldier. Throughout those long years he bore his trials with courage and dignity. Though compelled to live almost like an animal, he never lost his self respect or sense of humour. At the end he emerged weakened in body but with his spirit unimpaired. It was an outstanding performance.'

Thousands of Gunners suffered those long years of captivity. Of 156 men of 11th HAA Battery 44 died in captivity. Of 600 Gunners of 2nd HAA, 3rd HAA, 5th Searchlight, 7th, 9th and 11th Coast Regiments and 144th LAA Battery only 18 survived. Another who lived through the horrors of Changi was Captain James Clavell who became a famous author. His book *King Rat* was inspired by his experiences in that terrible place.

Not all of the men of the British, Australian or Indian Armies behaved to the highest standards in the battles for Malaya and Singapore or as prisoners, but extensive research and questioning of those who were there has revealed no serious case of misbehaviour by their Gunners, save for some minor pilfering in the early days in Changi prison. No doubt there were some who failed to measure up but they pale into insignificance in comparison with the great majority. In its dignity, courage and devotion to duty the Regiment had done very well indeed.

CHAPTER 5

THE LOSS OF THE NETHERLANDS EAST INDIES

FEBRUARY - MARCH 1942

(Maps 15 and 16)

Before leaving this part of the Far East theatre of war we must record the loss of Sumatra, Bali, Timor and Java because many Gunners were involved. Before the fall of Singapore the Japanese launched a three pronged attack on Java. On 20th January Lieutenant General Sano was ordered to capture Sumatra with his *38th Division*. On 9th February *229th Regiment* under Colonel Tanaka, who had behaved so cruelly in Hong Kong, left Camranh Bay under naval escort and sailed south. While he was doing so a stream of small boats was leaving Singapore carrying soldiers and civilians trying to escape to Sumatra. Some of the larger boats went by way of the Banka Strait and here met the Japanese escorts and were massacred. There were many acts of heroism as the survivors struggled ashore on the numerous small islands only to be killed or captured later on. But some got through and some even reached Ceylon. On 18th January 1942, 223 (Bomber) Group RAF left Singapore to reform at Palembang in eastern Sumatra; the group was renumbered 225 shortly afterwards. It needed anti-aircraft defence immediately and this was sent as we saw in the last chapter.

During the night of 13/14th February a Japanese convoy was sighted in the Banka Strait and attacked by all available aircraft, that is to say the aircraft which had been evacuated from Singapore to Sumatra. The Japanese aim was to capture the two airfields at Pangkalanbentang and Praboemoelih known as P1 and P2 respectively and also Palembang town, including the nearby oilfields (Map 15). These places were defended by a mixed group of Gunners, mainly in anti-aircraft units, and by Dutch troops. The Gunners were 6th HAA Regiment, 12th and 15th HAA Batteries with 12 x 3.7-inch HAA guns, 21st and 48th LAA Regiments and part of 35th LAA Regiment, 78th LAA Battery and two troops of 89th LAA Battery, a further 24 x 40mm Bofors guns. All regiments had only two batteries, none was fully equipped as they had been diverted from going to the Middle East and many of their guns and vehicles had gone to the wrong destination. However, there was enough equipment with which to function after a fashion. The layout, which was all in place by 3rd February 1942, was:

At P1 Airfield near Pangkalanbentang and Palembang:

15th HAA Battery (8 x 3.7-inch guns)

78th LAA Battery (12 x 40mm guns).

'B' Troop 89th LAA Battery (4 x 40mm guns).

At P2 Airfield near Praboemoelih:
12th HAA Battery (4 x 3.7-inch guns)
'A' Troop 89th LAA Battery (8 x 40mm guns).

Sadly the SS *Anting* was sunk by air attack while carrying the rest of 89th LAA Battery and all the 40mm ammunition but most of the men were rescued. Bombardier Plaville saved many lives by keeping men afloat until rescue came. More ammunition, including some Dutch rounds of a different design, were rushed to Sumatra from Batavia. The SS *Subadar* was hit when carrying most of the 3.7-inch ammunition and 10 of the 3.7-inch guns. She was beached and much was rescued.

Air attacks began straight away and many RAF aircraft were destroyed on the ground because there was no early warning at all. Then the commanding officer of 6th HAA Regiment, Lieutenant Colonel GWG Baass, set up his RHQ alongside that of the AOC No. 223 Group RAF which had by then arrived to co-ordinate the defences.

On 4th February Convoy WS 14 arrived at Batavia from Singapore with Headquarters 16th AA Brigade commanded by Brigadier HDW Sitwell. This formation consisted of 77th HAA Regiment and 21st and 48th LAA Regiments. These units had been at sea for eight weeks. On starting to unload, they were attacked by enemy aircraft. Tony Paley records that 'Sergeant Edward Sawyer, of the 79th [LAA] Battery was helping to unload at the time: "As we were unloading the guns some Japanese aircraft flew in low and started to bomb the ships. The *Exeter* opened fire with all her Ack Ack guns and I saw one plane come down." The situation around the docks was chaotic. Once ashore with their guns, the AA units were deployed around the harbour to provide air defence. It was then arranged that some of the British AA units would be dispersed to the important ports and aerodromes to provide the much needed air cover. Disaster struck the Gunners that day. Elements of 77th Heavy AA Regiment boarded an express train for Sourabaya. The train collided with a goods train. Three officers and twelve other ranks were killed and sixty officers and men were injured. This was a bitter blow so early in the campaign.' (Paley)

Initial deployments were as follows:

77th HAA Regiment was at Sourabaya, less 239th HAA Battery at Batavia.

21st LAA Regiment with 48th and 69th LAA Batteries and 'B' Troop of 79th LAA Battery were on airfield defence in eastern Java.

79th LAA Battery was ordered to Timor as part of 'Sparrow Force', a small Australian, American, British force sent to bolster the Dutch and Portuguese garrisons there. Its fortunes are recorded later.

48th LAA Regiment was at Batavia with its 242nd LAA Battery. Its 95th LAA Battery, which was sent to Sumatra via Oosthaven but returned to Java without disembarking when the Japanese overran the airfields at P1 and P2, and 49th LAA Battery, which was under 21st LAA Regiment deployed to defend the airfield at Kalidjati just north of Bandoeng.

The first major attack at P1 airfield and at Pladjoe oilfield near Pangkalanbentang was carried out by a Japanese parachute force which landed nearby on 14th February. Three aircraft were shot down by 15th HAA Battery. Then some Dutch troops and men of the RAF formed a local defence force. At this point all activity stopped and the Gunners awaited a ground attack. It soon came. First snipers, usually positioned high in the trees surrounding the positions, picked off anyone exposed to view. The Gunners soon dealt with them. A 3.7-inch round with fuse set at 1.5, fired into the trees over open sights and tore them to pieces. Later a Bofors gun was rushed by the enemy and captured but again a direct hit by a 3.7-inch shell destroyed the gun and its captors. Meanwhile the guns of 12th HAA and 78th LAA Batteries had been in action all day and had shot down 16 enemy aircraft. They had also defended the oilfields against ground attack until some Dutch troops arrived.

The situation at P1 airfield was by then precarious and it was decided to evacuate and move to Palembang. On the way 12th HAA and 78th LAA Batteries met a Japanese road block and a fierce fight took place. Gunner 'Geordie' Allen dealt with an enemy patrol with a Bren gun until Captain Jack Alpass found a way round. The Japanese then overran the airfield and pressed on to the oilfields at Palembang where they were again beaten off by the Gunners, who lost one officer and 16 men killed, 36 men wounded and one missing. Subsequent enemy attacks were held and hand to hand fighting went on around the deserted airfield with the anti-aircraft Gunners firing over open sights. They had been repeatedly attacked on all sides by parachutists with small arms and grenades. By last light all equipment had been destroyed and the survivors, determined to fight on, set off through the jungle to P2 near Praboemoelih.

The Japanese followed up and overcame the garrison at Pladjoe and dug in around the oil refinery. A counter-attack force was made up from the British anti-aircraft Gunners and after some fierce fighting they dislodged and scattered the enemy into the mangrove swamps; a splendid action showing high courage, morale and determination. The Dutch then took command of Pladjoe and Soengi Gerong refineries. But as more and more enemy arrived and with the news of the surrender of Singapore, the Dutch commander, on hearing that major Japanese forces had landed by sea and were advancing towards him, decided to pull out on 15th February. During the night 14/15th February Colonel Tanaka's *229th Regiment* had linked up with the hard pressed paratroopers at Palembang although they had suffered heavily from air attacks as they came ashore. The British and Dutch forces then left for Oosthaven from where they were to cross the Sunda Strait to Java. By this time 15th HAA Battery and the one troop of 89th LAA Battery were down to about two thirds of their strength.

On the road to Oosthaven several bridges had roofs constructed on them and these had to be sawn off to permit the gun tractors to cross. This took valuable time. Some bridges had been blown prematurely which caused some equipment to be destroyed and others to make wide detours, but somehow the majority got through. At Oosthaven Captain Bill Wightman of 78th LAA Battery was forbidden to take its guns to Java and had to destroy them on the quay side. 6th HAA Regiment, 78th LAA Battery and what was left of the two troops of 89th LAA Battery arrived in Batavia without guns and were organised to act as infantry but without any training to do so.

Wavell could see that the attack on Java would soon follow. He also knew that the 1st Australian Corps was on its way from the Middle East. It was destined for the Netherlands East Indies but it could not be ready for operations until about 21st March and that would be too late. He therefore recommended that it should be sent to Burma. In the event, it returned to Australia and then moved to New Guinea. On 15th February, the 2/40th Battalion moved from Darwin to defend Timor but was so heavily attacked from the air that Wavell ordered it to return. Its second attempt was successful. Then at 0940 hours 18th February enemy aircraft appeared over Darwin and began bombing and machine gunning everything they saw. Fire from the Australian anti-aircraft Gunners, 2nd, 14th and 22nd HAA Batteries (16 x 3.7-inch and 2 x 3-inch 20cwt guns, mostly uncalibrated) under Lieutenant Colonel JS Young RAA engaged as best they could but they failed to break up the attacks and all ships in the harbour were sunk. Later fresh waves attacked Darwin airfield and destroyed it. But the Australian Gunners continued to engage,

Gunner WT Hudson winning the Military Medal for fighting continuously with his Lewis Gun and destroying one of the attackers. It was a severe loss. 11 ships were sunk, 23 aircraft destroyed, 240 people killed and some 300 wounded. Five enemy aircraft were shot down by the guns.

Meanwhile enemy forces landed on the islands of Ambon on 31st January, Bali on 18th February and on the Dutch and Portuguese island of Timor on 19th/20th February as part of the general move against the Netherlands East Indies. The defence of Timor was in the hands of 'Sparrow Force', built round 2/40th Australian Infantry Battalion together with Dutch and Portuguese troops, neither of which were present in large numbers. On 20th February *228th Regiment* , which had fought in Hong Kong, landed on Timor (Map16). Two days before 79th LAA Battery RA, less 'B' Troop, under Major Jack Dempsey RA, had arrived at Koepang (Kupang) in Dutch Timor after an adventurous voyage under air and submarine attack. Two guns of 'A' Troop went to Klapalima to protect 2/1st Heavy (Coast) Battery RAA and 'C' Troop with the other two guns of 'A' Troop went to Penfui airfield. 'C' Troop deployed round the airfield and the two guns of 'A' Troop deployed to defend 'Sparrow Force' Headquarters on Force Hill, some 200 yards north of the airstrip. By midday 19th February the deployment of 'Sparrow Force' in Dutch Timor was:

Force Headquarters at Penfui Airfield, near Koepang, under Lieutenant Colonel Sir William Leggatt, CO of 2/40th Australian Infantry Battalion.

'A' & 'B' Companies, 2/40th Australian Infantry Battalion on beach positions between Klapalima and Oesapa Besar.

'C' Company, 2/40th Australian Infantry Battalion at Penfui Airfield.
HQ and HQ Company, 2/40th Australian Infantry Battalion at Babau.

'D' Company, 2/40th Australian Infantry Battalion was in reserve at Babau.

Detachments of 'B' and 'C' Troops, 18th Australian Anti-Tank Battery were with 'A', 'B' & 'D' Companies.

2/2nd Australian Independent Company was at Dili in Portuguese Timor.

2/11th Australian Field Company RAE was at Penfui, less a detachment at Tjamplong.

79th LAA Battery had 'A' Troop with two guns at Klapalima defending 2/1st Australian Heavy Battery and two defending Force Headquarters at Penfui with 'C' Troop defending the airfield.

There were some 200 men of the Dutch Army at Koepang and Tenau and a logistic base at Tjamplong (Champlong). Brigadier WCD Veale, an Australian Sapper, arrived to take command of all forces and the Dutch were commanded by Colonel NLW Van Straaten.

The Japanese attack on East Timor, regardless of Portugal's neutrality, came during the night of 19/20th February at Dili and the 2/2nd Independent Company, commanded by Major A Spence, fought hard at close quarters and even mounted a counter-attack to cover their withdrawal to Railaco and then into the hills from where they were to harass the Japanese for a further 18 months, being supplied by air and sea from Darwin. Next came reports of Japanese landings, also on the 20th, at the mouth of the River Paha on the south coast. This posed a threat to the airfield at Penfui where the understrength No 2 Squadron RAAF was stationed with its

Hudsons. The Sappers were ordered to blow their demolition charges at Penfui. 'D' Company was sent to Upura. At the same time 2/1st Heavy Battery at Klapalima was attacked from the air and 'A' Troop, 79th LAA Battery, opened fire but the heavy battery, serving in a coastal role, suffered direct hits. The Battery Commander, Major AJMcL Wilson RAA, and several Gunners were killed, others were wounded and both guns were put out of action. Thus 'B' Company and 'A' Troop's two guns were ordered to Babau. 'B' Company reported that enemy parachutists were landing some five miles east of Babau, which they entered at 1050 hours on 20th February. 'A' Troop which had just arrived immediately engaged over open sights but were forced back to Tarus where they linked up with 'D' Company. A counter-attack was ordered for 1630 hours to drive the enemy out of Babau, and it went in under the covering fire of the two Bofors guns, but it failed and the attackers were driven back to Ubelo.

That night Colonel Leggatt decided that, with the airfield out of action, Babau in enemy hands and only three days of supplies left, he had only one chance, to force his way through Babau and get to Tjamplong. There his force would replenish and then move into the hills to continue the fight with 2/2nd Independent Company. His plan was for the force to move that night to Tarus and to attack Babau from Ubelo next day. 79th LAA Battery would be spread along the column to provide air defence. On arrival the battery deployed around Tarus and the little force, to defend it against both air and ground attack. There were a lot of Japanese about all night. Lieutenant Charles Scott RA went round his guns to find several men out on patrol 'looking for Japanese'!

At 0830 hours on 21st February, 300 more Japanese parachutists were dropped near Babau and enemy air attacks started in earnest. 79th LAA Battery was in constant action and several aircraft were shot down. Sergeant Brockway claimed three himself. By 1030 hours 21st February the Australians were within 800 yards of Babau, but were pinned down by heavy fire. Two guns of 'A' Troop were then ordered right forward to engage the enemy and came under heavy fire themselves. Before long the detachments were driven from the guns and Major Jack Dempsey, Lieutenant Charles Scott and Sergeants Jones and Watson decided to counter attack to save the guns. Two Gunners engaged the tree tops, which were full of snipers, with Bren guns and effectively silenced them while Major Dempsey and the two Sergeants recovered the guns. It was a splendid action in the best traditions of the Regiment. They were then joined by a platoon of infantry and were very nearly in Babau so they held where they were while the remainder of the force consolidated at Ubelo. Then came the news that the Australians were in Babau after some heavy fighting and the whole force moved there that night.

By then they were all very weary, they had been in action non-stop for over 48 hours. But at 0800 hours on 22nd February they marched out of Babau towards Tjamplong. Again 79th LAA Battery was deployed along the convoy, but ammunition was very short. Soon they met Japanese preparing a road block and installing a howitzer at Usua. Two attacks to clear it failed. Leggatt then ordered a bombardment by all guns and mortars, to cover the infantry and the Sappers sent forward to destroy the block. The attack went in at 1700 hours and was a success, but there was still a large number of Japanese about as the little force moved forward with the gun tractors of 79th LAA Battery carrying the wounded. Leggatt was determined to press on, although his men were exhausted, because he knew that a strong Japanese force was approaching his rear from Koepang. It was imperative to get to Tjamplong to replenish. By this time they had destroyed some of the Bofors guns as there was no ammunition for them.

At 0600 hours on 23rd February a Japanese force approached their rear and ordered them to surrender as they were surrounded and about to be attacked from the air. Leggatt knew that he could not fight a battle and get to Tjamplong, his men were exhausted and almost out of ammunition, he could ask no more of them and at 0900 hours on 23rd February 1942 he decided to surrender. It had been a splendid effort against great odds and the men of 79th LAA Battery had given their all and earned the great praise of the Australian infantrymen. The battery then began a long period of captivity in the hands of the Japanese and were split up into groups throughout the Far East. Their story in captivity is told elsewhere but there is no doubt that they continued to maintain high standards wherever they were. In 1945 on his release from captivity, Lieutenant Colonel Leggatt wrote: 'This unit [79th LAA Battery RA] showed its excellent discipline during the four days of action. Their guns registered 18 hits upon enemy aircraft and reported 14 destroyed, including one four-engined troop carrier and a twin-engined flying boat. Dive bombing did not deter them in the least, only ammunition shortages prevented them from engaging all enemy aircraft presented.'

Meanwhile the Australians had deployed an anti-aircraft battery to Rabaul, which opened fire on Japanese attackers on 4th January 1942, and another to Port Moresby. It was at the latter that 30th Australian Infantry Brigade, 2/13th Field Regiment and 23rd AA Battery, with 4 x 3.7-inch and 3 x 3-inch 20cwt guns, were ready deployed by mid-March. Then 2/1st LAA Regiment just back from the Middle East joined them. The story of the gallantry of the Australian Gunners in New Guinea will be touched on later as part of the story of the war in the Pacific.

By this time Wavell had nothing to command and, with Burma by then in the charge of GHQ India, he dissolved his ABDA Headquarters, handing over the defence of Java to the Dutch. Brigadier HDW Sitwell was promoted to major general to command all remaining British Army units in Java while Air Vice-Marshal Maltby was to command the remaining air forces. But their task was hopeless. Some 10,000 escapees and evacuees had arrived from Singapore and Sumatra, they had little if any equipment and were mainly a liability. There were, however, quite a few aircraft of various types. Air Vice-Marshal Maltby set up his headquarters at Soekaboemi and began to activate some airfields in west Java, protecting them with British and Dutch units.

The Dutch had some 25,000 men on the island. There were 12 infantry battalions with some artillery and a few armoured cars. There was also a Home Guard of some 40,000 men but it was of doubtful quality. The British had 'B' Squadron, 3rd Hussars with 25 light tanks and the following artillery units:

Unit	**Batteries**	**Notes**
6 HAA Regt	12 & 15	No guns
77 HAA Regt	239, 240 & 241	
21 LAA Regt	48 & 69	
48 LAA Regt	49, 95, 242	
(6 HAA Regt)	78	No guns
(6 HAA Regt)	89 (two troops)	No guns

There was in addition 49th Battalion of 148th US Field Artillery Regiment.

The anti-aircraft regiments had been sent to protect airfields. By this time much of their equipment had been lost through enemy action and other causes. There were also two very good Australian units from 1st Australian Corps, 2/3rd Machine Gun and 2/2nd Pioneer Battalions. They had arrived from the Middle East before the request to divert the corps to Burma, and then on to Australia, had been received. The navies had some 16 assorted ships, British, Dutch, Australian and American, under Vice Admiral CEL Helfrich of the Dutch Royal Navy.

For several weeks the Japanese had been attacking Java from the air. The first action was when the guns of 77th HAA Regiment engaged enemy aircraft attacking the naval base at Sourabaya and shot down three. On 8th February Bombardier Elkins of 'B' Troop 79th LAA Battery, reported how his gun was directly attacked and had its sight bar damaged. He also reported hitting four aircraft attacking Malang on 11th February. Again this gallant troop, living up to the high standards of their comrades in Timor, found themselves in a duel with nine enemy fighters attacking some B-17s, which were on the ground re-fuelling, and drove them off. The naval base at Sourabaya and the port at Batavia had received particular attention from enemy aircraft, especially the fuel and ammunition dumps, and these commodities were already short.

The Dutch plan to defend the island was based on their belief that the Japanese would attack in two places; first, across the Sunda Strait in the west and second, at Sourabaya in the east (Map 15). A landing in the middle was considered unlikely. Thus they concentrated the bulk of their forces in the west, leaving the Home Guard to defend the middle. What was left plus the navy would defend Sourabaya. General Sitwell decided that, since the main British contribution to the defence of Java was the RAF, he would concentrate all he had to defend the airfields. 6th HAA Regiment, which had lost its guns in Sumatra and had taken command of the men of 78th and 89th LAA Batteries, was to do its best as infantry. He sent them to defend Tjililitan airfield while 77th HAA Regiment, less 239th HAA Battery, was to defend Sourabaya arriving there on 7th February. 21st LAA Regiment had one battery also at Sourabaya and one at Tjililitan airfield while its 79th LAA Battery, less 'B' Troop, was, as we have seen, lost in Timor. 48th LAA Regiment deployed 95th LAA Battery at Bandoeng airfield, 49th at Kalidjati and 242nd at Batavia. 'B' Squadron, 3rd Hussars and 49th Battalion, 148th US Field Artillery, and the two Australian infantry battalions were to form a mobile reserve under Brigadier Blackburn of Australia. This was to be known as 'Blackforce' and was to be located at Bandoeng.

On 26th February came reports of enemy shipping heading south through the Straits of Makassar and more leaving Muntok, on Banka Island, and the Allied naval force was ordered to attack them. As the fleet left Sourabaya, American aircraft attacked the Japanese convoys some 25 miles north of Bawean Island. After some delays Admiral Karel Doorman received news of the approach of the Japanese fleet at 1430 hours on 27th February. Doorman had five cruisers and nine destroyers while the Japanese had three cruisers and 14 destroyers. The engagement started at long range and the Japanese fired many torpedoes. HMS *Exeter* was hit and had to withdraw, then the Dutch destroyer *Kortenaer* was sunk. As the Japanese destroyers closed, HMS *Electra* was sunk, then followed a period of confusion when command and control of the multi-national Allied fleet broke down. At last light, contact was broken as HMS *Jupiter* blew up on a mine. But Doorman was determined to get at the enemy troop transports and steamed back into action meeting the Japanese cruisers at 2230 hours. But it was no good, the Dutch cruisers *De Ruyter*, with Admiral Doorman on board, and *Java* were sunk, the gallant Admiral going down with his ship.

The cruisers USS *Houston* and HMAS *Perth* got away to refuel at Batavia only to meet the Japanese Western Invasion Force at anchor as it was landing its troops at Bantam Bay 40 miles west of Batavia. They both engaged with all they had and sank several enemy transports before being engaged by the fleet escorts of three cruisers and nine destroyers. Both were sunk. Later the Dutch destroyer *Evertsen* ran into the enemy and was forced to beach herself. HMS *Exeter* and the destroyers HMS *Encounter* and USS *Pope* having effected some repairs and refueled at Sourabaya, tried to escape but were spotted by Japanese aircraft which directed their fleet to them. At 1000 hours on 1st March they met the concentrated fire of four cruisers. All three were sunk. Only four destroyers, all American, survived the Battle of the Java Sea and they were in harbour at Sourabaya. Later they escaped to Fremantle. The battle had delayed the invasion by 24 hours but at enormous cost. The landings occurred on the night 28th February/1st March.

On 1st March Sitwell ordered the following moves. Headquarters 21st LAA Regiment and two LAA troops to Bandoeng airfield; three LAA troops of the same regiment to Tjilatjap and two more to Jogjakarta; Headquarters 77th HAA Regiment with 240th and 241st Batteries from Sourabaya to Tjilatjap. In the course of this move one troop was cut off and lost at Sourabaya.

The eastern attack was made by the *56th Regiment* of *48th Division*, at Kragan at 0200 hours on 1st March. There was little opposition although allied aircraft attacked the landing craft with some success. But the enemy soon captured Tjepoe and began his advance to Sourabaya. By 7th March he was at the outskirts of the town and the Dutch garrison fell back to the island of Madoera. On 8th March the Japanese occupied Sourabaya, Malang and Tjilatjap. At the same time as these attacks were made, the western attack force landed the Japanese *2nd Division* at Merak and Bantam Bay while *230th Regiment* of *38th Division*, also of Hong Kong infamy, landed at Eretenwetan. Once again there was no opposition on the beaches although RAF Hurricanes attacked them as they landed. By 0800 hours on 1st March *230th Regiment* was in Soebang and heading for the airfields at Kalidjati and Tjikampek, cutting the road and rail links between Batavia and Bandoeng. The airfield at Kalidjati was captured after a bloody fight, the Japanese giving no quarter, and by 1230 hours the garrison was wiped out. The Gunners of 6th HAA Regiment had fought a bitter and unequal battle and paid the supreme sacrifice. Then on 4th March 239th HAA Battery and 242nd LAA Battery moved to Bandoeng. 'A' Troop of 12th HAA Battery of 6th HAA Regiment was overwhelmed and the Battery Commander, Major Neville Coulson, was killed in action. At this point the Regiment also lost its Commanding Officer, Lieutenant Colonel Baass. Major Joe Hazel took command, Major Gerald Moxon became second in command and Major Jack Alpass took command of 15th HAA Battery. The remains of this splendid regiment then concentrated at Garoet in central Java and awaited orders.

The landings at Merak and Bantam Bay by *2nd Division* were met with some opposition but nothing could stop the victorious Japanese and by mid afternoon they had captured Serang. They then advanced in two columns, the northern one directed at Batavia and the other towards Bandoeng. Batavia fell on the 5th March. 'Blackforce' was by then located at Buitenzorg and advanced to meet the Japanese at Leuwiliang on 2nd March where they held them all day and all night 2/3rd March. On the 3rd the 49th Battalion US Field Artillery fought hard and well and 'Blackforce' again stopped the enemy from crossing the river. Then, however, their rear was threatened as the enemy closed on Soebang. Accordingly 'Blackforce' withdrew to Buitenzorg with 'B' Squadron, 3rd Hussars and 2/2nd Australian Battalion guarding the rear while they did so. Their stand had enabled the garrison of Batavia to withdraw to Bandoeng. 'Blackforce' joined them there during the night of 5/6th March. The Dutch reckoned that it would not be possible to defend Bandoeng because it was so full of refugees, so the British moved into the hills to the south east of the town and resolved to fight on.

All available men of the Army and the RAF joined 'Blackforce', making it up to a strength of some 8,000. Then on 7th March the Dutch commander, Lieutenant General H Ter Poorten, ordered all resistance on the island to cease. The British were still assembling in the hills, they had only small arms and a few Bofors guns left. Few of the troops were trained in jungle warfare; food, ammunition and fuel were very short and there was virtually no medical support. Little help could be expected from local inhabitants and now none from the Dutch, who even withdrew their liaison staffs. By this time the Japanese knew exactly where the British were and that they were planning to fight on. Sitwell and Maltby considered that their position was hopeless, but they were still determined to fight for as long as they could. However they soon realised that to fight on after the surrender had been ordered would place them outside international law and bearing in mind the reputation of the Japanese they realised also that this action would make all prisoners liable to be shot. Accordingly, and with great reluctance, at 1430 hours on 8th March 1942 they ordered all British, Australian and American forces on the island to lay down their arms.

Thus, by 28th March, the whole of the Malay Peninsula and the Netherlands East Indies had fallen, allied Far East naval forces had been destroyed and the gateway to the Indian Ocean lay open. The Japanese had done all this in three months and were, as a result, in possession of rich resources with which to fight the war. They had been successful beyond their wildest dreams.

For the Allies the situation on 1st April was grim indeed. The men in the navies, the regiments and in the air squadrons had fought hard and well, so why had it all failed so very badly? Britain had been exhausted after the First World War, disarmament had been rapid and great faith had been placed in the League of Nations. The Army was reduced to little more than an imperial police force and the RAF to a tiny nucleus. The Royal Navy, which for over a century had controlled the seas, could hardly man a fleet, tiny by wartime standards. Politicians predicted no more wars and even ordered that, because they could not envisage a threat, no threat existed. Once publicly committed to this line they refused to heed the warnings as they began to appear and so nothing was done until it was too late. Reliance on warning time always fails because action is never taken in time for fear of provoking a potential enemy. There was no alliance or agreement with the USA after 1919; had there been then at least something might have been achieved. The failure to renew the treaty with Japan engendered deeply hurt feelings in that country. Then the 'no war for ten years' rule helped to inflict paralysis on thinking about the military future. The services fought each other for meagre funds and no training above unit level was carried out. Even in 1932, when events in the Far East showed that the chances of war were high, nothing was done. Indeed nothing of any consequence was done until 1934. Even then the services were told that the financial threat to the country was greater than the military so that still very little happened. Politicians cannot understand the complexity of war. They conveniently forget that it takes years to create the experience necessary to win in battle.

Armed forces must have the most up-to-date weapons available. They must have time to train at unit and at the operational levels and they must learn confidence and the will to fight and win. When the war started Britain did not have the weapons and did not have the time to train. Although the regiments fought with great gallantry, most had been split up to create new units, diluting them as they approached their moment of greatest trial. Initial defeat was almost inevitable. In addition it is vital that the three services learn to fight together. In the Far East, because of the nature of the ground, the islands and the long lines of communication, this was even more important. As it was they not only failed but actually operated against the interests of each other. Examples of this are the siting of indefensible airfields in north Malaya and in basing the defence of Singapore on aircraft and ships when there were insufficient of both.

Senior commanders, however, were not blameless. Brooke-Popham had predicted as late as September 1941 that war with Japan was unlikely and that in any case the Japanese, though numerous, were inferior. Then the Chiefs of Staff agreed to send the heavy warships *Prince of Wales* and *Repulse* to Far Eastern waters without escorts and without efficient air cover. They also planned to hold Hong Kong for a period, though knew it to be indefensible, and to defend Singapore without adequate air defence. When Percival sent back an estimate of what it would take to defend Malaya he was ignored because, of course, there was nothing available. Then again British intelligence was poor and in most cases wrong in its estimates. This was something which could have been rectified at very little cost, but again nothing was done. Even the most cursory monitoring of the way the Japanese operated in China would have shown the error of the estimates of the threat. Then again, the conduct of battle by the British was hopelessly ponderous and slow. Everywhere they were easily outflanked and overwhelmed by the same tactics time and time again. All this is of course not surprising because for decades the services had been ordered to believe that there would be no war and had been deprived of the facilities and training which they would need should war occur. In addition they were kept permanently overstretched as they struggled to meet even minor commitments, around the Empire and elsewhere, at unit level.

All this led to disaster and to the deaths of many young men. The losses were tremendous. The blow to national prestige, the strategic loss and the economic loss were huge. The ease with which a grossly underrated oriental power had defeated three western powers was to have a profound effect for many years to come. But in the end it was the awful loss of life and equipment that was so terrible. 166,500 men of the Commonwealth were killed, wounded or missing. Of these some 130,000 became prisoners of war. The sufferings of these men from the brutality or often sheer indifference of their captors has been told elsewhere. Ill treatment, starvation, lack of medical attention and their employment as slave labour led to the deaths of many and to the permanent impairment of many more. The Japanese lost some 15,000. But the tragedy was not yet over, as we turn now to events unfolding elsewhere.

CHAPTER 6

THE LOSS OF BURMA 15th JANUARY - 12th MAY 1942

(Maps 17, 18, 19, 20 and 21)

The defence of Burma was vital to the defence of India and of the great military base building up there (Map 17). Burma was also vital to provide lines of communication to enable the armies of China to be supplied from India. Burma is the size of France and Belgium put together. A great range of features, the Naga Hills in the north, the Chin Hills in the centre and the Arakan Yomas in the south stretch in a tangled mass of precipitous, jungle clad, almost impassable hills and steep rugged country running from the Himalayas in the north to the Indian Ocean in the south. This band of territory forms the border with India. In 1941 there were no roads and very few tracks which crossed from India into Burma, although efforts were being made to construct a motorable road from Kalemyo to Kalewa on the Chindwin. Another great band of mountains forms the Burma-China border, running south through the Shan States and on to Toungoo and through Tenasserim to Victoria Point on the Kra Isthmus. There are four great rivers in Burma; the Irrawaddy which flows through Mandalay and is joined by the Chindwin at Myingyan; the Sittang flowing through Meiktila to the Gulf of Martaban and finally the Salween which rises in China, flows though the Shan States and the Karen Hills to the sea at Moulmein. Throughout there were, in 1941, limited railways and roads, mainly in the river valleys, only a few went north of Mandalay. The monsoon period from May to October is very wet indeed and there was a permanent malaria epidemic in most of the country in 1941.

Burma, separated from India in 1937, had achieved a good deal of self-government as a Crown Colony but was still far short of independence. This did not satisfy everyone and there was a good deal of anti-British sentiment. In 1941 U Saw, the Prime Minister, was caught in Lisbon contacting the Japanese and was imprisoned in East Africa for the rest of the war. But the Karens in the south and the Nagas in the north remained staunchly loyal to Britain. After 1937 Burma was responsible for her own defence but came under the Commander-in-Chief Malaya for policy direction. The Commander-in-Chief India, who in 1940 was General Sir Claude Auchinleck, felt this was wrong and that since the defence of Burma was vital to the defence of India it should therefore come under him, and said so, but London did not agree. In his turn General Wavell, when he became Commander-in-Chief in 1941, did not like this arrangement either and said so too, but his request for a change was also turned down and so it remained until the Japanese attacked on 7th December 1941.

The Burma defence forces were very small as no threat to Burma from the east had ever been envisaged. In December 1941 military forces in Burma consisted of two British battalions, 1st Gloucestershire Regiment and 2nd Kings Own Yorkshire Light Infantry, four battalions of the Burma Rifles, mainly Karens, Chins and Kachins, and 2nd (Derajat) Mountain Battery which was located at Maymyo some 35 miles east of Mandalay. There were also six battalions of the Burma Frontier Force (BFF), mainly Burmans and converted from the old Burma Military Police. Finally there were some units of the Burma Auxiliary Force (BAF), mainly Europeans, Anglo-Burmans and Anglo-Indians. The BAF was mainly recruited to protect the Syriam oil refineries near Rangoon. They manned the Examination Battery at the mouth of the Rangoon River, which had 2 x 6-inch coast guns, and 5th Field Battery BAF which had 6 x 18-pounders. At the outbreak of war four extra regular and two extra territorial battalions were raised but at the expense of taking officers and NCOs from the two British battalions. 1st Heavy Anti-Aircraft Regiment BAF was formed and began to train but initially without any guns. By autumn 1941 that country was still without any capability of defending itself, being without effective artillery, engineers or weapons for its partly-trained and local infantry force although 5th (Bombay mountain battery arrived with 16 Indian infantry Brigade and 27th Mountain Regiment in November. There were only 16 Buffalo fighter aircraft, in the hands of 67 (Fighter) Squadron RAF, and one squadron of Tomahawk P.40 US fighters manned by the American Volunteer Group (AVG) operating from several airfields dotted around the country. Finally there were five motor launches of the Burma RNVR.

It was agreed, at a conference held in Singapore in October 1940, to despatch 13th Indian Infantry Brigade, under Brigadier AC Curtis, from India to Burma but it did not reach Rangoon until March 1941. It had with it 12th (Poonch) Mountain Battery, commanded by Major JGL Hume, and 23rd Mountain Battery, under Major TM Witherow, which arrived in June. The units at Maymyo were formed into 1st Burma Infantry Brigade, under the command of Brigadier GAL Farwell, and the new formation moved forward into the Shan States for frontier defence. Further south, in Tenasserim, four more battalions of the Burma Rifles were formed into the 2nd Burma Infantry Brigade commanded by Brigadier AJH Bourke. On 1st July 1941 1st Burma Division was formed under the command of Major General J Bruce Scott with its headquarters in Toungoo. It consisted of 1st and 2nd Burma and 13th Indian Infantry Brigades but had hardly any artillery, engineers or signals and was a division in name only.

Although numbers were increasing, operational capability was not, and the standard of training of the infantry in particular still left much to be desired. Then in November 1941, 16th Indian Infantry Brigade, Brigadier RK Jones, arrived from India and went to Mandalay in general reserve but it too was far from trained for war. So Burma was still not ready to defend itself. What is more, there was no headquarters or intelligence organisation capable of running operations, nor was there any form of civil defence structure. The General Officer Commanding Burma, Lieutenant General DK MacLeod, was told to protect the airfields in southern Burma if war came, in order to maintain the Imperial air route to Singapore and the lines of communication to China. He therefore put 1st Burma and 13th Indian Infantry Brigades in the Shan States because he saw the main threat coming from there. He held a central reserve and had garrisons at Tavoy, Mergui and Victoria Point. On 8th December 1941, as the Japanese attacked Pearl Harbour, Malaya and Hong Kong, the Chiefs of Staff transferred Burma to India Command and at the same time General Wavell was promised considerable reinforcement, particularly in anti-aircraft guns.

Wavell immediately ordered 45th Indian Infantry Brigade to move to Burma from India but was then told to send it to Singapore. He next decided to replace MacLeod with his own Chief of Staff in India, Lieutenant General TJ Hutton, a Gunner with considerable experience and in whom he had full confidence. Hutton arrived in Rangoon on 27th December 1941. Wavell had told Hutton to defend Rangoon and prepare for offensive operations into Siam and then went on to Chungking for discussions with Chiang Kai-shek. These discussions were to lead to considerable misunderstandings between Britain and China as to the best way to promote the war, mainly because Wavell found it impossible to get his points over to the Chinese leader. On his return Wavell was told, as we saw earlier, to set up a new Headquarters composed of American, British, Dutch and Australian staffs (ABDA) to be located in Java and to take full command of all operations in the Far East. But this left him without any direct communications with Burma, all signals being routed through Delhi which caused considerable delay. It was then decided in January 1942 to send 17th Indian Division with 46th Indian Infantry Brigade to Burma, but without 44th and 45th Indian Infantry Brigades which by then were en route for Singapore. So 48th Indian Infantry Brigade from 19th Indian Division was ordered to Burma with 17th Indian Division. Headquarters 17th Indian Division landed at Rangoon on 9th January 1942 under Major General JG Smyth with Brigadier GdeV Welchman as CRA and Major Roderick Lloyd-Price as BMRA.

Also in January reports of Japanese forces building up along the Siamese frontier began to reach Hutton. Rangoon had suffered its first air attack on 23rd December and civilian casualties were heavy, some reports say over 2,000. 1st HAA Battery BAF, which by then had 4 x 3.7-inch guns, and 3rd LAA Battery BAF with 8 x 40mm, were engaged and claimed three enemy aircraft shot down but they lost two 3.7s and one 40mm. Then on 31st December 8th Indian HAA and 3rd Indian LAA Batteries, the latter under Major CHT MacFetridge, arrived from India and were immediately deployed for the defence of Rangoon, Mingaladon airfield and the Syriam refineries. They brought a mixture of static 3.7-inch, 3-inch 20 cwt and 40mm guns. During these actions both 3rd Indian LAA Battery and 8th British HAA Battery which had just arrived (thus making two 8th HAA Batteries, one British and one Indian, and this can be confusing) claimed several downed aircraft but without radar or other adequate early warning their abilities were always limited. 3rd Indian LAA Battery was destined to play a major part in the campaign. The battery had been ordered to move to Burma by the commanding officer of 1st Indian LAA Regiment then at Malir near Karachi. Still untrained and manned mainly by mountain Gunners, it was given 20 British NCOs and 12 x 40mm Bofors guns for its move to Rangoon. The battery less one troop (there being three, each with four guns), was sent immediately to Mingaladon airfield; the third troop went to Moulmein. 27th Mountain Regiment, commanded by Lieutenant Colonel WG Constable, had arrived in Rangoon on 28th November 1941 with 5th (Bombay) Mountain Battery under Major WHH Wilberforce. Colonel Constable then took command of 2nd and 23rd Mountain Batteries, as well as 12th Mountain Battery which was in Moulmein. Army Headquarters was established in Rangoon with Brigadier JHB Birbeck as BRA; he had recently been CRA of 19th Indian Division. Major Rodney Burges was his GSO 2 (Ops) and Major Desmond Phayre was GSO 2 (AA and Coast Artillery). The Gunner order of battle in Burma during the 1941/42 campaign is at Annex G.

Hutton's appreciation of the situation showed that he realised that all depended on a successful defence of Rangoon. He knew that there was no road or rail link to India and all his supplies must come by sea. Yet Rangoon was vulnerable to land, sea and air attack. He therefore moved such stocks as he had to new depots in Upper Burma, around Mandalay, and stressed the importance of rapid work to make a road from Tamu to Kalewa which would link up with the road being built from Imphal to Tamu. This action did much to save the Army later on. Hutton's forecast of the Japanese attack route through Tenasserim was very accurate and he wanted to concentrate his effort there, leaving the Shan States to the Chinese Army. Accordingly he dispatched 16th Indian Infantry Brigade to Moulmein where it joined up with 2nd Burma Infantry Brigade. On 16th January 1942 the newly arrived 46th Indian Infantry Brigade, under the command of Brigadier RG Ekin, was sent forward from Rangoon to Bilin and Headquarters 17th Indian Division was to command these three brigades and become responsible for the area Mergui to Papun, a front of some 400 miles.

Major General JG Smyth VC, commanding 17th Indian Division, then sent 16th Indian Infantry Brigade, less 4/12th Frontier Force Regiment, to Kawkareik where it took under command 4th Burma Rifles and prepared a position on the Dawna Range guarding the eastern approach from Raheng. It in turn placed a company at Three Pagodas to guard the pass on the route from Bangkok. Their task was to stop any Japanese attack from either place. During January Moulmein and Tavoy were bombed. The Japanese Army was soon ready and on 15th January 1942, *112th Regiment* of *55th Division,* in *15th Army*, attacked Tavoy from Ban Pong, overwhelming 6th Burma Rifles and a section of 5th Battery BAF. This effectively cut off Mergui, so the garrison was withdrawn by sea. The Japanese now had the three airfields at Victoria Point, which they had already captured on 16th December 1941 when securing the Kra Isthmus, Mergui and Tavoy. Thus they could mount more effective air operations against Rangoon. Then on 20th January came the main attacks against 16th Indian Infantry Brigade at Kawkareik which fell back on Martaban with difficulty. Moulmein airfield was at this time defended by 8th Indian HAA Battery with 3 x 3-inch guns and one troop of 3rd Indian LAA Battery with 4 x 40mm guns. Air attacks started as the guns arrived and they were soon in action. The Japanese then headed straight for Moulmein which at this time was held by the partly trained 2nd Burma Infantry Brigade of five battalions, 12th Mountain Battery together with 8th Indian HAA Battery and one troop of 3rd Indian LAA Battery mentioned above.

Early on 30th January 1942 the Japanese attacked the seven mile perimeter of Moulmein (Map 18) from the south east against 8th Burma Rifles who had one section of 12th Mountain Battery in action with them and this section was soon hotly engaged, earning great praise from the hard pressed infantry. Meanwhile 5th Mountain and 8th Indian HAA Batteries were evacuated to Martaban. Then came new attacks against 3rd Burma Rifles which caused the garrison to fall back to the high ground just to the east of the town. Here the rest of 12th Mountain Battery came into action and all enemy attacks were held until last light. Smyth then had two options; to reinforce Moulmein from 16th Indian Infantry Brigade at Martaban or to withdraw. He consulted Hutton who agreed to a withdrawal but said the line of the Salween River, including Martaban, must be held.

During the night the Japanese landed in the north and were immediately engaged by 7th Burma Rifles but by then preparations had been made to withdraw. By 0200 hours 7th Burma Rifles were back at the Police Station and the troop of 3rd Indian LAA Battery had been lost. The Japanese had landed dressed as Burmese and had mingled with the retiring Burma Rifles only to surprise and bayonet many of the Indian LAA Gunners who fought fiercely, much of it hand to hand, to save their guns. Japanese artillery could, by then, bring down observed fire on the boats in the harbour, but only one was sunk. The brigade got out by first light behind a bridgehead held to the end by 4/12th the Frontier Force Regiment and 12th Mountain Battery which had sections covering the Post Office, Maingay and Mission Streets. Eventually, after more hard fighting the brigade arrived in Martaban with all guns less the 40mm Bofors, but it had lost a quarter of its strength. It had been a tough fight. Major Hume, commanding 12th Mountain Battery, reached the jetty to embark only to find one section of his guns missing. With a small party of Gunners and some infantry, he forced his way through the enemy to the section still in action in the town, and brought both guns and the men safely back, a splendid piece of dare-devil leadership. Second Lieutenant Mehar Dass, of 3rd Indian LAA Battery, heard that the enemy had not left sentries on the Bofors guns which they had captured, so he took a party of Gunners and managed to get back the one gun that, in the toughness of the fight, they had been unable to disable, but try as he might, he could not get it onto the steamer and reluctantly had to leave it behind. But he could not bear to leave his guns and so many of his men, and this gallant young Indian officer dived off the boat and swam ashore under heavy fire to disable the gun and try to save his men. He was not seen again, surely an action in the finest traditions of the Regiment. It had been the first experience of war for these men and they had done extraordinarily well and had taken a heavy toll of the enemy. The Japanese reports refer to 'a fierce resistance by a determined enemy.' Certainly the men of these two batteries had behaved with the greatest gallantry. It is worthy of note that it was this LAA troop, re-equipped, that was to do so well again right at the end of the campaign.

The action at Moulmein caused Wavell to send more troops to Burma. He ordered the move of 46th and 48th Indian Infantry Brigades to be speeded up, three more British battalions to be sent and 63rd Indian Infantry Brigade was to prepare for service in Burma. By this time 49th and 55th Chinese Divisions were moving into the Shan States to take up positions about Takaw.

Smyth's problem was how best to hold a line between Martaban and Pa'an some 30 miles to the north when a powerful Japanese force was concentrating at three crossing places even further north at Shwegun, Kamamaung and Papun some 100 miles away. He decided on a defence in depth ordering 16th Indian Infantry Brigade to hold the line Martaban - Pa-an - Kamamaung with Thaton. 46th Indian Infantry Brigade was to hold the line Bilin - Papun with 2nd Burma Infantry Brigade in reserve at Kyaikto watching the bridge over the Sittang river and maintaining his only link with Rangoon. Hutton then ordered 48th Indian Infantry Brigade to come under the command of 17th Indian Division and to move to Kyaikto as well. Wavell arrived at Rangoon on 4th February and stressed the importance of holding the current positions. He also ordered 7th Armoured Brigade, then on its way from Cairo to Malaya, to be diverted to Rangoon. With these extra forces Smyth sent 46th Indian Infantry Brigade forward to take over from 16th Indian Infantry Brigade which he pulled back to the Bilin area.

The Japanese crossed the Salween west of Martaban and established a road block at Paung. Orders to withdraw from Martaban did not get through but an attack was so obvious that the commander decided to destroy all equipment and break out cross country, which he did, reaching Thaton on 11th February. The guns of 12th (Poonch) Mountain Battery were got out in time by rail. 5th Mountain Battery, which had been at Moulmein but had been withdrawn early, took part in the fighting at Martaban, then sent one section from their harbour at Thaton to Pa'an Ferry. The remnants of that section, men only, rejoined at Thaton before moving to the Bilin River where they received two replacement guns. The other section of 5th Mountain Battery had already moved to cover the crossing at Pa'an with 7/10th Baluch Regiment and was attacked in strength by *215th Regiment* during the night 11/12th February. The fighting was hard, hand to hand and at point blank range but the little force stood its ground until over half had been knocked out. The story of the stand of 7/10th Baluch Regiment at Pa'an is one of the great acts of heroism of the old Indian Army. When the sun rose on 11th February the sound of battle had almost ceased except in 'C' Company. 'D' Company was no more and there were few left in 'A' Company. A Japanese officer standing on what had been 'B' Company position shouted for the remainder to surrender, to be answered by a defiant burst of machine gun fire. The guns of 5th Mountain Battery were in action by the remains of battalion headquarters and 'A' Company and were firing at advancing enemy at point blank range. The only hope was to link up the remains of 'A' Company with 'C' under the fire of the guns. This was done but in doing so the guns were lost to enemy infantry who got among the detachments with the bayonet. Only five officers and 65 men got away from the battalion and the battery. They had defended their position to the very last. The 5/17th Dogras were sent to their rescue but failed to get there in time. This meant that the Japanese were established across the Salween in two places.

On the afternoon of 13th February the Japanese shelled Duyinzeik and General Smyth realised the pace of their advance. He told Hutton that with the poor standard of training of his men, the acute shortage of artillery and with no air support he was in great danger of being cut off unless he pulled back to the Bilin river line as soon as possible. He reckoned he had only two battalions and his two mountain batteries fit for action. Fearing, as it turned out quite correctly, that he was being by-passed to the east, Smyth ordered 46th Indian Infantry Brigade to withdraw to the Bilin line at 1730 hours on 14th February. His plan was for 16th Indian Infantry Brigade to hold the line of the Bilin, 48th Indian Infantry Brigade to remain in reserve but holding the Thebyu river line while 46th Indian Infantry Brigade withdrew to Kyaikto leaving 5/17th Dogras in an outpost position east of the Bilin. This withdrawal was successfully carried out. By now Hutton was becoming concerned for the security of the Sittang river and the bridge at Sittang itself. He had given responsibility for the bridge to the commander of 17th Indian Division and ordered him to prepare it for demolition. The stage was now set for the defence of the Bilin river by 17th Indian Division opposed by the *33rd* and *55th Divisions,* each of two regiments each of three battalions.

Hutton then flew to see Chiang Kai-shek and received agreement that the Chinese 5th and 6th Armies, which were the equivalents of a British division, should come under his command. The former would move to the Toungoo area for the defence of the Burma Road while the latter would remain in the Shan States, so relieving 1st Burma Division for operations further south. Meanwhile 7th Armoured Brigade was due to arrive on 21st February but until it did, and until the Chinese moves were complete, the situation was critical on the Bilin river, for Smyth had an open left flank and no more reserves. Hutton warned Wavell that, although he would do all he could with the weary, part-trained 17th Indian Division on the Bilin, the Sittang was threatened and if that fell, Rangoon would be at risk.

At Bilin 28th Mountain Regiment, under Lieutenant Colonel AH Peskett, joined the division fresh from Madras and was a most welcome addition of firepower. It consisted of 15th (Jhelum) Mountain Battery, Major RJP Lock, and 28th Mountain Battery, Major JB Chaplin. The strength of each battery was four British and four Indian officers and 100 Indian other ranks with four 3.7-inch howitzers, and the vehicle establishment was three jeeps and seven 3-ton Chevrolet trucks. This distribution of vehicles was rarely, if ever, achieved and horses and mules were employed in most cases. Also at Bilin 5th Mountain Battery received two 3.7-inch howitzers still in grease to replace its losses with the gallant Baluchis at Pa'an.

The artillery order of battle by this time in Burma was indeed small and consisted of:

27th Mountain Regt	
2 (Derajat) Mtn Bty	4 x 3.7-in howitzers
5 (Bombay) Mtn Bty	4 x 3.7-in howitzers
12 (Poonch) Mtn Bty	4 x 3.7-in howitzers
23 Mtn Bty	4 x 3.7-in howitzers
28th Mountain Regt	
15 (Jhelum) Mtn Bty	4 x 3.7-in howitzers
28 Mtn Bty	4 x 3.7-in howitzers
1st HAA Regt BAF	
1 HAA Bty	4 x 3.7-in mobile and 4 x 3.7-in HAA guns
Indep Batteries	
3 LAA Bty	A few static 40 mm guns
3 Indian LAA Bty	12 x 40mm guns
8 Indian HAA Bty	4 x 3.7-in and 4 x 3-in mobile HAA guns
8 HAA Bty RA	8 x 3.7-in and 4 x 3-in mobile HAA guns
5 Field Bty BAF	6 x 18-pdr field guns
Rangoon CD Bty BAF	2 x 6-inch coast guns

By the time of the outbreak of war with Japan, India had already sent 4th and 5th Infantry Divisions to the Middle East and had completed most of her expansion plan for 1940 which involved the formation of 6th, 7th, 8th, 9th, 10th and 11th Infantry and 31st Armoured Divisions. She was now beginning her 1941 expansion programme which involved forming 14th, 17th, 19th and 20th Infantry and 32nd Armoured Divisions. Of these 6th, 8th, 10th and part of 32nd had been sent to Iraq, 9th and 11th to Malaya and 7th Division had already sent its 13th and 16th Infantry Brigades to Burma. By the end of 1941 India had 900,000 men under arms (with 300,000 overseas) and recruits were being taken in at a rate of some 50,000 per month. There was however a very great shortage of weapons. India still had only 36% of her requirements for 25-pounders, 23% of 2-pounders, 25% of 3.7-inch HAA guns and some 15% of her 40mm LAA guns. What is more, in the middle of forming 17th Indian Division, she had been forced to send 44th and 45th Indian Infantry Brigades to Malaya, so that the division had gone to Burma with only 46th Indian Infantry Brigade. 48th Indian Infantry Brigade had been sent from 19th Indian Infantry Division and 63rd Indian Infantry Brigade was soon to follow from 14th Indian Infantry Division. Thus 17th Indian Division was committed to action with two of its three brigades unknown to it.

The next great problem was the lack of road or rail communications between India and Burma. It soon appeared that the most feasible alignment for a road was to extend the Imphal track through Palel to Tamu on the Indo-Burma frontier and thence down the Kabaw Valley to Kalewa on the Chindwin. From there a road could be built to the railhead at Yeu. By the end of 1941 the Imphal road was 134 miles long, single carriage way, but metalled as far as Palel; thereafter there were only jungle tracks. Work then started in earnest to complete the link, with much being done by the Royal Engineers.

When Singapore fell on 15th February 1942 it became clear that India was at real risk. Accordingly the War Cabinet ruled that the defence priorities in the Far East must be Burma, India, Ceylon and Australia. Wavell recommended that 1st Australian Corps, then on its way to Java from the Middle East, should be diverted to Burma, that 70th British Division should be sent to Burma from the Middle East and that the defences of Ceylon should be strengthened by additional anti-aircraft artillery. But it was not to be. John Curtin, the Prime Minister of Australia, said that if Java fell the threat to Australia would become very real and he demanded that 1st Australian Corps should return home forthwith, which almost all of it did. Prompted by the need to secure the lines of communication across the Indian Ocean, steps were taken to build an airfield and fleet base on Addu Atoll in the Maldive Islands and to strengthen the defences of the Seychelles and Mauritius. Next, plans were put in hand to seize Diego Suarez in Madagascar which was controlled by the Vichy French. This action is described in Chapter 7.

To return to Burma; defences on the Bilin were far from strong. The river itself was fordable almost everywhere. General Smyth decided to put 16th Indian Infantry Brigade along the line of the river from the railway bridge in the south to Paya in the north. 1/9th Jats were to hold the right sector covering the main road and the railway. 8th Burma Rifles were to cover Bilin village in the centre and 2nd KOYLI were on the left covering Danyingon and Paya, with a detached company at Yinon. 1/7th Gurkhas were in reserve, with 5/17th Dogras still in an outpost position four miles south east of Bilin. 48th Indian Infantry Brigade sat in divisional reserve behind the Thebyu river while 46th Indian Infantry Brigade was manning the defences of Kyaikto. 5th, 15th and 28th Mountain Batteries and a section of 5th Field Battery BAF were forward with 16th Indian Infantry Brigade along the river line.

The Japanese plan was to advance to the Bilin with their *33rd Division* while *55th Division* crossed the Bilin estuary, moved by boat to Zokali and advanced to Taungzun and on to Kyaikto, so turning the right flank of the Bilin position. *33rd Division* moved fast and on 16th February it

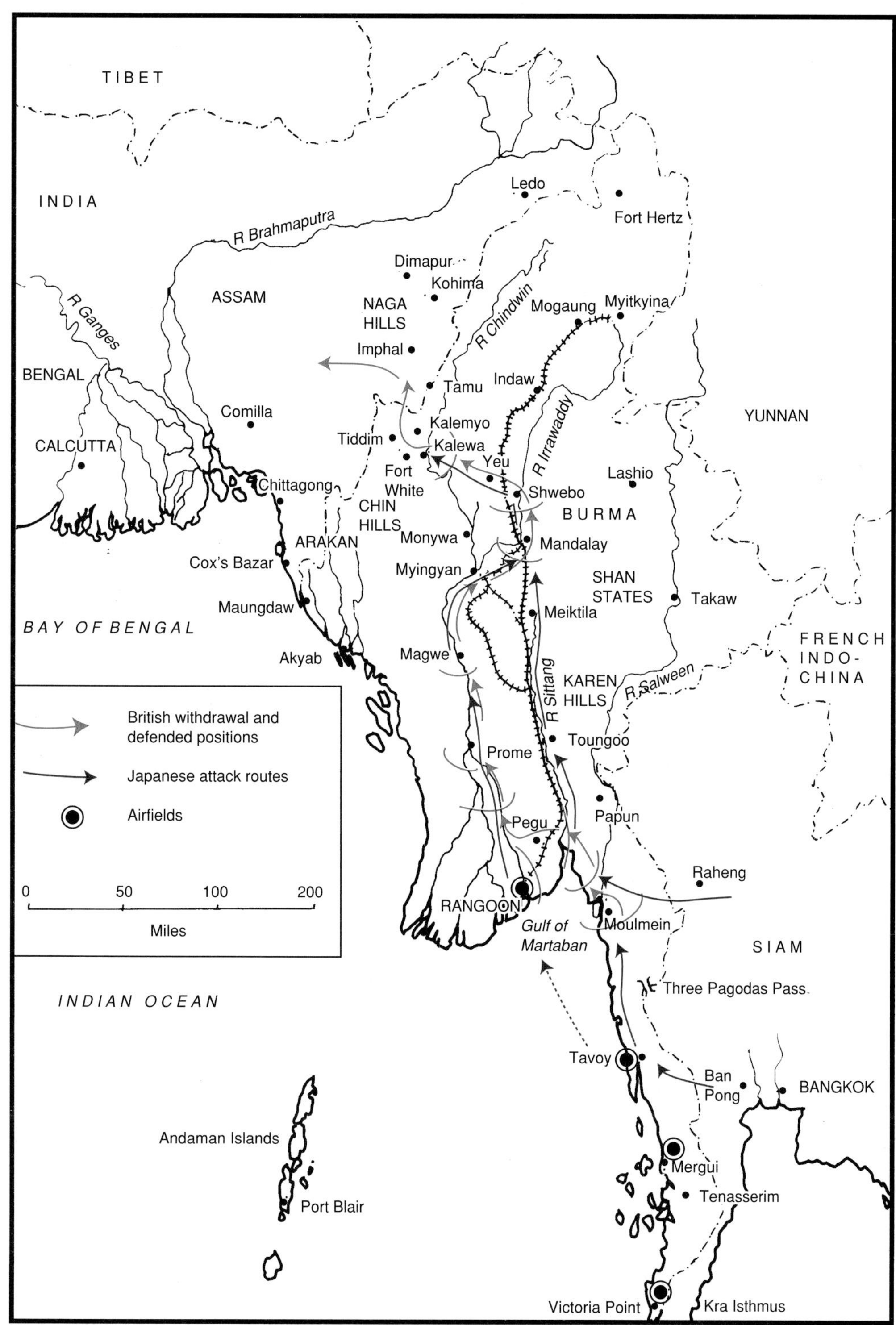
TIBET
INDIA
R Brahmaputra
Ledo
Fort Hertz
Dimapur
Kohima
ASSAM
NAGA HILLS
R Ganges
R Chindwin
Mogaung
Myitkyina
Imphal
BENGAL
Tamu
Indaw
Comilla
YUNNAN
Kalemyo
R Irrawaddy
CALCUTTA
Tiddim
Kalewa
Yeu
Fort White
Lashio
Chittagong
CHIN HILLS
Shwebo
BURMA
ARAKAN
Monywa
Mandalay
Cox's Bazar
Myingyan
SHAN STATES
Takaw
Maungdaw
Meiktila
BAY OF BENGAL
FRENCH INDO-CHINA
Akyab
Magwe
R Sittang
KAREN HILLS
R Salween
British withdrawal and defended positions
Japanese attack routes
Airfields
Toungoo
Prome
Papun
Pegu
0
50
100
200
Miles
Raheng
RANGOON
Gulf of Martaban
Moulmein
SIAM
INDIAN OCEAN
Three Pagodas Pass
Tavoy
Ban Pong
BANGKOK
Andaman Islands
Mergui
Tenasserim
Port Blair
Victoria Point
Kra Isthmus

Map 17 Burma

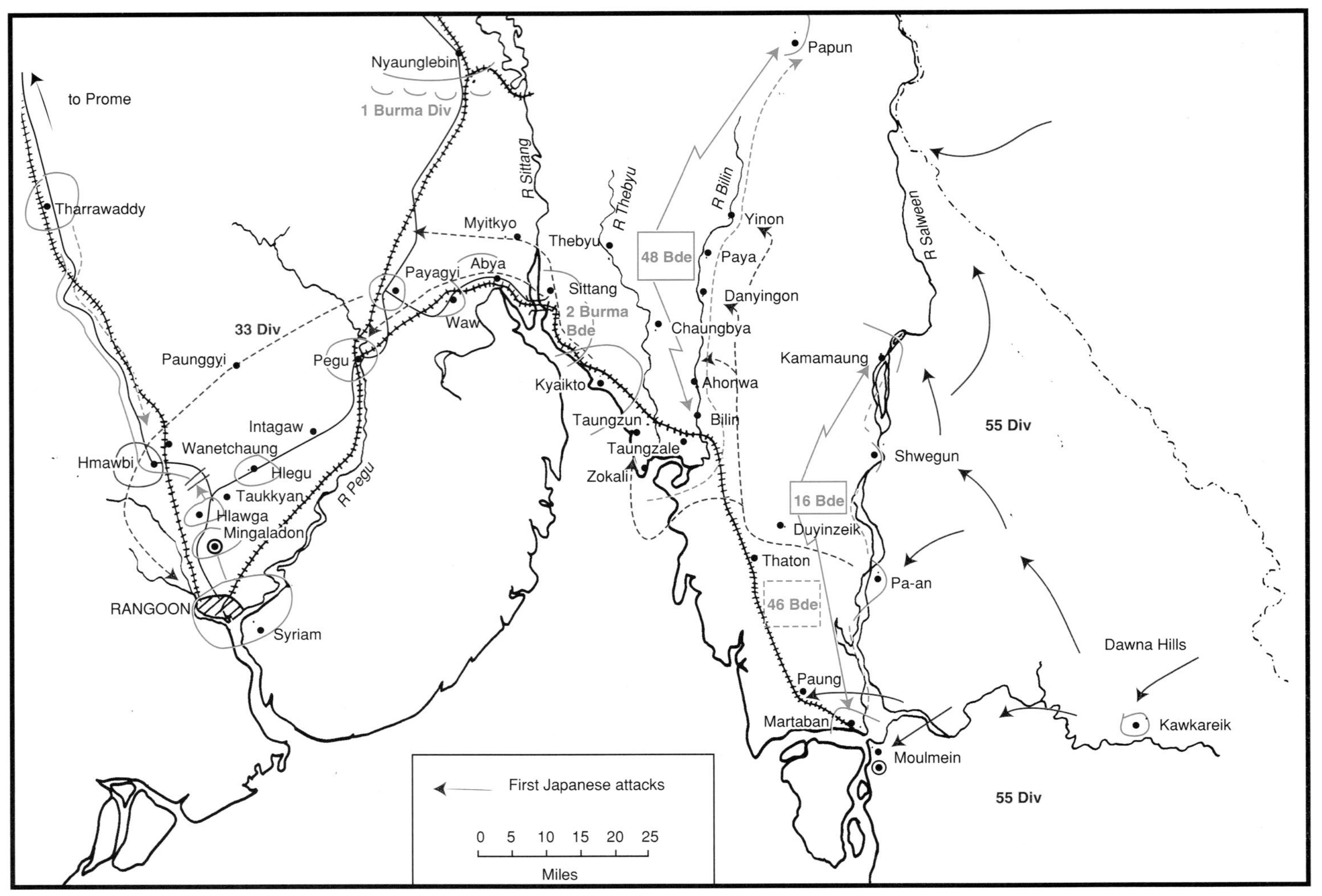

Map 18 Moulmein - Rangoon and the Bilin River. Dec 1941 to Jan 1942

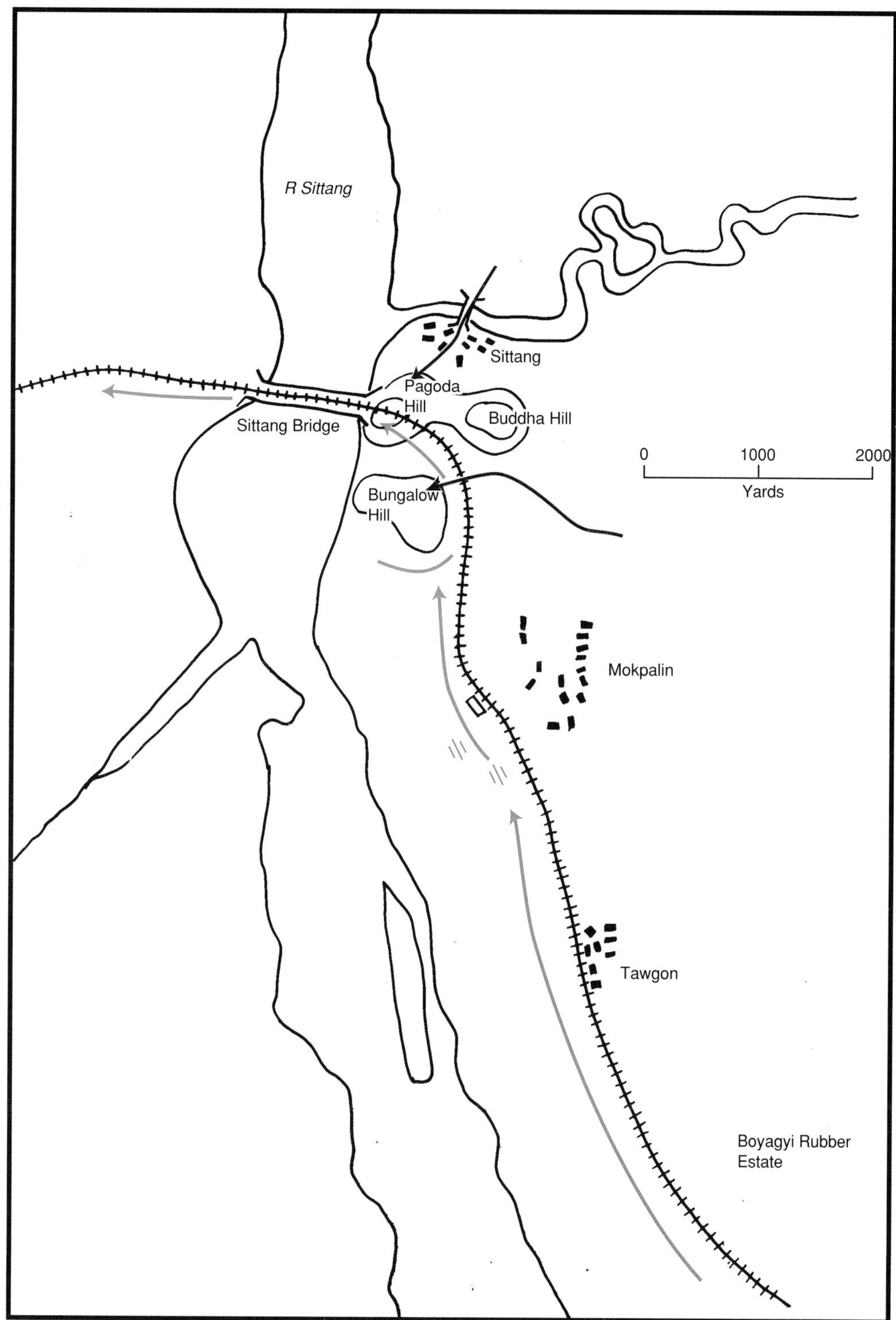

Map 19 Action at The Sittang Bridge

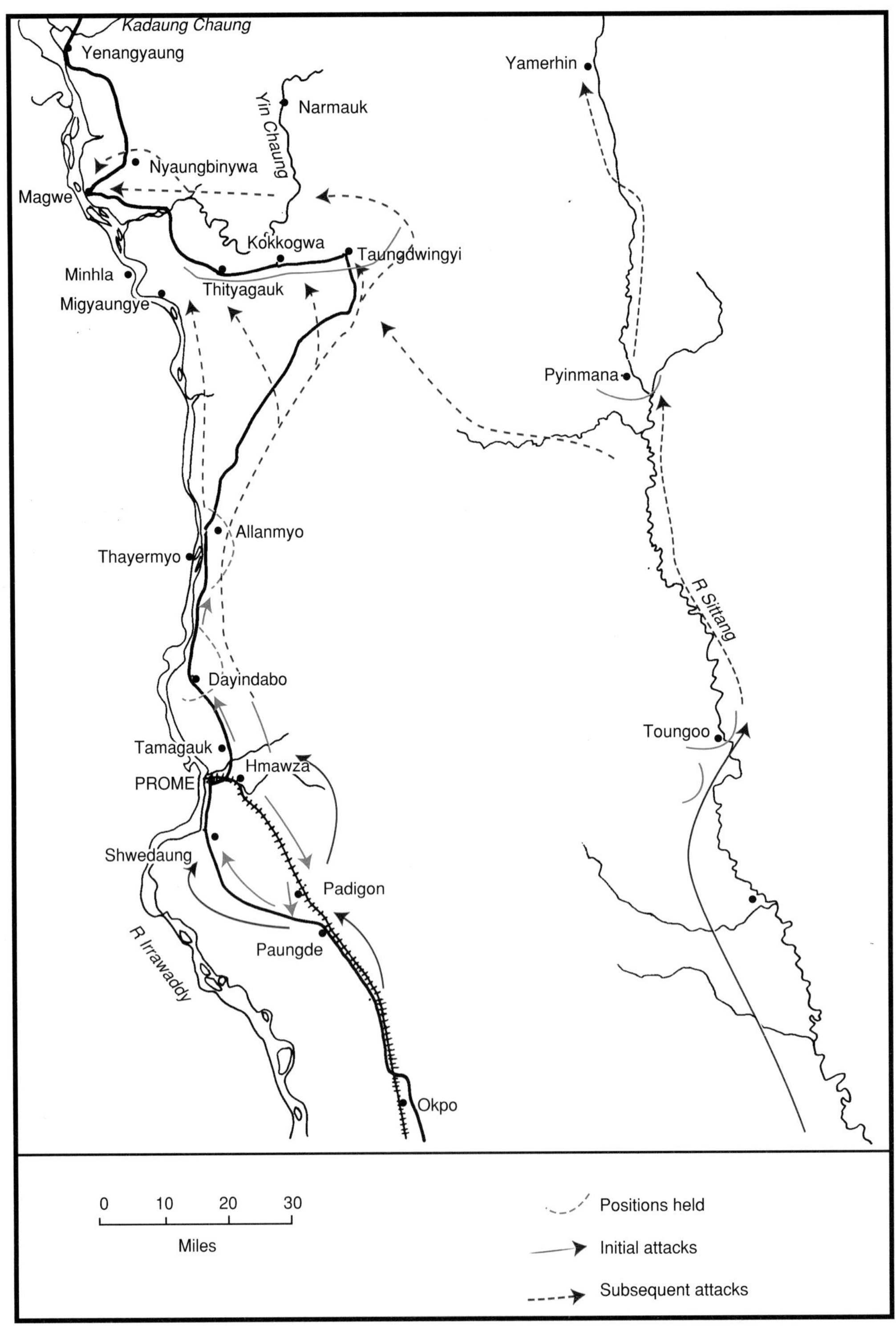

Map 20 Action at Prome and during the withdrawal to Yenangyaung

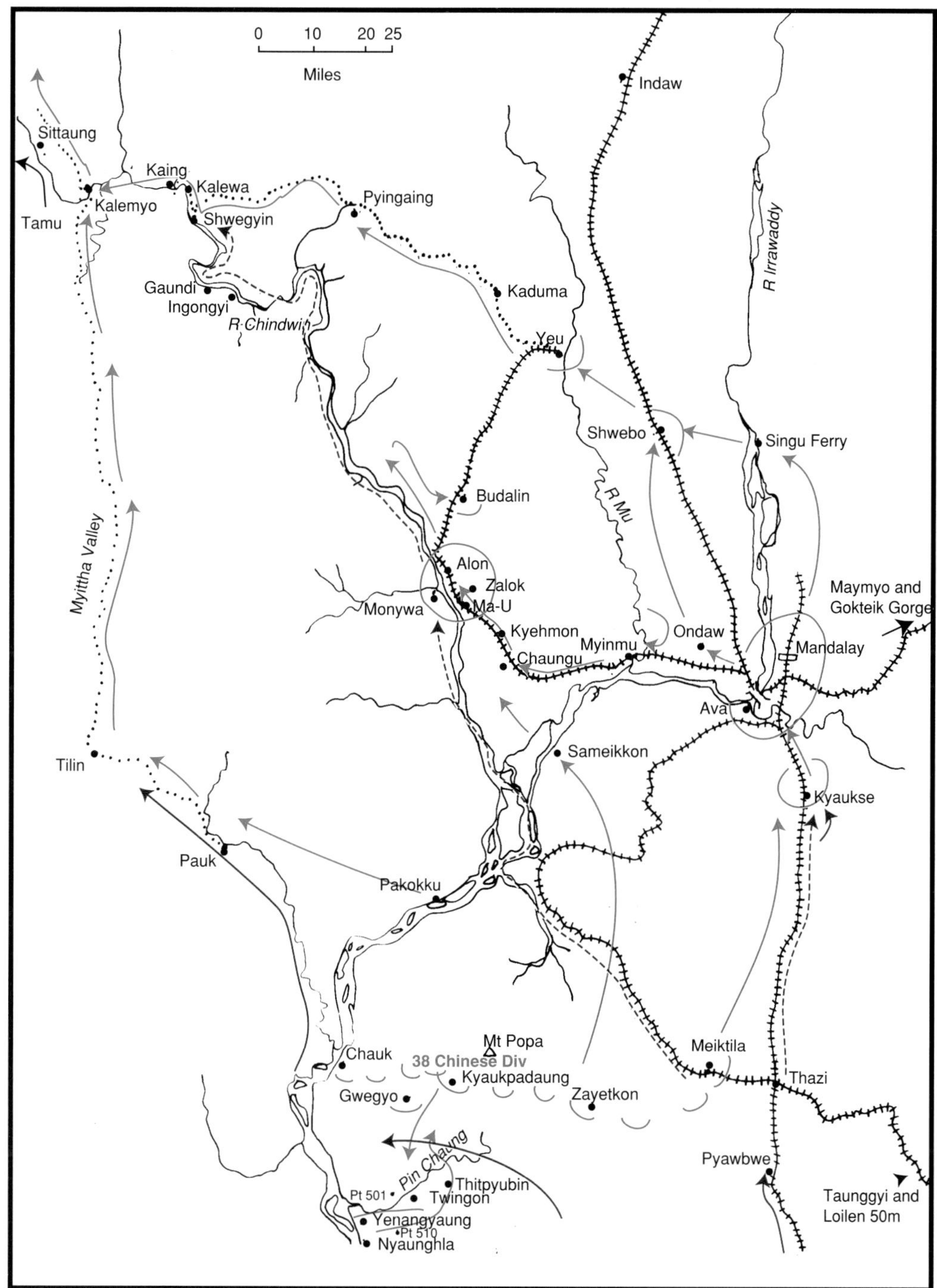

Map 21 The final retreat from Burma

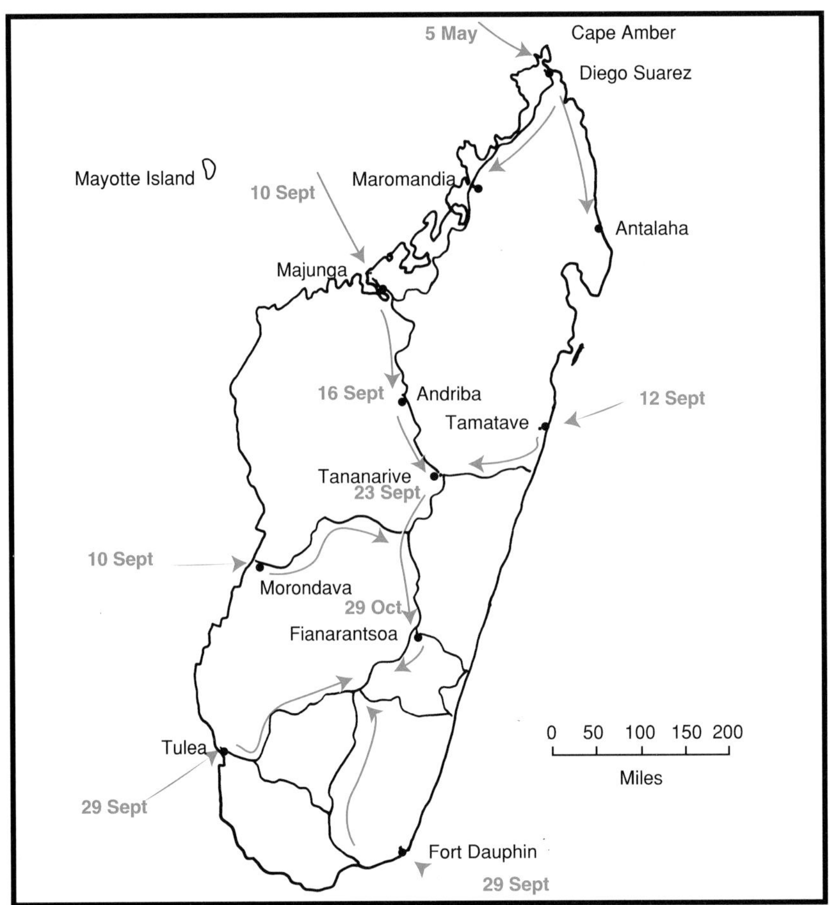

Madagascar

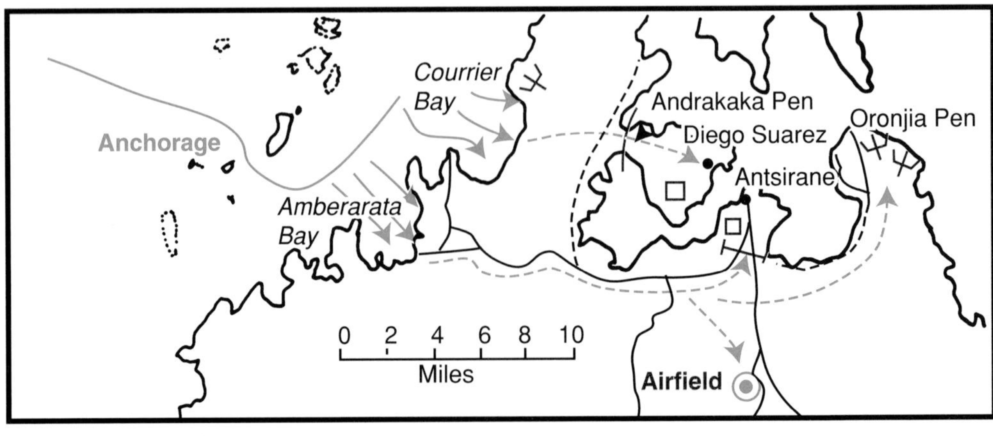

Dieggo Suarez

Map 22 Madagascar, 1942

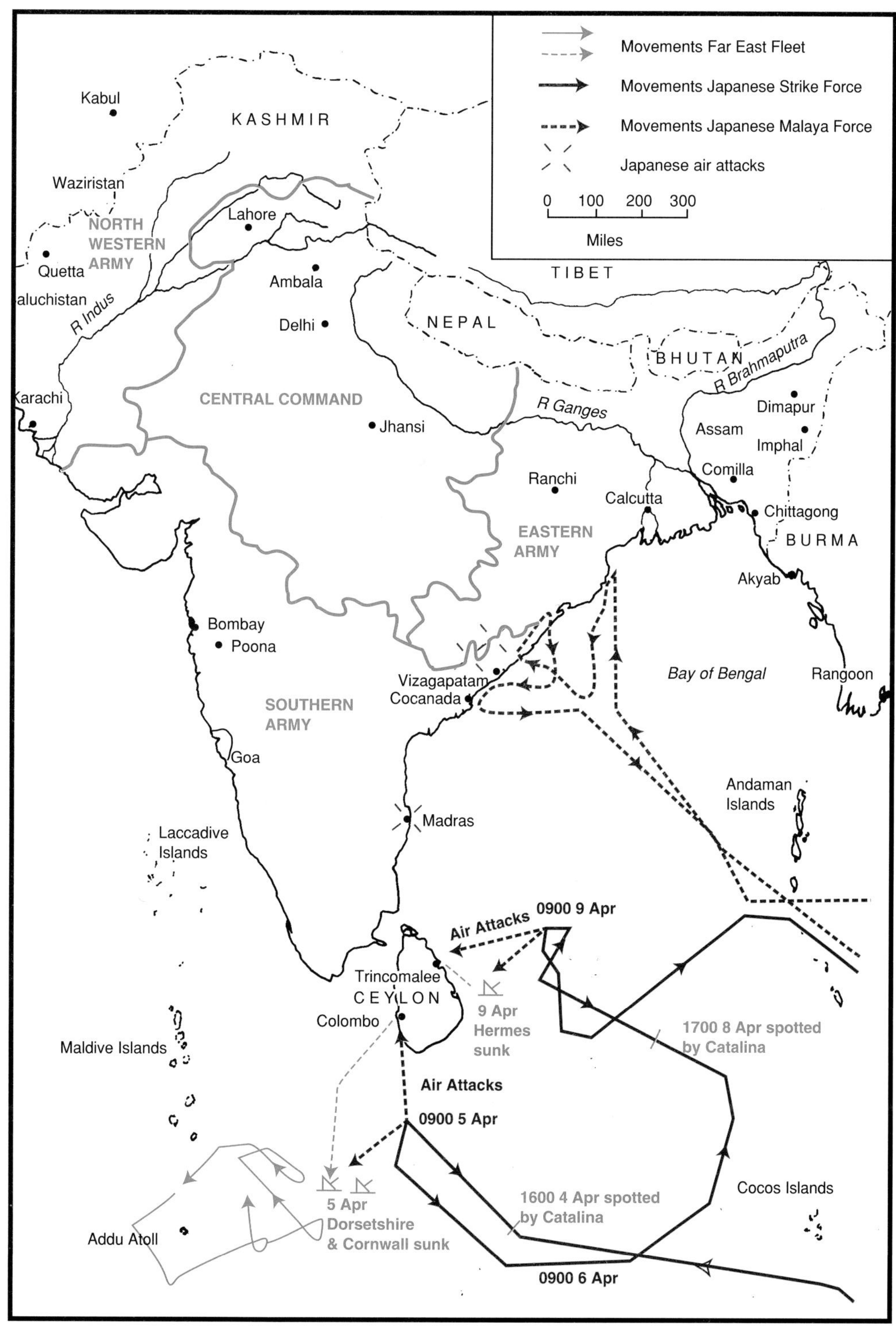

Map 23 India and Ceylon

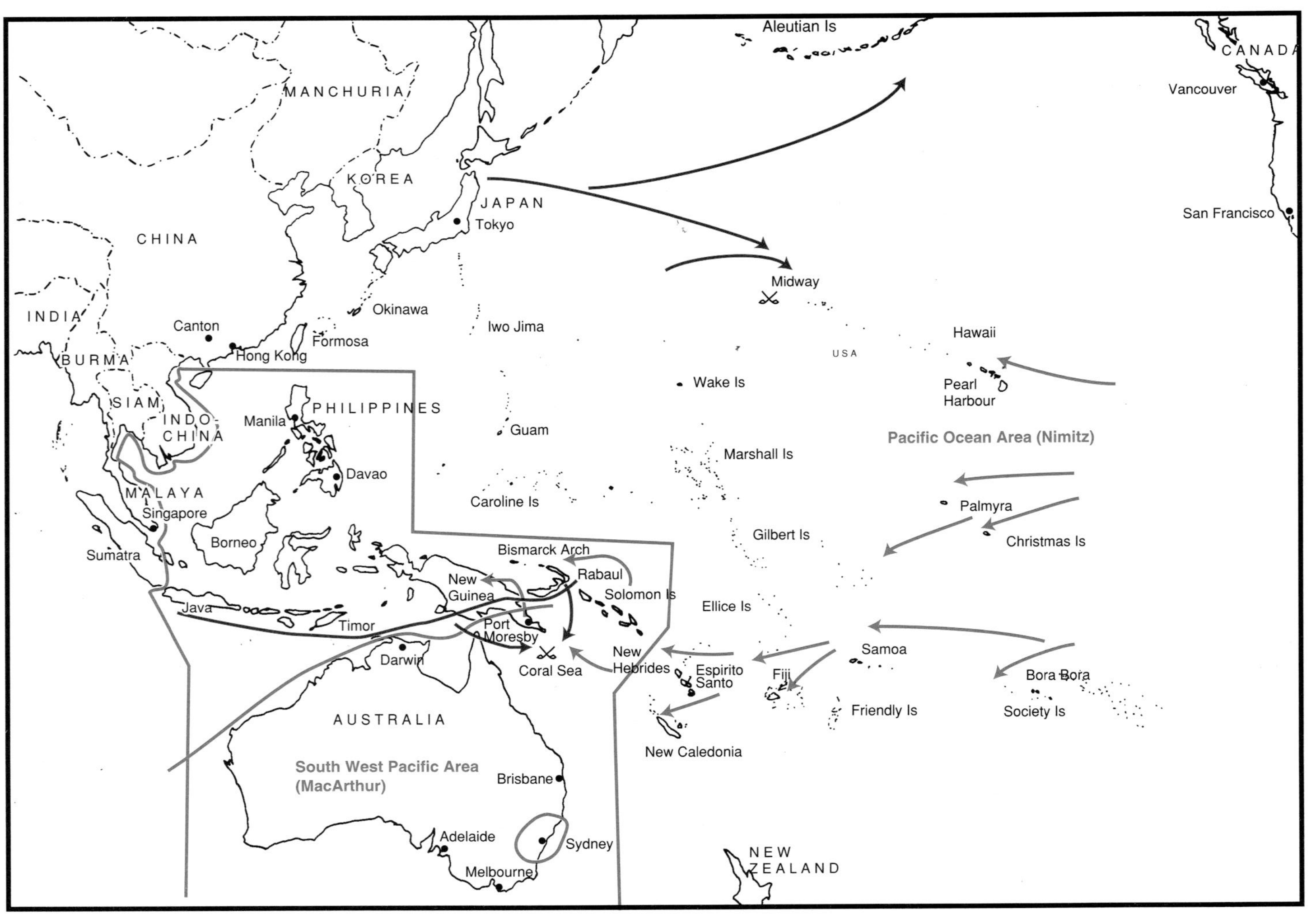

Map 24 Pacific Ocean Operations, 1942 - 43

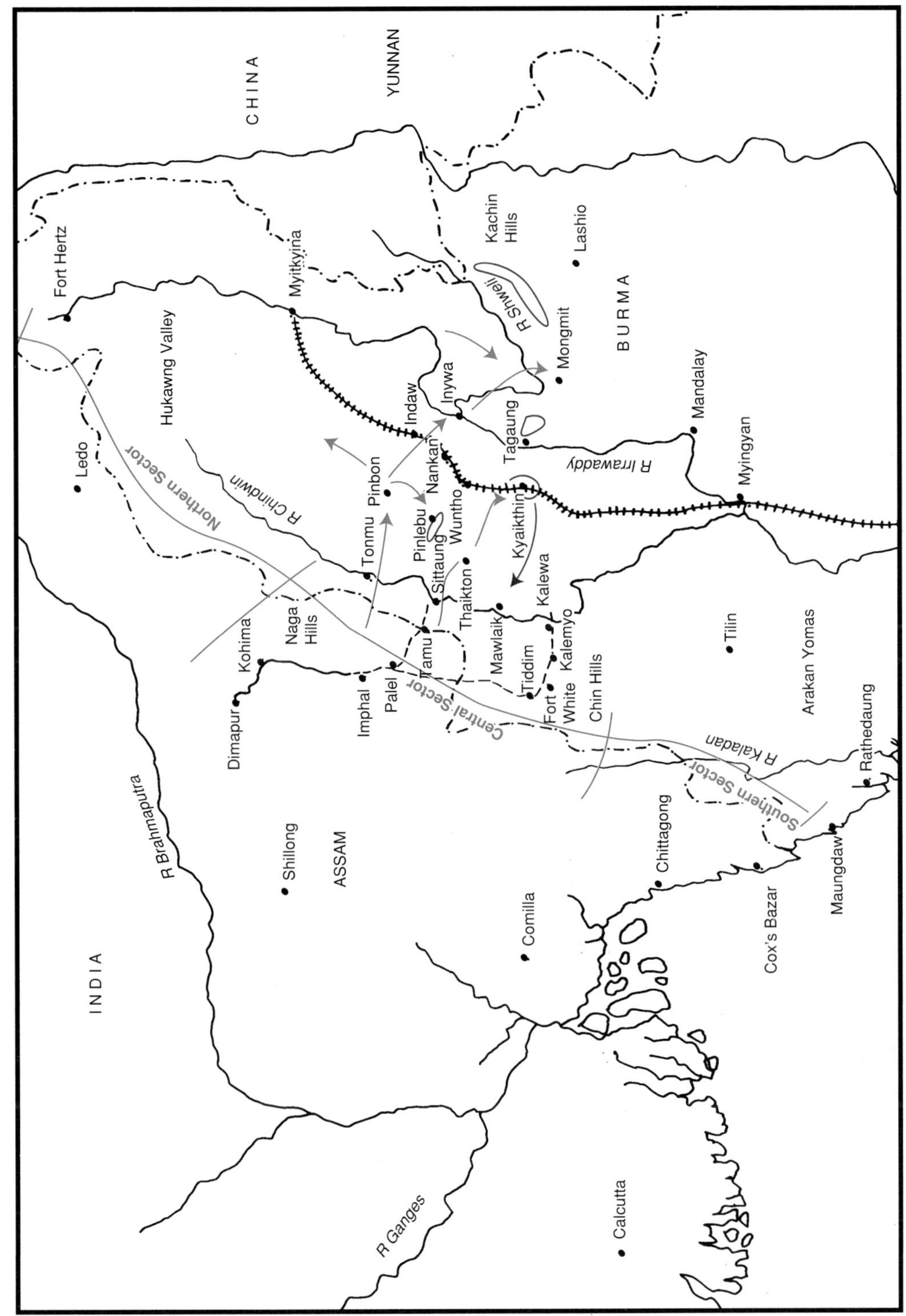

Map 25 The Assam Front 1942-43

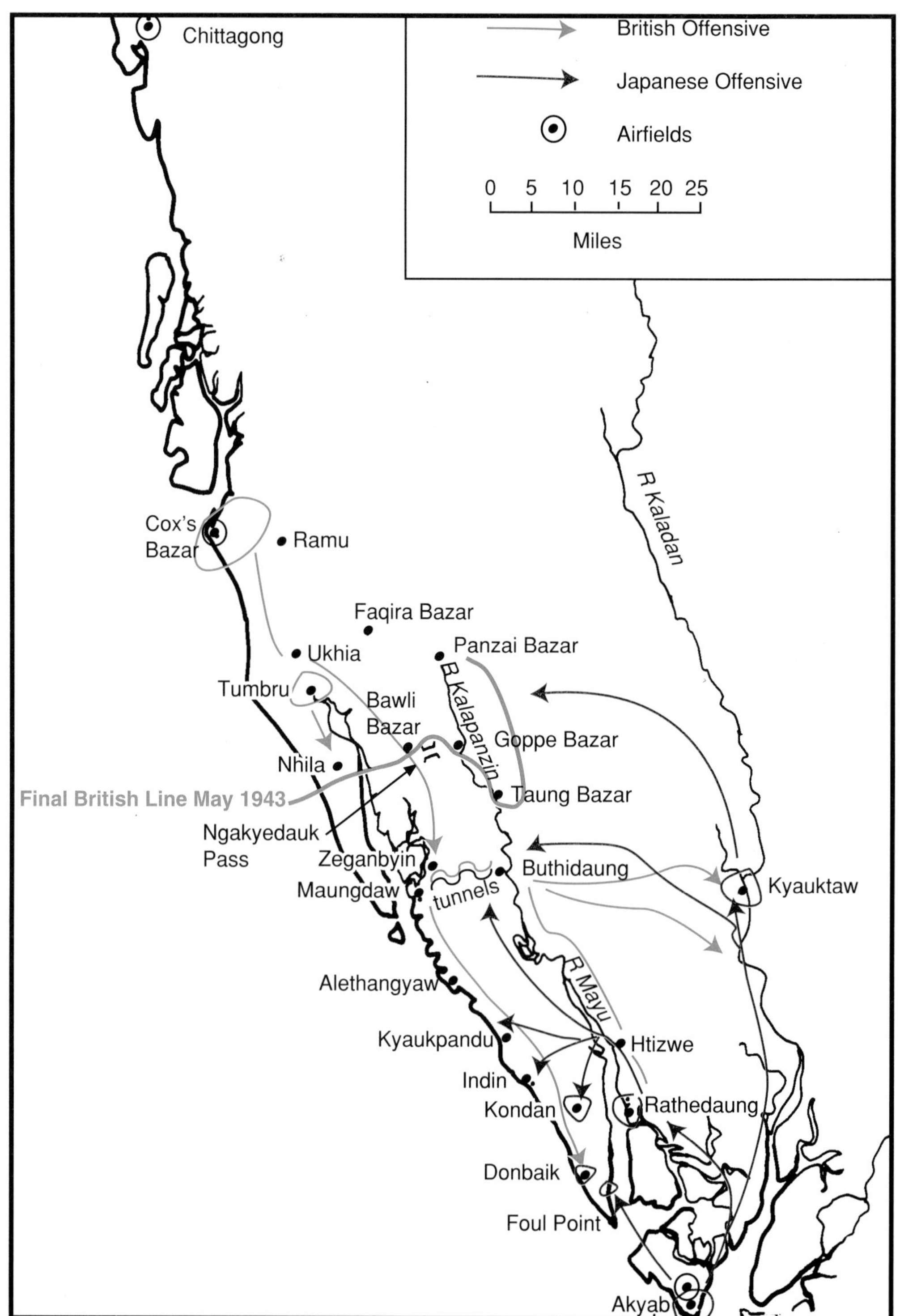

Map 26 The first Arakan 1942-43

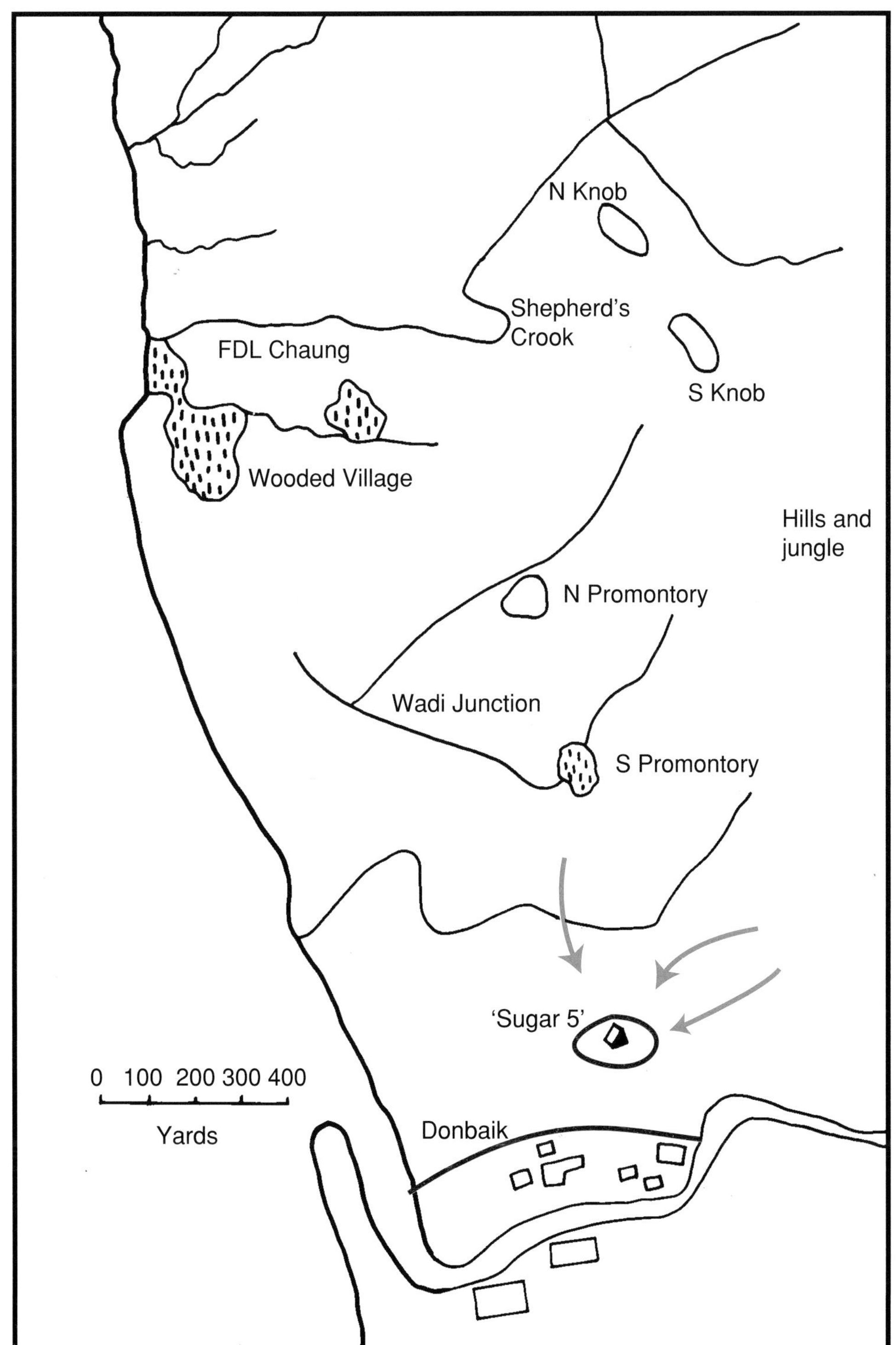

Map 27 Donbaik February 1943

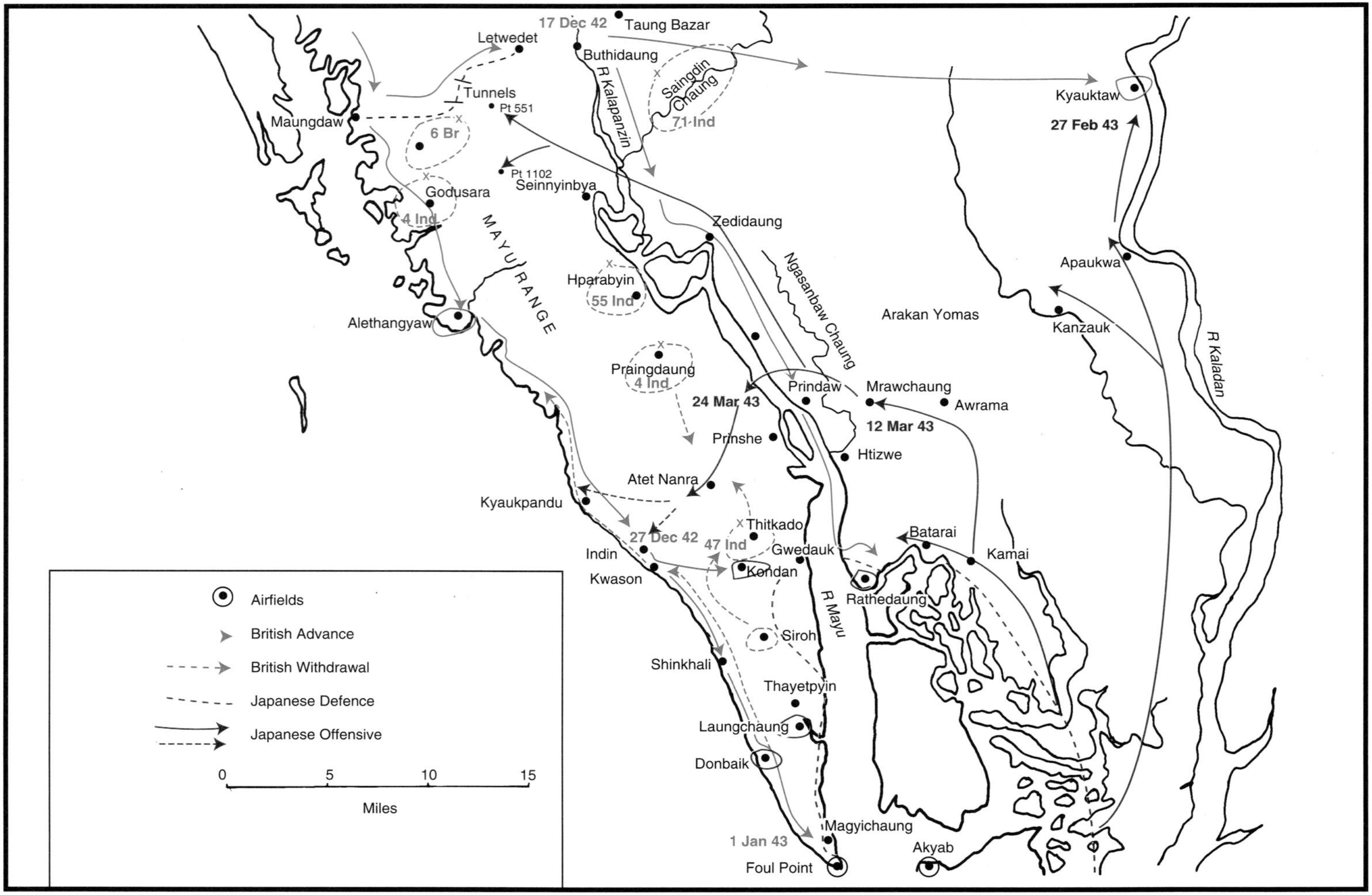

Map 28 The Arakan Front 1942–43

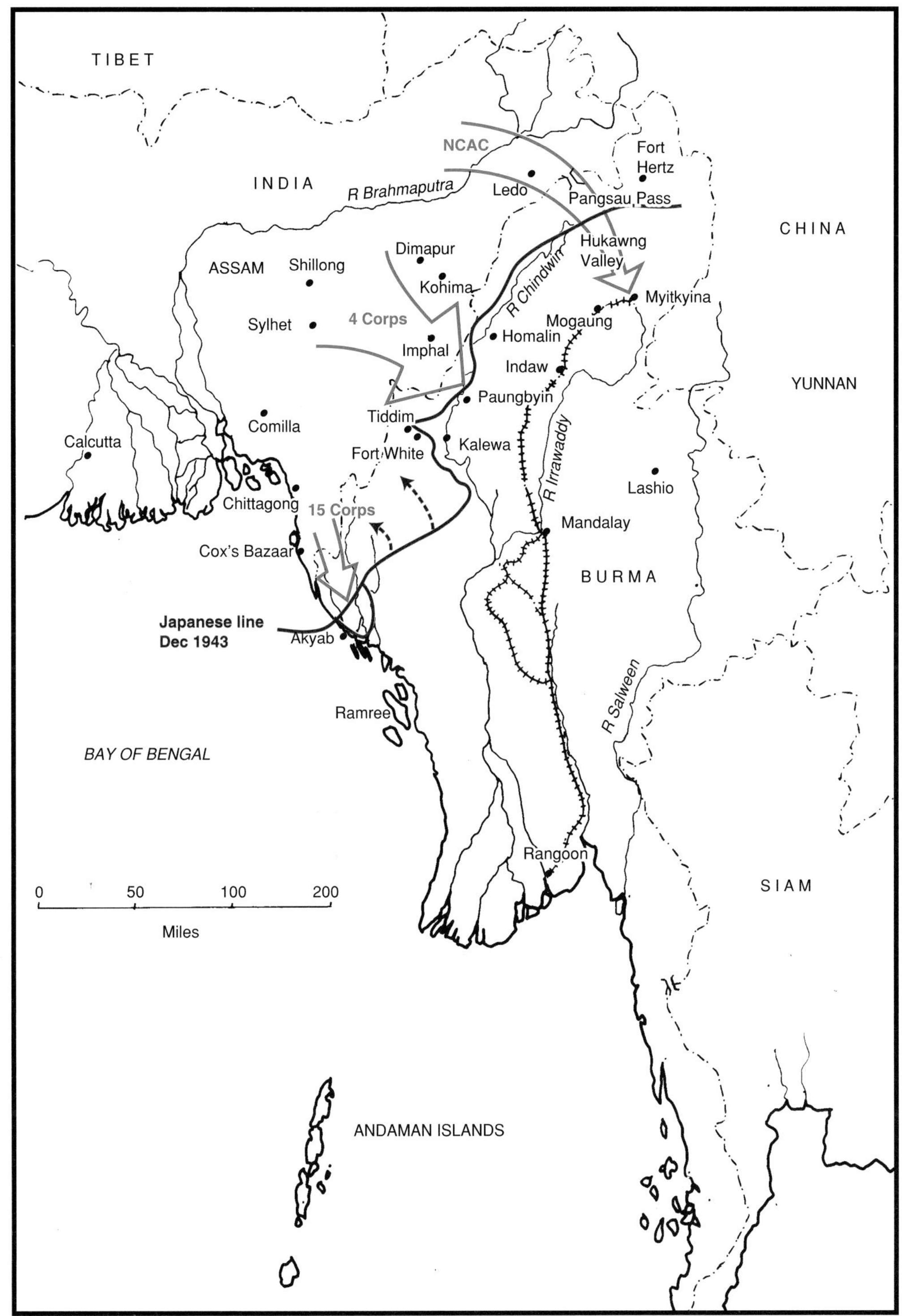

Map 29 S.E.A.C. plans for 1944

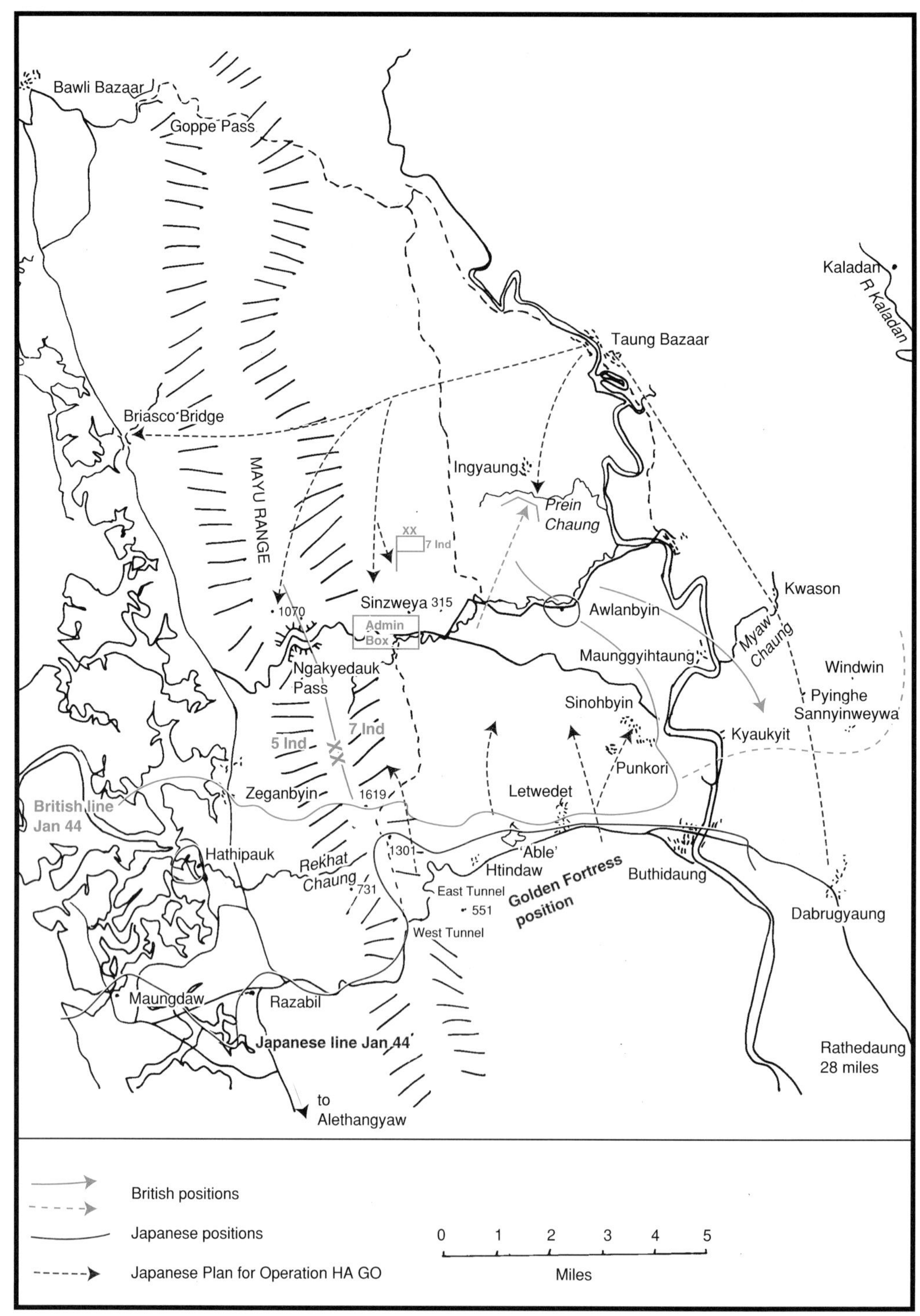

Bawli Bazaar
Goppe Pass
Kaladan
R Kaladan
Taung Bazaar
Briasco Bridge
MAYU RANGE
Ingyaung
Prein Chaung
XX
7 Ind
Kwason
Sinzweya 315
1070
Admin Box
Awlanbyin
Myaw Chaung
Ngakyedauk Pass
Maunggyihtaung
Windwin
Sinohbyin
Pyinghe
Sannyinweywa
7 Ind
5 Ind
XX
Kyaukyit
Punkori
Zeganbyin
1619
Letwedet
British line Jan 44
Hathipauk
1301
'Able'
Rekhat Chaung
Htindaw
731
East Tunnel
Golden Fortress position
Buthidaung
551
West Tunnel
Dabrugyaung
Maungdaw
Razabil
Japanese line Jan 44
Rathedaung 28 miles
to Alethangyaw
British positions
Japanese positions
Japanese Plan for Operation HA GO
0
1
2
3
4
5
Miles

Map 30 The second Arakan

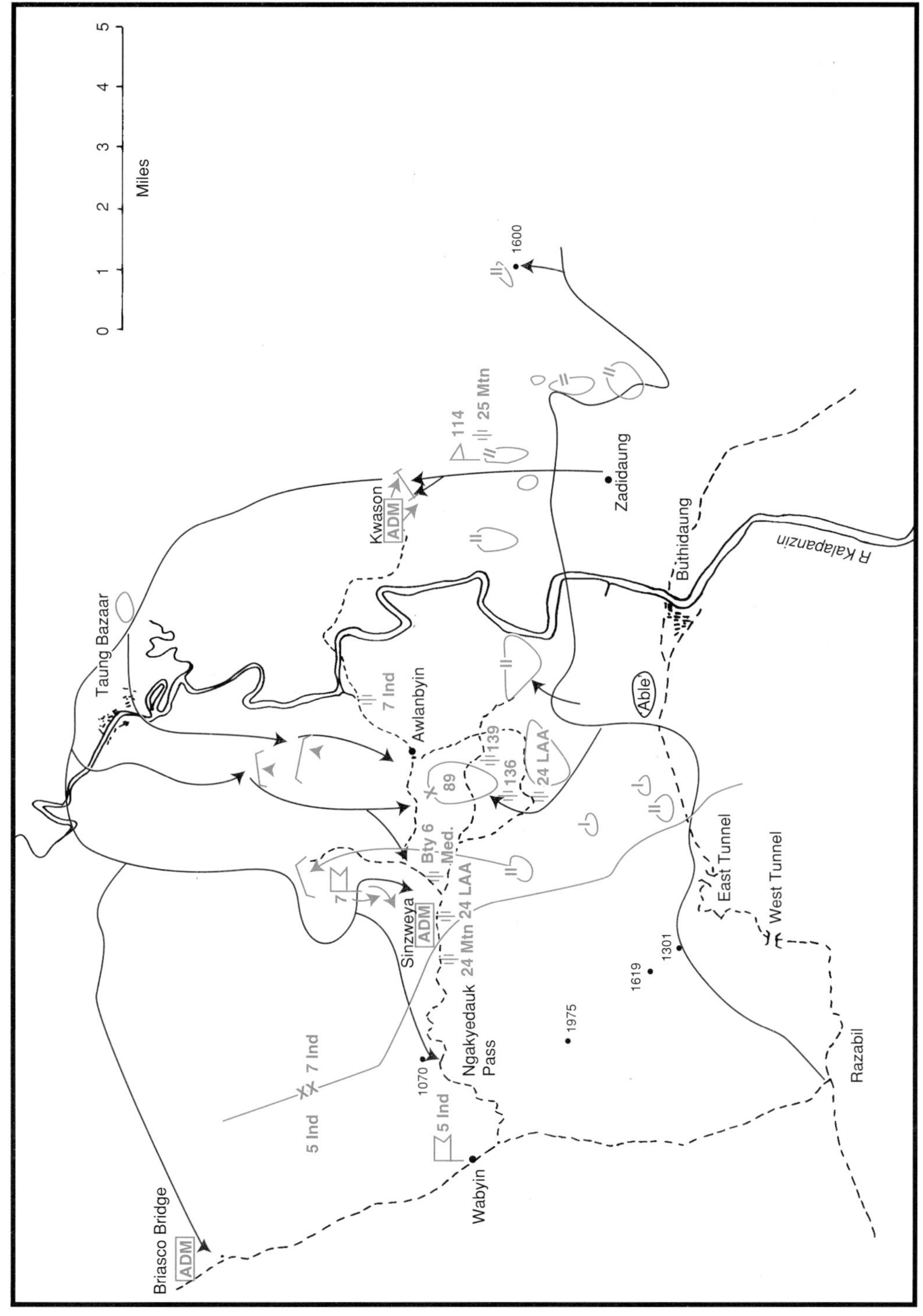

Map 31 Battle of the Admin Box • The Japanese Offensive 4th - 6th February 1944

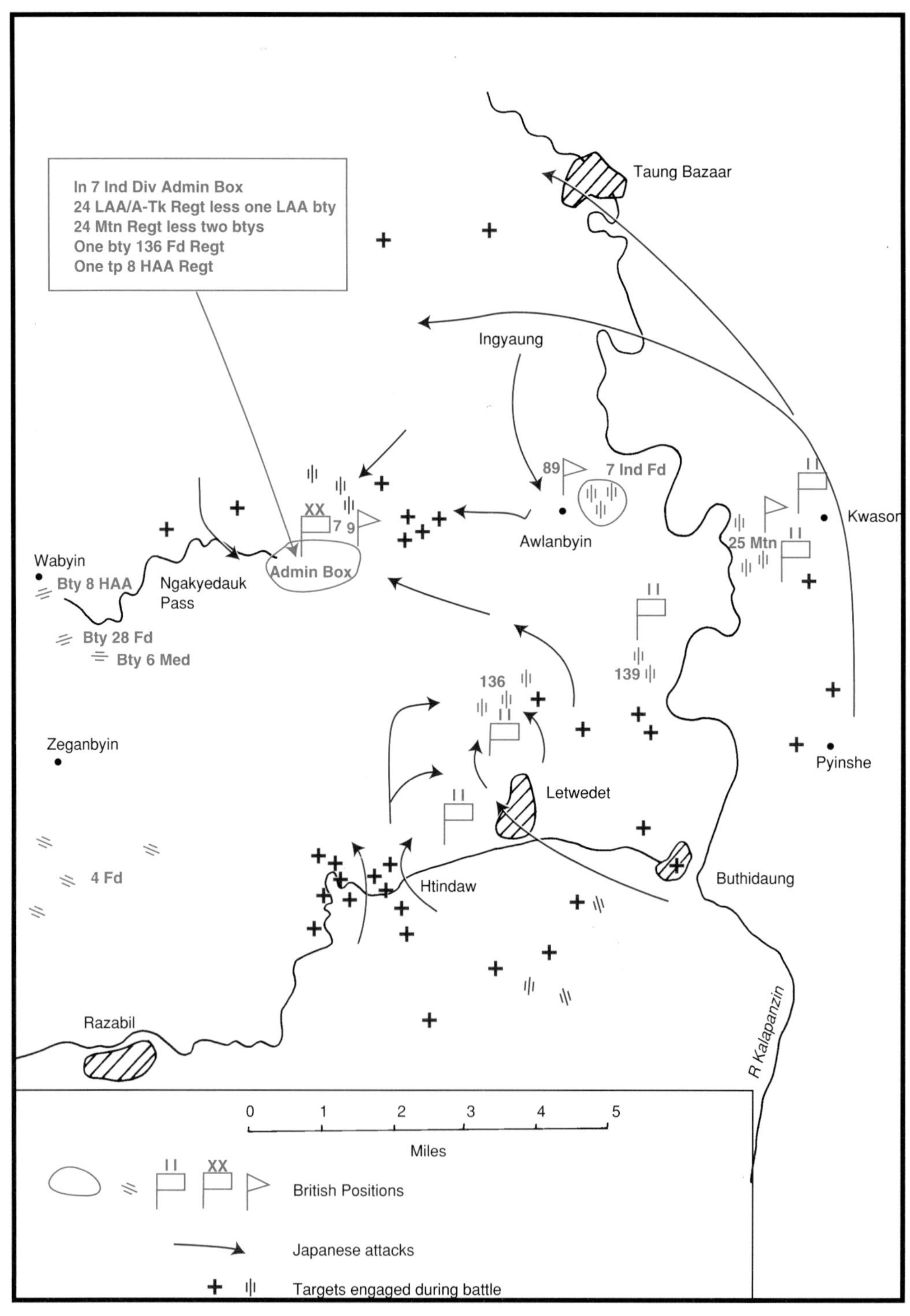

Map 32 7th Indian Division RA positions during The Battle of The Admin * Box 6th - 24th February 1944

reached the Bilin opposite Paya before the British could occupy their positions. It got across unopposed and occupied Danyingon. The KOYLI found them there when they arrived and could not dislodge them although they did manage to get one company into Yinon as ordered. Accordingly that night Brigadier Jones ordered 1/7th Gurkhas, his reserve, to capture Danyingon. This attack went in at 0800 hours and there was fierce fighting but the Japanese held their positions. General Smyth then ordered 1/4th Gurkhas with 5th Mountain Battery and all 16th Indian Infantry Brigade mortars to attack the village. This attack forced the Japanese out but they clung onto a small bridgehead west of the river and cut off the KOYLI company at Yinon.

To the south 5/17th Dogras were forced back to the west bank in disorder and lost most of their equipment and weapons and were of no further use until they reorganised. Smyth realising that a 15 mile front was too great for one brigade, ordered 48th Indian Infantry Brigade forward with its 2/5th Gurkhas to take command of the southern sector including 8th Burma Rifles, 1/9th Jats and the remains of 5/17th Dogras. They left 1/3rd Gurkhas at Thebyuchaung.

On the night of 17/18th February the enemy got across the river between the Jats and the Burma Rifles near Bilin just as Smyth began getting reports of large numbers of enemy around Zokali. He next learnt that 2/5th Gurkhas were holding the enemy at Bilin and that the Mountain Gunners had broken up an enemy counter-attack to recapture Danyingon. Nevertheless the situation on the left was of concern and he decided to move 4/12th Frontier Force forward onto that flank. By then he had no reserves left and could only order a company of 2/5th Gurkhas to cover the enemy approach from Zokali.

Hutton recognised that the tired men of 17th Indian Division were not going to hold onto the Bilin for long, especially with both flanks threatened by fresh troops. He ordered 2nd Burma Infantry Brigade with a company of 2nd Duke of Wellingtons to prepare the defence of the Sittang bridge crossing and he cabled Wavell about the situation that was developing. On the morning of 19th February Hutton visited Smyth at Kyaikto and realised the danger that 17th Indian Division might be unable to disentangle itself and get back behind the Sittang, which was essential for the defence of Rangoon. He therefore told Smyth to prepare for withdrawal and to order it when he felt it necessary. He also ordered 2nd Duke of Wellingtons and what was left of 7/10th Baluch to come under command 17th Indian Division and all available anti-aircraft units to move to defend the Sittang bridge from the west bank.

Meanwhile 4/12th Frontier Force were at Augale and on 19th February advanced towards Paya where they met and held several enemy counter attacks but after dark they withdrew, on orders, to Chaungbya. To the south the Japanese reached Taungale and Taungzun and air reports showed a continuous enemy build up in the Bilin - Ahonwa area. Smyth therefore decided that it was time to go and issued his orders. 48th Indian Infantry Brigade was to cover 16th Indian Infantry Brigade and then, along with 12th Mountain Battery it was to act as rearguard on the Thebyu river. All other troops were to take up a position on the line of the Kadat Chaung north of Kyaikto while 48th Indian Infantry Brigade withdrew to Kyaikto. The withdrawal was to start at 2230 hours on 20th February.

The action on the Bilin river had not been in vain. It had held the enemy for four days and had forced him to deploy most of his strength. It had also bought vital time for 7th Armoured Brigade to arrive, which it had done on 21st February. The essential task now was to get 17th Indian Division back across the Sittang for the defence of Rangoon. Unfortunately, that night one unit of 17th Indian Division sent the withdrawal orders over the radio in clear and this was intercepted by the Japanese. Lieutenant General Sakurai, commanding *33rd Division*, on receiving the plan, saw his chance and ordered *215th Regiment* to move at top speed for the Sittang Bridge and cut off the British. *214th Regiment* would also advance at best speed towards Mokpalin.

16th Indian Infantry Brigade got away under a thick mist during the early hours of 20th February and by last light had reached the Boyagyi Rubber Estate north west of Kyaikto where it was joined by 8th Burma Rifles and 1/9th Royal Jats. 48th Indian Infantry Brigade had more difficulty in getting away as it was still in contact. It was planned that it would get out at noon on the 20th under the cover of a heavy bombing attack by the RAF. This they did, although they suffered casualties from some British aircraft which mistook them for Japanese. By 1830 hours they were at the Thebyu river crossing where Hugh-Jones, the Brigade Commander, received orders from Smyth to get back to Kyaikto as soon as possible, which he did by 2230 hours. It was on the 20th that Smyth began to plan his withdrawal across the Sittang. From Kyaikto there was only one narrow unmetalled road to the Sittang Bridge, a distance of 15 miles. It ran through some dense jungle around Mokpalin. There was also a railway line which could be used for marching men. East of the bridge was Sittang village with the approach to the bridge itself guarded by Pagoda Hill and to its south, Buddha Hill and Bungalow Hill. The Sittang was a major obstacle with a fast current.

Smyth realised that the Japanese would almost certainly outflank him to the north. He also realised that in 3rd Burma Rifles, only 250 strong, he had a weak force holding the bridge (Map 19). His plan therefore was for 4/12th Frontier Force Regiment and the engineers of 369th (Malerkotla) Field Company, Bengal Sappers and Miners, to move at once to the bridge, prepare for its demolition and strengthen its defences. Divisional Headquarters would lead the withdrawal followed by 48th and then 16th Indian Infantry Brigades with 46th Indian Infantry Brigade acting as rear guard. At about 0500 hours 21st February a Japanese raiding party attacked Smyth's advanced headquarters at Kyaikto but was beaten off. The move got under way by 1000 hours on a very hot and dry day where the shortage of water added to the trials of the men and animals as they trudged along the dusty tracks. During the day there were many air attacks and many vehicles, including some ambulances loaded with wounded, were hit. Sadly some of these attacks came from Allied aircraft who again misidentified the columns as being those of the enemy. That evening 4/12th Frontier Force and the Sappers reached the bridge to find little had been done. Divisional Headquarters, 7/10th Baluch and 1/4th Gurkhas reached Mokpalin Quarries with 16th Indian Infantry Brigade at the Boyagyi Rubber Estate, all covered by 46th Indian Infantry Brigade's rear-guard position just west of Kyaikto. Smyth had already ordered all anti-aircraft guns, which amounted to 8th Indian HAA Battery's 3 x 3-inch guns and B Troop of 3rd Indian LAA Battery with 4 x 40mm, which had moved up from Zayatkwin airfield to replace the troop lost at Moulmein, to pull back quickly to defend the bridge from the west bank, which they had done. These guns were soon in action.

During the night 21/22nd February it was thought that the Japanese might try to seize the bridge by parachute assault, so Smyth sent 1/4th Gurkhas to the bridge, told them to take command of the company of Duke of Wellingtons, cross the bridge and prepare a counter-attack to recapture it if it were taken. He ordered 16th and 48th Indian Infantry Brigades to make best speed to the bridge and to get across as quickly as possible. Meanwhile Ekin's rearguard, 46th Indian Brigade, was in contact everywhere. Then at 0400 hours 22nd February, just as Headquarters 17th Indian Division set off from Mokpalin Quarries, the whole column came to a halt. A truck crossing the bridge had slipped off the decking over the rail tracks and become jammed in the girders. Once this was cleared and 1/4th Gurkhas were safely across, 7/10th Baluch, who had just reached the eastern end of the bridge, were greeted by bursts of fire as the enemy attacked from the north east, *215th Regiment's* advance guard had arrived. The detachment of 3rd Burma Rifles holding this area gave way at once and it seemed for a moment that the Japanese might capture the bridge. The Sappers had prepared only one span for demolition and stood by ready to blow it, but a quick counter-attack by 4/12th Frontier Force Regiment plus the weak 7/10th Baluch drove the Japanese away with the loss of 50 casualties.

At 1000 hours Smyth ordered Hugh-Jones, commanding 48th Indian Infantry Brigade, to take command of all troops in the bridgehead and he immediately extended the eastern perimeter to include Bungalow, Buddha and Pagoda Hills. The CRE ordered all boats to be destroyed and the only ferry was destroyed by enemy air attack. Meanwhile the Japanese attacked the column of transport from the east at Mokpalin, including the gun position of 28th Mountain Regiment and there was some close quarter bayonet fighting. Indeed so close was the fighting that the batteries, 5th, 12th and 28th, were continuously engaging targets at point blank range in the moonlight. 2/5th Gurkhas came to the rescue and counter-attacked the high ground to the east of Mokpalin railway station to protect the eastern flank during the withdrawal of the division. The battalion had to manage without artillery, which had not yet arrived, and it suffered heavily, but it did secure the route and the station. 1/3rd Gurkhas then arrived at Mokpalin and, assuming that the enemy was on the hills guarding the bridge, decided to attack them. They had not heard that these hills were in the process of being occupied by the bridge garrison from the north. By then the mountain batteries were arriving.

Back at the bridge, the head of the main column was arriving. The Sikh Section of 12th (Poonch) Mountain Battery under Lieutenant JOS Janson was leading and, because the bridge was still blocked when he arrived, he decided to use the ferry which at that time had still not been destroyed. This he did but was attacked from the air as he crossed. The boat caught fire and was then destroyed but not before they reached the far bank and the detachments saved the guns. The men carried the guns up the beach by hand and brought them into action covering the bridge from the western side. Later in the day Subadar Jowala Singh marched the mules across the bridge under heavy fire, but got them to the guns. He and Naik Dulip Singh were awarded the Indian Order of Merit for their gallantry that day. This little section had one man killed, seven wounded and seven mules wounded in this action. At Mokpalin the situation remained confused. The three batteries of 28th Mountain Regiment came into action with orders to help clear the way through to the bridge. 28th Mountain Battery did some shooting at the Pagoda at 450 yards over open sights and then the whole regiment engaged the Bungalow, Pagoda and Buddha Hills in support of the attack by 1/3rd Gurkhas. As this action started, troops from the bridgehead occupied Bungalow Hill where, hearing all the firing around Mokpalin and seeing the attack from the south, they assumed that it was the Japanese. The fog of war lay thick that day. Next the mountain batteries attacked Pagoda Hill. The bridge defenders, now certain it was the Japanese attacking the bridge, rapidly brought two more companies across the river. Some Japanese did indeed arrive and got onto Pagoda Hill, the bursting shells which hit them as they arrived were those of 28th Mountain Regiment engaging it for 1/3rd Gurkhas. This attack was remarkably successful and drove the Japanese off Pagoda and Buddha Hills after much bitter fighting. Not knowing that this had happened the bridgehead garrison attacked the hills that afternoon and secured them all, including Bungalow Hill.

As darkness descended on this confused situation, Hugh-Jones was told that the bridge demolitions were ready but with the enemy so close the Sappers could not guarantee to blow the bridge successfully under observation in daylight. He was also getting reports of chaos around Mokpalin and others that indicated that both 16th and 46th Indian Infantry Brigades were dispersed and no longer in any shape to fight and that all their guns had been destroyed. This was in fact not so. Indeed the Japanese had had such a bloody nose that day that they were not even following up in the south. At 0430 hours one of Hugh-Jones's staff got through to Brigadier Cowan at 17th Indian Division Headquarters, by then at Abya. He said that he could not guarantee to hold the bridge for more than an hour and that his information was that all his own troops on the east bank were in disorder and unlikely to make it. He said that he could not guarantee a successful destruction of the bridge in daylight under fire. Cowan referred to Smyth. What a decision! To blow now meant losing half his division, not to blow meant that there was a very high chance that the bridge would be captured at first light, and the way would be open to Rangoon. Smyth had no option, he ordered Hugh-Jones to blow the bridge at 0530 hours after the covering troops had been pulled back. The absolute rearguard was a group of staff officers with Tommy guns.

Then came the huge explosion, lifting the bridge into the air. The Sappers had done a good job. Two spans fell into the water and a third was badly damaged. There was suddenly complete silence, all firing on both sides stopped. Brigadier Jones, of 16th Indian Infantry Brigade and commanding the mixed force in the Mokpalin defensive box, realised that he was now cut off. He decided to hold and at the same time start to build rafts. At 1115 hours Japanese air attacks began on the beleaguered force, causing heavy casualties and setting the jungle alight. The Japanese renewed their efforts to wipe out the defenders and the little mountain guns engaged with devastating effect, firing shrapnel at fuse 0. But as ammunition ran out gun after gun was destroyed or its breech block was thrown down a well or into the river. Jones realised that he could no longer hold his positions and at 1400 hours ordered a general withdrawal. For some reason the Japanese were reluctant to follow up through the flaming wrecks of the vehicles and equipment as it was destroyed. The men rushed to the river bank and down the 30 foot bluff; the guns on the west bank, few that they were, fired non-stop to cover the stricken men on the other side; the scene was dreadful. Brigadier Ekin wrote afterwards;

'Here there was chaos and confusion; hundreds of men throwing down their arms, equipment and clothing and taking to the water . . . As we crossed, the river was a mass of bobbing heads. We were attacked from the air and sniped at continuously from the east bank. Although it was a disastrous situation there were many stout hearts and parties shouted to each other egging on others to swim faster with jokes about the boat race.'(Kirby Vol II).

Lieutenant Gilmour of 5th Mountain Battery was missing and many casualties occurred from drowning. Lieutenant Mackenzie of 28th Mountain Battery helped two Gurkha officers to move several wounded men across under fire, for which he was awarded the Military Cross. Somehow hundreds of men did get across the racing waters of the Sittang and lived to fight another day but for the moment they had no equipment at all, indeed many were naked. On 24th February 17th Indian Division mustered at Pegu (Map 18) with only 80 officers and 3,404 other ranks, only 1,420 of whom had any weapons at all. There were only a few guns and the men of 5th Mountain Battery and the section of 12th Mountain Battery were sent to Mandalay to re-equip with some 3.7-inch howitzers held there. 8th Indian HAA Battery and 3rd Indian LAA Battery moved to the defence of 17th Indian Division at Pegu where they were in constant action, shooting down six enemy aircraft in one day; a fine achievement. 3rd Indian LAA Battery less two sections had already re-deployed, one troop was at Rangoon docks covering the disembarkation of 7th Armoured Brigade and the other was at Pegu, the third had re-equipped and was at Hlegu. This troop was later ambushed and its troop commander was killed.

As tanks could not cross the canal bridge at Waw, Hutton decided to concentrate 17th Indian Division in the Pegu area. 46th Indian Infantry Brigade was broken up and its units used to make the others up to strength. 7th Armoured Brigade had by then arrived, consisting of 7th Hussars, 2nd Royal Tank Regiment, both equipped with Stuart tanks, 414th Battery RHA from 104th Regiment RHA (The Essex Yeomanry), and 'A' Battery 95th Anti-Tank Regiment RA. This brigade's last battle had been at Sidi Rezegh in the Western Desert in November 1941. On arrival it was given 1st Cameronians and 1st West Yorkshire Regiment. The brigade deployed with 2nd

RTR and the Cameronians around Thanatpin and 7th Hussars and the West Yorkshires around Payagyi and Waw.

As 414th Battery left Egypt, Lieutenant Colonel AG 'Hammer' Matthew, Commanding Officer of 104th Regiment RHA, said how sad he was to be losing a battery which had so distinguished itself in the desert. Major Tom Pereira was in command with Captain Shorter as Battery Captain. The troop commanders were Captain Chaplain and Lieutenant Sheppard; Lieutenant Simcox, Second Lieutenants Crump, Newbold, Ward and MacAlister ran the gun positions. 'D' Troop under Shorter was to work with 7th Hussars and 'E' Troop under Chaplain was to be with 2nd RTR.

Hutton warned Wavell that he might not be able to hold Rangoon even though he would do everything in his power to do so. But the Prime Minister and the Chiefs of Staff were not happy with what was happening and they suggested to Wavell that General Alexander should come out and take command forthwith. Wavell agreed and told Hutton that he wanted him to stay on as Chief of Staff. A lesser man would have objected but it is to Hutton's eternal credit that he agreed. By 23rd February the Chinese Army, in reality a division of three brigades, had moved south from the Shan States and was in the Sittang valley north of Pegu. It relieved 1st Burma Division which moved south, leaving behind 13th Indian Infantry Brigade which remained in the Karen Hills guarding the crossing of the Salween at Kemapyu. 2nd Burma Infantry Brigade was at Nyaunglebin and 1st at Kyauktaga, on the railway to Toungoo in the Sittang Valley, thus there was a gap between them and 7th Armoured Brigade some 35 miles to the south. Hutton told 17th Indian Division and 7th Armoured Brigade that their task was to cover Rangoon for as long as possible and then to retire to Prome to cover the oilfields, while 1st Burma Division would retire north to cover the deployment of 5th Chinese Army at Toungoo and the newly formed bases in central Burma.

It was now learned that the Australian Government could not allow 7th Australian Division to go to Burma. This meant that the only reinforcements planned were 63rd Indian Infantry Brigade and 1st Indian Field Regiment, which arrived on 3rd February, with 16 x 25-pounders in two batteries each of eight guns, plus 2nd Indian Anti-Tank Regiment with 20 x 2-pounders, together with six British battalions which would arrive over a period. On 25th February the Japanese made their last attempts to destroy Rangoon from the air and carried out attacks with over 170 aircraft. But the RAF and the AVG defeated them, destroying over a fifth of their strength but at heavy cost. Their 44 fighters were reduced to ten by 27th February. However, the Japanese did not interfere with operations around Rangoon from the air again. It had been an heroic effort on the part of the British and American fighter pilots.

By 27th February the Japanese were across the Sittang and at Mytitkyo clashes occurred with them and with renegade Burmans who had been armed by the Japanese for the first time. Hutton ordered 7th Armoured Brigade and a company of West Yorkshires to Tharrawaddy to guard the Rangoon - Prome road, 17th Indian Division to pull back to Hlegu and 2nd RTR to pull back to Pegu. Wavell was back from Java and was once again Commander-in-Chief India. He visited Burma and said that Rangoon must be held until all planned reinforcements had arrived. He also saw that Smyth was sick and very tired and he therefore ordered Cowan to assume command of 17th Indian Division. He then flew to Lashio for more talks with Chiang Kai-shek and on 3rd March met Alexander in Delhi as he arrived from England to take command. He also told him to hold Rangoon for as long as possible.

The Japanese Commander in Burma was Lieutenant General Shojiro Iida, commanding Japanese *15th Army*. He had heard of the British reinforcements and of the imminent arrival of the Chinese. He therefore urged maximum speed to capture Rangoon. His *33rd* and *55th Divisions* had already fought their way from Siam to the Sittang in some 34 days. They were very weary and had suffered heavily, but there was no one else. They were therefore ordered to make a super effort, to cross the Sittang on 3rd March and press on at full speed. There was a series of confused encounters around Payagyi on the night of 4th March before it was occupied by the enemy. It was evident that an outflanking movement from the north west was in progress. Hutton arrived at Hlegu on the morning of 5th March, on his way to visit 48th Indian Infantry Brigade, to be told that the road was cut near Payathonzu, south of Pegu. He also learned that enemy tanks were moving towards Pauggyi. Such a move could only have one mission, to cut the Rangoon - Prome road. Withdrawal of the Rangoon Garrison was looking hourly more hazardous. He discussed the situation with Cowan and they decided 48th Indian Infantry Brigade should move from Pegu to Hlegu and 16th Indian Infantry Brigade from Hlegu to Taukkyan. Then at noon General Alexander arrived in Rangoon to assume command. That afternoon he met Hutton and Cowan at Hlegu.

The situation facing him was not good. 1st Indian Field Regiment had arrived, 63rd Indian Infantry Brigade had disembarked but without any transport and was being concentrated at Hlawga, 12 miles north of Rangoon. 7th Armoured and 48th Indian Infantry Brigades were in contact with an aggressive enemy around Pegu and the Japanese appeared to be moving through the gap between 17th Indian and 1st Burma Divisions, heading for the Rangoon - Prome road. Air reconnaissance showed enemy boats threatening the Syriam oil refineries. Alexander then ordered 17th Indian Division to take 7th Armoured and 63rd Indian Infantry Brigades under command and to take the offensive in the Waw area. He then told 1st Burma Division to advance southwards from Nyaunglebin. While these orders were being issued the road north of Hlegu was opened and a reconnaissance party consisting of Brigadier J Wickham, commanding 63rd Indian Infantry Brigade, and his three battalion commanders reached Pegu. Pegu was defended by 48th Indian Infantry Brigade under Hugh-Jones. The brigade was positioned as follows:

- 1st West Yorks, less a company serving with a detachment of 7th Hussars at Tharrawaddy, covered the town from the east.

- 1st Cameronians, less two companies, occupied the town itself.

- 7th Hussars, less their detachment at Tharrawaddy, with a company of the West Yorkshires and 414th Battery RHA was deployed around the northern approaches to the town.

By this time 414th Battery was becoming expert in jungle operations. Captain Shorter was established as a high grade FOO and a deadly 'shot' with the guns, 'several times he enabled units of the brigade to disengage and escape encirclement by the accuracy of his shooting and his complete disregard for his personal safety.' (History 414th Battery RHA).

The Japanese attacked on 3rd March and reached the railway station after heavy fighting. 63rd Indian Infantry Brigade advanced from Hlegu to reinforce 48th Indian Infantry Brigade but found an enemy road block at Payathonzu at about 0930 hours. 2nd RTR then forced its way through and escorted the 63rd Indian Infantry Brigade reconnaissance party back to bring up their brigade. They were travelling in carriers when tragedy struck and the column ran into an ambush and snipers killed or wounded the whole party, which meant that 63rd Indian Infantry Brigade was facing its first ever action having just lost all its commanders, a most grievous blow. Meanwhile in Pegu a counter-attack threw the Japanese out of the town but hand-to-hand fighting continued for some time. On 6th March 7th Hussars were fighting near Payagyi when they met anti-tank guns. They were then told to pull back into Pegu and come under command of 48th Indian Infantry Brigade for its withdrawal from Pegu that night. They were to lead and they set off south at 2010 hours and cleared the road, after some pretty tough fighting, by 2200 hours, but failed to leave pickets to keep it open. The guns of 414th Battery RHA played a major part in dealing with the road block. However, when the infantry advanced down the road later the Japanese were back. They were cleared away by 1/7th Gurkhas and the column reached Intagaw at 0200 hours and finally reached Hlegu on 8th March but losses, particularly in officers had been severe.

General Iida was very satisfied with his progress and ordered *33rd Division* to race for Rangoon at top speed from the north west through Wanetchaung, Hmawbi and Hlawga.

Meanwhile the conditions in Rangoon were pretty chaotic. A very large proportion of the population had already left. Government and Army Headquarters had gone north, hospitals had been evacuated, mostly by train, nearly all the police had also gone, prisons had been thrown open and looting was rife. On the afternoon of 6th March, Alexander realised that there was no hope of saving the city and he ordered the denial scheme to be put into operation at 0200 hours on 7th March. As much as possible was done but it was a massive task and much was left intact. Much of the equipment of 8th HAA Battery RA was destroyed and the battery, together with 3rd Indian LAA Battery, took the remaining 3.7-inch, 3-inch and 40mm guns to the defence of the bridge at Hlegu where they were joined by the guns of 8th Indian HAA Battery from Pegu. Rangoon was soon engulfed in flames and thick black smoke which could be seen for miles around. The Royal Navy got all its vessels away and sailed for Akyab. The RAF sent 3,000 men to India and transferred the rest to airfields up country establishing 'Burwing' from the remains of 17 (Fighter) Squadron, 45 (Bomber) Squadron, 28 (Army Co-operation) Squadron and the AVG Squadron. 'Akwing' was established at Akyab from 135 (Fighter) Squadron, 67 (Fighter) Squadron and 139 (Reconnaissance) Squadron.

At dawn on 7th March the Rangoon Garrison, consisting of 1st HAA Regiment BAF, the Rangoon Field Brigade BAF, a detachment of the Royal Engineers, 1st Gloucesters, 12th Burma Rifles, one company 1/9th Royal Jats and some locally enlisted units, set off from the beleaguered city northwards up the Prome road to Tharrawaddy. They were led by an advance guard of one squadron 7th Hussars, 1st Indian Field Battery with its 8 x 25-pounders, and two companies of KOYLI. 17th Indian Division, with 7th Armoured Brigade under command, was to hold at Hlegu until the column had cleared Taukkyan and then it was to follow as rear guard. On reaching Taukkyan the column learned that the Japanese had established a block a few miles up the road. The Gloucesters supported by tanks and the guns of 1st Indian Battery attacked but failed, a second attack by 2/13th Frontier Force Rifles, brought up from 63rd Indian Infantry Brigade, fared no better. Meanwhile the advance guard, which had been allowed to pass the block by the Japanese reached Tharrawaddy to discover that the road had been cut behind them. It returned and decided to attack from the north and did so just as the Gloucesters were attacking and their 'overs' started to fall amongst them. At this point the advance party's radio failed and it could not contact the main body, so the attack was called off. Then came enemy air attacks and the guns of 8th Indian HAA Battery came rapidly into action off the line of march and claimed two out of six attacking aircraft.

The situation was desperate by last light and Alexander ordered 63rd Indian Infantry Brigade with all available artillery and armour to clear the block at all costs from the south next morning. The plan was for 1/10th Gurkhas to attack the block on the west of the road and 1/11th Sikhs to do the same on the east with the tanks and 2/13th Frontier Force Rifles advancing straight up the road. The assault was to be made under cover of an artillery attack by 1st Indian Field Regiment, with its 16 x 25-pounders, starting at 0835 hours. But the operation was beyond the untrained 63rd Indian Infantry Brigade. 1/11th Sikhs arrived at their start line early and saw a large enemy force crossing the Prome road to their north from east to west; this movement went on for three hours. Meanwhile 1/10th Gurkhas took all night to reach their start line and then became lost and dispersed in the jungle where they also saw a large force of enemy further to the west and moving south. Then shortly before the attack was due to start 2nd RTR reported the road clear. The artillery attack was called off and the move north continued. Clearly the road block had been put in place to cover the left flank of the Japanese *33rd Division* as it crossed the Prome road to attack Rangoon from the north west and not to cut off the retiring Rangoon Garrison as the British suspected. Such are the vicissitudes of war!

During 9th and 10th March the whole force was concentrated around Tharrawaddy covered by the ubiquitous 7th Armoured Brigade. At this time all five anti-aircraft batteries were together with the force, 3rd Indian LAA, 3rd BAF LAA, 8th HAA, 8th Indian HAA and 1st BAF HAA Batteries. They were then deployed into positions defending Shwedaung, Prome, Allanmyo and Magwe (Map 20). These moves were made through enemy infested country and they were constantly engaged in anti-air and ground actions. The action at Magwe was particularly fierce as the Japanese attacked it constantly with up to 250 aircraft a day.

The Japanese thought that the British had learned of their plan and had sent a force north to intercept *33rd Division*, hence the road block. They had not appreciated that they had crossed the path of the withdrawal from Rangoon. Accordingly they withdrew the road block to complete the attack on what they expected to be a defended Rangoon as soon as possible and in so doing missed a golden opportunity of destroying the whole British force in southern Burma. Finding Rangoon deserted they realised their error and raced back up the Prome road but they were much too late. The loss of Rangoon, however, was to alter the whole campaign. Burma was cut off from India except for air supply and a very limited road and track link in the north. Hutton's foresight had paid off, his forecasts though unpopular in London had been extremely accurate. He had moved most of the combat supplies north into new depots around Prome, Mandalay and Myitkyina and the Army was now able to withdraw onto them. This act alone did more than anything else to save the Army in Burma in 1942. The loss of the oil refineries was most critical and fuel was soon to become a scarce commodity. What is more the Andaman Islands had to be evacuated, leaving the airport at Port Blair for the Japanese to use and they were quick to do so. Finally China was cut off from her allies except by air.

Why had it happened? There are many reasons but most significant was London's refusal to place Burma under the command of the Commander-in-Chief in New Delhi until the war started. Had this been done a proper garrison could have been assembled. As it was General Hutton had an impossible task. The reinforcements that he badly needed were sent to Malaya and Singapore where they were lost. All he had were untrained troops whom he had to hurl into battle before they were ready in *ad hoc* groupings which did not know each other. He achieved more than could be expected. He tried to hold forward as ordered, when he knew he should have concentrated from the start on the Salween river line, but he bought time for 7th Armoured Brigade to arrive, the only trained formation available to him. History owes him more credit than he has been given, for without him disaster might well have struck much earlier. Once again the Army in Burma was desperately short of artillery, although the Mountain Gunners and later the Gunners of India and the UK did magnificently well wherever they could be employed. The *coup de grace* came when the Australian Government refused to allow 7th Australian Division to be diverted to Burma. Hutton realised the peril of holding Rangoon and losing all. Wavell, as always, was optimistic and never appreciated the superiority of Japanese tactics in the jungle and ordered the city to be held. That it was held for a while enabled the last reinforcements to arrive. Alexander tried again but soon realised the hopelessness of the situation and ordered the withdrawal.

1st Burma Division was moved across to Prome on the Irrawaddy from the Sittang valley. It had been involved in much fighting south of Toungoo. 27th Mountain Regiment had been involved in many operations. On 11th March 2nd (Derajat) and 23rd Mountain Batteries had joined in the attack on Pyuntaza which failed because of lack of firepower. On this occasion 2nd Battery was nearly overrun, but the attack was beaten off at point blank range by the guns and the Gunners with small arms. The battery fired 200 rounds in its defence that day. Lieutenant FW Graham went out with an OP but his line was cut and the party sent out to repair it was never seen again. On the 22nd March the division began to entrain at Toungoo for its move to the Irrawaddy, 23rd Mountain Battery was allotted the last train on the 24th. The Chinese 200th Division was moving in when a sudden Japanese attack occurred. The battery went straight into action alongside the Chinese infantry, who put up a gallant fight. The battery stopped an infantry attack at close range but found that the enemy had cut it off from the train and its transport. Lorries were set on fire and many members of the BQMS's staff were burnt in them. Then this splendid battery limbered up on its mules with speed and marched through the jungle, without escort, for a week before it rejoined the division.

Alexander decided that, to align himself with the Chinese at Toungoo, he must pull further back and concentrate his main effort around Prome itself. With the arrival of 1st Burma Division around Thayetmyo and Allanmyo, Burcorps was formed consisting of that formation, 17th Indian Division and 7th Armoured Brigade and on 19th March Lieutenant General WJ Slim arrived to take command at Magwe.

During the rest of March and early April 1942, the Japanese made good use of the port of Rangoon and reinforced themselves with the arrival of *213th Regiment* of *33rd Division*, two more air brigades giving them a total of some 420 aircraft, *56th Division* from Japan and *18th Division* from Singapore with more artillery, engineers and logistic troops. General Iida's plan was to advance through Pegu to Meiktila and Mandalay with *55th Division* starting mid-March, while *33rd Division* advanced to capture the Prome - Yenangyaung area by mid April. Then, on arrival, *56th Division* would attack northwards through Toungoo to Meiktila while *18th Division* sat in reserve. To meet this attack the Allies had in Burma two weak divisions; 17th Indian consisting of 16th, 48th and 63rd Indian Infantry Brigades and 1st Burma Division consisting of 13th Indian and 1st and 2nd Burma Infantry Brigades together with 7th Armoured Brigade and 5th and 6th Chinese Armies, each equivalent to a division, supported by some 150 assorted aircraft. Alexander decided to concentrate his forces in the Irrawaddy valley to protect the Yenangyaung oilfields and to leave 5th Chinese Army in the Sittang valley. 6th Chinese Army was in the Shan States guarding against a Japanese approach from Indo-China and could not help him. On 25th February 1942 Lieutenant General JW Stilwell, US Army, had arrived in India to command the Chinese forces in Burma.

The order of battle of the Gunners in Burma at this time was as follows:

Corps Troops:

414th Field Battery RHA (8 x 25-pounders) 7th Armoured Brigade
'A' Battery, 95th Anti-Tank Regiment RA (12 x 2-pounders) 7th Armoured Brigade
8th HAA Battery RA (4 x 3-inch guns)
8th Indian HAA Battery IA (4 x 3-inch guns)
3rd Indian LAA Battery IA (A and B/C Troops) (10 x 40mm)

1st Burma Division:

27th Indian Mountain Regiment IA
2nd (Derajat) Mountain Battery IA (4 x 3.7-inch howitzers)
23rd Mountain Battery IA (4 x 3.7-inch howitzers)
8th Indian Anti-Tank Battery IA (8 x 2-pounders)

17th Indian Division:

1st Indian Field Regiment IA
1st Indian Field Battery IA (8 x 25-pounders)
2nd Indian Field Battery IA (8 x 25-pounders)
12th Mountain Battery IA (4 x 3.7-inch howitzers)
5th Indian Anti-Tank Battery IA (8 x 77mm Skodas)

Army Troops:

HQ 28th Mountain Regiment IA*
1st HAA Regiment BAF
1st HAA Battery BAF (4 x 3.7-inch guns)
3rd LAA Battery BAF (8 x 40mm guns)
Detachment, Rangoon Field Brigade BAF

Lines of Communication Troops:

2nd Indian Anti-Tank Regiment IA less two batteries (8 x 2-pounders)
One troop, 3rd Indian LAA Battery IA (4 x 40mm guns)
Rangoon Field Brigade BAF, less detachment.

Note* 5th, 15th and 28th Mountain Batteries of 28th Mountain Regiment were re-equipping at Mandalay.

Throughout this period there was a considerable amount of air activity and the RAF and the AVG fought many hard battles to keep the enemy at bay but their losses mounted both in central Burma and at Akyab. It was the lack of any effective warning system that was the final straw and saw the destruction of the air force at Magwe and at Akyab. After this all aircraft were withdrawn to Assam and Chittagong, leaving the Army to manage with its guns and such air support as it could get from India.

By 19th March the enemy had closed on the Chinese at Toungoo. The fighting was bitter and hard. Stilwell found it difficult to get the Chinese to obey his orders and eventually on 26th March 200th Division, of brigade size, which was holding the town was forced to withdraw. They had done well but as they left they failed to destroy the bridge over the Sittang and the Japanese were able to exploit rapidly. Meanwhile in the Irrawaddy position 17th Indian Division under Major General DT Cowan, and 7th Armoured Brigade, commanded by Brigadier JH Anstice, were still in the Prome area (Map 20). On 26th March Slim told Cowan to stage a demonstration to co-ordinate with the Chinese defending Toungoo. Cowan ordered Brigadier Anstice to form a Strike Force consisting of 7th Hussars, 414th Battery RHA, 14th Field Company RE, 1st Cameronians, 1st Gloucesters, 2nd Duke of Wellingtons and one company of the West Yorkshires. It should, however, be noted that casualties had been so heavy that the infantry amounted only to about one and a half battalions. He was to attack and secure Okpo. But by the 29th all attempts to clear Padigon had failed although a foothold was gained at Paungde. Then came reports that the enemy were in Shwedaung behind them.

Cowan told Anstice to break off the action and fight his way back to Prome while he sent two battalions and 2nd Indian Field Battery to re-take Shwedaung from the north. To break out Brigadier Anstice ordered Major Pereira RHA, Battery Commander 414th Battery to take a force consisting of a troop of his battery, a troop of 7th Hussars and two companies of Gloucesters and remove the road block south of Shwedaung which they did. The whole force then closed up to attack a stronger block on the outskirts of the town and this took several hours of severe fighting. 414th Battery reported opening fire at 0715 hours, the guns having been registered by Captain Shorter by moonlight, before they could break through which they eventually did and what remained of the force rejoined the division at Prome. 414th Battery just managed to break out led by Captain Shorter in his tank. They had lost BSM Ward, Bombardier Donald and Gunners Ellis, Wilkinson and Storry killed, with BSM Eves, Sergeants Anderson, Davey, Goddard and Spencer, Bombardier Grundy and Gunners Morris, Moseley, Oakley, Ronson, Thornily, Turner and Watson wounded. One gun was towed out upside down by a tank, and two limbers, three tractors and five motor-cycles were lost. Gunner Saunders was awarded the Military Medal for attacking enemy machine guns with grenades and Lieutenant Simcox manned the last gun in action firing point blank at an enemy post, knocking it out (History 414th Battery RHA). The operation had failed and the Japanese forced the British back everywhere and were soon opposite Prome. The operation to help the Chinese had cost the British dear with the loss of some ten tanks, two guns, 21 officers and 290 men.

The enemy was closing in everywhere. A section of 12th Mountain Battery deployed with 5/17th Dogras was surrounded so closely on 28th March that in the dark an OP signaller felt a hand grabbing his equipment but he got away. Two days later the Japanese surprised the battery and overran it but a quick counter-attack by the Dogras saved the guns. It was at this time too that 15th Mountain Battery took over the equipment of 5th Indian Anti-Tank Battery, seven Skoda 77mm guns, transport and radios. 28th Mountain Battery was by then acting as infantry but had acquired one 3.7-inch howitzer. Near Prome one troop of 3rd Indian LAA Battery shot down five enemy aircraft.

It was by then clear that with the loss of Toungoo, the position at Prome was becoming untenable and Slim got permission to withdraw to the Thayetmyo - Allanmyo area. At this time 63rd Indian Infantry Brigade was at Prome, under Brigadier AE Barlow, 16th Indian Infantry Brigade was to the east of the town, under Brigadier JK Jones, 48th Indian Infantry Brigade was near Hmawza, under Brigadier RT Cameron, and 7th Armoured Brigade was at Tamagauk, under Brigadier JH Anstice. 1st Burma Division had 1st Burma Brigade at Dayindabo and 2nd at Allanmyo.

The expected attacks against Prome came at midnight 1/2nd April as *215th Regiment* in bright moonlight fought its way into the town and almost reached 63rd Brigade Headquarters and the gun areas. This forced Brigadier Barlow to withdraw. Meanwhile *214th Regiment* attacked Hmawza but was beaten off. 'At about midnight 1st April 12th Mountain Battery and 2nd Indian Field Battery were ordered to withdraw from Prome and the guns were safely got away. Later, after 63rd Indian Infantry Brigade had withdrawn, 2nd Indian Field Battery shelled Japanese positions in Prome from their positions to the north east.' (Official History Indian Armed Forces). Cowan then ordered both his forward brigades to pull back through 16th Indian Infantry Brigade while 7th Armoured Brigade covered the left flank. Next came reports of enemy once again working their way round to the rear and Cowan got permission to pull back to Dayindabo and in blazing hot weather the withdrawal began at 1130 hours on 2nd April. The dust and heat were intense, water as always was very scarce and the enemy air was active but the Japanese ground forces did not follow up and 17th Indian Division reached Dayindabo by last light. It was at this stage that Major General TJW Winterton took over from Hutton as Alexander's Chief of Staff. Hutton went to India to become GOC Western Command. At this time too Slim said that his plan was to defend the oilfields by holding the line of the Yin Chaung some 20 miles south of Yenangyaung. Prome was evacuated and the force moved back to a new line from Minhla to Taungdwingyi but the move of the air forces back to India was now being severely felt, as the RAF were no longer seen in the skies and their absence began to affect the morale of the troops who were by then suffering a very great deal.

The new front was 80 miles long, far too long to be held in depth. Alexander asked Chiang

Kai-shek for an extra division to help and one was promised but nothing ever happened. Thus his only option was to deploy in a number of widely-spaced brigade posts. The centre of the line was held by a Corps Strike Force under the command of Major General Bruce Scott and his 1st Burma Division, less 2nd Burma Brigade. The posts consisted of 48th Indian Infantry Brigade and 7th Armoured Brigade around Kokkogwa on the Yaume Chaung about ten miles west of Taungdwingyi, 13th Indian Infantry Brigade deployed about eight miles west around Thityagauk and 1st Burma Brigade at Migaungye on the Irrawaddy. Lieutenant Colonel MacFetridge recalls that 'At Taungdwingyi a gun detachment [of 3rd Indian LAA Battery] brought down, in brilliant style in full view of the cheering ground troops, an enemy bomber flying at extreme range, and was visited by the Divisional Commander who heartily congratulated the detachment. Not long after the action, the Troop Commander heard this successful engagement reported on the BBC news of the same day!' (MacFetridge).

There were big gaps in the line. The only road lay just behind it in easy range of Japanese guns. Soon enemy infantry made contact aiming straight for the oilfields and attacked Kokkogwa during a black dark night and a fierce thunder storm. They broke in as far as 13th Indian Infantry Brigade Headquarters but did not find it. At 0300 hours 12th April a company of 5th Royal Gurkhas restored the situation and the enemy sheered off to attack the nearby village of Thadodan. Here they came onto the gun position of 2nd Indian Field Battery but were beaten off in heavy hand-to-hand fighting with the guns firing at point blank range in a very gallant action indeed. Casualties were heavy on both sides. It was here too that Captain Shorter neutralised an enemy battery before a fresh attack came in on the night 12/13th April which was again repulsed with heavy casualties.

Meanwhile the Japanese advancing up the east side of the Irrawaddy captured Migaungye which exposed the right flank of Slim's position, forcing a further withdrawal to the line of the Yin Chaung south of Magwe. This was held by a weak 1st Burma Infantry Brigade and the divisional reserve made up of 5th Mountain Battery, 1st Cameronians, 7th and 12th Burma Rifles. At this time 17th Indian Division was between Taungdwingyi and Natmauk. Through the gap between the two divisions the Japanese were pouring troops, using much Burmese help in the form of guides and hand carts. The heat was scorching and the water still scarce. On 14th April 2nd KOYLI fought a hard battle on the Yin Chaung and just got away to Magwe but without any transport and only 150 strong. 1st Burma Rifles were next and fought hard for Magwe and were forced back to the Kadaung Chaung. At Magwe too 23rd Mountain Battery found itself cut off and surrounded and was preparing to spike its guns when two tanks of the 7th Hussars broke through and helped them out. During this period 8th Indian HAA Battery had been defending Magwe until they were told to load their three 3-inch guns onto barges and sail north 250 miles to Sagaing near Mandalay while its few vehicles set off on a long drive to join up with them. One troop of 3rd Indian LAA Battery also went to Mandalay and placed two guns at one end of the Ava bridge over the Irrawaddy, and was ordered to move every other day to the other bank. The other two guns were deployed on the North bank of the Myitngye river to defend the important road and rail bridges. 1st HAA Battery BAF and 8th British HAA Battery stayed on at Magwe until forced back to Yenangyaung.

The stage was now set for the battle for the oil fields of Yenangyaung. 5th (Bombay) Mountain Battery and one section of 12th (Poonch) Mountain Battery, having re-equipped at Mandalay, went by boat to Magwe. By this time Slim could see that the die was cast and at 0100 hours on 15th April he ordered the oil wells to be destroyed. On the following afternoon they went up in a huge sheet of flame resulting in total destruction. It was at the same time that 3rd Indian LAA Battery, Major CHT MacFetridge, was engaged with its troops spread across the whole battle area and he motoring everywhere to get the last ounce of value from his dispersed command.

On 15th April Major General Bruce Scott decided not to withdraw from his positions on the Yin Chaung and this was to have serious consequences, for it gave *214th Regiment* time to move round his left flank at Nyaungbinywa and cut his line of withdrawal to the Pin Chaung. All Scott could do was to put a force to the north east of Magwe while he pulled back to the Kadaung Chaung covered by 2nd RTR, 414th Battery and a company of West Yorkshires. Then came news that the Japanese had attacked and captured half of Yenangyaung from the north, which meant that 1st Burma Division was cut off and surrounded. It was at this time that, at last, the 38th Chinese Division was authorised to come under Slim's command and it moved to Kyaukpadaung (Map 21). This just enabled 1st Burma Division to find a way north under cover of an attack by two Chinese regiments and part of 7th Armoured Brigade. On 17th April the division's transport reached Gwegyo. 'Magforce,' made up of a mixture of units and built on Headquarters 7th Armoured Brigade, was then to attack and capture Nyaunghla with the help of 5th Mountain Battery at dawn on the 18th. At the same time 13th Indian Infantry Brigade was to seize Point 510 and exploit to Twingon, with 2nd and 23rd Mountain Batteries and a squadron of tanks under command. This was to clear the way for the division while 1st Burma Brigade was to act as rearguard. The country around Yenangyaung was barren, broken and intersected by dried up water courses. It was in this arid, shadeless land that the fighting took place. The troops were desperately short of water and rations, the temperature reached 115 degrees and the stench of the burning oilfields was all-pervading.

The attack began at 0630 hours 18th April. 1st Cameronians reached their objective but 7th and 12th Burma Rifles could make no progress. One reason was the acute shortage of artillery ammunition. 5th Mountain Battery had enough to keep only one gun in action. Meanwhile 13th Indian Infantry Brigade reached Point 510 and advanced towards Twingon only to find enemy in strength on Point 501, east of the village. Neither 5/1st Punjab nor 1st Battalion Royal Inniskilling Fusiliers nor the fire of the 2nd and 23rd Mountain Batteries could break through. By last light the 1st Burma Division was concentrated in a defensive box south of Twingon ready to break through if only a way over the Pin Chaung could be found. It was at Twingon that 8th HAA Battery was surrounded and overrun but recovered later when a 3-inch HAA gun was used to great effect over open sights. During the afternoon of 18th April, 38th Chinese Division attacked from the north under the fire of 414th Battery RHA, with the tanks of 2nd RTR and reached the northern bank of the Pin Chaung some distance east of the ford. There were several cases of mistaking Japanese for Chinese and vice versa which caused confusion. Just before dawn on the 19th, after a night made hideous with the jackal-howling of the Japanese around the perimeter, 13th Indian Infantry Brigade repulsed an attack from Twingon but as it became light casualties grew from enemy machine gun and mortar fire.

At last some good news. A squadron of 2nd RTR and a company of West Yorkshires thrust south across the Pin Chaung ford although just as they did, the West Yorkshires were ordered back to deal with a Japanese threat further north, but the tanks got through to the beleaguered division. The state of the men in 1st Burma Division was getting critical and many were simply dying from heat, lack of water and extreme fatigue. In this fighting, Left Section 5th Mountain Battery was caught by enemy gunfire as it was coming into action. With great courage Captain Magor managed to get his guns ready amidst the exploding shells and engaged the enemy at 600 yards, thanks to the gallantry of the two Numbers 1, Havildar Hari Singh and Naik Sheotaj Singh. The guns stayed in action with enemy shells and bullets falling all around them. Then Right Section came under fire and Havildar Ahmed Khan and another NCO were killed and Lieutenant Harler and several men wounded. The wounded were evacuated under fire by Subadar Hakim Khan IDSM who was killed in doing so and was later awarded a posthumous IOM for his gallantry. Major Wilberforce, the Battery Commander, then spotted an enemy gun, and though under gun and small arms fire himself, he knocked it out with Left Section. He then held on until the infantry had safely retired before pulling out himself. Major Wilberforce recalls, "With the vehicles stuck in the sand and their loads an appalling jumble of equipment, guns, everything, there was nothing for it but to set them alight and continue the journey on foot. Our experience was that whenever we were without mules (or a river prevented their use) disaster followed and the guns were lost." Havildar Ali Bahadur was awarded the IDSM for his bravery under fire for this action and Lance Naik Sultan Singh was commended for continually repairing the vital telephone lines also under fire. Captain Magor was wounded and next day the gallant Havildar Hari Singh was killed in action. Again and again the Mountain Gunners did their stuff when put to the test.

The gun mules suffered appallingly from wounds and lack of water and many died or had to be shot. Eventually when the break-out came, at all times under fire, the lorries carrying the guns of the splendid 5th Mountain Battery got as far as Kyaukpadaung where they tried to break out across country and got stuck in sand. With the Japanese everywhere and all round him, Major Wilberforce had no option but to set them and his beloved little 3.7s on fire and they were all destroyed.

Major General Bruce Scott now realised that his men could not endure the conditions any longer and decided to make a run for it even if it would be under fire. He formed up such guns as he had in front, with lorries carrying the wounded next, and moved along the track towards the Pin Chaung. They soon came under fire, a tank, two 40mm anti-aircraft guns and many vehicles were hit, some of the animals bolted as they got a smell of the water ahead, progress was agonisingly slow until it all ground to a halt with most of the vehicles bogged in soft sand. There was nothing for it but to abandon them and transfer the wounded onto the backs of the tanks. Somehow this gallant band struggled on, passed the village of Thitpyubin where they were machine gunned and yet they managed to get across the Pin Chaung and by nightfall 19th April they reached the Kyaukpadaung road. As they did so 38th Chinese Division attacked again, still with a troop of 414th Battery RHA and some tanks of 2nd RTR, and held the enemy until what was left of the brigade reached the outskirts of Yenangyaung. They then withdrew only to find themselves acting as rear guard to the stricken 1st Burma Division as it moved off to sort itself out around Mount Popa. It was here that 23rd Mountain Battery was given the fittest mules that remained so that it could join 38th Chinese Division in its task of holding back the enemy as he approached from the south. By the time they returned, not having been used, they found 1st Burma Division had moved on and they had a further 83 miles to march to re-join them. The mules had a very bad time indeed but without them the Mountain Gunners could not have achieved all they did. They surely deserved the greatest praise for their service at this time. At this stage 38th Chinese Division was put under the command of General Slim with the guns of 414th Battery RHA under its command. Was this the first time that British guns fought under Chinese command?

The price of the defence of the oilfields had been heavy for both sides. The British had lost about a fifth of their strength, 4 x 3.7-inch howitzers, 4 x 25-pounders, most of the 40mm and mortars and a section of 3rd Indian LAA Battery. Although 17th Indian Division sent a column to attack the right flank of the Japanese who were attacking 1st Burma Division around Natmauk, it was too late to be of real help. Also the fresh Japanese *56th Division,* under Lieutenant General Watanabe, was closing up on the Chinese in the Karen Hills at Loikaw and by last light on 18th April the road to Meiktila lay open. It was then essential to plug the gap at Taunggyi and the Chinese 200th Division was diverted to do so. The situation was serious everywhere and Wavell decided that, if Burma had to be evacuated, the Chinese and all troops east of the Salween should withdraw to the Chinese border while all British forces to the west of the river pulled back into India. Then 1st Burma Division would cover the approaches to India through Kalewa and 5th Chinese Army, with one British Brigade and 7th Armoured Brigade, would guard the Mandalay - Lashio road. But in the end it was agreed with the Chinese that it would be better if no British forces went with them to the Lashio area.

On 21st April Alexander issued orders to the effect that, in the event of a withdrawal from

Mandalay, all Chinese forces east of a line Pyawbwe - Mandalay would move north east under Stilwell's orders to defend Lashio. Meanwhile 22nd and 96th Chinese Divisions with 7th Armoured Brigade were to defend the Meiktila - Thazi area, while 1st Burma, 17th Indian and 38th Chinese Divisions were to defend the line, Meiktila - Zayetkon - Gwegyo - Chauk, and 28th Chinese Division would defend Mandalay itself. Wavell saw the danger of fighting with their backs to the mighty Irrawaddy and said that, if the defensive line ordered became untenable, preparations must be made to get Burcorps across that river west of Mandalay.

The Japanese *56th Division* reached Loilem on 23rd April and at this stage the whole of 6th Chinese Army pulled back into China. By then the 200th Chinese Division had reached the western outskirts of Taunggyi and eventually took it but only after Stilwell had offered 50,000 rupees as a bribe! This division then pressed on to Loilem which it found deserted and without further ado it also withdrew into China, leaving *56th Division* to set off for Lashio. Neither Alexander nor Stilwell knew of these events, but Stilwell then ordered 28th Chinese Division to move to Lashio and not to defend Mandalay, which by then lay open to attack from the north east. Accordingly Alexander sent a scratch detachment up to the Gokteik Gorge to give warning of any enemy approach from that direction.

By this time the Japanese were approaching Pyawbwe in strength and the Chinese 96th Division was showing signs of packing up. Meiktila was almost undefended in practice and Alexander decided that the time to cross the Irrawaddy had arrived. He gave orders that it should start on the night of 25/26th April and that Burcorps would act as rearguard while the Chinese divisions crossed first. At this time almost all available anti-aircraft guns were deployed for the defence of Mandalay. The three HAA batteries probably had between them 9 x 3-inch or 3.7-inch guns while 3rd BAF LAA Battery and the two remaining troops of the ubiquitous 3rd Indian LAA Battery had between them 16 x 40mm guns. Japanese aircraft maintained air attacks on the Ava bridge but it is to the eternal credit of these guns that the bridges were never hit, although the town was soon a burnt-out ruin.

The plan was to move on Kalewa by way of Yeu, the railhead on the Mu River and Shwegyin on the Chindwin. There was a rough track through the forest and the engineers set-to to improve it and steps were taken to provide stocks of supplies along the 120 miles of the journey. The real problem lay beyond that because the track from Kalewa to Tamu was certainly not passable to heavy vehicles. The task of opening this route was given to Colonel Gilpin RE who worked miracles to ensure that it was ready when it was needed. All unnecessary vehicles were dumped. Wavell was bent on saving as much of the Army of Burma as he could for the defence of India.

1st Burma Division, less 2nd Burma Infantry Brigade, crossed the Irrawaddy by the Sameikkon ferry without incident on 28th April and moved on to Monywa. 38th Chinese Division followed. Then came news of a Japanese threat towards Kalewa up the Myittha valley and Slim ordered 1st Burma Infantry Brigade to move to Kalewa directly by boat and then move to Kalemyo. 2nd Burma Infantry Brigade, which had crossed the Irrawaddy at Pakokku, would proceed to Tilin via Pauk and then withdraw up the Myittha Valley. 1st Burma Division had only 13th Indian Infantry Brigade so it was given 63rd Indian Infantry Brigade from 17th Indian Division. 1st Burma Division was to guard the approach up the west bank of the Irrawaddy and then follow 17th Indian Division and Corps Troops along the Yeu - Kalewa track.

Meanwhile 17th Indian Division was pulling back to cross by the Ava bridges at Mandalay covered by 7th Armoured Brigade still at Meiktila as the Japanese closed up on 27th April. At the same time 48th Indian Infantry Brigade had taken up a defensive position at Kyaukse to cover that approach. It had with it 7th Hussars, a troop of 414th Battery RHA, a troop of 'A' Battery 95th Anti-Tank Regiment and 1st Indian Field Battery. The brigade's position was on the southern edge of the town, which had been destroyed by Japanese air attack, and rotting corpses lay everywhere.

The brigade had about 1,700 men. Contact with the *18th Division* which had already fought in Malaya, Singapore and in the Philippines was made at 2200 hours on the bright moonlit night of 28th April. 1/7th Gurkhas astride the road and 2/5th Gurkhas east of it waited until the enemy was only 150 yards away and then drove him back with deadly small-arms fire. The Japanese tried to out-flank, but the 25-pounders of 1st Indian Field Battery found them and stopped them dead. The anti-tank guns of 'A' Battery dealt with the few Japanese tanks which were foolish enough to expose themselves. Three more times the Japanese attacked these splendid Gurkhas and each time they were driven back. Next morning, with some tank support, the Gurkhas cleared the area in front of them counting over a hundred enemy dead for the loss of one Gurkha. Then came orders to withdraw across the Irrawaddy that night. At last all arms were beginning to work together.

All day Kyaukse was shelled with guns heavier than anything used so far in the campaign. In spite of local attacks and enemy dive bombing, Brigadier RT Cameron conducted a model withdrawal at 1800 hours and there was a huge explosion as the road and rail bridges over the river Zawgyi were blown. The Gunners rained fire down on the enemy to cover the infantry as they pulled out. It was a classic operation carried out by all arms working well together. At this time the Chinese were in a bad way and 38th Division was withdrawn to Ava.

The Chinese 38th Division was returned to General Stilwell but on the 29th Lashio fell. By last light on 30th April all troops were across the mighty Irrawaddy and the magnificent Ava Bridge at Mandalay was blown. 48th Indian Infantry Brigade moved to Myinmu near the junction of the Irrawaddy and the Mu rivers. At the same time 8th Indian and 1st BAF HAA Batteries were ordered to Shwebo together with one troop of 3rd Indian LAA Battery to protect a landing ground there. They engaged some 27 enemy aircraft from this position but it was almost the end of the road for the 3.7s. After struggling with them through the length of Burma under appalling conditions and having taken a heavy toll of enemy aircraft 1st BAF HAA Battery was forced to destroy its beloved guns on 1st May and take to the road as infantry. 8th Indian HAA Battery struggled on as far as Yeu with their 3-inch guns but sadly they could get them no further and had then to do the same. That same day a troop of 3rd Indian LAA Battery went to Monywa and engaged enemy advancing up the Chindwin to great effect, sinking several barges before being ordered back to Yeu. Somehow 8th British HAA Battery got as far as Kaduma before it also had to destroy its guns as they too could go no further. This meant that the sole air defence for the Army were the six remaining Bofors guns of 3rd Indian LAA Battery! Then two of these slid over a cliff so that by the time the battery arrived at Shwegyin it had only four.

By 1st May Burcorps had 2nd Burma Brigade approaching Pauk and about to withdraw up the Myittha Valley. 1st Gloucesters, only some 150 strong, and 1st Burma Division, made up of 1st Burma and 13th Indian Infantry Brigades, were at Monywa. 17th Indian Division had 48th Indian Infantry Brigade at Myinmu, 16th Indian Infantry Brigade at Ondaw and 63rd Indian Infantry Brigade at Sagaing. 38th Chinese Division was east of the Mu river but north and east of the Irrawaddy with 7th Armoured Brigade. 96th Chinese Division was at Shwebo about to move to Mytkyina by rail and 22nd Chinese Division was crossing the Irrawaddy towards Shwebo at the Singu ferry. It is important to remember that in British terms these Chinese divisions were the equivalent of brigades. The Japanese had failed to trap the Allies in the loop south of the Irrawaddy and we now know that it was there that General Iida had ordered his four divisions to cut them off. *56th Division* was to capture Lashio and then advance to the Salween. *18th Division* was to move to Lashio. *55th Division* was to clear the Mandalay area while *33rd Division* seized Monywa and then Shwebo. We are next, therefore, most concerned with the action of *33rd Division*. Its *213th Regiment* was operating on the east bank of the Irrawaddy and had reached Myinggyan by 1st May. *215th Regiment*, in motor transport, was followed by *214th Regiment* operating to the west of the Chindwin in the Monywa area; some troops moved up the river in barges.

At this time Headquarters Burcorps was at Budalin. Headquarters 1st Burma Division was at Ma-U four miles south of Monywa. 1st Burma and 13th Indian Infantry Brigades were heading for Monywa and had reached Chaungu. Some six miles north of Monywa at Alon were some 2,400 clerks, wives and children awaiting boat transport up the Chindwin to Kalewa. It was at this stage that the Japanese attacked Monywa with artillery and mortars from the west bank but did not cross the river. Slim heard that the town was lost and realised that this would cut his withdrawal route so he ordered 1st Burma Division with 48th and 63rd Indian Infantry Brigades under command to recapture it while 17th Indian Division sent 16th Indian Infantry Brigade to Yeu to cover the approaches from the south. Then the Japanese occupied Monywa, 1st Burma Division's Headquarters was attacked but it got out and moved to Chaungu. 63rd Indian Infantry Brigade arrived first, detraining at Kyehmon early on 1st May. They immediately set off for Monywa, overcoming resistance at Ma-U on the way.

Alexander met Stilwell at Yeu that evening to review the situation and agreed that the time had come to pull back from the Irrawaddy. Stilwell agreed to release 7th Armoured Brigade and it was sent to Yeu to operate down the road to Monywa. This was their last meeting and, indeed, their last contact. Meanwhile Bruce Scott planned to attack Monywa with 63rd Indian Infantry Brigade astride the road from the south while 13th Indian Infantry Brigade made a night march across country and attacked from the east through Zalok. Each brigade was given a field and a mountain battery under command. 1st Burma Brigade was in reserve.

The attack went in as planned and 13th Indian Infantry Brigade did well, reaching Zalok by 0400 hours, and pressed on until it was held up by heavy opposition at Monywa railway station. 63rd Indian Infantry Brigade was held up on the southern edge of the town. 1st Burma Infantry Brigade then passed through them and made contact with 13th Indian Infantry Brigade who had just received a mysterious order which it ignored, to withdraw and pull out to Alon. While this was happening 1st Burma Division's transport managed to get through Zalok and Ettaw and reach Alon without too much trouble. At last light Bruce Scott could still not break into Monywa so he also went round the village and reached Alon also without any trouble. It was pretty certain that the order to 13th Indian Infantry Brigade to pull out came from the Japanese! But by last light on 2nd May, 1st Burma Division and 7th Armoured Brigade were concentrated at Alon and 16th Indian Infantry Brigade of 17th Indian Division was at Yeu. The road from Monywa to Yeu and the track from Yeu to Shwegyin were secure but the Japanese still had control of the direct route up the Chindwin to the vital Shwegyin-Kalewa crossing. To deal with this 16th Indian Infantry Brigade was ordered to move to Shwegyin to secure the crossing; and the whole withdrawal was accelerated.

On 3rd May 1942 1st Burma Division, now consisting of 1st Burma and 13th and 63rd Indian Infantry Brigades, began to withdraw towards Yeu, covered by 7th Armoured Brigade. The tanks of 2nd RTR with the guns of 'E' Troop, 414th Battery RHA went into action against enemy tanks and guns. Accurate fire by 'E' Troop silenced an enemy battery near Yeu. This move was then completed by nightfall with very little interference. On the same day Headquarters 17th Indian Division and 48th Indian Infantry Brigade followed on. The corps was by then ready for its final withdrawal from Burma. Meanwhile 2nd Burma Infantry Brigade had reached Pauk on 1st May and by the 12th it met transport 15 miles south of Kalemyo which took it to Tamu. The Brigade had covered 216 miles on foot in 14 days in the hottest time of year on very poor tracks. On 5th May 15th Mountain Battery was at Yeu where it received orders to dismantle its guns, destroy ammunition and move across the Chindwin.

Alexander was concerned to get back over the Chindwin before the monsoon broke. Stocks had been placed along the track but it was the wounded, some 2,300 in number, and the refugees that were to cause so much concern. It all went remarkably well even though the conditions were appalling. From Shwegyin all vehicles and guns had to be ferried across the Chindwin and then taken by river to Kalewa, because the tracks were not up to it. But there were only six river boats available and these would only carry 600 men and two lorries and two jeeps on each trip. Thus most guns and vehicles had to be abandoned and destroyed, leaving just enough transport to carry the wounded and vital supplies. The danger was an attack by the Japanese up the Chindwin from Monywa. A blocking position was created and air attacks called for. Fall back positions were also created at Kalewa and then Pyingaing, before final withdrawal.

13th Indian Infantry Brigade reached Shwegyin on 7th May and 1st Burma and 48th Indian Infantry Brigades were at Pyingaing. On the 8th Slim ordered 1st Burma Brigade to move to Indaw to protect the left flank while 63rd Indian Infantry Brigade and 2nd RTR, which had by then destroyed all their tanks and vehicles, crossed the Chindwin. So far so good, but there were ominous signs. The enemy bombed the boom barrier across the river at Gaundi and Shwegyin on 7th May where they lost two aircraft to the five guns of 3rd Indian LAA Battery, but here one more was lost leaving only four. By 9th May, *213th Regiment* had reached Kywe and Ingongyi, only eight miles south of the Shwegyin. Here Slim had ordered crossing operations to be conducted in a small basin about half a mile long and 400 yards wide and by 9th May this had become very congested with vehicles, guns, men, including the wounded, and animals. Enemy bombing meant that the Burmese boat crews would only work at night and the river had risen, putting the jetties almost under water. Thus the withdrawal was going very slowly at this bottleneck. At this time 7th Armoured Brigade had reached a point three miles short of the river at Shwegyin and this proved the final resting place for the tanks. The 25-pounders were given top priority to move forward and by great efforts were got to the bank of the Chindwin where they came into action.

It was, however, the herculean efforts of Major MacFetridge and the two guns of A Troop and two of C Troop of his splendid 3rd Indian LAA Battery that had fought at Moulmein some months earlier, that got them along the perilous mud track and into the Shwegyin basin. Three guns were put into action at the side of the track in a direct fire position with Second Lieutenants FD Webber and AD Knights acting as section commanders. One gun was deployed some 300 yards away in the anti-aircraft role.

Suddenly, early on 10th May, into this mass of men and equipment enemy infantry advanced from the south, covered by machine gun fire. They quickly seized a knoll which overlooked the jetty. This stopped embarkation but, by pressing in under a cliff some 200 yards upstream, three river boats managed to embark all the wounded and take them safely to Kalewa. Major General Cowan was at Headquarters 17th Indian Division at Mutaik and he ordered 1/3rd Gurkhas, by then only one company strong, and 1/4th Gurkhas to piquet the track from Mutaik to Shwegyin and sent 2/5th Gurkhas and a squadron of 7th Hussars to the basin. At 1300 hours a counter-attack by 1/7th Gurkhas supported by the fire of 1st Indian Field Battery, located in Mutaik and 3rd Indian LAA Battery in the basin itself, failed to dislodge the enemy, but did hold them at bay. Cowan realised that he could no longer use the ferries and that he must pull back through the jungle to Kaing. He ordered the 25-pounders of 414th Battery to act as rearguard for the last lap of that terrible march back into India.

The withdrawal began at once but only the barest equipment could be taken as the track was known to be exceedingly difficult. All remaining tanks, guns and vehicles had to be destroyed. 1st HAA Battery BAF, 8th HAA Battery, 15th Mountain Battery, 8th Indian Anti-Tank Battery and one troop of 5th Indian Anti-Tank Battery all reported that all guns had been destroyed in the area around Shwegyin. At 1700 hours the last 25-pounders, 3.7s and 40mm guns and mortars began firing off all ammunition at high rates. This held the enemy in check as the withdrawal got underway. At 1955 hours the rearguard began to leave their positions and the 40mm guns increased their rate of fire. The barrage by the three Bofors guns lasted 20 minutes and completely silenced the enemy, enabling the infantry to pull out without any more casualties. Not a man left the guns until the infantry were well clear. Then at 1755 hours every gun fired at the intense rate for ten minutes putting down a massive concentration on the positions just vacated by the Gurkhas and the Jats. As dusk came, Lieutenant Colonel BR Godley of the Jats walked up to the troop commander as he passed the lone line of guns guarding their rear as they withdrew and said, 'You saved the day, you know.' What higher tribute could there be? These were the last rounds fired in what had become the longest, cruellest and most difficult withdrawal ever conducted by the British Army. (MacFetridge).

12 (Poonch) Mountain Battery, less one section, was engaged in this area, outside the main battle. It was supporting 1/4th Gurkhas protecting the track leading to Shwegyin. A force of Japanese blocked the crossing and the battery came into action, fighting continuing all day. On 11th May the battery moved with 17 Div by a pack route, and crossed the river at Kalewa. It was remarkable that this battery and 3rd Indian LAA Battery were both engaged in the battles and at Moulmein and Shwegyin at the beginning and end of the campaign.

One unit war diary, quoted by the official history, records, 'The chief contribution came from the Bofors whose tracer shells lit up the descending darkness. It was a cheering sound the like of which we had not heard during our time in Burma. At 8.15 pm the guns ceased fire and five minutes later we received the order to go. As we left the Basin enormous fires were getting a good hold on the dumps of stores and ammunition, tanks and lorries. It was an eerie sight in the gathering gloom and distressing to think so much material had to be left behind. From the enemy there wasn't a sound. They had apparently had enough.' (quoted in MacFetridge). Although no-one realised it at the time, this was the last action of the campaign.

The last troops left Kalewa by boat during the night of 11/12th May and reached Sittaung on the 14th. All boats were then sunk and the men marched to Tamu. By 19th May the ordeal was over. But somehow the Gunners had managed to bring 28 of the 48 field, mountain and anti-aircraft guns they had had in Burma back to India. They were:

414th Battery RHA	6 x 25-pounders
'C' Troop, 2nd Indian Field Battery	4 x 25-pounders
27th Mountain Regiment IA	10 x 3.7-inch howitzers
28th Mountain Regiment IA	4 x 3.7-inch howitzers
2nd Indian Anti-Tank Battery	4 x 2-pounders

This was a truly remarkable feat, especially because they were often the last to leave each position. They had moved back over 1,000 miles in three months. The Army had lost some 10,036 casualties, of which 3,670 had been killed and wounded; the remaining 6,366 were reported either wounded or missing. The Japanese had some 4,597 killed, they lost 117 aircraft to the Allies 116. The first heavy rains fell on 12th May so they got out by the skin of their teeth. Dysentery and malaria took a heavy toll of the exhausted men. It had been a fine feat to get so many back still as a coherent whole. Nevertheless it was yet another defeat.

Why had it happened? Without doubt the primary cause was the sheer unpreparedness of the armed forces to defend Burma. There was a lack of men, guns, ships and aircraft. There was no organised intelligence or command and control system and what did exist was unfit for war. The Chinese arrived late and did not or could not respond when most needed. The Army in Burma was therefore asked to carry out a task which was way beyond its powers and capabilities. It was, in short, the same story again. Had it not been for some magnificent logistic work and planning, particularly by Hutton and for the presence of 7th Armoured Brigade, the story might have ended in another total disaster.

Strategically the loss of Burma was very serious. China was cut off, except by air, from India.

Yet if the Army had given in earlier or without such a fight, many more Japanese forces would have been released for operations against India. Burma had to be retaken and as soon as possible. 1st Burma Division went to Shillong to refit and became 39th Indian (Light) Division. 17th Indian Division also re-organised at Shillong to become 17th Indian (Light) Division. These two formations formed 4th Indian Corps under Lieutenant General GAP Scoones.

The few Gunners who took part in the first Burma Campaign had done well. Always too few, nearly always outgunned they stuck it out. The actions of 414th Battery RHA, the Mountain Batteries and of 3rd Indian LAA Battery were in the highest traditions of the Regiment, but indeed all units did remarkably well in appalling conditions and the fact that somehow they got so many guns back to India is to their eternal credit. We can be truly proud of what they achieved in Burma from December 1941 to May 1942.

For the last six days of the withdrawal 414th Battery RHA, along with the few remaining tanks, had acted as rearguard to the Army, first under 13th Indian Infantry Brigade and then under 16th Indian Infantry Brigade. The guns remained in action during the hours of daylight and then after dark followed the infantry back along the endless jungle tracks. They moved through Kalewa, Imbaung, Yezagyo, Khampat and Witok to Tamu where the monsoon broke with a vengeance. They eventually reached Palel on 18th May 1942. It was not until 11th June that the battery arrived at Dhond near Poona to refit and rest. Then at the end of August it received the order to expand and to become 14th Regiment RHA under its battery commander, duly promoted to Lieutenant Colonel, Tom Pereira, a just reward for a splendid job done.

3rd Indian LAA Battery were credited with destroying 22 enemy aircraft, one gun and a mortar during the campaign. Many more enemy aircraft were certainly hit and many enemy were killed and wounded. Eight guns were lost in action, 41 officers and men were killed and 17 wounded. The Battery was awarded two Military Crosses, one Distinguished Conduct Medal, one Indian Order of Merit, three Indian Distinguished Service Medals and five mentions in dispatches. It was a magnificent effort in every way. The Battery still lives (1999) as the 14th LAA Battery, Pakistan Artillery, and remembers with pride its action in Burma in 1942.

27th Mountain Regiment went to Ambala to refit but there was no rest for 28th Mountain Regiment which joined 23rd Indian Division for the defence of Assam and it remained at Shenam with 1st Indian Infantry Brigade. Here it picked up 16th (Zhob) Battery and later 13th (Dardoni) Battery.

Perhaps the best way to record the arrival of the Gunners back into India is in the words written by Brigadier G de V Welchman who had been CRA 17th Indian Division, throughout that long and gruelling journey:

'Few were not suffering from malaria and all that the men had to wear was the threadbare suit of drill they had worn throughout the long withdrawals. For shelter a tattered groundsheet was a luxury. But we shall always remember the typical words of cheer, sympathy and hope, 'Bad luck! Well done though. You did your best', or, 'Good, you've still got your guns with you.' - spoken by our Corps Commander, Lieut General W.J. Slim, as he was then, as he walked through that concentration of Gunners, the majority of whom were without the things that always mean so much to us all - the guns. Little has been told of the valiant efforts made to save those missing guns, the great work done by the Indian Mountain Batteries, prominent among them, 12th (Poonch), 2nd (Derajat) (FF), 5th (Bombay) and 23rd, the sterling support given by batteries of the 1st Indian Field Regiment, the unfailing co-operation of the 414th Battery RHA (The Essex Yeomanry) with the tanks of 7th Armoured Brigade and the Chinese Infantry of the 38th Chinese Division, the devotion to duty of the British, Indian and Burmese anti-aircraft artillery - 8th British and 8th Indian HAA Batteries, 3rd Indian LAA Battery and 1st HAA Regiment BAF; and the unselfish service in all kinds of roles of 2nd Indian ATk Regiment. But those who witnessed the deeds of these men will not forget them.' (Duncan).

1. The headquarters of a mountain battery of the HKSRA in Hong Kong in 1941. (IWM)

2. A 6-inch 26 cwt howitzer being used for training by HKSRA in a Malayan rubber plantation in 1941.

3. Indian mountain gunners with a 3.7-inch howitzer near Shwegyin, April 1942. (IWM)

4. Flooded British LAA battery, Assam/Burma border, Monsoon 1943. (IWM)

CHAPTER 7

MADAGASCAR, THE DEFENCE OF INDIA and THE EXPANSION OF THE AUSTRALIAN AND INDIAN ARTILLERIES

Including events in Ceylon, the Indian Ocean and the Pacific 1941-43

(Maps 22, 23 and 24)

Plans had been prepared as early as December 1941 to seize Madagascar in order to forestall any attempt by the Japanese to occupy it and disrupt the British sea lines of communication to the Far East. In March 1942 it was decided that the operation, codenamed IRONCLAD, would be undertaken because of the serious situation developing in Burma. The aim was to capture the Vichy French naval and air bases at Diego Suarez at the northern tip of the island and then to occupy the rest of the island (Map 22). D-Day was to be the best day between 4th and 8th May 1942 and the Port of Assembly was to be Durban. Help with shipping was to come from the Americans and Rear-Admiral EN Syfret RN, was appointed as commander with Major General RC Sturges, of the Royal Marines, as Land Force Commander.

The Land Force was to be called Force 121 and was to consist of 29th Independent Infantry Brigade Group, under Brigadier FW Festing, which included 1st Royal Scots Fusiliers, 2nd Royal Welch Fusiliers, 2nd East Lancashire Regiment, 2nd South Lancashire Regiment, 455th Independent Light Battery RA, under Major IW Mason Macfarlane, (which had four 3.7-inch howitzers and two 25-pounders) and 236th Field Company RE less one section. Next came No 5 Commando and 17th Infantry Brigade of 5th Division under Brigadier GWB Tarleton. 17th Brigade included 2nd Royal Scots Fusiliers, 6th Seaforth Highlanders, 2nd Northamptonshire Regiment and 9th Field Regiment RA, which was commanded by Lieutenant Colonel JR Lupton and consisted of 19th, 20th and 28/76th Batteries. The brigade was under orders for India with the rest of 5th Division and had sailed from the UK on 13th March by way of the Cape. The fleet and Force 121 met up at Freetown and began joint planning. Captain GA Garnons-Williams RN was to be Naval Assault Force Commander and Brigadier Festing was to be Land Force Assault Commander. The CRA was Lieutenant Colonel W Odling. Then came news that 13th Infantry Brigade under Brigadier VC Russell, also from 5th Division, would join the force at Durban as floating reserve. At Cape Town the force was met by the South African Prime Minister, Field Marshal JC Smuts, who advocated the capture of the ports of Tamatave and Majunga as well as Diego Suarez.

Rear-Admiral EN Syfret flew his flag in the carrier HMS *Illustrious* and was later joined by the battleship HMS *Ramillies* and the carrier HMS *Indomitable*. In addition there were two cruisers, HMS *Devonshire* and HMS *Hermione*, 11 destroyers, six corvettes, six minesweepers and an oiler.

For the carriage of the assault force and for the landing, there were three troopships, *Oronsay*, *Duchess of Atholl* and *Franconia*, five assault ships, two special landing ships, five MT ships and one hospital ship. There was much to be done at Durban to get the loading right for the landings. Then the force commander was told to include the towns of Tamatave and Majunga in his attack plans. To this end he said that he would need the full use of 13th Infantry Brigade. The reply from the Chiefs of Staff was that the move of 5th Division to India as complete as possible was of a higher priority, so this extra part of the plan was put into abeyance for the time being.

The fleet sailed in two groups on 25th April, 27 years to the day since the last great amphibious operation carried out by the Royal Navy and the British Army at Gallipoli in 1915. The Joint Commanders were on board the battleship, HMS *Ramillies*.

The harbour at Diego Suarez is about the size of Scapa Flow in the Orkney Islands and is located on the east coast of Madagascar at its northern end (Map 22 - Insert) To its west are Courrier Bay and Ambararata Bay, separated from the harbour by a narrow isthmus some two miles wide at its narrowest point. From this isthmus projects the Andrakaka Peninsula which at its nearest point is only 1,200 yards from the French naval base of Antsirane. The harbour entrance is in the east and is protected by the Oronjia Channel which was defended by three French coast artillery batteries. The bays to the west were also protected but by two batteries and, it was thought, a minefield. Although there were two good anchorages, the passage to the landing sites was very tricky, especially at night.

The aim was to storm and capture the naval base at Antsirane and the airfield some five miles to the south and to do so from the west across the isthmus. The main assault was to be carried out by 29th Independent Brigade Group landing on three beaches in Ambararata Bay. The brigade was on light scales but it had six light and six medium tanks and 455th Field Battery. As soon as it had landed it was to advance some 21 miles eastwards and capture Antsirane. Concurrently No 5 Commando and one company of 2nd East Lancashires were to land in Courrier Bay, silence the coast batteries and then advance to secure the Andrakaka Peninsula. 17th Infantry Brigade was to land as soon as 29th Infantry Brigade were ashore and attack Antsirane and the Oranjia Peninsula from the south. H-Hour was to be at 0430 hours on 5th May, which would be one hour and twenty minutes before sunrise.

The fleets were in position by noon on 4th May and at dusk the destroyers *Laforey*, *Lightning* and *Anthony* were sent ahead to mark and buoy the channel. Meanwhile the convoy, with minesweepers ahead, made its slow, silent and blacked out passage through the tortuous narrow route to the anchorage. At 2122 hours the moon rose in a clear sky and, as eyes strained eastwards, the dim outline of the coast could be seen. Shortly after midnight the convoy entered the buoyed channel and at 0154 hours on 5th May began to anchor as noiselessly as possible just out of range of the shore batteries. Had they known that the minesweepers had parted with their sweeps on a shoal at the entrance to the channel, they would have been more concerned because the channel had not in fact been swept. However there were no mines, at least not there.

While the assault craft were being loaded the minesweepers, now re-connected to their sweeps, swept an eight mile channel to the dispersal point in Courrier Bay, closely followed by HMS *Laforey* and the assault craft carrying No 5 Commando and the company of the East Lancashires. In this passage 17 mines were swept, two of which exploded but the defenders must have been sleeping heavily because nothing happened. At 0330 hours the assault boats headed for the shore in absolute silence. Surprise was complete. In a few minutes they were ashore and had captured the astonished batteries unopposed. They raced on and, although they met some opposition during the morning, by 0430 hours they were at the tip of the Andrakaka Peninsular looking for boats with which to cross to Antsirane. Meanwhile, by 0630 hours, 29th Infantry Brigade was ashore having had to silence only one machine gunner.

Captain WS Wright RA was Forward Officer Bombardment (FOB) with No 5 Commando and had with him three telegraphists RN and one signaller RN, he writes, '. . . A mile or so offshore was a string of small islands and rocky outcrops, the gaps between which were mined. In addition the whole bay was covered by a battery of 150mm coast guns in concrete emplacements. The plan was for the minesweepers to cut a way through the minefield and for the Commando to follow in LCAs and to take the coast battery, thus making it safe for 29th Infantry Brigade to land . . . Then about 0500 hours in bright moonlight we landed on the beach, walked up to the gun position and found it deserted . . . as dawn broke we investigated some buildings and found the gun detachments inside still in bed. An elderly French lieutenant was furious and seeing my three pips shouted out, "Vous etes trop jeun[e] pour capitaine." Thereafter the Commando moved eastwards as 29th Infantry Brigade took a wider sweep round towards Antsirane . . . We established an OP overlooking the harbour and saw a French warship. Leading Telegraphist Bradshaw (equivalent to Bombardier) said, "We should engage this one, it is flying the battle flag." I asked him what this meant and he said that flying the national flag from the foremast meant that the ship was prepared to fight. I considered engagement but because there was no sign of action I decided not to engage, but I think I was wrong.'

Across on the east coast HMS *Hermione* was carrying out a diversion by opening fire on the coastal batteries on the Oranjia Peninsula. Then at dawn aircraft from the two carriers dropped bombs, torpedoes, depth charges and dummy parachutists. Fighters attacked the airfield and achieved complete surprise, setting the hangars, still full of aircraft, alight.

By 0700 hours 29th Infantry Brigade was ready to move, led by the carriers and motor cycles of 2nd Royal Welch Fusiliers with 1st Royal Scots Fusiliers and 455th Light Battery following. It was a sweltering hot day as the force advanced along the single dusty road without meeting any opposition. Then at 1100 hours, at a sharp bend in the road, the lead motor cycles came under machine-gun fire from trenches and pill boxes on the high ground overlooking them. Brigadier Festing immediately ordered the infantry to attack supported by the 3.7-inch howitzers of 455th Light Battery. While this was being organised five British tanks came up, burst right through the astonished infantry and raced on towards Antsirane where four were disabled and the crews taken prisoner. All arms training still had some way to go!

Back at the beaches the landings continued even though the wind was getting up and more mines were found. By 1100 hours all 29th Infantry Brigade was ashore and at 1115 hours Brigadier Tarleton's 17th Infantry Brigade began to land. 9th Field Regiment landed at Courrier Bay but found on landing that there was no road south to link with the road to Antsirane. Thus the only option was for the regiment to go to the end of the Andrakaka Peninsula. But from there its guns could not reach the point where 29th Infantry Brigade was held up. As a result the brigade was short of firepower throughout its operations to capture Antsirane, where the French held out until 1500 hours. The brigade then advanced and came under fire from the main defences in the southern outskirts of the town.

At 2300 hours Brigadier Festing gave orders for an attack to go in at 0600 hours on 6th May. 2nd South Lancashires were to attack from the east and try to get behind the enemy, while 1st Scots Fusiliers were to attack in the centre with 2nd East Lancashires on their left, all supported by 455th Light Battery, the only guns in range. The eastern attack was very successful and got behind the enemy and captured many. But the frontal attacks failed partly because there were by then only five tanks left. 17th Infantry Brigade could not arrive until 1800 hours that day and 13th Infantry Brigade had just started to land. At this point Major General RC Sturges arrived and ordered a new attack with both brigades after dark, with a diversion into the harbour by some Royal Marines, taken there by destroyer, from the north. Both were to go in at 2000 hours.

At 2000 hours that evening HMS *Anthony*, with 50 Royal Marines on board, raced through the

Oranjia Channel at 22 knots. The shore batteries opened up on her but they soon ceased fire when HM Ships *Devonshire* and *Hermione* engaged them. Lieutenant Commander JM Hodges RN, commanding HMS *Anthony*, skilfully manoeuvred his ship and held her stern against the jetty at Antsirane long enough for the marines to jump ashore. They then raced into the town and captured the artillery headquarters and naval barracks against slight opposition. Meanwhile 17th and 29th Infantry Brigades had started their attack from the south and by 0300 hours Brigadier Festing reported that the town was in his hands. General Sturges then summoned the French to surrender but they took their time so the fleet were told to bombard the Oranjia Peninsula and this had the desired effect. Ten minutes later the white flag was raised. On 8th May 1942 with the mighty *Ramillies* and her escorts in the harbour the terms of surrender were signed. Diego Suarez and with it the route round the Cape of Good Hope to India had been secured.

Although Operation IRONCLAD had been successful there had been a price to pay. 100 men had been killed and 300 wounded and the French had lost 150 killed and some 500 wounded. By this time pressure was building up in India for the arrival of 5th Division: Burma had been lost and the threat to India was growing daily. On 20th May 13th Infantry Brigade sailed for Bombay and 17th Infantry Brigade followed on 12th June having been relieved by 22nd East African Infantry Brigade under Brigadier WA Dimoline. Negotiations began with the French in order to come to an agreement about the remainder of the island that was satisfactory to both sides and which would enable the British to reduce their garrison. These soon became protracted and unsatisfactory. Meanwhile the fleet dispersed, leaving *Ramillies*, three destroyers and two corvettes at Diego Suarez.

At 1030 hours on 29th May an unidentified aircraft flew over the harbour and this caused concern that the Japanese might attack. The fleet dispersed, but as it was doing so at 2025 hours, HMS *Ramillies* and a tanker were torpedoed. The tanker sank almost at once and *Ramillies* settled by the bows. By discharging oil and ammunition she overcame this and sailed for Durban. Depth charges were dropped by the corvettes but nothing was found. However, a day or two later and near Diego Suarez, two Japanese were found, they refused to surrender and were shot. Papers carried by them showed them to be the crew of a midget submarine.

At this stage Field Marshal Smuts again pressed for the capture of Tamatave and Majunga and he offered 7th South African Infantry Brigade to help. It was therefore agreed with Lieutenant General Sir William Platt, GOC-in-C East African Command, that if the current negotiations failed, Majunga should be captured. On 1st July Madagascar was placed under the command of General Platt. The island of Mayotte, in the Mozambique Channel 200 miles north west of Majunga, was captured and an airfield built there. But the French were clearly playing for time and had no intention of reaching an agreement, so plans were set in hand to capture Majunga and Tamatave, followed by an advance to the capital Tananarive. Landing craft were to come from India even though this would delay landings planned for the Arakan.

29th Infantry Brigade was to seize the harbour at Majunga on 10th September, then 22nd East African Infantry Brigade would pass through them and advance to the capital. 29th Infantry Brigade was then to sail round the island and land at Tamatave on 18th September and advance on the capital from the east. Meanwhile 7th South African Infantry Brigade would take over the garrison of Diego Suarez and advance south to take Maromandia and Antalaha. It was expected that the Vichy French would then capitulate. 22nd East African Infantry Brigade was landed successfully by 16th September and soon reached Andriba, only 100 miles from Tananarive. The Governor asked for an armistice but his terms were rejected on the 17th. Meanwhile 29th Infantry Brigade had landed as planned at Tamatave and had begun its advance. The Governor then declared Tananarive an open town and it was occupied by 22nd East African Infantry Brigade on 23rd September. But the Governor refused to capitulate, so operations continued to clear the rest of the island by force. On 29th September troops were landed at Tulear and Fort Dauphin and 22nd East African Infantry Brigade advanced south from the capital. The rains came and made progress slow and it was not until 29th October that Fianarantsoa was occupied. The Governor signed an instrument of capitulation on 6th November, but it had taken eight weeks after landing at Majunga to achieve it. Another Gunner unit to take part was 91st Field Regiment, commanded by Lieutenant Colonel W Buffey, which fought in the second part of the operation. A South African field regiment, one HAA battery and a LAA troop together with 56 (Uganda) Field Battery, EAA and two *ad hoc* sub units manning captured French equipment also played their parts.

The early months of 1942 were some of the most critical and anxious in the whole war. The Battle of the Atlantic was at its height, naval losses in the Mediterranean had been severe, General Auchinleck's Eighth Army was being forced back in North Africa and Malta was under heavy bombardment. As well as much of China, Hong Kong, Malaya, Singapore, the Philippines, the Netherlands East Indies and Burma had all fallen to the Japanese and now India and Ceylon were threatened. With Madagascar secure, Ceylon, as the link to India and Australia, required special attention.

While the Japanese were engaged in the occupation of Burma they were also intent on expanding their boundary in the southern Pacific and towards Australia. The island of New Britain, in the Bismarck Archipelago, formed part of the Australian Mandated Territory of Papua New Guinea. At the eastern end of the island is one of the finest natural harbours in the south Pacific at Rabaul. There were also airfields at Lakunai and Vunakanau. The Australian Government decided to send a garrison there and in March and April 1941 set about the installation of two 6-inch coast guns and searchlights, formed as Praed Point Battery, Rabaul, under the command of Major JRP Clark RAA. The core of the defences was provided by 2/22nd Infantry Battalion and in August a section of two 3-inch 20 cwt anti-aircraft guns was added to the garrison under the command of Lieutenant DM Selby RAA. The following month the garrison received further Gunner support from part of 17th Anti-Tank Battery under Captain G Matheson RAA. As well as other small supporting units, the RAAF was able to provide a few Hudsons and Wirraways. Japanese aircraft, of *24th Air Flotilla*, in considerable strength, raided Rabaul on 4th January 1942. Further intense aerial bombardment followed and Selby's guns kept Japanese aircraft at high level, thus reducing bombing accuracy, and on 20th January brought down one of the attackers. More modern Japanese machines caused the loss of most of the Australian aircraft available to the defence and the survivors were withdrawn. The airfields were put out of action by cratering. Further heavy air attacks followed and the 6-inch battery was destroyed by heavy bombing. With the approach of the *4th Fleet* the defenders took up their positions and Selby, with the greatest regret, destroyed his guns when ordered to do so, he and his men henceforth acting in an infantry role. Japanese landings, made by the *South Seas Force* took place on 23rd January under extensive air cover and the anti-tank gunners engaged landing craft but enemy troops continued to pour ashore and soon heavily outnumbered the Australians. Rabaul was in Japanese hands on the 24th and effective resistance ceased, though some defenders got away to the interior. Some 400 managed to get back to Australia.

By July 1942 the Australian Gunners had expanded under the direction of their MGRAA, Major General JS Whitelaw. There were by then ten Australian divisional artilleries, 33 field regiments, two survey regiments, three medium regiments, 12 anti-tank regiments, 37 coast batteries and some 80 anti-aircraft batteries. Of these 1st Australian Corps with two field regiments and seven anti-aircraft batteries was in New Guinea. 9th Australian Division with 2/7th, 2/8th and 2/12th Field, 2/3rd Anti-Tank and 2/4th LAA Regiments was in the Middle East. The rest of the artillery was in Australia. Even so it was considered that, with the Japanese in the Netherlands East Indies, the coast defence of Australia was not strong enough. Eight new coast batteries were raised and given the letters 'A' to 'H'. They were equipped with US 155mm M1917A1 guns. More were raised later and 'B' and 'E' Batteries went to New Guinea (Horner).

On 17th February 1942 the Pacific War Council decided that 16th British Infantry Brigade Group, part of 70th Division which was destined to move to Burma from North Africa, should go at once to Ceylon. Australia agreed that two brigades of 6th Australian Division, then embarking at Suez, should also be diverted to Ceylon with two squadrons of Hurricanes. Wavell, however, believed that the defence of Ceylon was mainly a naval and air force matter and that it was not wise to keep too many troops locked up there. He therefore proposed to send 70th British Division complete to India for operations in Burma and to send an East African brigade to Ceylon. Though the Chiefs of Staff agreed, they said that they could not provide enough naval and air forces for the island and that 16th British Infantry Brigade and an East African brigade must go there.

There were three areas of strategic importance in the Far East at this time: Ceylon, which controlled the reinforcement route to India and Australia; Bengal and Assam, which covered the Japanese threat from Burma; and the industrial region round Calcutta without which the war could not be supported. Wavell rated the threat through Assam as the greatest he faced and proposed to create a bastion in north east India for its defence. Meanwhile the Chiefs of Staff began to build up the Eastern Fleet under Admiral Sir James Somerville.

The Prime Minister had insisted that Vice-Admiral Sir Geoffrey Layton should be Commander-in-Chief Ceylon and that he should report direct to the Commander-in-Chief India. Churchill had been shocked at the state of the command structure in Malaya, Singapore and Burma at the start of operations. Under Layton, Lieutenant General Sir Henry Pownall was to be Land Force Commander with Air Vice Marshal JH D'Albiac as Air Officer Commanding Ceylon. Reinforcements soon began to arrive on the island. 34th Indian Division, with 99th and 100th Indian Infantry Brigades, arrived in December 1941 and 16th British Infantry Brigade disembarked on 14th March 1942, 21st East African Infantry Brigade arrived on 21st March and 16th and 17th Australian Infantry Brigades on the 23rd. Thus by the end of March 1942 there was the equivalent of two divisions on the island. There were also four fighter squadrons, three of Hurricanes and one of Fulmars, one bomber squadron, with Blenheims, and two detachments of Catalina flying boats. In addition there were three Fleet Air Arm squadrons, two of Fulmar fighters and one of Swordfish and Albacore torpedo spotter reconnaissance aircraft, at Trincomalee.

At the same time the artillery build up on the island began. In December 1940 there was only 6th Coast Regiment with its headquarters at Colombo, commanding 15th and 18th Coast Batteries and the Ceylon Garrison Artillery (CGA). The regiment manned 2 x 9.2-inch and 4 x 6-inch guns at Colombo and 2 x 9.2-inch and 3 x 6-inch guns at Trincomalee. The battle-tried 51st Field Regiment arrived from Egypt in February 1942 and joined 34th Indian Division. By March 1942 anti-aircraft defences consisted of 65th HAA, 2nd CGA HAA and 1st Royal Marines HAA Regiments and 22nd, 43rd and 55th LAA Regiments. Gun totals at that time were 32 x 3.7-inch, 4 x 3-inch, 3 x 12-pounder and 73 x 40mm (Routledge). The second of these LAA units, 43rd, went to 23rd AA Brigade and the third, 55th, to the Royal Marines AA Brigade. The growth of the artillery order of battle in Ceylon is given at Annex H.

Wavell went ahead with building his bastion in Bengal. He first moved 1st Indian Infantry Brigade from the North West Frontier to Imphal to protect the new Manipur Base and the Depot at Dimapur. 14th Indian Division, less one brigade, was sent to Comilla to protect the coast and the Calcutta industrial base. 109th Indian Infantry Brigade, less one battalion, was sent to Akyab. Finally he put 70th British Division, less 16th Infantry Brigade, and 23rd Indian Division at Ranchi under 4th Corps to act as a mobile reserve. At the same time Wavell said that he needed some 36 RAF squadrons to make sense of the defence of India, and over a period the Chiefs of

Staff made great efforts to provide them. A massive amount of work had to be done to construct airfields and the command and control and early warning systems, so vital to successful air operations. 10th US Air Force under Major General LH Brereton arrived on 5th March, with the main mission of keeping open the air supply route to China. In May 1942 it was agreed that 200 new airfields in Assam, Lower Bengal and the Ganges Plain would be needed, so the requirement for AA defence would be very great. Nearly 90 all-weather runways were ready by the end of the year. Japanese air raids commenced in October against Digboi, forward airfields in Assam and Calcutta itself. (Routledge).

The build-up of forces in India was to continue until the end of the war. The effect was the assembly of an enormous force which was in the end to defeat the Japanese. But in 1942 there was still a very long way to go. One of the great weaknesses was the poor standard of all arms training and rectifying this became top priority. In addition there was the great shortage of artillery which resulted in a major expansion of the Indian Regiment of Artillery.

Although there had been Indian Mountain Gunners for a long time, they were strictly part of the Royal Artillery until all six regiments were transferred to the Indian Regiment of Artillery on 8th August 1939. The Indian Artillery as such had its birth in 'A' Field Brigade which was raised in Bangalore on 15th January 1935. One of its young officers was one Paramasiva Prabhakar Kumaramangalam who was destined to become one of India's most distinguished artillerymen, always known throughout the British and Indian Gunners as 'K'. 'A' Brigade became 1st Indian Field Regiment. In May 1942 'B' Field Brigade which had been raised at Jhansi became 2nd Indian Field Regiment which fought with such distinction at Gazala in the Western Desert where 'K', commanding 7th Field Battery won a DSO. Later 2nd Indian Field Regiment was to join 20th Indian Division at Imphal. These Indian regiments were a great success and by November 1940 1st Indian HAA Regiment, 1st Indian Anti-Tank Regiment and 1st, 2nd, 3rd and 4th Indian Coast Batteries had been formed in what was now called The Regiment of Indian Artillery. In 1945 the Regiment was awarded the title 'Royal' for its distinguished service in the war and this title, The Royal Regiment of Indian Artillery remained until Independence, when it became The Regiment of Artillery in India and The Artillery of Pakistan in Pakistan. A long-standing Alliance still exists (2000) between the Royal Artillery and The Regiment of Artillery of India and The Artillery of Pakistan in memory of those days.

At this time the ports of Calcutta (2 x 6-inch guns), Vizagapatam (2 x 6-inch guns), Madras (2 x 6-inch guns), Cochin (2 x 6-inch guns), Karachi (2 x 6-inch guns) and Bombay (4 x 7.5-inch; 3 x 6-inch and 2 x 4.5-inch guns) were protected by coast artillery. A Coast Branch of the Indian Artillery was raised for this purpose which, besides finding the men for these batteries, sent a regiment to Addu Atoll in the Maldive Islands to man 6 x 6-inch and 1 x 4-inch guns and later it sent a battery to Diego Garcia. The Ceylon Garrison Artillery manned the guns defending the Seychelles and the Cocos Islands as well as those at Colombo and Trincomalee.

The expansion of the Indian Army went on. Soon to follow were 3rd Indian Field, 1st Indian LAA, 2nd Indian HAA and 2nd Indian Anti-Tank Regiments. On 1st January 1941 No 1 Technical Training Battery became the Indian Anti-Aircraft Training Centre at Drigh Road Camp, Karachi. It was from here that 8th Indian HAA Battery had departed for Rangoon when the call came in December 1941. One problem was the provision of officers, especially for the anti-aircraft units. Many had to come from the mountain batteries and more from British regiments. Then in January 1941 the Indian School of Artillery moved from Kakul to Deolali and opened a Cadet Wing for young British and Indian potential officers. OP Malhotra was on such a course and was eventually to become Chief of Staff of the Indian Army in 1978. Prem Singh Gyani, who was in fact commissioned from Woolwich in 1932, became the first Director of the Royal Regiment of Indian Artillery in 1947. Then, as in the rest of the Army, once the war had started, Indian cadets destined for the Gunners went to the Military Academy at Dehra Dun, doing a short course after which they were granted Emergency Commissions.

By this time there were many depots and training centres opening throughout India devoted entirely to the expansion of the Indian Artillery.

Establishment	**Date**
School of Artillery, Kakul, then Deolali	Jan 41 1924
Boys Depot and Training Centre, Deolali	Dec 1939
Cadet Wing, School of Artillery, Deolali	Jan 1941
AA Training Centre (AATC), Karachi	Jan 1941
No 1 AATC, (HAA),* Karachi	Jan 1942
Field Artillery Training Centre,*** Muttra	Dec 1941
Mountain Artillery Training Centre,*** Ambala	Dec 1941
No 2 AATC, (LAA),* Deolali	Jan 1942
Anti-Aircraft School, Karachi	Feb 1942
Coast Artillery School, Karachi then Bombay	1941
AA & CD Wing, School of Artillery,** Karachi	Spring 1941
No 3 AATC*, Deolali later Mehgaon (in late '42)	Apr 1942
Coast Artillery Training Centre, Bombay	Early 1942
Counter Battery School,**** Deolali	Aug 1942
Royal Artillery Depot, Deolali	Mar 1943
Coast Artillery Depot, Bombay	Sep 1943
Shillong Gunnery School (Assam)	Late 1943
AA Depot	Dec 1943
LAA Training Depot	Mar 1944
Nos 1, 2 & 3 AATC*s merged as the AATC***	Jun 1944

Notes:

* 1 and 2 AATCs merged with 3 AATC in 1944 and all three formed the AATC.

** Retitled AA School towards the end of 1941.

*** In 1946 these training centres were reorganised to form two all-branches establishments: RIATC for southern Indian classes at Pollachi near Coimbatore and, for northern Indian classes, at Ambala.

****This was a GHQ pool of CB officers and clerks and was probably informally known as the Counter Battery School.

Running parallel to the training structure was the raising of the regiments and there were problems. One was that of language, India having many of them. It was decided that all business should be conducted in Urdu but there were some largely Madrassi AA regiments that preferred English. Second was the urgency. This resulted in two Rajput, two Rajputana Rifle, two Sikh and one Punjab infantry regiments being converted to anti-aircraft Gunners. After some misgivings this worked well and, as in the UK, the units retained their infantry titles. The final list of units raised is at Annex J. Suffice it to say here that in the end there were 11 field, two medium, 10 anti-tank, 18 LAA, 19 HAA, 14 mountain, four coast and one survey regiments by the end of the war, a total of 79 and a prodigious feat.

Major General WHB Mirrlees was MGRA India at this time, having succeeded Major General WPJ Akerman in March 1942, and it was he who made all this happen in the first place. He therefore became the 'Father' of the Indian and Pakistan Artilleries. He devoted all his energies to their expansion and by his leadership and guidance endeared himself to a generation of Gunners of that great continent. He was aided by another, Brigadier JM MacNicholl, BRA Southern Army India, who also devoted much time and energy to the evolution of the Indian Artillery.

On 29th December 1942 Wavell was told by London to prepare an Indian Base for 34 divisions, 85 RAF and 15 USAAF squadrons with a total of 240,000 British troops. These were in outline:

- 2nd and 70th British Divisions.
- 32nd and 43rd Indian Armoured Divisions.
- 7th, 14th, 17th, 19th, 23rd, 25th, 26th, 39th Indian Divisions available for operations in India or Burma.
- 20th and 34th Indian Infantry Divisions for Ceylon.
- 11th East African and 81st and 82nd West African Divisions.
- Equivalent of a further 18 divisions to include:
    - One parachute brigade
    - Three tank brigades
    - Four independent brigades
    - One Long Range Penetration Brigade
    - Forces on the NW Frontier
    - Remnants of the Burmese Army
    - Chinese forces in India
    - Local forces in Assam and Ceylon

When Java and Sumatra fell, by 12th March 1942, the Japanese had completed the first phase of their strategic plan. The isolation of China by the defeat of the British in Burma was at that time going well. Rangoon had been occupied on 8th March but the presence of a British fleet operating from Ceylon threatened Japanese operations in the Bay of Bengal (Map 23). Vice-Admiral Nobutake Kondo, commanding the *Southern Fleet*, was therefore ordered to attack the naval bases in Ceylon and at the same time to attack shipping in the Bay of Bengal and pose a threat to India. His mission was to ensure safe passage for Japanese shipping to Rangoon and to impress the people of India with the might of Japanese military power. We now know that no invasion was planned but that could not be assumed at the time. The Japanese judged it to be very important to show their power at a time when they perceived that Anglo-Indian relations were deteriorating. In addition to the naval attacks Vice-Admiral Chuichi Nagumo's *1st Air Fleet* which had attacked Pearl Harbour, was to do the same to Ceylon. As before a Sunday, 5th April, was chosen for the attack in the hope of finding the fleet in harbour at Trincomalee and Colombo.

1st Air Fleet was borne by five carriers of the *Combined Fleet* when it left the Celebes on 28th March 1942, escorted by four battleships, two heavy cruisers and 11 destroyers. Seven submarines were already on patrol in the area. Meanwhile Admiral Sir James Somerville had assumed command of the Eastern Fleet on 27th March. He had the modernised battleship HMS *Warspite*, four old 'R' Class battleships, *Resolution*, *Ramillies*, *Royal Sovereign* and *Revenge*, the carriers *Indomitable*, *Formidable* and *Hermes* together with seven cruisers, 16 destroyers and three submarines. The fleet had been gathered together from all over the world and had not trained as a formation. Within 48 hours of his arrival to take command Admiral Somerville began to receive reports of the approach of a major Japanese fleet which might well be directed at Ceylon. His fleet was scattered, some ships exercising near the Maldives and the rest between Colombo and Trincomalee. He immediately ordered his Catalinas to find the enemy and then formed two forces, 'A' under his own command and 'B' under Vice-Admiral AV Willis. These he took to sea to the south of Ceylon. By 2nd April nothing had happened and his fleets were running short of fuel and water. He also reckoned that the threat from enemy submarines was increasing. He therefore sailed for Addu Atoll, leaving HM Ships *Dorsetshire* and *Cornwall* to return to Colombo to finish their re-fit and HMS *Hermes* and HMAS *Vampire* to go to Trincomalee to prepare for Operation IRONCLAD against Madagascar.

Soon the Catalinas confirmed the presence of Admiral Nagumo's *Striking Force*. Admiral Somerville had been ordered to keep his fleet intact for the defence of the Indian Ocean. He therefore again sailed to the south of Ceylon, hoping to get his aircraft in range of the Japanese. At the same time Vice-Admiral Layton was expecting attacks on Colombo and Trincomalee and he cleared both of all shipping. Sure enough the Japanese attacks came in at 0800 hours on Easter Sunday, 5th April 1942. Thunder clouds hung over the harbours and there were showers of rain. The first warnings of large formations of aircraft approaching came at 0740 hours. The enemy, consisting of 91 bombers and 36 fighters, first flew over Ratmalana airfield and then dived onto Colombo harbour, bombing and machine gunning everything they saw. Damage was light, however, owing to the dispersion of shipping. Hurricanes of the Royal Air Force and Fulmars of the Royal Navy took off and engaged the enemy and by 0835 hours the Japanese had gone. A small force of Blenheims took off to bomb their fleet but could not find them. The British lost two Catalinas, 15 Hurricanes, six Swordfish and four Fulmars, claiming 19 enemy aircraft shot down. The anti-aircraft Gunners claimed a further five, 43rd LAA Regiment claiming three of these.

HM Ships *Dorsetshire* and *Cornwall* had put to sea to join Admiral Somerville when they were attacked by waves of enemy aircraft and both were sunk, although 1,122 men were picked up after surviving for two days in leaking boats in shark-infested waters under a blazing sun. The Japanese then sailed north and by 9th April were in position some 200 miles east of Ceylon. A Catalina gave warning and Trincomalee harbour was cleared of ships, including *Hermes, Vampire* and escorts. Once again, at 0720 hours, radar reported large formations of unidentified aircraft approaching. This time there were 91 bombers and 38 fighters. 55th LAA Regiment reported engaging this attack. Soon bombs were falling on the dockyard and the air field. All fighters were scrambled and, although they destroyed several of the enemy, eight more were lost. At 0840 a squadron of nine Blenheims attacked the Japanese fleet but were immediately counter-attacked by Zero fighters which shot down five, the remaining four were all damaged before they returned. No hits were observed on the enemy. Then the Japanese sighted HMS *Hermes* and her escorts and attacked them with 90 bombers. The ships did their best with their guns but by 1030 hours *Hermes* was hit and listing with her flight deck awash. A few minutes later she turned over and sank. Then each escort ship was sunk in turn. Although the British did not know it at the time, these attacks were to mark the end of the Japanese threat to Ceylon. At dusk on 9th April Admiral Nagumo sailed for the Malacca Strait, his job well and truly completed. Indeed Admiral Somerville had also done well not to lose more ships.

Meanwhile Vice-Admiral Ozawa's *Malaya Force* had been taking a heavy toll of shipping in the Bay of Bengal. On 5th April he was off the coast of India at Cocanada and Vizagapatam. Everywhere he met un-escorted and defenceless ships which he sank with ease. 19 were sunk on 6th April alone, some 92,000 tons. At the same time Japanese submarines sank a further 32,000 tons along the west coast of India. The threat was increased by enemy air attacks on Indian towns and villages. All this caused much alarm everywhere. After an air attack on Madras there was so much panic that 19th Indian Division was ordered there to repel landings which were thought to be imminent.

Although this Japanese action was no more than a series of raids, London was alarmed as to what might happen next. Auchinleck was ordered to send more aircraft to Ceylon which he could not spare. The Chiefs of Staff recognised that the fleet alone could not protect Ceylon and that Southern India urgently needed more aircraft and anti-aircraft artillery. What was more, much of the fleet was about to leave for Operation IRONCLAD anyway. The Prime Minister signalled Wavell and said that he was going to get US ships for the Home Fleet in order to release several fast capital ships to Somerville; meanwhile Ceylon must be defended by aircraft and guns, the numbers of which would be further built up. Throughout all this, however, there were demands to protect convoys in the Mediterranean and as if that was not enough the Australians were asking for their two brigades of 6th Australian Division back from Ceylon. Then two brigades of 5th Division and 22nd East African Infantry Brigade were diverted to Operation IRONCLAD. Wavell exploded! He was being told with one voice of the vital importance of India and Ceylon and at the same time he was having all resources promised to him removed. He pointed out that he had only three incomplete divisions with which to defend Assam, Bengal and Orissa. He had seven brigades in Ceylon and only one partly trained division in the rest of India. All this while India had seven divisions overseas.

Churchill said that he fully understood Wavell's concern and promised that the Australian brigades would not be removed until they had been replaced by 5th Division, that 2nd Division would be sent out from England as soon as possible and that 29th Independent Infantry Brigade would be sent to India as soon as Operation IRONCLAD was complete. Accordingly Wavell planned to relieve the Australian brigades with one East African and one newly-formed (in India) British brigade. This would enable him to keep 2nd and 5th Divisions intact when they arrived in May and June respectively. Wavell described this period as 'India's most dangerous hour'.

Yet the Gunner build up in Ceylon did go ahead. In March 1942 2nd AA Regiment, Ceylon Garrison Artillery (CGA), consisting of 1st, 2nd and 3rd Heavy and 4th Light Anti-Aircraft Batteries, was formed. At the same time 1st Coast Regiment CGA, consisting of 1st, 2nd, 3rd and 4th Coast Batteries, was also formed to be followed by 53rd and 54th Coast Observation Batteries in June. In May 159th HAA Battery arrived with 76th LAA Regiment and both were attached to the RM AA Brigade commanded by Brigadier WFB Lukis. Also in May came 52nd HAA Regiment which went to Colombo, less its 271st Battery which went to Trincomalee. 162nd Field Regiment arrived in June and joined 34th Indian Division. Then in July 20th Indian Division, with 114th and 115th Field Regiments, arrived together with 23rd LAA Regiment and 63rd HAA Regiment, both of which went to Colombo. Finally 3rd Indian Anti-Tank Regiment disembarked in July to join 34th Indian Division. The full order of battle is given at Annex H.

It is appropriate at this stage to look at the development of another part of the Regiment, the task of which was to man the guns mounted on merchant ships. Their formation and initial story may be found in the previous volume of this series, 'The Years of Defeat 1939-1941'. When Japan attacked in December 1941 she quickly overran the traditional trade routes in the Far East. Shipping along the east coast of India was attacked and by 21st May 1942 Calcutta was almost closed as a port. The Commander-in-Chief India reacted and soon Indian Army reservists were manning machine guns on coastal shipping, but it was not enough. The Maritime Royal Artillery was ordered to extend its operations and to man the guns on merchant ships in Eastern waters. An Eastern Shuttle Service, or ESS, was set up to provide Gunners on all ships operating east of 60 degrees longitude.

The Maritime RA staff to establish this organisation, consisting of eight officers and 113 other ranks, sailed from England in March 1942 and by 5th July they had established a Headquarters in Bombay, with Port Detachments at Bombay, Karachi, Colombo and Fremantle. The plan was that the Eastern Shuttle Service would absorb all Maritime RA personnel who were operating at the time within its zone and create a pool at Bombay. But this plan did not work well because men in the zone at the time the organisation was set up had already been allotted to their ships in the UK, were usually on a return trip and were trained for the specific guns on their ship. Masters of ships, not surprisingly, would not give them up. Also some 500 Indian Gunners were appointed to this task but this also did not work well on ships which did not have an Indian crew. Accordingly, in December 1942, a new organisation was established for maritime operations world-wide as follows:

8th Battery MRA (Western Atlantic).
Headquarters and Port Detachment in New York, with Port Detachments in Halifax and Trinidad.

9th Battery MRA (Egypt).
Headquarters and Port Detachment at Port Said, with Port Detachments at Port Tewfik and Alexandria.

10th Battery MRA (Indian Ocean).
Absorbed the Eastern Shuttle Service with Headquarters at Bombay with Port Detachments at Bombay, Karachi, Calcutta and Colombo.

11th Battery MRA (South and East Africa).
Headquarters and Port Detachment at Capetown with Port Detachments at Durban, Simonstown, Port Elizabeth, East London, Mombasa and
Diego Suarez.

In addition No 1 West African Maritime Troop RA was sited at Freetown and No 2 at Fremantle, although this moved to Sydney in January 1943. It was now that the status of Maritime Gunners was properly defined. They were to be signed on as members of the ship's crew and were fully under the master for discipline whilst remaining under their Maritime Headquarters for leave, training, records and pay. They were always to wear the uniform of the Royal Artillery.

At this time there were, world-wide about 7,000 British merchant ships in operational use. Each had its own anti-aircraft and some had surface armament. Many ships had as many as 11 guns and several machine guns and Maritime RA normally found about half of the 20-30 men required to man them, the rest being found by the ship and trained by Maritime RA NCOs while at sea. The manpower ceiling for Maritime RA was 11,200 and this was not enough as commitments continued to increase. In the interests of completeness it is worth continuing the Maritime RA story in the Far East to the end of the war. The structure described above remained until the end of 1944 when 2nd Maritime Regimental Headquarters arrived at Bombay on 26th January 1945 and absorbed 10th Battery MRA. The Port Detachment at Colombo became No 6 Ceylon Troop Maritime RA and No 2 Troop at Sydney expanded into 12th Oceania Battery to cover Australia, New Zealand and New Guinea. These moves were part of the plan to prepare for the expected invasion of Japan.

One example of Maritime RA operations in the Far East is the action fought by the MV *Ondina* at 1155 hours on 11th November 1942, some 400 miles south west of the Cocos Islands in the Indian Ocean. On board were Bombardier F Ryan, Gunner W Nichol and Gunner W Kidd plus five naval ratings. The armament was 1 x US 4-inch QF gun, 1 x 20mm Oerlikon, 2 x twin Marlin machine guns, 2 x single Marlin machine guns and 3 x 0.303-inch Lewis guns. At 1125 hours *Ondina* was sailing in a calm sea in fine weather with the corvette HMIS *Bengal* when they saw two large Japanese armed raiders bearing down on them from the west which opened fire at 9,000 yards. *Bengal* steamed straight for them but was hit and set on fire and had to sheer off. The Gunners on *Ondina* engaged with their 4-inch and hit the lead vessel, an armed merchantman of some 20,000 tons, in the stern but she kept coming and firing. Then they hit her again, this time forward, and she began to sink. The other enemy ship began to close, engaging *Ondina* all the time, but by then *Ondina* had expended all her ammunition, so Bombardier Ryan organised the dropping of smoke floats to conceal her movements but she was then hit and began to list. 'Abandon Ship' was ordered and the Japanese ship, of about 15,000 tons, circled and machine gunned the crew of *Ondina* in their life boats, killing three and wounding two, and then made off. Bombardier Ryan states, 'At about 1630 hours the Second Officer, 3rd Engineer, the Gunlayer and myself re-boarded 'Ondina' and inspected the damage which was in fact not too bad. She had listed to starboard so we opened a water tank to bring her to an even keel. The crew then returned and we got under way. . . The Japanese raider sank at 1345 hours. The great danger on the gun deck during the action was caused by shrapnel.' Bombardier Ryan was awarded the Netherlands Bronze Cross and a Mention in Dispatches for this action.

Most actions fought by the Maritime Gunners were against enemy aircraft but this was one of the few anti-ship actions they fought and did so with the greatest courage and resourcefulness. Although they fought under the single 'Battle Honour' of the Royal Artillery 'Ubique', they also had their own special motto, 'Intrepid Per Oceanos Mundi', 'Boldly over the Oceans of the World.' There can be no doubt that everywhere they lived up to both. Their story will be continued in subsequent volumes of this series.

To keep operations in South East Asia in perspective it is next necessary to look briefly at the overall situation in the Pacific (Map 24). Rabaul in New Britain rapidly became an advanced base for the Japanese *4th Fleet*. It was covered by the Japanese *24th Air Flotilla* as it advanced towards Guadalcanal. To counter this the Americans occupied Samoa and New Caledonia and reinforced Hawaii, Christmas Island, Palmyra and the Canton Islands. They also constructed a fuelling base at Bora-Bora in the Society Isles. Then an American fighter squadron was deployed to Fiji where the garrison consisted of two New Zealand brigades. The Americans next increased their garrison at Port Moresby to a brigade and opened a naval and air base at Espirito Santo in the New Hebrides. Finally the US 41st Division was sent to Sydney in March 1942. Thus the Americans had established a string of bases from which they could operate.

Although the Combined Chiefs of Staff recognised that Germany was the prime enemy, they also recognised that the situation in the Far East had to be stabilised before a second front could be opened in Europe. On 22nd February President Roosevelt ordered General Douglas MacArthur to take command of all US, Australian and New Zealand forces in the Pacific. This vast area was then divided into two commands; The South West Pacific Area under MacArthur and the Pacific Ocean Area under Admiral Chester W Nimitz. Both were told to secure and hold key positions in their respective areas, to check any further Japanese expansion and to prepare for offensive operations at a future date. 32nd US Division was sent to Australia and the Pacific Fleet was built up in strength after losses suffered at Pearl Harbour. It was at this time that the growing US power in the area was demonstrated by air attacks on Tokyo and elsewhere in Japan. Although small in size these raids had effects out of all proportion to the damage inflicted. The Combined Chiefs of Staff also agreed that the defence of India and the Indian Ocean, including Sumatra, remained a British responsibility.

By April 1942 the Japanese had achieved all their strategic aims without the loss of a single major warship. It was an astounding performance. There was much argument in Japan as to where the next strategic targets should be. The air attacks on Tokyo showed gaps in their defences which needed to be rectified but it was decided that, whatever else they did, they must bring the US Pacific Fleet to battle and the best way to do this was to threaten Midway Island, because this would also threaten Hawaii. At the same time they must continue attacks along the islands in the south eastern Pacific.

Plans were accordingly made to attack Port Moresby, in New Guinea, and Tulagi, in the Solomon Islands and a Japanese fleet began to assemble at Rabaul. News of this reached Admiral

Nimitz in mid-April and he too began to assemble a fleet under the command of Rear-Admiral FJ Fletcher. The Japanese invasion fleet left Rabaul for Port Moresby with a powerful escort including carriers on 3rd May. They made contact with Fletcher's ships on 7th May just south of the Jomard Passage. The Americans were quick off the mark and launched their aircraft which attacked and sank the Japanese carrier *Shoho.* Next day they attacked again and hit the carrier *Shokaku* which suffered severe damage. It was not, however, all one way. Japanese aircraft from the *Shokaku* and *Zuikaku* hit the carrier *Yorktown* but did not do much damage. The carrier *Lexington* was hit by bombs and torpedoes but she survived in so damaged a state that she had to be abandoned. She was then torpedoed by an American destroyer. The Japanese turned back and Port Moresby was safe for the time being. The Battle of the Coral Sea was unique in that it was determined entirely by carrier-borne aircraft. The opposing fleets never exchanged a single shot. It was also the first check of what hitherto had been an irresistible Japanese advance.

Next came the Japanese attack on Midway. They planned a diversion against Dutch Harbor, towards the eastern end of the Aleutian Islands, using two light carriers. The main attack was to follow using the *First Mobile Force*, of the *Combined Fleet*, under Vice-Admiral Nagumo who had returned from his operations against the British in the Indian Ocean. The whole attack was under the direction of Admiral Isokoru Yamamoto, Commander in Chief of the *Combined Fleet*. Once again Nimitz got wind of what was afoot and he reinforced Hawaii with men and aircraft and assembled a fleet to the north of Midway.

On 26th May a great fleet left its ports in Japan and with much confidence sailed for Midway. They were first sighted by an American Catalina patrol aircraft on 3rd June and then on 4th June US radar picked up large formations of aircraft flying towards Midway from the north west. Nimitz immediately ordered an attack on the Japanese carriers while their aircraft were away attacking Midway Island where they did much damage, although the airfields remained open. However the first air attacks on the Japanese carriers fared badly. The Japanese fighters were still there and they took off and met the Americans as they approached and the Japanese anti-aircraft defences on their ships were also effective so that no ships were hit. Of the 41 American aircraft which attacked only six returned, but these had formed only the first wave. Admiral Nagumo then made an error; he ordered his remaining aircraft to rearm, substituting bombs for torpedoes, to carry out a second attack on Midway on the assumption that US carriers were not present. After these aircraft had left, the American second wave arrived over the largely unprotected Japanese fleet and this time the US aircraft were dive bombers. They quickly sank the carriers *Kaga* and *Soryu* and they left the *Akagi* drifting helplessly. They returned and sank her the next day. But the Japanese struck back and severely disabled the *Yorktown* which sank after a further attack by aircraft from the *Hiryu*, the last of the large carriers in Nagumo's force. She herself was sunk shortly afterwards. This was a tremendous defeat for the Japanese. They had lost their whole carrier fleet, some 250 aircraft and the cream of their pilots. Yamamoto ordered the fleet to withdraw. The Battle of Midway was a great American naval victory, it marked the beginning of the end, it was a battle from which the Japanese were never to recover. The defeat of the Japanese would ultimately lie at the hands of American forces in the Pacific.

But the war situation was still serious. The Germans were still advancing in Russia, the Eighth Army had lost Tobruk, Malta was still under heavy attack and there was concern that being cut off, China might drop out of the war. The Russians were clamouring for a second front and there was argument between the British and Americans about whether to land in North Africa or France in 1942.

At the Cairo Conference in August 1942 Wavell was told that he might have to send two divisions to Iraq because of the situation on the Russian Front. In the end it was settled that he would send 5th Indian Division and 7th Armoured Brigade, 'However', he said, 'This would adversely affect what I can do on Operation ANAKIM' (the plan to attack down the coast of Burma and capture Rangoon).

In July the Joint Chiefs of Staff authorised advances through the Solomons and along the coast of New Guinea to capture New Britain and New Ireland, with a first phase of seizing the Santa Cruz Islands and a second to seize the Solomons and Papua. Admiral Nimitz was to control the first and General MacArthur the second. Then came the news that the Japanese were building an airfield at Lunga Point on the island of Guadalcanal. Accordingly the American 1st Marine Division attacked them on 7th August and soon had the airfield in their hands. This was to become famous as Henderson Field until the end of the war. The Japanese reacted swiftly and sent a naval force to deal with the US Fleet at Guadalcanal. They clashed at 0150 hours on 8th August and sank several US warships but missed the troopships which successfully landed the rest of the invasion force. However the US Fleet was then forced to withdraw leaving the US Marines isolated without naval or air support and short of artillery and supplies of all kinds. The Japanese decided that they must take Port Moresby and Guadalcanal and landed a force at Lunga Point on 18th August escorted by a carrier group. The Americans met this with a similar force and a battle followed on 23rd August which was inconclusive. By mid-September, however, the Americans had managed to land another 4,000 marines, securing Guadalcanal although they lost the carriers *Wasp*, which was sunk and the *Saratoga* which was seriously damaged. This left US forces in the area with only the *Hornet* still fit for action.

By September 1942 the Australians were building up their forces in New Guinea. 1st Australian Corps had arrived on 11th August with 7th Australian Infantry Division fresh from the Middle East. Brigadier LES Barker was CCRAA and became CCRAA New Guinea Force, taking control over 2/13th and 2/14th Field Regiments and a troop of anti-tank guns. A coast battery and the anti-aircraft defences of Port Moresby came under the command of HQ New Guinea Force. By this time the Japanese had captured Rabaul and also Lae and Wewak and other places in eastern New Guinea. In the early days in that huge island the artillery played only a minor part largely due to the great difficulty of moving the guns over such forbidding terrain. A force was sent to defend Milne Bay which included, apart from the main formation, 7th Infantry Brigade, 4th Anti-Tank Battery, a section of 23rd HAA Battery, 2/6th HAA Battery, part of 2/9th LAA Battery and 9th Field Battery of 2/5th Field Regiment. Three airstrips had been constructed and two fighter squadrons of the RAAF were stationed there. The Japanese landed in Milne Bay on 25th August and, after some initial success, were beaten off. Interestingly, as the Japanese withdrew out of range of the 25-pounders, direct action fuses were transferred from their projectiles to those of the 3.7-inch HAA guns which were then used effectively in the ground role. On 6th September the Japanese evacuated.

The fighting faced by the Australians in the early days of the Papua New Guinea Campaign was as tough as could be met anywhere. The Gunners played their part. Meanwhile the anti-aircraft Gunners protected the vital base at Port Moresby. The fighting was savage and was conducted with great gallantry in appalling mountain, jungle and swamp conditions often in continuous rain. The Japanese advance southwards was met by Australian counter-attack after the enemy had reached to within 25 to 35 miles of Port Moresby. Part of 2/14th Field Regiment RAA moved forward along the Kokoda Trail to cover possible lines of attack. 7th Australian Division, however, pressed the enemy strongly over the Owen Stanley Range. Two 25-pounders were manhandled forward, with infantry assistance, and were able to engage. 7th Division continued to drive the Japanese back to the north. Port Moresby was raided repeatedly and anti-aircraft gunners were kept busy. Eventually the Australians and the American 32nd Division, which had been detached to assist in retaking Buna and other Japanese-held points on the northern shore of New Guinea, succeeded in their aim. Artillery presence had been increased by such measures as dismantling a

25-pounder to get it forward, to the use of 3.7-inch howitzers in the hands of 1st Australian Mountain Battery and to the movement of guns by sea. 2/1st Field Regiment organised two troops for movement by air which was something new. By the beginning of January the enemy in Buna had been destroyed. Operations continued and saw the use of Wirraway aircraft to direct artillery fire. There was only a relatively small number of guns present but effective concentrations were achieved. During this part of the campaign 2/1st Field Regiment fired an impressive number of rounds in supporting infantry operations or in putting down harassing fire. A major problem was the shortage of ammunition and General Herring later observed that a C-47 load of ammunition could be expended in a few minutes. (Horner).

We must now return to the war against the Japanese in Burma. Before turning to the operations planned for February to May 1943 in the Arakan, and by Wingate and his Chindits across the Chindwin, we need to look ahead to see what future planning was in progress. Wavell had been prevented from going onto the offensive in Burma in the dry season of 1942-43 because of lack of resources and casualties inflicted by malaria. He met General Stilwell in October 1942 to discuss the options. Stilwell said that Chiang Kai-shek had agreed to attack south from Yunnan with 15 divisions if the British/Chinese/Americans would attack from Burma by 1st March 1943, provided that air superiority could be achieved over Burma and the Bay of Bengal and that top priority be given to the construction of a good land route to China through Myitkyina and Ledo (Map 25). This latter proviso meant supplying by air a force as far east as Lashio to cover the road construction during the monsoon season, which would not be easy.

When Wavell reported this to the Chiefs of Staff they replied that Operation ANAKIM further south was, in their view, of greater importance than operations in northern Burma. Thus Wavell told Stilwell that, apart from long range patrol activity, he could not operate east of the Chindwin before the monsoon in May 1943. Chiang Kai-shek cabled to complain to Roosevelt who said that opening the road was most important and he would contact Churchill immediately. Churchill supported Wavell and the Generalissimo then cancelled all operations from Yunnan on 16th January while the President met the Prime Minister at Casablanca from 14th -23rd January 1943. Here they reaffirmed that the defeat of Germany remained first priority but an island by island advance in the Pacific to re-capture Rabaul should go ahead. The capture of Rangoon, Operation ANAKIM, was to be top priority in Burma and a provisional date for it was set at 15th November 1943. This would start with amphibious operations to seize Akyab coupled with limited operations from Assam in order to start work on the China road. Wavell, a Field Marshal from 1st January 1943, returned to India and pursued his plans to build up his forces and logistic base to support these operations.

It was now clear that only limited operations could occur until the start of the dry season in November 1943. Major operations would then be launched to recover Burma in the period November 1943 to May 1944. These operations would include an advance by 10,000 Chinese from Ledo to Mandalay while three British/Indian and three Chinese divisions, with one in reserve, would advance from Tamu-Kalewa also toward Mandalay. Meanwhile five British/Indian divisions would be available for amphibious operations to take place down the Arakan coast and eventually spearhead an attack on Prome which would lead to an attack on Rangoon in January 1944. However such operations would demand a build-up of the Far East Fleet and the air forces, British, Australian, New Zealand and Dutch.

Wavell's next move was to go to 4th Indian Corps in Assam to consider what moves were possible in the dry season November 1942 to May 1943. He found that much work had been done on the roads as far as Imphal but that this must next be developed through Tiddim to Kalewa, protected and assisted by 17th and 23rd Indian Divisions.

At the same time the Japanese were planning an advance into Assam with *15th Army.* The plan was for *33rd Division* with some units of *55th Division* to advance on the axis Kalewa, Imphal, Kohima and occupy Dimapur and Silchar. Events in the Pacific, however, caused them to put these plans on ice and remain on the defensive until Allied intentions became clear.

So we come to the end of the Spring of 1943, although we have carried the narrative forward to look at the strategic planning in progress to cover operations further into that year. There was not much time left before the onset of the monsoon in May but Wavell decided to conduct operations southwards to seize the airfields at Akyab as a preliminary to ANAKIM and to mount Wingate's first Chindit operation in north Burma. It is to these operations that we turn next.

CHAPTER 8

THE FIRST ARAKAN CAMPAIGN

SEPTEMBER 1942 - FEBRUARY 1943

and

THE FIRST CHINDIT OPERATION

FEBRUARY - MAY 1943

(Maps 25, 26, 27 and 28)

The Arakan is covered by dense jungle growing on steep parallel ranges of hills which approximately follow the line of the coast on the Bay of Bengal. There are paddy fields in the valleys intersected by small streams known as chaungs (Maps 25 and 26). The water and the banks of the rice fields are an impediment to all wheeled and tracked movement. There is a narrow coastal strip running from Maungdaw in the north, where it is some two miles wide, to Foul Point some 45 miles to the south, where it is only a few hundred yards wide. Inland the Mayu Range rises to a height of some 2,000 feet and, in 1942, was crossed by only one metalled road running from Maungdaw through two short tunnels by way of Letwedet to Buthidaung. Otherwise there were only a few jungle tracks. To the east of the Mayu Range is the Mayu River, known as the Kalapanzin in its upper reaches. Further to the east lie the great mass of the Arakan Hill Tracts and beyond them the Kaladan river. The chaungs in many cases were tidal and could not be forded at high tide. The only means of communication were a few tracks and the rivers, the tracks being virtually unusable during the monsoon. Wheeled traffic was brought to a standstill from May to October when the rain is almost unceasing, malaria is rife and leeches lurk everywhere. From November to April the climate is reasonably pleasant, although there can be a heavy dew and a mist in the valleys for much of each morning.

On 21st September 1942, 14th Indian Division, under Major General WL Lloyd, was ordered to move at once to capture Akyab with its port and airfield. He had 47th and 123rd Indian Infantry Brigades and was not to wait for his 55th Indian Infantry Brigade. His artillery consisted of 130th (Lowland) Field Regiment of 315th, 316th and 494th Field Batteries under Lieutenant Colonel RAG Nicholson, younger brother of General CGG Nicholson, which had arrived in India in May with 24 x 25-pounders and had moved to Chittagong with 55th Indian Infantry Brigade. Here 494th Battery was re-equipped with six 3.7-inch howitzers. He also had, under Lieutenant Colonel BC Barford, 23rd Mountain Regiment, which consisted of 3rd (Peshawar), 8th (Lahore), 17th (Nowshera) Batteries, and 2nd Jammu & Kashmir Mtn Bty (ISF). This regiment had arrived from Kakul with 16 x 3.7-inch howitzers. Almost immediately 2nd Mountain Battery went off to join 4th Indian Infantry Brigade at Imphal. Later, on 1st October, it was renamed 31st Battery. 14th Indian Division also had 44th LAA Regiment under Lieutenant Colonel FW Bancroft with 75th, 91st and 239th LAA Batteries each of 8 x 40mm Bofors guns. They had come from 1st Indian AA Brigade.

Lloyd decided to move by sea to Cox's Bazar, which he reached on 3rd October, and by the 23rd he had patrols operating in Maungdaw and Buthidaung. He was then ordered, on the 17th, to establish a brigade in the Maungdaw - Buthidaung - Rathedaung area, another in the Cox's Bazar - Tumbru area and the third, 55th, at Chittagong by 1st December. By this time the Japanese were on the move and had small forces at Kyauktaw on the Kaladan river from *231st Regiment* at Akyab. This regiment then sent its second battalion north by river launches and its lead element arrived at Buthidaung just as the first patrols of 1/15th Punjab of 14th Indian Division arrived. After a sharp action the Punjabis pulled back to Maungdaw, leaving the Japanese to occupy an outpost system on the line of the metalled road.

In spite of appalling weather 14th Indian Division continued its arduous advance southwards. By the end of November 123rd Indian Infantry Brigade was in the Zeganbyin - Goppe Bazar - Bawli Bazar area with 47th Indian Infantry Brigade along the precarious line of communications which ran through Ukhia to Cox's Bazar. 55th Indian Infantry Brigade was still in reserve at Chittagong. The engineers did all they could to improve the roads and a small fleet of boats was used to form a sea link along the coast. Wavell decided that a direct sea-borne attack against the enemy was out of the question because of lack of air cover, naval support and landing craft. He therefore ordered Lieutenant General NMS Irwin, Commander Eastern Army, India to seize Akyab by land approach and a short sea landing from the tip of the Mayu Peninsula against Akyab itself. He was to be reinforced by 6th British Infantry Brigade Group from 2nd British Division. This included 99th Field Regiment (Royal Buckinghamshire Yeomanry), under Lieutenant Colonel MSK Maunsell, with 393rd and 472nd Batteries but less 394th Battery which stayed in India. He was also given a small fleet of boats. Lloyd planned to attack the Japanese positions around Maungdaw and Buthidaung on 2nd December with 123rd Indian Infantry Brigade, keeping 47th Indian Infantry Brigade in reserve but sending one of its battalions to 123rd Brigade. He then had to delay for two weeks because of the very heavy rain and the need to secure his lines of communication. On 16th December the Japanese, feeling that their advanced force was too exposed, withdrew *II/213th Battalion* to the line Gwedauk - Kondan on the west bank of the Mayu River opposite Rathedaung, so that when the leading British patrols moved forward on 17th December, they found both Maungdaw and Buthidaung abandoned.

As the monsoon abated the RAF, with a small number of heavy and medium bombers, began to carry out attacks on Japanese airfields and lines of communication. Fighter squadrons were established at Calcutta and at Chittagong to defend those places and Allied shipping in the northern Bay of Bengal. Assistance was provided by 10th US Air Force using heavy bombers against Rangoon, Mandalay and even Bangkok. But by this time the fighter units, of the *5th Air Division*, had moved back into Burma to renew their air attacks. On 26th October they carried out a surprise air attack on Chittagong, following this with further raids in December. Calcutta was also attacked, between 20th and 28th December, causing hundreds of thousands to leave the city thereby seriously affecting the work of the docks and of the public services. The arrival of some Beaufighters with night fighting capability, soon proved very effective and these raids stopped for a time. On the whole, however, the Japanese continued to hold the initiative in the air. 224 Group RAF, at Chittagong, was ordered to support 14th Indian Division in its advance down the Mayu Peninsula to capture Akyab. By the end of the year 6th British Infantry Brigade had concentrated at Chittagong and begun to train for the sea-borne assault on Akyab.

The advance continued. West of the Mayu Range there was an unmetalled track as far as Alethangyaw but beyond this the road had to be built with the advance. Lloyd then heard that the Japanese were in Kondan but air reconnaissance could not confirm this. On 22nd December he therefore ordered 47th Indian Infantry Brigade to attack, clear them out of the way and then build a fair weather track to Foul Point. Meanwhile 123rd Indian Infantry Brigade was to advance down the eastern side of the Mayu River and capture Rathedaung, while one of its battalions, 8/10th Baluch was to cross the hills from Taung Bazar and seize Kyauktaw to protect the left flank. Unfortunately this plan separated the forces of 14th Indian Division by both the Mayu Range and the Mayu river and this was to affect subsequent operations.

Brigadier EH Blaker, commanding 47th Indian Infantry Brigade, ordered 5/8th Punjab to move down the east coast with engineer assistance. It reached Indin by 27th December and 1/7th Rajput moved over the hills to seize Atet Nanra and Prinshe by the 31st. Progress was good and by the end of the month Shinkhali and Thitkado had been occupied although 1/7th Rajput had met the expected opposition at Kondan. 1st Inniskillings, the brigade reserve, was brought forward to Alethangyaw.

1st Lancashire Fusiliers of 123rd Indian Infantry Brigade, was ordered to move down the Mayu river by boat and capture Rathedaung which it did on Christmas Day. But having done so the battalion returned to Htizwe to report the town empty only to retrace its steps on the 27th to find it strongly held. At Htizwe one section of 393rd Battery and 'E' Troop 472nd Battery, of 99th Field Regiment, joined the brigade. The failure to hold Rathedaung was to prove serious and on 31st December the battalion was ordered to attack the town and re-take it. By 1st January 1943 the carrier patrols of 47th Indian Infantry Brigade had reached Foul Point and occupied Magychaung although Kondan remained in Japanese hands. Lloyd then told Blaker to capture Kondan as a necessary step before the attack on Akyab could be launched. This was done on 4th January only to find that the enemy had pulled out. But the situation was deceptive. The Japanese were in fact strengthening their hold on the tip of the Mayu Peninsular. They had reinforced Rathedaung and sent a battalion to hold onto Laungchaung and Donbaik at all costs. Lloyd next told Blaker to clear all Japanese from the tip of the peninsula but he soon met determined resistance and fell back to Thayetpyin.

Further attacks on Donbaik under the fire of the guns of 23rd Indian Mountain and 130th Field Regiments failed to dislodge the enemy. On 9th January 123rd Indian Infantry Brigade again attacked Rathedaung under the fire of two mountain batteries, but this also failed. Further attacks on the 10th did no better. FOOs at this engagement were Captain BC Bonsor, Captain A Stewart-Liberty and Lieutenant D Fastnedge, all of 99th Field Regiment. Thus both brigades were within sight of their objectives but unable to break through. Irwin ordered Lloyd to concentrate all effort on the coastal approach and to break through there. In turn Lloyd told Blaker to mount a two battalion attack on Donbaik which he correctly estimated was held by one enemy company. He was to have 130th Field Regiment, less one battery (16 x 25-pounders) and 8th Indian Mountain Battery (4 x 3.7-inch howitzers). Yet again the brigade suffered failure and with heavy loss, particularly among the officers, when the attack went in on 18th January. On the same day 123rd Indian Infantry Brigade renewed its attack on Rathedaung, this time from the east and by night, but again met only failure.

Lieutenant General S Iida, commanding *15th Army*, realised the vital importance of holding the Akyab airfields, Rathedaung, Laungchaung and Donbaik and he ordered his *55th Division* to hold them at all costs with the support of *4th Air Brigade*. It was this action that was preventing British progress. However, *55th Division* was still at Prome and could not arrive in its entirety until early February so it was going to be a race against time. Could the Japanese hold the British advance with their very small forces until the balance of *55th Division* arrived?

Meanwhile the British renewed their attacks and brought forward all their reserves and the rest of their artillery (Map 27). 55th Indian Infantry Brigade, under Brigadier JM Hunt, moved up to take over the advance, taking under command 5/8th Punjab at Laungchaung and 1/7th Rajput at Indin in order to do so, giving the brigade five battalions. The artillery before Donbaik was increased by the arrival of a troop of 4 x 3.7-inch howitzers of 472nd Battery, 99th Field

Regiment, together with eight Valentine tanks of 'C' Squadron 146th Regiment RAC. 71st Indian Infantry Brigade, commanded by Brigadier GGC Bull, of 26th Indian Division, was moved forward from Chittagong to replace 6th British Infantry Brigade as 14th Indian Division's reserve, thus making them available for the Donbaik operation. Brigadier Hunt with all the tanks and artillery was to attack Donbaik on 1st February while Brigadier Hammond was to take Rathedaung on the 3rd. But at Donbaik the tanks did not arrive until after dark on 31st January and there was no time to marry up with the infantry or to reconnoitre.

At H-Hour on 1st February, the tanks moved forward behind the fireplan but three fell into a ditch and the attack failed. The infantry tried and tried again but an enemy bunker, by then known by its target number 'Sugar 5', held them every time. Captain Barney Brooke-Fox, FOO with 1/17th Dogra had 'Sugar 5' under observation and engaged with all he had but the 25-pounders and 3.7s could do little damage to such a well-built earthwork. Meanwhile at Rathedaung, 123rd Indian Infantry Brigade had attacked with three battalions under the fire of two mountain and one light batteries and great gallantry was shown by the infantry but by the end of the day the attackers were back where they had started from. The Japanese had obeyed their orders to the letter. They continued to hold and in doing so enabled Lieutenant General T Koga, commander *55th Division,* to concentrate his formation at Akyab. The task which now faced the British, which had been so achievable in December 1942, had now become most formidable.

Wavell decided to make one more attempt and told Lloyd to attack down the coastal plain with 6th British and 55th and 71st Indian Infantry Brigades. This he did on 18th February and yet, after severe fighting and heavy casualties, the Japanese still held their ground. Lloyd withdrew 55th Indian Infantry Brigade to Buthidaung for a rest before it was to relieve 123rd Indian Infantry Brigade at Rathedaung. 47th Indian Infantry Brigade was still between the Mayu Range and the Mayu river. It then became clear that the Japanese were beginning offensive operations to outflank 123rd Indian Infantry Brigade to the east. They had taken Kamai and Batarai. It next became equally clear that 55th Indian Infantry Brigade could not withdraw until about 26th February because 71st Indian Infantry Brigade could not get forward to relieve it in time. Lloyd reckoned that it would take at least two weeks to clear the peninsula, which would mean that the latest an amphibious attack could be mounted on Akyab would be 15th March after which the weather would deteriorate. He therefore wanted to go onto the defensive. Wavell, however, would not hear of it and ordered a concentrated attack on Donbaik by 6th British and 71st Indian Infantry Brigades as soon as possible. During this period the Japanese had not been idle; General Koga began planning to go onto the offensive himself. He first intended to destroy the British forces east of the Mayu River and then to cross and cut off the British around Donbaik. It was then that the British inability to reinforce their flanks because of the river began to have an adverse effect on their operations.

By 27th February it was clear that the Japanese were indeed outflanking 123rd Indian Infantry Brigade at Rathedaung and were moving round through Kanzauk and Apauka. Lloyd ordered a general withdrawal onto 55th Indian Infantry Brigade which by then was at Buthidaung and Htizwe. By 12th March the Japanese were at Mrawchaung and Awrama and the situation was serious. At dawn on 14th March the enemy launched heavy attacks on Kyauktaw from the north east and were only driven off at the point of the bayonet and by accurate artillery fire at point blank range. By early 15th March 2/1st Punjab and 10th Lancashire Fusiliers, with such artillery as they could manage, got back over the Ngasanbaw chaung and formed a defensive position on the north bank. Then 71st Indian Infantry Brigade moved south from Buthidaung to Taungmaw to cover the withdrawal of 55th Indian Infantry Brigade. This move meant altering the final attack on Donbaik ordered by Wavell.

Brigadier RVC Cavendish, commanding 6th British Infantry Brigade, had six battalions, his own four plus 1st Lincolns from 71st Indian Infantry Brigade and 5/8th Punjab from 47th Indian Infantry Brigade. He also had 99th and 130th Field Regiments. The former had 393rd Battery with 6 x 3.7-inch howitzers and 'F' Troop, 472nd Battery with 4 x 25-pounders, all of which had come over from the Rathedaung sector. There were by then three enemy battalions in the Donbaik - Laungchaung area. Close by Donbaik village was a mound, 50 feet in diameter at the base and 20 feet high, covered by scrub and a few trees. This was the notorious 'Sugar 5', its number as a target. Converted into a bunker by the Japanese, it provided extensive observation for several mortar positions and from January 18th to April 5th it was attacked repeatedly, by infantry, artillery and tanks, always without success. The last attempt was made in March when the attack went in at 0540 hours on the 18th.

'. . . the [1st] Royal Welch Fusiliers attacked, after the usual accurate but ineffective bombardment . . . But it was all to no avail - and 150 good men of the Royal Welch Fusiliers lay dead or wounded on and around the mound.' A night attack during the early hours of 19th March by 1st Royal Scots was no more successful.

'Incensed by this terrible loss of life and their inability to help the infantry, the Gunners decided to go to extreme measures to avenge their friends.

'Colonel Mark Maunsell, 99th Field Regiment, ordered work to start on two gun pits on the edge of the jungle, *80 yards* from the mound, while 130th Field Regiment worked out a covering fire plan. By March 22nd the pits were roofed in and ready and trenches dug to enable the 3.7-inch howitzers to be brought up. [For gallantry at Donbaik Colonel Maunsell was awarded the Distinguished Service Order, Arthur Stewart-Liberty the Military Cross and Sergeant Roberts the Military Medal]. . . At this stage an urgent call for more guns from the Mayu front took away Colonel Maunsell and 393rd Battery less a section, with one troop of 130th Field Regiment, and Colonel Ronnie Nicholson took command of the operation. At 0830 hrs on March 23rd he . . . gave the orders for the bombardment and covering fire to start. The two guns of 393rd Battery opened fire . . . smoke from 25-pounders covered the hills and the Jap mortar positions in a dense cloud . . . the Jap's retaliation was almost nil . .

'By 0945 hrs each 3.7 howitzer had fired 100 rounds . . . but the mound still stood with its heart untouched.' (RAG Nicholson in Duncan).

The operation continued, a 25-pounder firing armour piercing shot and aerial attack by Vengeance aircraft were to be employed but Japanese success in the Mayu valley forced withdrawal.

The guns at Donbaik were 24 x 25-pounders of 130th (Lowland) Field Regiment, 315th, 316th and 474th Batteries, 10 x 3.7-inch howitzers of 99th Field Regiment and 4 x 3.7-inch howitzers of 8th Mountain Battery of 23rd Indian Mountain Regiment. These guns fired some 43,000 rounds of which some 2,500 were fired at 'Sugar 5' alone by the 3.7-inch howitzers. 'After the battle on March 18th, Brigadier Cavendish commanding 6 British Brigade wrote to the CRA, [of 14th Indian Division] Brigadier Dalton, '. . . We all appreciate so much the way in which you did everything you could to help us. It was also outstanding, and has been remarked upon by everyone, that not one shell in all that complicated fire plan damaged our own troops.' It is also recorded that one FOO of 8th Mountain Battery found himself engaging Japanese positions only 30 yards from his OP and then between himself and the guns. Many hundreds of rounds were fired in this way and not one fell wide, saying much for the consistent accuracy of the 3.7-inch howitzer and the high standard of laying by the Indian Gunners. (RAG Nicholson in Duncan).

General Lloyd then ordered 6th British Infantry Brigade onto the defensive and released 99th Field Regiment, less two batteries, to move with 71st Indian Infantry Brigade then at Zedidaung.

It was at this stage that Lieutenant General Takishi Koga ordered his second phase to begin and started his move across the Mayu river to cut off the British by seizing Indin. Accordingly on the night of 24/25th March, one regiment of *55th Division* crossed the Mayu between Pandas and Thamihlaywa covered by *5th Air Division*. When Lloyd picked up these moves he told 47th Indian Infantry Brigade to attack them at Atet Nanra from the south and 4th Indian Infantry Brigade, which had just arrived, to attack them from the north with 31st Mountain Battery. But 47th Indian Infantry Brigade was too spread to concentrate in time and could only form an *ad hoc* force under Colonel BH Hopkins, second-in-command of 6th British Infantry Brigade. 'Hopforce' consisted of 1st Royal Berkshires, one company and one platoon of 1st Royal Scots, three brigade carrier platoons, one troop of 130th Field Regiment and a company of 10th Indian Engineer Regiment. 'Hopforce' was ordered back to the line Indin - Kyaukpandu to block the western end of the pass. (Letter, Michael Dimitriadi). 4th Indian Infantry Brigade was held up at Praingdaung and never got off the ground to attack from the north. It was at this stage that, contrary to all orders, Lloyd ordered a general withdrawal. This displeased Wavell and accordingly he sent Lloyd on leave, to be relieved by Irwin who took command of 14th Indian Division himself. Lloyd had been under great strain and he needed a rest.

At this time 47th Indian Infantry Brigade was at Sinoh and Irwin ordered it to Indin as soon as it could move, which it did successfully (Map 28). But by then the Japanese were infiltrating towards the west coast everywhere and were almost at Kyaukpandu. On 3rd April, 26th Indian Division, under Major General CEN Lomax, took full command of all operations on the Mayu Peninsula. Lomax told 6th British and 47th Indian Infantry Brigades to drive the Japanese from Atet Nanra and Kyaukpandu and then to consolidate south of Cox's Bazar with a view to offensive operations southwards. He had one brigade holding the Cox's Bazar - Maungdaw - Buthidaung area with a fourth at Chittagong. But it was already too late. The Japanese had occupied Point 251 north of Indin and had established a road block on the coast road thus cutting off both 6th British and 47th Indian Infantry Brigades. Cavendish ordered an immediate attack to clear the block using 1st Royal Scots and a troop of 130th Field Regiment from the south but it failed. Events were moving rapidly to a crisis. 4th Indian Infantry Brigade tried to attack from the north but could make no progress. It was found possible to by-pass the road block along the beach at low tide. Lomax ordered 6th British Infantry Brigade to concentrate at Indin and then to clear the route and link up with 47th Indian Infantry Brigade.

6th British Infantry Brigade's attack went in over the chaung to the north of Indin on the afternoon of 5th April. The brigade was ordered to withdraw through Sangan Chaung to Kwason. They marched all night, blowing up two bridges behind them as they went. The new position was manned by 1st Royal Berkshires and 12 x 25-pounders of 130th Field Regiment. By last light 2nd Durham Light Infantry and 1st Royal Welch Fusiliers held part of the Point 251 feature and 1st Royal Scots held Indin. 99th Field Regiment report firing a barrage for the DLI on Point 251 and three other enemy strong points. A combined Gunner/Infantry patrol was out all day with Captain Bonsor as FOO and this kept the force informed as to where the enemy were. The 12 x 25-pounders of 494th Field Battery of 130th Field Regiment and 4 x 3.7-inch howitzers of 472nd Battery of 99th Field Regiment were well within range of Indin at Kwazon, and brigade headquarters was in a small copse between these guns and the infantry.

During the night the brigade commander realised the vulnerability of his headquarters and considered moving it into the gun area for protection but decided not to, a sad decision as things turned out. Nicholson had said that he would stay at brigade headquarters but all his kit was in the gun area, so Cavendish told him to return there. Between the guns and the feature held by 2nd DLI and 1st RWF was another feature held by an *ad hoc* group of Sappers and Miners. In the early hours the Gunners heard the sound of firing to their north and stood-to. At 0430 hours Nicholson was called on the telephone by Cavendish who said that his headquarters was surrounded and the end was near, he could only speak softly as there were Japs everywhere. He said that Nicholson was now in command of all troops south of Indin and was to order the commanding officers of 2nd DLI and 1st RWF to attack Indin from the north. No sooner was this done than the enemy closed in with grenades and the bayonet. The headquarters was overrun and Brigadier Cavendish and most of his staff were killed or captured. Nicholson passed the orders to the two infantry commanding officers, those to 1st DLI went via Captain Barney Brooke-Fox, their FOO. The dawn attack which Cavendish had ordered was successful and drove the enemy out of Indin but tragically Cavendish, who had been taken prisoner, was killed, according to a Japanese account by British gun fire.

By this time, however, the enemy had overrun the feature held by the Sappers and Miners and they thus directly threatened the gun position. Nicholson ordered a weak company of 1st DLI to protect the brigade's east flank and this was joined by Captain Mike Lawrence of 494th Battery as its FOO. He then ordered Major AL Awdry's 3.7-inch howitzers of 472nd Battery to engage the Japanese in the old brigade headquarters position with shrapnel. Colonel Nicholson describes the events which ensued: 'As the first shells burst above the shore, pandemonium broke out. The copse and surrounding ground became alive with Japs who began to run towards the hills, while others fired. Major Awdry then got down to it in earnest and the LMGs of the carriers joined in, moving up as close as possible. The infantry - DLI, RWF and R Scots on the far side also joined in and the Jap suffered heavily. . . . I ordered my Adjutant, Tom Selby, to collect reps from all the little detachments in our area and arrange for them to meet at 1130 hrs at RHQ for orders. . . The next task, while the OPs kept the Japs at bay, was to make a road over the belt of loose sand, in order to reach the hard shore.' It was not possible to break out before 1500 hours, as it was necessary to cross a tidal chaung which was too deep to ford until the ebb occurred.

Colonel Hopkins took command of 6th British Infantry Brigade and, on Lomax's orders, withdrew the remains along the beach to Kyaukpandu during the night 6/7th April without difficulty. Nicholson's account continues:

'The column started to form up in the trees at Kwazon. Mike Lawrence, still out in his carrier and exhausted with malaria, stuck to his job and increased the rate of fire. The first guns came out of action. At 1445 we tested the chaung and selected the best place to cross. It was just possible. The guns in the north started their smoke screen and cases of the smoke shells fell near our Start Point. Soon a good "fog of war" was formed, and with a cheer the first vehicle passed Major Awdry, now controlling the start, crossed the improvised road and made for the chaung.

Would it cross or stick? It was a carrier and, mistaking the marked crossing place, it stuck. This looked like being the last straw, and to make matters worse Jap mortar bombs began to fall in the vicinity. The next vehicle approached the right spot, the gunners leaned out with their rifles at the "ready". If ever men prayed hard, we who watched did then.

'Lurching and heaving the good old "Quad" waded through, and the gunners, yelling like mad, opened fire with their rifles as they passed the ill-fated copse. Again we stood, our hearts in our mouths, to see if there was any retaliation. In the din going on it was not possible to distinguish shots, but the gun and quad went on and passed out of sight round a bend in the shore. The rest of the column filed by, everyone at the top of his form; even the four Jat machine gunners, completely bewildered, grinned back and waved to us as they got ready to fire their Vickers guns from the side of their truck. . . . The smoke screen continued to be fired by Major Charles Laughton, commanding the guns in the north, the officers and gunners loading and firing for over an hour to keep it going. By 1615 hrs the last vehicles, marching men and mules were on their way. Our little rearguard of carriers was waiting. We did our best to destroy the few vehicles which had stuck in the chaung. "Mike" Lawrence, firing until the Japs were within 1500 yards of the guns and keeping them off till the last, had gone by with his troops.

'The scene at Kwazon had ended, but the battle had moved on up the beach. Here at their appointed positions the guns of "A" Tp. 315 Bty. under Lt. EG Walker, and "P" Tp. 494 Bty. under Captain DJ Mundie, having passed the Bde. H.Q. copse, and coming into full view of the Japanese on the hills 800 yards away, halted, unlimbered and brought their guns into action. Firing over open sights they blazed away with every round of ammunition they had, HE, Smoke and AP crashed into the Japs, while the marching men, the mules and the lorries and trucks moved on to safety under cover of this fire.

'Then occurred the great moment of this hectic day. The DLI, RWF and the Royal Scots, weary and exhausted, moving out from Indin to the beach in their disciplined and well-ordered columns began to file past in the rear of the guns. The sight of the Gunners now under fire from the Japs, sending shell after shell in retaliation, was too much for the magnificent discipline of the Infantry. Taking off their helmets they broke ranks and rushed up to the guns. As in 1811 "An English shout arose", but on this 6th April, 1943 it was a British cheer - from Englishmen, Scotsmen and Welshmen - which rolled out over the Bay of Bengal above the din of battle. Cheering the Gunners again and again and clapping them on their backs the infantry showed, in this spontaneous action, their appreciation of the co-operation given by the men of the Royal Regiment. . . When the last shell had been fired the Gunners, revving up the "Quads", limbered up and went on their way rejoicing that they had at last defeated Colonel Tanahashi and his redoubtable troops of 112 Japanese Regiment, and lived again to fight another day with the 25-prs. they had brought through to safety. . . For their actions in these operations Capt. MR Lawrence and Bdr. McCulloch of 130 Field Regiment received the Military Cross and Military Medal respectively.' (RAG Nicholson 'Indin').

47th Indian Infantry Brigade attempted to fall back on Indin which it found to be in enemy hands. It therefore split up into small parties and also dribbled back along the beach to Kyaukpandu. It was no longer a fighting force and was sent back to India to reform. Once again the Japanese had triumphed and exactly according to their time table. They next turned their attention to the Maungdaw - Buthidaung Line. By now all regiments were reporting much increased sickness, especially malaria and jungle sores.

Lomax withdrew 6th British Infantry Brigade to the Dilpara - Kingyaung area and 4th Indian Infantry Brigade to the Lambaguna - Godusara area. 55th Indian Infantry Brigade was at Hparabyin with 31st Mountain Battery, and 71st Indian Infantry Brigade was back on the line of the Saingdin Chaung. On 14th April all troops in the Arakan, including Chittagong, were placed under the command of 15th Indian Corps, under Lieutenant General WJ Slim, who found morale low from constant failure, strain and malaria. He told 6th British Infantry Brigade to hold Maungdaw, the Tunnels and if possible Buthidaung. He put 36th Indian Infantry Brigade, also in Maungdaw, under their command. 55th Indian Infantry Brigade was withdrawn to new positions between Seinnyinbya and Kanthe. On 24th and 25th April the Japanese attacked Kanthe. Although they were repulsed they did manage to hold onto Point 1102.

Slim considered that the time had come to review the whole strategy for the area. He considered the airfields at Chittagong, Cox's Bazar and Ramu were vital. Although he considered Maungdaw an important pivot for future operations, he did not like it because of its exposed flanks. He therefore ordered a phased withdrawal to the area Cox's Bazar - Ramu. This would force the Japanese to operate at the end of long vulnerable lines of communication on ground which was open and better for Slim's tanks and artillery.

On 2nd May the Japanese at Point 1102 began their advance onto Point 551 which commanded the entrance to the Tunnels. 36th Indian Infantry Brigade was at Letwedet, with 71st Indian Infantry Brigade holding the tunnels themselves. By 4th May the enemy had taken Point 551 and had crossed the Buthidaung road at Milestone 4. Slim said that Buthidaung was not vital and ordered all troops both there and to the south to withdraw through the Tunnels. Then, in order to meet any possible outflanking movement through Taung Bazar, he placed 23rd British Infantry Brigade and 160th Field Regiment, both from 70th British Division at Chittagong, under Lomax's command. By evening 5th May it was clear that the position of 55th Indian Infantry Brigade was critical, accordingly 36th Indian Infantry Brigade was told to cover their withdrawal on the night of 6/7th May. 55th Indian Infantry Brigade was forced to destroy all its transport but it did withdraw intact, while 36th Indian Infantry Brigade fought a rear guard action at Letwedet before it also fell back. Lomax next re-deployed to defend Maungdaw. He put 4th Indian and 6th British Infantry Brigades in the coastal area with 99th Field Regiment. 71st Indian Infantry Brigade and 8th Mountain Battery were defending the Tunnels exits while 36th Indian Infantry Brigade and 31st Mountain Battery held the Ngakyedauk Pass. 55th Indian Infantry Brigade with 130th Field Regiment sat in reserve at Razabil, 23rd British Infantry Brigade with 160th Field Regiment was at Bawli Bazar, with 1/17th Dogras at Taung Bazar. Slim remained concerned that strong as his position was, it could be easily outflanked, a movement dear to the Japanese. He wanted to pull back to Cox's Bazar, but Wavell did not agree. However, a compromise was reached and it was agreed that the line Nhila - Bawli Bazar - Goppe Bazar - Taung Bazar should be held whatever happened.

Accordingly Lomax then issued orders to occupy this line. He put 26th Indian Division on the right, with 71st Indian Infantry Brigade at Nhila covering the Teknaf Peninsula and the Naf river, 36th Indian Infantry Brigade in the centre at Bawli Bazar and 4th Indian Infantry Brigade on the left at Taung Bazar and Goppe Bazar. 6th British Infantry Brigade was in reserve at Tumbru. 23rd British Infantry Brigade was at Faqira and 55th Indian Infantry Brigade at Panzai Bazar to protect the flank. By this time 14th British Infantry Brigade had been moved forward to Cox's Bazar as force reserve. The RAF was increasing its ability to support the Army in the field and had begun to cause a lot of casualties and damage to the enemy through the medium of 221 Group, in support of 4th Indian Corps, and 224 Group in support of 15th Indian Corps.

The failure in the Arakan was, however, to have wide repercussions. Although 6th British Infantry Brigade was well trained and experienced after its battles in France, it was losing up to 50 men per day with malaria. Training was poor at the operational level. Commanders had still not learnt that in the jungle, frontal attacks, unless accompanied by overwhelming firepower, would never succeed. In the jungle it was impossible to deploy sufficient artillery even if it was available or to employ sufficient air power because tactical targets could not be identified. But even so the standard of all arms training was not as good as it should have been. The rapid expansion of the Army had not helped, as regular units were cut in half to create new ones and the whole level of combat effectiveness was diluted. Mark Maunsell recounts how, 'he was ordered to tell an FOO with an Indian battalion to place its Commanding Officer under arrest and order the Second-in-Command to take over. The FOO said this was not possible because the Second-in-Command was crying at the bottom of his trench.' Again, the Commanding Officer of the Royal Welch Fusiliers wrote on 2nd April, 'The 130th [Field Regiment] are a very different proposition to the 99th. They will not put their SOS fire nearer to us than 200 yards, - useless, when we've been used to 40 yards; this is rather strange to say the least.' (Dimitriadi). The failures at Donbaik and Rathidaung, where there was much gallantry, were directly caused by lack of all arms experience at brigade level and above. These failures gave the enemy the chance, which he took with great skill, of moving onto the offensive and using his well known outflanking tactics. It is also true that, due to lack of experience in training at the operational level, British commanders were out of touch with reality and constantly gave orders which simply could not be obeyed and this sapped morale further and caused more casualties which, in turn, were then replaced by untrained reinforcements. It was a vicious circle, caused in part by the failure by politicians to understand the military art before the war.

Undoubtedly the plan to capture Akyab was justified when it was planned in 1942 but, as the initiative passed to the Japanese, Wavell should have recognised the situation and pulled back earlier to the Maungdaw - Buthidaung Line. As it was, by May 1943, the British Army found itself back where it had started from the previous October, but many men had paid the supreme sacrifice by then.

Nevertheless, by August 1943, a pattern of operations was emerging in the Far East. The Americans had seized the initiative in the Pacific and were planning major naval and amphibious landings in the Philippines (Map 24). In New Guinea Australian and American forces had taken the offensive, but the tide had not yet turned in South East Asia. Here the British had been pushed out of Burma, China was cut off, the Far East Fleet had withdrawn to East Africa and the attempt to recapture Akyab had failed. The only success was Wingate's first Chindit deep penetration operation.

In January 1943 Wavell had to decide whether, and if so how, to employ 77th Brigade which Wingate was busy training in the long range penetration (LRP) role (Map 25). Since it was no longer possible to co-ordinate its action with a Chinese attack from Yunnan because the Chinese authorities had decided against it, there was no real strategic reason to employ a large brigade behind enemy lines. Wavell estimated that the Japanese had four or five divisions in Burma by this time and that they would remain on the defensive for some time facing the British along the Chindwin and the Chinese along the Salween.

Wingate, however, put forward six reasons why his force should be used early in 1943. First, he wanted to test his concept; second, his brigade was ready and morale would be affected if its planned operations were called off; third, he would be able to test the likelihood of Burmese support for subsequent operations; fourth, he could remove any Japanese threat to Fort Hertz; fifth, he could prevent enemy filtration across the Chindwin and sixth, his operations would interrupt any possible Japanese offensive against Assam.

Lieutenant Colonel OC (Orde) Wingate, a Gunner with a considerable reputation for the conduct of unorthodox operations in Palestine and Abyssinia, had arrived in India shortly after the fall of Rangoon in February 1942. Wavell sent him into the jungle with Major JM (Mike) Calvert RE to reconnoitre north Burma and report back on the possibility of guerrilla type operations. This he did, returning to Delhi to say that specially selected and trained forces supplied by air could indeed conduct operations behind enemy lines with an effect out of all proportion to their size. Wavell agreed and allocated him 77th Indian Infantry Brigade for training in special operations in July 1942. Wingate selected as his emblem the mythological beast, the 'Chinthe' which soon became 'Chindit'.

The story of the first Chindit operation carried out from February to May 1943 does not concern us here in detail because, apart from the all-important figure of Wingate, there were very few Gunners involved. However, because Wingate was such a key figure in the history of the Regiment, it is important to recount what happened in outline.

On balance Wavell agreed with Wingate's six reasons and ordered 77th Indian Infantry Brigade, now also in the long range penetration role, to move to Imphal to start operations on 8th February 1943. At the same time he gave orders for 111th Indian Infantry Brigade to begin training for similar operations. 77th Brigade then came under the command of 4th Indian Corps and was supported by a detachment of 31 Squadron RAF, with C 47s (Dakotas), to organise and provide air supply.

Wingate was given the task of blowing up the Burma railway between Indaw and Kyaikthin. He therefore organised his force into two groups. Northern Group, under Lieutenant Colonel SA Cooke, had five columns, Nos 3, 4, 5, 7 and 8, consisting of about 2,200 men and 850 mules. This group was to cross the Chindwin at Tonhe, move by way of Pinbon and strike the railway around Nankan. Southern Group, under Lieutenant Colonel LA Alexander, had two columns, Nos 1 & 2, and 142nd Commando Company. It had some 1,000 men and 250 mules and was to cross the Chindwin at Auktaung, move by way of Thaiktau, blow the railway line at Kyaikthin and then cross the Irrawaddy near Tagaung and make for Mongrit. It was to act as a deception operation for Northern Group. Brigade Headquarters was to move with the Northern Group.

Southern Group's deception plan worked well but its No 2 Column was ambushed and forced to disperse. Its remnants made their way back to the Chindwin. By 1st March Northern Group had reached Pinbon without meeting the enemy. Wingate sent Nos 3 and 5 Columns, commanded by Majors JM Calvert and BE Ferguson respectively, to destroy the railway around Nankan which they did very effectively. No 4 Column was to ambush the road from Pinbon then rejoin Wingate at Indaw. Nos 7 and 8 moved south towards Pinlebu to demonstrate in such a fashion as to cause the Japanese to move troops away from the railway. All this went well and the enemy sent troops to Pinlebu and Pinbon. The air supply system was successful almost everywhere. However, contacts with the enemy became more frequent as they began to realise what was happening. Wingate wanted to seize the landing ground at Indaw and then cross the Irrawaddy and make for the Kachin Hills. This he did, crossing the great river unopposed two miles south of Inywa.

By this time the Japanese realised that they had a major force operating in their rear areas and decided to devote a major effort to destroy it in the area east of the Irrawaddy and west of the Shweli rivers. It was here that Wingate's appreciation of ground had been faulty. This area was more open and better served with tracks than he expected, thus the Japanese could move rapidly and he was soon in real danger. He still wanted to get into the Kachin Hills to assess the mood of the tribesmen but every time he tried to cross the Shweli, he found himself in trouble. Then on 24th March, 4th Indian Corps ordered him to withdraw to India. This he did successfully but with difficulty. Of the 3,200 men who crossed into Burma at the beginning of February, some 2,182 returned to India four months later but 1,018 casualties, some 32% of the force, was a high price to pay.

On balance, however, the first Chindit operation was a success. Wingate's plans have been criticised for being too inflexible, which caused some confusion when events developed differently from what had been expected. But the plan, with its successful built-in deception measures, was well founded. Perhaps too little effort was made to co-ordinate the actions of the southern group with those of the northern but, on the positive side, the actions showed that such operations would work. They showed that air supply in the jungle worked well and that considerable damage and disruption could be achieved behind enemy lines. Indeed so enthusiastic were Wingate and some of his supporters that they saw such operations as the panacea for the future conduct of the war in Burma. One great advantage of the first Chindit operation was that it forced the Japanese to re-think their whole strategy and concept of operations in Burma.

At Casablanca in January 1943 Operation ANAKIM was approved in principle. It was designed in order to recapture Burma at the end of the monsoon in November 1943. The idea was that British forces would advance from Assam and the Chinese from Yunnan coupled with sea-borne landings in the Arakan to seize the vital Akyab airfields. All would be directed at Rangoon. Then, at the 'Trident' Conference in Washington in May, it was realised that, along with operations planned for Europe in 1943, these plans were too ambitious, so a scaled-down version was authorised.

It was also agreed to create a new joint Anglo-American South East Asia Command (SEAC) with a British Supreme Commander and an American Deputy. On 20th October 1943 Field Marshal Viscount Wavell was appointed Viceroy of India, General Sir Claude Auchinleck having become Commander-in-Chief India on 20th June heading a separate but equal command to SEAC. Lieutenant General Sir Henry Pownall became Chief of Staff to Auchinleck. At the

'Quadrant' Conference, at Quebec in August, it was agreed that Vice-Admiral Lord Louis Mountbatten should become Supreme Allied Commander South East Asia and that Lieutenant General JB Stilwell should be his deputy while retaining his responsibilities as Chief of Staff to Chiang Kai-shek and for the command of all Chinese and American troops in Burma. At this conference it was also decided that the top priority of operations for 1944 must be the capture of north Burma and the re-establishment of land communications with China. Amphibious operations to capture Akyab and Ramree were also to be carried out, but as a second priority. Long term planning was to start to plan an advance through Burma, to land at Moulmein and to advance into Siam and Malaya and to recapture Singapore. The tide was certainly turning.

Auchinleck was to develop north east India and Assam into a major base for mounting operations into Burma. It was to include the construction of new roads and pipeline systems and the building or expansion of a huge number of airfields. In addition the Chiefs of Staff said that larger deep penetration, Chindit-type operations were to be mounted to pave the way for the advance. The new Chindit force was to consist of six brigades, the existing 77th and 111th and 14th, 16th and 23rd Brigades of the 70th British Division and the 3rd West African Brigade of 81st West African Division. The Gunners were to be well-represented. 51st and 60th Field Regiments, both battle experienced from the Western Desert, were to become infantry while four troops of 160th Field Regiment and four troops of 69th LAA Regiment were to operate with the force in their prime role with guns.

By August 1943 the frontier with Burma, some 700 miles long, was divided into three sectors:

Southern. This stretched from the Bay of Bengal across the Mayu Hills to the Kaladan valley and was based on Chittagong. It was held by Major General Lomax's 26th Indian Infantry Division.

Central. This ran from the Chin Hills to the Naga Hills which covered the approaches to Imphal and Kohima. It was based on Imphal and was held by Lieutenant General Scoone's 4th Corps of 17th Indian Light and 23rd Indian Infantry Divisions.

Northern. This was based on Ledo and covered the routes into northern Assam from Myitkyina. It was held by Lieutenant General Stilwell and his 22nd, 30th and 38th Chinese Divisions.

The Arakan and Central Fronts came under the commander of the Eastern Army, General Sir George Giffard, whose BRA was Brigadier GEW Franklyn and later Brigadier DW Bannister. The Army reserve at this time was 15th Indian Corps under Lieutenant General WJ Slim. The senior artillery appointments were then:

CCRA 15th Indian Corps	Brigadier GdeV Welchman
CRA 20th Indian Division*	Brigadier LA Harris
CRA 5th Indian Division**	Brigadier HK Dimoline
CRA 7th Indian Division**	Brigadier AF Hely
CRA 81st West African Division**	Brigadier JAE Hirst
CRA 2nd British Division***	Brigadier J D Shapland

* At Ranchi
** To arrive before the end of 1943
*** Undergoing amphibious training

By mid-November, and after much discussion, Mountbatten proposed seven separate but related operations for 1944, as follows:

1. The capture of the Andaman Islands by amphibious assault, Operation BUCCANEER.
2. The advance of 15th Indian Corps to seize the line Maungdaw - Buthidaung - Kyauktaw and the exploitation to Akyab.
3. The advance of the 4th Indian Corps to the Chindwin.
4. The advance of Stilwell's Chinese from Ledo to Mogaung - Myitkyina.
5. The advance of the Chinese from Yunnan to Bhamo and Lashio.
6. The capture of Indaw by parachute assault, Operation TARZAN, and the fly-in of a division.
7. Operations by the (Chindit) Long Range Penetration Groups to assist the attacks on Indaw and the operations by Stilwell's Chinese.

In the event the effect of operations in Europe and of the failure of the Chinese to agree to co-operate from Yunnan forced Mountbatten to adopt even less ambitious plans as we shall see.

By this time the Gunners in the Far East had expanded to a powerful force of some 28 field regiments (ten of them Indian), three medium regiments, ten LAA/anti-tank regiments, three anti-tank regiments, three LAA regiments, two HAA regiments, three light batteries, seven mountain regiments and a survey battery.

Much work was in hand to improve logistic stocks, communications and administration generally. Training was in full swing and much attention was given to fitness and medical precautions. Morale and welfare were improved to counter the feeling of being 'forgotten'. Before this programme started in 1943, for every man wounded in action there were 120 sick. Hospitals were overcrowded, dysentery was endemic and malaria serious. Feeding was also a problem with an army of so many diverse races, castes and religions. Provision of fresh meat of the right sort was a particular problem. But during 1943 all these problems were much reduced by great efforts by many people.

The work in hand to create a new and larger long range penetration force under Wingate's command continued. This new formation became 3rd Indian Division. Finding the right men was a real problem, as only the most experienced and the best would do. In training Wingate drove his new command hard and did not make many friends with those doing their best to help by his brusque remarks, but it was his drive and energy that got it ready for operations by 15th January 1944. Fired by Wingate's enthusiasm, 'Mountbatten had in turn persuaded General [HH] Arnold, head of the United States Army Air Force, to provide the 3rd Indian Division with an American force, known as No. 1 Air Commando, containing not only fighters and light bombers for close support, but transport aircraft, gliders, light planes for inter-communication and evacuation of the wounded, and the necessary maintenance organization. The pilots were carefully chosen and the commando raised and commanded by Colonels [PC] Cochran and [JR] Alison, both outstanding fighter aces, and . . . first-class organizers and leaders.' (Slim). The commando, consisting of 30 P 51 Mustang fighter-bombers, 12 B 25 Mitchell medium bombers, 13 C 47 Dakota and 12 C 46 Commando transports, 100 L 5 light aircraft, six helicopters and 225 gliders (Kirby), did much to develop the techniques of air supply which were to last long after the end of the war.

The American Chiefs of Staff were impressed by Wingate's description of LRP operations at the 'Quadrant' conference in August 1943 and set about recruiting some 3,000 men to be jungle-trained to form part of his force. These became the 5307th Composite Unit (Provisional), which was later known as 'Merrill's Marauders' after its commander Brigadier-General FD Merrill.

On 15th October 1943 Eastern Army became 14th Army and the former Eastern Command was recreated. The new army commander was Lieutenant General WJ Slim and his formation was spread out over 700 miles from the border with China, east of Fort Hertz, to the Bay of Bengal. This army formed part of 11th Army Group under General Sir George Giffard which also had responsibility for the defence of the rest of India and Ceylon.

By September 1943 the situation had changed a great deal. On the Southern Front the untried but well-trained 7th Indian Division, under Major General FW Messervy, had relieved 26th Indian Division and had concentrated astride the Mayu Range. The experienced 5th Indian Division, commanded by Major General HR Briggs, which had extensive battle experience from Eritrea and the Western Desert, moved to the west of the Mayu Hills. Both were in contact with Japanese outposts. On the Central Front 20th Indian Division, under Major General DD Gracey, which had been relieved in Ceylon by 11th East African Division, had relieved 23rd Indian Division, commanded by Major General OL Roberts, in the Kabaw valley. The Japanese at this time were at Yazagyo and Mawlaik. 23rd Indian Division moved into 4th Indian Corps reserve at Imphal. Early in October 63rd Indian Infantry Brigade of 17th Indian Division made contact with strong enemy probes around Fort White, Tiddim and Kennedy Peak and was reinforced by a battalion. Later 48th Indian Infantry Brigade, also from 17th Indian Division, was ordered up to Tiddim when 63rd Indian Infantry Brigade had been forced back to the area of Vengte. At this point 17th Indian Division took command of operations along the Tiddim Road.

On the Northern Front 38th Chinese Division met the Japanese *18th Division* near the junction of the rivers Tanai and Tarung in the Hukawng valley as it advanced to cover road construction.

Thus there was contact all along the 700 mile frontier. What is more the Japanese had the use of the Burmese airfields and this posed a serious threat to the Allies and to the air route to China. Allied airfields were a long way away in India, with too few aircraft and an inadequate warning system.

SEAC became operational in Delhi on 16th November 1943. Admiral Sir James Somerville was Commander-in-Chief Far East Fleet, General Sir George Giffard was Commander-in-Chief 11th Army Group and Air Chief Marshal Sir Richard Pierse was Air Officer Commanding-in-Chief. All had other tasks and other masters but all reported to Lord Louis Mountbatten on operations in South East Asia.

11th Army Group had Ceylon Army Command, made up of 11th East African Division and 99th Indian Infantry Brigade and some other bases in India, and 14th Army consisted of 15th Indian Corps on the Arakan Front, 4th Indian Corps on the Central Front and 33rd Indian Corps in reserve. 15th Indian Corps was by then commanded by Lieutenant General AFP Christison and comprised 5th and 7th Indian and 81st West African Divisions. 4th Indian Corps was commanded by Lieutenant General GAP Scoones and consisted of 17th, 20th and 23rd Indian Divisions. 26th Indian Division and 254th Indian Tank Brigade were in Army reserve. 33rd Indian Corps, not yet assigned to SEAC, was commanded by Lieutenant General MGN Stopford and had 2nd British, 19th, 25th and 36th Indian Divisions, 50th Indian Tank Brigade, 50th Indian Parachute Brigade, Special Force, and 3rd Special Service Brigade, consisting of 5th Commando and 44th Royal Marine Commando.

With the integration of Allied air forces in December 1943, Air Command South East Asia had 67 squadrons. The RAF at this time had 43, the RIAF three, the RCAF one, the R Neth AF one and the USAAF 19. Part of this command formed 3rd Tactical Air Force under Air Marshal Sir John Baldwin, a Strategic Air Force under Brigadier General HC Davidson, USAAF, Troop Carrier Command under Brigadier General WD Old, USAAF, and a Photographic Reconnaissance Force under Group Captain SG Wise. As we have seen, 3rd Tactical Air Force put 224 Group in support of 15th Indian Corps and 221 Group in support of 4th Indian Corps with Northern Air Sector Force in support of the Northern Front. Allied air forces had an effective strength of some 850 aircraft of all types whereas the Japanese in Burma had about 200.

On 15th April 1944 Headquarters SEAC moved from Delhi to Kandy in Ceylon where it was alongside Headquarters Far East Fleet, but Headquarters 11th Army Group remained in Delhi. General Giffard and the AOC-in-C, Air Marshal Pierse, could not move to Ceylon as both depended on India Command and both were deeply involved in Assam.

By November 1943, the war situation appeared to be improving. The Battle of the Atlantic had reached its turning point the previous summer, the successful North African campaigns had re-opened the Mediterranean route to the Far East, the Italians had surrendered and the Allies had captured Naples. The Russians were on the offensive and had recaptured Kiev. In the Pacific, offensive operations were successful everywhere. It was clear that the invasion of Europe would take place in 1944 and it was also clear that the defeat of Germany would remain the top priority.

Both Mountbatten and Chiang Kai-shek attended the next summit conference in Cairo on 22nd November 1943 codenamed 'Sextant'. It was agreed, after much argument, that Operation TARZAN, the re-capture of Burma, should be carried out in the dry season 1943/44 and that Operation BUCCANEER, the re-capture of the Andaman Islands, should follow as soon as possible. But it then became clear that there were not enough landing craft for BUCCANEER, the invasion of Europe, Operation OVERLORD and the invasion of the south of France, Operation ANVIL. Accordingly BUCCANEER was cancelled. Next the strategy for the defeat of Japan was agreed. Priority would be with the Americans in the Pacific where a ring of airfields would be seized within range of Japan from which bombers could operate in strength. Then once Germany was defeated, the British would send four divisions to Australia for service in the Pacific together with strong naval and air forces. Operations in South East Asia were reduced to the capture of upper Burma to re-establish the air and land routes to China and only then to extend operations southwards for the capture of Rangoon and onwards to Malaya and Singapore.

Although Mountbatten reduced the scope of Operation TARZAN, he included smaller amphibious operations against Akyab. It was then learned that after all Chiang Kai-shek would not move his forces out of Yunnan until the whole of Burma had been retaken. It was also learned that there were still not enough landing craft so the Akyab landings were also cancelled and it was decided to rely on a land advance southwards to capture the airfields there. Thus the plan was much reduced, as follows:

> The Northern Front was to advance to Mogaung - Myitkyina to cover the road building from Ledo.
>
> 4th Indian Corps was to consolidate the Imphal - Tamu road and to move east of the Chindwin in support of Wingate's penetration forces.
>
> 15th Indian Corps was to advance south and capture Akyab.

But the Japanese were also planning their future operations. Recognising that their initial successes had if anything over-extended them, they decided to push forward and create a safety net around their gains in a period of aggressive consolidation. They could see that, with Italy's surrender and with Germany bogged down in Russia, defeated in North Africa and facing imminent landings in France, they were very much on their own in the Far East. They decided, therefore, to consolidate where they were. There would be no more strategic offensives. Japanese forces must hold all gains at all costs.

Lieutenant General Renya Mutaguchi, commanding *15th Army* in Burma, recommended an advance to Imphal before any large scale British offensive could be launched. Accordingly *56th Division* was told to hold the Chinese on the line of the Salween River, *18th Division* was to stop the 'western' Chinese in the Hukawng valley thus preventing any advance from Ledo, and *15th*

Army itself, with *15th, 31st and 33rd Divisions,* was to seize Imphal and Kohima and advance beyond to ensure the defence of Burma. *55th Division* was to hold the Arakan and in particular the Akyab airfields. *15th Army's* plan was for *33rd Division* to take Imphal by way of the Kabaw valley, while *31st and 15th Divisions* would cross the Chindwin and advance on Kohima and then attack Imphal from the north. General Mutaguchi estimated that these operations would take three weeks. He then formed *33rd Army Headquarters* to control all operations in the north of Burma and *18th Army Headquarters* to do the same in southern Burma, to which he added the *2nd* and *54th Divisions. 5th Air Division,* of *3rd Air Army,* would provide air cover and D-Day would be 15th March 1944 but preceded by the advance of *33rd Division* towards Imphal starting on 8th March. There were great logistic risks in these plans but these were accepted in the belief that all operations would be complete by the end of the first week in April. But military operations have a habit of failing when they have known risks built into them because enough will go wrong anyway and this is what was about to happen.

By this time in the war the Allies had learnt many lessons about the handling of artillery in the jungle. First it was clear that close targets really meant close. FOOs had to be right in the very front positions otherwise they were almost useless. Targets were sometimes no more that 30-50 yards away so gun-laying had to be extremely accurate. It was not only the jungle that impeded movement, but the chaungs, paddy fields and swamps made wheeled movement extremely difficult. Tracks, such as they were, were very narrow and overgrown so that cumbersome and heavy vehicles found the going very difficult indeed. This was to some extent true with the 25-pounder which in its normal form was too heavy and too wide, but it was essential to have it available in all operations because of its range, flexibility, accuracy and hitting power.

The solution was to go for a mix of modified 25-pounders, 3.7-inch howitzers and 3-inch mortars. The British reduced the axle length of the 25-pounder and removed the platform. The result was known as the 'Jury Axle 25-pounder.' The Australians in New Guinea had similar problems and their solution was to build a smaller 25-pounder with a shortened barrel known as the 'Baby 25-pounder' This tended to be less stable on firing and had less range, though that was of relatively minor importance in jungle fighting anyway. Details of these two guns are at Annex L.

The British in Burma then re-organised so that the new light divisions would each have one light field regiment of 24 x jury axle 25-pounders, 2 x light mountain regiments (each of two batteries, each of 4 x 3.7-inch howitzers with mules and horses) and one battery of 16 x 3-inch mortars. They also had one LAA/anti-tank regiment of 24 x 40mm and 24 x 2-pounders. An infantry division was to have one field regiment of 24 x (normal) 25-pounders, 1 x jungle field regiment (of two batteries each of 8 jeep-towed 3.7-inch howitzers and one battery of 16 x 3-inch mortars) plus one mountain regiment (of four batteries each of 4 x 3.7-inch howitzers). It also had one LAA/anti-tank regiment of 24 x 40mm and 24 x 6-pounders. An armoured division was to have two field regiments (each of two batteries, each of 8 x 25-pounders, and one battery of 8 x 105mm Priest SP guns), one anti-tank regiment (of 36 x 6-pounders and 12 x 57mm guns) and one LAA regiment of 54 x 40mm guns. Finally, an assault division was to have three assault field regiments (each of one battery of 8 x 25-pounders, one battery of 8 x 105mm Priest SP guns and one battery of 6 x 3.7-inch howitzers).

Observation was also a major problem in jungle operations. A battery might need up to four OPs out at a time. Radios were noisy, a problem when OPs were close to the enemy, and unreliable so a great deal of line had to be used and this meant an increased establishment of signallers. Tanks were not suitable as OPs in the jungle. When closed down the FOO could not see and if he opened up he stood a good chance of being shot by a sniper. Thus consideration was given to the use of aerial observation at the end of 1943. This had begun in Europe and was proving highly successful in North Africa. Accordingly, in November, 656 Air Observation Post (AOP) Squadron RAF was formed in England. Its pilots were gunner officers and the ground crews mixed Army, RA and REME, and Royal Air Force. The squadron was warned for service in India and arrived at Bombay in January 1944 under the command of Major Denis Coyle. It went to train at the School of Artillery at Deolali using some Tiger Moths which were available before enough Auster Mark IIIs arrived to equip 'B' Flight. It was to be operational by the end of January. The establishment and details of 656 AOP Squadron are at Annex M. The story of the significant impact this squadron was to have on operations in Burma is told in subsequent chapters.

Finally there was the problem of 'bunker busting', as we saw in the operations at Donbaik. It was soon found that the best way to deal with Japanese bunkers was to use 25-pounders or 3.7-inch howitzers to blow away the cover, expose the target and establish its co-ordinates. Having done this, a 5.5-inch medium gun was brought up to within 800 yards or less. This gun would usually destroy any bunker in about 15 rounds. Later it was found that the same thing could be done with a 25-pounder provided it could get within 600 yards of the bunker and soften up the target first with some armour-piercing shot. The 6-pounder anti-tank gun could also be used but it had to be within 100-300 yards.

Large concentrations of fire had not been used so far in the Far East. Targets were normally engaged by individual troops of up to four guns. To increase this posed considerable survey problems. As we shall see, however, this was to change and guns were eventually used most effectively in large numbers in the Second Arakan, Kohima/Imphal and Irrawaddy crossing campaigns. However barrages and timed programmes were seldom successful as it was virtually impossible to predict the speed that infantry could achieve in following the fall of shot and, in any case, ammunition for them was seldom available. This meant that fireplans were usually FOO-controlled concentrations. Ammunition supply was always a problem in jungle operations and the solution was to use air drops as much as possible. This was done with considerable success.

So with a major build up of field, medium, anti-aircraft and anti-tank artillery, both British and Indian, the effect of the guns on the war in Burma was about to change. In the great battles to come in 1944 they were to play a major part and these were to be the battles that saw the turn of the tide from the long run of defeats into a long run of victories at last.

5. Maritime Artillery in training in 1943 (IWM)

6. A camouflaged 3.7-in Mountain gun, Arakan. (IWM)

7. Observing mortar and shell fire on Japanese positions, Arakan, March 1944. (IWM)

8. Indian mountain artillery ammunition column, March 1944. (IWM)

CHAPTER 9

THE SECOND ARAKAN CAMPAIGN

SEPTEMBER 1943 - JUNE 1944

and

THE SECOND CHINDIT OPERATION

NOVEMBER 1943 - MARCH 1944

(Maps 29, 30, 31, 32, 33 and 34)

One of the characteristics of Allied planning in South East Asia in 1943 was the constant need to change plans almost as soon as they were agreed. Because of the pressures from the European theatre, there were never enough landing craft or logistic stocks. At the 'Trident' Conference, in Washington in May 1943, the Combined Chiefs of Staff had to agree that for these reasons there could be no full scale Operation ANAKIM, the plan for a major offensive for the re-conquest of Burma over the period November 1943 to March 1944. Field Marshal Sir Claude Auchinleck, Commander-in-Chief India, was to plan for operations in the Far East, build up the Indian Army, the Indian logistic base and defend the North West Frontier, while Vice-Admiral Lord Louis Mountbatten, the newly-appointed Supreme Allied Commander, South East Asia, was to assume responsibility for the conduct of operations against the Japanese throughout the theatre.

Arising from the 'Quadrant' Conference in Quebec in August 1943, Auchinleck was told that the main effort in his theatre was to be an offensive to create a land route to China and to secure the air route. He was to plan a three-pronged attack to achieve this in 1944 consisting of advances from Ledo, the Chindwin andYunnan (Map 29). He was to plan for amphibious attacks to capture Akyab and Ramree, to secure airfields for operations in mid and southern Burma as a second priority. He was also to build up India as a base for future operations. Meanwhile the Americans and the Australians were to capture the Gilbert and Marshall Islands, Ponape and the eastern Caroline Islands, Palau and Yap, Guam and the Japanese Marianas (Map 24). In New Guinea, advances by the Australians and the Americans were to expand to the extent of taking or neutralising the eastern part of the island and achieve the same against the Admiralty Islands and the Bismarck Archipelago, Rabaul being neutralised if at all possible. Auchinleck was also to study subsequent operations against Sumatra, Singapore and the Kra Isthmus.

Against this strategy, Mountbatten first settled his immediate plans for the forthcoming offensive because time was already short (Map 29). Responsibility for the Northern Front rested with Lieutenant General JW Stilwell's Northern Combat Area Command (NCAC). He had 38th Chinese Division covering the construction of the Ledo road over the Pangsau Pass into the Hukawng valley, with 22nd Chinese Division in reserve. 4th Indian Corps, under Lieutenant General GAP Scoones, held the Central Front, with 17th Indian Light Division, Major General DT Cowan, at Tiddim and Fort White, and 23rd Indian Division, Major General OL Roberts, covering the approaches to Imphal and Kohima from the Kabaw Valley. The Arakan Front was the responsibility of 26th Indian Division, commanded by Major General

CEN Lomax. Both the Arakan and Central Fronts were under Eastern Army commanded by General Sir George Giffard. 15th Indian Corps, commanded by Lieutenant General WJ Slim, consisting only of 20th Indian Division, was in reserve at Ranchi. This structure was about to change.

As we have seen, throughout the summer of 1943 numerous plans of action for the 1943-44 campaigning season were discussed with London and Washington but in each case they had to be altered and reduced for logistic reasons. Mountbatten visited Chiang Kai-shek and obtained a promise that operations by a Chinese army would be possible but he learnt from Stilwell that all was not well with the Chinese formations in Yunnan, many troops suffering from malnutrition. At the same time those armies required extensive re-equipment, placing even greater strain on supplies and transport. Mountbatten also faced enormous logistic problems in India. The roads and the Indian railway could hardly sustain normal peacetime traffic, let alone the huge increases demanded by the build up of Allied armies and airforces. Then came the great expansion of the Indian Army which also demanded more and more logistic and movement support. Pipeline, road and rail construction and maintaining the air supply to China were taking up every possible facility, both military and civilian. On top of all this came even more demands for the logistic support for the offensive operations into Burma being planned for 1944. These were tasks of massive proportions. There was a great shortage of railway engines and some 200 airfields had to be built as well as new 'Logistic Reserve Bases.' The Indian economy was reaching breaking point, the crops failed in 1943, there was much unrest and a fair amount of anti-British feeling and finally, that year, there were massive floods in Bengal. The required tonnages of logistic stocks simply could not be created and moved and this included the amounts promised to Chiang Kai-shek, who complained bitterly. Morale began to suffer. Something had to be done to prevent a collapse.

Mountbatten's new Headquarters, South East Asia Command (SEAC) at Delhi, assumed full responsibility for operations on 16th November 1943. His Chief of Staff, Lieutenant General Sir Henry Pownall began work immediately. Inevitably there was some duplication of the work of Auchinleck's planning staff. The surrender of Italy in September had, however, released a number of warships which were sent to increase the Far East Fleet. General Giffard had the new 14th Army, formed from Eastern Army in October 1943, commanded by Lieutenant General Slim, and also Ceylon Command. The Allied airforces available are covered in the previous chapter.

On 22nd November came the 'Sextant' Conference in Cairo. Here it was agreed, as we have seen, that the plan to seize the Andaman Islands, Operation BUCCANEER should go ahead in the Spring of 1944. The plans to invade northern Burma, Operation TARZAN, a much reduced ANAKIM, and the Arakan should go ahead as planned. Chiang Kai-shek, who was present, said that air and naval superiority in the Bay of Bengal was essential and that plans must be made to seize the whole of Burma. He said this even though he would not allow Chinese forces to advance further than Lashio in order to help. Having agreed to TARZAN, in Cairo, he withdrew agreement once Churchill and Roosevelt had left for Tehran to meet Stalin. Back in India, however, Mountbatten managed to persuade the Generalissimo to accept the plan.

Then, as the weeks went by, it became clear that there would not be enough landing craft even for BUCCANEER and it too had to be cancelled. It had become clear that the landings in Normandy and the south of France not only had priority but they would take up all available craft. The question then was, would Chiang Kai-shek agree to attack from Yunnan without any amphibious operations in the Bay of Bengal? Meanwhile Mountbatten prepared a reduced Operation TARZAN, called PIGSTICK, which included a smaller amphibious landing on the Mayu Peninsula. But again he was told that there were not enough resources and this too had to be abandoned. Then came a bombshell. In reply to a letter from President Roosevelt urging him to attack from Yunnan in concert with Mountbatten, on 23rd December, Chiang Kai-shek said that he would not advance from Yunnan at all. This had a profound effect on all plans and forced Mountbatten to propose a set of relatively minor operations designed only to support the air route to China and the construction of a road route to Yunnan. He sent a team to London and then to Washington to present these plans to the Combined Chiefs of Staff. Included in them was a reduced plan to advance overland from the Arakan to seize the airfields at Akyab, a minor advance across the Chindwin and some long range patrolling by Wingate's larger special force, the Chindits of 3rd Indian Division. We must now pause and see what the Japanese had been up to and what had been happening in the Pacific.

General Mutaguchi realised from the first Chindit operation that his defences east of the Chindwin could be penetrated. He also realised that, given time, the Allies would advance against Japanese forces in Burma. He reasoned that the best way to prevent this was to seize the initiative himself, capture Imphal and advance into India. He therefore planned Operation U-GO for this purpose. Lieutenant General Masakazu Kawabe, commanding the *Burma Area Army,* issued his first orders on 12th August 1943. *56th Division* would hold the Chinese along the line of the Salween. *18th Division* would prevent any Allied advance from Ledo while *15th Army* consisting of *15th, 31st* and *33rd Divisions* would advance on Imphal and gain control of the Assam mountains. As a deception *55th Division*, under Lieutenant General T Hanaya who replaced Lieutenant General Takeshi Koga in November 1943, would advance on the Arakan front commencing three weeks earlier. This was Operation HA-GO. In the centre, *33rd Division* was to capture Fort White in November 1943 and then advance north up the Kabaw valley to Imphal. Meanwhile the main strike force, *15th* and *31st Divisions*, was to cross the Chindwin between Homalin and Paungbyin and then advance on Imphal and Kohima respectively. *31st Division* was to capture Kohima and then prevent the British from reinforcing Imphal from the north while *15th* and *33rd Divisions* captured it by a pincer movement from north and south.

At a conference in December 1943 the Japanese decided that, to ensure the safety of their position in Burma, it would be necessary to operate west of the line Naga Hills - Kohima - Imphal. Having satisfied themselves that they could cope with any Allied landings in the Bay of Bengal, that their air force could support the planned operations and that routes and logistics were satisfactory, *Imperial General Headquarters* authorised operations to begin as soon as possible after 15th January 1944. Kawabe issued his orders to *15th Army* on 19th January. The attack was to start by the middle of February and be completed by mid April. This would leave a month to consolidate before the monsoon broke. Because he was committing all available troops to the operation, Kawabe had no reserves so he was given the *2nd* and *54th Divisions*. Operations were then divided between three Army Headquarters, *28th* Army, commanded by Lieutenant General Shozo Sakurai in the Arakan, *33rd Army* to command *18th* and *56th Divisions* in the north and *15th Army* to concentrate on the main attack in the centre. *5th Air Division* was to provide the vital air support.

Lieutenant General Hanaya's plan was to anticipate the British advance, which he could see was about to start, by advancing to Bawli Bazar. He was then to attack Taung Bazar and the Ngakyedauk Pass. When these operations had drawn British reserves south, on the Central Front, *33rd Division* was to advance on Fort White and Tiddim a week before the move of *15th* and *31st Divisions* against Imphal and Kohima. D-Day for HA-GO was to be 4th February and, for the main operation U-GO, 15th March 1944.

Before following the course of these operations in detail it is necessary briefly to see what had been happening in the Pacific area (Map 24). On 18th September 1943 the Americans, in Vella Lavella in the Bismarck Archipelago, had been relieved by 3rd New Zealand Division, under Major General HE Barrowclough, which immediately went onto the offensive and drove the Japanese into a small pocket in the north west from where they were evacuated on 6th October.

The only remaining enemy on Bougainville lay between the Allies and Rabaul. They were attacked by the Americans on 1st November and the fighting raged on until March 1944.

The second phase of General MacArthur's moves in New Guinea involved two American divisions, the 32nd and 41st. Australian forces included 3rd, 7th and 9th Divisions and they were planning to capture Lae in September 1943. These operations were launched by a series of sea-borne attacks and the first Allied parachute drop in the Pacific campaign. The Japanese fought hard, conditions for both sides were appalling, and it was not until 15th October that the town fell and the advance along the north coast of New Guinea could begin.

On 20th November, 27th US Division, reinforced by 2nd US Marine Division, attacked the Gilbert Islands. Casualties were high in spite of a very heavy naval and aerial bombardment and the fighting went on until 22nd/23rd November, when the last few Japanese surrendered. New Britain was attacked by the Americans on 15th December and the western end of the island was seized by 23rd January 1944. MacArthur then attacked the Admiralty Islands which he succeeded in capturing by 24th March. Slowly Rabaul was being surrounded by the capture of each small island in turn and soon it was completely cut off. Meanwhile Admiral Nimitz had captured the Marshall Islands, his forces landing there on 1st February 1944, but there were over twenty islands in the group. Each had to be captured separately and the Japanese fought hard for every one and it took until the end of April to clear up all resistance. By that time the net was beginning to close around the Japanese in the Pacific.

Now back to the Arakan (Map 30). Throughout the period of all this planning in 1943, contact with the enemy had been maintained on each of the three sectors of the Assam front. Giffard, at 11th Army Group and Slim at 14th Army had been developing their plans to launch 15th Indian Corps in the Arakan to attack the main enemy position along the Maungdaw - Buthidaung line about the middle of January 1944. In anticipation of this 114th Indian Infantry Brigade of 7th Indian Division took over the forward position astride the Mayu Range in August 1943 and the following month divisional headquarters moved from Ranchi to Ukhia. 5th Indian Division followed. The artillery order of battle of 15th Indian Corps for the battles about to start in the Arakan is at Annex O.

The enemy defences were very strong and were based on the Tunnels and Point 551, with a forward strong point on Point 1301. Razabil in the west and Letwedet had been made into fortresses by the Japanese. The ground was hilly, scrub covered and thick in tiger grass. Defences were dug deep into the hillsides and were immune to all but direct hits with big shells. In November 1943 the position was held by *143rd Regiment* with outposts at Hathipauk and Awlanbyin. Facing it, the British front was held by 26th Indian Division until September, when it was withdrawn into reserve around Chittagong and 5th and 7th Indian Divisions moved forward to prepare for the advance.

5th Indian Division, commanded by Major General HR Briggs, deployed to the west of the Mayu Range with 123rd Indian Infantry Brigade, Brigadier TJ Winterton, in contact with the enemy on the line Zeganbyin - Point 1619, and 161st Indian Infantry Brigade, Brigadier DFW Warren, lying back in depth. 9th Indian Infantry Brigade was still in India at the beginning of December and would move to the Arakan later where Brigadier GC Evans took command on 4th February 1944. All three brigades of 7th Indian Division, commanded by Major General FW Messervy, were east of the Mayu Range by mid November. 28th Jungle Field Regiment was with 5th Indian Division and 139th Jungle Field Regiment with 7th Indian Division, each with one battery of 16 x 3-inch mortars and two batteries each of 8 x 3.7-inch howitzers. 139th Regiment had to remain to the west of the Ngakyedauk Pass (pronounced 'Nukchidowk' but soon known to everyone as 'Okeydoke') until the Sappers had built a 'jeepable' road. The pack batteries of the mountain artillery regiments were deployed with 25th Indian Mountain Regiment on the west side of the pass with Brigadier FJ Loftus-Tottenham's 33rd and Brigadier WA Crowther's 89th Indian Infantry Brigades which were waiting to cross. A battery of 25th Indian Mountain Regiment was with 114th Indian Infantry Brigade, Brigadier MR Roberts, of 7th Indian Division but they were to the east of the pass, having crossed the Mayu Range in mule pack. The addition of 139th and 136th Field Regiments, the latter moving forward towards the end of October, gave 7th Indian Division something approaching its proper level of artillery support, the gallant mountain batteries being all it had until then. Available also was 6th Medium Regiment, located some 80 miles south of Chittagong, consisting of 18th and 19th (Niagara) Medium Batteries, each with eight 5.5-inch guns.

By this time 81st West African Division, commanded by Major General CG Woolner, had reached Chiringa on the coast and was ready to advance down the Kaladan valley. The division had been formed in West Africa after the defeat of the Italians in March 1943. It had 3rd (Nigerian), 5th (Gold Coast) and 6th (Mixed) Infantry Brigades. Its artillery consisted of three independent light batteries (each with 4 x 3.7-inch howitzers) numbered 3rd, 5th and 6th as were the brigades. Later these were formed into 101st Light Regiment. In addition they had 21st LAA/Anti-Tank Regiment, which had four batteries each with four 40mm Bofors guns. It never received any anti-tank guns. The division arrived in India in September 1943. At this time its artillery was all man-portable or, as it was known, 'head-loaded'; the larger gun parts and the ammunition being carried on leather stretchers. The establishment of one battery was seven British officers; three British warrant officers, six British NCOs and 980 Africans, most of whom were unarmed 'gun-carriers.' Just before departing for the Kaladan operation all this was changed. 3rd (Nigerian) Infantry Brigade went off to join the Chindits, but did not take its light battery. At the same time the light batteries were given jeeps and their organisation altered so that they each had two gun-troops each of 2 x 3.7-inch howitzers jeep-towed and one troop of 8 x 3-inch mortars, 'head-loaded.' These had been given base-plates which increased their range from those of the infantry mortars from 1,650 to 2,400 yards. Only one troop of 6 x 40mm Bofors guns took part in the Kaladan operation.

The two brigades of 81st West African Division marched from Chiringa on the coast south of Chittagong, which became the West African Base and Divisional Rear Headquarters, some 74 miles to Satpaung. It had to build its own jeep track as it went through some of the world's worst country. This was completed in some four weeks, with no mechanical equipment and very little use of explosives. The weather was scorching hot on the mountains and extremely cold in the valleys at night and there was always the rain. It was a magnificent feat and the track became known as 'West Africa Way'. Later a separate track of another 25 miles had to be built for the guns and this was known as 'Gunners' Way.' By this time the batteries were independent again and RHQ 101st Regiment had been disbanded. The CRA was Brigadier HB Jolly and his job was to co-ordinate the work of the batteries and act as an RHQ if ever two batteries were deployed together. The order of battle of the artillery of the East and West Africans in the Far East is at Annex P.

In the Arakan, 33rd and 89th Indian Infantry Brigades were ordered to move across the Ngakyedauk Pass and then south towards Letwedet while 114th Indian Infantry Brigade cleared the enemy from Awlanbyin, which they did after some tough fighting. The brigade then moved across the Kalapanzin river and advanced to the Myau Chaung. By the middle of December the Ngakyedauk Pass was fit for jeep traffic and 139th Jungle Field Regiment was able to move into the Kalapanzin valley to help 33rd Indian Infantry Brigade who were under considerable pressure. 136th Field Regiment crossed on 2nd and 3rd January. By this time all 25th Indian Mountain Regiment had also crossed the pass and had joined 114th Indian Infantry Brigade east of the Kalapanzin. 24th Indian Mountain Regiment was back with 5th Indian Division to the west of the Mayu Range. Also at this time, 6th Medium Regiment, less one battery which remained west of the Mayu Range, moved into the 'Admin Box'. '19th Medium Battery was dug in at the western end of the pass in order to support 5th Indian Division. Then on 14th January it was ordered to cross the pass to join 7th Indian Division. 'C' and 'D' Troops were deployed in the 'Admin Box'. Captain Fisher went out as FOO with 4/15th Punjabis.' (History 19th Medium Battery).

81st West African Division had started its advance down the Kaladan on 18th January. 6th (WA) Infantry Brigade led on the east bank with the two mortar troops of two of the light batteries south from Daletme. 5th (WA) Infantry Brigade was at Satpaung. The first action came on 24th January just south of Paletwa, but it was a minor affair and the guns were not involved. The advance towards Kaladan Village was continued down the Kaladan by 6th (WA) Infantry Brigade and down the Pi Chaung by 5th (WA) Infantry Brigade.

While these operations were in progress there was still uncertainty as to which strategic plan was to be adopted in Burma. On the Central Sector the orders for Operation TARZAN, the plan for a move into northern Burma, were much the same as those for Operation GRIPFAST, a lesser version of the same thing, and were similar enough for planning to proceed. On the Arakan Front it was more difficult because Operation PIGSTICK envisaged a sea landing at Akyab by 2nd British Division to act as an anvil for the 15th Indian Corps hammer as it advanced south. Operation CUDGEL involved an advance by 15th Indian Corps without the 2nd British Division landings and was considerably different. When Mountbatten had had no reply from the Chiefs of Staff about the availability of landing craft for PIGSTICK by 6th January 1944, he could wait no longer and he cancelled it and TARZAN and ordered GRIPFAST and CUDGEL to be adopted.

Once the Ngakyedauk Pass was open to vehicles, early in January, 7th Indian Division built up an administrative area and supply point at Sinzweya, which became known as 'The Admin Box' (Map 30). By the middle of the month 5th Indian Division was deployed, with 123rd Indian Infantry Brigade on the western slopes of the Mayu Range north of the Rekhat Chaung, 161st Indian Infantry Brigade astride the Bawli Bazar - Razabil road north of Hathipauk, and 9th Indian Infantry Brigade, which had by then arrived, was in reserve. 7th Indian Division had 89th Indian Infantry Brigade on the eastern slopes of the Mayu Range around Point 1619, 33rd Indian Infantry Brigade facing Letwedet and 114th Indian Infantry Brigade to the east of the Kalapanzin between Maungyihtaung and Kwason. Both divisions were in contact but 7th Indian Division had no reserves.

On 6th January the Japanese had evacuated both Hathipauk and Maungdaw but the latter did not fall until a fierce attack by 161st Indian Infantry Brigade and 24th Indian Mountain Regiment, Lieutenant Colonel RHM Hill, with 11th and 20th Mountain Batteries but less 12th Mountain Battery and a section of 2nd Mountain Battery, onto Point 124, had succeeded. This was followed by an attack on Maungdaw itself by 2nd West Yorks and 12th Mountain Battery, under Major AB Howard, whose rapid and accurate concentrations chased the Japanese from village to village and enabled the West Yorks to mop up with great speed. This type of rapid gunfire was clearly too much for the Japanese. On the 19th General Christison, commanding 15th Indian Corps, received his orders from Slim and he, in turn, issued orders for 5th Indian Division to attack and capture Razabil and for 7th Indian Division to attack and capture Buthidaung. These operations were to be phased, so that the small armoured force and the corps artillery could support each in turn. 15th Indian Corps plan was:

> 7th Indian Division would first capture the 'Able' feature which overlooked the Tunnels - Buthidaung road, Htindaw and Letwedet using the Corps Artillery.
>
> 5th Indian Division using 25th Dragoons, the Corps Artillery and RAF support, was to capture Razabil.
>
> 7th Indian Division would then capture Buthidaung.

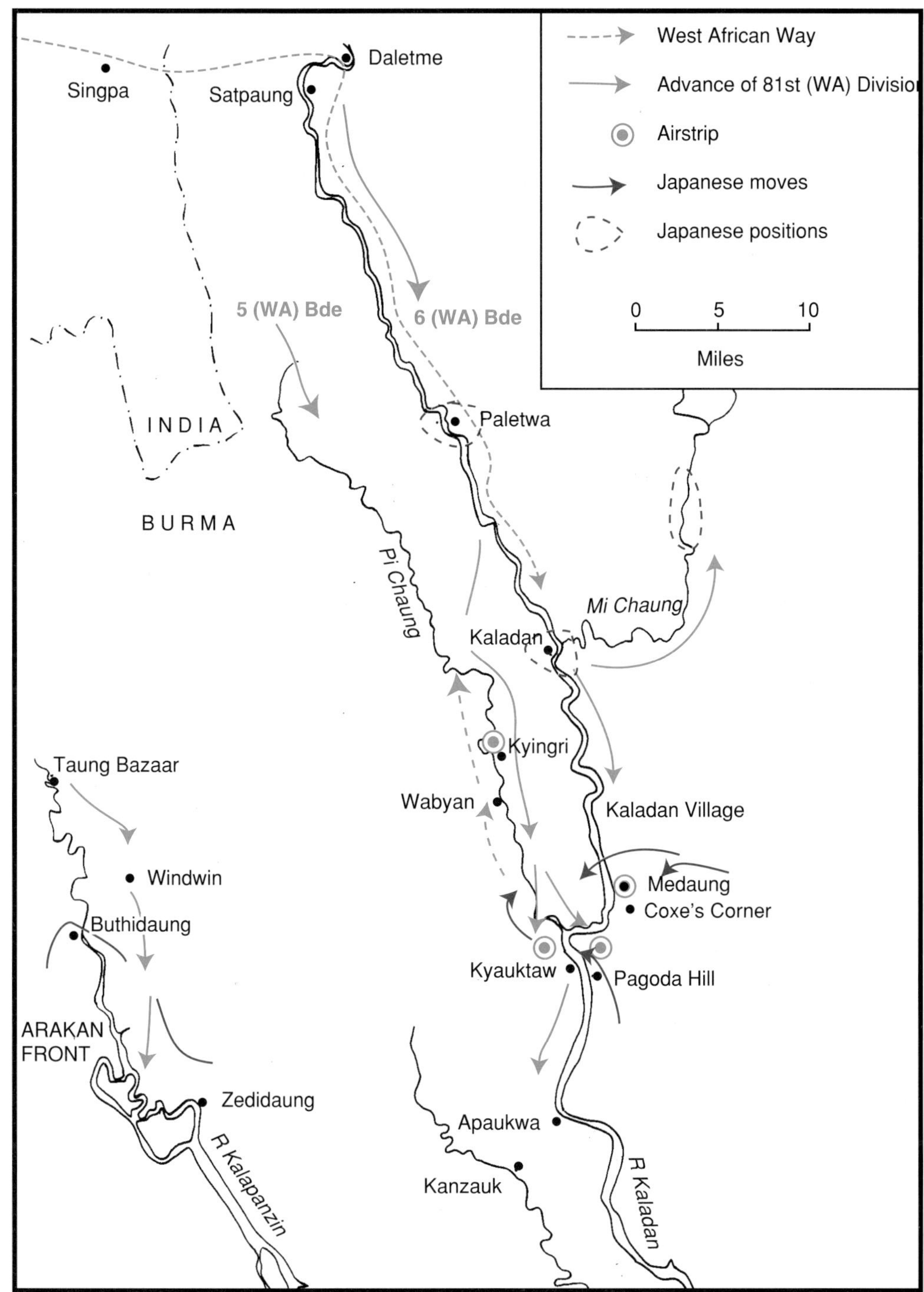

Map 33 The Kaladan Valley Front, January to May 1944

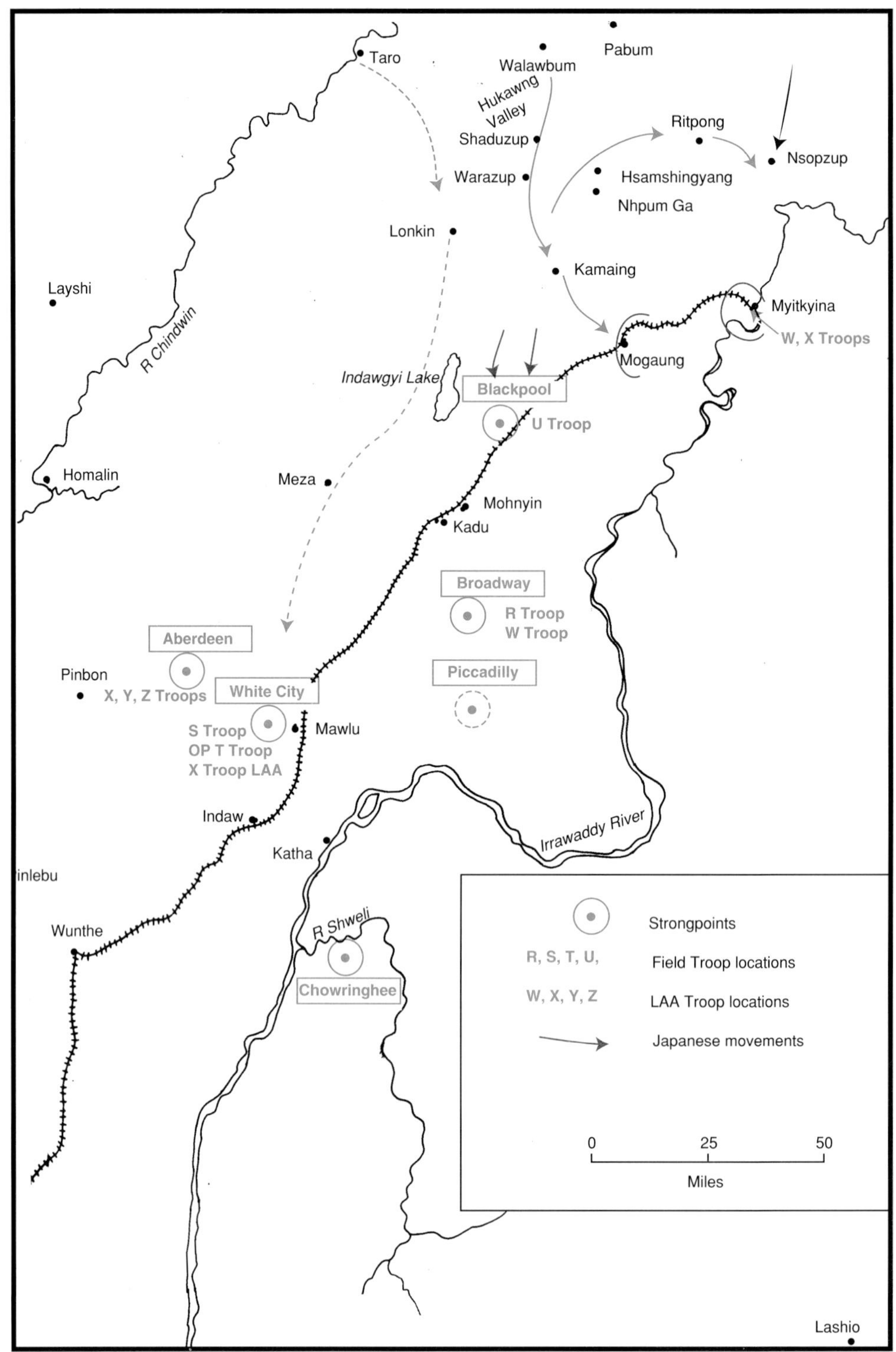

Map 34 Area of second Chindit Operations 1944

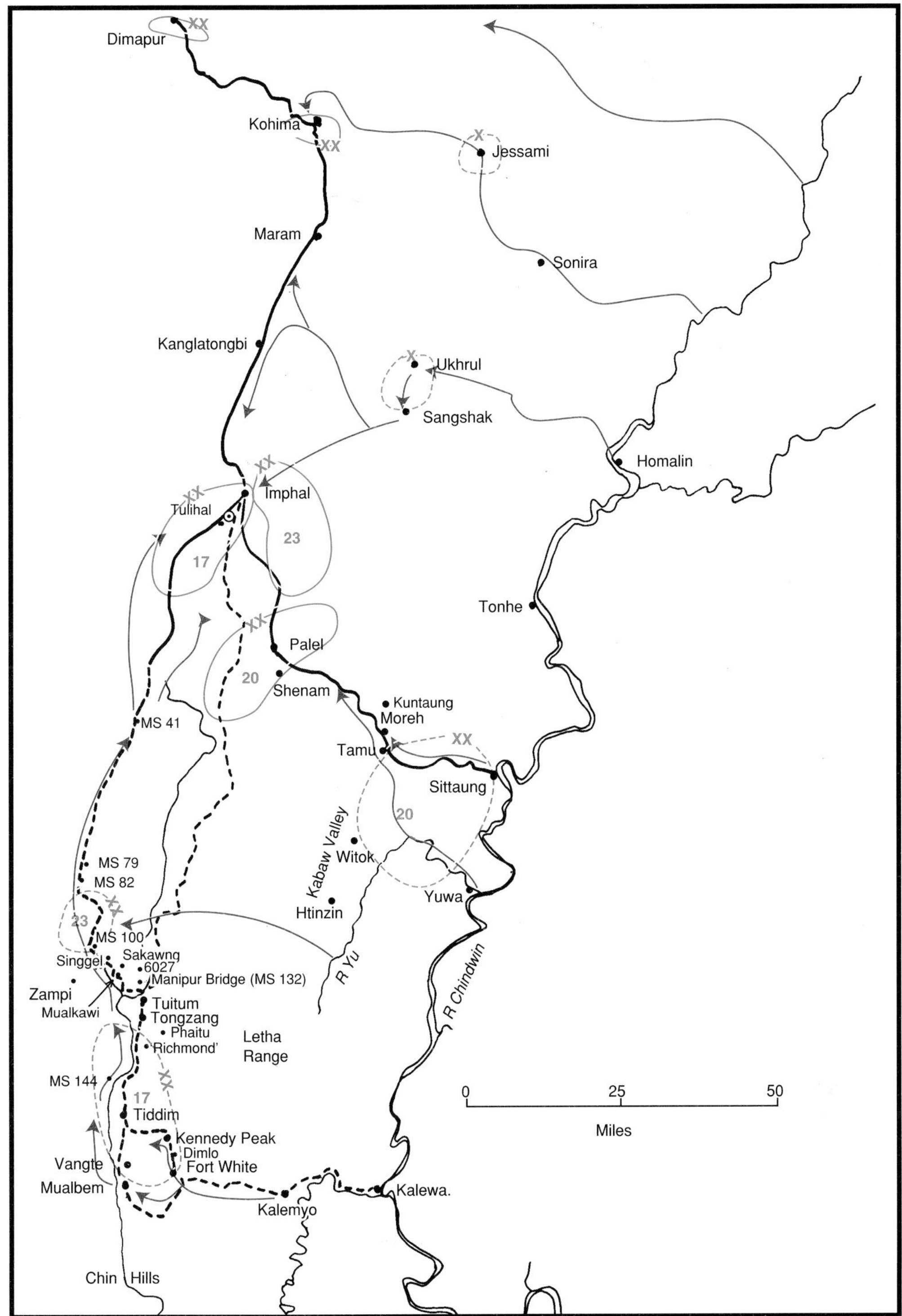

Map 35 The Tiddim Road battles November 1943 - February 1944

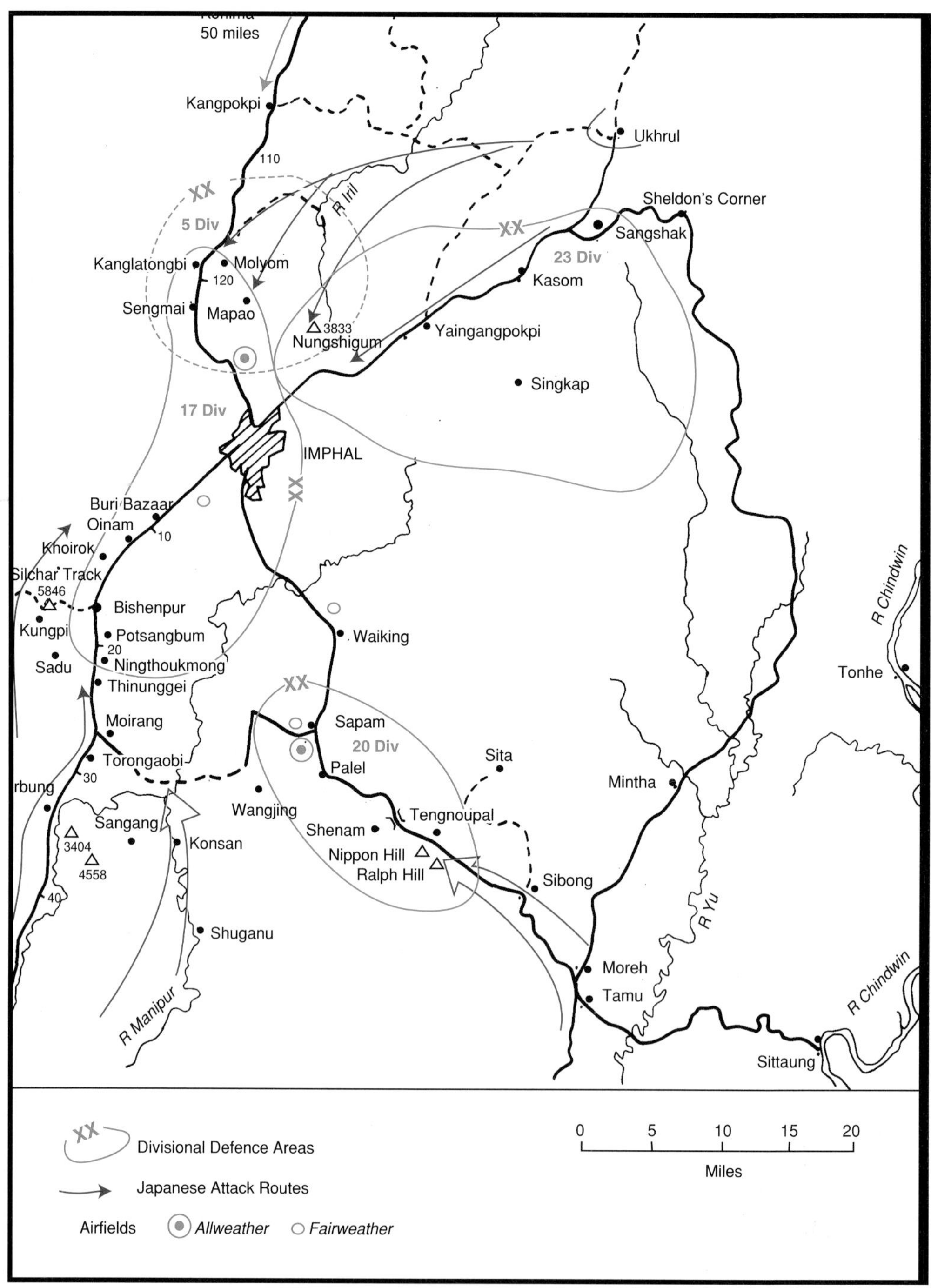

50 miles
Kangpokpi
Ukhrul
110
5 Div
R Iril
Sheldon's Corner
Sangshak
23 Div
Kanglatongbi
Molyom
120
Kasom
Sengmai
Mapao
3833
Nungshigum
Yaingangpokpi
Singkap
17 Div
IMPHAL
Buri Bazaar
Oinam
10
Khoirok
Silchar Track
5846
Bishenpur
Kungpi
Potsangbum
20
Waiking
Sadu
Ningthoukmong
Thinunggei
Tonhe
R Chindwin
Moirang
Sapam
20 Div
Torongaobi
Palel
Sita
30
Mintha
Wangjing
Sangang
Tengnoupal
Shenam
3404
Konsan
4558
Nippon Hill
Ralph Hill
Sibong
40
R Yu
Shuganu
Moreh
Tamu
R Manipur
R Chindwin
Sittaung
Divisional Defence Areas
Japanese Attack Routes
Airfields
Allweather
Fairweather
0
5
10
15
20
Miles

Map 36 The Imphal Battlefield

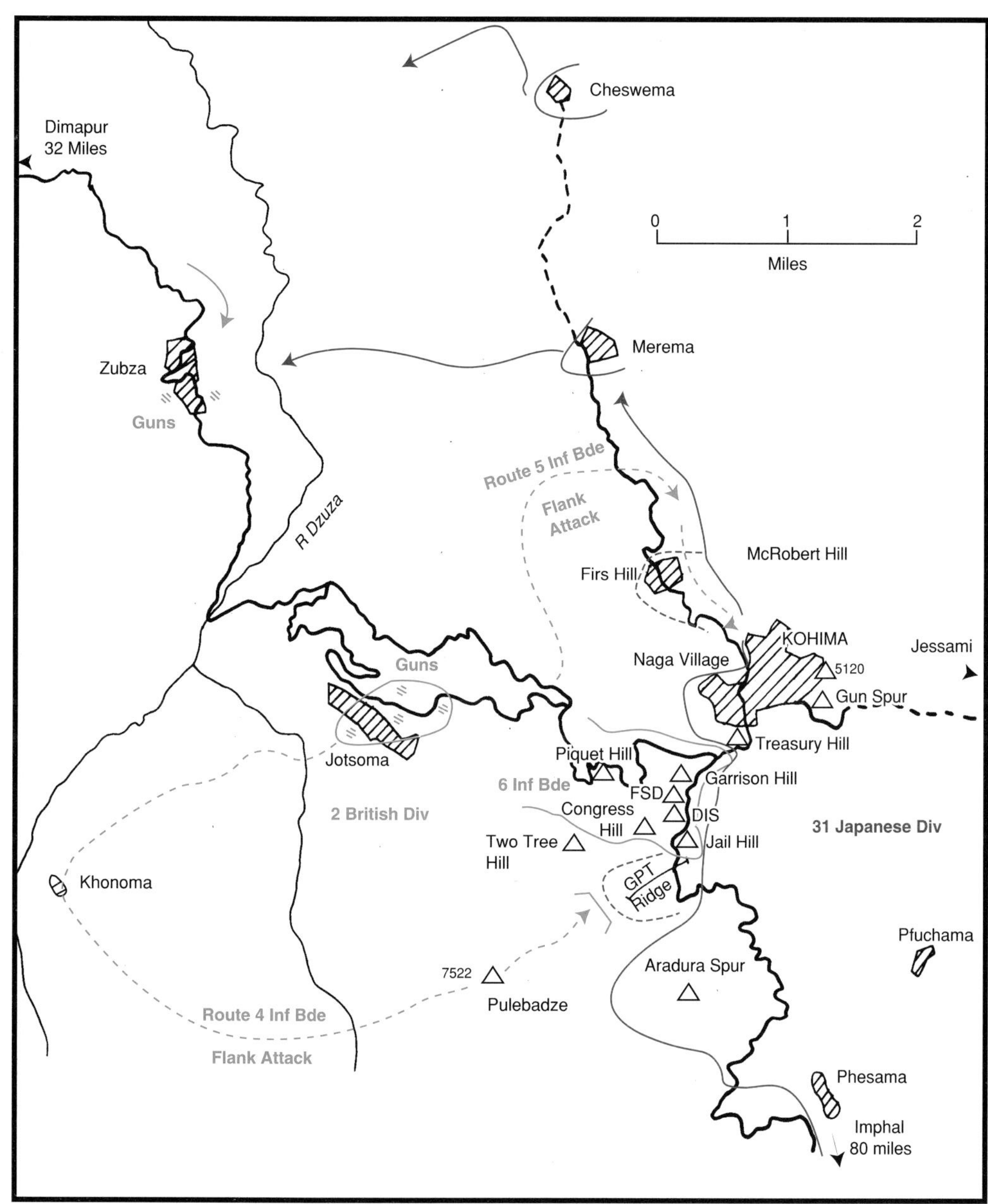

Map 37 The Kohima Battlefield

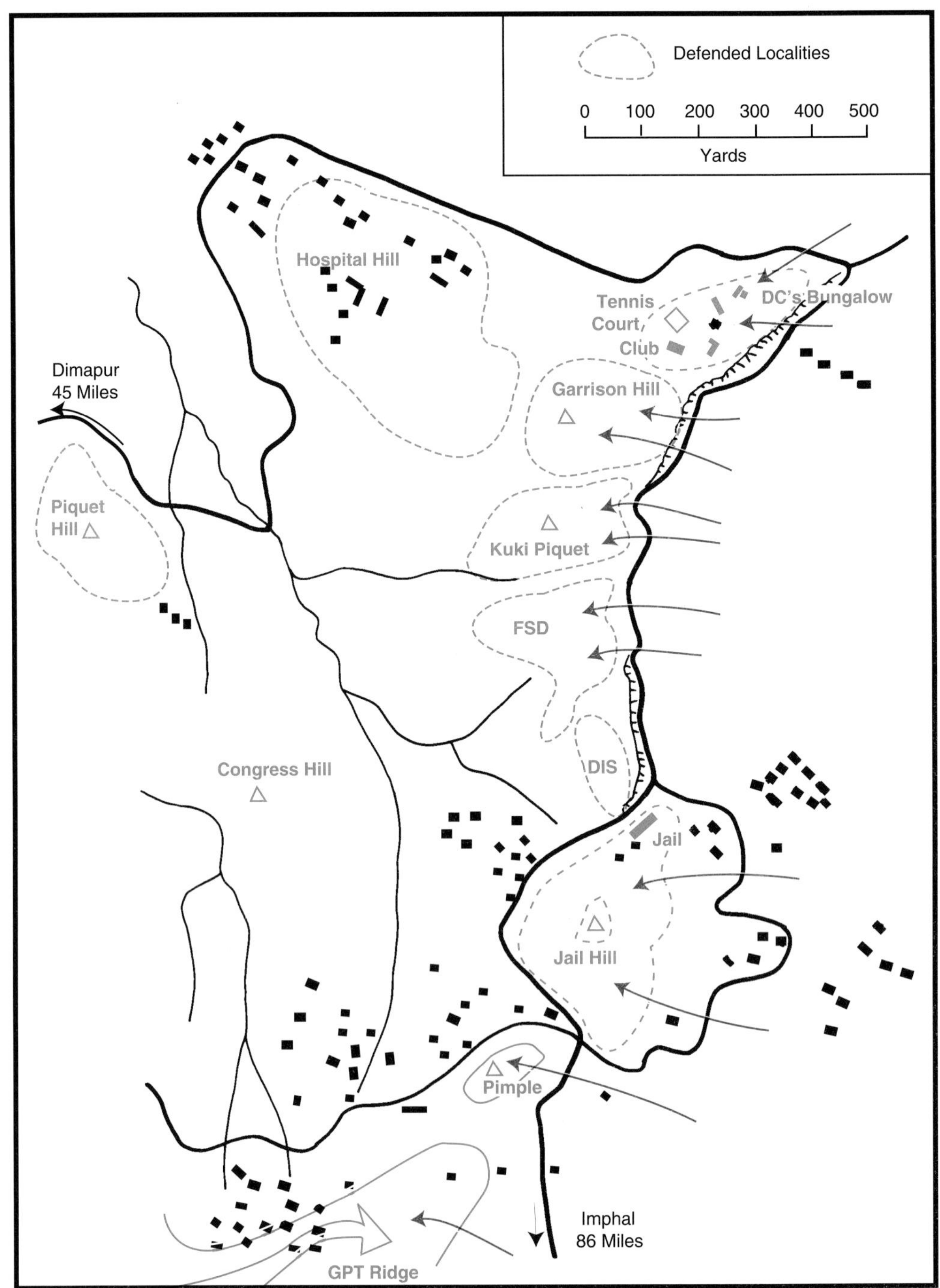

Map 38 Kohima Ridge

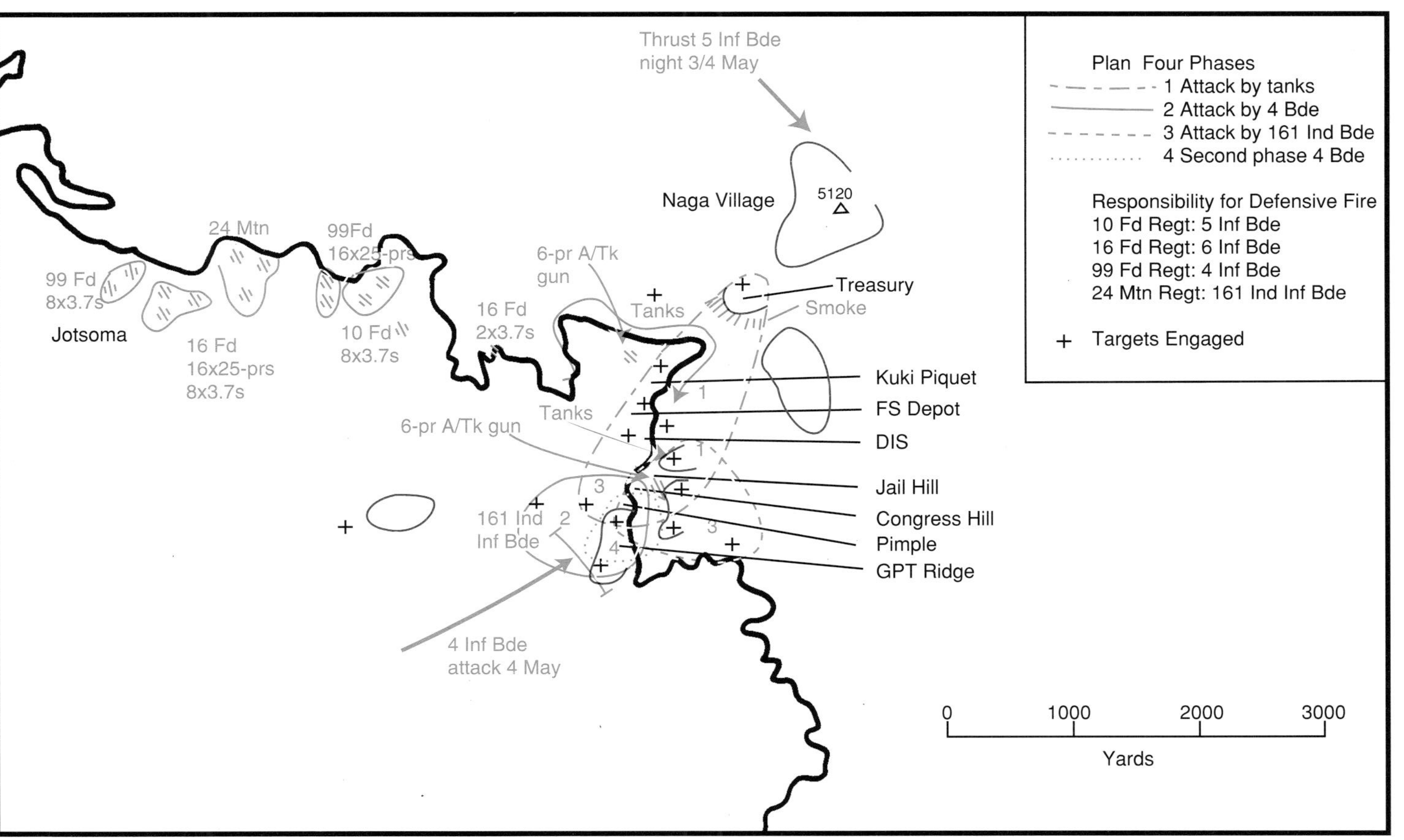

Map 39 Fire plan for 2nd Division attack at Kohima 4 May 1944

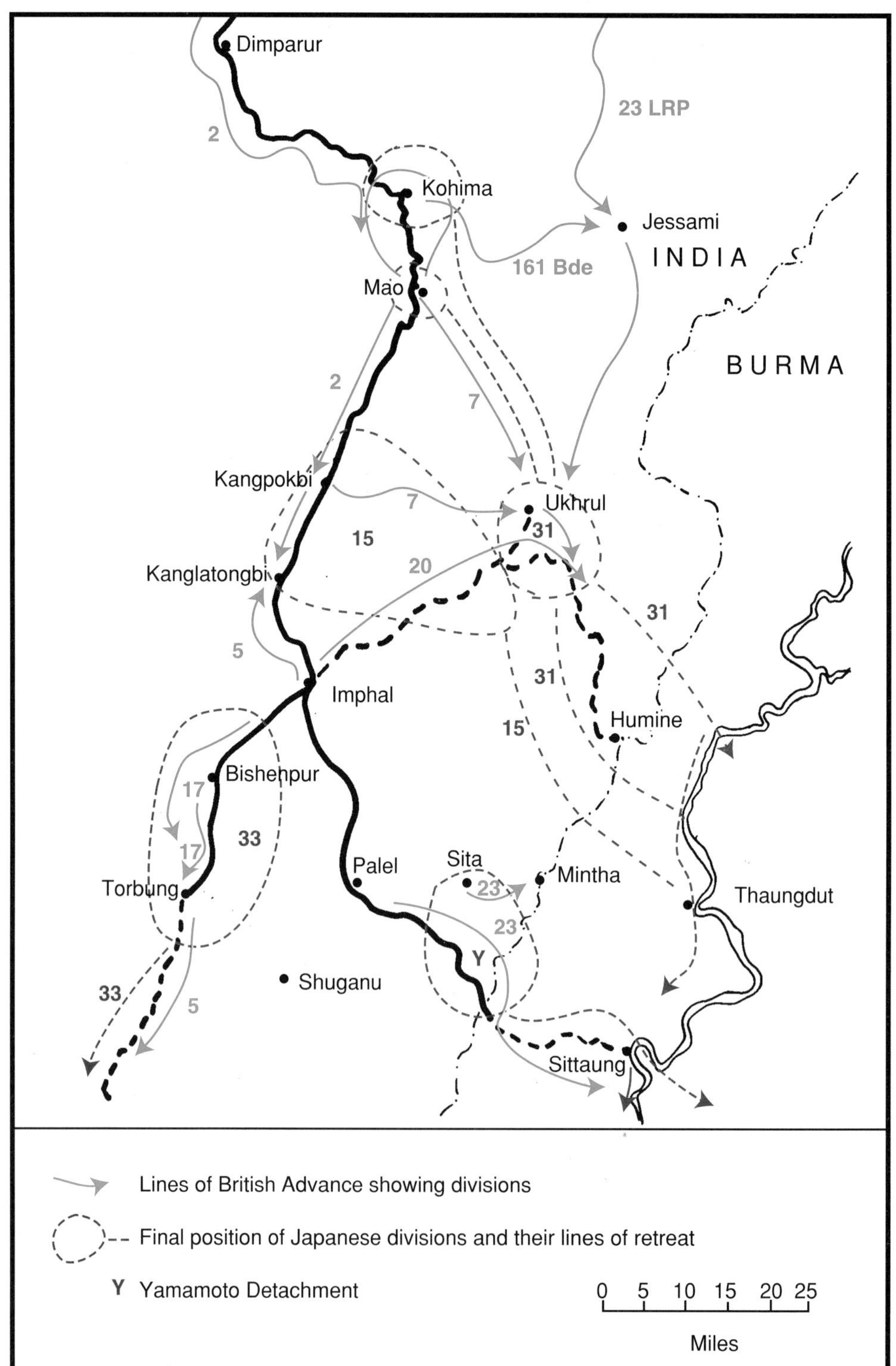

Map 40 The British counter-offensive at Imphal June-July 1944

Both divisions would then exploit to the line Indin - Rathedaung.

Simultaneously 81st West African Division would advance down the Kaladan Valley.

Messervy's plan for 7th Indian Division was for 89th Indian Infantry Brigade, with the Corps Artillery commanded by Brigadier AF (Tim) Hely, CRA 7th Indian Division and Major R McCaig his BMRA, to capture the Japanese position on 'Able.' At the same time 114th Indian Infantry Brigade was to infiltrate through the hills to the east of the Kalapanzin river and capture Dabragyaung from where it could cut the Buthidaung - Rathedaung road when necessary. 33rd Indian Infantry Brigade was to engage Letwedet so closely that the Japanese there could not interfere with 89th Indian Infantry Brigade on 'Able.'

It was at this time that 656 AOP Squadron arrived with two Flights, 'A' and 'C', each of six Auster IIIs. Squadron Headquarters was located alongside Headquarters 15th Indian Corps while 'A' Flight was allocated to 5th Indian Division and 'C' Flight to 7th Indian Division. Both flights soon began to demonstrate their value to all operations.

114th Indian Infantry Brigade began to advance during the night 14/15th January 1944 and by last light on the 15th it was established along the line Kyaukit - Pyinshe - Windwin. By 20th January, 4/14th Punjab was at Sannyinweywa and by the 21st 4/5th Gurkhas were close to Dabragyaung. There was heavy fighting everywhere because unknowingly the brigade had met with an enemy making their initial moves for their HA-GO offensive. As a result 1st Somerset Light Infantry failed to take Pyinshe Kala. Meanwhile further west, the RAF bombed 'Able' for three days before the corps artillery and 89th Indian Infantry Brigade attacked.

Although preliminary operations against the Japanese defences had been carried out in November and December, it soon became clear to Messervy that he was going to have to mount a specific operation to capture the 'Able' feature. This was the north eastern bastion of the main enemy position known as 'Golden Fortress'. The southern side of it gave observation over the Tunnels and the Buthidaung road. The job was given to 89th Indian Infantry Brigade which consisted of 2nd KOSB, 7/2nd Punjab and 4/8th Gurkhas. 136th Field Regiment, with 24 x 25-pounders, 139th Jungle Field Regiment, with 16 x 3.7-inch howitzers and 16 x 3-inch mortars, and 19th Battery of 6th Medium Regiment, with 8 x 5.5-inch guns, were to be made available. Brigadier Crowther, the brigade commander, ordered Lieutenant Colonel Mattingley and 2nd KOSB to carry out the assault supported by Major RD Powell of 364th Field Battery of 139th Regiment, on the night of 18/19th January 1944. Robin Powell was an authorised OP in direct communication with HQRA, that is to say he had authority to fire all guns in range. The plan was in three phases. Phase 1 was to capture two smaller features, 'The Pimples'. Phase 2 was to capture the north east corner of 'Able' following an intensive bombardment and Phase 3 was the occupation of the remainder of 'Able' feature.

Soon after dark on the 18th January a patrol reported no enemy on the 'Pimples.' It was then decided to go straight for Phase 2 but at the appointed hour. The battalion advanced across the paddy fields when, right on cue, the bombardment began. It was the heaviest and most concentrated artillery attack so far in Burma, 100 guns on a 500 yard front. 19th Medium Battery history states, 'Zero Hour was 2230 hours and few members of the battery will forget the dramatic scene of our eight guns firing simultaneously and shattering the pitch darkness and silence of the night. This was the first introduction of the Japanese to the 5.5-inch shell.'

The infantry followed closely. But, heavy as the fire was, as the guns lifted and dawn began to break the enemy came to life and opened fire with machine guns. However, by keeping an open formation the KOSB casualties were light. The OP parties were with the lead companies which were soon held up by concentrated machine gun fire. Colonel Mattingley himself led an attack on one enemy position with a Bren gun and silenced it, while Captain John Harvey, FOO with 'B' Company brought down the fire of 364th Battery so close and with such accuracy that it destroyed another. Soon the Phase 2 objective was taken and Powell describes his elation at seeing the Buthidaung road just before reporting to HQRA. Then furious digging-in took place before the expected counter-attack.

Next day Colonel Mattingley saw enemy building up for the counter-attack and called for fire. Robin Powell recalls that 'I consulted Dick McCaig at HQRA at once and he sanctioned five rounds gunfire from all available guns by predicted shooting on the target indicated. This was the signal for one of those accidents of war which are inescapable and probably more frequent than is sometimes supposed. The first round of the five from one of the 5.5-inch guns landed in the compressed area of Battalion HQ. To experience and survive one and to know that there will be four more shells to follow without having the time or chance to stop them, counts as one of the least pleasant experiences of my life. When the dust had settled after the salvo ceased and the remaining four medium shells had done their worst, the toll of casualties was headed by the instant loss of Colonel Mattingley and a number of Jocks who received a direct hit in the temporary dressing station where they lay. In addition, the KOSB Signals and Intelligence officers, and many other HQ staff were wounded, and included was one of John Harvey's signallers. I have always hoped that the rest of the artillery strike found its mark on the Japanese and justified poor Mattingley's last request of his Gunners.' (Major RD Powell). Sometime later, enemy guns started to engage the Borderers heavily with light artillery from 'Pimples'. Accordingly the brigade commander, Brigadier Crowther, ordered 7/2nd Punjab to assault the enemy who had moved onto 'Pimples' with Lieutenant Mick Blagg as FOO during the night of 21/22nd January. This was done, though the Punjabis suffered severely. This was followed by a furious artillery duel between the Japanese artillery and 364th Battery all night of 22/23rd January. Then a final attack on the 24th secured the whole feature except for an enemy force still holding the north east corner. This was cleared on the 29th and 4/1st Gurkhas of 33rd Indian Infantry Brigade took over the defence with the support of the guns of 136th Regiment.

To the west of the Mayu Range the attack on Razabil had been postponed until 26th January so that the Corps Artillery could swing back across to 5th Indian Division (CRA, since June 1942 in the Western Desert, was Brigadier ECR (Bob) Mansergh, with Major John Mermagen as his BMRA) after the battle for 'Able'. This attack went in after some not very accurate bombing by the Strategic Air Force, both USAAF and RAF aircraft taking part. In spite of this and the weight of the artillery attack, the infantry succeeded only in getting a foothold on the lower slopes of the Razabil Ridge by last light on the 26th. They struggled on and the Gunners attacked each strong point in turn but, even though apparently destroyed, as soon as the fire lifted, each enemy position came to life again. The Gunners engaged at Razabil were 24th Indian Mountain Regiment, 4th Field, 7th Indian Field and 28th Jungle Field Regiments, one troop of 6th Medium Regiment and one battery of 8th (Belfast) HAA Regiment with 3.7-inch AA guns in the ground role. Some of these guns were controlled by the newly-arrived Austers of 'A' Flight, 656 AOP Squadron. Also available was the fire of the Lee/Grant tanks of the 25th Dragoons. The batteries of 24th Indian Mountain Regiment were engaging targets very close to the infantry, their FOOs with the leading sections. OPs were established within grenade-throwing range of enemy trenches and the signallers had a very hard time keeping the line through. Defensive fire was used frequently to stop local counter-attacks which came in every night. One FOO had to spend three nights in such a position, inside the enemy's stronghold, but he carried out some extremely useful shoots. There is no doubt that these Mountain Gunners played a most significant part in the struggle for Razabil, but the Japanese held and further attacks were postponed.

Christison next decided to swing his main effort back to the east and give 7th Indian Division as much help as possible to attack Buthidaung from 'Able.' 9th Indian Infantry Brigade, with 24th Indian Mountain Regiment, moved forward to relieve 89th Indian Infantry Brigade, which was then to withdraw to the area of Awlanbyin and rehearse an attack on Buthidaung with 25th Dragoons. A Corps Artillery Group consisting of 6th Medium Regiment, less one battery, 7th Indian Field Regiment and one battery of 8th (Belfast) HAA Regiment, was formed. The group, commanded by Lieutenant Colonel FR Wetherfield the commanding officer of 7th Indian Field Regiment, was moved over the Ngakyedauk Pass during the first three days of February. In 7th Indian Field Regiment, 16th Battery was commanded by Major 'Chota' Lloyd, 17th Battery by Major Bob Measey and 18th Battery by Major Mark Runganadhan. These regiments deployed, started digging in and stocking up with ammunition. OPs were forward and observing the strong Japanese positions they were about to attack. At the same time a Counter-Battery Team, a meteor (meteorological) party and 'C' Flight of 656 AOP Squadron had arrived. At the same time Headquarters 15th Indian Corps took control of the 7th Indian Division Administrative area at Sinzweya, leaving the division free to concentrate on the forthcoming battle. To keep the enemy guessing the Reconnaissance Regiment of 81st West African Division, which was with the Armoured Group, kept up a series of raids along the Arakan coast using the few landing craft that were available. During this period 'C' Troop 19th Medium Battery suffered a serious premature which killed one member of the detachment while engaged on HF tasks.

By the first few days of February both Giffard and Slim were convinced that the Japanese were about to attack somewhere. Slim issued orders that, if they did and if any British formation was cut off, it was to form a defensive box and fight it out while it was supplied by air. He then issued further orders to ensure that joint Army-Air plans and resources existed so that air supply was ready, should it be required.

Unknown to the British, however, the Japanese *28th Army Headquarters* had given the order to launch *55th Infantry Division* onto Operation HA-GO to start on 4th February. Its aim was to draw British reserves south before the main Japanese attacks were made in the centre to capture Imphal. So we come to the battles of the Second Arakan Campaign which started with what has come to be known as 'The Battle of the Admin Box' (Map 31). The ground over which the bulk of it was fought was an area about ten miles square, bounded in the north by a line from Taung Bazar to the Briasco bridge on the Bawli Bazar - Maungdaw road, in the west by the crest of the Mayu Range, in the south by the line of the Tunnels - Buthidaung road and in the east by the line of the Arakan Hill Tracts. Down the centre of this area ran the tidal Kalapanzin River which varied from 50 to 150 yards in width and had a rise of some eight feet at high tide. Most of the chaungs were tank obstacles. Sinzweya, the centre of 7th Indian Division's Administrative Area, was to become the focal point of the battle. It lay in an amphitheatre about a mile long and half a mile wide, surrounded by jungle-covered hills. The Ngakyedauk Chaung ran along the southern edge of the box and to the west the ground rose steeply to the main ridge of the Mayu Range. Ammunition Hill was in the middle; it was so called because of the many ammunition dumps around it. 114th Indian Infantry Brigade had its own administrative area at Kwazon, east of the river. In the dry season, which then obtained, there were thick mists in the morning which often did not clear until well into the day. The Japanese made best use of the knife-edged ridges along the top of the hills which were extremely difficult to hit with artillery, and the reverse slope was impossible to hit in most cases. The only answer was to fire along the axis of the ridge, but this was not always possible.

On the evening of 3rd February 15th Indian Corps was deploying and grouping for its attack on Buthidaung which was to start on the 6th. Headquarters 15th Indian Corps was some three miles south of Bawli Bazar. To the west of the Mayu Range 5th Indian Division had its headquarters at Waybyin. It had 161st Indian Infantry Brigade with 4th Field Regiment facing Razabil. To its left was 123rd Indian Infantry Brigade deployed along the line of the Rekhat Chaung and up to the crest of the Range as far as Point 1619, with 28th Jungle Field Regiment. Its 9th Indian Infantry Brigade had taken over from 89th Indian Infantry Brigade over to the east of the hills in 7th Indian Division's area. 9th Indian Infantry Brigade had one battalion overlooking Htindaw and 2nd West Yorks was in reserve alongside brigade headquarters. The third battalion was still guarding Maungdaw on the coast.

7th Indian Division had its headquarters about a mile north east of Sinzweya in the Laung Chaung. 33rd Indian Infantry Brigade was holding a four mile front with 4/1st Gurkhas holding 'Able,' where Captain Pat Griffin of 136th Field Regiment had an OP. 1st Queens were facing Letwedet and 4/15th Punjab holding the line up to the Kalapanzin River. Brigade Headquarters was at Tatmakhali and both 136th Field and 139th Jungle Field Regiments were alongside it. 136th Field Regiment was by then commanded by Lieutenant Colonel GR (Geoffrey) Armstrong who had served with 11th Regiment HAC in the Western Desert. 136th Field Regiment had 347th Battery, Captain JB Frith, 348th Battery, Major AN Boucher and 500th Battery, Major RC Blair. 114th Indian Infantry Brigade had two battalions poised to cut the Buthidaung - Rathedaung road to the east of the river. Brigade Headquarters was on the Pyinshe Kala Ridge about a mile north of the village with 25th Indian Mountain Regiment, under Lieutenant Colonel LHO Pugh, nearby. It was Colonel Pugh who had planned and led a successful attack onto some German merchant vessels in the harbour at Goa in 1943. The horsed squadron of the Gwalior Lancers manned outposts east of Taung Bazar out to Point 1600. 89th Indian Infantry Brigade was licking its wounds with 25th Dragoons just south east of Sinzweya. 7th Indian Field Regiment was on its own just to the south of the Ngakyedauk Chaung near Point 147. 6th Medium Regiment, less one battery was immediately north of the chaung and just east of Sinzweya. 24th LAA/Anti-Tank Regiment, commanded by Lieutenant Colonel RB 'Bunny' or 'King' Cole, was deployed to protect the whole administrative area. The regiment also ran special re-supply jeep convoys over the Ngakyedauk Pass. It had 12 x 40mm Bofors and 12 x 57mm (6-pounder) anti-tank guns.

Meanwhile 81st West African Division had put 5th (WA) Infantry Brigade on the Pi Chaung, 6th (WA) Infantry Brigade at Kaladan village, with 11th (EA) Scout Battalion out on the left flank (Map 33). 7/16th Punjab was at Paletwa and in touch with 'V' Force. In the Arakan, 'V' Force consisted of platoons of the Tripura Rifles and a large number of locally-enrolled civilians whose chief task was to obtain information about the Japanese. The division had a Dakota airstrip at Medaung and had flown in a troop of six 40mm Bofors to protect it. There was much activity on both sides as both made preparations for their forthcoming attacks. There was a considerable amount of counter-battery fire and many Japanese air attacks. Such was the situation when the battle began.

The Japanese plan is shown on Map 30. Briefly, Lieutenant General T Hanaya, commanding *55th Division*, divided his force into four columns. The first, under Colonel T Koba comprising *I/111th* and *III/114th Battalions* was to guard Akyab. The second, under Colonel Yoshida consisting of the *I/144th Battalion* was to guard the coast south of Godusara. The third, under Colonel Doi, comprising the *I/143rd* and the *III/143rd Battalions* was to hold the line west of the Kalapanzin and the fourth, under Major General Tokutaro Sakurai, consisting of *112th Regiment*, commanded by Colonel S Tanahashi, together with *II/143rd, I/213th Battalions* and *55th Reconnaissance Battalion* was to break through the British to the east of the Kalapanzin, seize Taung Bazar, swing south west and block the Ngakyedauk Pass and cut the coast road. At this stage Colonel Doi was to attack northwards from the Htindaw - Letwedet area. *7th Air Brigade*, of *5th Air Division,* with 34 fighters and ten bombers, was to cover the operation.

At 0400 hours on 4th February listening posts around Headquarters 114th Indian Infantry Brigade heard sounds of large bodies of men and animals moving past them and the Somersets reported in similar fashion soon afterwards. Although there was an assumption that the noises were made by Indian supply parties, patrols were sent out by brigade headquarters. At 0530 hours patrols made contact with the Japanese and identified *112th Regiment*. As the mist began to clear at 0700 hours, more patrols saw large bodies of men approaching Kwazon. The guns of 19th and 23rd Mountain Batteries of 25th Mountain Regiment caught them in the open and caused heavy casualties, forcing them to disperse. At one moment 23rd Mountain Battery was engaging enemy over open sights with two guns firing forwards at 600 yards and two firing directly to the rear at 300 yards. 19th Mountain Battery reports. '4th Feb. The morning of the Jap infiltration. We caught 120 of them over to our rear at 1,600 yards, Zero 145 degrees. Jap planes overhead all morning, Jap troops using 'Rising Sun' flags for recognition purposes. . . . [5th February] Half our guns now face north and half south. The remnants of the Japanese party which we beat-up yesterday are on top of the hill about 2,000 yards from me here.' Brigadier Roberts, commanding 114th Brigade, told Messervy that he thought it was no more than a large patrol and that he could deal with it. Then came a report from the Gwalior Lancers that a force of over 800 enemy were marching six abreast with flags flying passing to the north of brigade headquarters and heading for Taung Bazar. Lieutenant Colonel Pugh and his Intelligence Officer established an OP and swung round two guns of 23rd Mountain Battery and brought heavy fire to bear on the centre of the column causing many more casualties. Meanwhile 19th Medium Battery reported engaging enemy east of the Kalapanzin. At the same time '[4th Feb] Between 0830 and 0930 the LAA guns (N Tp. 24 LAA A/Tk Regt.) protecting the Battery were attacked by Jap fighter bombers. Two bombs fell close to the Battery C.P. and wounded Gunner Lunt F. so severely that he died at midday in the M.D.S.' (Dunne). 7th Indian Field Regiment also reported being laid on Zero Lines at bearing 180 degrees and then being ordered to engage Taung Bazar at bearing 360 degrees at 80 rounds Gun Fire!

Dick McCaig wrote to the former Captain Rex Boys in 1997 'I was Brigade Major RA 7th Ind Div and I remember very clearly the morning of 4 Feb 44 when you came into my "office" at Div HQ. We had early had vague information of much movement during the night through our eastern Brigade - thought then to be locals fleeing from the Japs due to the impressed coolies shouting "don't shoot". And there was word from Taung Bazar of some Japs having appeared there.

We were both well aware of the absolute ban on flying you over enemy territory, but you were keen to go and have a look. Unwisely, in the event, I did not intervene. After long study of the map I walked out with you to your plane, swung your prop for you, & you took off. (McCaig letter to Boys 6 Jul 1997).

Rex Boys recalls '. . . I took off for the [Kalapanzin] river, which was quite close, and flew up and down the banks seeing nothing. For the first time, I realised how little one could observe through dense forest even at low altitude. The whole area could have been teeming with Japs for all I could tell. Then I flew south to Taung Bazar. There was no longer a union jack on Tony's [Irwin] *basha*. At once the Japs came swarming out of the village huts and began to shoot at me . . . but I had no guns to call on. I was about to turn back when I realised I had lost control of my aircraft, which went crashing into the ground from about 500 feet. It happened very suddenly: no time to think. . . I was unconscious, and the first thing I dimly realised was that I must get out quick. I opened the door and tumbled out bottom first, dragging my broken legs after me, and lay beneath the wing, losing consciousness again.

When I came to, I was aware of shadowy figures creeping around under the trees. These, as Tony Irwin was later to inform me, were Texas Dan and his mates, all set to earn the reward that 'V' Force offered for rescuing pilots who had force landed. Seventy-five rupees was the official rate, but in the confusion of the Japanese attack, accounting procedures went by the board and Texas Dan was thought to have got away with nearly a thousand. I would not have quibbled.

(Boys). His Burmese rescuers carried Captain Boys on a bamboo pole until he could be transferred to a sampan and then to 54 Field Ambulance, commanded by Major Crawford, which had delayed its withdrawal having been warned of Boys's plight.

In 19th Medium Battery, 'On Feb. 5th Jap. aircraft were again active but no bombs were dropped. Throughout the day there was intermittent Jap. shell fire within a few hundred yards of Battery posn. either 105 or 150 mm. This crept closer to D Tp. posn. and at 1530 hours 3 shell in quick succession fell in H Sub section gun pit. The detachment were standing by ready to fire on a predicted shoot and the casualties were therefore heavy. Serjeant [HE] Gibbons, the No. 1, was killed outright and Gunner [J] Anwyl. Bdr. Clark J.M. died almost immediately. Gunner [ES] Davidson and Gunner [J] Hamill were severely burnt and were immediately removed to the M.D.S., where they were when it subsequently fell into Jap. hands. They did not survive. [in fact Major Dunne later writes that 'Gnr. Hamill survived until the M.D.S. was again in our hands though he died soon after. He reported that the Japs had shot Gnr. Davidson in bed.']. . . Meanwhile D Troop O.P. was supporting 4/15th Punjab with fire into Sinohbyin village. He was eventually forced off his own OP - a feature north of Sinohbyin village - with the infantry, as a result of a strong Jap. attack, but established his O.P. in the vicinity. He was to remain there for the next five weeks, through to the Battery by wireless only.

Gunner Anderton a signaller, was seriously wounded by rifle fire in the shoulder while maintaining the O.P. line on Feb. 4th. and was evacuated by infantry carrier to the M.D.S.' (Dunne).

Messervy, realising that this was something much bigger than patrol activity, sent 89th Indian Infantry Brigade north to Ingyaung and Prein Chaung to intercept them and severe hand-to-hand fighting took place. That evening, 4th February, Slim ordered 26th Indian Division to send 71st Indian Infantry Brigade to 15th Indian Corps and Giffard, who was at Headquarters 5th Indian Division as the news came in, went to Headquarters 7th Indian Division and spent the night 4th/5th February there. 2nd and 20th Indian Mountain Batteries, commanded by Majors P Hartley and TH Harrison respectively, were ordered to the Briasco Bridge to join 26th Indian Division. Throughout 5th February, 89th Indian Infantry Brigade held its ground against fierce attacks. Then came reports of large numbers of the enemy moving westwards towards the Mayu Range. Slim ordered the whole of 26th Indian Division to come under the command of 15th Indian Corps and Christison ordered it to move to Bawli Bazar as quickly as possible. On returning to his own Headquarters, Giffard ordered 36th Indian Division, Major General FW Festing, to speed its move to Chittagong while Christison ordered 71st Indian Infantry Brigade to move to the Goppe Pass and attack the Japanese now operating in 7th Indian Division's rear areas. By evening it looked as if the situation was under control. 25th Dragoons were also ready at Sinzweya. So far there was no enemy movement from the south.

During 6th February the situation rapidly deteriorated (Map 31). First, at dawn, an enemy force raided 5th Indian Division's Administrative Area at Briasco Bridge. Then at 0700 hours an enemy force at battalion strength broke into Headquarters 7th Indian Division. There was severe hand-to-hand fighting and they were driven out but not before the Signal Centre had been broken into and the cyphers compromised. Eventually orders were given that everyone was to destroy all papers and any valuable equipment and make their way back to Sinzweya as best they could. The Commanding Officer of 24th LAA/Anti-Tank Regiment, Lieutenant Colonel Cole, was in command of the defences in part of this area. The defence of the whole area known as the 'Administrative Box' came under the command of Brigadier GC Evans, commander of 9th Indian Infantry Brigade, on the orders of General Christison. Evans, late the Royal Warwickshire Regiment, had arrived in the Arakan on 4th February and almost immediately received the corps commander's orders from his divisional commander, Major General Briggs, to take command of 7th Division's Administrative Area, to put it in a state of defence, and hold it at all costs. This he did superbly.

At dawn on 7th February the enemy attacked northwards into 33rd Indian Infantry Brigade sector and, in doing so, got into 139th Jungle Field Regiment's area and overran a mortar position. Slim appreciated that the Japanese could not maintain themselves for long so far behind British lines as long as those lines stood firm. He therefore told Christison to tell 5th and 7th Indian Divisions to stand fast and that they would be supplied by air. It was this decision, together with the leadership afforded by Brigadier Evans, that saved the day. Then in the early afternoon Messervy and some of his staff appeared on foot at Sinzweya, weary and bedraggled, and set up a headquarters using the radios of Cole's 24th LAA/Anti-Tank Regiment. Later when Brigadier Tim Hely and his BMRA Dick McCaig arrived, Headquarters Royal Artillery re-opened and established contact with its regiments. Messervy told Brigadier Evans to retain command of the local garrison and to bring 19th Medium Battery of 6th Medium Regiment inside it. He told Brigadier WA Crowther of 89th Indian Infantry Brigade to cover 7th Indian Field Regiment with 4/8th Gurkhas. 24th Indian Mountain Regiment, with 11th Mountain Battery commanded by Major AMS Fergie, and one section of 12th (Poonch) Mountain Battery, under Major AB Howard, were also in the 'Box'. The Sikh section of 12th (Poonch) Mountain Battery was some distance away and was under constant attack. However, it fought its way through an ambush with great determination before reaching a smaller 'Box' occupied by the 'B' Echelon of 3/14th Punjab. Lieutenant Bagshawe was awarded a Military Cross and Driver-Havildar Mukand Singh the Military Medal for outstanding bravery during this action. Captain WL Worthington, adjutant of 24th Indian Mountain Regiment, was killed that day while collecting documents from dead Japanese.

It was on 6th February that 136th Field Regiment reported its first brush with the enemy. At about 0315 hours movement was heard around 500th Field Battery's guns and soon a sharp small arms engagement at close range began with a strong enemy patrol and a number of them attempted to rush the command post but were driven off. By dawn they had gone, leaving six dead behind, but the battery lost Gunner D Elliott killed and Bombardier Trainer and Gunner Lock wounded. It was later that morning that 362nd Battery mortars were attacked in a re-entrant and the battery was forced to abandon them. Then at 0340 hours on 7th February, 348th Battery was attacked but drove off the enemy after a fierce fight. By last light on 6th February 19th Medium Battery was inside the Box at its eastern end and was still protected by 'N' Troop 24th LAA Regiment. Alan Fuller recalls that 'The Japs seemed to appear everywhere and 17 Battery were called upon to engage targets from all round the clock. Crest clearances were a great problem then, often solved by shooting away the tops of trees. There was a certain amount of confusion due to the presence of Japs everywhere, sometimes referred to, I believe, as "the fog of war". No sooner had I occupied one OP than it was time to move with my Company and this time it was to the FFR [Frontier Force Rifles]. On features to the left and right of me were Captains Ralph Gauge and Ronnie Blackburn in their OPs.' (Lewendon, 7th Indian Field Regiment).

Brigadier Tim Hely's account of the battle at divisional headquarters needs to be told in more detail, backed by the memory of Major Dick McCaig, his Brigade Major. 'The bursting of mortar bombs and grenades and the staccato rattle of tommy-guns and automatic weapons warned HQ 7th Indian Division that Sunday, February 7th, 1944, was to be no ordinary day. The Japs, who for some days had infiltrated through our 14 mile front in large numbers, put in a dawn attack on Divisional HQ. Signals took the first knock, and although they suffered heavily, they re-organised and held their ground.' (Duncan). Under their commander, Lieutenant Colonel Pat Hobson, they held off the Jap attack at the jungle entrance to Div HQ for over five hours losing some seven officers and 30 men in doing so, a splendid effort. 'HQRA were word-perfect in their defence positions and manned their slit trenches under [Captain] Julian Grant, the IO, and Sergeant Ditchfield, an experienced campaigner of Middle East days.' British and Indian side by side waited for the Jap to attack. Communications were immediately opened to all regiments by wireless in the operations trench, and Dick McCaig, the Brigade Major [RA], soon had the regiments completely in the picture about what was happening. No other communications were then working.' (Duncan) The battle continued spasmodically throughout the morning. Sergeant Ditchfield stopped several enemy rushes with his Bren gun. Captain Grant discovered that the GOC and most of the divisional HQ Staff had left very early during that part of the attack which fell directly on them. At about 1030 hours Lieutenant Colonel Hobson came to the HQRA trench to see Brigadier Hely. 'Before leaving, it would be about 11.30 am, I handed over control of the RA net to the outstation 24th LAA/ATk Regt in the Admin area . . .' (McCaig). It was decided to destroy everything and move to the Sinzweya Box. At no time was radio communication lost. 'The General and Tim [Hely] were at King Cole's RHQ . . . HQRA withdrew from the old Div HQ in two successive formed parties always fully under control. . . Throughout, the RA wireless net to our regiments remained through and in action. For some considerable time this was the only communication forward from Div HQ. But above all the gallant and magnificent stand for many hours by 7 Div Sigs not only saved all our skins, but probably imposed a quite vital day's delay in the Jap advance on our Admin area. . . The debt we all owe 7 Div Sigs has never been properly acknowledged.' (McCaig).

On 7th February the BC of 19th Medium Battery records that 'The Japs had unfortunately had access to Pt. 315, a long jungle-covered hill running North and South only 400x [yards] from the Battery at its nearest point. This was engaged at 1220 hours when movement on its face was seen, and also a hill feature in exactly the opposite direction at the long range of 2000 yards.' (Dunne).

About 1700 hours, in the Admin Box, the GOC, Frank Messervy, the CRA, Tim Hely, Pat Hobson, McCaig and several others were beginning to get control again. Dick McCaig reports seeing Brigadier GC Evans standing 'on a little windswept mound. He was quite brief. The gist of what he said was "There will be no withdrawal, we will fight it out. Dig in, face out, and shoot the Jap down. No movement whatsoever during the night. Any penetration and we will come out in the morning with the tanks and the W Yorks and restore the position".' Dick McCaig goes on, 'That was the psychological moment when our fortunes in this war changed, and it was Geoff Evans who did it.'

Tim Hely continues, 'Gunners soon showed their versatility. HQ 24th LAA Regiment became HQ 7th Indian Division. Gunner signallers and sets were soon working to all brigades and, as our communications with outside regiments had never been broken, we were in a comfortable position. Ammunition for the guns in the Box was there for the taking, since the corps ammunition dump was in the centre of the valley'.

'Outside the Box, 136th Field Regiment, under Geoff Armstrong, and Harry Hall's 139th Field Regiment were safely with 33 Brigade. 25th Indian Mountain Regiment, under Lewis Pugh, was with 114 Brigade; and 7th Indian Field Regiment was rather isolated some distance away, [with 89th Indian Infantry Brigade] while 24th Indian Mountain Regiment, under Humphrey Hill, were on the Box perimeter. The first two regiments had tremendous tasks. Not only did they shoot for their own brigade, but also, turning their guns round, they shot day after day and night after night for the beleagured Box. They were particularly useful for counter-battery tasks, of which there were many.' (Hely in Duncan).

'The Japs soon consolidated their positions round the Box. They occupied the hill features and could look down on all the activities of the garrison. Battle took place daily for the immediate hills, and it was with great difficulty that these were held. Cole's LAA boys, moving their Bofors around, shot Japs off many hill positions over open sights and supported infantry counter-attacks.

Jack Thompson of 24th LAA . . . soon discovered some mortars in the corps dump. Collecting odd cooks and drivers, he manned these mortars and used them very effectively.' George Golding also of 24th Regiment formed an infantry company of Gunners and did a magnificent job throughout the 16 days of the siege, on one occasion had 100 dead Japanese within 50 yards of his position. The enemy once engaged the guns of 8th (Belfast) HAA Regiment with machine guns, causing casualties. The Ulstermen became very angry; lowering their long 3.7s they blasted the hillside whence the fire had come until there was no reply. They had avenged their dead whom they buried on the gun position. Later the enemy fired incendiaries into the ammunition dumps causing major fires. Colonel 'King' Cole, Gordon Cock, Dan Houghton, (Staff Captain RA), ably assisted by the medium regiment, and the ground crew of 'C' Flight 656th AOP Squadron did magnificent work in putting them out, Houghton receiving a wound that almost cost him his leg. The gallant Cole was also wounded and, although greatly weakened by loss of blood, he refused to remain in the Dressing Station but continued to carry out his duties.' (Hely in Duncan). The citation to Colonel Cole's immediate DSO personally presented to him later by Lord Louis Mountbatten read, 'His organising ability was most marked. Throughout this period his coolness, cheerfulness, efficiency and encouragement to the Administrative troops was a great stimulant to the garrison. The example set by this officer, and his complete indifference to his own safety, undoubtedly did much towards the successful defence of the 'Admin Box'. His conduct throughout was deserving of the highest praise." He and his splendid regiment did more than most to defeat the Japanese in the 'Battle of the Admin Box.'

By dawn on 7th February the situation looked better with 89th Indian Infantry Brigade about Awlanbyin. A sort of perimeter held mainly by artillery posts provided some sort of defence of the 'Administrative Box' area. 2nd West Yorks and 25th Dragoons provided a mobile reserve around Ammunition Hill and did magnificent work wherever they went. The first attacks on Sinzweya came in during the night 7/8th February along the eastern edge of the 'Box.' It was here that the Japanese mercilessly killed the wounded and the doctors when the Dressing Station was overrun. It was here that Gunners Davidson and Hall were having their wounds dressed as the Japanese burst in. Neither survived. Lieutenant GW Robertson of 136th Regiment was in the 33rd Brigade Dressing Station, at the mouth of the Ngakyedauk Chaung, recovering from malaria, and managed to organise some defence and get a number of patients away to safety. For his personal courage and coolness on this occasion he was awarded the Military Cross. The same night an attack on Sinohbyin was repulsed but the attackers dug-in in their positions inside the perimeter and it took three days to eject them. By the 8th the *Sakurai* Column, consisting of *112th Regiment*, *II/143rd Regiment*, *Ist/213th Regiment* and *55th Engineer Regiment*, had closed the Ngakyedauk Pass and this meant that the 'Administrative Box' was encircled around Sinzweya except for its eastern flank. This area, containing most of 7th Indian Division, was some seven miles wide and four miles deep. 33rd Indian Infantry Brigade and one battalion of 9th Indian Infantry Brigade were facing south with 89th Indian Infantry Brigade facing north and west. During the night 7/8th February the gun position of 'C' Troop, 17th Battery 7th Indian Field Regiment, was attacked. 'On the flank of both 'C' and 'D' Troops there was a British Light AA gun. The Japs surprised this gun detachment, killing many of them. They then charged the nearest 'C' Troop gun, some carrying explosives on short poles, hoping to blow up each gun.

Fortunately, the camouflage nets had just been lowered again after firing, preventing the Japs from penetrating the gun position, and were fired upon by our gunners from inside. At the same time a platoon from the KOSB who were just setting out on patrol attacked them from behind and practically the whole Jap force was killed. . . [next morning] a long line of dead Japs had been laid out. All were much taller than usual, and were from the Japanese Imperial Guard.' (Alan Fuller in Lewendon [Ed] 7 Ind Fd Regt].

114th Indian Infantry Brigade was still east of the Kalapanzin river guarding the eastern flank. In fact the area contained a number of smaller 'Boxes', each with all round defence with patrols operating between them. The RAF were quite splendid and in the five weeks of the siege they flew 714 sorties and dropped 2,300 tons of supplies to different formations. It was a magnificent effort and the services of 31 Squadron undoubtedly saved 7th Indian Division. It was on 8th February that 31 Squadron, led by Brigadier General Old, USAAF, the commander of Troop Carrier Command, made its first supply drop to 7th Indian Division. In addition the newly-arrived Spitfires were soon dominating the air by day to such an extent that the Japanese hardly dared approach. Two Vengeance bomber squadrons kept up an incessant tactical bombing programme, on one occasion flying 269 sorties in one week. At the same time Dakota aircraft, of 62 Squadron, were dropping supplies to 81st West African Division and to troops in the Chin Hills and around Fort Hertz in the north as well as training to supply the Chindits in their major operation which was just starting. Further support came from the Strategic Air Force and 224 Group RAF operating with 15th Indian Corps. Air supply had arrived as a major component of the land battle in Burma and all who were there have the greatest respect for those splendid Dakotas of 31 and 62 Squadrons and their intrepid air crews. The question to be answered, however, was whether 7th Indian Division could be relieved of the need for air supply so that the Chindit operation could be launched on time because the same aircraft were needed for both operations.

The enemy force which had crossed the Mayu Range by way of the Goppe Pass had cut the Bawli Bazar road near the Briasco Bridge and threatened 5th Indian Division's supply line. They had then swung south and reinforced their comrades holding the Ngakyedauk Pass. General Briggs, of 5th Indian Division, reported a strong enemy road block near the top of the pass beside Point 1070. Christison told Briggs to clear it up. At the same time he told 81st West African Division to advance south from Kaladan and threaten Kanzauk in the Japanese right rear.

During the night of 8/9th February, the Japanese manhandled some guns onto a hill overlooking Sinzweya and engaged Ammunition Hill at point blank range and caused fires and explosions. It took a counter-attack with tanks under a massive bombardment to drive them off. Slim by this time deduced that the Japanese plans were going astray and that if he could hold he would defeat them. Any thought of amphibious operations later on were cancelled and 36th Indian Division, which had been preparing for them, was allotted to 15th Indian Corps. Christison ordered it to send its 29th Infantry Brigade to Bawli Bazar to relieve 36th Indian Infantry Brigade of 26th Indian Division. This left 5th Indian Division available to clear the Bawli-Maungdaw road and the Ngakyedauk Pass. On 13th February patrols of 7th Indian Division met patrols of 26th Indian Division at Taung Bazar; the tide was indeed turning.

At 0300 hours on 9th February, in the moonlight, the men of 347th Field Battery saw the gleaming bayonets of a large body of Japanese coming down the hill towards them. They immediately engaged over open sights and the effect was devastating. Then suddenly the Gunners saw, to their horror, that there were a number of Sikhs among the dead Japanese. They were mortified, but realised that the enemy were using the Sikh withdrawal as a cover for their attack. At 1700 hours on 9th February 'F' Troop of 136th Regiment was attacked. The enemy first rushed a Bofors gun which was again close to the 25-pounders. The gun detachment fought at point blank range until the Japanese final charge before pulling back. Number 2 Gun of 'F' Troop then destroyed the Bofors and the Japanese who were on it. But 'E' Troop was next in danger and Lieutenant McCulloch was able to use 364th Battery to engage the attacking enemy while 'E' Troop pulled out to come into action further back, setting zero lines by using the Pole Star as aiming point. By this time five troops of 136th Field Regiment's 25-pounders, 364th Field Battery's eight 3.7-inch howitzers and five Bofors guns of 24th LAA Regiment were all located in a valley just south of 'Happy Valley', which became known as 'Gun Valley'

9th February was a bad day for 19th Medium Battery whose history says that a section of 'D' Troop was moved on orders of higher authority to a position where it could be shelled by a concealed enemy 70mm gun over open sights. 'The section had just come into action when the Jap gun opened rapid fire, quickly getting direct hits on both A.E.Cs. - one caught fire and Gunner [L/Bdr A] Bluer and Gunner [V] Bates were killed. The other A.E.C. withstood the direct hit and remained serviceable. L/Sjt Gardner, Gnrs. Houghton, Sayers, Williams R. and Wise were wounded though fortunately not seriously enough to prevent their rejoining the Battery fairly quickly.

The guns were got out of action with some difficulty owing to the fact that their tyres had been burst by shellfire. . . The CPO, Lieutenant [L] Curtis played a prominent part and notable assistance was given by the BC and BSM of 205 A/Tk Bty.

On the afternoon of Feb.9th. supplies were dropped from the air in the Battery Area. This was the first time the Battery saw Dakotas in action and it was an extremely heartening experience for all ranks, it greatly reduced their sense of isolation.

Gunner Beattie was less heartened than the remainder of the Battery as he had the misfortune to have his shoulder dislocated by a sack of sugar dropped without a parachute.' (Dunne).

The pattern for defence in the 'Box' was developed over the 16 day siege. There was very little cover, the enemy could see into most positions and he conducted suicide attacks most nights; in the morning Japanese bodies on the wire were a common sight. Casualties began to mount. The pressure on OPs was very great as they were right on the perimeter, could seldom rest and were constantly engaging the enemy. Most batteries had four or five OPs out all the time and to man and supply them was a considerable strain. There was no shortage of ammunition which was dropped in on most days. Indeed the air drops became so accurate and regular that all manner of stores and equipment arrived by this method, including mail and a pair of spectacles for the GOC, General Messervy! In his book *The Sparks Fly Upward*, Geoffrey Armstrong, commanding officer of 136th Field Regiment, writes 'Spare parts of all kinds were another must. By a thousand to one chance a breech mechanism cartridge extractor, indented for by radio for A1 gun of 136 Regiment, was actually parachuted into the very gun pit two days later. The Dakotas [C 47], later joined by the larger Commando [C 46] planes, would arrive in threes or fours, that being a convenient number to be in the dropping area at once, and the time available on target. The pilots displayed great skill and resourcefulness and seemed unperturbed by any fears as to their vulnerability. On the only occasion on which we saw one being attacked by a Jap fighter, as it completed its drop and began to ascend, the Jap was knocked out of the sky by one of our Bofors guns. It was just closing on the Dakota and, in fact, the Bofors had "trained" on it and had to wait for the Dakota to get clear. It came down in flames.'

The enemy offensive reached its climax on 14th February with attacks all around the area of the 'Box'. The whole of Point 1070 was captured by the Japanese as was part of the 'Able' position. The pressure on the garrison of Sinzweya was by this time very great. It had been under constant attack and bombardment for almost ten days. Accordingly Messervy moved 89th Infantry Brigade back into the 'Box' to defend the eastern flank. By then 4th and 71st Indian Infantry Brigades, which had 20th and 27th Indian Mountain Batteries under command, of 26th Indian Division were poised to attack Point 315 from the north. Then patrols of 114th Indian Infantry Brigade found Kyaukit abandoned and patrols of 33rd Indian Infantry Brigade found the strong point at Punkori also abandoned by the enemy. On 18th February 5th Indian Division increased its pressure on the Ngakyedauk Pass from the west. But the Japanese were still fighting hard and were dug in around Point 129 and, across the river, on the ridge north of Kwazon, so the fighting raged on. We now know that, from 15th February, the shortage of supplies was a serious problem for the Japanese. Slim was right, they were in real difficulty. But the fighting remained tough. Five enemy 75mm shells hit 19th Medium Battery's position, killing the Battery Captain, Captain RL Taylor, and wounding Lieutenant J I'Anson, BQMS Johns, Bombardier Key, Gunner Wilde and Officers Mess Cook Budhu. But the guns remained in action all day including the engagement of the enemy immediately in front of Lieutenant DA Darroch's OP. (Dunne)

Nevertheless an attack on Point 315 on 21st February by 4th Indian Infantry Brigade failed and another fanatical attack by the Japanese very nearly reached 7th Indian Division's Headquarters for a second time; the enemy were taking desperate measures. But it was also on the 21st that the enemy position on the pass at Point 1070 fell, although they still clung to the route further up. One Japanese bunker on the slopes of the Point 1070 feature could not be silenced. Accordingly a 5.5-inch gun of 'B' Troop, 6th Medium Regiment, was placed in a pit dug by the Sappers with two tanks shielding the front. The bunker was then engaged over open sights at a range of 600 yards and at an angle of depression of 11 degrees. One ranging round was followed by 20 rounds Gun Fire and the bunker ceased to exist. Then on 23rd February, after a short sharp clash with the last Japanese posts, patrols of 89th Indian Infantry Brigade from the east met those of 123rd Indian Infantry Brigade from the west. The following day the pass was re-opened and the air supply of 7th Indian Division ceased. We now know that General Hanaya, commander of the *55th Division,* ordered Operation HA-GO to be abandoned on 24th February. He told the garrison on Point 315 to hold out until the force at the Briasco Bridge had returned which they did, abandoning that position during the night of 25/26th February just as 4th Indian Infantry brigade were about to attack yet again. The fighting dragged on as parties of enemy fought their way through the British positions. The guns were in constant use and were centrally controlled by HQRA to ensure maximum effectiveness everywhere. On 25th February a group of some 1,200 enemy was seen just south of the 'Admin Box' by an infantry patrol. The BMRA ordered an 'Uncle' target using 7th Indian and 136th Field and 6th Medium Regiments from the east of the Mayu Range and 1st Medium and 130th Field Regiments from the west. Next morning some 300 bodies were found and many more must have been wounded. Again, on 27th February, Captain Pat Griffin was heavily engaged helping 4/1st Gurkhas on the 'Able' feature. During the siege 136th Field Regiment had ten men killed, nine wounded and five missing .

The battle of the Ngakyedauk Pass, or the 'Admin Box', cost 15th Indian Corps 3,506 casualties, of which over half were in 7th Indian Division. It was a vital battle which marked the turning point in the war in South East Asia. In his message to 15th Indian Corps, Slim wrote 'The Battle of the Arakan was the first occasion in this war in which a British force has withstood the full weight of a major offensive, held it, broken it, smashed it into little pieces and pursued it. Anybody who was in 7th and 5th Indian Divisions and was there has something of which he can be very proud.' In *Defeat Into Victory*, Slim expands on this, 'This Arakan battle, judged by the size of the forces engaged, was not of great magnitude, but it was, nevertheless, one of the historic successes of British Arms. It was the turning-point of the Burma campaign. For the first time a British force had met, held, and decisively defeated a major Japanese attack, and followed this up by driving the enemy out of the strongest possible natural positions that they had been preparing for months and were determined to hold at all costs. British and Indian soldiers had proved themselves, man for man, the masters of the best the Japanese could bring against them. The RAF had met and driven from the sky superior numbers of the Japanese Air Force equipped with their latest fighters. It was a victory, a victory about which there could be no argument, and its effect, not only on the troops engaged but on the whole Fourteenth Army, was immense.' Finally the operation had shown that large formations in the jungle could be supplied by air provided they held their ground and did not move. It also demonstrated for all to see the impact of well-handled artillery on jungle operations. The gun layout and fireplans used are set out in Map 32.

Christison was determined to press on and it is a measure of the high morale of 15th Indian Corps that he was able to do so only five days after the re-capture of the Ngakyedauk Pass. He ordered 81st West African Division to attack southwards and seize Apaukwa which they did (Map 33). The light guns had been in action with 1st Gambia Regiment south of Kaladan Village on 12th February and again a few days later at the crossing of the Pi Chaung. They were again engaged with 4th Nigeria Regiment in the capture of Kyauktaw and Apaukwa. Again, on 2nd March, they fought with 5th Gold Coast Regiment near Kyauktaw. Then on 3rd March the Japanese counter-attacked at Pagoda Hill just south east of Kyauktaw. There was a spirited fight at Cox's Corner when the guns were again in action and to considerable effect but then the Japanese got behind them and forced General Woolner to pull back to Wabyan on the west bank of the Pi Chaung into a divisional box in the Kyingri Loop where a Dakota strip was built and again six Bofors guns were flown in to defend it. This position was shelled by the Japanese and the 3.7-inch howitzers did their best to reply. Later the West Africans were driven back up the Kaladan Valley. This was a serious reverse but Christison was determined to attack south after his success in the defence of the 'Admin Box' (Map 30). He ordered 7th Indian Division, with 33rd, 89th and 114th Indian Infantry Brigades, to capture Buthidaung forthwith and 5th Indian Division to attack Razabil. 26th Indian Division, under Major General CEN Lomax, was to secure the area of the pass and stand by to relieve 7th Indian Division after the fall of Buthidaung. He told 81st West African Division to come forward again into the Kalapanzin Valley.

Messervy ordered 33rd and 89th Indian Infantry Brigades to isolate Letwedet and capture Buthidaung, while 114th Indian Infantry Brigade were to prevent enemy east of the river from assisting those in Buthidaung. 33rd Indian Infantry Brigade was to attack Buthidaung from the west under an attack by the Corps Artillery of over 100 guns. These were 136th, 139th and 7th Indian Field Regiments and 6th Medium Regiment from the east of the Mayu Range, and 130th Field and 1st Medium Regiments from the west, 72 x 25-pounders, 16 x 3.7-inch howitzers and 32 x 5.5-inch guns; 120 guns in all. Two features called 'Rabbit' and 'Poland' had first to be cleared and at 1015 hours 7th March the guns opened fire on them with 1/11th Sikhs and 4/15th Punjab advancing close behind the bursting shells. Success was complete and quick. Consolidation followed and then, at 2300 hours, the guns opened fire on Point 142, the next objective, and this too was quickly overrun by 4/15th Punjab. Guns and infantry were at last working well together each having complete confidence and respect for the other. In these attacks some 14,500 rounds were fired and the infantry suffered only 60 casualties. On 6th March Captain HLK Fisher of 19th Medium Battery fired 380 rounds busting bunkers on the 'Massif' feature and, on the same day, he was relieved by Captain Gething, of 18th Medium Battery, after five continuous weeks in an OP within a few yards of the enemy. (Dunne).

Messervy decided to press on and launched 1/11th Sikhs against Buthidaung at dawn on the 9th March, having beaten off a Japanese counter-attack with combined guns and infantry during the night. On the 9th, 1st Lincolns attacked two features called 'Spit' and 'Polish' with Captain AR Fuller, of 'C' Troop 17th Field Battery 7th Indian Field Regiment, as FOO. He recalls that, 'About two hours before dawn the Lincolns, with fixed bayonets, set off in two waves towards our wooded starting point for the attack and reached it in one and a half hours time. Gunner Govindon, my orderly, fixed his bayonet so as not to be outdone, but I preferred my Thompson sub machine gun. The signallers having to carry wireless sets, batteries, etc, were unarmed.

The 25th Dragoons soon noisily took up their position in front of us. As it became light our regimental guns put up a tremendous barrage on "Spit" and "Polish", blowing apart most of the jungle on that position. It was then the turn of the Grants to move forward and open fire, and we followed behind the Grants for protection. There was a certain amount of machine gun fire from the Japs which was largely silenced by the fire from the Grants of 25th Dragoons. Just before the attack Vultee Vengeance dive bombers made mock attacks on the position, and a 'Mike' target engaged the Japanese nearby on Indauk. This was all most impressive as we approached the position behind our barrage.

My O.P. party was in the second wave of the attack following about 30 yards from the front wave. We were held up by rows of dannert wire (probably removed from Singapore) but as we climbed through it three Japs looking thoroughly scared came running towards us and one of them fired at us and missed. Our O.P. party, particularly Gunner Govindon, quickly despatched them to their ancestors.' (Major AR Fuller in Lewendon [Ed] 7th Indian Field Regiment).

Next day 1/11th Sikhs came under heavy artillery fire but this was silenced by the British guns and a most effective smoke screen enabled them and some tanks of 25th Dragoons to move forward. But the Japanese were not yet beaten. Alan Fuller, by then with 5/16th Punjab, who had just relieved the Lincolns, was attacked on 'Spit' and 'Polish' which they had at last captured. He could not get through by radio so, 'I fired my Verey Light Pistol "red over green over red". . . Immediately I was relieved to hear the guns, in the distance, answer my SOS target call just in front of our position. . . The SOS fire was due to cover an area of 200-300 yards in front of our position. The change in the wind force caused the shells to burst in the trees and stumps of trees just over our heads, but fortunately the shell splinters were falling very close just in front of us. . . Next morning the Japs left many dead, close to our trenches. Sniper fire prevented them from being counted, but they were estimated at 150.' (Major AR Fuller in Lewendon [Ed] 7th Indian Field Regiment). After the taking of Buthidaung the regiment was ordered to withdraw to its monsoon defended area. Shortly before this took place it was saddened by the loss of its second-in-command, Major CHB Grotrian, to a land mine and the severe wounding of its commanding officer, Lieutenant Colonel FR Wetherfield, by a mortar bomb.

The artillery attack at Buthidaung is well described by Robertson in his book, *The Rose and the Arrow.* He writes, 'At 22.20 the guns opened up on Cain, Rabbit and Poland - all hell was let loose. In the Kalapanzin Valley the guns of 136th, 139th, 7th Indian [Field] and 6th Medium and from west of the Mayu 130th Field and 1st Medium fired simultaneously. 72x25-pdrs., sixteen 3.7-inch howitzers and 32x5.5-inch guns poured a torrent of shells onto the two features for twenty minutes. The noise of the guns firing and the shells exploding echoed and re-echoed off the many ridges of the Mayu in a fantastic volume of sound. It was a very bright moon that night but the continuous flashes from each of the gun areas looked like bursts of summer lightning.

All this noise ceased as abruptly as it had started, to be replaced by a new sound. In the Gun and Happy Valleys we were roughly five thousand yards, say three miles, from the forward Infantry of 1/11th Sikhs whose attack went in the moment the fire of the guns ceased. But we could hear their shouts and war cries as they went in with the bayonet. . . nothing could have withstood the ferocity of their attack . . .'

The capture of Buthidaung was the signal for 26th Indian Division to take over from 7th Indian Division which it did, putting 4th Indian Infantry Brigade on the eastern slopes of the Mayu Range and 29th Infantry Brigade between them and the Kalapanzin River. 114th Indian Infantry Brigade stayed on a little longer in order to drive the Japanese out of Kyaukit, which it achieved by 22nd March, and then left to rejoin 7th Indian Division on its way to the Central Sector. There was more fighting on this front including the attack on Point 162, 'The Massif', but the Japanese were defeated and had no further offensive capability. This was just as well since the situation was rapidly deteriorating on the Central Front. It was at this time that Major General WHB Mirrlees, MGRA India, visited regiments on the Arakan Front. He was responsible for all Gunners, British and Indian, east of Suez and it was due to his drive and energy that the enormous build-up of artillery had gone so well and because of his direction that standards of gunnery remained so high in spite of the speed of the expansion. The Regiment owes him a very great deal for what he did for the Far East Gunners in 1943, 44 and 45. It is interesting to note that, as at 30th June 1943, there were 64,452 Gunners in India Command whose total all arms and services strength was 211,307. Thus the Gunners accounted for some 30% of the strength of the Far East Army. The strength of the Royal Regiment World-wide on that day was 699,993.

On 9th March, 5th Indian Division began operations to capture Razabil and the Tunnels (Map 30). Briggs had under command 81st West African Reconnaissance Battalion and 44th Royal Marine Commando which he used to raid Alethangyaw to draw Japanese attention that way. 'A' Flight 656th AOP Squadron RAF took part in this operation. He then moved 161st Indian Infantry Brigade round to the south of Razabil through Maungdaw to a position south east of the town between the Buthidaung and Alethangyaw roads. Finally he planned a deception to let the Japanese think that the main operation would once again be a frontal attack by 123rd Indian Infantry Brigade, 15th Indian Corps Artillery and the RAF. 161st Indian Infantry Brigade met no opposition and was in place by dawn on 11th February. In the end, so powerful was the artillery attack, involving 200 guns, that 123rd Indian Infantry Brigade had no difficulty in overrunning Razabil. 161st Indian Infantry Brigade then faced east and attacked the Western Tunnel and 2nd Indian Mountain Battery went right forward to engage the enemy over open sights. It was during these operations that Major S Clark commanding 19th Indian Mountain Battery was awarded an immediate Military Cross for gallantry during an attack by 4/5th Gurkhas. Next, 29th Infantry Brigade attacked from the north and, although there was some opposition at Points 1070, 731 and 1301, by the 15th March the enemy had abandoned their positions completely. Then 36th Indian Division completed its take over from 5th Indian Division which also left for the Central Sector.

In the Kaladan valley (Map 33), 81st West African Division sent a group back across the Kaladan River to clear up an enemy force on the Mi Chaung. For this, once again, jeep tracks had to be cut for the guns. It was here that they fired for the last time before being withdrawn on 9th April, reaching the base at Chiringa on the 20th. It had been found that, although they did their best the effort needed to keep wheeled vehicles going in the jungle was just not worth it. Only mortars could be manhandled through thick trackless jungle and only mortars took part in the rest of this operation. In May, 41st Mortar Regiment, head-loaded, was formed from half 21st LAA/Anti-Tank Regiment, the other half forming a special force of infantry. This regiment, under Lieutenant Colonel JA MacNabb, consisted of three batteries, 101st, 102nd and 103rd, each of 8 x 3-inch mortars. Each battery had a strength of 318 men, although about 100 of these were ammunition carriers with three or four rounds per man. The regiment was ready for action in September.

During February there was still much discussion between Mountbatten's Headquarters, London and Washington about the strategy to be adopted in South East Asia. Mountbatten favoured Operation CULVERIN, which involved sea landings in Sumatra and Malaya to cut off the Japanese in Burma. However this would demand many more resources, especially landing craft and naval escorts. What is more, such operations would not improve the air or land routes from India to China so essential to keep China involved and to ensure that her airfields would remain available for air operations against Japan. Mountbatten sent a group of officers first to London and then to Washington (this was known as 'The Axiom Mission') to sort this out and in the end it was resolved that he must abandon CULVERIN and advance with 4th Indian Corps as soon as possible to seize the Shwebo- Monywa area. His mission was, 'To develop, maintain and protect the air route to China.'

Also during the first two months of 1944 Wingate was preparing for his next Chindit offensive. He became obsessed with the idea that Long Range Penetration (LRP) operations of the type he was planning were the answer to the defeat of Japan and that conventional ground forces were only needed in a supporting role (Map 34). His plan, Operation THURSDAY was confirmed by Headquarters 14th Army on 9th January whereby he was to deploy three LRP brigades astride the Japanese lines of communication behind the Chindwin and around Myitkyina and the Hukawng Valley to assist Stilwell. But Wingate envisaged doing more with his force. His first detailed plan, issued on 16th January, envisaged that 111th Brigade, under Brigadier WDA

Lentaigne, would be flown into an area south of Pinlebu on 1st March with orders to cut the Wuntho - Pinlebu rail and road communications and then operate in the Mu river valley north of Pinlebu. 77th Brigade, commanded by Brigadier JM Calvert, would fly into the Kaukkwe River valley between 7th and 12th March and establish road blocks between Mohnyin and Mawlu. 16th Brigade, led by Brigadier BE Fergusson and containing 51/69th RA - men of 51st and 69th Regiments - acting as infantry, would cross the Chindwin on 16th February and march in by way of Taro and Lonkin, attack Indaw and then destroy the railway in the Bongyaung - Meza area. Wingate reckoned that he needed up to four battalions, each with a troop of 25-pounders and a troop of 40mm Bofors guns, to defend his strong points. At a meeting with Slim he was promised one such group.

The Gunners in the second Chindit operation were in two categories. The first consisted of the re-roled 51st Field and 69th LAA/Anti-Tank Regiments, all Territorials, as Chindit infantry and they were to form Columns 51 and 69 in Brigadier Fergusson's 16th Brigade. 60th Field Regiment, also a Territorial unit, was allotted, again as infantry, to Brigadier Perowne's 23rd Brigade as Columns 60 and 88. This brigade was employed separately, raiding Japanese communications west of the Chindwin. The second category concerned the provision of artillery for the operations themselves. This was done by creating four special lightweight, four-gun, jury axle 25-pounder troops from 160th Field Regiment, to be known as R, S, T and U Troops, and a similar four troops each of six lightweight 40mm Bofors LAA guns from 69th LAA/Anti-Tank Regiment as W, X, Y and Z Troops. These were all to play a significant part in the operations and some were present at all the Chindit strongholds of 'Broadway,' 'Aberdeen,' 'White City,' and 'Blackpool.' See Annex Q.

Wingate demanded three more garrison battalions to guard his bases once established. He went direct over the heads of Slim and Giffard to Mountbatten but was told that he must find these from his own resources. He would get 3/9th Gurkhas and all the guns but no more battalions. Wingate considered resigning but then decided against it. He was also firmly reminded that his tasks in order of priority were first, to help Stilwell's advance on Myitkyina by drawing off Japanese forces opposing it; second, to create a favourable situation for a Chinese advance from Yunnan and third, to inflict maximum confusion and damage to Japanese forces in north Burma. Wingate decided to keep his plan for 16th Brigade, to order 77th and 111th Brigades to fly in and each to prepare a landing strip as soon as they arrived for the build-up of their brigades. 3rd West African, 14th and 23rd Brigades were to be held in reserve for relief or for exploitation but could not be moved without authority of Fourteenth Army. At his final conference at Imphal on 31st January, Wingate told his commanders that the secret of success was concentration of effort into an area within a 40 mile circle of Indaw. In essence they would be cutting the communications of the *18th* and *31st Divisions*. 16th Brigade was to deny to the enemy the Naba - Indaw and Banmauk areas. 77th Brigade would be flown into two points in the Kyaukke Valley to be known as 'Broadway' and 'Piccadilly'. A third landing area would be prepared in a bend in the Shweli River east of the Irrawaddy called 'Chowringhee'. The first troops would land by glider and take small bulldozers with which to make Dakota landing strips as quickly as possible. Then the rest of the brigade would air land. 111th Brigade would land at 'Broadway' as soon as 77th Brigade landing was complete.

On the afternoon of Sunday 5th March 1944 Lieutenant General Slim, Brigadier General WD Old, USAAF, commanding the US/British Troop Carrier Command, Air Marshal Sir John Baldwin of 3rd Tactical Airforce, Colonel P Cochrane, USAAF, of No 1 Air Commando, and Major General Wingate gathered together at Lalaghat to see Calvert depart with 77th Brigade. Much depended on non-interference by the Japanese air force and much had been done in the past month to destroy it in the air and on the ground and with great success. Then, just before take-off, they were shown some newly-arrived air photographs which showed the proposed landing area at 'Piccadilly' was covered in tree trunks! Had the plan been blown? But both 'Broadway' and 'Chowringhee' were clear. After considerable deliberation it was decided that they should proceed but, since 'Chowringhee' was across the Irrawaddy and Calvert did not want to split his force as it landed, they decided to stake all on 'Broadway'. The advance guard of four Dakotas each towing two gliders took off in quick succession. As they flew through the night skies apprehension both on the ground and in the air was high. After all, it was a great gamble. The first glider got down as planned and soon a flare path was established but several of the rest crashed into some deep ruts. Calvert, who was safely down, realised that the main body would soon take off and he knew he must stop them until he had cleared the strip, so he sent the codeword 'Soya Link', which meant trouble on the ground. But he was soon able to send 'Pork Sausage', which meant all was well. These two code words represented all that was worst and all that was best in British Far East rations! Of the 62 gliders that set off that night eight were recalled, eight crash landed but 35 landed at 'Broadway'. Of these 35 all but three were wrecked but 400 men were down with enough equipment to start constructing the airstrip. Soon L 5 light aircraft were landing and taking off the injured. The first Dakota landed at 1800 hours on 6th March and by dawn on the 7th, 62 more had landed some 900 men, 100 animals and 20 tons of stores. Wingate went with them and in the next three nights 272 Dakota sorties were flown, bringing in all of 77th Brigade, 3/9th Gurkhas, a troop of four 25-pounders and a troop of six 40mm Bofors guns. It was a magnificent effort and so far with no interference from the enemy.

Wingate then decided that, to avoid congestion at 'Broadway,' he would land 111th Brigade forthwith at 'Chowringhee'. Accordingly the advance party took off on the night of 6/7th March and all but one glider landed safely. Unfortunately the one that crashed carried the airfield construction equipment, but more was sent and by midnight on 7th March the strip was pronounced ready for use, a magnificent effort by the American Engineers and the Sappers. During the next two nights 118 sorties were flown and the brigade was down, plus two other special force groups. Wingate visited 'Chowringhee' on 8th March and recognised the danger of the vulnerable, open, waterless area it was in. He decided to abandon it and to fly 111th Brigade to 'Broadway' after all. This was done on the night of 10/11th March and again without any interference from the enemy. Thus in seven nights 650 Dakota and glider sorties had been flown, 9,000 men, 1,350 animals, 250 tons of stores and two four-gun 25-pounder troops together with two six-gun 40mm Bofors gun troops had been successfully landed and still no reaction from the Japanese. Wingate was delighted and issued an order of the day saying so in his own special style.

Then on 9th March Wingate heard that Giffard was planning to use his reserve LRP brigades elsewhere and he flew to Slim determined to offer his resignation, such was his nature. Slim reminded him that there was never any question of him needing his reserves except for relief or exploitation, neither of which would come for some months, and he would ensure they were ready by then. However Slim said that 14th Brigade would remain available and, as he left, Wingate resolved to find a use for it as soon as he could. On return he planned a second stronghold to be called 'Aberdeen' to be established in the Meza valley.

The Japanese had been completely surprised by the size and scale of the landings. Lieutenant General Renya Mutaguchi, commanding *18th Division*, considered for some time that they were small, as did *15th Army*, and that local troops could clear them up as they occurred. But by 12th March he realised that they represented something much more serious and that he would have to take special measures to deal with them. By this time his operations against the 4th Indian Corps had started and he did not want anything to interfere with them.

On 9th March Calvert, with his 77th Brigade, set out to cut the road and railway north of Indaw. A second special force set out to rouse the Kachin guerrillas into action. Shortly afterwards 111th Brigade also departed. The defence of 'Broadway' was in the hands of 3/9th

Gurkhas, 'R' Troop of 160th Field Regiment, 'W' Troop of 69th LAA Regiment, which arrived between 6th and 8th March, and six Spitfires which sadly were soon either shot down or destroyed on the ground because they lacked adequate early warning. 'W' Troop destroyed five Japanese aircraft but most of 'Broadway's' attackers flew high and out of range of the 40mm guns. By 15th March Calvert had established a block at Henu called 'White City' where he was soon attacked but held for several days, successfully cutting the communications to Myitkyina. It was here that after some adventures Captain SR Nicholls RA landed with his 'S' Troop of 25-pounders also from 160th Field Regiment. He reported taking off at dusk on 5th April to land later in a very muddy paddy, to be met by Brigadier Calvert himself. Calvert said that they could not enter 'White City' and must spend the night in the Thazi wood. The rest of his troop got down successfully as did 'X' Troop 69th LAA Regiment which brought ten 0.5-inch AAMGs and two 2-pounder anti-tank guns.

Next day they all moved into the perimeter where Major Duxbury, CRA Special Force, visited Nicholls. Captain Arthur Mendus of 'T' Field Troop was also there. He was appointed to 16th Brigade which was at 'Aberdeen.' It had been decided not to send his troop there but, between 24th and 26th March, they did send 'X', 'Y' and 'Z' LAA Troops, 'X' being still armed with 0.5-inch AAMGs, and they were constantly in action. Mendus therefore stayed with Nicholls's 'S' Troop. The troop came into action and Nicholls established an OP on a nearby hill some 350 yards away which he shared with the Staffords' mortar OP. Then suddenly, on that first afternoon, came an air attack and enemy gun fire, some of it air burst. Nicholls saw the flashes of the enemy guns and decided to retaliate. But just as he found the range he ran out of ammunition. Going to find some he ran into Calvert who said once again, 'We *are* pleased to have you'. Nicholls observed, 'This sounded as if I was an honoured guest at his party and he assumed that I was enjoying it as much as he was! (Nicholls)

By now the Japanese were attacking both 'Chowringhee', which had been abandoned, and 'Broadway', which was defended, from the air. Meanwhile 111th Brigade crossed the Irrawaddy and established an airstrip at Aikma on the Meza river.

While these landings were taking place, 16th Brigade had been toiling southwards towards its operational area. Fergusson attacked Lonkin and then moved to capture Indaw and established 'Aberdeen' near Taungle. At Taungle he met Wingate who told him he planned to use 'Aberdeen' for both 111th and 14th Brigades. He also told Fergusson to attack Indaw on the 24th and said that 14th Brigade would fly in on the 23rd and assist. Wingate then flew to Comilla to meet Slim to get permission to deploy 14th Brigade. Slim agreed but not to Wingate's task for it, which by then was to cut communications to the Japanese *15th Army* and, in any case, he did not have enough aircraft to fly it in yet. Wingate then sent a signal direct to Mountbatten for onward transmission to London complaining bitterly that he was being hampered by lack of aircraft and that, if only he could be given them, he could provide a major victory. Mountbatten passed this on but with a footnote saying that, whereas he certainly needed more aircraft, he did not believe that the Chindits alone could provide a major victory. He also knew that the Japanese were about to make a major attack on Imphal and Kohima and that he must fly in more troops quickly to meet it as well as maintain the LRP brigades already deployed. Eventually some 80 aircraft were produced from the Middle East but these could not arrive until early April.

After his interview with Slim, Wingate nevertheless ordered 14th Brigade to begin its fly-in to 'Aberdeen' and then to move to attack enemy communications between Wuntho and the Chindwin. At the same time Slim ordered 5th Indian Division to be flown to Imphal from the Arakan. Thus neither could be done at best speed. Wingate visited 'Broadway', 'White City' and 'Aberdeen' and then flew to Imphal. That evening, 24th March, he left Imphal for his own headquarters in an American B.25 bomber which crashed into the mountains to the east of

Imphal and Wingate was killed. It was a sudden and great tragedy but, before assessing Wingate, it is important to see what happened on the ground immediately after his death. First, Slim was shocked, for he admired Wingate in spite of the problems he frequently caused. He appointed Lentaigne to command the Special Force. Lentaigne appointed John Masters, his Brigade Major, to command 111th Brigade and to continue its task to attack Japanese communications between Wuntho and Indaw. He then went to Special Force Headquarters at Sylhet to assess the situation. Most operations were, as far as he could see, proceeding according to plan. 16th Brigade was about to attack Indaw, but the Japanese had discovered their approach and it failed. When he discovered that 14th Brigade had indeed landed but were not going to help 16th Brigade as Wingate had promised, Fergusson decided to move to Alezu and concentrate his weary brigade. Lentaigne stopped 14th Brigade and flew to Comilla to see Slim. At this point we will leave the Chindits but we will return to them as their story unfolds.

Wingate is the only commander to get a major assessment in the Official History. There can be no doubt that he was a remarkable man. No one could have achieved all that he did in Palestine and Abyssinia without very special qualities indeed. We will of course never know what might have happened to the Chindit operations had he lived. At the time of his death he had, against many odds, created a remarkable fighting machine but, in doing so, he had angered many. He had such firm and unshakeable beliefs of his own that he could irritate those above and below him. His true motives at the time of his death are still not known. He was clearly planning operations which were not precisely akin to his orders. He had ordered 14th Brigade into Burma against Slim's wishes and had committed it to a task outside his remit. He had also ordered 16th Brigade to do the one thing he had so often said his forces must never do, attack a prepared position, this one at Indaw.

Without doubt he owed his *entrée* into Burma operations to Wavell, who had been impressed with his original thinking in Abyssinia. He gave him the resources and opportunity to test his theories in the jungles of Burma. What is more, he appeared on the scene with a series of new ideas at a time when gloom was widespread. These appealed to Churchill who always leant towards the unorthodox. He also proposed action at a time when British prestige badly needed it. This coupled with his determination and confidence in himself appeared to be the solution to many problems. His trip to the 'Quadrant' conference where he convinced both the British and American Chiefs of Staff, and his ruthless ability to use this support placed him in a unique position to get what he wanted. This he exploited to the full.

The history of war shows that in the end there is seldom a short cut to the defeat of major armies by major armies, although nuclear weapons may come close to it. Wingate was convinced that there was, and that his philosophy of the indirect approach would not only win in Burma but could go on to defeat Japan in the Far East if employed vigorously enough. There is equally no doubt that properly handled special forces can play a part out of all proportion to their size in support of major armies and in this the Chindits were a great success. Whatever else, Wingate was a great leader of men, he was a sound thinker and could provide many original ideas. He thoroughly understood guerrilla warfare but he was not so good when his guerrilla activities turned into more conventional operations. Although a first rate leader, he was not, in fact, a very good commander, and often gave confusing orders. Indeed, it is possible that he did not always tell his subordinates all that was in his mind, so that on several occasions they were not clear about their long term objectives. This could matter when things begin to go wrong and a subordinate is cut off. But there can be no doubt that the Chindits did contribute to the Japanese defeat; they also expanded the concepts of air deployment and air supply of large forces in combat. Wingate died at the height of his career. He will never be able to bask in the words of his supporters and there are many, nor will he have to face his critics of whom there are also many.

He will always be a controversial figure but he will always be one of the most illustrious sons of the Royal Regiment of Artillery.

Before turning, in the next chapter, to the great battles about to break out around Kohima and Imphal, it is important to record briefly what General Stilwell and his American-Chinese forces were doing in the Northern Sector (Maps 29 and 34).

By 1st February General Stilwell had secured the crossings of the Tern river at Taihpa Ga. During the month he had been reinforced by Merrill's Marauders, who had been training with Wingate and his Chindits, and the 1st Chinese Provisional Tank Unit. His next task was to destroy the Japanese *55th* and *56th Infantry Regiments* defending Maingkwan. His plan was to use the Marauders for a wide outflanking movement and cut off the enemy at Walawbum while the 22nd Chinese Division and the tank unit made a frontal attack. By 22nd February the Marauders were in position but the Chinese moved too slowly and the Japanese concentrated on the Marauders, who were driven off after some severe fighting. Nevertheless the operation cleared the Hukawng Valley and work could begin to carry the Ledo road forward to Maingkwan. However, time was short if Stilwell was to get to Mogaung and Myitkyina before the monsoon set in at the end of April.

After discussions with Slim on 3rd March, it was agreed that the British at Fort Hertz should advance to Sumprabum and a battalion of the Burma Rifles was flown there. Slim said that he would try to achieve surprise by a swift attack on Myitkyina from the north through Naura Hyket Pass. Stilwell then heard from Chiang Kai-shek that there would be difficulties with any advance by his forces from Yunnan. Meanwhile Stilwell ordered his Chinese to advance south down the road to Kamaing and the Marauders to move east to Pabum. His Chinese were held up at Shaduzup on 26th March. The Marauders swung south and cut the road at Warazup, forced the enemy to withdraw and enabled the Chinese to continue their advance. But then the Japanese made major advances and Stilwell was forced to withdraw to the airstrip at Hsamshingyang where the 3rd Marauders and two 75mm pack howitzers formed a strong point. 2nd Battalion Marauders was, meanwhile, cut off without water at Nhpum Ga. But the Japanese then withdrew to Myitkyina, leaving the Marauders worn out but safe.

On 6th March Mountbatten visited Stilwell who said that, when he reached the Mogaung - Myitkyina area, he would require an additional Chinese division. He then asked Mountbatten to bring pressure on Chiang Kai-shek to attack from Yunnan to pin down Japanese forces on the Salween. Mountbatten approached London and Washington but nothing that the Prime Minister or President could do would persuade the Generalissimo to agree until an ultimatum from General Marshall stated that if he did not make a move, all aid would be cut! On 14th April Chinese forces were ordered to attack from Yunnan. At this time long term arrangements were in hand to construct US airbases in China for subsequent attacks on Japan. Then Chiang Kai-shek got wind of a major Japanese offensive from the north to expand their control of south-east China and take the new American airfields there. This attack, Operation ICHI-GO, was launched and on 17th May 1944 the Japanese crossed the Yellow River and on the 27th they advanced against the airfields of south-east China, just as Chiang Kai-shek had agreed to attack from Yunnan.

But we must leave the dramatic events beginning to develop in China and the Pacific and return to operations on the Central Front in Burma and to the exploits of the Chindits still operating with success behind enemy lines. By March 1944, it will be seen that the Royal Regiment was playing a major part in all operations in South East Asia. The Gunners in the Arakan did much to ensure that the Japanese were defeated for the first time in the war. The field Gunners were incredibly adaptable as their various structures and organisations showed. The anti-aircraft Gunners began to get the measure of Japanese aircraft but were also frequently employed in the ground role. The ubiquitous mountain Gunners were simply 'Everywhere' and acquitted themselves in the very highest traditions of the Regiment. In particular the Gunner signallers distinguished themselves during the second Arakan. The story of the overrunning of 7th Indian Divisional Headquarters on 7th February might have been very different if HQRA had not maintained full control of all its regiments throughout the battle, thus enabling Divisional Headquarters to function. There was much more yet to be done before victory came, but the Gunners of the 'Forgotten Army' were providing that thread of stability and cohesion which is so essential in any operation.

Perhaps the gallantry of the Gunners in the 'Battle of the Admin Box' is best summed up by Brigadier MR Roberts, commander of 114th Indian Infantry Brigade at the time of the battle, when he wrote 'If any unit deserves "Admin Box" as a battle honour it is 24th LAA/Anti-Tank Regiment. Not only were they ubiquitous, but they took on anything that flew or walked, and at the end of it all, they could still with truth be described as "King Cole and his merry men", and there is not a unit in the 7th Division that will grudge them this tribute.' (Roberts).

CHAPTER 10

THE BATTLES OF THE TIDDIM ROAD and THE CHINDITS

FEBRUARY - MARCH 1944

(Map 35)

Throughout the months of February and March 1944 there was fighting all along the Central Sector by 4th Indian Corps, especially in the Kabaw Valley and the Chin Hills. In the Tiddim area stood 17th Indian Light Division with 129th Light Field Regiment, raised in Edinburgh in 1938. By 1944 it was commanded by Lieutenant Colonel CFJ Younger. There were also 21st and 29th Indian Mountain Regiments and 82nd LAA/Anti-Tank Regiment. The division was advancing towards Kalemyo and had surrounded enemy strong points covering Fort White. In the Kabaw Valley 20th Indian Division, with 9th Field and 114th Jungle Field Regiments and 23rd Indian Mountain and 55th LAA/Anti-Tank Regiments was trying to clear the route to Yuwa and was meeting strong resistance. 23rd Indian Division, less 49th Indian Infantry Brigade but with 158th Jungle Field Regiment, 3rd Indian Field Regiment, 28th Indian Mountain Regiment and 2nd Indian LAA/Anti-Tank Regiment, together with 234th Indian Tank Brigade, was in corps reserve at Imphal. 49th Indian Infantry Brigade, with the Kohima Garrison under its command, was at Ukhrul covering the approaches from the south east.

It was during some of the fighting in February that Major General Cowan told 129th Field Regiment that their accurate and close engagements supporting a company of 7/10th Baluch contributed very greatly to the repulse of repeated Japanese attacks and the infliction of heavy casualties. During this period 129th Field Regiment was doing trials with the 'Jury' axle, the narrow wheel-base 25-pounders, and these were going well but so was an idea of their own, to mount their 25-pounders on a Jeep axle, an idea suggested by Lance Bombardier CC Jones, whom the commanding officer put forward for an award, as this too was a great success. More details of the 'Jury' axle 25-pounder and of the 'Baby 25-pounder' favoured by the Australians in New Guinea are at Annex L.

Before following the progress of operations it is worth spending a few words on conditions in Burma for the Gunners. In 'Notes From Theatres of War No 19; Burma 1943/44', the War Office stressed the importance of artillery in all jungle operations. They referred to some of the heavy concentrations fired in the Arakan. 'In an attack onto the western approaches to Buthidaung, seven thousand shells were fired on a 500 yard front and the enemy left his well dug-in positions and ran.' It stressed the extra time needed to register a target in the jungle and that timed fireplans seldom worked because it was impossible to calculate the speed of infantry movement in the jungle. Shooting had to be observed or at least 'On call.' Also, many targets were very close to our own troops. This meant that a very large number of FOOs was needed and they had to be right forward with the leading infantry sections. The importance of DF around the objective was also stressed. Local all-round defence of gun positions was vital. Sooner or later most gun positions would be attacked by enemy infantry.

Mortars were of great value but lacked range. The 3.7-inch howitzer was excellent but also lacked range. In the end little could beat the 25-pounder with the 'Jury' axle and, using the No. 231 fuse, it could usually deal with a bunker by direct fire if it could get close enough. But the prime 'bunker buster' was the 5.5-inch gun also with the No. 231 fuse. The 3.7-inch HAA gun was most effective in the ground role with the No. 117 fuse and long range and the Bofors 40mm gun was excellent in both the ground and air defence roles. Sound ranging worked well when there was time to lay out a sound ranging base. Counter-battery fire also worked well but the Japanese dug their guns in so effectively that the fire seldom did much damage. Air Observation was not understood for some time but as soon as it was it became very useful and soon demonstrated its enormous effectiveness in the Arakan battles of February/March 1944.

The various trial organisations referred to in Chapter 8 had settled down to six as follows:

- The mechanised field regiment had three batteries, each with 8 x 25-pounders and the usual vehicles.
- The mountain regiment had four batteries, each with 4 x 3.7-inch howitzers in mule pack.
- The jungle field regiment had two batteries, each of 8 x 3.7-inch howitzers, and one battery of 16 x 3-inch mortars. The whole regiment was jeep towed or carried.
- The light field regiment was a normal field regiment but with jeeps and animals only for movement.
- The assault field regiment was specially designed for sea assault landings and had a mixture of 25-pounders, 3.7-inch howitzers and American SP 105mm Priests.
- The light anti-aircraft/anti-tank regiment had two batteries, each of 12 x 40mm Bofors guns and two batteries, each of 12 x 57mm or 6-pounder anti-tank guns.

The 3.7-inch howitzer was chosen for the jungle field regiments because of its accuracy when engaging the very frequent close targets and for its high angle capability. Each detachment had three jeeps, one to tow the gun and two for towing trailers for stores and ammunition. The guns were given towing eyes and pneumatic tyres. The first unit to be converted into a 'jungle regiment' was 27th Field Regiment in July 1942. Trials were a success and in July 1943, 28th, 114th, 134th, 139th, 158th and 160th Field Regiments started to convert and were complete by September 1943. Although the change over caused few problems, it was not popular because the Gunners liked their new and very effective 25-pounders. The conversion to mortars was even more unpopular. It was not until after the Kohima/Imphal battles that the jungle regiments were ordered to revert to three batteries each of eight 25-pounders again. The 'jungle regiment' had, however, worked well, except that the mortars did not really fit the pattern of concentrating fire and it was always hard to find a job for them without splitting them up. They could be effective if they happened to be in the right place at the right time, but they did eat up ammunition. Later, even the 3.7s were often out of range for an 'Uncle' or 'Victor' target. Then came the 'jury axle' 25-pounder with a narrow wheel base and, if required, no shield (or platform), which was 'jeep towable' and airportable. It had longer range and a greater variety of shell and, as a gun/howitzer, it was the answer to all these problems. See Annex L.

Nevertheless, Japanese prisoners reported that British mortars were very effective and most feared, that British shelling was very accurate, that harassing fire was very effective by day and by night and finally that, as soon as British shelling started, Japanese soldiers would go to ground and would not come up until the fire lifted. It also became clear that guns would often have to leave their positions to engage specific targets, especially when 'bunker busting' but it was vital that they always returned to protected dug in positions at night. FOOs had to be highly competent and pretty good as infantrymen as well but to do their job properly they had to be escorted.

In November 1942, 24th LAA and 82nd Anti-Tank Regiments had amalgamated to form 24th and 82nd LAA/Anti-Tank Regiments and joined 7th and 17th Indian Divisions. Then in August 1943, 33rd LAA and 69th (Duke of Connaught's) Anti-Tank Regiments did the same, joining 19th Indian and 70th British Divisions respectively. It was 69th that became so involved with the Chindits. A month later 55th LAA and 56th (King's Own) Anti-Tank Regiments amalgamated to join 20th and 5th Indian Divisions. Finally in November 1943, 122nd LAA Regiment combined with 100th (Gordon Highlanders) Anti-Tank Regiment to form amalgamated regiments for 36th Indian and 2nd British Divisions respectively. This structure worked well, especially as the air threat was never too serious and few tanks were met. Thus the regiments were available for many tasks and the Bofors guns were very effective against ground targets.

A word on health, because it was a vital factor. Malaria took a toll of very large numbers of men, far more than battle casualties. Much was due to ignorance. When new anti-malarial discipline was enforced, such as the wearing of long trousers, the rolling down of shirt sleeves, the provision of mosquito nets and of course Mepacrine tablets taken daily, it receded rapidly as a problem. But there was always dysentery, scrub typhus, beri-beri and typhoid to contend with, although much could be done by good hygiene and water discipline. Lastly there were leeches, which had to be burnt off the skin with a cigarette or some salt, as well as snakes, scorpions, cockroaches and ants.

By late February 1944 it was clear that *33rd Division* was operating around Tiddim and that preparations for an offensive were being made (Map 35). This was confirmed by the identification of *18th Heavy Artillery Regiment* at Kalemyo and much boat traffic on the Chindwin. Accordingly Lieutenant General Scoones, Commanding 4th Indian Corps, ordered 23rd Indian Division to put a brigade at Kuntaung, to withdraw labour units from the front line areas and for 17th Indian Division to capture Fort White. This it tried to do with 48th Indian Infantry Brigade and a heavy artillery attack but failed. The Gunners were deployed by the CRA, Brigadier JH de Robeck. 21st Indian Mountain Regiment, Lieutenant Colonel PER Dawson, was with 48th Indian Infantry Brigade and 29th Indian Mountain Regiment, Lieutenant Colonel G Horsfield, with 63rd Indian Infantry Brigade. The CRA kept 129th Jungle Field Regiment and 82nd LAA/Anti-Tank Regiment under his command but deployed them around the Tiddim-Kennedy Peak area.

HQRA 17th Indian Light Division's Operation Order No 1 of 1st January 1944 grouped artillery for these operations as follows:

48th Indian Infantry Brigade

Artillery Commander: Lieutenant Colonel Dawson.

One battery, 129th Field Regiment.
One LAA section, 82nd LAA/Anti-Tank Regiment.
21st Indian Mountain Regiment, less 37th Mountain Battery.

63rd Indian Infantry Brigade

Artillery Commander: Lieutenant Colonel Horsfield.

One LAA Section, 82nd LAA/Anti-Tank Regiment.
29th Indian Mountain Regiment plus 37th Mountain Battery.

Fighting went on throughout January and February 1944 in the Tiddim - Fort White - Mile Stone 22 area, with guns constantly in action covering infantry patrols. In January Subadar Fateh Khan of 9th Mountain Battery, 29th Indian Mountain Regiment was awarded the Military Cross for gallantry as an FOO when he took command of disorganised infantry and then, with complete disregard of direct enemy fire, he engaged the enemy with his guns and defeated them. His citation states, '. . . and this was not an exceptional case. This VCO has, throughout this period, remained in the forefront of all battles.'

Several attacks were made on the bunkers at MS 22 in February using field and medium guns and 2- and 6-pounder anti-tank guns in direct fire by several FOOs but to no avail. It had not been easy to get 246th Medium Battery up the steep mountain tracks but, once there, its fire was significant. The main battle for MS 22 took place on 25th and 26th February. After 246th Medium Battery engaged the bunkers for three hours using fuse No. 231, the rest of the divisional artillery, 21st and 29th Indian Mountain and 129th Field Regiments joined in. As patrols of 1/7th Gurkha Rifles approached under cover of the guns they came under machine gun fire but this was silenced by a 2-pounder anti-tank gun placed in position for just this task. This plan was repeated on 26th February. This time the assaulting infantry got right up to the bunker when the FOO of 129th Field Regiment, who was with them, was killed by a sniper and the officer with the anti-tank guns was wounded. 'A' Company 1/4th Gurkhas attacked the 'Gibraltar' feature, with Lieutenant James Proctor of 21st Indian Mountain Regiment as FOO to outflank the MS 22 bunker but they too ran into real problems and suffered heavy casualties. Then 'B' Company attacked and again Proctor acted as FOO, but again without success and they were forced to withdraw, with Proctor and his two signallers killing at least five enemy with their rifles and bayonets as they covered the infantry pulling back with gunfire. For his great gallantry in this action Proctor was awarded the Military Cross and his citation concludes, 'His great courage and total disregard of his personal safety in hand to hand fighting against superior enemy forces and his outstanding example of courageous and skilful FOO work . . . had already become a source of great inspiration throughout the regiment.' For the same action one of his signallers, Naik Bacham Singh, won the Military Medal and the other was awarded a Gallantry Certificate.

The British had 17th Indian Light Division in contact around Tiddim and 20th and 23rd Indian Divisions further north around Imphal. The Japanese had *33rd Division* advancing towards Tiddim and *15th* and *31st Divisions* further north sitting back from the Chindwin waiting to attack. Thus two almost equal forces faced each other. The trick was to see if one side could deceive the other and concentrate in time to win. Scoones reckoned that the enemy would first try to cut off 17th Indian Division by attacking its line of communication and then go hard for Imphal. He therefore decided to withdraw to the Imphal Plain and create a strong reserve for a counter-attack. 17th Indian Division was ordered to be prepared to pull back, if a major threat developed, leaving a brigade at Tiddim for as long as it could hold, while 20th Indian Division was ordered to withdraw to the Shenam Pass south east of Palel in similar circumstances. Scoones also pulled back as many administrative units as he could to the Dimapur railhead. The problem was to identify when the enemy would make a major attack.

After watching the fly out of 77th Brigade with Wingate on 5th March, Slim went to Headquarters 4th Indian Corps at Imphal and discussed Scoones's plans, which he approved. He told Scoones that he had ordered 25th Indian Division to take over from 5th Indian Division in the Arakan and that he had told 5th Indian Division to fly to join 4th Indian Corps between 13th March and 14th April. Scoones then spent the next few weeks perfecting his administrative plans for the defence of the Imphal Plain. He created a series of logistic boxes based on the airstrips and ensured plans existed for their defence. These were often built up around the gun positions.

Before looking at operations in the Kennedy Peak - Tiddim Road area, we must not forget the Maritime Gunners manning the guns on the merchant ships bringing the vital supplies and reinforcements into the Far East Theatre. One tragic event that occurred at this time was the murder of the crew of the SS *Behar* which shows the acute danger run by these members of the

Regiment. The SS *Behar* sailed from Melbourne on 29th February 1944 bound for Bombay with a cargo of war stores. By mid-morning 9th March she sighted an enemy cruiser approaching when she was just south west of the Cocos Islands. It turned out to be the Japanese cruiser, *Tone*. The cruiser closed rapidly and opened fire while still out of range of the *Behar's* guns. She soon scored so many hits that the *Behar* capsized and sank. The *Tone* picked up the crew, except for Gunner Stanley Pycroft aged 21 who was killed in action by his gun, and sailed on for Batavia. Here Rear Admiral Naomasa Sakonju said that the prisoners were to be disposed of immediately even though Captain Mayazumi of the *Tone* begged for their lives. 36 were put ashore, but 72 were taken to sea and, on the night of 18/19th March 1944, each prisoner was felled by a blow to the stomach, kicked in the testicles and beheaded. In 1948 Admiral Sakonju was tried for this crime, found guilty and executed. Amongst many others murdered on that awful night were Sergeant Charlie Ratcliffe, Bombardier Neil Brodie and Gunner Alex Rodney, all of 1st Maritime Regiment RA, and Bombardier Arthur Bower and Gunner Alfred Street of 4th Maritime Regiment RA.

By early March 1944, 17th Indian Light Division, Major General DT Cowan, had 48th Indian Infantry Brigade under Brigadier RT Cameron in the Kennedy Peak - Vengte area and 63rd Indian Infantry Brigade, commanded by Brigadier GWS Burton, in reserve between Kennedy Peak and Tiddim. He also had 'Tonforce', of two battalions plus 9th and 38th Mountain Batteries, in the Tonzang area. 20th Indian Division under Major General DD Gracey had 100th Indian Infantry Brigade, Brigadier WAL James, in the Witok - Htinzin area, 32nd Indian Infantry Brigade, under Brigadier DAL Mackenzie, facing south east astride the Yu River and 80th Indian Infantry Brigade, Brigadier S Greaves, astride the track facing Sittaung. All three brigades were patrolling actively. Divisional Headquarters was at Tamu and the Divisional Administrative area was at Moreh. Finally, 23rd Indian Infantry Division, under Major General OL Roberts, had 1st Indian Infantry Brigade, Brigadier RC McCay, near Kuntaung with a battalion forward at Tonhe. 49th Indian Infantry Brigade, under Brigadier FA Esse, was still at Ukhrul and 37th Indian Infantry Brigade, Brigadier HV Collingridge, was at Kanglatongbi with 254th Indian Tank Brigade.

On 9th March reports began to come in of large enemy forces crossing the Manipur river near Mualbem. There was much small scale fighting. An OP of 1st Royal (Kohat) Mountain Battery, of 21st Indian Mountain Regiment, covered a party of infantry withdrawing past it with particularly effective fire. Then 'Tonforce' at Tonzang was attacked. Cowan immediately told 63rd Indian Infantry Brigade to go back to Tonzang, take 'Tonforce' under command and clear the route. Next came reports of large enemy forces west of Tiddim moving north. Clearly they had crossed the Manipur river and were trying to cut the Tiddim road. Cowan ordered 9th Jat, a machine gun battalion, back to the Manipur Bridge where they found three infantry companies, an engineer squadron and a mountain battery. Scoones decided he must help 17th Indian Division get out or they would be cut off. At this time 493rd Battery, Major Peter Brown, of 129th Field Regiment, was deployed within 50 feet of the crest of Kennedy Peak at a battery height of 8871 feet, proudly claiming to be the highest guns in the World! Getting there had been a major test, as each gun had to be pulled to the top by a line of jeeps and every available man on the drag ropes. As we have seen 246th Medium Battery of 8th Medium Regiment, less 'C' Troop, had also reached the summit with the aid of bulldozers. This regiment was moved back to Imphal on 11th March and was next in action at Kanglatombi. Are these Regimental records?

While these operations were in progress 100th Indian Infantry Brigade at Witok came under pressure. Scoones was convinced that the enemy offensive had begun and ordered a general move back to the Imphal plain positions. 17th Indian Division was to pull out on the night of 13th March. 37th Indian Infantry Brigade with a squadron of tanks was told to go down the Tiddim road as far as MS 82 to help 17th Indian Division in its withdrawal. 49th Indian Infantry Brigade was ordered to hand over Ukhrul to 50th Indian Parachute Brigade, under Brigadier MRJ Hope-Thomson, which had just arrived, and to join 37th Indian Infantry Brigade at MS 82. It had with it 28th Mountain Battery of 28th Indian Mountain Regiment. 17th Indian Division began to fall back and reached Tonzang by 15th March without too much difficulty but trouble was soon to come. The enemy had created four road blocks at Tuitum, MS 128, MS 132 and the Manipur Bridge.

The Japanese then pushed on westwards and attacked the 'Peacock' OP at Point 7953 and then the village of Phaito and the 'Richmond' feature. This put them in a position to cut the road, which they did on the night of 13/14th March at the Tuitum Saddle. On 15th March 1/10th Gurkhas and 29th Indian Mountain Regiment attacked the position but failed to dislodge them. It became urgent to clear the block, as the divisional column was closing up from the south. Accordingly, Colonel Younger reports, 'Regiment in action at MS 144. Fireplan for the attack on Tuitum roadblock: 493rd Battery firing from the north and 311th and 312th from the south, two 6-pounder guns of 82nd LAA/Anti-Tank Regiment were forward at Tuitum firing over open sights. 1/3rd and 1/10th Gurkhas took the position with only three casualties.' This fireplan with guns firing from north and south gave the Japanese no reverse slope protection. In addition Hurricanes had bombed and strafed the enemy position. 38th Mountain Battery report this battle as follows, '1/3rd Gurkhas attacked a small feature covering the road block under the mortar fire of 38th Mountain Battery which they seized but they lost contact with brigade headquarters except through the Gunner radio. The main position was attacked at 1330 hours 15th March by 1/3rd and 1/10th Gurkhas but failed. 129th Field Regiment arrived in range that night and next day a new attack was preceded by RAF bombers, the 25-pounders of 129th Field Regiment, the 3.7-inch howitzers of 21st and 29th Indian Mountain Regiments, the mortars of 38th Mountain Battery, 2 x 2-pounders, 2 x 40mm guns and one 25-pounder right forward sniping direct into enemy bunkers. The attack was a success. 1/3rd Gurkhas reached their objectives by following within 50 yards of the falling shells and found all the Japanese either dead or dying in their trenches. In this action Subedar Mohammed Khan of 29th Indian Mountain Regiment was awarded the Military Cross for the accuracy of his direct fire, and his leadership and devotion to duty under close enemy fire which was an inspiration to all ranks.'

The division moved on. Lieutenant Colonel Younger again, '17th March. Regiment at MS 126 fired many DF tasks onto enemy attacks as they tried in vain to re-take the Tuitum position, and did great execution.' The Tuitum position was by then the rearguard while operations continued to clear the route further north. Colonel Younger continues, '19th March. Still at MS 126. Continued rearguard actions. 312th Battery moved to MS 120 for attack on Point 6027. . . 23rd March. 493rd Battery at MS 126 continued to cover the rearguard until MS 109 was recaptured. 311th and 312th Batteries at Maulkawi village still engaging Point 6027 and covering 48th Brigade's encircling movement to capture MS 109. Also attacked 5800 feature, 7617 Spur, MG Spur, Spur at MS 107 and MS 105 to cover the moves of the infantry. Much CB and HF fire as well.' (Monthly news letter, March 1944, to the MGRA India).

Then the enemy, who had suffered heavy casualties from the artillery, suddenly fell back and opened the way to the Manipur Bridge. 37th Indian Infantry Brigade had linked up with the hard pressed Jats at MS 100 where they had held for two days. The division was nearly through and 20th Indian Division was conforming by its move back to the Shenam Pass.

Slim asked Mountbatten for more aircraft to speed up the move of 5th Indian Division from the Arakan just at the time Wingate was also asking for more for the move of 14th Brigade. Until these aircraft could arrive Mountbatten diverted others from the Chinese air bridge on 16th March and the move of 5th Indian Division started on 19th March. On the 18th Giffard had decided that 2nd British Division should move to Chittagong forthwith and join 14th Army there, although this did not, in the end occur. 7th Indian Division was to follow 5th Indian Division at best speed. Finally 23rd Brigade was allotted to 14th Army for use in emergency.

Meanwhile 17th Indian Division was struggling back from Tiddim, but General Cowan had acted swiftly. When the order to move came, 48th Indian Infantry Brigade and 129th Field Regiment less 493rd Battery, were deployed along the Letha Range of hills. As we have seen Cowan ordered 63rd Indian Infantry Brigade and 29th Indian Mountain Regiment to go to Tonzang as soon as possible while 48th Indian Infantry Brigade with 129th Field Regiment was to cover the rear at Tiddim. The actual rearguard was 2/5th Royal Gurkhas and 6th Mountain Battery. The forces at Fort White were pulled back by midnight on 13th March when Tiddim was evacuated and all roads cratered. Attacks were frequent and at one stage an *ad hoc* 'Mountain Commando Battery' was formed under Lieutenant Evans.

While all this was happening, further north an enemy column was seen approaching Ukhrul and a spirited action began at Sheldon's Corner just as 123rd Indian Infantry Brigade, of 5th Indian Division, landed some 40 miles away at Tulihal airfield. This brigade was sent immediately to join 23rd Indian Division where it became the divisional reserve. Slim went to Imphal where he learnt from Scoones that the critical battle to get 17th Indian Division back past MS 96 was about to be fought, Ukhrul was under heavy pressure, the enemy were close on the tail of 20th Indian Division and reports were coming in of strong enemy forces heading for Kohima and Dimapur. Slim realised that he would soon have two major battles on his hands and he ordered Headquarters 33rd Corps, commanded by Lieutenant General MGN Stopford, to move forward to Comilla and be ready to plan a counter-stroke to deal with the situation fast developing at Kohima. 1st Burma Regiment was diverted from its move to Fort Hertz to Dimapur as were 161st Indian Infantry Brigade of 5th Indian Division and 24th Indian Mountain Regiment, under Lieutenant Colonel RHM (Humphrey) Hill, which was just about to arrive from the Arakan. The stage was set for what was to become some of the most cruel, bitter and fierce fighting of the whole war in battles which were to be crucial to the outcome of the war in South East Asia.

Meanwhile, in the 17th Indian Light Divisional area, enemy patrols began to close on OP and piquet positions east of Tonzang which had been occupied by 'Tonforce.' It soon became clear that this was the major thrust. Lieutenant Colonel Younger of 129th Field Regiment, in his monthly letter to Major General Mirrlees, MGRA India, described the battle that followed. 'During the first ten days of March attacks on enemy positions in the Fort White area continued. 312th Battery had relieved 493rd in the Kennedy Peak/Dimlo area, 311th in the Tiddim area with 493rd Battery covering the Manipur river crossing on the Tuitum feature.' It was then recognised that a greater danger lay to the north around MS 100 and that the critical supply dump at MS 109 was also threatened.

The battles of Singgel, near MS 100, and Sakawng, near MS 109, were fought to clear the withdrawal route; Singgel by 37th Indian Infantry Brigade of 23rd Indian Division which had 6th Field Regiment with them; this battle was not over until 25th March. MS 100 was still held by 9th Jat. After many probing attacks the Jats were rescued but the Japanese still held two road blocks at MSs 99 and 97. 48th Indian Infantry Brigade was ordered to re-take MS 109 and the Supply Dump and open the road for the final phase of the withdrawal. Brigadier Cameron decided to do this by a right flanking movement through Sakawng village which he reached on 21st March. 129th Field Regiment had 311th and 312th Batteries at Mualkawi alongside the guns of 21st Indian Mountain Regiment. The first phase went in on 22nd March with artillery attacks by 37th Mountain Battery's mortars but it failed. Brigadier Cameron then planned a more ambitious attack for the 23rd with 311th and 312th Field Batteries as well. The guns opened fire at 0615 hours on the 23rd and after severe fighting the enemy were driven off those positions which covered the approach to MS 109. During this fight two FOOs, Major EN Hunter of 129th Field Regiment and Captain PW Winfield of 37th Mountain Battery, ranged the guns onto the objective when a platoon of 9th Borders was only 15 yards from it! They did this by slowly dropping the range and explaining the great delicacy of the operation to the layers. The task was also eased because the guns were to a flank which removed the 'zone' and enabled corrections to be applied in azimuth with great accuracy. Nevertheless, both were wounded by their own splinters but the fire was extremely effective and the position was taken with almost no further casualties.

With 1/7th Gurkhas under Lieutenant Colonel Jim Robertson leading, the brigade set off to clear the route and rescue the vital Supply Depot at MS 109. In soaking rain they cleared another Japanese position on the way. Meanwhile 129th Field Regiment, less 493rd Battery which was still with the rear-guard, and two Bofors guns from the rump of 82nd LAA/Anti-Tank Regiment, most of which had by then been converted into infantry, and 21st Indian Mountain Regiment, pounded the enemy position. 2/5th Gurkhas went to cut off the Japanese from the north and hit their position near MS 104, known as 'The Knoll.' At 1430 hours on 25th March the Gunners attacked 'West Knoll' with maximum firepower and then 'C' Company 2/5th Gurkhas attacked it with great gallantry, but were held. They called on the Gunners again, and a second artillery attack rained down. Eventually they were successful but only by using the rest of the battalion as well as all the guns, plus those of 1st Mountain Battery firing over open sights. The cost, however, was high, 37 Gurkhas were killed and 67 wounded. Such was the price of success, but the Japanese had had enough. To their surprise, on the morning of 26th March, the Gurkhas found 'Bunker Hill' spur which covered the Depot, deserted. General Scoones signalled Cowan, 'Congratulate all ranks on progress and sterling fighting qualities.'

It was at this time that Cyril Hoskins, then a surveyor with 129th Field Regiment, had a horrifying experience. After the fighting on 24th March ammunition was low, down to five rounds per gun. Air drops failed as the parachutes all drifted into the Japanese lines. Accordingly he and another Gunner, John Hinchcliffe, were told to drive up the road towards Imphal and see how far they could get before they met the enemy. They were chosen because they were surveyors, therefore good at map reading, and there was no survey work going on at that time. They were in an 8 cwt truck and after some miles they stopped beside a stationary Red Cross ambulance. They found that the driver had been shot and two wounded Gurkha soldiers had been killed on their stretchers. They drove on until they reached MS 109.

Here they were challenged by a British major who was surprised to learn that the road to the south was open and he immediately reported it to 17th Indian Division by radio. 'He said that he had driven down with his radio operator and then he showed us the horror he had found. At MS 109 had been a clearing hospital which the Japanese had captured. They had hung all the wounded on to the trees and bayoneted them to death, there were at least 20. We took down the bodies and placed them in a basha hut.' (Hoskins). Once again they were reminded of the barbarous nature of their enemy.

On 26th March Lieutenant Colonel Younger of 129th Regiment reported, 'Moved to MS 109 area. Engaged MS 102 and enemy guns at Khuabum, Zampi and Maulkawi, two enemy mountain guns knocked out. . . March 29th. 312th Battery moved to MS 98 and covered the withdrawal of the division to MS 82. 311th and 493rd Batteries to MS 82. . . March 30th. 312th Battery moved to MS 82. 311th, 312th and 493rd Batteries engaged on counter-battery tasks and harassing fire. Fired in support of 37th Indian Infantry Brigade of 23rd Indian Division through whom we have now passed. . . 1st April. All three batteries deployed near MS 79 and engaged enemy around MS 72.' There was in fact a tough fight by the infantry to break through a road block at MS 72 but it was successfully cleared. On 2nd April Colonel Younger wrote 'Regiment marched to MS 41. No firing for the first time in 21 days. . . 4th April Regiment marched to MS 4 north of Imphal and is grouped with 5th Indian Division.' During the three weeks of the withdrawal 129th Field Regiment fired 6,990 rounds.

As it moved back at the end of the Tiddim Road battles, 21st Indian Mountain Regiment learnt that Captain Bernard Aldred had been awarded the Military Cross for consistent bravery in action under fire both as Gun Position Officer and as FOO between 5th January and 6th April 1944.

Next we must look further to the north to see what was happening as the Japanese *15th* and *31st Divisions* closed on Imphal and Kohima respectively. By 22nd March 4th Indian Corps was in contact on a 180 mile arc stretching from Layshi in the north, by way of Ukhrul and Tamu, to Tuitum on the Tiddim road in the south, and a major threat was developing towards Sangshak only six miles north east of Imphal. Scoones ordered the newly-arrived 5th Indian Division, less 161st Indian Infantry Brigade, to cover the Imphal-Kohima road. 161st Indian Infantry Brigade was to keep the Dimapur-Imphal road open and Colonel HU Richards, Commander Kohima Garrison, was to hold it at all costs. For this all he had initially was 1st Assam Regiment.

At Sangshak was 50th Indian Parachute Brigade, under the command of Brigadier M Hope-Thomson, with 152nd (Gurkha) and 153rd (Indian) Parachute Battalions, 4/5th Mahrattas of 49th Indian Infantry Brigade, half of the Kalibahadur Regiment, a Nepalese unit, 15th (Jhelum) Mountain Battery under Major RJP Lock, 583rd Mortar Battery, a detachment of 4th Field Company and a field ambulance. Two OPs were manned, one in the church and one with 4/5th Mahrattas. The guns and mortars were in action on a small feature about 100 yards by 50 on the highest part of the position. There was very little room.

The Japanese force spotted approaching Sangshak was the leading *II/58th Battalion* of *31st Division* heading for Kohima by way of Mao. Major General M Miyazaki, commander of *31st Infantry Group* in Lieutenant General Kotoku Sato's *31st Division* on reaching Ukhrul, strayed south into *15th Division's* area to deal with this threat to his flank. It was a mistake he was to regret. His first attack at Sangshak was made at 1600 hours on 22nd March but was defeated, although the defender's outposts fell back around the guns. Heavy attacks were made all night, especially against No 1 Gun of 15th Mountain Battery which was more exposed than the rest. The mortars, which were well dug in, engaged with great success. There was sniping all day on 23rd March and air drops and air strikes were carried out in support. The OP in the church was attacked and a signaller was wounded but the OP party wounded and captured a Japanese officer, a rare event. The guns inflicted heavy damage on enemy forming up at Sanjing village nearby. On 25th March No 2 Gun of 15th Mountain Battery fought a duel with an enemy gun and silenced it to the cheers of the infantry. That evening Major Lock was wounded in the face but stayed at his post. A Naik and a Gunner were killed at No 1 Gun and eight more wounded including Lieutenant Malhotra. The enemy pressed very hard on the 26th and broke into the position. A new perimeter was made round No 2 Gun and a very strong resistance was put up by Havildar Surwan Dass of 15th Mountain Battery, some officers of 152nd (Gurkha) Parachute Battalion and some Gunners from No 3 Gun under Naik Ali Akbar. Gunners Gheba Khan and Ayub Khan fought like tigers with small arms and grenades and, with the encouragement of the wounded Major Lock, somehow this splendid little band held on.

Major Lock then led a gallant attack to clear No 1 Gun position with Major Smith, commanding 583 Mortar Battery, himself a former mountain Gunner. When the enemy were ejected later, it was seen that Major Lock had bayoneted three Japanese in the gun pit. He and Smith had both been killed trying to clear a trench just beyond it. Attacks and rushes continued. Havildars Surwan Dass and Mohan Lal charged again and again with grenades and a Bren, and on one occasion Mohan Lal brought back a wounded British officer. The infantry used the guns as a rallying point for a final rush alongside the Gunners with Brens and grenades. Havildar Mohan Lal brought back the sights of No 1 Gun and at the same time saved the life of another Gunner who lay wounded in the gun pit. The Gurkhas counter-attacked and saved the guns but only No 2 was fit to fire and at 1600 hours it fired 70 rounds at enemy guns at Lingshang while the detachment was being sniped by enemy infantry. The Japanese guns were silenced.

At 1830 hours the little garrison was ordered to withdraw. The guns were stripped of essential parts after shells were rammed down the barrels 'fore and aft' and exploded. After the action Lieutenant Kidd of 15th Mountain Battery concluded his report saying, '2230 hours. The battery with its wounded marched out in a block behind 152 [Gurkha Parachute] Battalion.' After four days struggling through the hostile jungle they reached Waithou and then Imphal. The defence of the guns at Sangshak by the men of 15th Mountain Battery and 583rd Mortar Battery must equal any in the annals of the Regiment. The awards of the IDSM to Havildar Surwan Dass and Havildar Mohan Lal were richly deserved but in any other place at any other time the awards would certainly have been more numerous. As it was, Major Lock, Lance Naik Mathra Das, Gunner Fida Hussain Shah, Gunner Gian Chand and three cooks were killed around the guns. Four Gunners were captured, six were wounded and six were missing, a total of 22 casualties. But their gallantry and that of 152nd (Gurkha) Parachute Battalion was not wasted and was to play a significant part in the great battles to follow. The time they gained was to allow the deployment of 161st Indian Infantry Brigade to Kohima in time to stem the Japanese attacks. Had they not attacked Sangshak it is highly possible that the Japanese would have broken through at Kohima. It had been a costly error. Seldom have so few, by their gallantry, devotion and courage, played such a significant part in a major battle.

By 1st April, 161st Indian Infantry Brigade had 4/7th Rajputs at Dimapur with 24th Indian Mountain Regiment, under Lieutenant Colonel Humphrey Hill, less 20th Mountain Battery, and 1/1st Punjab at MS 16 between Dimapur and Kohima. They formed an all-round defensive position and were soon to be surrounded. At Kohima were the 4th Royal West Kents and 20th Indian Mountain Battery commanded by Major RC (Dick) Yeo. The outposts of 1st Assam Regiment were still out at Jessami and Kharasom.

Before describing the great battles of Kohima and Imphal it is necessary briefly to get up to date with what was happening elsewhere.

50 miles to the south 20th Indian Division was still defending the Kabaw valley. 32nd Indian Infantry Brigade was in the Tamu area, 80th Indian Infantry Brigade was between Kongkhang and Sibong and 100th Indian Infantry Brigade was at Moreh. On 27th March General Slim decided to send 2nd British Division to Dimapur. On 28th March the leading elements of *138th Regiment* of *31st Division* attacked 1st Assam's outposts at Jessami. On the night 30/31st March the Imphal-Kohima road was cut at Maram. On the 28th, 20th Indian Division withdrew to the Palel/Shenam area. The move of 2nd British Division began with 4th British Infantry Brigade and 16th Field Regiment moving by rail to Amarda airfield near Calcutta and then by air to Dimapur. Meanwhile 17th Indian Light Division had deployed to the north of Imphal with 63rd Indian Infantry Brigade at Kangpokpi where it relieved 9th Indian Infantry Brigade of 5th Indian Division. This division then went to Nungshigum to meet an enemy threat to Point 3833. 123rd Indian Infantry Brigade repelled an enemy attack on Yaingangpokpi. 23rd Indian Division was holding Wangjing with 1st Indian Infantry Brigade astride the Tiddim Road at Torbung with 37th and 49th Indian Infantry Brigades. It still had 32nd Indian Infantry Brigade in reserve at Palel.

33rd Indian Corps began to organise the defence of the Kohima Sector. Major General RPL Ranking, the commander of 202nd Line of Communications Area, was ordered to defend Dimapur/Kohima. 1st Burma Regiment was to defend the Base at Dimapur, 161st Indian Infantry Brigade was to be his mobile reserve and was ordered to be concentrated at Nichuguard forthwith. This left the Kohima garrison very thin on the ground, but help was coming. On 1st April 5th British Infantry Brigade, under Brigadier VFS Hawkins, of 2nd British Division, began to arrive at Bokajan about 10 miles to the north. Also on that day Headquarters 33rd Indian Corps opened at Jorhat. Meanwhile 221 Group RAF at Imphal was working with both 4th and 33rd Indian Corps. Fourteen squadrons were made available. Nine had Hurricanes, of which four were equipped as fighter bombers, three had Vengeance light bombers and two had Spitfires. In addition there was a Beaufighter squadron for night fighter work. At the same time the enemy swung his air effort to this front but it was never as great as it had been in the Arakan. By and large the RAF controlled the skies and during March they flew some 4,500 sorties for the loss of 16 aircraft. Two LAA batteries of 55th LAA/Anti-Tank Regiment withdrew with 20th Indian Division to Imphal. 67th HAA and 28th and 78th LAA Regiments were also deploying to defend the airfields and airstrips around Imphal. Here 165th LAA Battery shot down three enemy fighter bombers with 175 rounds, while 24th LAA Regiment shot down two in the Shenam Pass. Altogether 12 enemy aircraft were shot down during this period. Meanwhile 100th LAA/Anti-Tank Regiment joined 2nd Division at Dimapur.

Mountbatten, in assessing the situation facing him, reckoned he would soon be balanced enough to hold the enemy. He told General Stilwell to continue with his operations to capture Myitkyina. Stilwell said he would get there by about 20th May. The Chindits were told to operate against the enemy in the Mogaung valley to assist. He told the Chiefs of Staff in London that the best way his command could help American operations in the Pacific was to develop the air route to China and this meant seizing a major airfield. He warned that, until he had defeated the present Japanese attacks, his advance into Burma would slow down. Essential to the development of the air route was the capture of Myitkyina and the build up of an air head and a fuel base there. At this time Slim estimated that it would take until June to mop up all Japanese west of the Chindwin.

Meanwhile, in the Arakan, operations were by no means over. 25th Indian Division had taken over from 5th Indian Division to the west of the Mayu Range, with 51st Indian Infantry Brigade south east of Maungdaw, 74th Indian Infantry Brigade was also in that area. 72nd Infantry Brigade of 36th Indian Division was in the West Tunnel area with 29th Infantry Brigade, commanded by Brigadier HC Stockwell, in reserve at Bawli. The Gunners were:

15th Indian Corps:

CCRA, Brigadier L Harris

1st Medium Regiment. Lt Col RAH Soames.
6th Medium Regiment. Lt Col WG Fox.
8th (Belfast) HAA Regiment. Lt Col JC Cunningham
36th LAA Regiment. Lt Col PA Brooke
5th (Mahratta) Anti-Tank Regiment,

25th Indian Division:

CRA, Brigadier R O'Carrol-Scott.

8th Field Regiment. Lt Col JCH Mead.
27th Jungle Field Regiment. Lt Col CL Corsar
5th Indian Field Regiment. Lt Col RA Crooks
7th Indian LAA/Anti-Tank Regiment. Lt Col PGP Bradshaw

36th Indian Division:

CRA, Brigadier GE Barrington

130th Assault Field Regiment. Lt Col HCB Hall
178th Assault Field Regiment. Lt Col KM Wright
122nd LAA/Anti-Tank Regiment. Lt Cols CD Oliver/JW Calver

81st West African Division:
CRA, Brigadier HB Jolly

1st (WA) LAA/Anti-Tank Regiment. Lt Col OW Holleyman
3rd Independent (WA) Light Battery
4th Independent (WA) Light Battery
6th Independent (WA) Light Battery

In the Kaladan valley 81st West African Division, under its GOC Major General CG Woolner, was building a Dakota strip at Kyingri on the Pi Chaung. General Christison then ordered 25th and 36th Indian Divisions to complete the capture of the Maungdaw - Buthidaung road and hold it through the monsoon. This meant driving the Japanese from their strongholds at Point 551 and the West Tunnel area. 81st Division was told to move to the Kalapanzin area. Meanwhile 114th Indian Infantry Brigade was still east of the Kalapanzin river around Kyaukyit and in contact with aggressive Japanese patrolling. Then on 26th March, after a heavy bombardment, 72nd Indian Infantry Brigade captured the West Tunnel area but the Japanese were still strong inside the tunnels. They were not finally driven out until 4th April. 6th Medium Regiment was heavily involved in these operations.

The battle for the Tunnels was not without incident. 24th Field Battery of 27th Field Regiment reports, 'The battery was in action at Kanbyin in the West Mayu foothills. Captains Harris, Clarke, Whitehead and Affleck occupied OPs with 17/5th Mahrattas. On 5th April a Mahratta company was driven off Point 904 by a surprise attack in the middle of the day. Captain Clarke had just moved to a fresh OP. There were several casualties and the attack revealed a weakness of patrolling and general alertness. A counter-attack was organised for the April but at dawn that day another Mahratta position, known as 'Bird' and including Captain Whitehead's OP, was attacked.

From the History of 19th (Niagara) Medium Battery we learn that 'The attack duly went in on Apr 7th and from the KANBYIN feature it appeared like the finale of a tattoo. The fire plan came down perfectly and during the final stages, the tanks of the 25 Dragoons moved into position covering SPIT and POLISH from the East and South East to give the infantry close support. One tank was hit and set on fire by Jap 47mm A/Tk guns . . . Three of these Jap guns were subsequently captured. The 1 Lincolns then went in and in spite of strong opposition and heavy casualties secured SPIT and POLISH. 168 Jap bodies were found on the objective many killed by Artillery fire. More bodies were subsequently found by our infantry when digging in.' It was in the afternoon of 7th April that the battery was ordered back to the 'Admin Box' 'whence it was to send out troops and sections as required for specific jobs.'

Whitehead says that the morale of the Mahratta company he was with was low when they were attacked later. After a short engagement the only men left on the position were the company commander and the OP party, who were forced to withdraw. A new position was taken up at the north end of 'Bird' by a company of 8th Hyderabad, with Captain P Sherston-Baker as FOO. That night the enemy pressed his attack hard and by morning it was the same story. The OP party were the last to leave. Bombardier Rose was wounded by a grenade. Eventually the position was re-captured with the fire of 5th Indian and 8th Field Regiments, 24th Jungle Field Battery and one battery of 1st Medium Regiment.

Soon East Tunnel area was also captured but it became clear that the Japanese were determined to hold Point 551 and if possible they were going to re-capture Buthidaung. Christison decided not to bother about the defence of Buthidaung but to capture Point 551 as soon as possible. It was a very strong position and held by a determined enemy. Accordingly Major General CEN Lomax, commanding 26th Indian Division, allotted his full Divisional Artillery (Annex U) plus 1st and 6th Medium Regiments, two batteries of 36th Indian Division, one squadron of tanks from 25th Dragoons and one from 149th Regiment RAC to this task.

The infantry attack went in at 0800 hours on 15th April following heavy air and artillery attacks but after fierce fighting which went on until the 30th, the objective had still not been taken. It was during this fighting that 30th Indian Mountain Regiment, commanded by Lieutenant Colonel TWR Hill, distinguished itself. 33rd Mountain Battery, Major IMG Williams, was involved in a close action over open sights and acquitted itself well. During the fighting on 15th April Lieutenant JG Downes of 33rd and Captain NJ Deane of 32nd Mountain Batteries were killed while directing fire alongside the infantry as FOOs during the attacks on Point 551. Captain TR Harris and Lance Sergeant S King, of 24th Field Battery, were with the 14/10th Baluch in this operation as FOO party and the latter won a Military Medal for recovering wounded from the middle of the enemy position. Major ALO Buxton and Captain P Sherston-Baker, also of 24th Field Battery, each won the Military Cross for gallantry during this operation. Some 12,000 rounds were fired in all.

Meanwhile 34th Mountain Battery, under Major Hadfield, had been operating with 25th Indian Division. By now the monsoon was imminent and a re-organisation took place to hold the line as it was. Nevertheless it was decided to have one more go at capturing Point 551 and the night of 3/4th May was chosen. Success came more easily than expected by the end of 4th May. The Japanese tried a counter-attack but failed and after that they began to pull back everywhere. However, all was not well in the Kaladan valley and 81st West African Division had been pushed back again to the Pi Chaung where it held. The monsoon broke on 15th June but by then 15th Indian Corps was in possession of the vital Maungdaw road over the Mayu hills to Point 551 overlooking Buthidaung.

We left the Chindits in their strongholds recovering from the shock of the death of Wingate (Map 34). 77th Brigade, commanded by Brigadier Calvert, was based on 'Broadway' but operating from 'White City.' 16th Brigade, under Brigadier BE Fergusson, worn out after its long march, had failed to capture Indaw and was reorganising at 'Aberdeen.' 111th Brigade, now commanded by Lieutenant Colonel John Masters, its former Brigade Major, was concentrating for operations against Japanese communications on the Chindwin. 14th Brigade, under Brigadier T Brodie and 3rd (WA) Brigade, Brigadier AH Gillmore, were being flown into 'Aberdeen' for operations against the railways about Indaw. 23rd Brigade was no longer available and had been re-allocated to 14th Army.

Major General WDA Lentaigne, now GOC 3rd Indian Division/Special Force, realised that without 23rd Brigade he could not capture the all-weather airfield which he desperately needed and which he believed was at Indaw. He also knew that the enemy would try all they could to drive him out of 'White City.' He therefore ordered more artillery to 'White City.' As we have already seen this amounted to the six Bofors guns of 'X' Troop, the four 25-pounders of 'S' Troop and the two 2-pounder anti-tank guns. He also ordered 6th Nigeria Regiment to take over its defence. Slim then directed that the sole remaining task of the Chindits was to assist the advance of Stilwell on the Northern Front. Thus Lentaigne came to the conclusion that he must evacuate the Indaw area before the monsoon started. He must move closer to Mogaung and Myitkyina. He therefore decided to open a new strong point at 'Blackpool' some 50 miles north of 'White City.' 16th LRP Brigade which had been in the field the longest would be flown back to India and 'Broadway,' 'White City,' and 'Aberdeen' would be closed. He would then attack Mogaung with 3rd (WA), 14th, 77th and 111th Brigades. Once 'Blackpool' was established, it was agreed that the Chindits should come under the command of General Stilwell.

The Japanese attacked 'White City' on the night of 6/7th April with three battalions and artillery, but were driven off. Captain SR Nicholls, commanding 'S' Field Troop, describes many engagements against enemy guns and mortars at this time including a successful location and engagement of a 150mm mortar which was causing problems. He also co-operated with the RAF by marking targets with coloured smoke and engaging some enemy anti-aircraft guns on their behalf and went out with Calvert on his patrols to deal with any Japanese attacks. The enemy attacked again on the 10th but were again defeated, suffering heavy loss. Enemy guns bombarded the OP of 'S' Troop and mortally wounded Captain Arthur Mendus the OP officer of 'T' Troop, who had done such magnificent work. Later on the guns were attacked from the air and Sergeant Joyce was killed. There were no more attacks, except from the air, until 'White City' was evacuated in early May. It was at 'White City' that the Bofors manned by the men of 'X' Troop, 69th LAA Regiment, accounted for six aircraft destroyed, seven probables and eight damaged for only 1,073 rounds fired. While these operations were progressing, 77th and 111th Brigades were destroying enemy supply dumps, 21 in all, at Pinbon, and wrecking 16 railway bridges. They were also causing chaos by establishing road blocks. So successful were all these operations that Lentaigne decided to attack Indaw after all. This was done successfully by 16th LRP Brigade but the airfield was not found to be all-weather so it was destroyed.

Then the move north began. 111th Brigade established 'Blackpool', some five miles south west of Pindaw, by 7th May 1944. 16th Brigade, meanwhile, flew back to India and 'Aberdeen' was abandoned. 'White City' was abandoned on 9th May and 'Broadway' on the 13th. During the evacuation of 'White City', Captain SR Nicholls reported going out as an OP with an infantry patrol to cover the move and engaging several targets before the guns had to cease fire to be loaded onto aircraft for the evacuation. No 1 Gun, Sergeant Baird, was to stay to the last to cover the last aircraft as it took off and then it was to be destroyed. At this point, Major Peter Mead RA arrived to co-ordinate ground-air control. He hated the idea of leaving a gun behind and at midnight he told Nicholls to get the gun to the airstrip as fast as possible. Somehow they did, dismantled it and No 1 Gun, which had defended the rear to the very end, left on the last but one aircraft to take off. The force from 'White City' flew to Sylhet airfield in Assam, a splendid job well done.

Captain Nicholls also records the story of 'R' Troop, which was the first of the four troops to land. It had landed at 'Broadway.' The Troop Commander, Captain Guy Hepburn, had flown out on 5th March by glider but it became unstable and the towing Dakota had to cut them loose. Their pilot skilfully got them down on a sandbank by a river in the moonlight. They dodged Japanese patrols until they reached the Chindwin, some 650 yards wide, which they had to swim, and eventually got back to Lalaghat, having marched between the *15th* and *31st Divisions* preparing for their forthcoming offensive.

Meanwhile 'R' Troop had flown in to 'Broadway' with the GPO in charge. It was soon in action by the airstrip. Guy Hepburn flew in by Dakota only to find that his GPO had been killed in an air crash. The first attack came in on 27th March and 'R' Troop's baptism of fire was the defence of their gun pits with small arms. Next day the troop engaged two enemy 70mm guns in action across the airstrip over open sights and destroyed both of them. There were no further attacks, except by air, until the force was evacuated with its guns on 13th May. 'W' Troop of six Bofors also landed at 'Broadway.'

The guns from 'Aberdeen' were moved to 'Blackpool.' Before leaving, the Bofors guns of 'Y' and 'Z' Troops had a field day on 4th May when they destroyed five out of 12 attacking aircraft. Captain Nicholls reported 'On the night of 2nd May Captain Philip Young RA, the commander of 'U' Field Troop, with Lance Sergeant AC Wright flew to 'Aberdeen. Here they met Major JM Masters (later to become a well-known novelist) and who was Brigade Major of 111th Brigade. When Masters took over the brigade, on Wingate's death and Lentaigne's promotion, Young and Wright accompanied him to the site selected for 'Blackpool' on 7th May. Young found an OP on the highest point to the right of his gun line. The garrison was made up of the Cameronians and the King's Own Regiment, later reinforced by 3/9th Gurkhas. On the first night they were attacked and this included the fire of an enemy 105mm gun. That night Major Duxbury, the Chindit CRA, was flown in but was killed by shell splinter in the back fired from that gun.' The attack was driven off although Young's guns had not yet arrived.

Captain Young managed to get the infantry to help him dig gun pits ready for the guns which were due to fly-in shortly. One of the gliders loaded with a bulldozer was hit and dived into the ground, killing all on board. The first Dakotas to land were also engaged and damaged and the weather was appalling as the monsoon began to break. However, on the night of 13/14th May, the troop, less one gun whose Dakota had to return to base, landed. Lieutenants PA Large, and RW Swann arrived with the guns and a No 22 radio set. The three guns were assembled and towed into position by dawn on the 14th. At 0525 hours the area was heavily shelled and again at 0934 hours. However work continued and the three guns were 'Ready' by 0742 hours and the telephone line was through to the OP by 0950 hours. The range to the Japanese 105mm was calculated at 1,750 yards and it was engaged at 0530 hours on 15th May. Captain Young then registered useful targets on the road and railway near Pinbaw. That night an attempt was made to free-drop 25-pounder ammunition but it all arrived damaged. At midnight the troop engaged Pinbaw. The gun position was shelled and attacked from the air several times and suffered several casualties but, being unable to retaliate because they were so close, it was not possible to ascertain Japanese positions. The enemy 'were leaning up against our wire, so close that to attack them with aircraft would be very dangerous to us.' (Masters)

The following night Philip Young went out on a patrol to find the 105mm gun and pinpoint its position in the foothills south west of Pinbaw. The patrol discovered enemy in strength but Young went on alone and found the gun's position. The patrol returned at 0430 hours on the 18th. At 1600 hours the gun engaged the 105mm and called in air strikes. That night the fourth gun arrived and was ready for action on the 19th. On 20th May, Lieutenant Large went out with infantry to set an ambush but bumped into the Japanese and suffered more casualties. Large lost his No 48 radio set. At 1100 hours on the 21st the guns engaged infantry forming up in the paddy fields many times. The shortage of ammunition was becoming a problem. The Japanese were using trains drawn by motor vehicles fitted with flanged wheels and a rail target was successfully engaged. The *53rd Division* was beginning to deploy fully and the guns engaged troop movements and vehicles. On 23rd May the Japanese attacked in force and got onto OP Hill which then became the front line. Enemy shells set fire to the scrub in front of the Cameronians whose job was to protect the guns. 'Philip Young in the OP saw two 70mm infantry guns the other side of the airstrip and managed to target the [infantry] 3" mortars on to them. Both were destroyed. In the valley the Japs were trying to reconnect the railway and the guns prevented this and fired on other enemy movement. However, ammunition was fast running out. Just before 11.00 am Captain Philip Young was killed by mortar fire on OP Hill.' (Nicholls).

Masters thought this might be a prelude to a major attack and he ordered the guns to swing round and engage over open sights. Then it began to rain; the monsoon had broken. Enemy shelling continued at an increased rate and fell in a great fury on the King's Own. Everyone was dead tired and wet but the battle raged on and slowly the enemy pressed forward against the gallant Cameronians.

Shortly after dawn on 25th May the enemy swarmed onto OP hill where Philip Young's body still lay. A counter-attack was mounted but the position could not be held. Lieutenant Large took command of the troop and established a new OP behind the guns. Soon he too was wounded. By then the guns were under small arms fire, Lieutenant Swann and 18 men lay wounded, one died. Masters decided that 'Blackpool' was untenable and ordered the position to be evacuated up the Namkwin Chaung. The guns were stripped of sights and breech blocks and all fit men were told off to carry some 350 wounded. (Nicholls).

The horrors of the withdrawal, as they struggled over the jungle covered mountains in appalling monsoon conditions, were an extreme test for everyone. The Japanese mortared them as they left but did not follow up on foot. No rations were issued for three days and the wounded suffered terribly. At Indawgyi Lake 14 wounded men of the troop and three sick were evacuated by seaplane. There were now no officers left in 'U' Troop, so Lieutenant DA Foxall of 69th LAA Regiment took command of the 18 Gunners who remained and they formed the Brigade Headquarters Defence Platoon. They were eventually flown out to India by Dakota from Tincawk Sakan airfield, 50 miles north of Kamaing on 17th July. They had certainly done all they could. As a footnote, the guns of 'U' Troop were recovered three months later by 36th Division as it advanced south from Myitkyina. (Nicholls)

Stilwell had told Lentaigne that he intended to capture Mogaung from the north with 22nd and 38th Chinese Divisions and that he wanted the Special Force to patrol vigorously against the town from the south. Calvert soon reported that there were some 4,000 enemy in Mogaung, and Stilwell told him to attack it. In reality the loss of 'Blackpool' meant that the only course now open was to withdraw the Chindits to India. They were by then a spent force and not strong enough to attack prepared positions.

Stilwell's 22nd and 38th Chinese Divisions had reached Nanyaseik and Lawa by 27th April. He then ordered a special column of Marauders and Chinese to move off on 12th May to capture Myitkyina, but the Japanese were determined to hold Kamaing at all costs until the monsoon. Further east 4th Burma Regiment had advanced south from Fort Hertz and captured Sumprabum on 19th March and by the end of April it was in contact at Nsopzup. The Marauders could therefore sweep round this flank and captured Ritpong on 9th May and they reached and captured the airfield at Namkwi, four miles from Myitkyina, on the 16th, but this was not secure until Myitkyina itself had been captured. At this time 'R', 'S' and 'T' Field Troops were concentrated some ten miles south of Sylhet in Assam and were preparing to fly in and help the Americans at Myitkyina airfield. The members of 'U' Troop came to Sylhet in small parties, mostly from hospital, but the guns were not called for by Stilwell. Lentaigne offered to help from the south and Stilwell again declined but then failed to take the town himself. He was determined not to call on British help. He allowed the flying in of 'W' and 'X' Troops of 69th LAA Regiment only, and this as a result of the insistence of Major General GE Stratemeyer, commanding the British and American air forces which made up Eastern Air Command.

In August the guns of 'R', 'S' and 'T' Troops were handed in and the men went to Bangalore for rest. They had certainly done their stuff. Their gunnery had been excellent, although they had always been short of ammunition. They had fought magnificently both with the infantry and in the defence of their guns and they had co-operated with the RAF and USAAF, indicating targets for them and getting them to spot the fall of shot. Of the 12 guns which had deployed with the Chindits, five were lost. Four officers out of 11 were killed and two wounded. The LAA troops had performed equally well, and above all, the Bofors guns on their light-weight two-wheeled chassis had given no trouble at all. There is no doubt that the Chindits held many Japanese forces who were badly needed at Imphal and Kohima and they caused much disruption to Japanese communications and logistics. They also helped Stilwell seize and hold Myitkyina. The Gunners had certainly played an important part in Chindit operations. The Commander, Wingate, was a Gunner, two columns, Nos 51 and 69, were formed from Gunners and commanded by Gunners. Four troops of field and four troops of LAA guns accompanied the force with great success. They all did more than they were told to do and did it with great gallantry. That they had an impact on the war in Burma is beyond doubt but whether that impact was worth the amount of effort will be argued for ever. The complete list of Chindit Gunners is given at Annex Q.

So far the role of air observation in the Far East has not been covered in any detail. 656 (AOP)

Squadron RAF was formed at RAF Station Westley in England on 31st December 1942 under Major DW (Denis) Coyle RA. Its role, like that of its sister squadrons, was to observe and correct the fire of artillery and also to conduct reconnaissance as ordered. The aircraft were Austers and the pilots consisted of 23 Royal Artillery captains per squadron. The ground crews were 90 Gunners and REME and 80 Airmen. The first aircraft arrived in 656 AOP Squadron in February 1943 and the squadron moved to RAF Stapleford-Tawney for training before embarking for the Far East at Liverpool on 12th August 1943. Once in India the squadron was based first at RAF Juhu. Training went on throughout the rest of the year, including observation of fire at the School of Artillery Deolali. 'A' Flight of two Auster IIIs, the first of six, arrived in Bombay while 12 more went direct to Calcutta to be ready for operations without having to fly across India first. On 12th January 1944 the squadron, consisting of 'A' and 'C' Flights, moved into action in the Arakan. It left 'B' Flight at Juhu with Headquarters 33rd Indian Corps for amphibious training.

The squadron was based at Chota Maunghnama, an emergency fighter strip just south of Chittagong. 'A' Flight was allotted to 5th Indian Division and 'C' Flight to 7th Indian Division. 'C' Flight flew its first AOP operational reconnaissance sortie on 25th January 1944. The ground crew of 'C' Flight, under Bombardier Roe, moved into 7th Indian Division's 'Admin Box' and had a very exciting time putting out fires around Artillery Hill and the ammunition dump during the Japanese attacks in February. The airstrip on which the squadron was located turned out to be close to the point where the Japanese had decided to break through and cut the coast road so it became very unhealthy and caused much time to be spent on local defence. The CCRA 15th Indian Corps, Brigadier L Harris, recognised the danger to the squadron and ordered it back to Cox's Bazar. Squadron Headquarters was then set up alongside Headquarters 15th Indian Corps at Bawli Bazar and flights were commenced in support of 5th, 26th and 36th Indian Divisions as they tried to release 7th Indian Division fighting for its life in the battles of the 'Admin Box' on the east side of the Mayu hills.

An airstrip was laid out alongside Headquarters 114th Indian Infantry Brigade, east of the Kalapanzin. The squadron commander, Major Coyle, tested it on 18th February and led in a dozen light aircraft, mostly American L 5s fitted with stretchers to fly out casualties. This marked the start of aerial casualty evacuation for all formations. It was very much appreciated by everyone and saved many lives. Soon it became almost automatic for brigades to lay out a light aircraft strip wherever they went. The aircraft were kept busy and were out every day, correcting the fall of shot for the guns as well as carrying out reconnaissance and other missions. Army flying had really arrived in the Far East.

When the Japanese attacks on the Imphal front started, the squadron was ordered north at short notice. It left 'A' Flight with 15th Indian Corps to cover the Arakan front and flew 900 miles to join up with 'B' Flight, which had flown in from India, to support 33rd Indian Corps at Imphal. Meanwhile, 'A' Flight, with Captain Ted Maslen-Jones and Captain Frank McMath were each responsible for one side of the Mayu hills and were kept very busy. McMath operated from a wind-swept strip in the old 'Admin Box' and did the squadron's first night shoot to cover the withdrawal of 4th Indian Infantry Brigade. Maslen-Jones operated deep behind enemy lines in support of 44th Royal Marine Commando as they outflanked Razabil.

During the operations to clear the Tunnels in April, 'A' Flight was particularly active. Its diary for 7th April states '1 Lincolns attack 'Spit & Polish.' Kingston flew a sortie over the area and corrected 30th Medium Battery [presumably 19th Medium Battery is meant] who were firing just in front of own troops. Tanks, dive bombers and Hurricane strikes all very spectacular and successful. After the fireplan was over Kingston had two medium batteries for opportunity targets but nothing seen. Lincolns found 85 dead and two guns on the feature. Own casualties, 15 dead and 30 wounded. McLinden carried out four CB sorties but the Jap doesn't fire when we are up, which is most annoying. Own troops capture eastern tunnel.'

The pilots were averaging some 40 hours flying per month. They engaged the enemy with every type of gun from 3-inch mortar to 3.7-inch guns of 8th (Belfast) HAA Regiment. These latter were very long range and very accurate; the very first shoot with them destroyed an enemy field gun. These Northern Irish Gunners were as keen as mustard and loved firing for the AOP. They were also very hospitable and the AOP pilots visited them frequently.

The squadron, less 'A' Flight, was by then at Headquarters 33rd Indian Corps at Jorhat in the Brahmaputra valley. 'B' Flight had already arrived by flying some 1,500 miles across India and was located at Imphal airfield, which was intensely busy as it operated some 300 Dakotas, Skymasters, Wellingtons and a squadron of fighters. Meanwhile 'C' Flight was deployed to Dimapur to cover operations at Kohima, but flying operationally over the Kohima mountains was virtually impossible because the absolute ceiling of the Auster III was 7,000 feet and most of the hill tops were way above this. Also the nearest possible strip was 30 minutes flying time away. Then at the end of April, when the monsoon started, there was very little the squadron could do and it was decided to withdraw it, less 'A' Flight still in the Arakan, to Ranchi for deep servicing. By the middle of May, 'A' Flight also badly needed proper servicing and it returned to squadron headquarters. The squadron had had its baptism of fire in the jungle, there was much to think about, but there was no doubt at all that its operations had been an unqualified success.

By this time in the war co-operation with the RAF was improving and it fell mainly to Gunners to work out how to do it. Lieutenant Colonel Ralph Bury, a Gunner who had been engaged in Army/Air co-operation since 1940, was Senior Air Liaison Officer at Headquarters 224 Group RAF covering 15th Indian Corps in the Arakan. At Headquarters Allied Land Forces South East Asia, Colonel 'Jock' McNeil was co-ordinating the Army/Air operations as Colonel GS (Ops Air). He had already had much experience in North Africa. The problem was how to provide precise target data to pilots in almost impossible country. The solution was the establishment of Visual Control Posts (VCPs). These were manned by an RAF pilot and a Gunner Captain, plus driver and signallers. They were located at battalion or even company headquarters and could deploy forward as required. The VCP would get its orders and then move to where it could see the target. Once this was located and agreed, the Gunner would mark it with coloured smoke and the RAF officer would talk the pilot down towards it until he could see it. The system worked well, especially when a 'cabrank,' usually of four aircraft, remained overhead awaiting a call. One 'cabrank' could usually provide a period of some 20 to 30 minutes duration over the target area. The organisation used in the Arakan is given at Annex S.

So the stage was set for the great battles about to start, which became known as the Battles of Imphal and Kohima. Second Arakan had marked the first major defeat of the Japanese in battle in South East Asia, and Imphal and Kohima were to mark the turning point of the war in this theatre. It had been all defeat until the Arakan; from now on it was to be victory all the way. But first there was some very hard fighting to do, indeed some of the hardest anywhere in the whole war. Kohima has been described as the nearest thing to Passchendaele in the Second World War and was to rank with the other great battles of the war such as Alamein, Stalingrad, Cassino and D-Day. It had taken three years of war, many defeats and many casualties to rectify the shortcomings of pre-war defence policy. Now at last the stage was set to win.

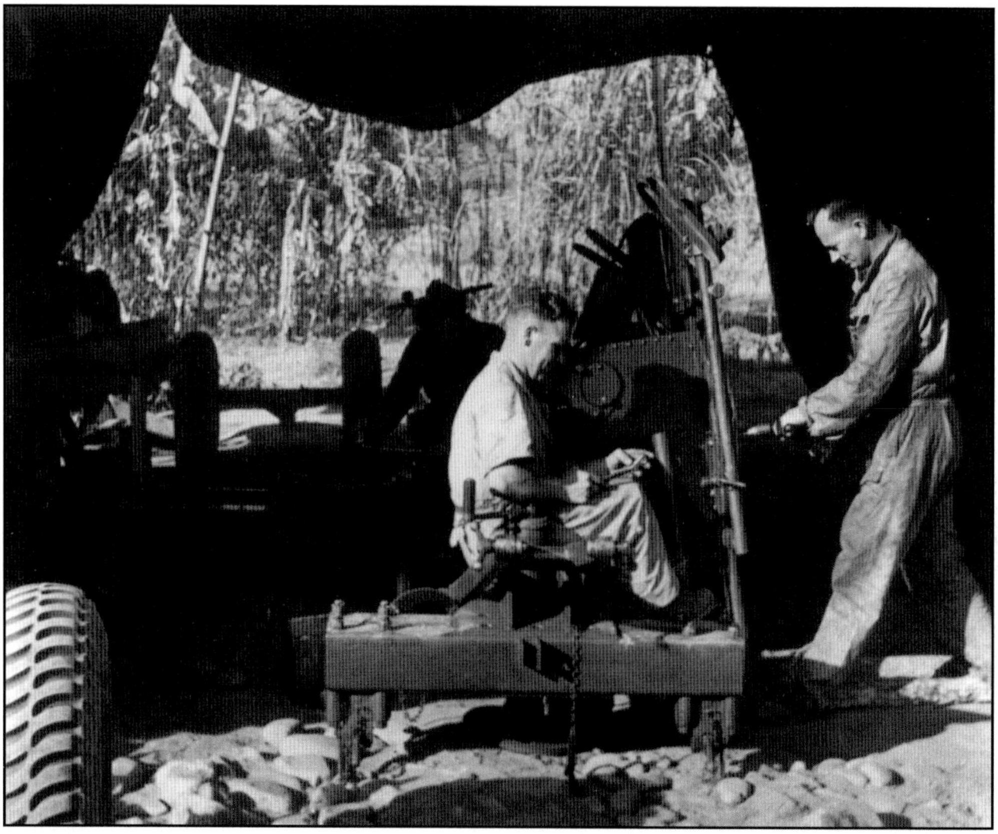

9. Repairing a 40 mm Bofors LAA gun in a REME workshop on the Central Front, March 1944. (IWM)

10. Church Knoll, Kohima from the north end of Naga Village, May 1944 (IWM)

11. A C 47 (Dakota) about to drop supplies near the Siang River. (IWM)

12. A C 46 (Commando). (IWM)

13. An L5 aircraft about to evacuate a casualty, Ramree Island. (IWM)

14. An Indian 3.7-inch howitzer firing near Meiktila. (IWM)

15. Indian mountain gunners, Arakan 1944. (IWM)

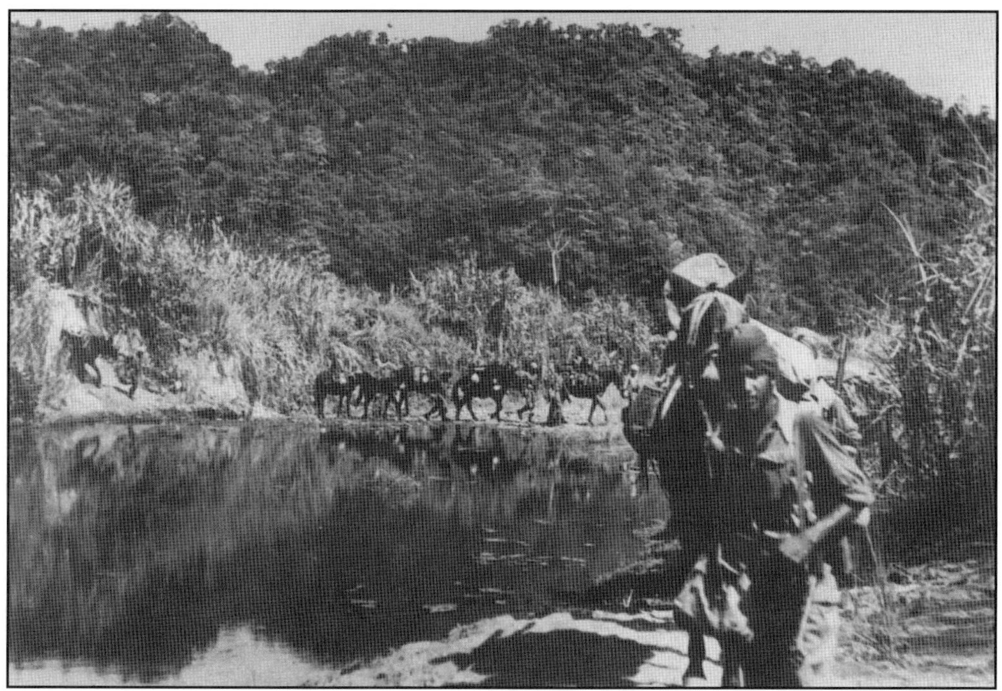

16. 30th Indian Mountain Regiment crossing the Pi Chaung near Ridaung, November 1944. (IWM)

17. A Nakajima Ki 43 'Oscar', a fighter used extensively in Burma by the Japanese Army. (IWM)

18. A 40mm Bofors LAA gun of 36th LAA Regiment, Arakan, December 1944. (IWM)

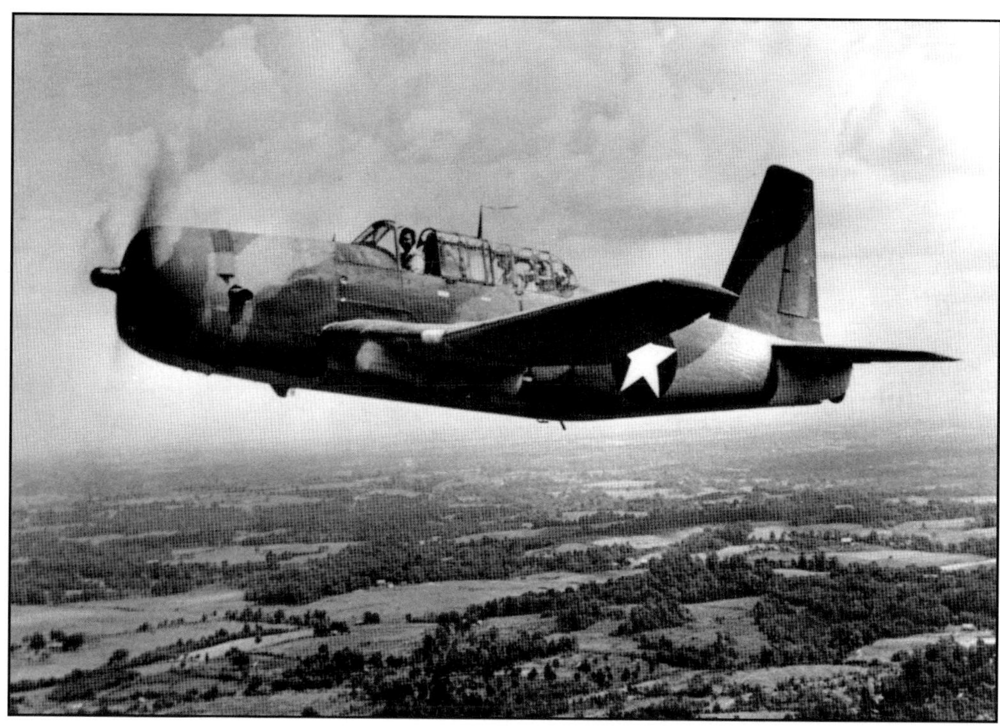

19. A Consolidated Vultee Vengeance dive bomber. (IWM)

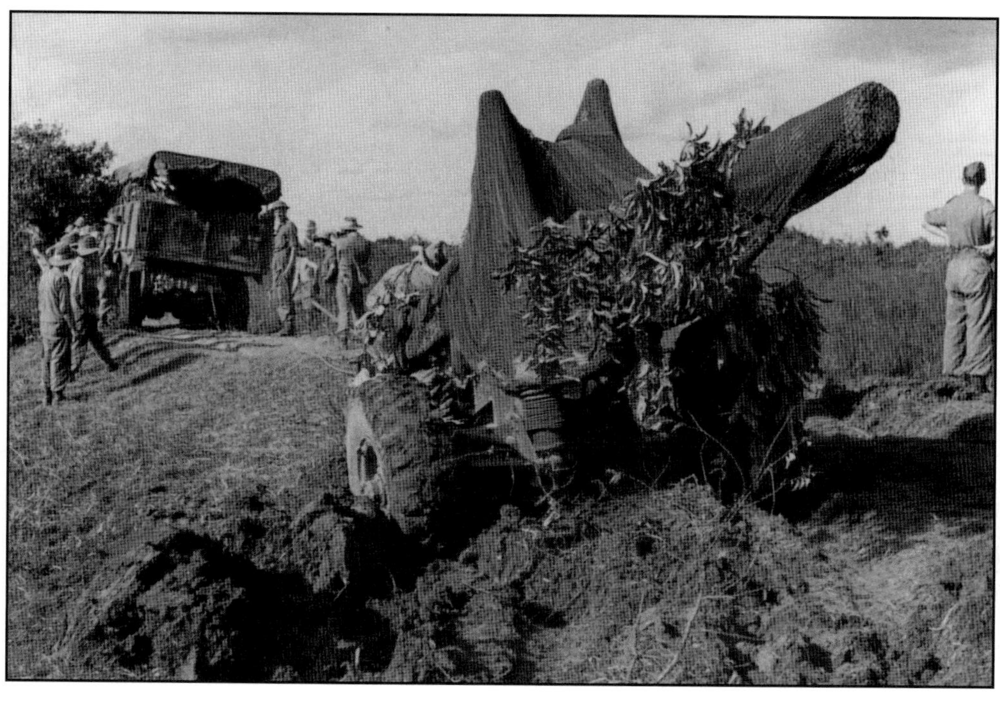

20. Winching a 5.5-inch gun near Payan, late 1944. (IWM)

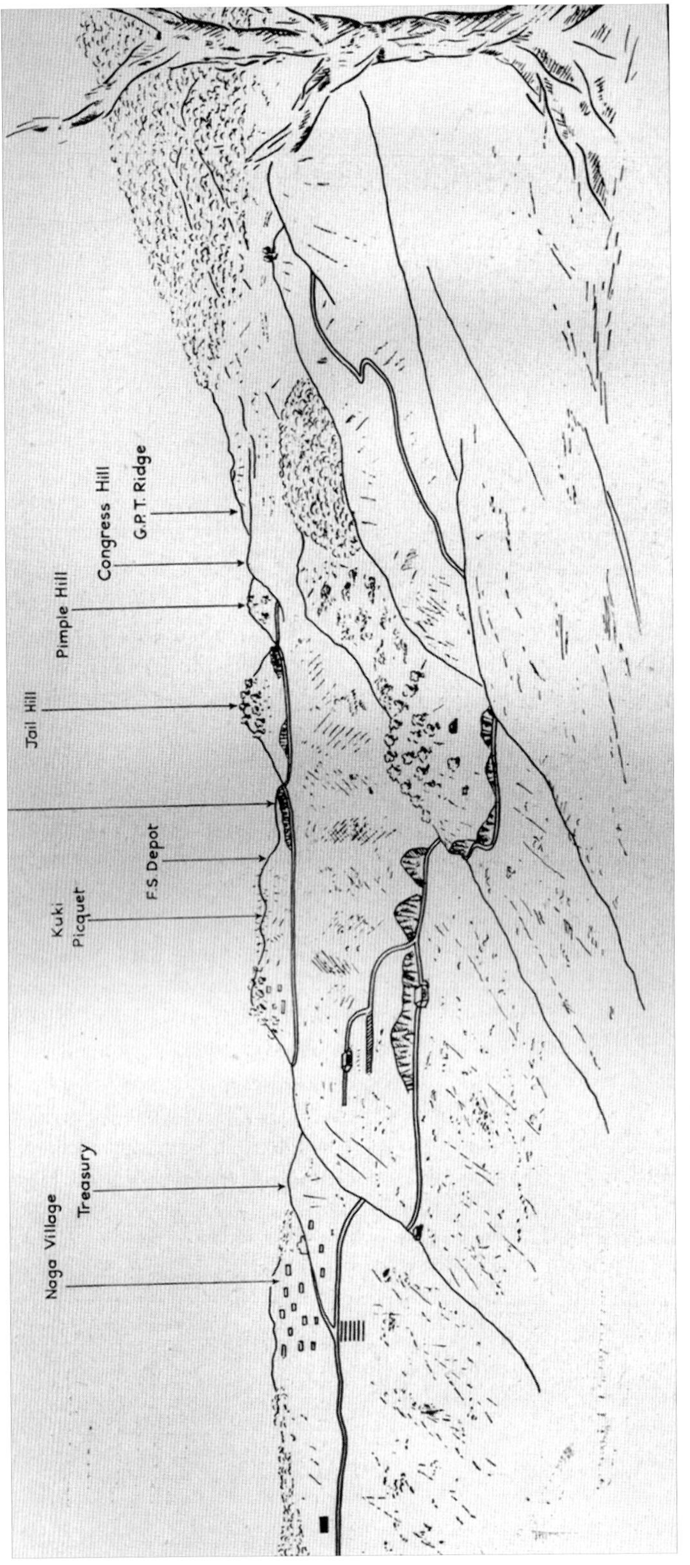

21. Kohima. Panorama showing objectives for Operation Key, 4th May, 1944

CHAPTER 11

THE BATTLES OF IMPHAL AND KOHIMA

APRIL - JULY 1944

(Maps 36, 37, 38, 39 and 40)

Slim told Stopford that, on his arrival at Jorhat, 33rd Indian Corps was to prevent the Japanese getting into Assam, to keep open a line of communication with 4th Indian Corps around Imphal and then to destroy all enemy west of the Chindwin. Stopford reckoned correctly that his enemy would be *31st Division*. He realised that it would not be easy to hold Kohima and Dimapur until 2nd British Division arrived. Thus he organised the defence around 161st Indian Infantry Brigade, commanded by Brigadier DFW Warren. The brigade had just arrived from 5th Indian Division in the Arakan where it had been heavily involved and had with it 24th Indian Mountain Regiment under Lieutenant Colonel Humphrey Hill. Stopford did not necessarily have to fight at Kohima but he recognised its strength as a position and he did not want to give it up unless he had to (Maps 36 and 37). For centuries it had guarded the route from Burma into Assam. *31st Division* had already cut the Imphal road at Mao and it then began to close on Kohima from that direction and from Jessami in the east, while its patrols were active to the north and north west of the town. At this time 161st Indian Infantry Brigade and 24th Indian Mountain Regiment were concentrating at Nichuguard but 5th British Infantry Brigade of 2nd British Division was arriving at Bokajan and 23rd Brigade was on its way to Mariani.

On arrival, Lieutenant Colonel Hill went to the Depot at Dimapur and 'borrowed' transport and 5,000 rounds of 3.7-inch howitzer ammunition in some 3-ton trucks, since as yet his guns had none. It was foresight which was to pay off and probably saved Kohima, as it was some weeks before the normal re-supply system began to work and the rounds were needed immediately. Brigadier DJ Steevens was CCRA 33rd Indian Corps and was responsible for the build up of the corps artillery for the forthcoming battle. Brigadier HSJ 'Pat' Bourke, CRA 2nd Division, arrived at Dimapur and he too went foraging. He found two 5.5-inch guns in the Ordnance Depot there. These were manned by some men from 4th Field Regiment and he gave them to 16th Field Regiment. They joined 72/86th Battery as 'G' Troop. They fired some 1,500 rounds during the siege. 10th Field Regiment, commanded by Lieutenant Colonel DG Cannell, was the first Gunner regiment to arrive after 24th Indian Mountain Regiment and it was soon in action at Zubza. When 100th LAA/Anti-Tank Regiment arrived, it sent its 221st and 222nd Anti-Tank Batteries to Imphal and then deployed 163rd and 164th LAA Batteries as infantry for the defence of Dimapur.

The first attack on Kohima was launched after dark on 4th April 1944 by *IInd Battalion* of the *58th Regiment* from the direction of Mao and was directed against GPT Ridge. Meanwhile *Ist Battalion 58th Regiment* had swept round through Kezoma, moved through Naga Village unopposed and reached Cheswema. The men on Garrison Hill soon got a taste of battle. They had one 25-pounder which came into action, although there is no record of who manned it. It was quickly knocked out and then they were on their own. Major General RPL Ranking, who commanded 202nd Lines of Communication Area and who was now in general command of the Dimapur/Kohima area and had Colonel HU Richards as Kohima Garrison Commander, suggested to Stopford that, as 5th British Infantry Brigade was arriving, he should send at least part of 161st Indian Infantry Brigade forward to Kohima. Stopford agreed and decided to send the whole brigade. At dawn on 5th April 4th Royal West Kents and 20th Mountain Battery, under Major RC Yeo, moved off from Jotsoma. As they came into action later that day, near Garrison Hill, the enemy attacked Jail Hill at the other end of the ridge while the Deputy Commissioner's Bungalow (the Deputy Commissioner being Mr Charles Pawsey) was mortared.

Brigadier Warren decided that there was not enough room for his whole brigade in Kohima and occupied Jotsoma, some two and a half miles away. From here his artillery, 24th Indian Mountain Regiment (2nd, 11th and 12th Mountain Batteries) could deal with the enemy as they attacked, and did so with great effect. Meanwhile the guns of 20th Mountain Battery came into action in a very exposed position under enemy rifle fire on Garrison Hill. Several targets were engaged but this drew more enemy fire onto them and the infantry asked the guns to stop firing. Fire orders were then sent to the batteries at Jotsoma from four OP officers of 2nd and 20th Mountain Batteries, Captain Peter Kendall, Lieutenant Dickerson and Lieutenant JS Punia, all of whom had slipped into Kohima before it was cut off, and of course the Battery Commander, Major Dick Yeo. These four kept a 24 hour watch throughout the siege, no call for fire was ever refused and, thanks to the foresight of Humphrey Hill, there was no shortage of ammunition. Together they probably did more than most to ensure that all Japanese attacks failed. Lieutenant Dickenson fixed up an abandoned motor car to charge radio batteries otherwise this could have become a major problem. At one stage Dick Yeo had all four OPs hard at work along the Kohima Ridge.

Enemy attacks began in earnest on 7th April and went on through to the following day. '8th April. Six or seven enemy guns are thought to have taken part last night. Some 800 rounds fired. This concentration preceeded attacks onto DCs Bungalow . . . Right Section 20th Mountain Battery was in action near the Bungalow and was ordered to a new position. Lieutenant DPR Dickenson RA was wounded. Guns in action all night. One 25-pounder arrived from Dimapur at the MS 42 position with a detachment from 4th Field Regiment and came under command . . .' Then on 9th April, 'Three enemy guns spotted by flashes and engaged as a destructive shoot with very good results. Party of Japs seen moving towards Zubza. Jap bunkers located. Lieutenant DJ Richards engaged 150 enemy as a 'Mike Target.' Locals later reported 60 casualties.' (War Diary 24th Indian Mountain Regiment).

All the Company Commanders of the 4th Royal West Kents were soon good at calling for fire themselves, Kenyon of A Company, Winstanley of B, Shaw of C and Eastern of D. On 10th April the Japanese mounted a ferocious attack and overran 20th Mountain Battery, but not before two guns were buried and two were pulled back to Summerhouse Hill near the DC's Bungalow and the Hospital. Major Yeo and six men were wounded that day.

The battle for the Ridge raged through the early days of April and the mountain Gunners played a major part in them. Brigadier CE Lucas Phillips wrote; 'Here the 3.7s very soon had the approaches to the Ridge 'recorded' with absolute precision. Again and again they broke up enemy attacks just as they were being launched, by day and by night. Their response to an infantry demand for 'defensive fire' was swift and exact. The DFs on the tennis court were as close as 20 yards from the infantry. Not once during the whole siege did a shell land on the infantry within the perimeter, despite frequent switches and alterations of range at night. This was due, not only to good direction of fire, but also to what Humphrey Hill called 'the deadly accurate laying of our Indian Gunners' . . . Nor was this all. Before very long, the ears of the Gunner officers became so well attuned that they could tell from the Japanese noises just where and when the assaults were to be made and were able to anticipate the infantry demands before they were made. On several occasions Lieutenant Colonel HJ Laverty, commanding the Royal West Kents would call, 'Gunner! DF No 6,' to receive the reply, 'Its on the way, sir!' There can seldom ever have been a better example of infantry/artillery co-operation. Thus while it can never be said that one unit was the sole battle-winner at Kohima, for many were to play a vital part, it is none the less certain that 24th Indian Mountain Regiment was one of them, and without them, Kohima could never have been held.' (Lucas Phillips). None of this in any way plays down the gallantry, skill and courage of the Infantry who were magnificent from start to finish.

As the guns of 2nd British Division pulled into action beside the mountain Gunners at Jotsoma, the OPs inside the perimeter called on them as well so that the total fire being brought down onto the Japanese was for ever increasing. It is recorded that some 3,500 rounds were fired on one DF Task alone over a period of five hours. 2nd British Division had been training for amphibious operations against Akyab when the call came. They had three field regiments, 10th, 16th and 99th, each had one battery of six 3.7-inch howitzers, one of eight towed 25-pounders and one of eight Priests. These last consisted of American 105mm howitzers mounted on a Sherman tank chassis. The units were known as 'Assault Field Regiments.' But when ordered to Dimapur two changes were made. First the 3.7-inch howitzer battery in each regiment was increased to eight guns and second, the Priests were handed in and replaced by eight towed 25-pounders. Thus at Kohima, 10th Field Regiment had 30th Light and 46th and 51/54th Field Batteries, 16th Field Regiment had 27th Light and 34th and 72/86th Field Batteries and 99th Field Regiment had 393rd Light and 394th and 472nd Field Batteries.

As the guns arrived it was clear that there were hardly any gun areas around Kohima. In the end only two could be found. The first was at Jotsoma where 24th Indian Mountain Regiment was already in action, but the range to Kohima was only 3,500 yards. The second was at Zubza where the range was 8,500 yards and too far for the mountain guns. Here 10th and 99th Field Regiments deployed in tight, packed gun positions with guns wheel to wheel, but their two 3.7-inch batteries had to move forward to Jotsoma. 16th Field Regiment arrived and came into action at MS 32, with 27th and 72/86th Batteries facing north to cover operations on that flank being carried out by the Royal Scots. Later both 16th and 99th Field Regiments also moved forward into Jotsoma, but it took time to get them into action. 34th Field Battery, with its 25-pounders, reported having a whole troop on the drag ropes of each gun in turn to get them onto their platforms.

By nightfall 5th April, 4th Royal West Kents were deployed on Garrison and FSD Hills. Two companies were pulled back from GPT Ridge. By capturing this feature the Japanese had also taken the main water supply to the garrison and this was to become a major problem. Casualties were mounting fast. The enemy next attacked Jail Hill where their first bayonet charge was broken up by the guns of 24th Indian Mountain Regiment but in the end they forced the Royal West Kents back through the DIS to the FSD feature. Then came attacks from the *IInd* and *IIIrd Battalions* of *58th Regiment* onto Naga Village after a heavy bombardment. 'When the barrage lifted *58th Regiment*, in wave after screaming wave, came at their objective with the storm in full spate, halted and checked by the extraordinary accuracy of 24th Indian Mountain Regiment's 3.7s from Jotsoma directed by Yeo and his three OPs.' (Colvin). The Japanese took Naga Village on 8th and 9th April and then swarmed across to the DC's Bungalow as far as the tennis court. Present were the Gunners of the section of 20th Mountain Battery but they stood firm. 'Two Punjabi Mussulmans died defending their guns with their last Bren round.' (Colvin). By this time Kohima was cut off, as a Japanese force had reached Piquet Hill and another had reached Zubza. Their arrival at Zubza marked the high water mark of the 'March on Delhi'.

It was on 10th April that Slim ordered a major offensive. Scoones was to hold south of Imphal and was then to attack *15th* and *33rd Divisions* in turn, Stilwell was to continue his advance on Myitkyina while Stopford was to hold Kohima, with a view to advancing to the Chindwin. On the 12th the enemy attacked Hospital Hill with great ferocity but were held by the gallantry of 'C' Company of the Royal West Kents. Lieutenant Punia was the OP with them on Hospital Hill that day and with great skill he brought the fire of his guns to within 15 yards of the company, so repulsing the attack.

By evening 9th April, 5th British Infantry Brigade, under Brigadier VFS Hawkins, was ready to advance from Bokajan and 6th British Infantry Brigade, commanded by Brigadier JD Shapland, was arriving. Accordingly Stopford ordered Major General JML (John) Grover, commanding 2nd British Division, to take over operational control of the Dimapur/Kohima area from Major General Ranking. Grover's first task was to break through to Kohima and, by midday on 11th April, 7th Worcesters were attacking the enemy position at Zubza with a squadron of 150th Regiment RAC. Several tanks in 'C' Squadron of this regiment were manned by Gunners of 99th Field Regiment and they saw a good deal of action. But the Japanese fought hard. It took three days to overrun them and this only with a fresh battalion, 1st Cameron Highlanders, and 32 guns of 10th Field Regiment and 72/86th Battery of 16th Field Regiment. Time was running out for the Kohima garrison; could it hold until relief reached them?

The garrison at Kohima was suffering from serious water and ammunition shortages and casualties were increasing rapidly. Attempts were made to air drop what was needed but it was impossible and most of what was dropped fell in enemy lines. By 13th April the situation was desperate and on that day enemy artillery scored two direct hits on the Royal West Kents' Dressing Station on the western end of Garrison Hill, doing appalling damage. It was also on this day that *124th Regiment* was located at Phekekrima and 23rd Brigade was released to Stopford to deal with it. During the night of the 17th April Kuki Piquet fell and this meant that the tiny garrison on Garrison Hill was facing the enemy on three sides but it was fighting desperately. Thus at daylight on the 18th, just as the gallant remnants of the little force on Garrison Hill prepared for their last battle, they heard and saw the crash of concentrated British artillery on the enemy as he formed up in front of them and soon tanks and infantry approached along the road from Jotsoma. The Japanese were forced back and the siege was raised. Captain BAT Hammond of 16th Field Regiment reports of this action, 'My own 'C' Troop of 34th Field Battery was on the front edge of Zubza. Its job was to blind the track between Naga Village and Merema. Being clearly visible from the guns, I ordered each No 1 a responsibility for a quarter of the smoke screen we were to put down at 'Gun Control' over open sights. It was a perfect day for smoke, cool, damp and windless; our screen lasted from 0800 hours until dusk with only a few feed rounds per hour.'

Operations continued on the flanks. 'On 19th April Lieutenant Colonel R.J. Uniacke sent Lieutenant D.H. Woodcock on an artillery patrol escorted by a platoon of the Royal Scots to engage enemy by-passing Kohima by way of Zubza.' (Woodcock)

'The fireplan for the attack by 1st [in fact 2nd] DLI onto 'Terrace Hill' was registered and fired at 1130 hours 18th April and later 1/1st Punjabis, less two companies, entered Kohima Garrison.' (War Diary 24th Indian Mountain Regiment). 24th Indian Mountain Regiment report 17 killed and 22 wounded by this time. Then during the night 18/19th April they report, 'A Jap battalion attacked a company on 'Terrace Hill' and after suffering many casualties occupied it. Heavy concentration fired onto 'Terrace Hill' and 'Twin Trees.' Major AB Howard acted as FOO with 1st DLI as they counter-attacked 'Terrace Hill' and he shot two Japs with his rifle before he was wounded and evacuated. General pounding of all enemy positions on 'Treasury', 'Jail Hill,' 'Congress Ridge,' 'DCs Bungalow,' 'DIS' and 'FSD' all day. Then on 20th April, relief of Kohima Garrison by 1st/1st Punjabis' complete. 35 Gunners with Major TH Harrison, Second-in-Command, relieve 20th Mountain Battery but Major RC Yeo and Lieutenant DPR Dickenson staying to hand over OPs. Today our first 3.7-inch howitzers with pneumatic tyres arrived.' (War Diary 24th Indian Mountain Regiment).

Tragically Major TH Harrison was killed in action at his OP on 22nd April by a direct hit by a mortar bomb on his trench and Dick Yeo returned to take command again. He then learnt that he had been awarded the DSO, and Dickenson and Subadar Walidad of 11th (Dehra Dun) Battery, the Military Cross. Havildar Major Mahomed Khan and two more Gunners from 20th Battery were killed during the last days of the siege. Meanwhile 268th Indian Infantry Brigade, formerly of 44th Indian Armoured Division, was ordered to Dimapur, where it arrived on 8th May.

The Kohima Garrison was evacuated to Dimapur with all its casualties. 161st Indian Infantry Brigade concentrated at Jotsoma and 6th British Infantry Brigade took over the defence of Kohima itself. The heroic stand of the Kohima Garrison under Colonel Richards, in particular that of the Royal West Kents and 24th Indian Mountain Regiment, played a vital part in the ultimate defeat of the Japanese. 4th British Infantry Brigade, Brigadier WH Goschen, had by then arrived and it was ordered to protect the road back to Dimapur while, on 23rd April, 5th British Infantry Brigade deployed to attack and capture Naga Village from the north, this being the start of a left hook by that formation. With them went Captain IF (Ian) Carpenter of 72/86th Battery, 16th Field Regiment, who was to win a Military Cross for gallantry, and Bombardier Hobbs his OP Assistant who was to win the Military Medal. At the same time, *124th Regiment* pulled out from the Wokha area and moved round to attack Kohima from Aradura.

While this, the first battle for Kohima, had been raging, 4th Indian Corps was re-grouping around Imphal. 5th Indian Division was ordered to re-occupy the high ground around Kangpokpi and clear the road back to Imphal. 23rd Indian Division was to occupy Ukhrul and threaten *15th Division*. 17th Indian Division was to take over all operations on the Tiddim Road while retaining 63rd Indian Infantry Brigade at Kanglatongbi. It was also to take command of 32nd Indian Infantry Brigade at Moirang, with 37th Field and 6th Mountain Batteries and 48th Indian Infantry Brigade. On 6th April, 9th Indian Infantry Brigade, having been relieved by 63rd Indian Infantry Brigade at Kanglatongbi, had moved to deal with enemy at Nungshigum. But the threat to the former was too strong and 63rd Indian Infantry Brigade was forced back to Sengmai. On 7th April, 3/9th Jat was driven off the summit of Point 3833, Nungshigum Hill. The position was quickly regained, however, with the help of the fire of the guns of 4th Field and 28th Jungle Field Regiments and an air strike. The Japanese could see the great value of this hilltop position overlooking Imphal and regained it again by ferocious new attacks on the 11th. It was the closest they ever got to Imphal and they were only four miles from 4th Corps Headquarters. They had to be removed and a major attack with air strikes, artillery and the tanks of 3rd Carabiniers, was launched by 1/17th Dogra. It was re-taken but at a heavy cost to both sides.

Meanwhile 37th Indian Infantry Brigade of 23rd Indian Division relieved 123rd Indian Infantry Brigade of 5th Indian Division at Yaingangpokpi and 1st Indian Infantry Brigade occupied Singkap. 49th Indian Infantry Brigade went to rejoin 23rd Indian Division at Yairipok. 32nd Indian Infantry Brigade then pulled back to Bishenpur, leaving 3rd Special Service Brigade to cover the Sappers trying to open a new road from Silchar to Bishenpur.

23rd Indian Division set off to attack *15th Division* at Kasom from the south on 16th April. This was carried out by 1st and 37th Indian Infantry Brigades and the divisional artillery, 158th and 3rd Indian Field, 28th Indian Mountain and 2nd Indian LAA/Anti-Tank Regiments. By now 8th Medium Regiment had arrived from the Tiddim Road battles and it deployed its 246th Medium Battery less 'B' Troop, under 23rd Indian Division at Waithou, 'B' Troop was on the Ukhrul Road under 5th Indian Division, 247th Medium Battery less 'C' Troop, was at Moreh under 20th Indian Division with 'C' Troop in 'Sardine Box' just west of Imphal airfield. From its positions 246th Medium Battery fired 2,885 rounds in 30 days. 8th Medium Regiment was commanded by Lieutenant Colonel HB Jolly who, at various times, also commanded Imphal Keep Artillery and the artillery group of 32nd Indian Infantry Brigade at Bishenpur.

By 21st April, 23rd Indian Division had closed with the enemy and some tough fighting took place. *15th Division* pulled back. Meanwhile 5th Indian Division was trying to advance up the Iril Valley against the enemy at Kanglatongbi. This advance was being carried out by 123rd and 9th Indian Infantry Brigades. They hit strong enemy positions at Mapeo which were clearly going to need a lot of artillery to dislodge. The Japanese later said that 19th April was the day they realised they were not going to take Imphal with the forces they had. On that day they ordered their forces there onto the defensive. Scoones realised that the crisis of the battle had passed on the summit of Nungshigum on 21st April.

Operations were still in full swing to the south. 80th Indian Infantry Brigade, of 20th Indian Division, had driven the enemy off 'Nippon Hill', employing the whole of the divisional artillery, on 12th April; the units involved being 9th Field, 114th Jungle Field, 23rd Indian Mountain and 55th LAA/Anti-Tank Regiments. It had then defeated the inevitable counter-attacks but during the night of 16th April the Japanese stormed back with heavy artillery attacks and drove 80th Indian Infantry Brigade off again. They did however fail to drive the brigade out of Sita. Next they made a major drive to get through the Shenam Pass by frontal attacks with tanks and artillery. They swarmed over the 'Crete East' position and the 'Cyprus' position had to be abandoned, but 'Crete West' and 'Scraggy' held and became the scene of hard fighting for the next three months and marked the limit of the Japanese penetration towards Palel.

On the Tiddim Road, 32nd Indian Infantry Brigade's position at Bishenpur was very strong. Its right lay on Point 5846 on the Silchar Track and Wireless Hill. Its left was protected by the marshes around Ningthoukhong. However, on 16th April the enemy occupied Wireless Hill and Kungpi, but these were re-captured in a gallant tank attack by the Carabiniers. By then the enemy had been identified as *214th Regiment,* and it had reached Khoirok. *215th Regiment* was coming straight up the Tiddim Road. The threat increased and the British were suffering heavy losses, especially in tanks. The enemy tried to make more use of his air power but to little avail. The RAF and USAAF ruled the skies and his losses were heavy both by day and by night. Up to 21st April the Hurricanes had flown 2,000 sorties and dropped over 300 tons of bombs, while the Vengeance squadrons dropped some 550 tons in 1,700 sorties, all for the loss of 20 aircraft. Thus by 21st April 1944 the Japanese had been held everywhere, but they had not yet been defeated. 55th LAA/Anti-Tank Regiment shed its anti-aircraft batteries to become 111th Anti-Tank Regiment on 1st September 1944 and destroyed four enemy tanks, losing one gun on 17th April. 55th LAA Regiment then moved into the Artillery Box at Bishenpur where they claimed 12 enemy aircraft destroyed.

General Mutaguchi realised that *15th Division* needed help and he told General Sato, of *31st Division*, to send a regimental group to its aid. Sato planned to send *124th Regiment* less its *IIIrd Battalion* which was to hold Naga Village (Map 37). His *138th Regiment* was to send its *Ist Battalion* with *124th Regiment,* while that formation was holding between Cheswema and Merema and harassing the Kohima - Dimapur Road. *58th Regiment* was to capture Garrison Hill at Kohima. This plan was taken by an officer of the Cameron Highlanders from the body of a Japanese soldier he had just shot and Grover acted fast. He ordered Brigadier JD Shapland, 6th British Infantry Brigade, to clear the Japanese from the Kohima Ridge. Stopford released 161st Indian Infantry Brigade to Grover and told him to attack, accept risks and use all available brigades. Grover ordered 4th British Infantry Brigade, under Brigadier WH Goschen, to move to Jotsoma and leave a battalion at Zubza. He told 5th British Infantry Brigade, under Brigadier VFS Hawkins, to clear the Merema Ridge and then attack Naga Village as we have seen. Medium Tanks of 149th Regiment RAC and the divisional artillery, of 10th, 16th, and 99th Field and 100th LAA/Anti-Tank Regiments, were also available. But Sato was also acting and was at that time giving orders to attack Garrison Hill.

On the afternoon of 22nd April, 1st Royal Berkshires, with two troops of tanks and under the fire of the divisional artillery, advanced on the DC's Bungalow but the tanks could not cope with the steep slopes and the infantry suffered heavily. Officer casualties were particularly high and Major Harry Grenfell, second-in-command of 10th Field Regiment had a foot blown off by a mortar bomb. Also on that day Captain BM (Barney) Ward tells how he was ordered to report to Major Bryan Bonsor on Garrison Hill because he needed another OP. On arrival he recalls registering DFs on Kuki Piquet, FSD and DIS before being told to move to a new position overlooking the Kohima - Imphal Road. That night seven companies of *58th Regiment* attacked the DC's Bungalow Spur, Garrison Hill and Kuki Piquet. Four enemy companies were almost wiped out by the combined firepower of the infantry and the artillery, but 2nd Durham Light Infantry, who faced the attack, lost 105 men and a third of its officers trying to restore the situation. Barney Ward reckons he would have been one of the casualties if he had not been moved. During the night of 23/24th April, 24th Indian Mountain Regiment's diary states, 'Enemy penetrated perimeter near Lieutenant Mandar Singh's OP and his party accounted for five Japs with their small arms. The position was restored after a counter-attack.'

On 24th April General Grover decided that a double encircling movement would best shift the enemy on his front. He therefore ordered 4th British Infantry Brigade plus 143rd SS Company at Jotsoma to move via Khonoma and attack GPT Ridge from the south west with the support of the divisional artillery under Lieutenant Colonel JWH James, commanding officer of 99th Field Regiment. 161st Indian Infantry Brigade was to take over all 4th British Brigade's other tasks. On the left 5th British Infantry Brigade was to press on through Naga Village from the north. The divisional artillery moved forward into cramped positions around Jotsoma to cover both these operations.

General Sato, commanding *31st Division*, in his command post on Point 5120, saw that a major operation was being mounted against him. Accordingly he held *124th Regiment* back from its move to join General M Yamauchi's *15th Division* and and he held back *I/138th Regiment* to help his *58th Regiment* in its attacks onto Kohima ridge. It was probably this disregard for his orders by Sato that saved Imphal, but it was also to halt 4th British Infantry Brigade's right flanking operation onto Aradura Spur, prolong the battle of Kohima, and because it meant that GPT Ridge was not re-captured for some time, it left the British with a serious water shortage.

By 24th April the whole of the Kohima battlefield was under the observation of the OPs of 10th, 16th and 99th Field Regiments. They all knew each other well and also knew all the infantry commanding officers and company commanders. They were treated as a pool on whom anyone could draw. They deployed wherever they were needed and moved freely between battalions where they were greeted as close friends. This long period together of the regiments of 2nd British Division through the Dunkirk battles, the defence of England and the training in India, was to prove one of its greatest strengths in the testing times to come and remains a great lesson of combat. The artillery of 2nd British Division in its battle at Kohima 'embraced all the skills of the arts of gunnery handled by an efficient unified team.' (Woodcock). *Ad hoc* late groupings can be fatal in battle. At this time Major Bryan Bonsor was on Garrison Hill acting as artillery commander, since his commanding officer was preparing for operations with 4th British Infantry Brigade.

We should at this stage look at the action taking place around Imphal because the two battles impinged so much on each other (Map 36). 63rd Indian Infantry Brigade held Sengmai until relieved by 89th Indian Infantry Brigade of 7th Indian Division, by then beginning to arrive. 123rd and 9th Indian Infantry Brigades captured the Mapao position but the enemy clung to Molvom. 49th Indian Infantry Brigade had occupied Kasom and 23rd Indian Division captured Shongpel. Further south, in the 20th Indian Divisional area, there was a determined attack on 'Scraggy' on 27/28th April but it was driven off. On the Tiddim Road, 32nd Indian Infantry Brigade at Bishenpur was still under considerable pressure. There was tough fighting for the vital water point on Point 5846 and the enemy pressed forwards to Potsangbum - also known as 'Pots and Pans' - on the Tiddim Road itself. When 89th Indian Infantry Brigade had relieved 63rd Indian Infantry Brigade it moved south to assist 32nd Indian Infantry Brigade. Now back to Kohima (Maps 36 and 37).

General Sato's *31st Division* was planning a four battalion assault onto Kohima Ridge while others secured its flanks at Naga Village and Aradura. But Mutaguchi knew that there was no more help and he knew that his supplies were fast running out. He also recognised the seriousness of the situation and cancelled the commitment, which had not been met, to send a regiment to Imphal. Things were beginning to go very wrong for the Japanese. On 26th April the Japanese attacked the advancing 5th British Infantry Brigade on the Merema Track. At the same time they attacked Kuki Piquet with great ferocity, causing considerable casualties to the 2nd Dorsets who were at the time forming up to attack DC's Bungalow Spur. This they did at dawn on 27th April and soon had one company digging in at the spur overlooking the road. This splendid action enabled a troop of tanks of 149th Regiment RAC and another of 45th Cavalry to fight their way around the corner and up the Merema track to join 5th British Infantry Brigade in their attack on Naga Village from the north. Another troop tried to come to the aid of the other company of the Dorsets held up at the 'Club' but torrential rain prevented them climbing up the slope. The forward company of the Dorsets held mainly due to the magnificent fire of the 25-pounders of the 2nd Divisional Artillery, controlled by Major Bryan Bonsor, often firing as close as 25 yards in front of their trenches. But the Dorsets suffered over 70 casualties from constant Japanese attacks. Nevertheless this Spur was never lost; it was a magnificent effort by a splendid battalion and the guns.

On 28th April, The Emperor of Japan's birthday, further attacks were made against Garrison Hill but these were repelled by concentrated artillery fire and stubborn resistance by the infantry. Captain John Moreton of 99th Field Regiment, later Sir John Moreton, was FOO that day and, although wounded, brought down his fire with the greatest accuracy. For his coolness, judgement and courage on Garrison Hill that day he was awarded an immediate Military Cross. His citation not only describes his gallantry under fire but illustrates the nature of the fighting. He was wounded in the shoulder on the morning of 28th April by a sniper as he was firing a sten gun at the enemy in the area of the DCs Bungalow. Despite his wound he insisted on carrying on. On the night of 28/29th April the enemy attacked Garrison Hill again and broke through to within ten yards of 'A' Company Headquarters of 1st Berkshires where Moreton's OP was located. He then did great damage to the enemy by the gunfire he brought down. He put himself in great peril every time he spoke on the radio owing to the very close proximity of the enemy. Captain Moreton remained at his post all night, killing a Japanese officer three yards from his position, and was also engaged in a grenade slinging match with the enemy for several hours. All this in spite of the pain of his wounds. 'Throughout he showed great coolness, judgement and courage of the highest order.' That day also 143rd SS (Commando) Company with Captain Boyd-Thomson of 99th Field Regiment as FOO moved onto the 'Pimple' feature. He was joined by Captain Beamish of the same regiment on the 29th. Sadly on 3rd May, Boyd-Thomson was out on a patrol with 143rd Company and was never seen again.

24th Indian Mountain Regiment reported, '29th April. Major AMS Fergie at his OP on 'Piquet Hill' directed the fire of some tanks onto enemy bunkers. Several earthworks were destroyed. He then fired DF Tasks onto Kuki Piquet all night . . . 30th April . . . One section of 3.7-inch howitzers of 27th Light Battery, 16th Field Regiment, came under command this regiment, and were in action on Piquet Hill. They engaged enemy bunkers with good results. In the early evening the enemy put in a two company attack on 'Twin Trees.' Captain TGJ Murray brought down heavy fire and the attack was broken up.' (War Diary 24th Indian Mountain Regiment).

On the right flank 4th British Infantry Brigade was struggling along mountain paths made so slippery by the rain that in places men, shivering and wet through, had to crawl to make any progress up the steep slopes. Lance Corporal GT Gordon, Royal Signals, of Lieutenant Colonel JWH James's RHQ party, 99th Field Regiment reports; '. . . we assembled at six o'clock on the evening of 23rd April, each with the following load - large pack containing one half of a blanket, one gas cape, pullover, towel, spare socks, a 48 hour light scale ration, rifle, 50 rounds, two primed grenades, a stout stick and a full water bottle - quite a load as we were soon to realise. The wireless sets were made up into man-pack loads each requiring three people. Our RHQ party consisted of the CO, his batman, Lieutenant [HW] Sebag-Montefiore [later Bishop of Birmingham], the Survey Officer, four Gunners and we four of the Signals Section. In addition each Battery had a small OP party. . . The infantry consisted of the R. Norfolks and the R. Scots with a half company of 143rd SS who were to be scouts. There was the brigadier with a skeleton HQ, part of the Brigade Signals section, a section of Field Ambulance, half a dozen engineers and the Gunners OP parties including ourselves.' (Gordon).

At the same time, on the left flank, 5th British Infantry Brigade attacked, but failed to capture, an enemy position at Firs Hill while on the right flank, after spending a night at Khonoma and two more in the open in heavy rain, on 29th April the two lead battalions of 4th British Infantry Brigade reached Pulebadze. The brigade was ordered to occupy Aradura Spur, block the Imphal Road and then attack GPT Ridge. On the left, 5th British Infantry Brigade was to attack Naga Village forthwith while 6th British Infantry Brigade was to make a frontal attack and capture FSD and Jail Hill. At this time there was a shortage of artillery ammunition. Then it was realised that the Japanese were present in strength at Aradura, because *124th Regiment* had not moved to join *15th Division*, so Grover ordered 4th British Infantry Brigade to attack GPT Ridge from the west instead. This involved cutting a track through the jungle which took three days. On 3rd May with 2nd Norfolks in the lead good progress was made but there were snipers everywhere. The next day the Norfolks, covered by the fire of 16th and 99th Field Regiments, got onto GPT Ridge with some 77 casualties. One of these was Lieutenant Colonel James, the commanding officer of 9th Field Regiment. Corporal Gordon heard later that he had been hit by 'A burst of automatic from a sniper right across his back - he had actually seen the Jap in the trees and, as he turned to point him out to his batman with a tommy gun, they got him.' (Gordon)

On 11th May both FOOs of 16th Field Regiment, Captain PE Stainton and Lieutenant J Riddle, serving with 1st Queens, on Garrison Hill were wounded and the latter's OP Ack, Sergeant Hatton, was killed and his signallers wounded. Lieutenant Colonel RJ Uniacke, commanding 16th Field Regiment, had his third lucky escape when a grenade fell beside him. Fortunately it fell in soft ground and did him no harm when it exploded.

Meanwhile 4/1st Gurkhas of 33rd Indian Infantry Brigade of 7th Indian Division had got onto 'Two Tree Hill.' Enemy patrols and snipers were everywhere. They killed Brigadier Goschen and Lieutenant Colonel IH Hedderwick of 4/1st Gurkhas and, as we have seen, had already killed Lieutenant Colonel JWH 'Jimmy' James of 99th Field Regiment, and the fighting raged on. These were all very serious losses in the middle of a battle.

On 4th May the tanks and 2nd DLI attacked Jail Hill and DIS under a fireplan by 16th Field Regiment. Captain R (Bob) Makepeace and Captain CM (Michael) Raine both of 34th Battery went forward in tank OPs while Lieutenant TC (Busty) Davis was in a carrier (Map 39). The tanks did well and got to Jail Hill but the carriers had a rough time going round the DC's Bungalow, being shot up from Treasury Hill, and only a few got to DIS. Busty Davis's driver, who was wounded, won the Military Medal saving his crew. At about 1100 hours Bob Makepeace said to Colonel Uniacke over the radio that he had had a track blown off by a 47mm shell but he had knocked out the gun and was about to be towed by a tank. Then silence. Later it was found that

Japs had dropped a phosphorous bomb on the tank which had brewed up, and when Makepeace and the crew jumped out they had all been killed by a machine gun. By 5th May the Berkshires and the Durhams formed a composite battalion on Garrison Hill and FSD. On the 7th an attempt to capture Jail Hill by 1st Queens had to be abandoned and the battalion was withdrawn under a smoke screen fired by their FOO Lieutenant Findlay of 99th Field Regiment. Meanwhile, on 3/4th May, the Camerons tried very hard to capture Naga Village and Point 5120, sadly without much artillery to help. For long afterwards the Camerons were convinced that, had they had the fire of the guns, they could have taken the village that day. After all, with the greatest gallantry, they nearly did so on their own.

On GPT the Norfolks, under the inspired leadership of Lieutenant Colonel Robert Scott, reached their objectives by 0900 hours on 4th May (See Map 39 for the fireplan for this attack). Captain RE Brook-Fox was FOO with them and immediately registered some DFs. At 1000 hours a mortar bomb hit Brigade Headquarters and Major AL Awdry and Lieutenant CP Richardson of 99th Field Regiment, amongst others, were wounded. By 1100 hours that day, Captain Hazell had established an OP with the Norfolks and Lieutenant Richardson, although wounded, with the Royal Scots. Then on 6th May, while bringing down fire on an enemy attack at close range, Captain RE Brooke-Fox was wounded. On 8th May 99th Field Regiment reverted to 6th British Infantry Brigade but they still had an OP at Naga Village with 5th British Infantry Brigade.

Major DD (David) Law, commanding 27th Light Battery of 16th Field Regiment wrote, concerning events on or about 4th May, 'While I was at 6th Brigade Headquarters, 2nd Dorsets were around the tennis court, they had found a 25 pounder near the bungalow [presumably the one knocked out on 5th April]. Two artificers from 16th Field Regiment came up and repaired it within 24 hours. It was decided to use it over open sights at a Jap bunker on Kuki Piquet. A small supply of HE and AP ammunition was humped up Garrison Hill, avoiding snipers. The gun was manhandled up over some difficult exposed ground under cover of darkness. At first light we fired DF 1 from our two batteries for 3 or 4 minutes and then we waited for the Japs to re-ocuppy their bunker. We then fired about five AP rounds with the 25 pounder followed by the HE. I was in command! The Japs came rushing out of the bunker, two had no clothes on. They were machine gunned. Later a company of Royal Berkshires took the position.' (Letters at the RAI). It has to be pointed out, however, that there are others who dispute the existence of a 25 pounder at this spot and argue that the gun in question might have been either a 6 pounder or a 3.7 inch howitzer.

On 4th May 24th Indian Mountain Regiment reported OPs deployed as follows:

Captain G Green	Garrison Hill
Subadar Walidad	Garrison Hill
Major Nettelfield	The Cutting
Lieutenant BK Mehta	The Cutting
Jemadar Pehalwan Khan	The Cutting
Major AMS Fergie	Piquet Hill
Lieutenant Colonel RHM Hill	Punjab Ridge

They also had Captain Green with the RWFs in their attack on 'Summer House Hill' on 5th May 'which was a very sticky show.' (War Diary 24th Indian Mountain Regiment).

A word here about the action of 100th LAA/Anti-Tank Regiment. The LAA batteries protected the guns during daylight and there were some air attacks as well. There were no Japanese tanks but the anti-tank batteries also had mortars which were extensively used. On two occasions two 6-pounders were moved right forward for direct fire tasks, once on Garrison Hill and once on GPT Ridge with the Norfolks. It was at about this time that 136th Field Regiment, by then at Ranchi, was ordered to send five complete OP parties to help 2nd British Division at Kohima, such were the casualties. This they did and among them were Captains KM Bevins and SP Youlden, who both went to help 25th Indian Mountain Regiment which had arrived with 7th Indian Division. Captain Youlden, of 347th Field Battery, won a Military Cross for his action against Naga Village and his OP Assistant, also of 347th Field Battery, won a Military Medal for keeping communications open against all odds. Captain Bevins, though stricken with typhus, somehow kept going.

5th British Infantry Brigade had got as far as Point 5120 but had been unable to hold it and were concentrated at the west end of Naga Village. Stalemate had been reached by both sides. It was on 7th May that a Gunner, Major General CGG Nicholson, took command of Headquarters 21st Indian Division. With this he took full responsibility for the security of the rear areas with 252nd, 253rd and 257th Sub-Areas and 268th Indian Infantry Brigade, leaving Major General John Grover to concentrate on the battle at Kohima. Meanwhile Headquarters 7th Indian Division had arrived and taken command of 33rd and 161st Indian Infantry Brigades, 114th Indian Infantry Brigade was on its way from the Arakan, but for artillery 7th Indian Division had only 25th Indian Mountain Regiment. Around Imphal all divisional areas were strengthened and Headquarters 20th and 23rd Indian Divisions changed places thus rectifying the poor deployment of their brigades which had become mixed up. 5th Indian Division advanced up the Kohima road and 17th Indian Division strengthened the area around Bishenpur.

It was in the middle of this battle that 24th Indian Mountain Regiment received a message from 5th Indian Division to say that for their gallantry in the battles for the Ngakyedauk Pass in the Arakan Jemadar Kartar Singh had been awarded the Military Cross and five other ranks a Certificate of Gallantry. These awards were in addition to those already mentioned in Chapter 9.

At *15th Army*, Lieutenant General Mutaguchi had also received reinforcements. He reckoned that he could not now take Kohima or attack Imphal from the north or the east but he could from the south along the Tiddim Road, where *33rd Division* was still very effective and was by then under the command of the forceful and experienced Lieutenant General N Tanaka. He decided to reinforce him with *14th Tank Regiment, the II/18th Heavy Artillery Regiment* and *Ist Anti-Tank Battalion. 151st Infantry Regiment*, less its *Ist Battalion*, was sent to Mutaguchi as *15th Army's* reserve. He told Tanaka to break into Imphal from the south.

Meanwhile things were stirring again at Kohima. Brigadier FJ Loftus-Tottenham attacked Jail Hill and DIS with his 33rd Indian Infantry Brigade on 11th May. The fireplan by the 2nd British Divisional Artillery started at 0440 hours and lasted for 25 minutes, then it lifted onto Treasury Hill while the tanks moved forward to FSD. Lieutenant Jimmy Riddle of 16th Field Regiment was also on Jail Hill that day as FOO with 1st Queen's and he too was having a rough time in the open. His OP Assistant, Sergeant Hatton, was killed and the rest of his party were all wounded. But he kept on engaging the enemy wherever he could. 'At the same time 24th Indian Mountain Regiment ranged all its batteries onto DIS to cover the attack by 4/15th Punjab at dawn on 11th May. Lieutenant RA MacDonald and Lieutenant SR Mehta were FOOs, with Major Nettelfield alongside the Commanding Officer of the Punjabis. The attack started at 0510 hours and soon DIS was reported captured but Lieutenant Mehta had been seriously wounded in the head while controlling fire, his signaller had been killed and two others wounded.' (War Diary 24th Indian Mountain Regiment). On the same day 16th Field Regiment reported that Captain Stainton was wounded while serving as an FOO on Garrison Hill.

What was left of 4th and 6th British Infantry Brigades was ordered to clear up GPT Ridge, FSD and Kuki Piquet, while 5th British Infantry Brigade was finally to capture Naga Village and Point 5120. But this was not achieved until 19th May and then only partially, and only then with the direct fire of three 5.5-inch guns of 5/22nd Medium Battery of 1st Medium Regiment. These were dragged up to Treasury Hill where they each fired some 200 rounds at the defences at 800 yards range, doing much damage, but the Japanese were still there. Meanwhile 33rd Indian Infantry Brigade's attack onto Jail Hill started well until it was swept by flanking machine gun fire from GPT Ridge and FSD.

At GPT, the tanks hit a road block near FSD and were held. The Gunners fired HE and smoke to enable the hard pressed infantry to dig in. By 1900 hours the situation was getting desperate and again casualties were mounting. Then a thick mist descended from the hills, men could stand and dig, wounded could be evacuated, ammunition could be rushed forward and the crisis passed. That night in cold rain the infantry and the FOOs spent a miserable time. Next morning the road block was cleared and the tanks eased forwards but progress was slow. Neither 4th nor 5th British Infantry Brigades made much progress and Brigadier JA Theobalds, who had taken command of 4th British Infantry Brigade on 7th May, was killed and Brigadier VFS Hawkins, of 5th British Infantry Brigade, was wounded. By last light on 12th May the Japanese still clung to the reverse slopes of GPT Ridge, FSD and Kuki Piquet and were still in the deep redoubts on top of Jail Hill and DIS.

Loftus-Tottenham called for one last effort. They all spent another miserable night clinging to the rim of Jail Hill but before dawn on 13th May the enemy began to crack. With the exception of those facing the DC's Bungalow, the Japanese began to slip away and 33rd Indian Infantry Brigade followed hard, taking no small toll of them as they departed.

The final battle was to take place on the tennis court by the Bungalow. There 2nd Dorsets, with a Lee tank of 149th Regiment RAC winched into position by the Sappers, a 3.7-inch howitzer and a 6-pounder anti-tank gun, destroyed the remaining bunkers whose occupants fought grimly to the end. The 3.7-inch howitzer of 20th Mountain Battery, was brought into position by Major Bryan Bonsor of 99th Field Regiment. 24th Indian Mountain Regiment reported, 'One gun of 20th Mountain Battery was put in a sniping position over the DCs Bungalow and had a most successful shoot. Japs ran out of the bunkers and about 60 were killed in the open . . . then the tennis court area fell into our hands. Pieces of Right Section's guns were recovered (they had been buried earlier in the battle).' Major Bonsor was awarded a well deserved Military Cross for his action in the defence of Garrison Hill and the DC's Bungalow. His citation reads, 'Major BC Bonsor was RA Liaison Officer at my Tac HQ on Garrison Hill during the latter part of the operations. His complete disregard for danger and his personal safety was the subject of comment by all. His aggressive use of his guns was the delight of the Infantry and on 13th May for the attack on the DC's Bungalow he obtained and put into action personally a 3.7-inch Howitzer which he fired direct at 200 yards into the flank of the enemy position. The gun position was in the open and exposed to enemy mortar and gun fire. His initiative was responsible for killing about 40 Japs by 3.7 howitzer shell fire and to a great measure [he assisted in] the final capture of the objective.' (Signed) JD Shapland Brigadier [6th British Infantry Brigade].

The Dorsets were then able to cross the tennis court and finally destroy the last enemy in the bunkers. It was a fine example of all arms training, a tank winched into position by the Sappers, the guns and of course the Infantry. With this act the whole of Kohima Ridge was at last clear, but it had been a grim task. It had been 39 days since the first attack and the cost to both sides was high, both victor and vanquished had lost very heavily. 33rd Indian Infantry Brigade lost some 400 men in taking DIS and Jail Hill alone. On the night of 13/14th May, 4/1st Gurkhas captured Treasury Hill and this finally broke the Japanese effort. They could take no more. Little food for weeks and ammunition rapidly running out, they had endured terrible conditions under constant and ever increasing shelling. 2nd British Division, which had borne the brunt of the fighting after the gallant stand of the Royal West Kents had held the line at the crisis of the battle, was, after a couple of days rest, reinforced for the great march to victory which was about to start. 268th and 114th Indian Infantry Brigades took over the defence of the position. Before leaving Kohima, 2nd British Division did as the local Nagas did before they left a battlefield, it left its Memorial behind. On it were inscribed words that were to mark its great sacrifice at Kohima. They are the words now used annually in the National Act of Remembrance:

'When you go home,
Tell them of us and say,
For your tomorrow,
We gave our today.'

The battle of Kohima had been one of the toughest, hardest fought, close-quarter battles of the Second World War. There was no quarter asked or given, much of the fighting was at the point of the bayonet and it went on relentlessly round the clock, often in pouring rain and always in oppressive heat when water, food and medical supplies were in very short supply. *31st Division* was determined to break through and it spared nothing in its countless attempts to do so but 2nd British Division and 161st Indian Infantry Brigade were equally determined that they would fail. For the Gunners it was a true test of their shooting. FOOs had to be in the forward section posts. They had acute crest clearance and meteor problems and they had to shoot down to within 20 yards of their positions, sometimes down to 15 or even 10 yards in front of their comrades in the Infantry. By sheer professionalism, coupled with the greatest courage and gallantry, they achieved these incredible results. Time and time again they broke up enemy attacks. Non-Gunners may not fully realise just what an achievement this was, particularly as it was done without a single shot falling in error throughout the whole battle. It meant that the battery team from FOO to the command post and out to the gun detachment and above all the gun layer must be a well oiled machine of the very highest standards. Nor must they flinch because of enemy action, fear, fatigue, wound or lack of food and water. The FOO had to understand precisely the performance of each gun almost as a living person and the individual capabilities of his men. Several times an FOO would call for a specific gun and specific gun layer for a particularly tricky task. The OP Acks must be mentioned as well for the way in which they supported their FOOs and, on occasion, took over from them when they were incapacitated.

The role of the guns at Kohima was decisive. Without them the battle would have been lost and their action on those jungle clad hills of Assam must go down in history as another of the Regiment's finest hours, but they could not win alone. No words are capable of expressing the supreme gallantry of the Infantry at Kohima, for the Gunners who were there are the first to say that it was the Infantry who won the battle.

The second Battle of Bishenpur began on 13th May when 48th Indian Infantry Brigade, with 21st Indian Mountain Regiment, both of 17th Indian Light Division, marched round the east of the Logtak Lake to Wangjing and swung through Suganu to block the Tiddim Road at Torbung. Then on 14th May Brigadier RT Cameron of 48th Indian Infantry Brigade was ordered to seize a road block at Torbung with his brigade and 21st Indian Mountain Regiment. The brigade group carried out a circular march through Waikong and Shugam and on to Komsan. Here the Sappers put a bridge over the Manipur river. At 0530 hours on 15th May 2/5th Gurkhas arrived at Sangang with seven miles to go to their start line for an attack on the Point 3404 feature. First Sangang had to be taken in what turned out to be a stiff fight. Then 1/7th Gurkhas, with Captain Jimmy Proctor as their FOO, set off for MS 33 on the Tiddim Road and a road block was established. That night they were attacked by tanks but these were driven off by the guns and some PIATs and many enemy were killed. This was the action that cut *33rd Division* in half. By

0630 hours on 16th May 2/5th Gurkhas were overlooking the road from Point 3404. Hard fighting was to follow to hold the road. The enemy attacked as planned and by 21st May both 17th Indian and *33rd Japanese* Divisions were cut in half and both divisional headquarters were threatened.

Lieutenant Evans was in an OP on Point 3404 when the Japanese made another attempt to break through from the south. They attacked in waves and were mown down by the guns of 1st and 6th Mountain Batteries and the mortars of 37th Mountain Battery, all controlled by Lieutenant Evans and Lieutenant Mohammed Aslam. Next morning 105 bodies were counted. On 20th May an attack on Point 3404 was defeated but British casualties were mounting. Nevertheless the road block held and the guns were constantly in action covering aggressive infantry patrolling. Lieutenant Kenyon was FOO at the block itself. Then on 24th May Brigadier Cameron decided to abandon it and set up a new road block at Moirang.

The situation facing 17th Indian Light Division was serious and an *ad hoc* group, known as 'Woodforce', was sent south from 20th Indian Division comprising 7/10th Baluch, 9/12th FF Regiment, 1/4th Gurkhas, two troops of 3rd Carabiniers, two troops of 7th Light Cavalry and a battery of 114th Jungle Field Regiment. This force deployed around 17th Divisional Headquarters and held for four days.

On the night of 24th May, heavy rain played havoc with the move and 6th (Jacob's) Mountain Battery was attacked and lost three of its four guns. It had been moving with 37th Mountain Battery and ran into an ambush. Jemadar Hakim Ali brought No 3 Gun into action and killed 12 Japanese. Lieutenant Taylor, of 6th Battery, and Lieutenant Melvin, of 37th Battery, set off to find some mules and succeeded but on returning found that two guns had sunk into the morass, four men had been killed and 11 were wounded. Jemadar Hakim Ali was awarded a Military Medal for his gallantry in this action and the next night the one remaining gun of 6th Battery was recovered and was in action at Moirang where it knocked out two enemy tanks but Lieutenant Taylor was killed. Major Edward Garnett, the Battery Commander, returned to his guns and organised the dressing and evacuation of the wounded before he raised a scratch gun team who brought down effective fire on the enemy. This was a prime factor in breaking up an enemy attack and it cheered 2/5th Gurkhas. For this action Major Garnett was awarded the Military Cross.

It was not until 29th May that 48th Indian Infantry Brigade made contact with 63rd Indian Infantry Brigade at Potsangbum. Afterwards it became clear that, had the Torbung Road block been left in position a few more days, Tanaka would probably have had to call off his attack on Imphal because of the dire straits his men were in by then. Such are the fortunes of war.

Meanwhile, to the north of Imphal, 5th Indian Division had made slow progress but by 20th May it had captured Kanglatongbi. The slowness in opening the Kohima - Imphal Road was causing comment in London and Mountbatten raised the issue with Giffard. Giffard had to explain that it would take time and that the southern threat by *33rd Division* had first to be destroyed. He also explained the very bitter and savage nature of the fighting which was not understood outside the battle areas. Nevertheless he flew to see Stopford to find out what was to be done (Map 40). Stopford's plan for 33rd Indian Corps was for 2nd British Division to advance down the main road to Imphal. The CRA, Brigadier Pat Bourke, had already ordered 27th and 30th Light Batteries to get forward using any means possible. Captain BAT Hammond recalls that 'I saw one 3.7 under tow by the battery water truck with the detachment clinging to the tank and another behind an OP carrier'. 7th Indian Division was to advance from Naga Village by way of Chakhabama and Kezoma, with 23rd Brigade directed on Kharasom and Ukhrul. With the latter went one section of 5th (Bombay) Mountain Battery. All artillery was to be under Corps control except for the mountain guns because of the problem of finding gun positions for them. Accordingly, on 24th May, Stopford gave orders for 2nd British Division to attack Aradura

Spur with the support of the corps artillery on 26th May and then to advance to Imphal through Mao. Meanwhile 7th Indian Division attacked Naga Village under the fire of the mountain guns but after heavy fighting the enemy still clung to Point 5120. In the end they pulled back exhausted once the mediums were brought up. 1st Medium Regiment, commanded by Lieutenant Colonel RAH Soames, reported that on 25th May 1944 'In sp 7 Ind Div operation to clear Naga village 5/22 Med Bty were put under command RA 7 Ind Div . . . a single gun was brought into action . . . The gun moved up during night 24/25 . . . and went into action at first light. 110 rds were fired at bunker posns at 1500 yds range using charge III and fuze 231. One bunker was destroyed and several badly damaged . . . OP . . . was hit by a 75mm shell and . . . Captain AC Booth-Jones was wounded, . . . Gnr Ivison E killed and . . . L/Bdr Moore F wounded. (War Diary 1st Medium Regiment).

24th Indian Mountain Regiment described the final action around Naga Village as follows: '29th May 0530 hours. Major AB Howard with 33rd Brigade. Lieutenant JS Punia on 'Treasury Hill' with 7/2nd Punjabis who have relieved 4/1st Gurkhas. Enemy guns and mortars active. Lieutenant G Green reports 4/1st Gurkhas on 'Basha Hill.' Major P Hartley moves with battalion to 'Nose.' 4/15th Punjabis attack 'Church Knoll' after concentration fired. 'Hunter's Hill' and 'McRobert' engaged as 'Mike Targets.' Fireplan 'Naga' fired at 1310 hours. 'Church Knoll' captured. Smoke indication for air strikes by 12th Mountain Battery very successful. Heavy enemy shelling. One signaller killed and two wounded. Fresh OP party, Lieutenant PA Densham moved in. Two attacks during the night. Both repulsed. 4/1st Gurkhas continue operations against bunkers on 'Green Spur' with Sappers and pole charges.' (War Dairy 24th Indian Mountain Regiment).

2nd British Division did not get under way until 27th May. 6th British Infantry Brigade first captured the western end of Aradura Spur and then 4th and 5th British Infantry Brigades advanced one on each side of the road with tanks moving along it. Captain JO (John) Moreton and Lieutenant Findlay were FOOs for this attack. A Japanese counter-attack on the 28th destroyed 6th British Infantry Brigade's Tactical Headquarters and Brigadier Shapland was wounded, the fourth brigadier of 2nd British Division to become a casualty in a month. The Royal Welch Fusiliers had pulled back in a hurry leaving behind brigade and battalion headquarters and some OPs of 99th Field Regiment. Next 4th British Infantry Brigade attempted a frontal attack on Aradura Spur but failed and over half the tanks and a Sapper squadron were lost on the steep slithery slopes, in heavy rain on a minefield. Both 1st Royal Scots and 2nd Norfolks had suffered heavily and the attack was called off, while the guns held the enemy in their trenches. The corps artillery then switched to attack Naga Village in front of 7th Indian Division where Captain Barney Ward was FOO. But again frontal attacks failed and casualties were heavy. When 161st Indian Infantry Brigade took 'Firs Hill' and 'McRobert Hill' the Japanese had had enough and pulled out. By last light on 31st May 1st Queens had at last occupied Naga Village. 114th Indian Infantry Brigade came forward and the orders for a general advance were given on 2nd June. The advance went well until 114th Indian Infantry Brigade met resistance at Kezoma and 161st Indian Infantry Brigade also came under fire at Kekrima. Then 4th British Infantry Brigade found that the enemy on Aradura Spur had gone and on 5th June, 5th British Infantry Brigade occupied Phesama Ridge with the Worcesters and Lieutenant Richardson of 99th Field Regiment as FOO.

The Japanese situation was by then grim. *31st Division* had held until it could do so no more. Sato told the rear parties of *124th* and *138th Regiments* to hold as long as they could to cover the rest of the division which was to make its own way out. It was these parties that fought so hard at Naga Village and on Aradura Spur until they too abandoned the position on 4th June. No one could have done more. Even so, on 5th June Lieutenant General Masakazu Kawabe, commanding the *Burma Area Army*, went to Mutaguchi's headquarters and urged him to open new attacks against Imphal through Palel and provided him with his last reinforcements of infantry and artillery. On 3rd June, Mountbatten was ordered to continue operations throughout the monsoon and to do all he could to improve the air link to China. On 9th June he ordered Giffard to clear the Dimapur - Kohima - Imphal Plain - Tamanthi area of all enemy forces and to prepare to exploit across the Chindwin in the Yuwa - Tamanthi area after the monsoon. He also stated that 82nd West African Division would arrive in India in August, that 19th Indian Division would become available and that 36th Indian Division would move north and come under General Stilwell's command in July.

Back at Kohima, the breakout was at last under way. 'On 6th June, D-Day in Europe, Capt JF Thom, [394th Battery] moved down the Imphal Road with an armoured column and the next day he and Capt Moreton had reached MS 55. An extensive harassing fire plan was arranged for Kigwema for the night 7/8th June.' (White).

'9th June. At first light 34 Bty moved up into action just short of Viswema and the transport was sent back for 72 Bty. The gun position was on a small spur running out from the road with a flat top about 80 x 80 onto which we packed 24 guns and RHQ. There was a steep drop off the road and a difficult track was bulldozed down it. . . Just before the road passed by the village there was a road block of boulders and mines covered by an ATK gun. The CO of 1/8 Lancashire Fusiliers, Willie West, was killed by a mortar bomb in his jeep. . . [10 June] In the evening [an OP] was registering DF when a shell failed to clear the crest and hit the roof of a house in the [Royal] Scots area. By bad luck their RAP was just alongside and it wounded four, including the doctor and padre, so I had to go up and see their CO to try and restore confidence in us, which was not a pleasant job.' (Uniacke).

On 11th June Captain Ian Carpenter, FOO with the Lancashire Fusiliers, was wounded in the neck. On 20th June, while moving fast to keep up with the tanks, Major RLT Burges, second-in-command of 16th Field Regiment, got the gun reconnaissance parties too far forward at MS 81 and they came under machine gun fire and were only saved by a smoke screen. Nevertheless this move ensured that momentum was maintained. Then a road block was bumped at MS 88 and all guns piled into action in a lay-by at MS 87. It was a tiny area some 200 x 60 yards, but into it went a troop of 3rd Medium Battery, 4 x 5.5-inch guns; 27th Light Battery, 8 x 3.7-inch howitzers; 34th Field Battery, 8 x 25-pounders; and outside on the grass verge beside the road were the eight more 3.7s of 30th Light Battery. It was raining hard and everyone was dead tired but exhilarated at the advance. At dawn next day a 40 minute barrage was fired to cover the Royal Scots and Norfolks as they cleared the block. (Uniacke).

In 99th Field Regiment, Major Bonsor and Captain Moreton were at MS 59 and 393rd Field Battery was in action at MS 48 and 472nd Field Battery was on its wheels. On the reverse slope of the 16th Field Regiment gun position, some 100 mortars of the brigade and 100th LAA/Anti-Tank Regiment came into action. Captain Hammond describes the scene, 'My 'C' Troop was the rearmost troop and was right on the crest, just 28 yards behind 'A' Troop. Looking to the rear from the CP there was a veritable forest of mortar barrels.'

On 12th June the deluge began and lasted four days and turned every stream into a torrent, swept away culverts, bridges and tracks and brought all operations north of Imphal to a standstill. Yet in the Shenam Pass area *33rd Division* began another attack and eventually succeeded in capturing 'Scraggy' after what was perhaps the heaviest bombardment put down by the Japanese in the whole Burma Campaign (Map 36). But 37th Indian Infantry Brigade still held the Shenam Pass. 49th Indian Infantry Brigade was at Shuganu and 1st Indian Infantry Brigade, with two batteries and a squadron of tanks, was at Wanjing. *33rd Division* continued its attacks up the Tiddim Road and got well past Bishenpur to the northwest in the hills. Bishenpur was held by 63rd Indian Infantry Brigade, while 32nd Indian Infantry Brigade was at Point 5846, with 48th Indian Infantry Brigade and 'Woodforce' in reserve.

In his letter to the MGRA dated 3rd June 1944 (the material in square brackets is inserted for the sake of clarity), Lieutenant Colonel CFJ Younger, commanding 129th (Lowland) Field Regiment, wrote 'A strong threat to Imphal developed towards the beginning of the month [May] with the reinforced Jap 33rd Division pressing up the Tiddim Road'.

The forces to hold this move by the enemy finally amounting to four brigades supported by four field batteries, two mountain regiments, one mountain battery, one medium battery and one HAA battery in a ground role, and latterly one jungle field Battery.

The artillery, less the Jungle Field Battery, was deployed in two Boxes on the west side of the Tiddim Road between MS 14 and 16. In the Northern Box, Mediums, the HAA and five Field Troops. In the Southern Box, [129th] Field Regiment headquarters and three Field Troops.

Both Boxes had perforce to be defended by the Gunners themselves.

Considerable Jap shelling from all natures of gun has been experienced during the month, together with several air raids on gun areas, and determined gun busting expeditions by the enemy.

As regards the latter, the N Box was attacked by a pukka gun busting party on the night of 7th May of some 50 men. The attack was repulsed with small loss and one Major and some 20 Jap ORs killed.' [Over the next two or three days *Ist* and *IInd Battalions* of *214th Regiment* were wiped out].

Experience has shown that, with some warning, artillery units behind wire can stand off small and medium scale attacks by Jap infantry, provided guns are deployed with this in view and perimeters are kept small enough to be covered by the weapons and the men available . . . there is a limit to the time that a Field Regiment can continue to fire its guns by day and night, hump ammunition, dig in and make bunkers, put out wire or panjis, carry out patrols, man listening posts, and at the same time stand-to for long periods at night, without the technical performance of the guns becoming impaired. . .

Major EN Hunter, evacuated wounded on 23rd March, has received an immediate award of the MC.

Captain DWBM Gordon [was killed at Bishenpur on 12th May] in hand to hand fighting when an infantry position was overrun [and at Ningthoukhong on 31st May] Captain AH Ashcroft and [on 3rd June] Captain WK Bellhouse [were killed by shell and mortar fire]. Four men have been killed and five wounded.' (Younger).

In his subsequent report to the MGRA India, for June 1944, Lieutenant Colonel Younger writes 'During the month support has been given to the following operations. First, operations by a composite Brigade, WOODFORCE, to clear the area in the hills west of the road Buri Bazar-Bishenpur. Second, operations by 48 [Indian] Brigade to counter a thrust on our forward positions on the plain in the Ningthoukhong and Potsangbam. Third, operations, again by 48 Brigade, to clear the Silchar track from its junction with the Tiddim Road to Point 5846 which is some five miles to the west, where we have a Brigade established.' In August he reported that 'Our ammunition expenditure for the month [July] was 21,682 rounds. During the whole operations, including the Tiddim battles, we have been in action for 244 days and have fired 121,253 rounds in all.' (Younger).

As the rain died away north of Imphal, 2nd British and 7th Indian Light Divisions again began to make progress. On 15th June, in 99th Field Regiment 'A Troop 393 [Field Battery], were in action at MS 63 and Capt [EH] Hazell was established in an OP . . . RHQ Fwd Tac [HQ] was at Khuzama. A fire plan was registered on Bickford Spur on the morning of the 16th and the feature was captured during Operation Leonard later. The infantry moved forward to MS 65. Lt [CP] Richardson was with the Royal Berks, Lt [GJ] Goodchild and Capt Hazell with the RWF and Capt. [JF] Thom with the DLI.

On the 17th Lt. CC Coventry established an OP . . . Heavy harassing fire was put down on Mao Songsang and the next day (18th) it was captured.' (White).

By 18th June they had reached the Mao ridge and by the 19th had cleared the Maram Ridge. The Japanese were by then in headlong retreat. On 22nd, Captain Hazell, now with the Camerons, was caught in an enemy ambush and was wounded as was Gunner Dennison. Gunner Watts was killed. Then, at 1030 hours 22nd June 1944, came an historic meeting. 2nd Durham Light Infantry and a troop of tanks of 149th Regiment RAC, accompanied by Lieutenant DH Woodcock RA, of 16th Field Regiment, leading the 2nd British Division met up with a patrol of 1/17th Dogra and some tanks of 3rd Carabiniers from 5th Indian Division at MS 109. Major Bonsor and Captain Thom were present at the opening of the road on 22nd June 1944 at MS 109. That evening General Grover, of 2nd British Division, met General Briggs, of 5th Indian Division, and on the 23rd the first, free, two way running on the Kohima - Imphal road began. The battle of Imphal was also over.

Slim next decided that 33rd Indian Corps was to capture Ukhrul and operate to the north of Imphal while 4th Indian Corps concentrated on the approach of *33rd Division* up the Tiddim Road. 20th Indian Division passed under the command of 33rd Indian Corps and 5th Indian Division moved to 4th Indian Corps. By 26th June Mutaguchi recognised that *31st Division* had no more fighting capacity and must be rested and that success at Imphal was no longer possible. He requested permission for *15th Army* to pull right back to Tiddim, but this took time to sanction. By 28th June, in appalling weather, 33rd and 89th Indian Infantry and 23rd Brigades were closing on Ukhrul. Realising that their escape route was being attacked, the Japanese fought hard. 25th Indian Mountain Regiment, commanded by Lieutenant Colonel Lewis Pugh, was heavily involved. One of his men was killed in a patrol action and Pugh asked for volunteers to recover his body. Sweeper Ram Sarup and two drivers said they would do it and the Sweeper, protected by the rifles of the drivers and under heavy automatic fire, succeeded in his task. For his gallantry, Ram Sarup became the first Sweeper to be awarded the IDSM. The regiment shot the infantry into Ukhrul over open sights taking a heavy toll of the enemy. Colonel Pugh recalls, 'Directed by FOOs with the leading infantry, 25th Mtn fired shell after shell into the buildings, often no more than 40 yards in front of the leading Infantry. Smoke rose from the burning village and fragments of houses flew high into the air. The roar of musketry, the crash of our own shells, and those of the enemy who was shelling the whole area indiscriminately, thundered in echo from the neighbouring hills and rolled up the deep narrow valleys. By midday contact was made with troops attacking from the west, and by evening with 89 Bde from the south-west. Pockets of resistance remained but organised defence had ceased. That night, in the glow of the burning village the remaining enemy were liquidated'. (Pugh).

In 20th Indian Divisional area the conditions were terrible. The columns struggled through blinding rain, swollen torrents, deep cloying mud and along treacherous slippery paths. They were hungry because air supply was impossible and the temperature change from the valleys to the mountain tops was causing illness and extreme fatigue. There was no cover or comfort for the sick or wounded and dysentery and scrub-typhus set in. From 3rd to 7th July the Japanese held on grimly. Then they broke for the Chindwin and 20th Indian Division followed. Colonel Pugh again, 'The next four mile march was one of the worst ever undertaken. The river at the bottom of a 2,000 foot valley was flanked by paddy fields and the rain fell in torrents. All day the mules struggled through a morass till late at night. Some drowned in the mud, some were so exhausted that they fell, unable to get up or walk and had to be destroyed. Officers and men laboured waist deep in mud and water but by 2200 hours the last man and animal had struggled in.' Everywhere they found dead, dying or disease ridden and starving Japanese, scenes of indescribable horror of men who had gone on until they had dropped, abandoned guns, vehicles, weapons and equipment, bodies filled every hole, rut and pothole. And all the time the rain poured down. The end had come and it was decided to withdraw 7th and 20th Indian Divisions to better conditions to enable them to recover.

On 28th June RHQ 99th Field Regiment, together with 472nd and 394th Batteries, 'moved south [of Bishenpur] to come under the command of 17th Indian Division. 393 remained in action at MS 93¼ under 10 Field Regiment RA. On the 30th, 394 fired in a fire plan on Nunggang and registration continued during the day . . . [July 4th] Our troops occupied Nunggang. 393 at this period was experimenting with a baby 25 pounder and a 25 pounder mounted on a Jury Axle. . . [July 6th] 393 carried out firing tests with the modified 25 pounders . . .' (White).

On 8th July 24th Indian Mountain Regiment recorded in their War Diary, 'Imphal. Major General HR Briggs, GOC 5th Indian Division, inspects the regiment and formally welcomes it back to the division. Dinner given in his honour with Brigadier ECR Mansergh, the CRA, Lieutenant Colonel FBB Noble HLI, the GSO 1 and Major JHF Mermagen, the BMRA, present.'

Headquarters 33rd Indian Corps opened at Imphal on 1st July. During the first week of July Major General CGG Nicholson, destined to become Master Gunner St James's Park, assumed command of 2nd Division from Major General John Grover who had led it for so long and so wonderfully well. His departure was deeply regretted by those serving in the division at the time.

Planning began for the offensive into Burma and it was agreed that, after a period of rest, reinforcement and training, this could start in November. Manpower was very short and plans were made to reduce the number of anti-aircraft units and to use the officers and men to bring the infantry up to strength. This was done, and although the Gunners involved deeply resented this move, they entered their new life with vigour and remained an eternal credit to the Regiment. General Slim established a Forward Tactical Headquarters at Imphal from where he could plan the re-conquest of Burma. On 11th July he recommended that 11th East African Division should move from Ceylon to Imphal and that 17th and 23rd Indian Divisions should return to India to rest, while 19th Indian Division should move from India to Chittagong.

On 23rd June Lieutenant Colonel Richard Uniacke was told that his 16th Field Regiment was to move to join 23rd Indian Division south of Imphal. Accordingly, taking Major Rodney Burges, his second in command, and Chris Morris, his adjutant, he went to Headquarters 4th Indian Corps in Imphal where they had a good lunch. They then went to Headquarters 23rd Indian Division where they met Brigadier Mike Andrews, the CRA and his BMRA, Major PB (Peter) Gillett whom they knew well of old. Here they heard the division's plans.

Fighting continued in the Shenam Pass. Major General Ouvry Roberts, commanding 23rd Indian Division, decided to attack the Japanese and drive them out once and for all. There had been tough fighting around a series of strong points. One, known as 'Scots Knob', had been held by the Japanese in the face of a determined attack on 27th June by two companies of 6/5th Mahratta Light Infantry supported by 16th Field Regiment in the shape of Captain BAT Hammond and Captain DH Woodcock as FOOs; 100 rounds per gun were fired by 34th and 72/86th Batteries. Hammond's two signallers, Gunners Humphrey and Fishwick were wounded, the former mortally. Woodcock's OP Ack and signallers stayed with him throughout the withdrawal and kept him in touch with the Mahratta battalion. Woodcock was by then involved in close-quarter fighting and was within 25 yards of an enemy bunker. He managed to direct the fire of a tank onto it, when he was hit in the right leg and thigh by a burst of machine-gun fire and had to be helped down the hill. His OP Ack, Bombardier Hobbs, had already won a Military Medal at Kohima when Captain Carpenter won his Military Cross and his services again showed the importance of this type of well trained first-class assistance.

Throughout the war, the work of the OP Officer's Assistants, known as 'OP Acks', was of the highest order. Normally young bombardiers, they frequently took over command when their OP

Officer was killed or wounded, performing feats which, pre-war, were usually regarded as way beyond their rank and experience.

'Scots Knob' was then attacked for the second time, on this occasion by 5/6th Rajputana Rifles. Captain R de R Channer, an FOO in 158th Field Regiment, reported how his section of 25-pounders broke up three Japanese counter-attacks once the position had been taken. He describes how he was able to drop his rounds right in front of the infantry because his guns were firing at right angles to their position, thus the zone of the gun did not apply - an ideal situation for a Gunner but not always easy to create.

Roberts had his own 9th Field Regiment, consisting of 19th, 20th and 28/76th Batteries, and 158th Field Regiments with 581st, 582nd and 583rd Batteries, and was reinforced by 16th Field Regiment of 2nd British Division, 1st Medium Regiment, 19 Battery 7th (Rajput) Indian HAA Regiment and 43rd Survey Battery, all under his CRA Brigadier RW Andrews. 1st Indian Infantry Brigade was to seize 'Nippon' and 'Ralph' Hills, while 49th Indian Infantry Brigade would move round the flank via Sita and Sibong Ridge and establish a road block. When all this was achieved 37th Indian Infantry Brigade, with a squadron of 149th Regiment RAC, was to drive straight down the road and destroy all enemy this side of the Chindwin. D-Day for 37th Indian Infantry Brigade attack was to be 24th July. It was during the preparations for this operation that 16th Field Regiment were caught in a terrific storm which caused the river near the gun position to rise a foot in ten minutes and to continue rising until all guns and equipment had to be abandoned and the men had to run for it. All manner of ways were tried to recover the situation and by 21st July all was saved. Two elephants, indented for by 72/86th Battery, arrived for the recovery task, but just too late!

It was also during this operation that Captains RH Franks of 23rd and Lieutenant JF Kenyon of 5th (Bombay) Mountain Batteries of 25th Indian Mountain Regiment, who were with the leading infantry, brought down devastating fire which smothered machine gun, rifle and grenade fire, giving the infantry time to deploy for attack. They then brought down fire within 20 yards of the infantry as they attacked and the position was captured with very few casualties. Both officers were exposed to enemy fire for nine hours but their action saved the day. Both were awarded the Military Cross and Lance Naik Mahomed Ajaib was awarded the Military Medal.

17th Indian Division at last stopped Tanaka on the Tiddim Road and on 29th June he accepted defeat. But there was still some fighting to do. An account of 99th Field Regiment reports that 'Major Bonsor and Lt Sebag-Montefiore went to 32 [Indian Infantry] Brigade on the Silchar Track. . . The northern edge of Thinunggei was registered by both Batteries.' Both were heavily engaged throughout 10th, 11th and 12th July. Then on the 13th a fireplan was used for an attack by 63rd Brigade on Commando Hill. This action went on daily until 17th July when Thinunggei was captured and 'Major Awdry and Lieutenant Kay registered HF and SOS targets there.' The enemy was now giving ground and by the 23rd the regiment was at Moirang, where a section of 8th Medium Regiment joined them. 'D Troop's position was at a height of 2,650 feet.' Then on 28th July they were sent back to rest at last and to a camp near MS 84 on the Kohima - Imphal Road. (White).

At much the same time 24th Indian Mountain Regiment had 2nd Mountain Battery at Bishenpur. They were relieved by 12th (Poonch) Mountain Battery on 23rd July. As they moved off they were told that Lieutenant DPR Dickenson and Gunner Teja Singh had been awarded the Military Cross and the Military Medal respectively for gallantry in action at Kohima.

5th Indian Division was then ordered to pass through 17th Indian Division and drive the remains of *33rd Division* south, using two squadrons of tanks and the artillery of both 5th and 17th Divisions to do so. The enemy fought hard at Ningthoukhong and it required a heavy artillery attack to dislodge him. 5th Indian Division then took up the advance and cleared the route as far as Torbung. 17th Indian Division retired to Imphal prior to leaving for well-earned rest in India. On 4th July the Japanese authorised the abandonment of the offensive and all their divisions fell back. 23rd Indian Division's advance went on as planned because there was still opposition and each Japanese post had to be dealt with separately. On 31st July 23rd Indian Division was told to hand over to 11th East African Division. It was all over. 4th Indian Corps went to Ranchi to rest and prepare for the forthcoming offensive. Headquarters 33rd Indian Corps assumed control of the whole of the Central Front. By 31st July 2nd British Division was resting at Maram, 7th Indian Division was at Kohima, 17th Indian Division at Imphal and 20th Indian Division at Wangjing. 5th Indian Division was still chasing the Japanese down the Tiddim Road and had reached MS 42. 11th East African Division, having taken over from 23rd Indian Division, was sorting itself out at Palel where 2nd Indian Field Regiment joined it.

Throughout the Kohima and Imphal battles the Japanese air force had been active but the Royal and US Army Air Forces had dominated the skies. Nevertheless the air defence of the Army was of immense importance. In 4th Indian Corps area 67th HAA, 28th and 78th LAA Regiments operated under corps command while 55th, 56th, 82nd, 100th LAA/Anti-Tank and 2nd Indian LAA Regiments were with the divisions. Within divisions the main task was the protection of the gun areas, supply points and headquarters. The corps regiments were used almost entirely to protect the airfields and airstrips, headquarters and supplies in the Imphal plain. About 60 enemy aircraft were destroyed by the combined action of the RAF and the guns. 67th HAA Regiment claimed ten, 55th LAA/A-Tank Regiment 12 and 82nd LAA/A-Tank Regiment three. The anti-aircraft guns were also used in the ground role frequently. Lieutenant Denis Howard of 67th HAA Regiment wrote, 'Early in June 1944 I had two mobile 3.7-inch HAA guns sited in the AA role at Kanglatongbi which is about 20 miles north of Imphal. None of us had had any instruction or practice at firing in the ground role. During one battle the infantry were up in the hills trying to get the Japs out of a bunker. Tanks were being winched up but could not get their guns to bear. Out of the blue I got a radio message from some unknown chap with the infantry saying that he 'had heard about our flat trajectory and would I please fire?' 'Good heavens.' I said, 'What do you want me to fire at and what happens if I hit you?' 'Don't worry,' came the reply,' Try that bushy topped tree at map reference . . . .' I did, he corrected me and on the third round he cheered like mad as I had got a shell right into the slit of the bunker! Some time later we did it again at Bishenpur but we still had no range tables. By December we were practising properly conducted ground shooting exercises.'

It had been a tough fight. The Allied Forces, composed of British, Indians, Burmese, Africans, Americans and Chinese had suffered 29,200 casualties between November 1943 and July 1944 of which some 8,000 were lost in the Arakan, 5,000 at Kohima, some 13,000 in all the Imphal battles and some 3,200 with the Chindits. The Japanese had suffered much, much more. They lost some 53,500 of which some 30,500 were killed, missing or died of other causes. Of the remaining 23,000 the great majority were suffering from wounds, malnutrition, disease or more than one of these. They had suffered a very great defeat. There is no doubt that it was the infantry which bore the great strain of this victory. General Giffard wrote to General Slim on 28th July, 'The Infantry can be justly proud of their great successes achieved by hard and skilful fighting. Equally distinguished in their own sphere, the 'Gunners', whether British, Indian or African, have shown once again their courage, devotion to duty and determination at all costs to support the infantry and to destroy the enemy. They have fought, too, as infantry with outstanding success. The gallantry of the OP Parties with the leading infantry has been most marked. The determination of the regiments and the batteries to get forward whatever the obstacles and difficulties, has resulted in guns of every type, including medium, coming into action in positions which in the early stages of the campaign no one would have dreamt of trying to reach.' He goes on to congratulate the Royal Armoured Corps, the Indian Armoured Corps and the Royal, Indian and African Engineers, stressing the vital importance of all arms and services working together and adds 'I have not forgotten the immense debt which the Army owes to the Air. It is no exaggeration to say that without the really magnificent assistance given by the Eastern Air Command, the Army could never have won its victories.' (quoted in Kirby).

The Royal Regiment had grown up in the jungle. It was bigger, involved in every aspect of the battle, confident in its ability to overcome the problems of terrain, climate, disease and shortages. It had developed its own structures and techniques for the special circumstances of the jungle and those needed to fight the Japanese. Above all it had the measure of its enemy. At last every British commander recognised that firepower is a fundamental constituent of modern war. Alone it cannot win, but others cannot win without it. They had come to recognise that it must be a fundamental ingredient of any plan and then that it is only effective if used concentrated and controlled by observers and artillery commanders at every level of command, using its great flexibility to adjust as the battle develops.

The war was not yet over, the Japanese still had plenty of fight left in them; the difference was that the Allies now knew that at last they were winning.

CHAPTER 12

THE OTHER FAR EAST FRONTS and PLANNING THE OFFENSIVE FOR THE CONQUEST OF BURMA

AUGUST - DECEMBER 1944

(Maps 24, 41, 42 and 43)

In March 1943 the Japanese had moved their *Headquarters Southern Army* to Singapore. When the US threat in the Pacific developed, this Headquarters was moved to Manila and *Headquarters 7th Area Army* was created in Singapore to control *16th, 25th, 29th and Borneo Garrison Armies*. Its task was the conduct of operations in the Andaman and Nicobar Islands, Sumatra, Java and Malaya. Burma was the responsibility of *Burma Area Army*, under Lieutenant General Hyotaro Kimura who replaced Kawabe in August 1944 and acquired as his Chief of Staff, Lieutenant General S Tanaka, formerly commanding *18th Division* in north Burma.

In outline, Japanese land forces in south east Asia were as follows:

***Southern Army*, Manila, FM Count H Terauchi.**

***HQ 7th Area Army*, Singapore, Lt Gen K Doihara, May 1944**

29th Army	Malaya, Andaman and Nicobar Islands
25th Army	Sumatra
16th Army	Java
Borneo Garrison Army	Borneo

***HQ Burma Area Army*, Rangoon, Lt Gen H Kimura, November 1944**

15th Army	*15, 31, 33, 53 Divs*	Lt Gen S Katamura
28th Army	*54, 55 Divs 72 Bde*	Lt Gen S Sakurai
33rd Army	*18, 56 Divs*	Lt Gen M Honda
Area Army Reserve	*2, 49 Divs, 24 Bde*	

In January 1944 the British Far East Fleet, which had been badly run down to reinforce the Mediterranean and D-Day preparations, was being built up again. Three battleships, and the fleet carrier *Illustrious*, had arrived and plans were afoot to increase the fleet by a further ten cruisers, 24 destroyers and escorts, two flotillas of submarines and another fleet carrier, HMS *Victorious*. The submarines immediately began to dominate the west coast of Malaya and the Straits of

Malacca and sank many Japanese ships. This caused some increase of Japanese submarine activity in the Indian Ocean and this in turn caused the British to increase long range flying boat patrols by 222 Group RAF at Colombo and 225 Group at Bangalore. German submarines were operating off Aden and these were working with the Japanese further east and as a result British losses at sea began to increase. Then in April 1944 the Japanese sent five battleships, three fleet carriers, 18 cruisers and 26 destroyers to Singapore and it looked as if a new threat to the Indian Ocean was developing. However it soon became clear that this was a withdrawal from the Pacific rather than preparations for an attack in the Indian Ocean.

The US fleet carrier *Saratoga* joined the British Far East Fleet in March and a combined and highly successful attack was made on the Japanese airfields at Sabang Island and Lhoknga on Sumatra (Map 41). A similar attack was carried out on Sourabaya on 16th May, also with complete success. Then the Andaman Islands were attacked on 21st May. On 5th July the fleet carriers *Indomitable* and *Victorious* arrived at Colombo. Admiral Sir James Somerville decided to carry out a combined air attack and bombardment of the Japanese air base at Sabang. This he did on 25th July, again with great success although the Japanese air defence artillery and coastal guns fought back hard, destroying several aircraft and hitting three ships. This action marked the first occasion for quite some time that British naval guns had opened fire on the Japanese. There was, thereafter, no more trouble in the Indian Ocean.

Land operations throughout SEAC had depended on air superiority. So far we have dealt with the use of air power only in support of ground operations by Brigadier General WD Old's Troop Carrier Command and Colonel Cochrane's 1st Air Commando. The battle to ensure control of the skies was raging throughout the theatre at the same time. Throughout 1942 and well into 1943 the Japanese had had air superiority. However this began to change when the British and US Army Air Forces were integrated in December 1943 and when new long-range fighters such as the Thunderbolt, the Mustang and the Lightning began to arrive and make their presence felt. Air Chief Marshal Sir Richard Pierse, Allied Air C-in-C South East Asia, had as the first priority for Air Marshal Sir John Baldwin's 3rd Tactical Air Force, the protection of the air route to China and of the construction of the land route from Ledo to Myitkyina. The second priority was to give maximum support to land operations in the Arakan and around Imphal, mainly with Hurricane, Spitfire and Vengeance aircraft, and the third to use the Strategic Air Force to attack enemy shipping, airfields, bridges, railways and other nodal points in the Bangkok, Moulmein, Port Blair and Rangoon areas.

The result of these air operations was that when the Japanese land attacks began in Burma, in February 1944, the *5th Air Division* had only two of its air brigades, the *4th* and *7th* and two additional air regiments, with 131 aircraft of which 81 were fighters. At this time Eastern Air Command, under Major General GE Stratemeyer USAAF, excluding transports, had 735 aircraft, 464 RAF and 271 USAAF, comprising 480 fighters, 80 light bombers, 80 medium bombers, 64 heavy bombers and the remainder were for reconnaissance and liaison. 100 of these aircraft were allotted to the protection of the air bridge to China but this still left the Allies with a superiority of some 3:1. 3rd Tactical Air Force, consisting of 221 and 224 Groups RAF, was detached to work closely with 4th, 15th and 33rd Indian Corps on the Assam and Arakan Fronts. The Strategic Air Force was made up of American heavy and medium bombers, Liberators and Mitchells, together with Liberators and Wellingtons of the RAF. From March to July 1944 the Japanese flew 1,750 sorties while the Allies flew 29,660, for the loss of 130 RAF and 40 US aircraft. From the opening of the Japanese Imphal offensive the Allies were, therefore, able to establish air superiority over any area when required. By mid-June 1944 their air superiority was absolute throughout most of Burma. In May, Transport Command was abolished and all transport operations came under 3rd Tactical Air Force and 10th USAAF was created to look after Stilwell's Northern Combat Area

Command (NCAC). Then Eastern Air Command, under Major General Stratemeyer, consisted of the Strategic Air Force, 3rd Tactical Air Force, 10th USAAF, the Photographic Reconnaissance Force and 293 Wing RAF with Beaufighter night fighters and Spitfires.

We left the Japanese making good progress in Operation ICHI-GO, their invasion of China proper (Map 41). They reached Hankow successfully but were held by Chinese forces at Changsha with the help of General Chennault's 14th USAAF. His main task was to protect the airfields around Chengtu for subsequent use in operations against Japan: Operation MATTERHORN. But the threat to the heart of China was developing fast. The Japanese pressed on and overran Honan Province and by May they were crossing the Yangtze and heading for Changsha. Chiang Kai-shek urgently requested the release of MATTERHORN stocks and resources to assist in meeting this threat, plus all supplies reaching China by the air bridge from India. The US Chiefs of Staff authorised the temporary use of 7th Heavy Bomber Group of the Strategic Air Force in India, to move fuel to 14th USAAF at Chengtu so that it in turn could give maximum support to the Chinese. However, the Chiefs of Staff refused the use of the bombers of 7th Heavy Bomber Group to attack the advancing Japanese, since they did not believe they would be successful and, in any case, they were needed for raids against Japan which were about to start.

The first air attack on Japan since the Doolittle raid in 1942 was made on 15th June 1944 to coincide with the attack on Saipan, but caused little damage. A second and more successful raid was made against Kyushu on 7th July. Vice President Truman visited China in July and assessed that the ground threat to China was very real. The President accepted that drastic measures were needed. On 8th July Chiang Kai-shek agreed that Stilwell, recently promoted to general, should assume full command of all Chinese and American Forces in the China theatre, but not yet.

While all this was taking place, the Chinese 11th Army launched its offensive from Yunnan with 12 divisions, some 72,000 men, across the Salween on 10th April 1944 (Map 42). 20th Army was to move down the Shweli river and capture Tengchung and then move towards Myitkyina. 11th Army was to capture Lungling and Mangshih astride the Burma road and then attack Bhamo. Facing them was the *56th Division* under Lieutenant General S Matsuyama. He had about 11,000 men. His plan was to cover the Hpimaw, Mamien, Tatangtzu, Hungmushu and Lameng Passes with a strong screen, place his main body at Lungling and a reserve at Bhamo. By 9th June the Chinese 87th and 88th Divisions were attacking Lungling and by the 22nd, 20th Army had debouched into the Shweli Valley and was soon investing Tengchung. But, very soon, the Chinese attack was beginning to lose momentum. It did, however, set about reducing the walled cities of Tengchung, which barred the way to Myitkyina and Lameng and lay astride the Burma Road. Although by the end of August the Chinese had succeeded in each case, they were spent and could go no further. The great Chinese offensive across the Salween, which figured so largely in the Allied plans for the re-conquest of Burma, had hardly made any impact on the Japanese and had failed. Matsuyama had done his stuff well.

We must next turn our attention to General Stilwell and his attack from Ledo. His aim, when we last considered his position, was to capture Kamaing, Mogaung and Myitkyina and link them by road to Ledo. He had under command Merrill's Marauders who were worn out, his original 22nd, 30th and 38th Chinese Divisions, two newly arrived and very untrained 14th and 50th Chinese Divisions and 3rd (WA), 14th, 77th and 111th Brigades. At the end of May he had 22nd and 38th Chinese Divisions with 149th Chinese Regiment, which had some tanks, investing Kamaing. The Chindits were preparing to attack Mogaung and the rest of his force was investing Myitkyina. *53rd Division* had been opposing the Chindits and was then ordered to move to Myitkyina. *18th Division* was holding Kamaing but, on 28th May, 112th Chinese Regiment cut it off at Seton and soon 113th Chinese Regiment was at Lawa. Thus cut off, *18th Division* was forced to pull out and on 16th June 22nd Chinese Division occupied Kamaing. Stilwell had achieved his first objective. The remains of *18th Division* got out through the hills to Sahmaw but by then it was only about 3,000 strong and had lost all its guns.

Stilwell's plan to capture Myitkyina by *coup de main* had failed. His forces were desperately short of supplies and the Marauders were virtually unfit for duty. Two attacks on 31st May and 1st June also failed, as did more throughout June. 'Morrisforce', of two battalions, had been operating as part of the Chindits to stir up the Kachin tribesmen. It had started to attack Myitkyina from the south and reached Waingmaw but could not hold it. After that it was ordered, by Brigadier-General HleM Boatner, the American commander at Myitkyina and Stilwell's chief of staff, to attack Maingna which it did, suffering many casualties, but was unable hold it. 'Morrisforce' was down to a strength of about two companies. On 25th May General Stilwell met Major General WDA Lentaigne to discuss how they could best operate together. Lentaigne explained that it was impossible to hold strong points in areas where the enemy could bring his artillery to bear. He would therefore have to abandon 'Blackpool' and 'White City.' When he said this he did not know that, as he spoke, Masters was being driven out of 'Blackpool'.

After some argument Stilwell agreed to the abandonment of 'Blackpool' but only in emergency. He then accused Lentaigne of not mounting an attack on Mogaung more quickly and later asked him to explain why 'Morrisforce' had not arrived at Waingmaw. After some argument they agreed that 77th Brigade would attack Mogaung as soon as possible and that the other brigades would protect the Indawgyi Lake until all Special Force casualties had been evacuated by flying boat. Stilwell next complained to Mountbatten that the Special Force was not carrying out his orders. Mountbatten sent Slim to see him to sort it out. After his visit Slim reported that all was now well and that 77th Brigade and 'Morrisforce' were doing what was wanted of them. He recommended that once the Myitkyina/Mogaung situation was sorted out, two LRP brigades should be withdrawn and that two should stay until 36th British Division could get there. This formation was the former 36th Indian Division renamed on 1st September 1944. Stilwell agreed. But it was to take all June before some 500 Special Force casualties had been flown out by Sunderland flying boats from Indawgyi Lake and before the remainder had been moved by raft up the Indaw river to Kamaing from where they too were flown out. This had taken much time and effort and again Stilwell was not pleased.

111th Brigade was moved in appalling monsoon weather. At one stage the men struggled for two miles waist deep in water, to the Padiga area which it reached on 19th June and set off again to contain the remains of *18th Division* at Sahmaw. 77th Brigade was about to attack Mogaung from the south in conjunction with 38th Chinese Division attacking from the north. 3rd (WA) Brigade was to move north of Sahmaw while 14th Brigade moved to Taungni and Pinbaw. But Masters, with 111th Brigade, could make no progress against stiffening Japanese opposition and his men were at the end of their tether. At this stage, early June, Stilwell returned to the charge demanding that Lentaigne explain in writing why no attacks had yet been carried out. Again Lentaigne explained the very light nature of his force which was by then being asked to carry out major operations against positions held in strength by tanks and artillery which were beyond their capability, especially as the Chindits by then had no artillery. In addition they had been in the field for some four months, casualties had been heavy and his men were approaching exhaustion.

The Japanese had detected 77th Brigade's move against Mogaung and had reinforced it considerably. Nevertheless, by 12th June the brigade was within a mile of the town but the fighting was hard and they had fought themselves to a stand-still. They were down to 550 men and many of these were sick. Calvert decided to hold his gains and wait for the Chinese reinforcements promised by Stilwell. But it was not until 25th June that a combined attack by 77th Brigade and 114th Chinese Regiment could be mounted, since the Chinese had taken their time. However, it succeeded after very heavy fighting although at a cost of another 150 casualties to the Chindits. So tough was the fighting that two Victoria Crosses were won. Nevertheless, Stilwell's second objective had been captured by the magnificent fighting qualities of the Chindits and Calvert's splendid determined leadership. But with only 300 men left there was now no option but evacuation. By this time 77th, 111th Brigades and 'Morrisforce' had been in continuous action for four months and between them they had only some 400 effective men left. The move out began on 7th July when 77th Brigade and 'Morrisforce' moved to Warazup to be flown back to India.

In the meantime 3rd (WA), 14th and 111th Brigades were containing the enemy at Sahmaw and Taungni. After further disagreement with Stilwell, 111th Brigade, now down to one company in strength, was evacuated on 30th July. Stilwell and Boatner simply could not understand what these men had been through. The Chindits never stopped trying to carry out the orders they were given but these orders were beyond their capability. By 15th July 72nd British Infantry Brigade, the first from 36th British Division, began to land at Myitkyina airfield. Its task was to concentrate at Mogaung and then attack the enemy at Sahmaw. 3rd (WA) and 14th Brigades were to hold the flanks and take over the defence of Sahmaw so that 72nd British Infantry Brigade could go on and take Taungni. This was all complete by 9th August and it allowed the remainder of the Chindits to be flown out. Their long ordeal was over and the last of them arrived back in India by 27th August. The five brigades had sustained 3,628 casualties, some 18% of their total strength, but sickness produced very much higher casualty figures. By 3rd August Myitkyina had also fallen and Stilwell had captured all his three objectives and could concentrate on developing the road and pipeline from Ledo.

Apart from 'W' and 'X' LAA Troops at Myitkyina airfield there were very few Gunners involved towards the end of the Chindit operations. Most had been with Fergusson's 16th Brigade which had had such a gruelling march into Burma and had returned to India from 'Broadway.' The four 25-pounder troops and two of the LAA troops had already returned to India but their presence was sorely missed towards the end. Some artillery would have made a great difference to the final operations against Mogaung and Myitkyina, which were way beyond the capabilities of the Chindits by that time. Nevertheless the Chindit Gunners did all that was asked of them and more.

Next we must turn briefly to operations in the Pacific Area, notably New Guinea (Map 41). With the occupation of the Marshall Islands by the Americans and the encirclement of Rabaul, the Japanese recognised that they faced serious problems. They first reinforced the Marianas, the Bonin and Palau Islands. Next they changed their command structure so that command of all operations was given to Admiral Nagumo from his Headquarters on Saipan. He had a much reduced *4th Fleet, 14th Fleet and 31st Army*. Further south *17th Army* remained cut off in Rabaul and operations elsewhere were controlled by *18th Army*. Finally two divisions were sent to reinforce western New Guinea. Everything depended on control of the sea and this was fast slipping out of Japanese hands.

American strategy was for MacArthur to continue his advance westwards along the north coast of New Guinea with the Australians. His objectives were to seize Halamahera and then to cross to the Philippines. Nimitz was to support MacArthur and move westwards towards Japan through the Marianas and then towards the Philippines through the Palau Islands. In New Guinea 7th Australian Division met up with the Americans near Bogadjim on 13th April 1944. By 25th April, 11th Australian Division had relieved 7th and was advancing beyond Alexishafen and by June patrols had reached the Sepik river. MacArthur next decided to establish a major naval and air base at Hollandia but this meant advancing beyond the range of land-based aircraft. Thus it was decided first to seize the Japanese airstrip at Aitape as a preliminary operation. Combined attacks went in on 27th April when some two assault divisions were landed to the west of Humboldt Bay and at Aitape. Complete surprise was achieved and the operation, the largest of its kind in the war so far, was a great success. The Japanese were soon forced back to Halamahera. But there was a lot more fighting to defend Aitape and to seize Biak, Wakde and Noemfor Islands. When this was done the Japanese were forced right back to western Vogelkop where they were cut off and mopped up by the Australians. The Americans built an air base early in July 1944 at Sorong and MacArthur was poised for his return to the Philippines.

Admiral Nimitz planned to attack the Marianas by seizing the islands of Saipan, Tinian and Guam. D-Day for the attack on Saipan was 15th June and was to be carried out by 5th Fleet and 2nd, 3rd and 4th US Marine Divisions, with 27th US Division in reserve. It involved 500 warships and a massive air and sea bombardment. By last light on 15th June, 20,000 Marines of 2nd and 4th Divisions were ashore and a beachhead had been secured but that night Admiral Spruance, commanding the operation, received the news that the Japanese Fleet was approaching. It was being shadowed by US submarines. Spruance cancelled the landings at Guam, landed his reserve, 27th Division, at Saipan, withdrew all transport ships and prepared for battle. The details of the Battle of the Philippine Sea do not concern us here but, in the end although both sides lost many aircraft, the Americans chased the remains of the Japanese Fleet away towards Okinawa. In Saipan, after Vice-Admiral Chuichi Nagumo and Lieutenant General Yoshitsugu Saito, the Saipan and Tinian garrison commanders, had both committed suicide and the Japanese had carried out a suicidal charge by 3,000 men, the island was captured at the cost of some 3,500 American lives. Next came Guam. After the heaviest naval bombardment of the war so far, the Americans landed three Marine divisions. The fighting was very hard and it was not until 12th August that the island fell. Tinian fell on 24th July. The net was closing fast, and the Americans were the undisputed masters of the Pacific.

After securing Morotai and the Palau Islands the Americans prepared for their assault on the Philippines at Leyte by carrying out intensive air attacks from carrier-based aircraft on all areas which might help in their defence, especially the airfields on Formosa. When the American Fleet was seen approaching Leyte on 17th October 1944, Admiral Soemu Toyoda, as Commander in Chief, ordered the *Combined Fleet* to attack it. This involved moving *1st Striking Force* from Singapore and *5th Fleet* from Okinawa. The details of the Battle of Leyte Gulf which then occurred do not concern us here either, but suffice to say that it was the last major action fought by surface ships in the war. The Japanese lost three battleships, four carriers, nine cruisers and eight destroyers, while the Americans lost one light carrier, two escort carriers and three destroyers. The Japanese had again suffered a heavy defeat. By 22nd October the Americans were established on Leyte but it was to be a long hard slog in appalling weather before the island fell on Christmas Day.

Next was Luzon. By this time US long-range bombers were attacking Japan from airfields in the Mariana Islands. Admiral Nimitz's next objectives were to be Iwojima and then Okinawa, while MacArthur captured Mindoro Island. It was now that the Japanese *Kamikaze* attacks became a real menace; several major ships were sunk and the US Fleet had to reorganise its anti-aircraft defences to cope. Nevertheless 6th US Army, consisting of 1st, 11th and 14th Corps, was successfully landed on Luzon on 4th January 1945 while the US Fleet moved into the China Sea and attacked the remains of the Japanese fleet in ports along the Chinese coast, including Hong Kong. Again the fighting on land was tough and it was not until 1st February that the airbase at Clark Field was re-captured. On 31st January, 11th Airborne Division was dropped with many more reinforcements. Manila fell after hard house-to-house fighting on 4th March and this meant that the Americans controlled all strategic points in the Philippines, although there was much mopping up still to do and this involved more hard fighting.

In Burma (Maps 42 and 43), Mountbatten had issued his orders on 9th June. General Giffard, of 11th Army Group, was told, first, to hold his present positions on the Arakan Front during the monsoon and then to attack and capture Akyab as early as possible in the next dry season. On the Central Front he was to re-establish communications on the Dimapur - Kohima - Imphal road by not later than mid-July, then to clear all Japanese forces from the area Yuwa - Tamanthi and prepare to exploit across the Chindwin after the monsoon. Stilwell was told to capture Mogaung and Myitkyina and establish an airhead with effective road and pipeline links with Ledo. As we saw in the previous chapter most of this had been accomplished by the end of August 1944. Giffard said that, given the right forces, he could be ready to resume the offensive by 1st November, but he would prefer to delay the capture of Akyab and give priority to the Central Front.

It was at this point that Mountbatten was asked to submit his plans for the capture of Rangoon. For this he developed plans for Operations CAPITAL and DRACULA. Plan CAPITAL foresaw a general advance from north to south to the line Pakokku - Mandalay - Lashio by all available British, American and Chinese forces. The first phase would start in November 1944. The second to start in February 1945, would be the exploitation to Rangoon. This plan had a good chance of success and would ensure the rapid creation of air, road and pipeline links to China, but it would take time to capture Rangoon and there would be heavy logistic penalties because of the long and complex lines of communication for a force of this size. Operation DRACULA proposed that an amphibious/airborne assault would be made on Rangoon and then an exploitation northwards to Pegu would be coupled to a vigorous offensive southwards by 14th Army. Such a plan would cut the Japanese lines of communication and ensure that their forces in north Burma withdrew. It would capture Rangoon sooner and would have fewer logistic penalties. For this plan, however, he would need more resources, particularly landing craft.

Mountbatten asked the Combined Chiefs of Staff for direction by 1st September and they summoned him to London early in August. Churchill still favoured an amphibious operation against Sumatra, but could live with DRACULA. The Chiefs were wary of getting bogged down in central Burma but accepted that something had to be done to maintain the initiative and to protect the lines of communication to China. However, the extra resources would not be available unless the war in Europe ended in 1944. After protracted discussion it was agreed that the first two phases of CAPITAL should be carried out as soon as possible, that is to say, as far as the capture of the line Pakokku - Mandalay - Lashio, with a first phase to capture the line Kalewa - Shwebo - Mogok. Then in March 1945 forces would be released to enable DRACULA to be launched.

General Sir Alan Brooke wrote to Dill in Washington, 'I am quite clear in my own mind that strategically it is right for us to use all our forces in close co-operation from Australia across the Pacific in the general direction of Formosa. By operating our forces alongside of MacArthur we can pool resources at sea and in the air for various closely connected steps. Whereas by retaining our forces in the Indian Ocean we operate independently, incapable of close co-operation, with the result that operations will be more protracted.' (Fraser). Churchill was opposed to this strategy but Brooke insisted, accepting only that an invasion of Malaya should be part of it. It was this far-sighted direction of national effort that made Brooke the master of strategy for the war and arguably one of the greatest generals Britain has ever produced, in the same mould as Marlborough and Wellington. He too was to become Master Gunner St James's Park at the end of the war.

After the 'Quadrant' Conference at Quebec in September the Combined Chiefs of Staff sent the following orders to Mountbatten with the full agreement of Churchill and Roosevelt:

> '1. Your object is the recapture of all Burma at the earliest date. Operations to achieve this object must not however prejudice the security of the existing air supply route to China, including the air staging post at Myitkyina and the opening of overland communications.

2. The following are approved operations:

(a) The stages of Operation 'Capital' necessary to the security of the air route, and the attainment of overland comunications to China.

(b) Operation 'Dracula'. The Combined Chiefs of Staff attach the greatest importance to the vigorous prosecution of Operation 'Capital' and the execution of Operation 'Dracula' before the monsoon in 1945, with a target date of 15th March.

3. If 'Dracula' has to be postponed until after the monsoon of 1945, you will continue to exploit Operation 'Capital' as far as may be possible
without prejudice to preparations for the execution of Operation 'Dracula' in November 1945.' (Kirby)

Much work had to be done to ensure the logistic viability of the great Armies now expanding in India. Including the Indian Army, this involved provision for some 2.67 million men, the transport, ordnance, training structure not only for them but also to support China over the 'Hump' and the operations now being planned for Burma in 1944/45. This was the job of the Commander-in-Chief India, General Sir Claude Auchinleck and his Principal Administrative Officer, Lieutenant General Sir Wilfred Lindsell, a Gunner of great experience who had been Quarter Master General to the BEF under General Gort in France. To help him he had Major General Ashton Wade who had been commissioned into the Royal Artillery in 1916 at 'The Shop' but had later become 'The Father' of the Royal Corps of Signals. At GHQ India in 1945 he was Deputy Adjutant General and responsible for the massive build up of manpower necessary for both the British and Indian Armies.

New railways, ports, pipelines, airfields and roads had been and were being constructed. It was a massive undertaking but in November Lindsell was able to state he had enough capacity to support all that was envisaged, with some spare for the unforeseen. He assured SEAC that all supplies foreseen as needed at Chittagong, Dimapur and Ledo would be provided. It would, however, be necessary to follow the advancing Army with a new road from Imphal through Tamu and down the Kabaw Valley and onwards to Kalewa. At least five divisions could be maintained using this route, plus some air supply. They would require some 12,125 tons per day. Further north, success demanded the completion of the construction of the Ledo - Myitkyina road extended to meet the old Burma Road so that the required supplies to Stilwell's forces, plus 65,000 tons per month for China, could be moved. This was anticipated to be complete by the end of November. Until it was, 36th British Division, then operating along the railway north of Indaw, was without its artillery and transport and was supplied entirely by air. It was not until 5th November that the first of five convoys totalling 315 vehicles with guns, left Ledo and travelled by way of Mogaung to join the division at Mohnyin before the end of November.

36th Indian Division had been formed in India in 1943 and was initially trained for amphibious operations. It had two infantry brigades and 130th (Lowland) and 178th Assault Field Regiments, the former with 315th, 316th and 494th Field Batteries and the latter with 122nd, 366th and 516th Field Batteries. In each case one battery had 8 x towed 25-pounders, one had 8 x SP 105mm Priests and the third had 6 x 3.7-inch howitzers. It moved to the Arakan in March 1944 but the SP batteries were converted to towed 25-pounders. It was withdrawn to India in May 1944.

The division was re-organised and became 36th British Division on 1st September 1944, its brigades still all British. It moved to the northern front initially without artillery but eventually it was to have a powerful divisional artillery as follows:

CRA: Brigadier GH Inglis.
130th (Lowland) Field Regiment. Lt Col JDC Thomson
315th Fd Bty, 8 x 25-pounders
316th Fd Bty, 8 x 25-pounders
494th Fd Bty, 8 x 3.7-inch howitzers
178th Field Regiment. Lt Col KM Wright.
122nd Fd Bty, 8 x 25-pounders
516th Fd Bty, 8 x 25-pounders
366th Fd Bty, 8 x 3.7inch howitzers
122nd (Royal Warwickshire) Anti-Tank Regiment. Lt Col CD Oliver.
168th A/Tk Bty, 12 x 6-pounders & 12 x 3-inch mortars
321st A/Tk Bty, 12 x 6-pounders & 12 x 3-inch mortars
402nd A/Tk Bty, 12 x 6-pounders &12 x 3-inch mortars
32nd Indian Mountain Regiment. Lt Col R de C Yeo.
12th (Poonch) Mtn Bty, 4 x 3.7-inch howitzers
17th (Nowshera) Mtn Bty, 4 x 3.7-inch howitzers
28th Mtn Bty, 4 x 3.7-inch howitzers
3rd Meteorological Detachment

During the period from August to November certain reorganisations had to take place to be ready for a new style of offensive operation. One lesson of the campaign so far was that formations designed for one type of operation only did not always work because the precise operation for which they were organised and trained seldom occurred. General Giffard therefore proposed a standard infantry divisional structure. This was to consist of three infantry brigades each of three battalions, to be increased to four where possible, a reconnaissance battalion, a divisional headquarters battalion and a machine gun battalion. The artillery was to consist of two field regiments, one mountain regiment and one anti-tank regiment. Anti-aircraft artillery would all be held at corps level and then allotted as required by the CCRA. In support there were to be engineers and signals as at present. Scales of transport were to be drastically reduced and would include three mule companies. This reorganisation was to occur *in situ*. It had already occurred in 36th British Division.

There was another problem, especially in the infantry, and that was the acute shortage of manpower. By this time the army in Burma had a shortage of some 11,200 men, which could not be made up by the current flow of reinforcements. It was therefore decided to continue the conversion of Gunners to Infantry. The first step was to disband three British light anti-aircraft units and the anti-aircraft batteries in the divisional LAA/Anti-Tank regiments. This measure, with a few other adjustments, would produce some 3,500 men. 55th LAA/Anti-Tank, formerly 55th LAA Regiment noted sadly in its War Diary, '. . . so ended five years of active service in the AA role in France, Norway, Ceylon and Burma.' In the end, 24th, 55th, 56th, 82nd, 100th and 122nd LAA/Anti-Tank Regiments became Anti-Tank only. 59th, 60th, 78th and 118th LAA Regiments were converted to infantry. 63rd, 70th and 95th HAA Regiments and 8th Indian HAA Battery returned to India and were broken up to provide reinforcements elsewhere in the army. This again caused much sadness but in war such measures are often necessary and it is to their credit that the men involved, mostly by then very experienced, got down to their new roles with vigour. Their services as Gunners are not forgotten.

In Special Force, 3rd (WA) Brigade and six British battalions, including 51st and 60th Chindit Regiments Royal Artillery, were also disbanded and their men used to reinforce the remainder. The distinguished service of 51st and 60th Field Regiments in the Western Desert, most notably at Sidi Rezegh, and of course in Burma as Chindits, must not be forgotten. They had brought the very greatest credit to the Regiment during the Second World War by their gallantry displayed in the toughest fighting. This, however, enabled 23rd, 77th and 111th Brigades to be made up to full strength and 14th and 16th Brigades to remain in cadre until reinforcements became available. But even with these measures severe shortages remained. Both Operations CAPITAL and, particularly, DRACULA needed airborne units but did not foresee the use of long range penetration forces. The airborne units were therefore created by re-roling 44th Indian Armoured Division, which already contained 50th Indian Parachute Brigade, and then by converting and adding 14th Brigade re-roled as an air-landing brigade. The two formations then formed 44th Indian Airborne Division.

Such had been the damage to the Chindits as a force that it soon became clear they would not be ready for operations until late 1945 or early 1946. Some units had sustained losses from all causes of up to 90% in four months. Mountbatten therefore reluctantly recommended that Special Force should be broken up. This was eventually agreed by the War Office on 5th February 1945 and 77th Brigade became 77th Indian Parachute Brigade and joined 44th Indian Parachute Division along with 50th Indian Parachute and 14th Air Landing Brigades. 23rd and 111th Brigades were broken up. 16th Brigade became a reserve infantry brigade and 3rd (WA) Brigade was re-constituted and rejoined 81st West African Division. At the same time the many small clandestine forces operating in the theatre were organised into Force 136, a part of Special Operations Executive, and were placed directly under ALFSEA command.

At the same time, the organisation for running joint land/air operations was re-shaped. First 221 and 224 Groups RAF became mobile, dedicated to provide offensive air support for land operations to an accredited Army headquarters. They were no longer to be involved with air defence or air transport operations. Headquarters 3rd Tactical Air Force was disbanded and Headquarters RAF Bengal/Burma was formed in Calcutta to control all other air operations. 221 Group RAF, under Air Vice-Marshal SF Vincent, was to be responsible for close air support for the Central Front and was to be located alongside Headquarters 14th Army, while 224 Group RAF, commanded by Air Vice-Marshal the Earl of Bandon, was to do the same for the Arakan Front and was to be located beside Headquarters 15th Indian Corps. Air transport was to be centrally controlled from a new Combat Cargo Task Force Headquarters established at Headquarters Eastern Air Command.

By the end of the first week of August 1944, the situation in 15th Indian Corps, Lieutenant General AFP Christison, had remained static since June (Map 44). 25th Indian Division, commanded by Major General HL Davies, was at Maungdaw but had sent one brigade to cover the Tunnels. 26th Indian Division, under Major General CEN Lomax, was at Ukhia with a brigade in the Taungu - Goppe - Bawli area. 81st West African Division, under Major General CG Woolner, less 3rd (WA) Brigade, was in reserve at Chiringa while 82nd West African Division, commanded by Major General CMcIS Bruce, which had just arrived, was training at Ranchi.

On the Central Front, (Map 43) 33rd Indian Corps, commanded by Lieutenant General MGN Stopford, was continuing to drive south towards Kalemyo. 5th Indian Division, commanded by Major General GC Evans, had reached MS 49 on the Tiddim road south of Imphal and was in contact with the Lushai Brigade operating to the south west. On the Tamu Road, 11th East African Division, under Major General CC Fowkes, was taking over from 23rd Indian Division, covered by 5th British Infantry Brigade, of 2nd British Division, commanded by Major General CGG Nicholson. It was intended that General Fowkes would advance down the Kabaw valley and then move to the Chindwin at Sittaung. 2nd British Division was training at Maram, 7th Indian Division, under Major General FW Messervy, was doing the same at Kohima as was 20th Indian Division, under Major General DD Gracey, just south of Imphal. 254th Indian Armoured Brigade was at Kanglatongbi. Headquarters 4th Indian Corps, 17th and 23rd Indian Divisions, 23rd Brigade and 3rd Commando Brigade had all been pulled back to India for rest, reorganisation and training.

The Chinese New 1st Army, consisting of 30th and 38th Divisions, and the Chinese New 6th Army, made up of 14th, 22nd and 50th Divisions, were training at Mogaung, Kamaing and Myitkyina (Map 42). 36th British Division, Major General FW Festing, was at Mogaung. It consisted of 26th, 29th and 72nd Indian Infantry Brigades and its divisional artillery, as we have seen, was under Brigadier GH Inglis. Festing's 72nd Indian Infantry Brigade was at Kamaing and he had just been told that, as soon as his 29th Indian Infantry Brigade and some artillery arrived, he was to attack and capture Pinbaw. Three Chinese batteries, under an American officer, were allotted to him. Then 366th Light Battery, of 178th Field Regiment, with 6 x 3.7-inch howitzers, was parachuted in alongside Headquarters 29th Indian Infantry Brigade, under Brigadier HC Stockwell, on 18th August to assist in its intended taking of Pinbaw.

The bombardment of Pinbaw by 45 bombers and 42 fighters of 10th US Air Force lasted some three days. By the evening of 27th August, the infantry found that all resistance had ceased. Stockwell was authorised to advance and by 13th September he had captured Namma and made contact with the enemy some four miles further to the south. Stockwell's rapid advance was carried out at a faster rate than that of road repair behind him and he relied entirely on air supply provided by 10th Air Force. Meanwhile much work was going on to develop the base at Myitkyina, the Ledo road and the pipeline. Further east the Chinese Yunnan Armies were still besieging Tengchung, Pingka and Lameng and engaging the Japanese who were holding Lungling on the Burma Road.

On the Central Front (Map 43), *15th* and *31st Divisions* were withdrawing in disorder to the Chindwin and *1st Indian National Army Division* had disintegrated. Only *33rd Division* and the *Yamamoto Detachment* retained any cohesion on the Tiddim and Tamu roads. On 6th August Slim ordered Stopford to clear away all enemy from west of the Chindwin and to establish a bridgehead to the east of that river as soon as possible. In turn, Stopford ordered 5th Indian Division, Major General Evans, to drive the enemy off the Tiddim road and to establish bridgeheads over the Myittha and Chindwin rivers at Kalemyo and Kalewa. 11th East African Division was to secure Sittaung and send a brigade to Kalewa, which would be supplied by air as vehicles could not operate in the Kabaw valley during the monsoon. On 10th August Fowkes was ready and 5th British Infantry Brigade was released to rejoin 2nd British Division at Maram. 268th Indian Infantry Brigade was withdrawn to Imphal. 'V' Force was reorganised so that its Assam Zone was given to 33rd Indian Corps, its Lushai Zone to the Lushai Brigade and its Arakan Zone to 15th Indian Corps.

On 12th August 11th East African Division set off. Its 25th (EA) Infantry Brigade, with 302nd (EA) Field Regiment, less one battery, advanced on Sittaung against minor resistance but reached the ruins of the village on 4th September, where it found scenes of the greatest horror. The village was filled with corpses, abandoned vehicles and equipment. 26th (EA) Infantry Brigade advanced south down the Kabaw valley unopposed to Htinzin where appalling weather forced them to a temporary halt. Mr EF Given, then a troop officer in 303rd (EA) Light Regiment, which had converted from 25-pounders to 3.7-inch howitzers in August, found the 'road' down the Kabaw Valley impassable because of the monsoon floods. In mid September his troop's guns were parachuted to him. One lost a part but the other three survived and this event must represent a very early, perhaps the earliest British example of guns being dropped by parachute. As the 3.7-inch howitzer could be quickly dismantled and reassembled it would seem to be ideal for this role. 21st (EA) Infantry Brigade sat at Palel in reserve. It was known that Lieutenant General N Tanaka and his *33rd Division* had been told to hold the line Mawlaik - Kalewa - Gangaw, while the remains of

15th Division held the area around Pinlebu and linked with *53rd Division* facing 36th British Division around Mohnyin. Then 268th Indian Infantry Brigade, of five battalions, relieved 25th (EA) Brigade north of Tamu to cover the Chindwin from Sittaung to Tamanthi, some 150 miles north.

In early September 26th (EA) Infantry Brigade advanced to Yazagyo and met opposition; 21st (EA) Infantry Brigade advanced to Htinzin and then the weather deteriorated to such an extent that these two brigades were completely cut off for ten days. Such help as they could get came by air drop but the condition of the wounded and sick became serious, as they could not be evacuated. Despite this, by 30th September 26th (EA) Infantry Brigade had pushed on some five miles south of Yazagyo and 21st (EA) Infantry Brigade were at Mawlaik. Both were in contact with the enemy but casualties and sickness were taking a heavy toll and it was clear that no further progress was possible until artillery could be got forward. Although conditions improved in October, the track down the Kabaw valley was still a sea of mud up to 18 inches deep. The Sappers did all they could and constructed corduroy roads but it was taking three weeks to get one wheeled vehicle from Tamu to Yazagyo, a distance of about 50 miles. Some 25-pounders had to be winched for part of the way from tree to tree. It was a mammoth task and was the price to be paid for campaigning in the monsoon season, but it was done. With 11th East African Division were 8th and 17th (Nowshera) Mountain Batteries and a section of 2nd (Derajat) Mountain Battery under Lieutenant JS Punia, who had fought so bravely at Kohima. The division also received some light tanks from 254th Indian Tank Brigade. To the division's front, the RAF continued to hammer the enemy, attacking supply points and those targets indicated by leading troops.

Following up this very difficult advance came the anti-aircraft Gunners who were to become so important in the defence of the bridgeheads over the Chindwin. '. . . 52nd and 101st HAA and 44th LAA Regiments moved east from Imphal to Tamu and down the pestilential Kabaw valley to the Chindwin to meet 5th Indian Division at Kalemyo at the end of November. 11th East African Division, with its AA support, then turned east up the Chindwin to Kalewa, an important ferry centre which was to be the site of a crossing by 33rd Indian Corps. A bridgehead was secured here and preparations began for a major water crossing by 2nd British and 20th Indian Divisions. Not only were ferries, barges and launches to be used but amphibious vehicles such as the DUKW were also to be employed and the Royal Engineers constructed a 1,100 foot Bailey Bridge on pontoons. Both 52nd and 101st HAA Regiments were employed for bridgehead protection at Kalewa and Kalemyo, supplemented by 44th LAA Regiment. Enemy air attacks had been slight up to this point, but now the Japanese made a determined attempt to knock out the Bailey bridge. It was covered by intense concentrations of fire; attacks were broken up, six aircraft were destroyed and the bridge remained intact.' (Routledge).

It was much the same for 5th Indian Division advancing down the Tiddim road. Everything came to a halt during the downpours, often for several days at a time then, as the rain slackened, some movement was possible. All the way *33rd Division* left small rearguards which fought hard. Progress was about two miles a day and only then because of herculean efforts by the Sappers. By 22nd August, 9th Indian Infantry Brigade with Major AB Howard's 12th (Poonch) Mountain Battery, which had been leading since July, reached MS 83. Major Howard wrote, 'The enemy was on the run and we chased them with our guns as far and as fast as we could, firing HF by night and either small concentrations or opportunity targets by day. As each battalion leap-frogged through we took over support and continuously harried the retreating Japs. Physically the operation was not very exhausting and it was great to be able to chase our enemy who had chased us so far and so furiously in 1942. During this operation another Military Cross was awarded.' (AB Howard).

Now 161st Indian Infantry Brigade with 20th Mountain Battery, under Major P Kendall, took the lead and by the end of August it had reached MS 100, the scene of such heavy fighting in the

Spring. The next problem was to seize a crossing over the Manipur river which was in full spate. The two mountain batteries were moving on a pack basis and were using all available mules and drivers.

Major General Evans decided to move 123rd Indian Infantry Brigade with 11th Mountain Battery by road from Torbung right round through Imphal and Palel to Shuganu. The force was to take a battery commander and FOO of 28th Field Regiment as well. It was then to move on a pack basis across country and attack the Japanese holding the Manipur crossings at Tuitam, Tongzang and Tiddim from the rear - how sweet was revenge - while the rest of the division attacked from the west. By 11th September the brigade had reached a position near Tuitam and by the 13th they found the bridge, which they were so hoping to capture intact, had been destroyed. The river was a swirling torrent, 100 yards wide with rapids in which nothing could live. 161st Indian Infantry Brigade, now with 2nd Mountain Battery, commanded by Major J Nettelfield, closed up from the west and realised that their only hope was to get a line across. But it failed and although one man, Captain Zia-ud-Din of 1/1st Punjab, managed to swim across no-one else did. Nevertheless against all odds the Sappers established two cable ferries by 18th September and much of 161st Indian Infantry Brigade got across, although it proved impossible to get the 3.7-inch howitzers over.

Meanwhile 123rd Indian Infantry Brigade found Tongzang held in strength and with the fire of 11th Mountain Battery tried to attack but could make no impression until 1/17th Dogras cut the road behind the enemy and they fled into the hills, leaving their 105mm guns behind. Next day the river rose, the current increased to 16 knots, several men were drowned and the ferries had to be closed. Major General Evans had to be evacuated with typhoid and Brigadier DFW Warren of 161st Indian Infantry Brigade was promoted to take over command of 5th Indian Division. He and Stopford had to accept that the river could not be bridged until after the monsoon and that they would have to construct large rafts to get the tanks and guns across. This they did and it was again a magnificent achievement by the Sappers.

For the advance on Tiddim the division had six tanks of 3rd Carabiniers, 28th Field Regiment, under Lieutenant Colonel RA Collins, one battery of 4th Field Regiment, 24th Indian Mountain Regiment, by then less 12th (Poonch) and 17th (Nowshera) Batteries which had left to form 32nd Mountain Regiment for service with 36th British Division, and three field companies of engineers. Both 4th Field Regiment and 56th LAA/Anti-Tank Regiment returned to Imphal at this stage. By then the only contact with the division was by air drop and all sick and wounded had to be held and carried by the division. Scrub typhus started to increase. This called for skilled nursing if victims were to recover and to their eternal credit many nurses volunteered to go forward to do so. It was the pilots of 656 AOP Squadron who flew them in. The flight which took an hour was over some of the most inhospitable country in the world but the girls, who were novices in the air, did not turn a hair when they saw where they had to land. The Tiddim airstrip was at about 6,000 feet and consisted of 300 yards bulldozed off the top of a mountain spur with an almost sheer drop of 3,000 feet at each end. (Maslen-Jones)

Warren's plan was first to capture Tiddim, Fort White and Kennedy Peak with 123rd Indian Infantry Brigade, while 161st Indian Infantry Brigade held a secure base at Tongzang and 9th Indian Infantry Brigade held the river crossing site. He also had the Lushai Brigade with 5th (Bombay) Mountain Battery. This brigade was to seize Falam and Haka, to patrol to the river to Myittha and thus protect that flank. Next he would pass 9th Indian Infantry Brigade through 123rd Indian Infantry Brigade and it would then advance to capture Kalemyo.

After four months re-equipping with Auster IVs and training hard at Ranchi in India, 656 AOP Squadron had returned to the Burma Front. Squadron Headquarters, with 'A' and 'B' Flights, went to Imphal and 'C' Flight moved to 15th Indian Corps in the Arakan. An advance party consisting of Captains EW Maslen-Jones, George Deacon and Frank McMath with Corporals

Brown and Quinn, both RAF Fitters, set off on the 400 mile journey, stopping to refuel at Jessore on the way. On his arrival at Imphal the commanding officer reported to Headquarters 14th Army and was told to re-deploy to Palel. 'A' Flight, consisting of the three pilots mentioned above and 'Pip' Harrison was ordered to deploy immediately to join 11th East African Division at Tamu in the dreaded Kabaw valley. On 5th November 'A' Flight moved across the border into Burma and arrived at the strip at Yazagyo. HQRA briefed it that the Japanese were falling back but that resistance was stiffening as they approached Indainggyi and the Myittha Gorge. Since ground observation was almost nil and FOOs were having to get within 20 to 30 yards of their targets, AOP was to be tried for the forthcoming attack.

At 1000 hours on 8th November Frank McMath took off to engage enemy bunkers only to meet about a dozen enemy fighters dive bombing the gun position he was using. He steered away, dropped very low in the valley, flew around and waited, not being noticed. Some Spitfires appeared and chased the Japanese away and McMath controlled his first divisional shoot. The drill was simple, he had received a quick briefing by HQRA before take off. Contact, once in the air, was made with the FOO on the ground who gave the details of forward troops and the target after which he went straight into an engagement with the 25-pounders of 302nd (EA) Field Regiment. A safe opening round in a place where he hoped it would be seen and then a process of firing subsequent rounds until a short bracket of 100 yards was achieved; then 'Gunfire.' At any stage the ground FOO could take over and the pilot was ready for another task.

The strip was some 10 minutes flying time from Indainggyi, but was still very vulnerable to Japanese patrol activity so they had to pay close attention to local defence. Flight headquarters moved in at this time and all concerned took anti-malarial and anti-scrub-typhus precautions very seriously. Food was simple, sufficient and monotonous but LAC Whitlock, the flight cook, did wonders with it and became a hero of the campaign. They were visited by Brigadier DJ Steevens, the CCRA, who was to become a great supporter of the AOP. Then it was decided to use a strip near divisional headquarters at Honnaing, the problem was that it was under enemy observation, so it could only be used for a few minutes at a time. An aircraft would land, the pilot would switch off and go to be briefed by the BMRA while his machine was rapidly refuelled. He would then jump in, start up and take off. No aircraft was damaged using this technique but frequently a shell landed just as the aircraft was climbing away.

'The main task at this time was the location of enemy guns. This was perhaps our most difficult task as the Japanese Gunner's fire discipline was so strict that at the first sign of an Auster in the sky they almost invariably stopped firing. Their camouflage and the natural cover of the jungle were so perfect that they were virtually invisible.' (McMath). But in the next few days Captains Maslen-Jones and Harrison each destroyed a gun due to some carelessly uncovered tracks which led to them. This restricted enemy fire a great deal and soon the whole flight advanced to Honnaing. Shortly after the fall of Indainggyi the flight prepared an advanced strip some 15 miles away near Neyinzaya Chaung, but remained at Honnaing. As before they dug trenches immediately to accommodate everyone. Supplies were air dropped and again they were flying constantly. ' 'Pip' Harrison and I flew forward on a daily basis to take orders from the Brigade Major, Royal Artillery, and carry out our sorties before returning our aircraft to relative safety each evening.' (Maslen-Jones).

Then came the attack on the Myittha Gorge, Captain Frank McMath recalls that '. . . the call for Air Observation reached the Flight, and I was sent up in Radio communication with 1/3 Medium Bty, and 302 and 303 East African Field Regts, which gave me a firepower of 8 x 5.5 hows. 24 x 25-pdrs. and 24 x 3.7 in mountain guns.

As this was about the biggest thing we had tackled so far, George [Deacon] rigged up a wireless set at the strip so that he could listen to the shooting and hear how the afternoon's sport was going.' Time went by and 'Mac' didn't return, the guns had stopped firing and it was clear that something had happened. Ted Maslen-Jones took off at last light to search for 'Mac,' but failed and returned to land on a strip illuminated by vehicle headlights. Then a jeep turned up and it was 'Mac' who recounted his story. ' At first the dense jungle had beaten me completely and I could see nothing but tree-tops, but after I had searched vainly for some minutes and the FOO of 303 Regt had fired a shell into what he believed to be the centre of the enemy position, I discovered one bunker well hidden at the base of a great tree. Immediately I called for fire from the Mediums, choosing a fuze which would give instantaneous explosion even if the shells hit tiny branches.

"Hullo Baker 6, . . . Troop Target map reference 452715, Fuse 119 - over", and checked the eager reply from the gunners back in the Kabaw valley.

In less than a minute they reported ready to fire: "Ready 6,200, 25 seconds - over." (the Range and Time of Flight of the shell), and I answered with a sharp command: "Fire! - over." Instantly the gunners reported "Shot 3 - over" and I glanced at the second-hand of my clock so that I should know the exact moment when the shell would land and could use the intervening time for putting the aircraft into a place where I could best watch the explosion. This is a simple enough manoeuvre, although calling for a certain amount of care that one doesn't fly into the trajectory of the shell just as it comes along.'

A great white burst of smoke showed that the round fell short of the target. After a couple of adjustments a round exploded right in the middle of the suspected area, and only a few yards from the one bunker I had spotted, so I summoned all four guns of the Troop by: "6400, 5 rounds Gun Fire - over" . . . The twenty shells I had ordered caused tremendous havoc and a pall of smoke which hid the exact extent of the damage . . . Then I saw that the devastation was simply amazing, turning that tiny piece of jungle into a close imitation of one of Paul Nash's paintings of the European battlefields.' Mc Math was flying at 600 feet at 80 mph slowly turning to one side then the other to unsight any Japanese who might be trying to shoot him down. 'As I circled slowly round and round only a few hundred feet above the trees, I made out more and more of the weapons pits, and crawl trenches which had lain hidden in the undergrowth and which could well be holding a very formidable force. 303 Regiment then had to be brought onto the target, as it was far too large for the Mediums to deal with alone. . . By this time I had been flying for 1½ hours and as my petrol capacity was somewhere about 2½ hours . . . I was beginning to think about going home. . . the Infantry Commander on the ground . . . made his plan for an all-night bombardment, followed by a dawn assault. This meant bringing 302 Regt's 25 pdrs on to the target which proved no easy task as they were widely dispersed in the Kabaw and each troop of 4 guns had individually to be corrected.

At half-past five I had a gallon and a half left, and one more troop to shoot, and so beginning to fear a forced-landing, I climbed up to a safer height of 1500 feet or so. At last the job was finished and all three regiments could now shoot straight into the Jap positions for ever if they wanted to, so I turned for home with less than one gallon of petrol, but a comforting height beneath me, and Honnaing strip just visible in the distance about 10 minutes flying away.

. . . suddenly the engine began coughing, the petrol gauge dropped to zero, and a moment later the engine failed altogether. . . I glided down and watched the trees coming up rapidly towards me, but all the time the edge of the jungle was drawing nearer. Could I make it? . . . I pulled on all my flaps suddenly and shot 20 feet into the air and sailed over the last branches . . . I let the flaps up with a bang. Instantly the aircraft stalled and sank quite gently into the [elephant] grass which, being 12 feet tall and as thick as the finest cornfield, cushioned me beautifully.' McMath was unhurt though his aircraft required the attentions of RAF rear workshops. A bunch of LAA Gunners rushed through the undergrowth. Their battery was close to 3rd Medium

Battery which he had just been ranging and it was from them that he borrowed the jeep which drove him home.

Next came the attack on the Myittha Gorge by 11th East African Division. Observation on the ground and from the air was worse than ever. The job of 'A' Flight was to keep one aircraft airborne in contact with the lead FOO who was with the lead company. On meeting the enemy the Austers would swoop down and try to locate the enemy positions; sometimes they did and sometimes they did not. The problem was locating our own forward troops so they began putting up huge orange umbrellas and this worked well. The pilot could then blast the jungle ahead of the infantry whether he saw the target or not. The second task was to range the divisional artillery constantly onto any likely enemy position early each day, so that fire could be called at any time either directly or with reference to the recorded point. Thirdly they engaged any enemy they could see, something they did with vigour. 'On 22nd November all four pilots flew two sorties each, with a total flying time of 16 hours. We virtually had to take it in turns, so narrow was the battle front. During the day we carried out between us a total of twenty-three shoots using No 3 Battery of 1st Medium Regiment and the two East African field regiments. Captain Ian Walton also ranged and put down smoke markers for an air strike by Hurri-Bombers. Interestingly the record shows that the coordinates for all this activity at the entrance to the gorge were within an area not more than five miles square, and the majority were concerned with a feature called Telegraph Hill. (Maslen-Jones).

As the division approached Kalewa, 'A' Flight was told to engage that place with a troop of 3.7-inch HAA guns from 101st HAA Regiment firing at their extreme range of 19,400 yards. 'I knew a lot about these guns, as they had been the equipment of our old friends from Belfast [8th HAA Regiment] in the Arakan. . . We planned the shoot extremely carefully, timing it for the time when all the weather conditions would help the shell along a bit further, as, to be quite frank, we were all a little doubtful whether we could reach the town at all. (McMath). The pilot eventually found the remains of the town which had been destroyed by Japanese, British and American aerial bombardment. 'The first round from the HAA troop sent up a great spout of water from the very point where the brown rapid waters of the Myittha swirled into the clear blue Chindwin, that is about 500 yards plus and about 200 yards to the right of the track-junction which I was aiming at. . . we fired salvo after salvo into the town . . . the purpose had really been to direct guns on to this track bottle-neck, rather than attempt to destroy the town, so that throughout the following nights shells could be fired spasmodically to worry the enemy in his night movements, which is what nearly all his big troop movements were. This type of firing is called Harassing Fire and is always marvellously effective. In this case we had proof of our success when a Jap Officer's diary was captured later, in which he said, "For some days the evacuation from Myittha Gorge through Kalewa has been made hell by the accurate enemy shelling which came down all night and gave us no rest, but a terrible fear."' (McMath). On 21st November 'A' Flight moved to Hpaungzaik five miles west of the Myittha Gorge. Kalewa fell on 2nd December 1944.

The provision of air defence for these operations was not easy. Nevertheless 67th HAA and 28th LAA Regiments forced their way down the Tiddim road, together with 91th LAA Battery, of 44th LAA Regiment, and 56th and 82nd LAA/Anti-Tank Regiments. Most of their shooting was against ground targets eliminating strong points but they also provided vitally important working parties and vehicles to assist the move of the whole force forwards. It was at this stage that 28th LAA Regiment returned to Imphal to be broken up to provide infantry reinforcements. At this time too 163rd LAA Battery of 56th Regiment converted to 3-inch mortars. But 67th HAA Regiment forced its way forward magnificently, its great Matador gun tractors skidding and winching their way along the tracks with their 3.7-inch HAA guns. It helped with long range accurate ground fire to reduce the enemy garrison at Tiddim and then almost incredibly, '. . . [it]

climbed the high ground of the Kennedy Peak feature with 5th [Indian] Division, no easy task as tracks had to be bulldozed to take heavy vehicles, the steep slopes required vehicles and guns to be winched up them and enemy bunkers had to be blasted clear by concentrated fire. Supplies of all kinds, including AA ammunition, were delivered by air to maintain the advance and this was done with great efficiency.' (Routledge).

Operations by 5th Indian Division got under way on 29th September but *33rd Division* was holding the area in strength and was well equipped and supplied. Clearly it was going to take longer than expected. Warren tried a flank attack through Dollaung while the rest of the brigade moved along the track with the tanks. The Japanese fought hard, in spite of heavy air attacks particularly on their positions at Kennedy Peak and Vital Corner. 'His rearguard waited in concealed defence positions that commanded the winding road, opening fire on our lead infantry section and killed or wounded several men. If the rifle company failed to oust the enemy, then Howard's mountain guns battered the position with whatever ammunition the limited air drops had provided.' (Brett-James). This went on until 16th October when, under heavy artillery attack, the Japanese pulled out overnight. Tiddim was captured and a light airstrip was created so that at last the long-suffering sick and wounded could be flown out. After a further gallant push in still terrible conditions, this splendid division pressed on and captured first Vital Corner and then Kennedy Peak. From the cold mist at the top of that great hill, the men could see the broken remains of Fort White, their next objective. But the enemy had had enough and progress was swift. At the entrance to Kalemyo stood a sign post which said 'To Tiddim 48 miles.' It was here that 5th Indian Division was pulled back to rest in the Naga Hills around Maram and their place was taken by 20th Indian Division.

All was ready, from Tiddim to Myitkina, to execute Operation CAPITAL as soon as the weather permitted.

The Japanese had more problems to cope with. The Tojo Government had fallen in July 1944 and General K Kosio and Admiral M Yonai formed a new one. New orders were issued to defend the Philippines, Formosa and the Ryukyu and Kurile Islands while the armies in China were ordered to capture the American airfields (Map 41). *11th Army* began to advance on 29th August and had soon captured Kweilin and Tanchu.

In Burma, (Map 43) General M Kawabe, at *Burma Area Army,* re-organised so that Honda, with *33rd Army* consisting of the newly-arrived *2nd* and *18th,* and *56th Divisions*, could take the offensive on the Salween Front. *53rd Division* was sent to Mutaguchi's *15th Army* to reinforce the shattered *15th, 31st and 33rd Divisions*. At the end of August, Lieutenant General Heitaro Kimura replaced Kawabe and Lieutenant General S Katamura replaced Mutaguchi at *15th Army*. Lieutenant General S Tanaka was succeeded by Lieutenant General E Naka at *18th Division* and went to be Chief of Staff to Kimura. Headquarters *Southern Army* was told to hold southern Burma at all costs and to try to sever Allied communications with China as a second priority. Honda's plan was to attack astride the Burma Road towards Lungling with *2nd Division* on the right and *56th Division* on the left. This operation began on 3rd September but by the 7th there was stalemate after very heavy casualties had been suffered.

Kimura deduced that he must hold the Yenangyaung oilfields and the rice growing areas of the Irrawaddy delta, if he was to supply his forces. Thus he must hold the line, Mandalay - Yenangyaung - Ramree Island. He therefore ordered *33rd Army,* Honda, with *18th* and *56th Divisions* and *168th Regiment* of *49th Division*, to hold the right sector from Lashio to Mandalay and *15th Army,* Katamura, with *15th, 31st, 33rd* and *53rd Divisions*, to hold the line of the Irrawaddy from Mandalay to Pakokku with a division in reserve at Meiktila. *28th Army,* Sakurai, with *54th, 55th Divisions* and *72nd Independent Brigade*, was to hold the Arakan coast as far as Rangoon. *2nd Division* and *49th Division*, less two regiments, formed the Army reserve at Taunggyi.

Planning for Operation CAPITAL was moving on apace. 14th Army's plan was in four phases; the first, to capture Kalemyo and Kalewa; the second, an airborne operation at Yeu to open the road for artillery to be got forward for the attack on Mandalay; the third, the capture of Mandalay and the fourth, consolidation and exploitation. But it was clear that the parachute division would not be ready in time and should anyway be kept for Operation DRACULA, the assault on Rangoon. The parachute element of the plan was dropped. Clearly there was going to be a massive Sapper task to get 14th Army forward and then to maintain the routes for logistic traffic. Even so there would be a need for large air support operations, both operational and logistical.

By this time the Chiefs of Staff had concluded that, because of the toughening resistance in Italy, in October 1944, they could not authorise the transfer of forces to the Far East in time for DRACULA in March 1945. They therefore ordered Mountbatten to carry out CAPITAL and exploit as best he could until the end of the monsoon in November 1945. Mountbatten decided that he should go onto the offensive in the Arakan, clear the Japanese out and thus release his own forces for DRACULA. Having met Churchill in Cairo, Mountbatten was authorised to attack in the Arakan in January 1945 and to start planning for landings on the Kra Isthmus and the Andaman Islands.

Because of General Stilwell's multiple appointments and his refusal to serve under Giffard and 11th Army Group, Mountbatten asked for changes to his command structure and permission to create a new Anglo/American Headquarters, Allied Land Forces South East Asia (ALFSEA). At this time, however, the Americans were having trouble with the Chinese to get them to agree to Stilwell's becoming Commander-in-Chief. In China itself the Communists wanted rid of Chiang Kai-shek with the concommitant possibility of civil war. The Japanese, however, were still pressing on south westwards from Hengyang and north westwards from Canton. This was not a time to take risks. The Japanese had captured Lingling and were threatening the two largest US airbases in China at Kweilin and Liuchow. The Yunnan Armies were also under threat and, on 15th September 1944, Chiang Kai-shek threatened to withdraw them unless Stilwell attacked from Myitkyina within a week. President Roosevelt sent a strong message to the Generalissimo on the 19th in which he said that the whole of the offensive in Burma, to open a safe route to China, would be in jeopardy unless the Chinese thrust forward in Yunnan. Stilwell himself delivered this message and this angered Chiang Kai-shek so much that he ordered him to be removed. Stilwell left on 27th October.

General Stilwell's departure enabled Mountbatten and the US Chiefs of Staff to reorganise. The Americans divided the China-Burma-India Theatre with Lieutenant General DI Sultan, US Army, who had replaced Stilwell in command of the American and Chinese forces in Burma-India Theatre, NCAC and in Yunnan. Lieutenant General AC Wedemeyer, US Army, was to act as Chief of Staff to Chiang Kai-shek and become Commanding General China Theatre. This was approved by the Combined Chiefs of Staff, as was Mountbatten's creation of a new land forces HQ, ALFSEA which replaced 11th Army Group on 12th November 1944. On that day Lieutenant General Sir Oliver Leese became Commander-in-Chief ALFSEA and took command of all British, American and Chinese forces in Burma. His Main Headquarters was in Kandy alongside Headquarters SEAC and his Advanced Headquarters was at Barrackpore close to Headquarters Eastern Air Command. A new Lines of Communication Command came into being at Comilla. Meanwhile Admiral Sir Bruce Fraser took command of the newly-named British Pacific Fleet and Air Chief Marshal Sir Keith Park became Air Commander-in-Chief. Finally, in December, Lieutenant General FAM Browning took over from Pownall as Chief of Staff, owing to the latter's ill health.

The Japanese advance in China went on relentlessly. By 4th November 1944 they had captured Wunchan and were advancing on Liuchow. Nanning was occupied on the 24th and Tuhshan early in December. Then the Japanese reasoned that they were secure in China, that they had removed the key American airfields and could concentrate on the American advance in the Pacific. But all was not well for them in China; the move of supplies over 'The Hump' to the Chinese Army was increasing with the development of the base at Myitkyina. General Wedemeyer was concerned that a threat might develop to Kunming at the Chinese end of the 'Hump' route and he requested the move of 22nd and 38th Chinese Divisions, one to Tuhshan and one to Chungking, to secure the approaches to both. Wedemeyer then wanted more aircraft and the Generalissimo warned that he would move more Chinese forces back to China if the Japanese advance was not stopped. Mountbatten, in turn warned that such moves would severely threaten the forthcoming Burma offensive. The American Chiefs of Staff considered support for Chiang Kai-shek, in view of the crisis developing in China, was of greater importance than an offensive in Burma and they supported Wedemeyer.

In the end it was 14th and 22nd Chinese Divisions that were flown out to Kunming with two air commando troop-carrying squadrons of the USAAF. In return 20th Bomber Command was evacuated from Chengtu to Calcutta and could be used for limited operations within SEAC. It has been necessary to outline these events in the Pacific and China because they were to have considerable impact on what was, and what was not, possible in Burma in 1944/45. By December the main forces of 14th Army on the Central Front stood poised to advance. 15th Indian Corps in the Arakan, by then under the direct command of ALFSEA, was also ready to resume the offensive. The stage was set for the final act.

The Royal Regiment had grown in size and experience and was in great form as it faced the battles yet to come. Its strength on 31st December 1944 in the whole of India/Burma command, excluding the Indian Artillery but including officers employed outside the Regiment on the Staff, was:

Field Artillery	3,012 officers	24,723 other ranks
HAA Artillery	1,487 officers	15,942 other ranks
LAA Artillery	1,297 officers	18,645 other ranks
Searchlight Artillery	116 officers	712 other ranks
Coast Artillery	173 officers	526 other ranks
Employed elsewhere	2,272 officers	
Totals	8,366 officers	60,548 other ranks

A grand total of 68,914 all ranks.

On this same day the world-wide strength of the Royal Regiment of Artillery was 672,686 all ranks. Thus some 10% of the Regiment was serving in the Far East.

CHAPTER 13

ARAKAN

OCTOBER 1944 - JANUARY 1945

and

THE OFFENSIVE FROM THE CHINDWIN TO THE IRRAWADDY

JANUARY - FEBRUARY 1945

(Maps 43, 44, 45, 46 and 47)

We will first follow operations on the Arakan Front from October 1944 to January 1945 (Map 44). Christison's 15th Indian Corps held a line running from Godusara - The Tunnels - Ngakyedauk - Taung Bazar - Goppe Bazar - Mowdok. 25th Indian Division, commanded by Major General GN Wood and based at Maungdaw, held the right sector from Godusara to the Ngakyedauk Pass with 51st, 53rd and 74th Indian Infantry Brigades. Under his CRA, Brigadier AJ Daniell, he had 8th and 27th Field Regiments, 33rd Indian Mountain Regiment and 7th Indian Anti-Tank Regiment. Next was 26th Indian Division, under Major General CEN Lomax at Ukhia, in reserve except for one brigade forward under 25th Indian Division covering Taung and Goppe Bazars and the track to the Kaladan at Ngofewngrowa. He had 4th, 36th and 71st Indian Infantry Brigades. His Gunners, under Brigadier the Baron de Robeck, were 160th British and 7th Indian Field, 30th Indian Mountain and 1st Indian Anti-Tank Regiments. Major General FJ Loftus-Tottenham's 81st West African Division was based at Chiringa with his forward troops covering the Mowdok area. He had 5th and 6th (WA) Infantry Brigades only, his 3rd (WA) Brigade was still with Special Forces. His Gunners were 21st (WA) Anti-Tank Regiment, 41st (WA) Mortar Regiment and 101st (WA) Light Regiment. Finally 82nd West African Division, commanded by Major General CMcIS Bruce, was at Ranchi waiting to be called forward. It had 1st, 2nd and 4th (WA) Infantry Brigades and his CRA, Brigadier RHM Hill, had 22nd (WA) Anti-Tank, 42nd (WA) Mortar and 102nd (WA) Light Regiments. Finally 50th Indian Tank, 3rd Commando and 22nd (EA) Infantry Brigades were awaiting orders to join 15th Indian Corps.

Christison planned to advance with, from right to left, 25th Indian, 82nd West African and 81st West African Divisions to capture the line Donbaik - Rathedaung - Myohaung, where he expected to meet determined resistance. This was Plan ROMULUS. Then, having drawn the Japanese into battle, he intended to land 26th Indian Division and 3rd Commando Brigade by amphibious assault to seize the Myebon Peninsula and Akyab. This was Plan TALON. This plan meant that 81st West African Division, in the Kaladan valley, had to make a considerable advance to line up with the others before operations could start in earnest. Accordingly Loftus-Tottenham started to move in mid-October. By 30th November, against considerable opposition, he had created a firm base between Kaladan - Tinma and Kyingri. He was up against Major General T Koba's *Matsu Detachment* of three battalions of infantry and one of artillery.

By early December, 30th Indian Mountain Regiment had been reduced to three batteries, 27th, 32nd and 33rd. It shed its 34th which, with 19th (Maymyo) Mountain Battery, formed 33rd Indian Mountain Regiment, for 25th Indian Division, under Lieutenant Colonel R Ellis. 27th Mountain Battery had come under attack at Goppe Bazar in October and had engaged over open sights to drive the attackers off. Lieutenant Lowe, a Canadian officer, was killed while working as FOO with the infantry in this operation. 33rd Mountain Battery had a similar experience at Taung Bazar a few days later, when Lieutenant Charangit Singh distinguished himself beating off the enemy with direct fire and causing over 70 casualties. At this stage 27th Mountain Battery joined 26th Indian Division while 30th Mountain Regiment, with 32nd and 33rd Mountain Batteries, joined 81st West African Division after a march of three weeks into the Kaladan valley. Its strength was ten British and six Indian officers, 436 men, 26 horses, 118 mules and 187 transport mules attached. The conditions were appalling and the animals suffered greatly.

81st West African Division was advancing down the Kaladan valley, with 6th (WA) Infantry Brigade and 101st Mortar Battery in the Pi Chaung and 5th (WA) Infantry Brigade on the Kaladan itself. 41st (WA) Mortar Regiment, under Lieutenant Colonel JA Macnabb, provided covering fire. It consisted of 101st, 102nd and 103rd (WA) Mortar Batteries, each with eight 3-inch mortars. (Nomenclature can be confusing as 101 was also the number of 81st West African Division's light regiment and 102 the number of 82nd West African Division's light regiment). On 10th January 4th (WA) Infantry Brigade of 82nd West African Division came under the command of 81st West African Division for the capture of Myohaung. On 20th January one gun of 33rd Mountain Battery became lost in the jungle and was ambushed and captured. It was found a few days later undamaged.

The advance of 82nd West African Division has been well recorded by its CRA, Brigadier Hill, and he gives a good idea of the complexities of operating artillery in the depths of almost impassable jungle. On arrival in India the 82nd West African Divisional Artillery reorganised so that it had 102nd Light Regiment, under Lieutenant Colonel MC Munro, with 24 jeep-drawn 3.7-inch howitzers and 22nd Anti-Tank Regiment, under Lieutenant Colonel Fraser, with 36 x 57mm/6-pounder guns which were tractor drawn. This regiment had a secondary role as infantry which it adopted most of the time. 42nd Mortar Regiment, commanded by Lieutenant Colonel A Liddell, had 24 x 3-inch mortars, head loaded. There was a small jeep-mounted HQRA.

82nd West African Division concentrated at Razabil, leaving 22nd Anti-Tank Regiment in the infantry role defending Bawli Bazar and the Goppe Pass. 4th (WA) Infantry Brigade advanced south down the east bank of the Kalapanzin towards Buthidaung with 101st Light Regiment, less one battery but with 105th (WA) Mortar Battery under command. On the way tragedy struck when Major Reekie, Lieutenant Palmer and Sergeant Rowley, all of 105th (WA) Mortar Battery, ran into an ambush and were killed, an awful start to operations. On 14th December, 2nd (WA) Infantry Brigade was advancing on Buthidaung astride the road from the west and 1st (WA) Infantry Brigade was clearing the jungle to the south. The artillery grouped with 82nd West African Division for this operation was 5th Indian Field Regiment, with 24 x 25-pounders, 102nd (WA) Light Regiment, with 24 x 3.7-inch howitzers, one troop of 27th Field Regiment with 4 x 25-pounders and a Medium Group consisting of 6th Medium Regiment, less one battery, with 12 x 5.5-inch guns and one troop of 36th LAA Regiment with 6 x 40mm guns. All these guns were in action in the Htindaw Bowl alongside divisional headquarters including HQRA. Captain Jimmy Jarrett was the AOP pilot of 'C' Flight 656 AOP Squadron which was also alongside HQRA and he did a great deal of flying and target registration. There was also a section of 2nd Survey Battery which did splendid work providing information from its OPs and succeeding in keeping all guns on a corps grid throughout the Kalapanzin advance, no mean achievement. The guns were covering as far forward as Buthidaung which, after very slight opposition, fell and both brigades soon had a bridgehead over the Kalapanzin river, but 1st (WA) Infantry Brigade had some tough fighting in the hills using the guns frequently. By this time 4th (WA) Infantry Brigade was at Kindaung and the Sappers had assembled some 640 river craft at Buthidaung which they then launched into the Kalapanzin. This was to be the main supply route for the force as it moved south.

It was during the fighting in the Kaladan valley that Havildar Umrao Singh, of 33rd Indian Mountain Battery, 30th Indian Mountain Regiment, won the Victoria Cross for extreme gallantry in action. A section of 33rd Mountain Battery under Lieutenant VN Matthews was posted to a forward company position of 8th Gold Coast Regiment. The aim was to counter enemy shelling. Then at 2200 hours on 15th December the enemy put in a strong attack which lasted several hours. Havildar Umrao Singh's citation reads:

'In the Kaladan valley, in Burma, on December 15/16th 1944, Havildar Umrao Singh was in charge of one gun in an advanced section of his battery, when it was subjected to heavy fire from 75mm guns and mortars for one and a half hours prior to being attacked by two companies of Japanese.

When the attack came he so inspired his gun detachment by his personal example and encouragement to fight and defend their gun that they beat off the attack with losses to the enemy.

Though twice wounded by grenades in the first attack, he again held off the second enemy attack by skilful control of his detachment's small arms fire, and by manning a Bren gun himself, which he fired over the shield of his gun at the Japanese who had got to within five yards' range. Again the enemy were beaten off with heavy losses. Third and fourth attacks were also beaten off in the same manner by the resolute action and great courage of Havildar Umrao Singh.

When the final attack came, the other gun having been overrun and all his ammunition expended, he seized a gun bearer [a metal bar] and, calling once again on all who remained, he closed with the enemy in furious hand-to-hand fighting and was seen to strike down three Japanese in a desperate effort to save his gun, until he was overwhelmed and knocked senseless.

Six hours later, when a counterattack restored the position, he was found exhausted beside his gun and almost unrecognisable with seven severe wounds, and ten Japanese round him.

By his personal example and magnificent bravery Havildar Umrao Singh set a supreme example of gallantry and devotion to duty. When recovered, his gun was fit to fire and was in fact in action again and firing later that same day.' (Duncan)

Havildar Umrao Singh was the fourth Gunner to earn the Victoria Cross in the war and was to be the only other rank in the Royal Artillery or Indian Regiment of Artillery to do so. The action took place near Tinma some 30 miles east of Buthidaung. Seldom, if ever, has there been such a magnificent example of the courage of one man to save his gun against such enormous odds. His action brings great credit to the Regiment and is a lesson in what is meant by defending the guns, the Colours, to the last. He was decorated by His Majesty King George VI, Colonel-in-Chief of the Royal Regiment of Artillery, at Buckingham Palace on 15th October 1945. He visited England again in 1970 and was present at the VJ Celebrations in London in August 1995.

The Medium Group and 5th Indian Field Regiment moved forward into action near Buthidaung on 20th December. The latter crossed the river at Kindaung and moved some miles south, but on 13th January 1945 it was ordered back to Razabil. Similarly 101st Light Regiment moved as far south as Kindaung and then handed over its jeeps to 102nd Light Regiment before returning to re-join 81st West African Division at Chiringa. By 7th January 4th (WA) Infantry Brigade was at Kanzauk. It then moved 60 miles further south to Apauka where 22nd Anti-Tank Regiment came forward and took over the defence. By 16th January HQRA and 102nd Light Regiment had also arrived at Apauka, but the going had been tough, with the hard-used jeeps struggling along with the guns in tow and all the officers and men walking alongside.

The general advance had begun on 11th December with a move down the coastal plain by 74th Indian Infantry Brigade, Brigadier JE Hirst, of 25th Indian Division, supported by Arakan Coastal Forces vessels from Maungdaw and the destroyers *Napier* and *Nepal*, the whole commanded by Captain EW Bush RN. By 15th December the advance had reached Myinhlut and received a seaborne re-supply. Such opposition as it had met was dealt with by the guns of the army and the Royal Navy. By 20th December it was closing on Indin. 53rd Indian Infantry Brigade was advancing down the east side of the Mayu Range and met opposition at Seinnyinbya which it dealt with but later met a strong dug in enemy position at Hparabyin. Across the river 2nd (WA) Infantry Brigade had got to Kindaung where it ran into heavy opposition particularly from enemy artillery. Further east 4th (WA) Infantry Brigade, Brigadier AHG Ricketts, was mopping up in the Kalapanzin valley while 6th (WA) Infantry Brigade had moved from Tinma towards Myohaung. At Kru they hit an enemy position and 101st Mortar Battery, Major GTMdeM Morgan, engaged at short range, marking the target for Hurri-bombers and then firing a smoke screen. He advanced with the lead infantry and, by controlling the fire with great skill and by his energy and professionalism, kept up the momentum. For this action he was awarded the Military Cross. Some weeks later, in the same action that Havildar Umrao Singh had won his Victoria Cross, Lieutenant Tony Verity of 101st Mortar Battery had found himself commanding a platoon of 1st Gambia Regiment and beating off a ferocious enemy attack. He did so well with the infantry that he did not get back to his battery for over a month. The battery was next in action at Thaure before being ordered to proceed to Myohaung. Astride the Mayu Range 25th Indian and 82nd West African Divisions were up against the *Sakurai Detachment*, consisting of three infantry battalions, a reconnaissance regiment and a mountain artillery battalion, commanded by Major General T Sakurai.

Progress was good and it was decided to bring forward Plan TALON, the assault on Akyab, to a date between 20th and 27th January 1945. By 23rd December, 74th Indian Infantry Brigade was in Donbaik, scene of so much fighting in 1942 - 43, and found it deserted. 53rd Indian Infantry Brigade held the Japanese at Hparabyin while 51st Indian Infantry Brigade moved round to take them in the rear. The Japanese were to get a taste of their own tactics. Over on the Mayu river 4th (WA) Infantry Brigade had passed through 2nd (WA) Infantry Brigade, overcome resistance at Taungmaw and was closing on Htizwe.

It was at this time that Major General Wood, at 25th Indian Division, noticed a general move of Japanese forces towards the Kaladan. Unknown to him at the time this move was a result of Major General T Sakurai's receiving agreement to withdraw. He had been told to move east behind the *Matsu Detachment* which was facing north at Myohaung, evacuate Akyab and rejoin *55th Division* at Prome. Thus 74th Indian Infantry Brigade reached Foul Point, without any opposition, on 27th December. 53rd Indian Infantry Brigade crossed the river and occupied Rathedaung while 51st Indian Infantry Brigade cleared the rest of the peninsula. 81st West African Division had, however, run into stubborn opposition from the *Matsu Detachment* at Thayettabin, but the advance had been so successful that Joint Force Headquarters again brought forward the assault on Akyab to start with a landing by 3rd Commando Brigade under a heavy aerial and naval bombardment at 1230 hours on 3rd January. The brigade was to be accompanied by a squadron of tanks, 6th Medium Regiment, a battery of 8th (Belfast) HAA Regiment and a battery of 36th LAA Regiment. 74th Indian Infantry Brigade was to follow up, crossing by landing craft from Foul Point. It was then to pass through the commandos and capture the whole of Akyab Island. This speed up of the plan caused some logistic problems, but 15th Indian Corps opened an FMA (Forward Maintenance Area) at Foul Point, stocked from Maungdaw and Chittagong by coastal craft and this saved the day.

Naval support was to be supplied by Rear-Admiral AD Read's Bombardment Force, made up of the cruisers *Newcastle*, *Phoebe* and *Nigeria*, and 224 Group RAF had laid on an attack by some 200 aircraft. All was ready when a dramatic event occurred. Captain CJB (Jimmy) Jarrett RA of 'C' Flight, 656 AOP Squadron was flying over Akyab in readiness to observe for the naval bombardment the following day. He could see no targets and no sign of enemy at all and, as he flew lower and lower, the local inhabitants started waving to him. He landed on a rice field and was told that the Japanese had gone. He took off and flew back to report to the CRA 25th Indian Division, Brigadier John Daniell, who took him to the divisional commander, General Wood. Jarrett eventually met the corps commander, General Christison. It was agreed that, if he could bring back 'a spokesman', they would accept that this was not some deep deception plan on the part of the Japanese. Jarrett flew back and collected 'a spokesman', partly because he 'had a magnificent old college crest in gold on a smart blue blazer.' Jarrett left his batman, Gunner 'Derk' Carter, behind, having appointed him 'temporary military governor'. Carter was then treated royally and was feted with chicken and coffee by the elders. Later Jarrett was awarded a well-earned DFC for this and many other daring exploits from the air. General Christison and Air Vice-Marshal the Earl of Bandon flew in to Akyab to be mobbed by the inhabitants. They immediately ordered the landing to take place as ordered but without the bombardment, which was called off thanks to Jarrett. (Jarrett in Duncan). By 4th January Akyab was occupied without a shot being fired and work immediately began on the airfield. A few days later Hurricanes were operating against the Japanese in the Kaladan valley where 81st West African Division faced an enemy force of some three infantry and one artillery battalions, with air support, near Thayettabin.

The fighting at Thayettabin was tough. On 14th January, 101st Mortar Battery itself under fire from some 37mm guns, reported getting a cry from the infantry that the enemy were on top of them and they were hard pressed. Captain Michael Clarke, on duty at the time, ordered "five rounds gunfire" from 14 mortars and the enemy dispersed. Next day he got a message from the infantry, 1st Gambia, 'Thank God for the guns, Mike, you did a good job last night.' On the 15th the Gambians attacked again, Major Tom Morgan advancing with them controlling a fireplan of 16 mortars from 101st and 102nd Mortar Batteries designed to follow the air strike. The Japanese pulled out of their positions as the attacking infantry approached. (Clarke).

Provision of air defence artillery to cover the offensives on all three fronts was, again, not easy. The air threat was not high but high enough that it could not be disregarded. CCRAs kept air defence resources under their own control allotting units to divisions for specific tasks. For example Brigadier C Goulder, CCRA 4th Indian Corps, ordered 69th LAA Regiment, which had found the special troops for the second Chindit operation, to detach its 207th LAA Battery to go under command of 19th Indian Division which was to move forward to link up with NCAC. Brigadier DJ Steevens, CCRA 33rd Indian Corps, grouped 101st HAA and 44th LAA Regiments with divisions, keeping 52nd HAA and 2nd Indian LAA Regiments under his own command. 2nd British Division was given 226th HAA Battery of 101st HAA Regiment and 75th LAA Battery of 44th LAA Regiment to provide route protection and cover for airstrips and gun areas. 20th Indian Division was allotted 297th HAA, less a troop, and 239th LAA Batteries from the same regiments and they had no easy time covering the rough route to Monywa and then to the Irrawaddy crossing sites. For the crossings themselves, CCRA 33rd Indian Corps concentrated all his four regiments under his own command. 101st Regiment had two batteries in the AA role and one troop of 297th HAA Battery which manned 2 x 7.2-inch howitzers. 44th LAA Regiment placed one battery with each division to protect the crossing sites themselves. Meanwhile on the Arakan front 15th Indian Corps had 8th (Belfast) HAA Regiment and 36th LAA Regiment. These regiments were again allocated to tasks as they arose by the CCRA, Brigadier LA Harris. Finally the defence of the support area airfields in Chittagong, East Bengal and Bawli was the responsibility of 13th AA Brigade, consisting of 70th British and 6th and 7th Indian HAA

Regiments, 35/12th Indian HAA Battery, 77th British and 3rd, 6th and 8th Indian LAA Regiments and 10th Indian LAA Battery.

Before turning to the main attacks on the Central Front we must look at the progress of Northern Combat Area Command (NCAC) (Map 42). We left them, under General Stilwell, with Major General FW Festing's 36th British Division the only formation in contact with the enemy, at Namma, and the Chinese New 6th Army, less 14th Chinese Division, with 50th Chinese Division at Hopin and 22nd Chinese Division in the hills ten miles south east of Mogaung. The Chinese New 1st Army was east of the Irrawaddy, with 38th Chinese Division facing Bhamo, still held by the Japanese, and 30th Chinese Division was to the east of that place. 14th Chinese Division and Mars Force, an American divisional-sized formation still being formed, were in reserve. Stilwell knew he was up against *53rd Division* with *56th Division* still facing the Chinese Yunnan Forces in the Lungling - Mangshih area. *18th Division* was at Namhkam and *2nd Division* at Muse with two battalions holding Bhamo.

Stilwell's plan was to launch 36th British Division followed by 50th Chinese Division on the right, down the west side of the Irrawaddy to seize the Indaw - Katha area. In the centre 22nd Chinese Division was to seize the old Chindit airstrip at 'Broadway,' then it was to cross over the Irrawaddy at Shwego and occupy Skidaw. On the left, 38th Chinese Division was to seize Bhamo and Namhkam. The advance began on 16th October but 36th British Division soon hit trouble when its 29th British Infantry Brigade met a well-prepared position at Mawhun. This was not captured until 31st October and the advance resumed but resistance was stiffening. Festing asked General DI Sultan, who by then had replaced Stilwell, to get the 50th Chinese Division to come forward to protect his line of communication which was being threatened and this he did. By 12th November, 72nd British Infantry Brigade, by then in the lead, struck the main enemy position just north of Pinwe, identifying the enemy as *119th* and *151st Infantry Regiments.*

Festing decided to attack on 22nd November but realised that support from the 50th Chinese Division was doubtful. He asked that it should protect his flank from enemy known to be at Auktaw. 72nd British Infantry Brigade attacked as planned and soon the Japanese began to give way. 29th British Infantry Brigade took over the lead on the 27th and found that the enemy had abandoned Pinwe, but the fighting had been hard, 36th British Division suffering some 400 casualties. Nevertheless Indaw, Naba and Katha were occupied by 13th December and contact was made with 19th Indian Division at Banmauk. Sultan then ordered Festing to advance astride the Irrawaddy as soon as his third brigade, 26th Indian Infantry Brigade, arrived. He was then to cross the Irrawaddy and clear crossings of the Shweli River south of Mabein and then take Mogok.

Meanwhile 22nd Chinese Division had advanced without opposition and crossed the Irrawaddy at Shwegu, which it occupied on 7th November. Leaving a regiment to hold Shwegu, it pushed on and by 30th November its 65th and 66th Chinese Regiments were at Si-u. It was at this stage that General Sultan was ordered to send 14th and 22nd Chinese Divisions back to China. He thus pulled out 22nd Chinese Division and replaced it with 475th US Infantry Regiment from Mars Force. One of its three battalions stayed at Shwegu and made patrol contact with 36th Division at Katha. The remaining two battalions arrived at Si-u on 10th December just in time to repel a Japanese counter-attack from *18th Division*. Honda then moved *18th Division* to Mongmit, less its *55th Regiment* which was to defend Namhkam.

On the left, 38th Chinese Division had advanced on Bhamo taking Myothit on 28th October. The division then encircled the town but the Japanese were determined to fight. The garrison consisted of some 1,200 men, four field guns and a few mountain guns and was well supplied. 30th Chinese Division had, meanwhile, moved to Namyu to ensure that Bhamo could not be relieved. They were just in time because the Japanese were planning a move to save Bhamo and attacked viciously on 9th December, overrunning some of 30th Chinese Division's artillery units.

The Chinese counter-attacked and there was heavy fighting. By 14/15th December the garrison, reduced to about 900, broke out along the river bed in the early morning mist, and reached Namhkam, on which the rest of the Japanese force withdrew to the same place.

It was on 29th October that 11th Chinese Army attacked from Yunnan. Two divisions, supported by 14th USAAF from China, attacked Lungling while 200th Chinese Division cut it off to the south. Lieutenant General S Matsuyama, commanding *56th Division,* withdrew to Mangshih on 3rd November, but the Chinese did not follow up until pressed by General Wedemeyer and then they moved but slowly. They occupied Mangshih on 20th November and Chefang on 1st December but would go no further. The Japanese fell back, avoiding battle and laying waste to the land. With these moves the right and centre wings of NCAC had completed their tasks for the first phase of Operation CAPITAL, though the Chinese 1st Army still had some way to go to capture Namhkam. By then 36th British Division was at Indaw and Katha, 475th US Infantry Regiment at Si-u, 30th and 38th Chinese Divisions in the Bhamo - Namyu area and the Chinese Yunnan Army at Chefang. However, General Sultan realised that he still had a gap to fill before he could link the Ledo road to the old Burma Road and so complete the land route to China. He first moved 50th Chinese Division towards Namhkam and decided to stop and re-group. We will leave him there and turn to the exploits of 4th and 33rd Indian Corps on the Central Front (Map 43).

On 19th December 1944 33rd Indian Corps, under Stopford, had the Lushai Brigade at Gangaw, 2nd British Division, commanded by Major General CCG Nicholson, crossing the Chindwin at Kalewa, 20th Indian Division, Major General DD Gracey, with 80th and 100th Indian Infantry Brigades, west of the river at Kalemyo and Khampat and 32nd Indian Infantry Brigade across at Chingyaung. 4/10th Gurkhas of this brigade were already some eight miles east of Pyingaing. In 4th Indian Corps, under Messervy, 268th Independent Indian Infantry Brigade was at Yeshin and in touch with 33rd Indian Corps at Chingyaung. 19th Indian Division, commanded by Major General TW Rees, was already on the line Kangon -Wuntho -Nankan and was in contact with 36th British Division at Kunbaung and Meza. 7th Indian Division, under Major General GC Evans, was in reserve waiting its turn at Kohima but had one brigade at Tonhe and 28th (EA) Infantry Brigade at Imphal. The only formation in contact with the enemy was the Lushai Infantry Brigade at Gangaw and it had no artillery.

The enemy continued to withdraw everywhere. *15th Army* had *53rd Division* across the Irrawaddy at Tigyaing and *15th Division* was also across at Thabeikkyin. *31st* and *33rd Divisions* were struggling back in the area of Yeu. Their rear guards were fighting hard and often took a lot of getting out, frequently demanding major air strikes and artillery attacks.

19th Indian Division, which had not so far seen action, had started to cross the Chindwin on 4th December 1944. It had advanced rapidly to the Irrawaddy brushing aside resistance. After about three months training and resting, 2nd British Division crossed the Chindwin by the 1,154 foot Bailey Bridge, built by Indian Sappers in only 28 hours, at Kalewa on 19th December and pressed on towards Shwebo. 20th Indian Division crossed at Mawlaik, just north of Kalewa, on 3rd December and fought its way south down the east bank of the Chindwin against considerable opposition. It captured Monywa on 22nd January before clearing the west bank of the Irrawaddy around Myinmu.

In December 1944 14th Army received eight more 7.2-inch howitzers. Two went to 4th Indian Corps Artillery to be manned by 67th HAA Regiment until 20th March 1945 when they were handed over to 52nd HAA Regiment. Both were handed in to the Ordnance Field Park at Pegu on 11th May 1945. 15th Indian Corps also had two, known as 'Aunt' and 'Uncle', which were issued to 6th Medium Regiment although they were manned by a troop of 101st HAA Regiment throughout 1945. These guns were engaged in action at Akyab, Kawndaw, Rangoon and on the

Irrawaddy crossings. Movement was always a problem and often extra recovery vehicles and bulldozers were required to get them into their firing positions.

Sergeant E Parnell of 187th Heavy Battery of 67th HAA Regiment gives a vivid description of these great guns. 'We took over two of these guns at Imphal in December 1944. A detachment of 32 men was formed. I was GPOA. We did some training in the paddy fields on the Ukhrul road. Shells were carried on a frame by four men and then rammed home by six. The cordite charge was in four cotton bags, the whole being used for Charge Super and the bags discarded down to Charge 1. On firing the gun ran back on large steel ramps behind the wheels and rolled forward to be stopped by two wooden chocks. There was only 4 degrees of top traverse by handwheel. The rate of fire was one round every one and a half minutes on a good day. The detachment left Imphal on Boxing Day 1944 and went by stages via Tamu and the Kabaw valley to the Irrawaddy bridgehead at Pagan. The normal use was for the gun to go forward at first light to join the infantry who would point out targets, usually a bunker which was taken on over open sights. Often an air strike or an attack by smaller guns would be used to blow away the bunker camouflage.

We reckoned on firing about four rounds before the Japanese mortared us. This put the gun-layer under some pressure to get an early hit and there was much criticism at each miss! A hit on a bunker resulted in earth, logs and Japs flying 50 feet into the air and before it could all land the gun was rapidly coupled up to its tractor and got away before a mortar bomb arrived! Some targets were taken on using the AOP. It was a US L5 aircraft that gave us a direct hit on a Japanese 155mm gun which was under a building on stilts at Chauk.' (Parnell, letter of 17th July 1991 held by the RAI).

136th Field Regiment of 7th Indian Division reported concentrating at Tamu including 347th Battery with 'jury axle' 25-pounders. They were under orders to move to join the Lushai Brigade at Gangaw. 'Incidentally, the spectacle of this vast Fourteenth Army concentrating and "approaching to contact" is most impressive, thrilling and inspiring. Bumping through the dust on every track to the CHINDWIN and beyond are every type of formation and unit, every class and colour of soldier, every kind of weapon and vehicle, guns, tanks, transporters, lorries, jeeps, bulldozers and sapper contrivances, mules, horses and even elephant bridging teams, all on the move. Airstrips come into operation over night, and overhead go the bombers, fighters, "bully" bombers and Austers. What a circus! One battery was got onto Juries, almost on the move by methods which could hardly be described as "3rd or 4th Echelon modifications" ' (Extract from Monthly Newsletter CO 136th Field Regiment (Lt Col GR Armstrong) December 1944).

Lieutenant Colonel RJ Uniacke, commanding 16th Field Regiment in 2nd British Division, wrote of the period of his advance to Ondaw, Ywathitgyi and Mandalay:

23rd [November 1944]'We got orders here [Yazagyo] for the breakout from 11 Div bridgehead. 6 Bde were to be in the lead and I was to support them with my regiment plus a 3.7 how battery (393 Bty of 99th [Field Regiment]) [under Captain John Moreton] and a mortar battery (170 Bty of 100th A/Tk Regt - who doubled as mortar batteries) under command.

16 [December] We finally left the conc [concentration] area at 2245 that night and crossed the CHINDWIN at dawn next morning on what was then the world's longest Bailey pontoon bridge. The road was terrible on the other side and there were continual blocks so that we took 6 hours to do 10 miles and arrived at SHWEGYIN in the afternoon. This was where transport was finally abandoned in the 1942 retreat and there were numbers of abandoned and stripped vehicles, Stuart tanks and 25 prs, all looking like bleached skeletons in their cream coloured desert paint. They belonged to 7 Armd Bde who were the rearguard.

23rd. We reached PYINGAING (Pink Gin) without having met a Jap. We had expected to fight for it but the only sign of opposition were hundreds of trees across the road and blown bridges.

24th. Contact was made in the afternoon, the leading tanks and infantry being fired on while they were moving across a dry river bed. An unlucky burst from a MG caught the Bn Comd Post killing the tank Sqn Comd (3 DGs [Carabiniers]) and seriously wounding the CO of 1 R Berks (Robinson) and we pulled back into boxes for the night. The Padre, in no way deterred by the battle, held a carol service in the gun position before blackout.

27th. . . . the R Berks coy on Brown Hill was shot at from Jungle Top confirming that they were Japs . . . the story ended happily for us as we harassed them effectively during the day so that they did not fire again. (We also 'stonked' them heavily for 20 mins with 25 prs, 3.7 hows, 3" mortars and Vickers MMGs!).

5th January 1945 I got orders to move down south to the YE-U area and join 4 Bde who were going to cross the MU river south of YE-U . . . and continue the advance on SHWEBO.

6th. We set off at dawn to cross the MU river. . . 8th. The R Scots carried on . . . and at midday their CO John Masterson-Smith [Lt Col J Masterson-Smith] decided to have a full scale fire plan from my regt, a 3.7 how bty and a medium bty . . . The fire plan finally came down at 1700 and was successful in getting the infantry in [to Payan]. . .

20th. A patrol made contact at WETTHABOK [some 40 miles south of Shwebo] on the main road and a plan was made for an attack early next day.

21st. The attack soon after dawn was successful. Infantry and tanks formed up under cover of a smokescreen and went in under a 15 min concentration from the regt plus a light battery. . . In the afternoon I moved the regiment up to the area behind WETTHABOK and they were again shelled when moving in. Fortunately it was inaccurate again though it got everyone digging in quicker than usual. A Jap patrol was seen soon after dark in moonlight and it moved into the gun area. Four were killed, which made the gunners very perky. It was certainly a good advertisement for [Major] Rodney Burges' defensive layout.

1st February. The Air OP was up at 0800 ([Pip] Harrison) and registered 11 guns with 45 rounds in our sortie lasting $1^{1}/_{2}$ hours, which says a lot for the work at the gun end and, above all, for Harrison's shooting. He was a first class shot and had a most cheerful voice on the air. It was always a pleasure having him shooting us.

4th. At 1030 the first of three sqns of Thunderbolts started their bombing. All three sqns dropped their pair of 250 lbs bombs per plane and then started their striking runs. They were well controlled by the VCP at the Bde Comd Post, which was in touch with the Bn Comd so he was able to say exactly what he wanted and when they were to stop.

10th. Part of the deception plan is to give an impression of an artillery build up and I had various guns attached for periods, a section of 6" Hows, a troop of 5.5" guns and a 3.7" HAA gun. . . The HAA gun could just reach MANDALAY so we put a few shells over so that we could say we were the first to shell MANDALAY.' (Uniacke).

By mid December 656 AOP Squadron had Squadron Headquarters at Palel, 'A' Flight at Kalewa, 'B' Flight near Pilebu and 'C' Flight in the Arakan. Everywhere flying hours were mounting. 'B' Flight was advancing fast with 2nd British Division and it was far from easy for the ground crews to keep up.

99th Field Regiment, also in 2nd British Division, recorded, 'New Year dawned with 99th Field Regiment RA, less 393 [with 16th Field Regiment] and 394 [with 10th Field Regiment], at Pyingaing Myauk, and 393/394 Batteries in hides in the area of Kaduma.

2nd January 1945 . . . 394 had moved up to support the Dorsets in their crossing of the Mu River at Ye-U. D Troop had established a good OP on a bridge. 394 came into action at Thantha with Capt JF Thom at C Troop OP and Capt HW Sebag-Montefiore at D Troop OP. They engaged an enemy gun at 1520 hours. Meanwhile, the regiment had moved from Tawgin to another hide.

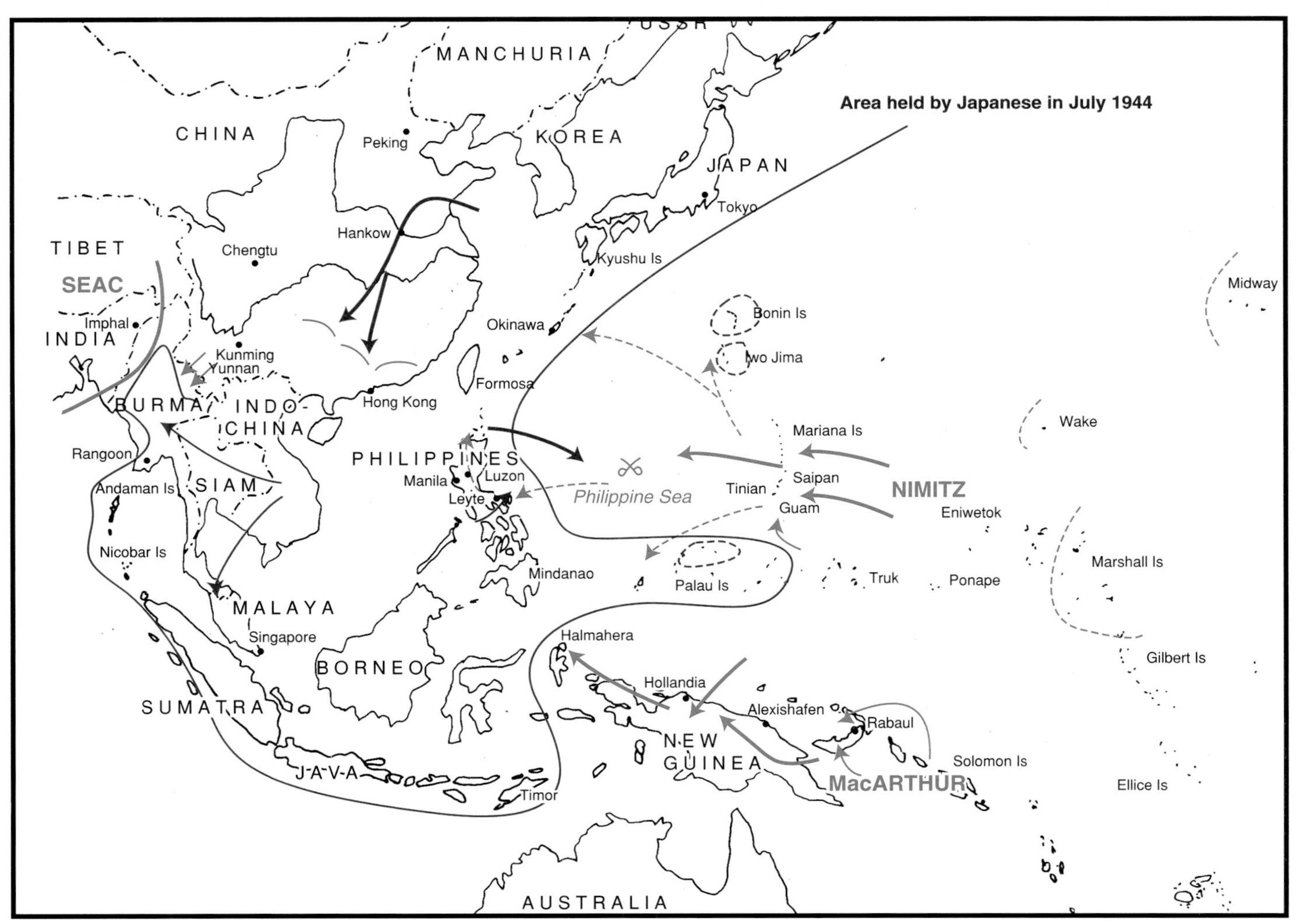

Map 41 Pacific Operations March-July 1944

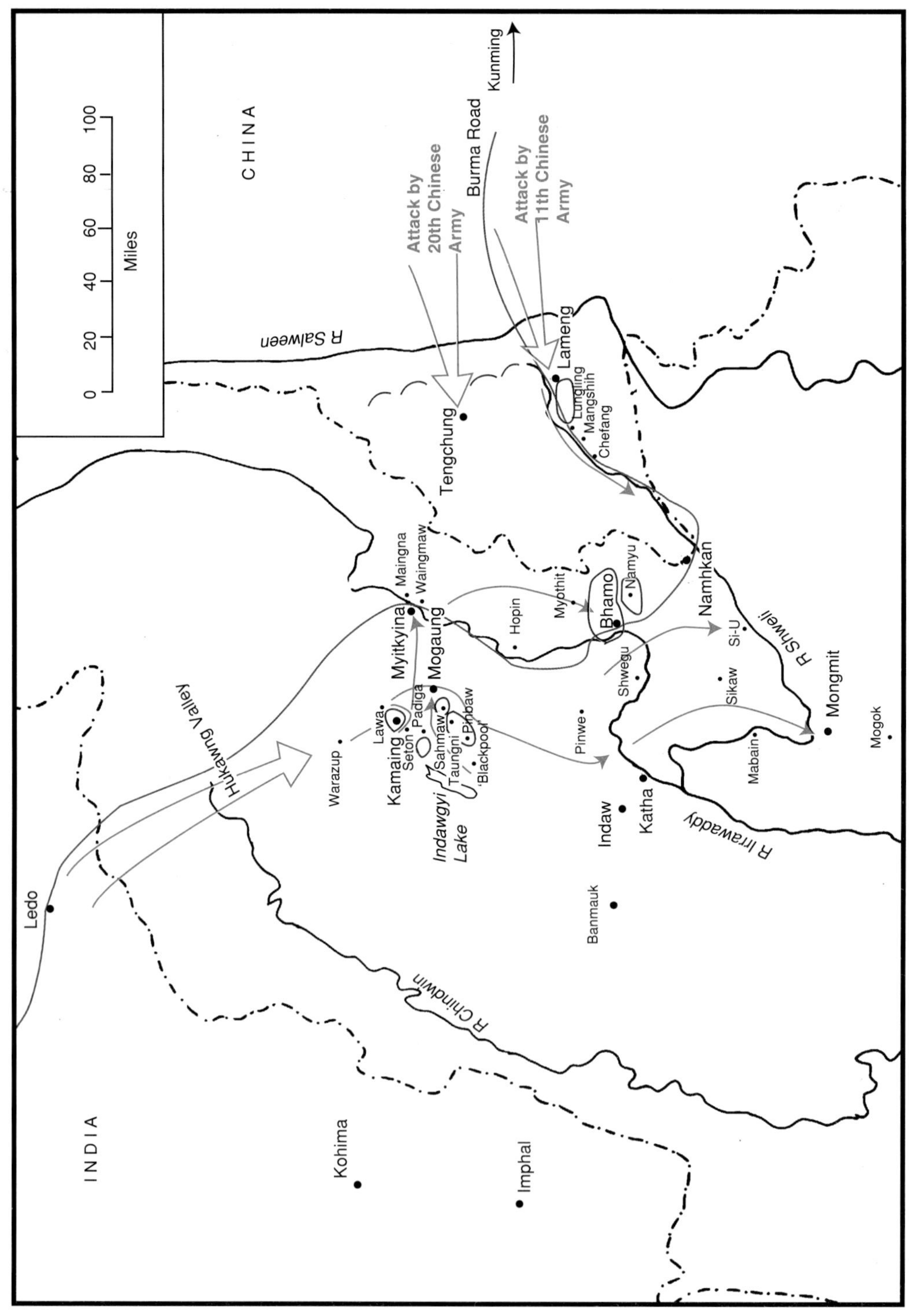

Map 42 The Chinese attack from Yunnan and Stilwell's and Chindits' capture of Mogaung and Myitkyina August 1944

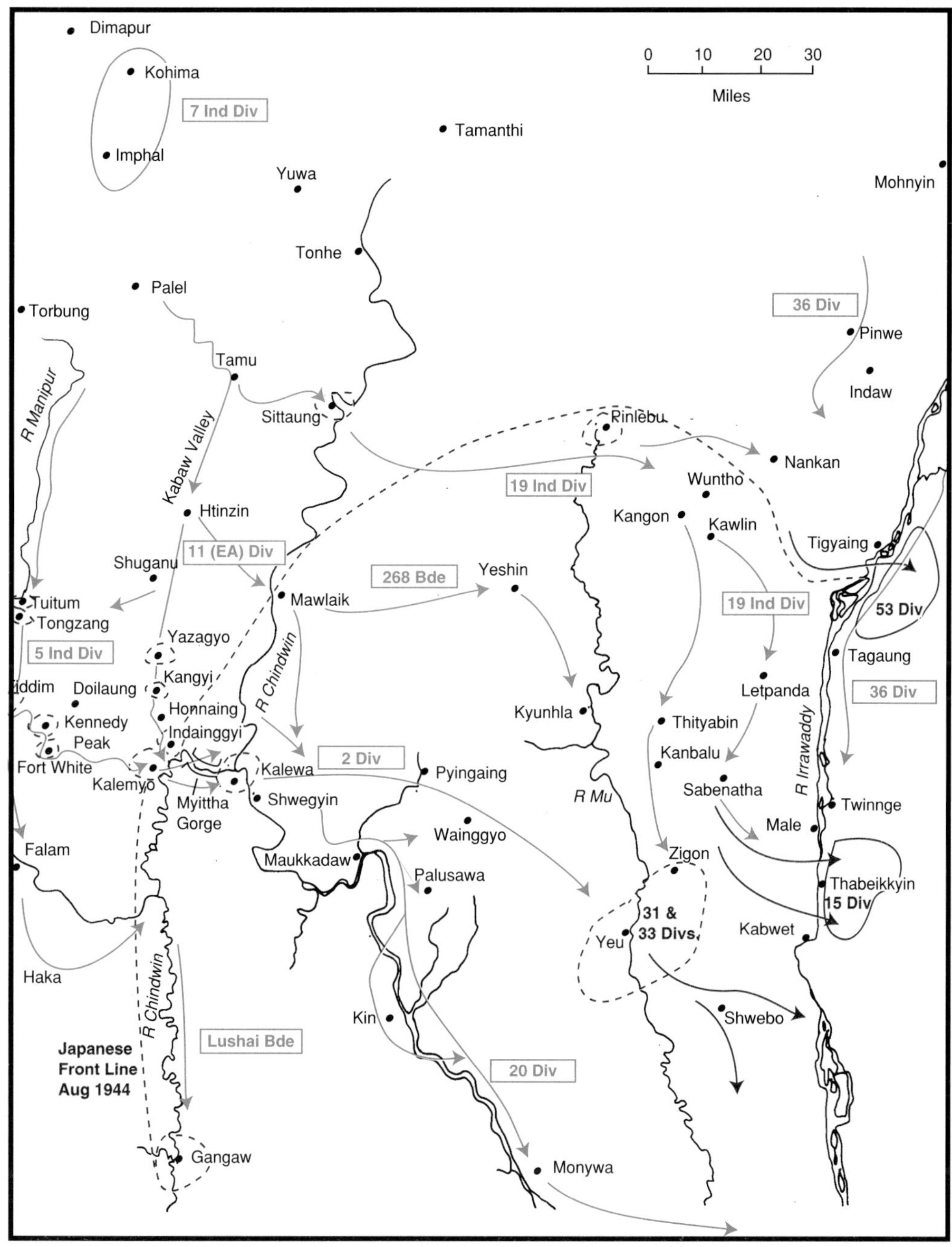

Map 43 Operations to clear enemy from west of the Chindwin and plans for the advance

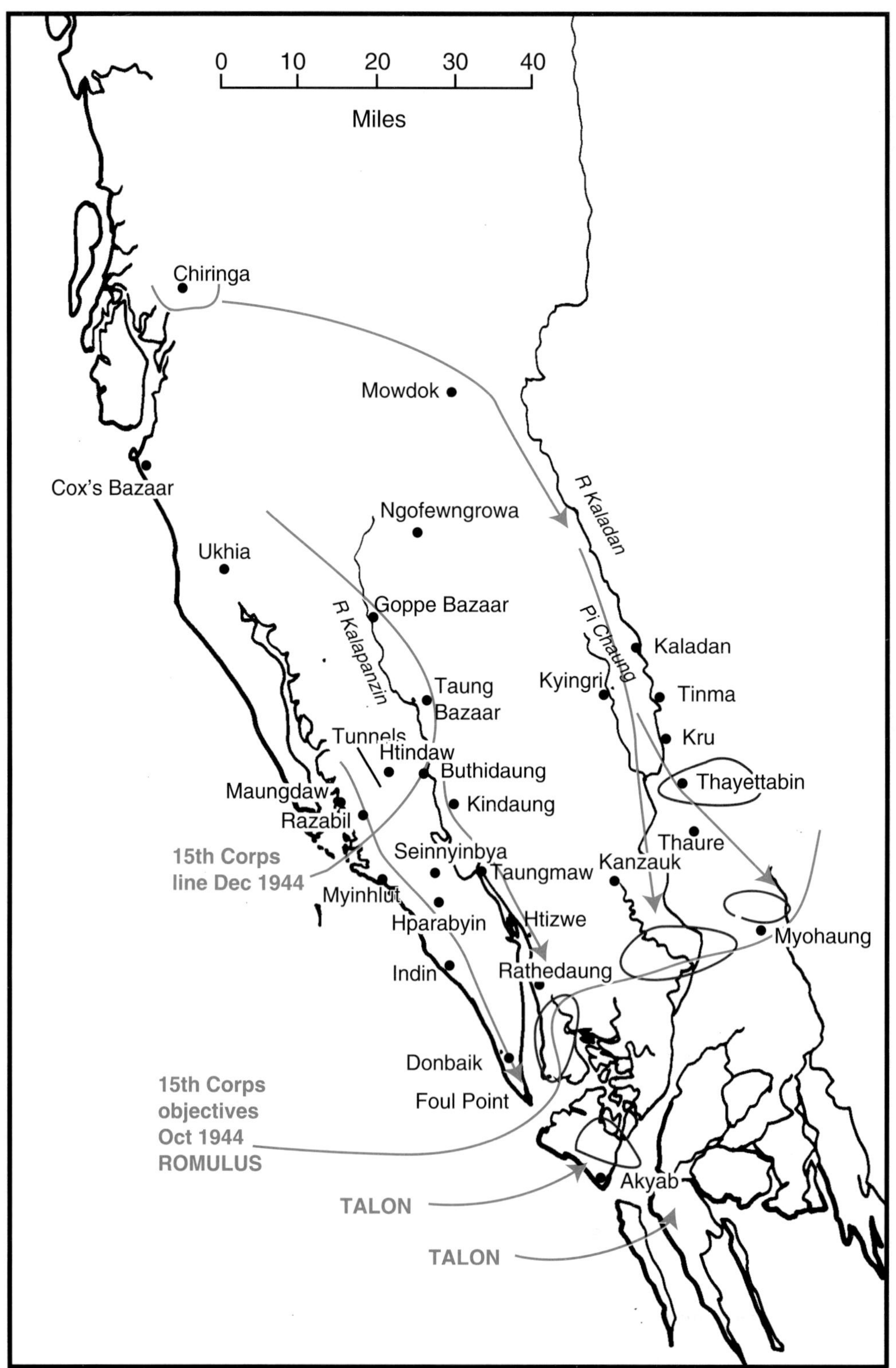

Map 44 Third Arakan, January 1945

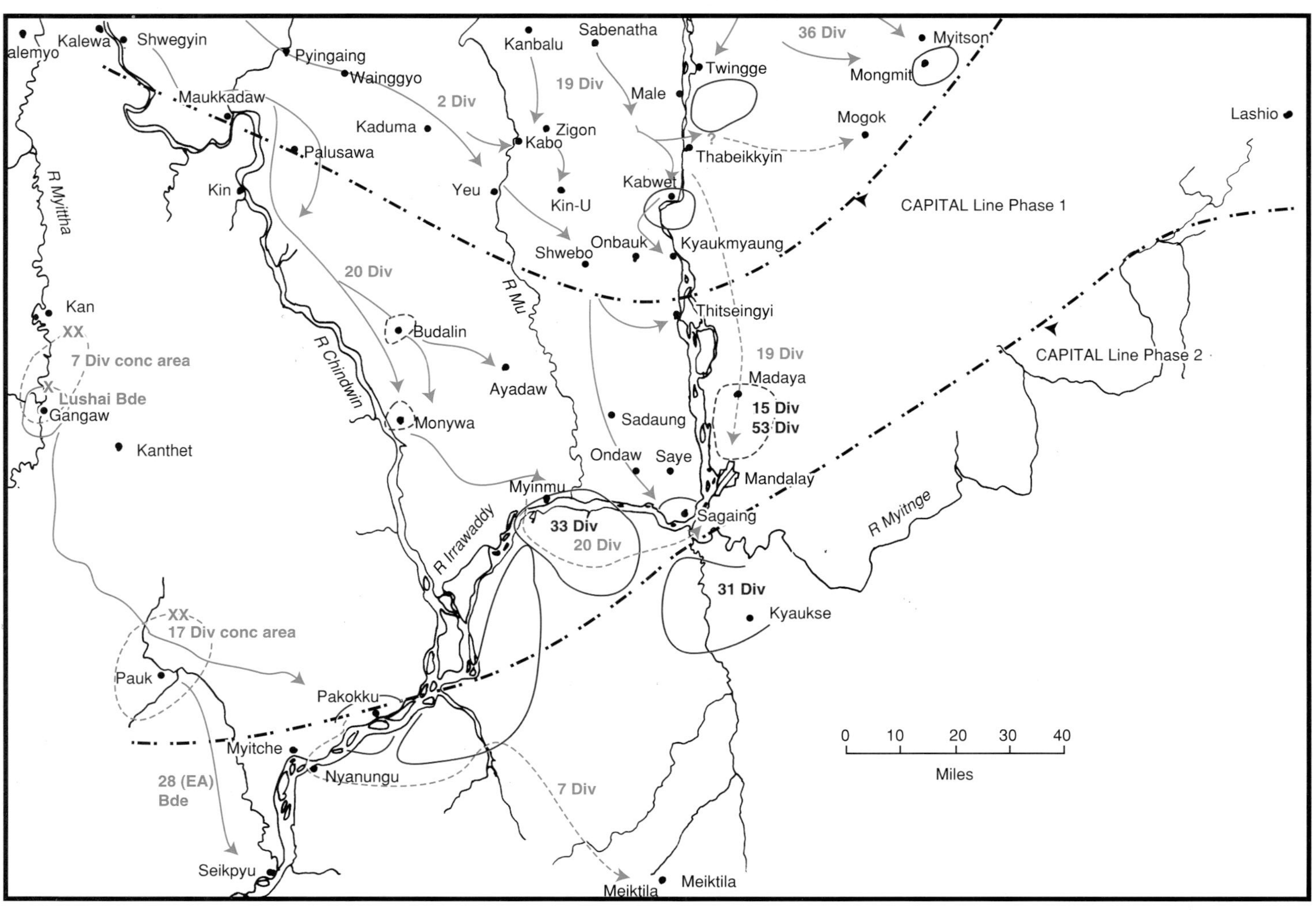

Map 45 The advance to the Irrawaddy December 1944 to January 1945

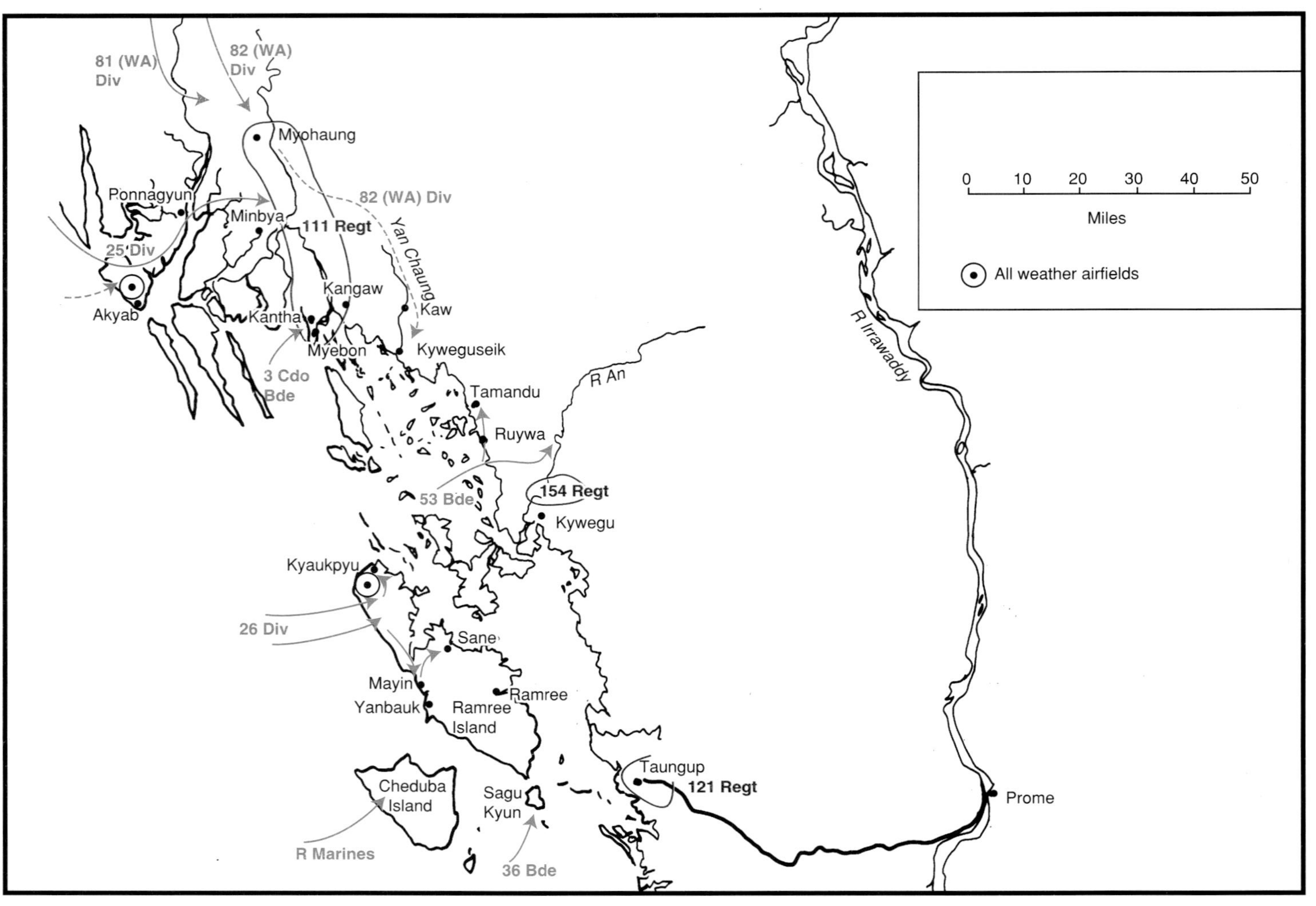

Map 46 Battles of South Arakan

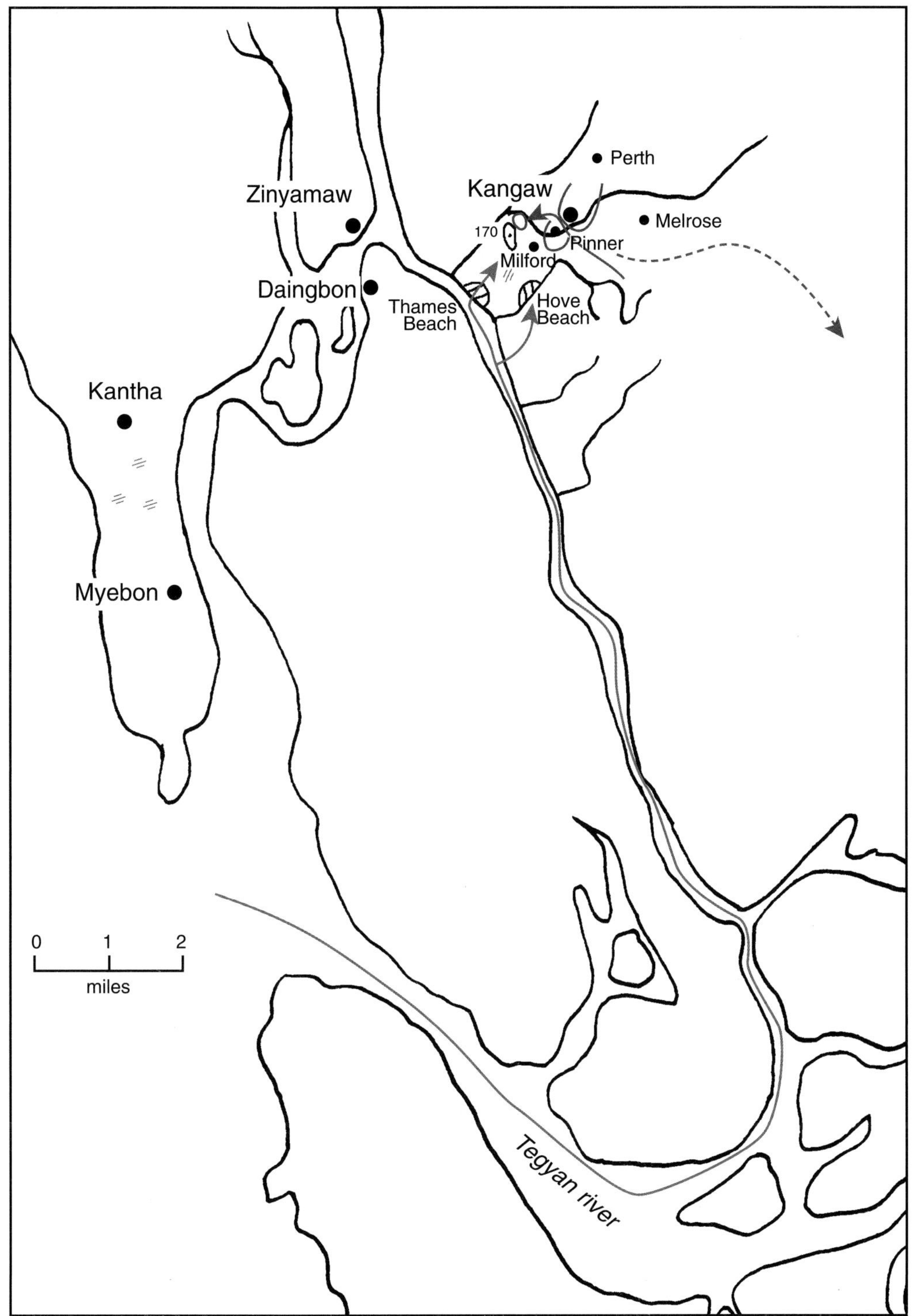

Map 47 Attack on Kangaw

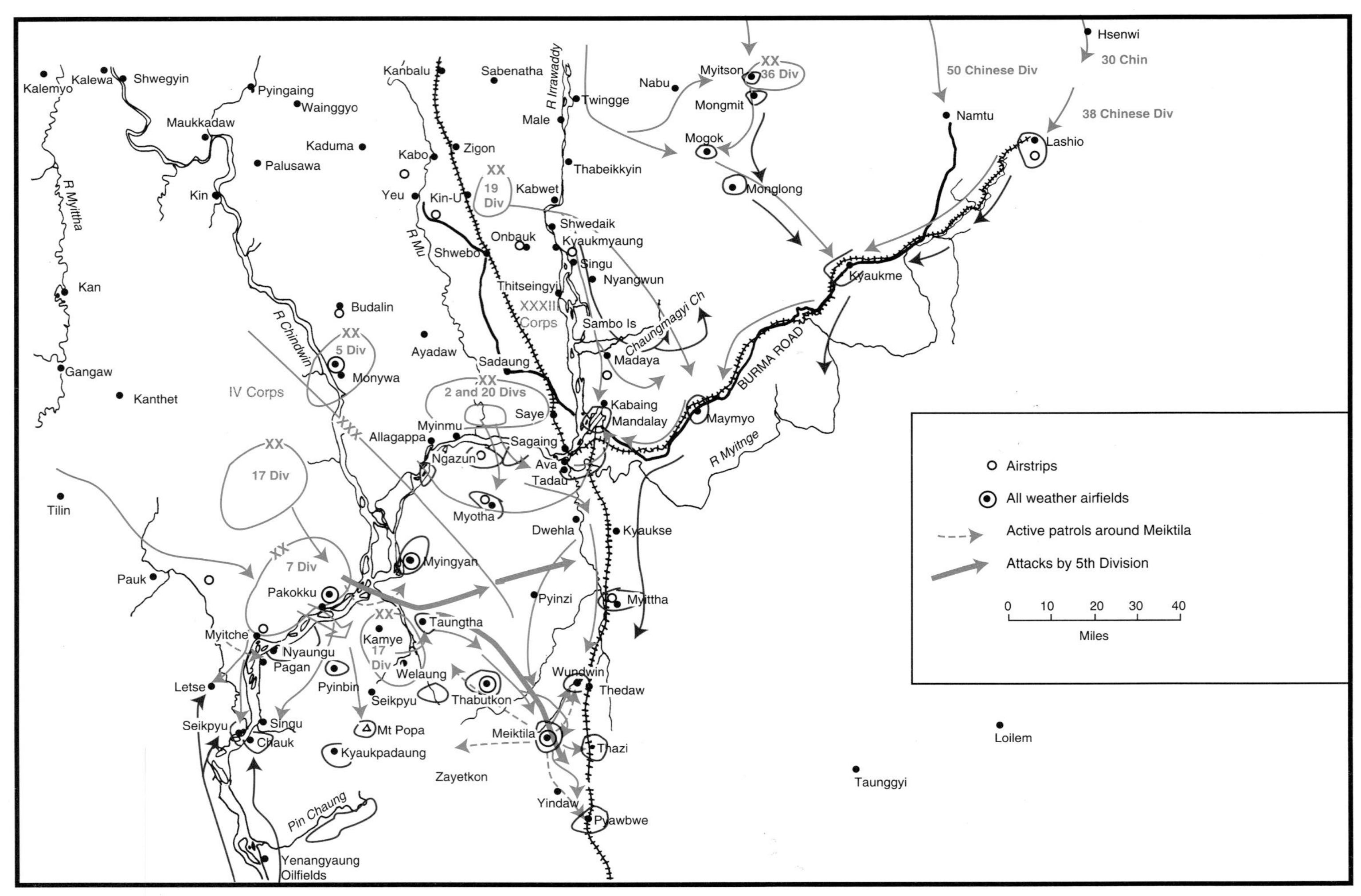
Airstrips
All weather airfields
Active patrols around Meiktila
Attacks by 5th Division
0 10 20 30 40
Miles
Hsenwi
30 Chin
50 Chinese Div
38 Chinese Div
Namtu
Lashio
Myitson
XX
36 Div
Nabu
Mongmit
Mogok
Monglong
Kyaukme
BURMA ROAD
Maymyo
R Myitnge
Kalemyo
Kalewa
Shwegyin
Pyingaing
Wainggyo
Maukkadaw
Kaduma
Palusawa
Kin
R Myittha
Kan
Gangaw
Kanthet
Tilin
Pauk
Budalin
XX
5 Div
Monywa
R Chindwin
IV Corps
XXX
Kanbalu
Sabenatha
R Irrawaddy
Twingge
Male
Zigon
Kabo
Yeu
Kin-U
XX
19 Div
Kabwet
Thabeikkyin
Shwedaik
Kyaukmyaung
Onbauk
Shwebo
R Mu
Singu
Nyangwun
Thitseingyi
XXXIII Corps
Sambo Is
Chaungmagyi Ch
Madaya
Ayadaw
Sadaung
XX
2 and 20 Divs
Saye
Kabaing
Mandalay
Myinmu
Allagappa
Sagaing
Ngazun
Ava
Tadau
Myotha
Dwehla
Kyaukse
Myittha
XX
17 Div
XX
7 Div
Pakokku
Myingyan
Pyinzi
Taungtha
XX
Kamye
17 Div
Welaung
Myitche
Nyaungu
Pagan
Pyinbin
Seikpyu
Thabutkon
Wundwin
Thedaw
Letse
Seikpyu
Singu
Chauk
Mt Popa
Kyaukpadaung
Meiktila
Thazi
Zayetkon
Yindaw
Pyawbwe
Pin Chaung
Yenangyaung Oilfields
Loilem
Taunggyi

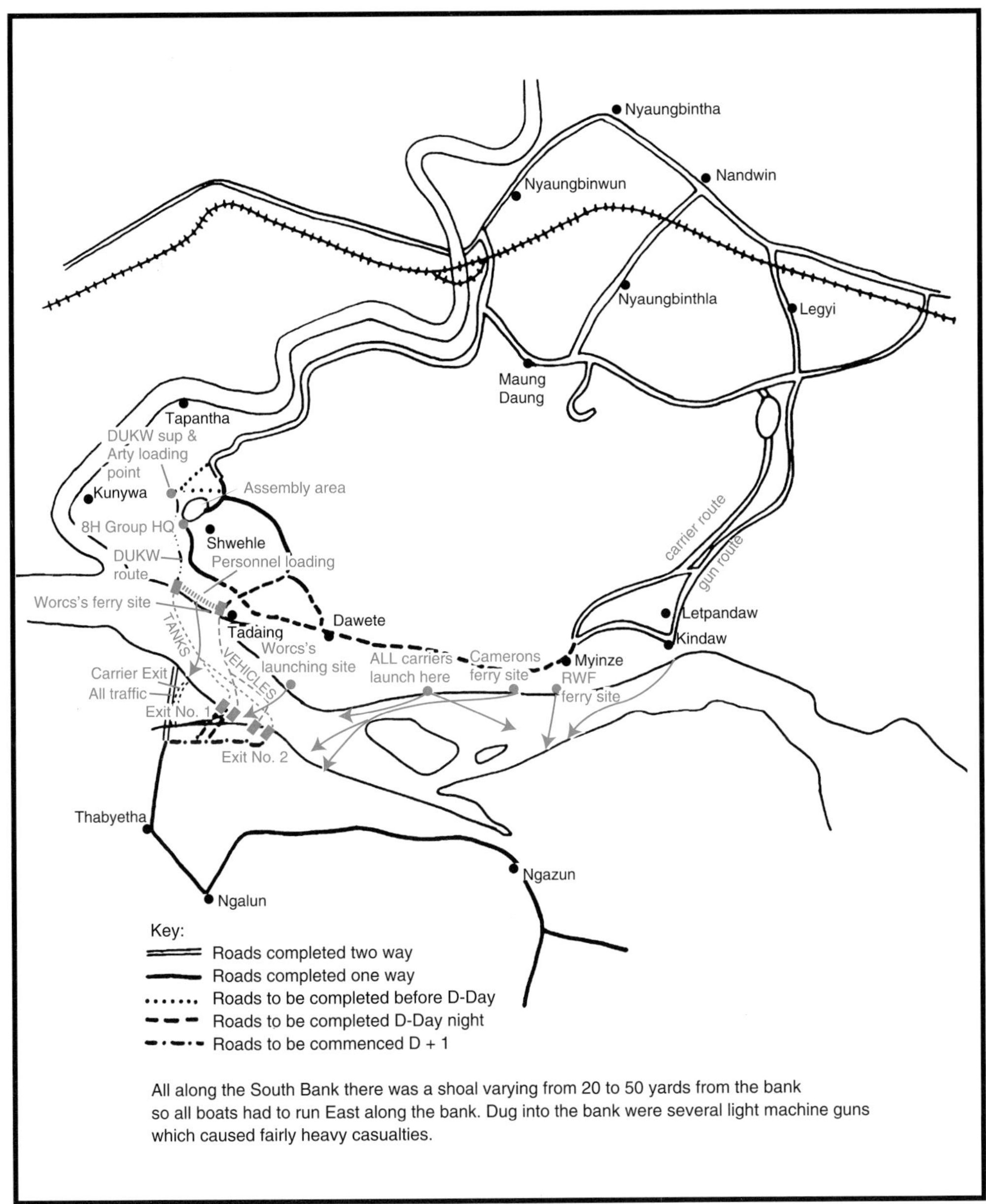

Map 48a 2nd Division: outline plan for the Irrawaddy Crossing, 25th February 1945
Taken from a sketch map now in the possession of 2nd Armoured Division.

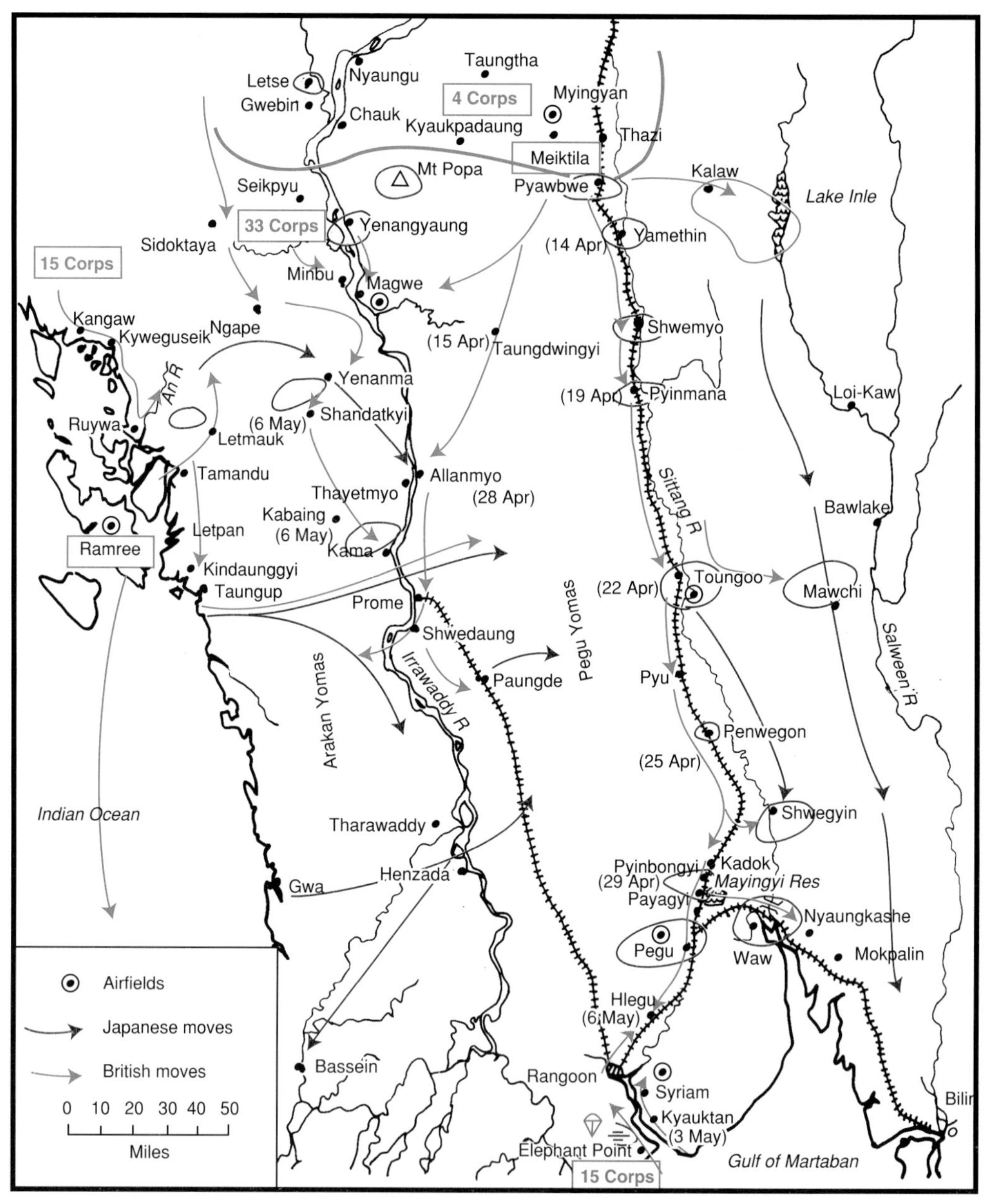

Map 49 The Battles of the Irawaddy and the Rangoon Road

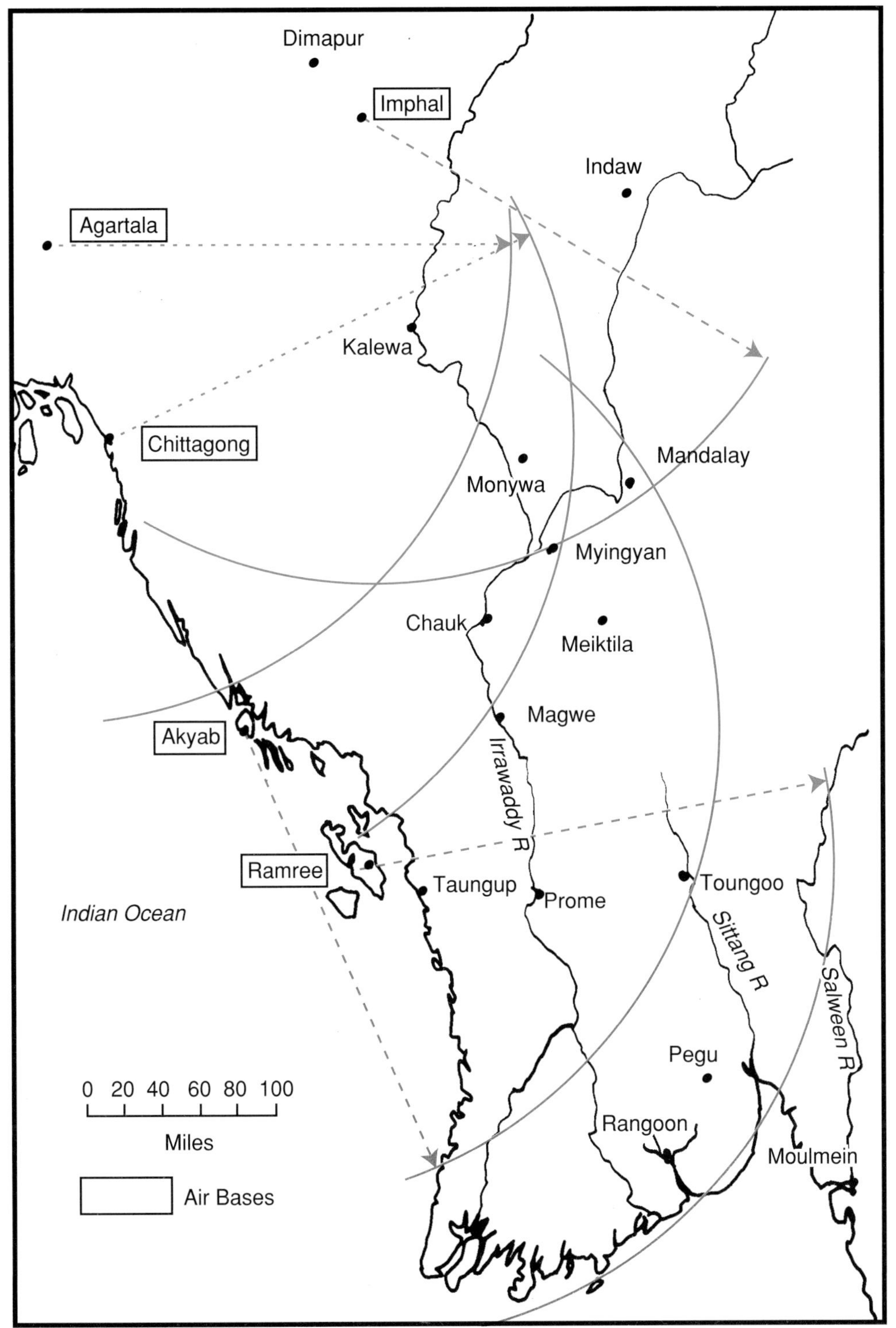

Map 50 Economic radius of transport aircraft from air bases

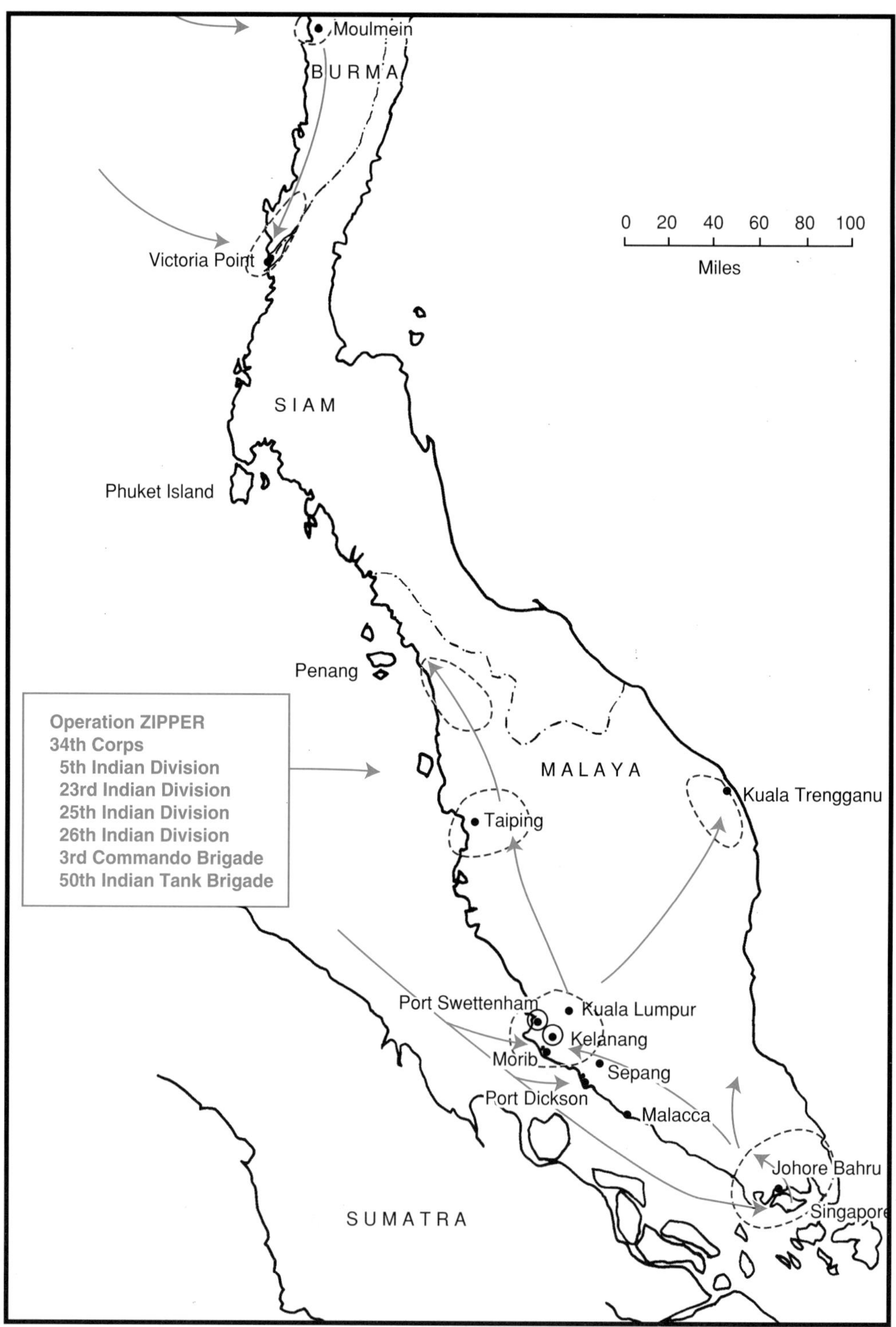

Map 51 The re-occupation of Malaya September 1945

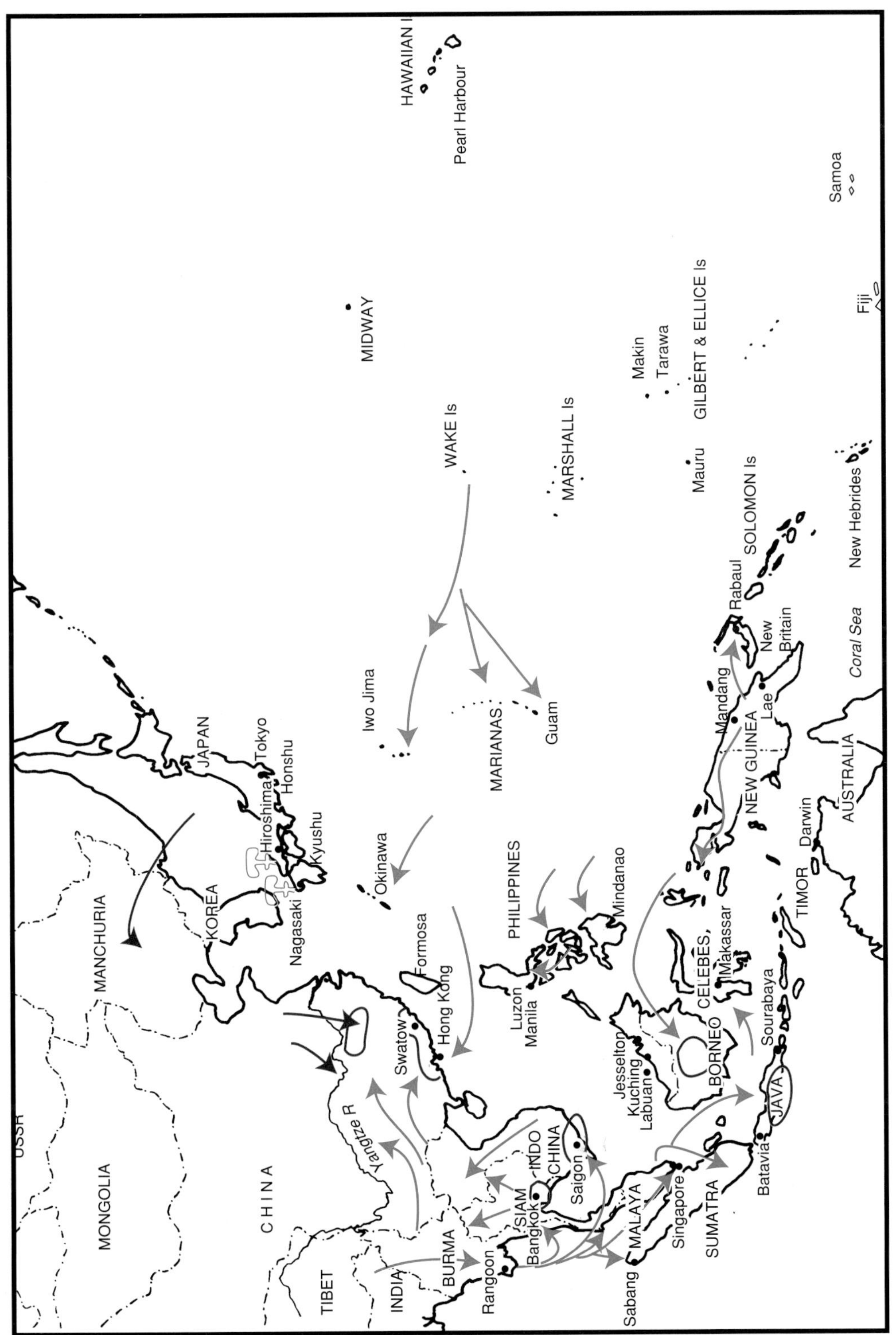

Map 52 The Pacific Theatre, the end of the War August/September 1945

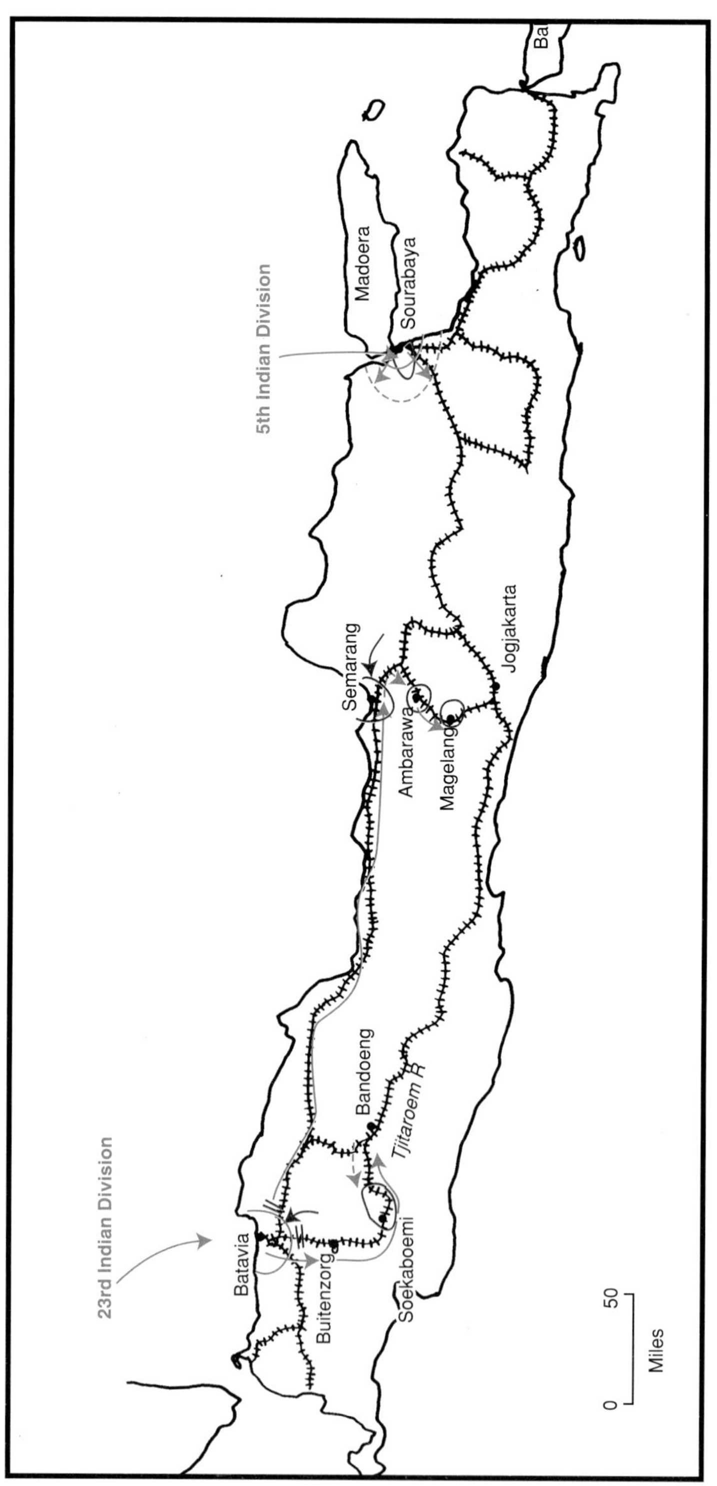

Map 53 Java 1945-46

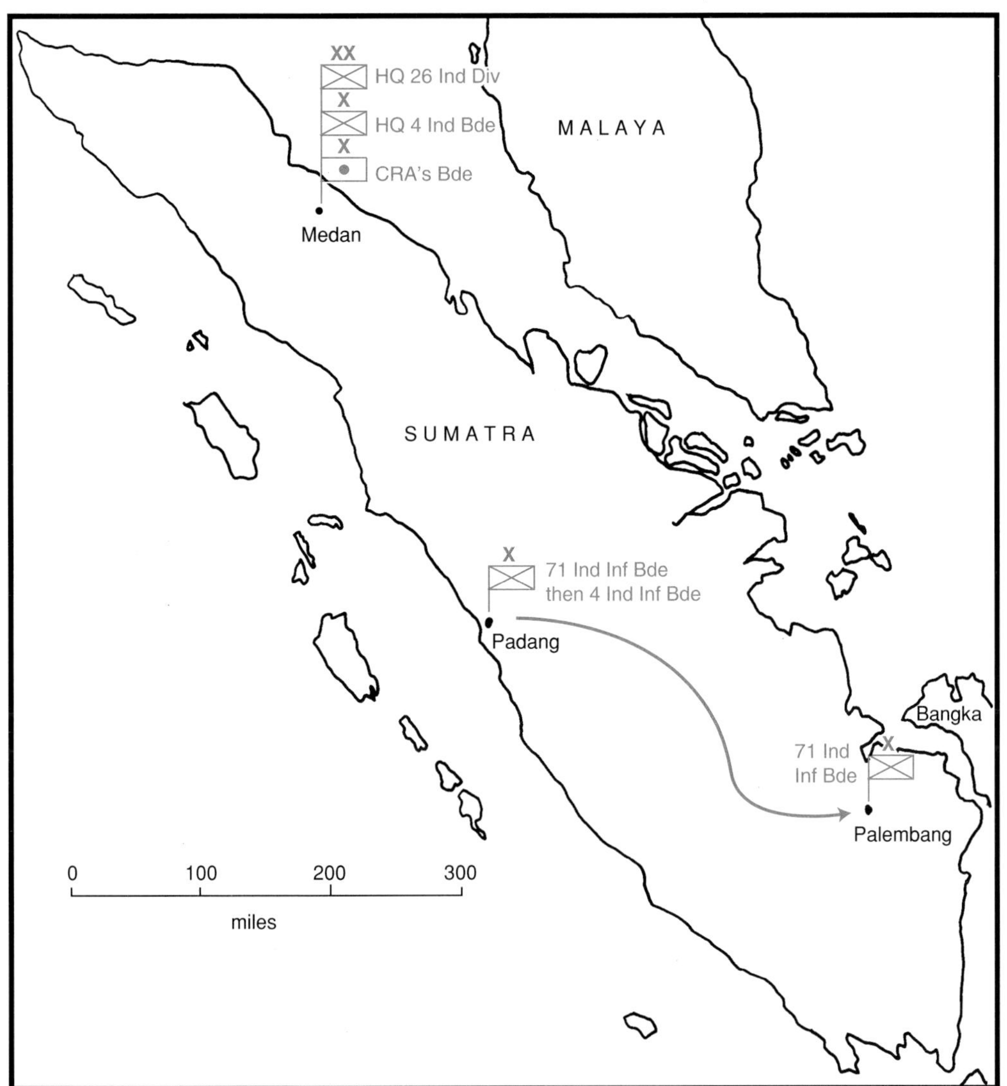

Map 54 Sumatra July 1946

4th January . . .an action occurred in which Capt JF Thom acted with great courage which led to his award of the Military Cross.' (White).

In his book *Straight On For Tokyo*, Lieutenant Colonel OGW White, CO of the Dorsets, writes: 'Just at that moment "A" Company came up on the set. It was the Gunner forward observation officer Jimmy Thom, from 99th Field Regiment, who gave me a reasonably clear picture of the situation on the left flank. "A" Company had advanced a certain way across the open when company headquarters and the rear platoon came under very heavy mortar fire from a position in a banana plantation to the east and slightly forward of Gun Copse. John Bowles had been killed instantly and this platoon (No 9) temporarily disorganised. The leading platoons (Nos 7 and 8) were, however, pushing on towards their objectives. I asked Jimmy Thom if he could command foot soldiers and receiving a reply to the effect that he would have a "bloody good try" I instructed him to take over "A" Company and press on. This remarkable yeoman of Buckinghamshire not only took over "A" Company and reorganised the reserve platoon, which had suffered some few casualties, but continued to direct his own guns and brought down most effective fire from his battery on the mortar position which had been so troublesome. For his gallant part in this battle Jimmy was awarded an immediate Military Cross. (quoted in White). Thom's citation concluded, 'Captain Thom displayed exceptional courage, cool judgement and outstanding leadership. By his personal example and energy in assuming command of a force other than of his own arm of service whilst still fighting his guns, he was undoubtedly instrumental in the success of the battalion attack.'

'A' Flight, 656 AOP Squadron, had the problem of supporting three divisions all in contact with the enemy. It arranged for No. 1 Section under Captain Frank McMath to work with 19th Indian Division, No. 2 Section under Captain Ted Maslen-Jones with 20th Indian Division and No. 3 Section under Captain 'Pip' Harrison with 2nd British Division leaving No 4 Section under Lieutenant Ian Walton to work with Headquarters 33rd Indian Corps.

By 16th January 99th Field Regiment moved through Shwegyin and Pyin-U to Sadaung (Map 45). The regiment was with 4th British Infantry Brigade but 472nd and 393rd Batteries were under 16th Field Regiment with Captain CP Richardson of 472nd Battery and Captain DJ Mayne of 393rd Battery as OPs for the attack on Wetthabok by the Norfolks. Major E Butler-Henderson and Captain Gibbings were also with the Norfolks. On the 24th 'D' Company came under heavy fire from a 75mm very close-by and were taking casualties. Captain Colin Richardson worked his way forward under heavy shell fire until he could see the gun and could shout fire orders to his signaller. He then brought down such effective fire that the gun was silenced and many lives were saved. For his gallantry in this action and on several other occasions he was awarded the Military Cross. His citation concludes, 'Captain Richardson displayed a high example of courage and sense of duty which was an inspiration to all men holding the feature and by his brave action was undoubtedly responsible for the saving of many lives.' Sadly this brave young officer was killed in action on 3rd February still doing his duty as FOO. 472nd Battery was then present with 16th Field Regiment in the attack on Ywathitgyi. After the air strikes and following the fireplan the two battery commanders of 393rd and 394th Batteries were advancing alongside 'B' and 'C' Company Commanders when Captain JOH Beamish was mortally wounded.

On 2nd February the Air OP registered targets to the east of the village of Ywathitgyi. The fireplan, fired by 10th, 16th and 99th Field Regiments, lasted for eight minutes and the whole area erupted in flames. The Royal Scots moved in with Major Bonsor, Captain Weatherby, Captain Thom and Captain Hazell all from the 99th Field Regiment providing the firepower. The attack was a complete success. During this attack Gunner J Saunders was OP Signaller with the OP Party accompanying 1st Royal Scots when his FOO was mortally wounded. He immediately evacuated him to a safe area in spite of heavy small arms fire. He then assumed the duties of FOO and brought down a most effective fireplan. 'His coolness under fire and his immediate assumption of the duties of a Gunner officer had a considerable influence on the course of the battle.' (From his citation for the Military Medal). It should be noted that Gunner Saunders had already served with great bravery on 'Garrison Hill' with an isolated platoon near the DC's Bungalow at Kohima when, in spite of being continuously sick with dysentery, he refused to leave his post at the OP.

99th Field Regiment was in continuous action, mainly with the Norfolks, clearing up enemy to the west of the Irrawaddy at Saye, Ywathitgyi and Byedayaw until its turn to cross the Irrawaddy came at the end of the month. On 16th February Lieutenants CC Prince, RDG Rigg, MR Gwynne-Howell and AH Nash joined the regiment.

The first task of 4th Indian Corps was to capture Pakokku, establish a bridgehead over the Irrawaddy and seize Meiktila, but it had major logistic problems. The road from Kalemyo to Pakokku, some 230 miles and the only route for administrative traffic, was unmetalled, narrow and tortuous, with many steep hills, hairpin bends and very weak bridges. Thus, to begin with, all maintenance had to be by air until the Sappers could open the route. 33rd Indian Corps was to capture the weir at Kabo intact as it controlled the vital water supply for operations on the plains. It was then to seize the Monywa - Yeu - Shwebo area and finally get across the Irrawaddy ready to attack Mandalay. It too would have to depend on air drops until airfields could be opened at Budalin, Yeu and Shwebo. Again the Sappers would have the major task of opening the route Kyigon - Yeu to establish a reliable forward maintenance area. Until that could be done maximum use would have to be made of river traffic from Kalewa to Shwegyin. Deception was to be a major part of the plan and orders were given out only on a need-to-know basis. It was particularly important to conceal the move of 7th Indian Division and strict radio silence was imposed within that formation as it advanced south of Kalemyo. Maximum use was made of line, jeeps and light aircraft. When 4th Indian Corps Headquarters moved forward, a dummy HQ was left behind which made some discreet security slips on the radio indicating that it had not in fact moved at all. The ruse was successful.

Within 33rd Indian Corps, 20th Indian Division was to capture Monywa and be ready to cross the Irrawaddy and attack Mandalay from the south. In the centre 2nd British Division with 19th Indian Division on its left was to capture the Kabo Weir, advance and capture the airfields at Yeu and Shwebo and prepare to attack Mandalay from the north. Between these two divisions was 268th Independent Indian Infantry Brigade. 254th Indian Tank Brigade was to follow up as soon as the road conditions allowed. The first task for the Sappers was to open the road to Kan so that tanks and guns could be got forward to the Lushai Brigade. 7th Indian Divisional Engineers were reinforced by an AGRE and set to work. The tanks were at this time concentrated at Witok. 136th Field Regiment arrived as soon as the road was open and on 10th January 1945 the attack on Gangaw began. 347th Battery put down yellow smoke for the air attacks ranged by the Air OP. After heavy air and artillery attacks the Lushai Brigade captured the village and soon, in great secrecy, 7th Indian Division was concentrated in the Gangaw area. 'One most interesting effect produced by the advent of the 25 pr was the confidence it gave the local villager. Streams of information poured in as soon as the guns had made themselves heard, and it proved to be good information. Evidently in the eyes of the Burman the presence of field guns means the British have come to stay, and it is not another fly-by-night Wingate column.' (Lt Col GR Armstrong, Monthly News Letter for January 1945).

'After four years of training since Dunkirk, the regiment was off at last . . . In the [19th] Divisional Area, from Tamu northwards, there was no road to the river bank for MT or guns. The Infantry and 26th Indian Mountain Battery, supporting 62 Brigade, were soon over the Chindwin going hard after the Jap. "No road for the Guns? - well make one" and we did. . . Officers and men of 115 Fld., 33 A/Tk. and 4 Ind Fd Regts, dug, drilled, blasted and bulldozed, working in reliefs at high pressure. Twelve days later, Harry Lees (BC 239 Bty) got the first 25-pr over the road, crossing the Chindwin with his battery on Dec. 7. Infantry from 98 (Indian Infantry) Bde made four miles, the Gunners eight, and General "Pete" Rees in expressing his gratitude and praise ordered the road to be called "Gunner Way."

Over the road, across the 500 yard wide Chindwin went the guns of the Div Arty on the three ramshackle rafts available, to catch up the Infantry.

Eastwards through Le-U, Kya-In, Sinlanaung, Pinbon then SE through Pinlebu, Kawlin, we drove, moving every day, and in our "spare" time clearing strips for AOPs and Dropping Zones for food and P.O.L., ferrying infantry and acquiring and repairing sufficient Jap vehicles to make us 100% mobile.' ('The March of 115th Field Regiment').

20th Indian Division reached Maukkadaw on 26th December and headed for Wainggyo and Palusawa where it made contact with the enemy. Meanwhile 6th British Infantry Brigade, followed by 5th, both of 2nd Division, had reached Pyingaing on the 24th. 268th Independent Indian Infantry Brigade was at Yeshin with patrols out as far as Kyunhla by 26th December. On the same day 19th Indian Division was on a line Thityabin - Letpanda where it met increasing opposition from *31st Division*, the old enemy at Kohima, who fought like tigers to cover the withdrawal of *15th Division* across the Irrawaddy. But by the 29th Kanbalu and Sabanatha were secured and by 5th January the division was on the Zigon - Male road. It was at Zigon on the 26th that 115th Field Regiment, under Lieutenant Colonel RAG Nicholson, whose brother was commanding 2nd Division, reported that its 239th Field Battery had fired the regiment's first rounds in anger since leaving Dunkirk. It had then pushed on, leapfrogging forward by batteries, constantly in action against enemy rearguards. Ammunition was always short because it all had to be dropped from the air. 'Late on Jan 3rd the CO, leading OP Parties, got ahead of the leading Infantry [4/4th Gurkha Rifles]. His jeep was suddenly brought to a halt by machine gun fire at 20 yds range from the Sindawchaung. Thanks to an improvised bullet proof "windscreen" of teak and bricks, the CO, batman and driver were able to retaliate with Stens and grenades. Gnr FD Alderson, batman, by unhooking the trailer regardless of enemy fire, enabled the jeep to reverse, narrowly missing a mine. A fine GF Target then presented itself to 240 Bty. The shoot was so ably conducted by Major K Walker that the Jap position was completely smashed by the time the leading Gurkhas arrived. Jap flags were subsequently presented by them to the CO and Major Walker, and Alderson received the MM.' ('The March of 115th Field Regiment').

With the objective of Shwebo and the Irrawaddy, the regiment advanced pushing the enemy until it reached Kin-U on 7th January. 'Captain T Hubbard, 480 Bty, was severely wounded while directing the fire of a section of 25 prs which had been brought up to within 700 yards of a Jap position [supporting the leading company of 2nd Berkshires]. Capt Hubbard, while endeavouring to pin-point the enemy MGs engaged and destroyed an enemy post with grenades. He was later rescued by his Major, Robin Winchester, in a carrier and was awarded the MC for this and previous gallant actions.' ('The March of 115th Field Regiment') The sudden appearance of this rapid and accurate fire soon cleared the enemy from the Kin-U cross-roads and the advance continued.

Further south, 20th Indian Division hit very bad country, re-crossed the Chindwin, moved down the west bank to Kan, crossed back over the river and started its advance on Monywa. 32nd Indian Infantry Brigade hit strong enemy positions at Budalin and in heavy rain cleared them after some tough fighting on 10th January. Ted Maslen-Jones of 'A' Flight, 656 AOP Squadron briefed Hurri-bombers for this attack and ranged the guns of 9th Field Regiment at the same time. The Hurri-bombers were effective and left the town burning. The guns did the rest, with the infantry mopping up. 32nd Indian Infantry Brigade then set out for Monywa which it reached on 14th

January. 100th Indian Infantry Brigade was directed at Ayadaw, with 80th Indian Infantry Brigade following in reserve.

2nd British Division captured Pyingaing on 28th December, 6th British Infantry Brigade raced off to Kaduma and sent 1st Royal Welch Fusiliers, with some tanks and Sappers, to seize the Kabo Weir which was captured intact. The divisional reconnaissance battalion captured the airfield at Yeu which was soon brought in to use. 5th British Infantry Brigade passed into the lead and occupied Yeu against sniping and shell fire. The retreating Japanese blew the bridge over the Mu river but a Bailey bridge was soon emplaced by the Sappers to enable the advance to continue. On 5th January 1945 Stopford ordered 2nd British Division to attack Shwebo, while 19th Indian Division was to occupy Kin-U and Kabwet and simulate a main crossing of the Irrawaddy at Thabeikkyin. Having crossed, it was to advance to Mogok. Nicholson sent 4th British Infantry Brigade down the Yeu - Shwebo road to block the western outskirts of Shwebo itself, while 5th British Infantry Brigade attacked the walled town from the north. 6th British Infantry Brigade remained in reserve at Yeu. Meanwhile Rees sent his 98th Indian Infantry Brigade to capture the airfield to the east of the town and his 64th Indian Infantry Brigade to seize the airfield at Onbauk and then to cut off the town from the south, while 62nd Indian Infantry Brigade was sent to capture Thabeikkyin. The fighting was very hard against the last remnants of *15th Division* but all objectives were seized by 7th January. By the 9th Shwebo was occupied by 5th British Infantry Brigade but part of the garrison escaped. Meanwhile 19th Indian Infantry Division captured Kyaukmyaung and got a battalion across the Irrawaddy during the night. The separate parts of 14th Army were by then working well together at the operational level and all arms and services were functioning as a team but it had taken over three years of combat and many casualties to achieve this standard.

It was at Kyaukmyaung that Captain DK Payne of 33rd Anti-Tank Regiment crossed the Irrawaddy in a rubber boat after dark to act as OP for the regiment's 12 mortars. He had with him Sergeant Gillingham, Bombardier Wright and Gunners Cowan and Woollard and a No. 48 radio set. Once across they joined 3/6th Rajputana Rifles. They made a sangar on the top of the hard rocky 'Pear Hill' and registered DF within 25 yards of the wire. There was an OP from a mountain regiment there too. On the first night they were shelled very heavily. This shelling was confirmed by SEAC as some of the heaviest so far in the Burma campaign. The regiment's own guns replied and it was here that it learned of the Japanese trick of synchronising their own time of flight with its own guns firing to give the impression that our shells were dropping short; for a while it believed them! That night too there were 'jitter parties' right up to the wire. 'The second night we were attacked with great ferocity by infantry but 33rd Regiment's mortars and the Raj Rifs together chased them off with heavy casualties. The third night there was a repeat of the shelling and another even bigger assault. The infantry company commander asked the OPO to bring the DF closer. The latter pointed out the danger and company commander accepted it, but the Japanese kept coming. All the OPO could do next was to drop his regiment's mortar bombs on his own OP. It worked and the enemy fled though the OPO's radio was put out of action by his own fire, but the OP party all survived. The attacks went on for several days, getting weaker and weaker, and it seemed that the Japanese had no flexibility. The OP party became very tired and dirty but eventually were relieved.' (from an account attached to 33rd Anti-Tank Regiment Diaries). 33rd Anti-Tank Regiment reported at length on the 3-inch mortar in action. Normal ammunition could reach 1,600 yards and with Super Charge, 2800 yards, but Super Charge produced very big safety zones. The regiment, originally a Liverpool LAA unit, consisted of 78th, 274th and 275th Anti-Tank Batteries and was commanded by Lieutenant Colonel CL Overton.

Both 19th and 20th Indian Divisions began to prepare for the main crossing of the mighty Irrawaddy. It was here that enemy aircraft attacked in larger numbers than had been seen for some time and destroyed a number of Dakotas on the ground. Landings had to be restricted to night-time only until 15th January. 99th Field Regiment lost some vehicles and suffered some casualties from these attacks. Further south a strong enemy position was located between Monywa and Ayadaw stretching to the Sagaing hills. On 19th January, 4th Indian Corps began its move forwards. It was to capture Pakokku, cross the Irrawaddy and then seize Meiktila, 28th (EA) Infantry Brigade was leading to mask the presence of 7th Indian Division behind it. 114th Indian Infantry Brigade was their lead brigade moving behind 28th (EA) Infantry Brigade with 89th Indian Infantry Brigade, 23rd Mountain Battery and a platoon of 62nd Field Company Madras Sappers and Miners, directed at Pauk by way of Kanthet. 'The move forward, known to the Gunners as the Irrawaddy Handicap, and described as "a most enjoyable and hectic drill order with a real enemy", lasted eleven days. . . The leading battery of guns was always accompanied by an anti-tank troop and an engineer platoon in mechanical transport to make diversions, lift mines, strengthen bridges and clear road-blocks, while other artillery and engineer reconnaissance parties accompanied the leading infantry, the former to note gun positions and air OP landing strips well ahead, the latter to estimate engineer requirements and look for and mark mined areas and water points.' (Roberts). 'By the end of the first week in February,' reports Ted Maslen-Jones, 'we had recorded all the main features on 20 Division's potential bridgehead which included strategic villages and road intersections on a wide front. The largest village, called Kalaywa, was opposite the proposed crossing point at Myinmu.' Tactical headquarters was at Allagappa and a good landing strip was found nearby. By this time Tactical Headquarters 14th Army was at Nandaw with Headquarters 656 AOP Squadron alongside.

By 3rd February 7th Indian Division was well past Tilin, with 114th Indian Infantry Brigade directed at Pakokku. '347 Bty were detached on Feb 1 and sent off with 28 EA Bde in 2 columns against Seikpyu. They have just returned after a most exciting three weeks and have had plenty of good targets. The brigade were simulating a division and drew that Jap 49 Div on to them in some force. The Jap attacked company positions very strongly and OPs had narrow escapes bringing down closer and closer DFs to get the infantry out. (Lt Col GR Armstrong's Monthly News Letter for February to the MGRA India).

17th Indian Division was told to prepare for a crossing of the Irrawaddy at Nyaungu and was then to move into the Pauk - Kan area. Slim realised that once across the Irrawaddy it would be the dry season and there would be little water for animals, however the going would improve for tanks and vehicles, thus he wanted to get as many vehicles forward as the roads and air lift would permit. He wanted to get a force into Meiktila to cut off the Japanese in Mandalay and seize their supply dumps, but he did not want the enemy to realise what was happening. This was to be done by 17th Indian Division passing through 7th Indian Division once they were across the river. Indeed the advance of 17th Indian Division remained undiscovered by the Japanese. Slim set a target date of 8th February for 4th Indian Corps to cross the Irrawaddy.

The advance of 33rd Indian Corps had been so fast that it began to outrun its supplies and a pause was ordered to allow them to catch up. Stopford changed his plan slightly, ordering 2nd British Division to attack Sagaing while 19th and 20th Indian Divisions attacked Mandalay from the north and west respectively. On 16th January Slim warned that there were signs of a Japanese counter-offensive and ordered 20th Indian Division to capture Monywa and then Myinmu as soon as possible. It was to take under command 7th Indian Light Cavalry, with its light tanks, part of 11th Indian Cavalry in a reconnaissance role, a troop of 1st Medium Regiment and 101st HAA Regiment, less a battery, for use in long range attack. 2nd British Division took under command the Carabiniers, with their medium tanks, and another troop of 1st Medium Regiment. Finally 19th Indian Division took under command a squadron of 11th Indian Cavalry, one battery 1st Medium Regiment and one battery 101st HAA Regiment, also being employed in the ground role. 150th Regiment RAC, 268th Indian Infantry Brigade and a troop of 7.2-inch howitzers were to remain in corps reserve.

By 17th January 20th Indian Division had 100th Indian Infantry Brigade in Ayadaw while 32nd and 80th Indian Infantry Brigades had surrounded Monywa by the 19th. By the 22nd it had been taken, leading elements had reached the Irrawaddy at Myinmu and many Japanese were lost trying to escape across the river. 2nd British Division seized Sadaung and captured Ondaw on 24th January. Its patrols reached the Mu river and met up with those of 20th Indian Division, Captain HW Sebag-Montefiore of 99th Field Regiment making one of the first contacts. On 31st January, 4th British Infantry Brigade with tanks and artillery began its attack on Sagaing and Saye while 5th British Infantry Brigade hit enemy positions at Thitseingyi. Meanwhile 19th Indian Infantry Division was consolidating bridgeheads over the Irrawaddy at Thabeikkyin and Kyaukmyaung. Further north the Japanese still had a bridgehead on the west bank of the river at Kabwet. It was here, on 10th January, that 275th Anti-Tank Battery and 'F' Troop 207th LAA Battery were part of a subsidiary crossing at Thabeikkyin which involved the elimination of an enemy bridgehead on the west bank at Kabwet. Captain APL Tottenham of 239th Field Battery penetrated 5,000 yards as an FOO behind enemy lines to good effect on this occasion.

98th Indian Infantry Brigade reinforced by one squadron of 11th PAVO Cavalry, 1st Medium Regiment, 240th Field Battery and one troop of 33rd Anti-Tank Regiment, set off to deal with the Japanese bridgehead. It was here that 'D' Troop 22nd Battery of 1st Medium Regiment found themselves in full view of the enemy and engaged two bunkers with the GPO acting as observer. They scored several hits, then the GPO corrected his fire and landed a round right inside a bunker. Both were destroyed. After heavy aerial and artillery attacks and some tough fighting which cost the Royal Berkshires over 100 casualties, the Japanese had had enough and pulled out. At Kyaukmyaung 62nd Indian Infantry Brigade was six battalions strong but had to fight hard to defend its bridgehead which, after much hand-to-hand combat, it did.

115th Field Regiment report this same incident as follows, 'After meeting 2 Div at Shwebo on Jan 10 1945, 19 Div. began the battle for the crossing of the Irrawaddy between Seiktha and Singu. 98 Bde Group, including 115 Fd Regt, 275 A/Tk Bty and FTp 207 Bty LAA carried out a subsidiary crossing at Thabeikkyin, 25 miles up-stream and were also involved in eliminating the enemy bridge-head on the West Bank at Kabwet. Ammunition for the operations being limited to 8 rpg per day, recourse was again made to use of guns in a direct fire role combined with air support. 25 prs, 6 prs, 5.5s and LAA guns were all used in this role at both places, destroying effectively those bunkers left untouched by aerial bombardment. The LAA Tp also brought down one aircraft in the only Jap air attack at Thabeikkyin. A "Counter-Gun" patrol led by Capt. APL Tottenham, 239 Bty, penetrated 5000 yards behind the Jap lines in an attempt which, though unsuccessful, was a fine example of endurance, courage and skill.' ('The March of 115th Field Regiment').

By 1st February the Japanese were all behind the Irrawaddy and preparing their positions. Because 19th Indian Division had two bridgeheads at brigade strength at Thabeikkyin and Kyaukmyaung, Lieutenant General S Katamura, commanding *15th Army*, was convinced that this was where the main crossings would be and that subsequent operations would link up with 36th British Division north of Mongmit. He therefore ordered *53rd Division* to assemble at Madaya and contain and destroy these two bridgeheads with the aid of *15th Division*. These were, however, no longer divisions as such, they had suffered appalling casualties and in the end he had to send both together, and together they failed. Katamura then realised that 14th Army might cross further south and broke off these operations, ordering *53rd Division* to join *31st Division* around Kyaukse. *33rd Division* was around Myinmu. He was very much on the defensive. It was at this stage that *Southern Army Headquarters* ordered *2nd Division* and *5th Air Division* to Indo-China. This was to have dire effects on Japanese operations in Burma.

By 1st February 1945 14th Army was up to the Irrawaddy from Myitche to Thabeikkyin but there were two Japanese enclaves at Pakokku and Sagaing which were about to be attacked by 7th Indian and 2nd British Divisions respectively. Both 7th and 20th Indian Divisions were planning assault crossings and 19th Indian Division was strengthening its two crossings to the north. 17th Indian Division reinforced with armour was poised to strike towards Meiktila. Slim had gained the initiative and, with his great air superiority, he was able to strike wherever he wanted on a 200 mile front.

On the northern front (Maps 42 and 45) General Sultan's plan had to be changed when 14th and 22nd Chinese Divisions returned to China. He decided to leave 36th British Division to advance down the east side of the Irrawaddy towards Myitson. 50th Chinese Division moved to Si-u to relieve 475th US Infantry Regiment which in turn went further east to cut the old Burma Road at Namhpakka with the rest of Mars Force. 30th and 38th Chinese Divisions were ordered to move at once and capture Namhkam. By late December 1944 the forward brigades of 36th British Division had reached Tagaung on the Irrawaddy and Kunchaung on the Shweli without meeting opposition. Pressure was put on 11th Chinese (Yunnan) Army to seize Wanting but it was very reluctant to move forward from Chefang. However, by mid-January, it moved as required. It by-passed Wanting and met stiff opposition at Mongyu. After a hard fight it forced all Japanese back to Namhpakka. By this time 1st Chinese Army had surrounded Namhkam and General Honda, commanding *33rd Army*, recognised the threat developing to his left flank from 36th British Division and 14th Army's bridgeheads over the Irrawaddy.

By 28th January 1945 the Burma Road from Ledo to China was declared open and the first direct convoy from Ledo arrived at Kunming, with supplies and weapons for the Chinese Army, to a great civic welcome on 4th February. But this also caused the Chinese to withdraw all their forces from Yunnan, less those under General Sultan's command, back further into China. They then took no further part in the Burma campaign and this action ended operations on the Salween Front. The move, however, was not too serious. 1st Chinese Army, essentially 30th and 38th Chinese Divisions, was still there and was directed to link up with 50th Chinese Division around Lashio which would then advance to Hsipaw while 36th British Division advanced to Kyaukme. Mars Force would remain to secure the Burma Road.

By 10th February the Japanese had pulled back to Namtu, Hsenwi and Lashio. 36th British Division passed through Twingge on 18th January after a stubborn fight and 29th British Infantry Brigade moved off along the east bank of the Shweli river to attack Mongmit. Meanwhile 72nd British Infantry Brigade met a determined rear guard at Mabein. Festing ordered this brigade to secure crossings over the Shweli at Myitson. Its progress was slowed up by active enemy rear guards, but it reached Bahe, where 26th Indian Infantry Brigade, took over the lead and went on to reach Myitson on 31st January. Its first attempt at crossing failed and Festing realised he had met strong enemy forces guarding the approach to Mongmit.

The advance to the Irrawaddy had been so swift and successful that 14th Army was seriously outstripping its supply chain. The follow-up roads were not yet ready and more transport aircraft were urgently needed if the momentum was to be maintained. Furthermore the army was very nearly beyond the economical use of transport aircraft based in Assam. Accordingly Mountbatten proposed to the Chiefs of Staff that he should capture Ramree Island as soon as possible and then maintain 14th Army from the airfields at Chittagong, Akyab and Ramree, stocking them by sea from India. Even so, he said he would need another 140 transport aircraft. At this time the combined strength of the British/Indian/African portion of ALFSEA was 971,828, made up of 127,139 British, 581,548 Indian, 44,988 East African, 59,878 West African and 158,275 civilian labourers. Of these 260,000 were being maintained in combat at the end of the long lines of communication on the Irrawaddy and all the way back to India. Supply remained a huge task and it is the greatest tribute to the administrative and logistic staffs and units that it never failed as it did so signally with the Japanese.

On 20th January Mountbatten issued new orders. 14th Army was to capture Rangoon before the monsoon. 15th Indian Corps was to capture Ramree and Cheduba Islands, establish a bridgehead at Taungup and then open the Taungup - Prome Road. The lines of communication would be re-organised with a series of subsidiary headquarters to control their development and the forward movement of combat supplies. Plans were made to make more use of clandestine operations with Force 136 and to raise a force of Karen Levies. After the 'Argonaut' Conference at Malta in January 1945 the Combined Chiefs of Staff issued new strategic orders to Mountbatten on 3rd February as follows:

> '1. Your first object is to liberate Burma at the earliest date . . .
> 2. Subject to the accomplishment of this object your next main task will be the liberation of Malaya and the opening of the Straits of Malacca. . .
> 3. In view of your recent success in Burma and of the uncertainty of the date of the final defeat of Germany, you must aim at the accomplishment of your first object with the forces at present at your disposal. . .
> 4. You will prepare a programme of operations for the approval of the Combined Chiefs of Staff.
> 5. In transmitting the foregoing directive the CCS direct your attention to the agreed policy in respect of the use in your theatre of United States resources deployed in the India-Burma theatre.' (Kirby)

During the last few months of 1944 the Eastern Fleet had been very active in the Indian Ocean, attacking targets in Sumatra in September and the Nicobar islands in October. On 22nd November this fleet was reduced in size and renamed the East Indies Fleet under Vice-Admiral Sir Arthur Power consisting of the battleship *Queen Elizabeth,* the battlecruiser *Renown*, eight cruisers, five escort carriers, 24 destroyers and other ships, a total of about 70. The rest of the fleet formed the British Pacific Fleet under Admiral Sir Bruce Fraser and consisted of the battleships *King George V* and *Howe*, the fleet carriers *Indefatigable*, *Illustrious*, *Victorious* and *Indomitable,* five cruisers, and three flotillas of destroyers. Thus by February 1945 Allied command of the Indian Ocean was complete and safe for the amphibious operations planned for the Akyab peninsula.

During February 134th Medium Regiment, under Lieutenant Colonel TED Kelly, arrived with 16 x 6-inch 26 cwt howitzers and was attached to 19th Indian Division, a most welcome addition.

Lieutenant General S Miyazaki, commanding *54th Division,* had abandoned Akyab but had been told to hold the An and Taungup Passes (Map 46) to protect the rear of the *15th Division* operating in the Irrawaddy valley. He decided to base his defences on Kangaw, with *154th Regimental Group,* and Taungup, with *121st Regimental Group.* The *Matsu Detachment*, which was in essence *111th Regimental Group*, was to cover the Kaladan approach and then to fall back on Tamandu, Kywegu, Myebon and Ramree.

In the first few weeks of January 1945, 27th Field Regiment, under Lieutenant Colonel Charles Corsar, was at Chittagong preparing for amphibious operations in Operation DRACULA. On 10th January the regiment saw its first Z Craft, a lighter built in India, some 100 feet long, very beamy and with a draught of about three feet. Four 25-pounders on gun platforms were secured to its metal deck. The officers who went on board HMS *Enterprise* (E' Troop) were the Battery Commander of 37/47th Field Battery, Major John Russell, Captain MacGregor, 'E' Troop Commander, Lieutenant Harold Worland the CPO, Lieutenant Ted Goodall the GPO and Lieutenant SA Guild, the Troop Leader. Sergeant Crump was the Signals

NCO and Bombardier Proud was CPOA. The vessel was commanded by a naval officer and the crew taken from IWT Arakanese. *Enterprise* sailed on 11th January. 'F' Troop's Z craft was HMS *Fighter* and had to wait as all was not yet ready. *Enterprise* reached Cox's Bazar that evening and next day was on her way to St Martin's Island where the guns were calibrated. On 13th January she sailed to Akyab and then to Hunter's Bay off the Myebon Peninsula where she arrived early in February.

Lieutenant Colonel Corsar recalls that 'The difficulties of mooring in suitable positions in the narrow, tidal and often swift-flowing chaungs were very real, but the RNR, RA and IWT combination overcame them as they arose. The vessels moved up and down these largely uncharted waterways, sometimes well ahead of any covering troops, seeking, and usually finding, opportunities to harass the Jap, who must often have wondered how shells pursued him when the nearest reported artillery was miles away.' (Corsar in Duncan).

It was decided to assault Ramree Island with 26th Indian Division and Cheduba Island with a Royal Marines detachment on 21st January. Meanwhile 25th Indian Division and 3rd Commando Brigade exploited eastwards from Akyab occupying Ponnagyun and Minbya where 53rd Indian Infantry Brigade hit strong enemy positions and a posthumous Victoria Cross was won by Lance Naik Sher Shah of 7/16th Punjab in the fighting. On 15th January 3rd Commando Brigade landed on the Myebon Peninsula under cover of aerial attack and gunfire from 37/47th Field Battery on 'Z' landing craft.

'At 0600 hours 15th January we moved towards the Beach. . . We fired at 0900 hours. The War Diary states it was a fireplan registered by an Air OP. . . I remember we were rocking slightly [the vessel being only partially beached] as we fired. The layers did very well as no comment came back from the sharp end.

By 1100 hours we were fully beached on the black volcanic sand and engaged another target, a dug in position. . .

The BC's jeep was put ashore and, being the only regimental jeep ashore, was taken by Major Aubrey Buxton who was RA rep with 3rd Commando Bde. Around midday the Supremo Lord Louis Mountbatten arrived in a jeep and, driving alongside, got onto its bonnet and climbed over the rail. He asked me where our OC was. Major Russell had gone forward to the gangplank where we had expected him to stop. The troop was gathered at No 1 gun and addressed by Lord Louis. He said that this was a historical occasion and wished us good hunting.' (Guild).

The first wave of the attack had with it three Bofors LAA guns of 36th LAA Regiment, one 5.5-inch gun of 1st Medium Regiment and a battery of 8th Field Regiment; these were the only guns to land in the assault. 3rd Commando Brigade secured a bridgehead in the face of some opposition and 74th Indian Infantry Brigade passed through them and captured Kantha. 82nd West African Division, now under the command of Major General HC Stockwell, moved east from Htizwe and cut off the Japanese in the Lemro valley and occupied Myohaung on 25th January. Christison then attempted to cut off the *Matsu Detachment* at Kangaw by amphibious assault using 25th Indian Division, less 74th Indian Infantry Brigade which was to hold Myebon and Kantha. At the same time he ordered 82nd West African Division to pursue the enemy down the Hpontha - Kani track and along the Yaw chaung to Kyweguseik. 81st West African Division was to mop up around Myohaung and then withdraw to Chiringa. At this point 30th Indian Mountain Regiment, less 27th Mountain Battery, came under the command of 82nd Division. Lieutenant Colonel TWR Hill was awarded the OBE and Major IM Williams and Captain RC Pillar the MBE for their part in the division's operations so far. An operation was mounted into the Lemro valley and for the first time 41st (WA) Mortar Regiment concentrated to deal with a strong enemy position at Ywathit. There was a good deal of shooting until patrols of 81st Division met those of 82nd and the battle of Mohaung was over.

At Myebon 37/47th Field Battery had landed and the Z Craft went back to Akyab for more of 8th Field Regiment. Guild recalls, [18th January] 'The CRA's list which I still have in my diary is as follows:

1. 1 gun and 1 Quad, being the balance of V Bty, Wireless Batteries, & cable in 2 Jeeps & Trailers.
2. RHQ 8th Fd 4 Jeeps and Trailers and if room at the end 2x15 cwt trucks. RHQ to bring tactical staff only not administrative men.
3. The CRA's Jeep and Trailer with his Liaison Officer.
4. 2 x 12 volt 22 Wireless sets and portable batteries for Major Buxton.
5. Maj Buxton's Jeep.
6. W Bty (8th Fd) Complete, 8 guns 8 quads 2 jeeps. If no room then to cut down W Bty to 4 quads, cut out ammunition and the 2 x 15 cwt trucks.' (Guild)

On 20th January 'E' Troop re-embarked and prepared for the assault on Kangaw.

The assault on Ramree Island by 26th Indian Division was to be supported by the fire of HMS *Queen Elizabeth*, the cruiser *Phoebe* and the destroyers *Rapid* and *Napier*, the sloop *Flamingo* and the RIN sloop *Kistna*, by Thunderbolts and Mitchells of 224 Group RAF and by 85 Liberators of the Strategic Air Force. 71st Indian Infantry Brigade with 160th Field Regiment, two batteries of 36th LAA Regiment and one squadron of 146th Regiment RAC landed unopposed just west of Kyaukpyu at 0940 hours 24th January 1945. By mid-afternoon a bridgehead had been secured. 4th Indian Infantry Brigade, with 7th Indian Field Regiment, landed on the following day and occupied Kyaukpyu, leaving 71st Indian Infantry Brigade free to advance south along the west coast. Mayin was occupied on the 25th and Yanbauk on the 26th against stiffening opposition. At the same time the Royal Marines, who landed at Cheduba, found it deserted. On Ramree Island 71st Indian Infantry Brigade swung north to capture Sane on 1st February while 36th Indian Infantry Brigade with 27th Mountain Battery seized Sagu Kyun Island. Ramree town was captured on 9th February after a stiff fight by a combined attack of 4th and 71st Indian Infantry Brigades. By 17th February all resistance had ended but some 500 Japanese defied all efforts to cut them off and made it back to join their own forces on the mainland. The airfield on Ramree was quickly brought into action and was defended by 22nd HAA Battery of 8th (Belfast) HAA Regiment and two troops of 36th LAA Regiment.

Next was the attack on Kangaw (Map 47) by a fleet of some 50 landing craft of many sorts, including 'Z' Craft each fitted to take a troop of 25-pounders to provide covering fire as they approached the landing beaches. The guns could not in fact fire while the craft was under way so it had to be anchored or beached first. They approached silently and were not seen until 1240 hours on 22nd January. The RIN sloops *Narbada* and *Jumna* shelled the area around the landing beach, medium bombers of No. 224 Group laid a smoke screen to cover the landings, while 1st Medium Regiment and the 25-pounders of 'W' Field Battery of 8th Field Regiment on the Myebon Peninsula and the 25-pounders of 24th and 37/47th Field Batteries of 27th Field Regiment on the Z Craft attacked Point 170 which dominated the beaches. The Air OP played a major part in this attack, both observing fire and reporting progress.

At 1303 hours 3rd Commando Brigade landed on 'Hove' beach and soon captured Point 170. 1st and 5th Commandos were quickly ashore and consolidated around Point 170. Next 51st Indian Infantry Brigade landed under heavy fire. The going was appalling, soft, slippery mud flats which prevented the use of any vehicles, all stores having to be carried in man pack. What is more, resistance increased rapidly and accurate enemy artillery engaged the beaches and the positions on Point 170. The enemy probably had at least a battalion of 105mm howitzers and some captured 25-pounders in action. They produced some of the heaviest and most concentrated fire yet experienced in the Arakan. Every effort was made to locate them, including the use of AOP, but it was impossible. Nevertheless Brigadier Daniell, CRA 25th Indian Division, managed to fire several 'Uncle' targets with all his guns save one battery and one troop but with the assistance of a troop of mediums.

On 24th January, 'E' Troop, 37/47th Field Battery struggled ashore with its guns up the log track laid for the purpose. The gun position was under enemy observation and it was impossible to dig. Shells were soon falling all around them. An OP was established on Hill 170 with the Commandos. On the 25th the battery organised a fireplan, including RAF Thunderbolts, to get 19th Hyderabad onto the 'Milford' feature while a Japanese 75mm shelled them. On the 26th more of 51st Indian Infantry Brigade and a troop of tanks of 19th Lancers struggled ashore with great difficulty. 37/47th Battery's OP saw one tank bellied, mud up to the top of its tracks. On 28th January over 1,000 enemy shells fell onto the attacking force but damage was slight as the shells penetrated deep into the mud. The guns of 27th Field Regiment, especially those of 24th and 37/47th Batteries, engaged with hardly a gap in their firing. Slowly Kangaw was surrounded but the Japanese sent reinforcements and there was very tough fighting at close quarters around Point 170 which dominated the battlefield. The fighting became savage. It was here that Captain LK Macgregor and Bombardier Sleet, of 37/47th Field Battery, were killed and where Bombardier Morris was awarded a Military Medal. Lieutenant GA Knowland of 1st Commando won a posthumous Victoria Cross. Major John Russell, commanding 37/47th Battery, went up to the OP to help but was soon wounded. He was later awarded the Military Cross. Nevertheless the position held, but the cost was heavy, some 2,000 Japanese killed and 600 British and Indian troops killed or wounded. By this time 74th Indian Infantry Brigade was approaching from the north and 2nd (WA) Infantry Brigade, with 34th Mountain Battery, had reached Kani. 4th (WA) Infantry Brigade were at Kaw. The Japanese then pulled back to Tamandu.

On 8th February Tamandu (Map 46) was attacked from the air and on the 16th, 53rd Indian Infantry Brigade and a troop of 7th Indian Anti-Tank Regiment landed unopposed at Ruywa. Cover was provided by two batteries of 27th Field Regiment and a troop of medium guns which had been landed on an offshore island, and by bombardment by the sloops *Narbada*, *Jumna* and *Flamingo* together with airstrikes. Captain Boyd of 'C' Flight 656 AOP Squadron found himself directing the fire of HMIS *Nabada* when she was dive bombed and he found himself dodging both Japanese fighters and the ships anti-aircraft guns! Captains Annett, Clarke and Large were FOOs with 74th Indian Infantry Brigade which had passed through 53rd Indian Infantry Brigade to take Tamandu. There were some fierce engagements using the guns of 24th and 37/47th Batteries now ashore at Ruya. By 17th February the bridgehead was secure and 2nd (WA) Infantry Brigade landed. It was then urgent to clear up the enemy in the An valley, since air supply to 15th Indian Corps was to be drastically reduced. 22nd (EA) Infantry Brigade had arrived to garrison Ramree Island, thus freeing 25th Indian Division to return to India for a rest and 26th Indian Division for operations on the mainland. 33rd Indian Mountain Regiment also returned to India, 34th Mountain Battery reached Calcutta on 11th April and 19th (Maymyo) Mountain Battery in May, where the regiment was made up to strength by the addition of 35th Mountain Battery. 27th Field Regiment, of 25th Indian Division, which had fought so long and so hard, was told to remain behind and prepare for a sea-borne landing at Rangoon; rather a blow when it saw the rest of the division depart for leave.

The air support organisation continued to develop. Each brigade and HQRA had a VCP (Visual Control Post) of the RAF from which aerial attacks could be directed and which linked them to the Army Air Support Control Unit, manned by the RAF and the Royal Signals, at Corps Headquarters. Targets were pointed out by FOOs. Throughout these operations, liaison with the Royal Navy worked well. A Bombardment Control Headquarters (BCHQ) was established on the

Force Headquarters Ship. Afloat was the naval Senior Bombardment Liaison Officer (SBLO). With the CRA was a naval Bombardment Liaison Officer (BLO) who would advise on the capabilities of the naval guns available and control the deployment of the Forward Observers Bombardment (FOBs) who were Gunner officers.

We have already seen how the great advance to the Irrawaddy had succeeded beyond everyone's dreams. The strategy was right and Slim held the initiative. The situation looked bleak for the Japanese but they were still fighting as hard as ever and Slim knew that the problem would only get more difficult as he forced his enemy back onto their supplies while he lengthened his own lines of communication in some of the World's wildest and most inhospitable country. The first test was to cross the mighty Irrawaddy and assault Japanese positions which were increasing in strength as the days went by. The monsoon would start in May and it was already almost March. He must capture Rangoon before the rains came. Mountbatten's strategy had secured his first objective, the supply route to China; next he had to concentrate on the conquest of Burma and begin to plan for operations to conquer Malaya, Singapore and the Netherlands East Indies.

Throughout these operations the men of the Royal Regiment had acquitted themselves well. Everywhere they were involved in the destruction of enemy strong points, in providing covering fire to get the infantry and tanks onto their objectives and in ensuring that any enemy aircraft that managed to get through were dealt with. They had to observe fire from the air and provide observation ashore for the ships of the Royal and Royal Indian Navies. The guns had to struggle forward under appalling conditions achieving well nigh-impossibilities with winches and drag ropes. They had learnt the lessons of the jungle, they were determined to be up with the hunt and they always were. The forward observers were simply outstanding. They had to be constantly within a few yards of the targets they were engaging. Their job was to stay in action as battalions changed and to provide a source of unfailing communications and information which gave cohesion to the tactical battle. Air observation was here to stay, thanks to the splendid work and devotion to duty of the officers and men of 656 AOP Squadron. Throughout, Gunner communications, frequently the only means of reaching the forward troops, reached a very high standard indeed.

Yet so far it had not been essentially an artillery battle. The infantry were magnificent and it was they who did the close quarter fighting and who suffered the casualties. All Gunners who were there salute their comrades in the infantry and this made them the more determined to ensure that they spared nothing to ensure that the guns were always there ready to do all in their power to reduce the risks to the gallant men of the infantry regiments. Artillery/Infantry co-operation was at its very best, although several Gunner commanders said that, at the start of operations, the infantry had tended to be very arrogant about the Gunners, one had called them a 'dispensable luxury.' But this did not last once the real fighting started. No infantryman at any level would be keen on making a move without a Gunner commander beside him. Those infantrymen who fought in Burma speak about the Gunners with the greatest respect and gratitude and what they achieved together in those testing days. They shared the most appalling conditions equally. Major BLN Ditmas of 129th Field Regiment wrote 'We were not Gunners first and foremost . . . we were almost as much infantry as Gunners. At the OP there was often hand-to-hand fighting. At the gun positions shelling, bombing and direct infantry attack were always a major consideration. The threat came from the 'jitter party,' operating by night, trying by every possible means to locate our positions and infiltrate into them . . . We risked the shell and bomb and concentrated in our gun positions until our perimeters were reduced to the minimum and could be defended by ourselves. . . Sometimes a field regiment, a medium battery and a LAA troop with all their transport occupied a 500-yard square.' (Ellis).

As D-Day for the crossing of one of the World's mightiest rivers approached there was much excitement and apprehension. Clearly co-ordinated firepower was going to be critical and the Gunners were well aware of this. The plan was good, their morale was high, they were confident in their ability to win, but they also knew that they were still up against a fanatically determined enemy who would fight to the finish. They were going to do it, but it was not going to be easy.

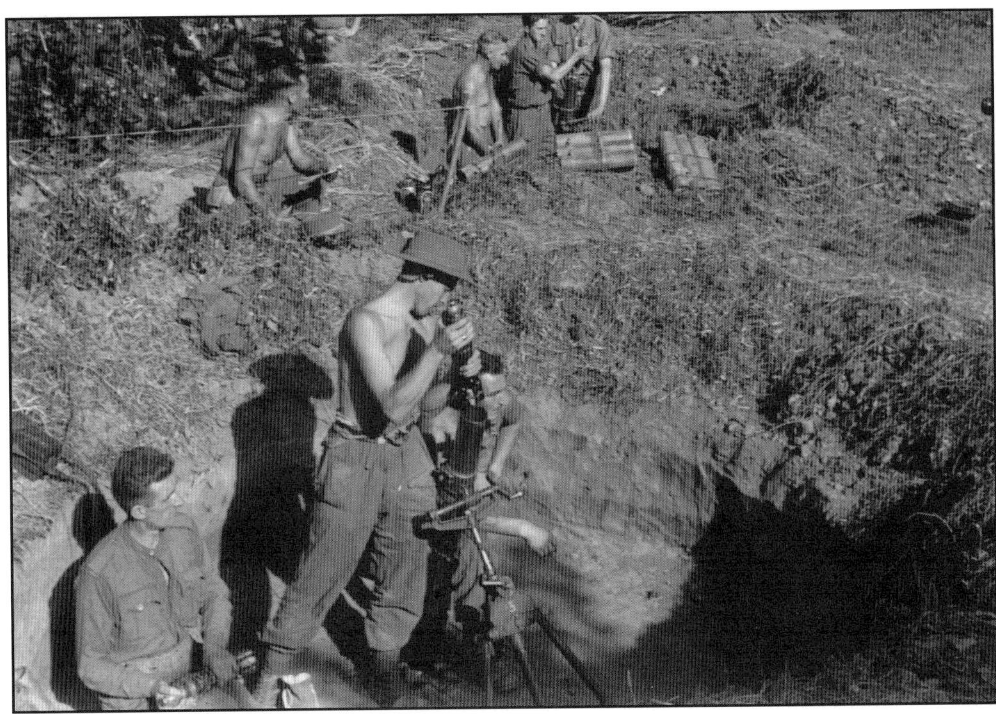

22. An infantry 3-inch mortar in action December 1944. (IWM)

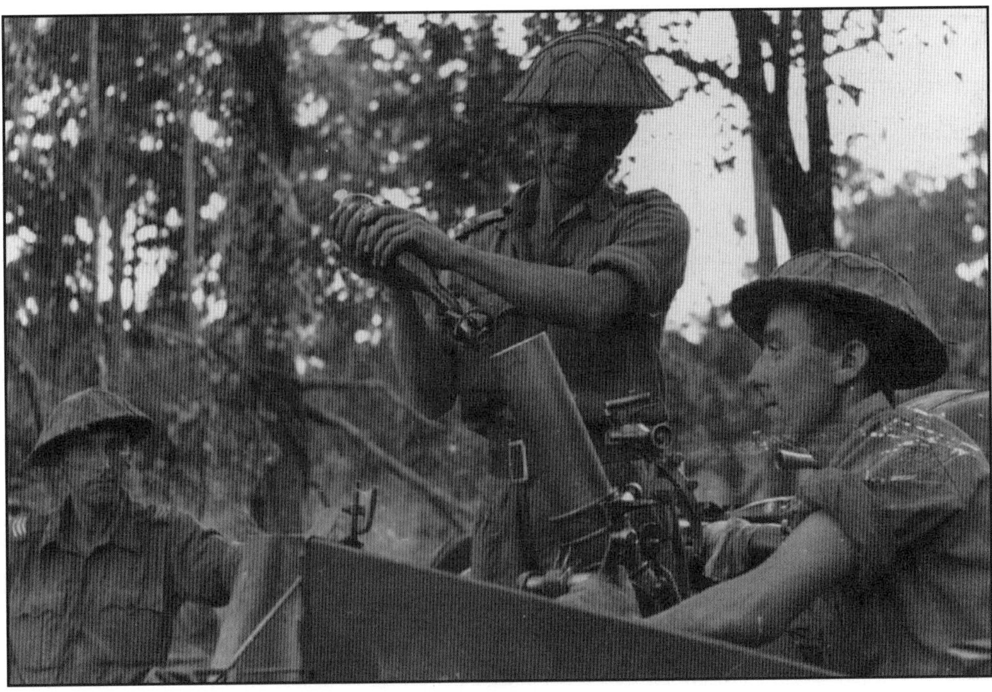

23. 3-inch mortar of 33rd Anti-Tank Regiment RA (Gordon Highlanders) mounted in a carrier, Waingyo, January 1945. (IWM)

24. A 40mm Bofors of 36th LAA Regiment, perhaps at Akyab, January 1945. (IWM)

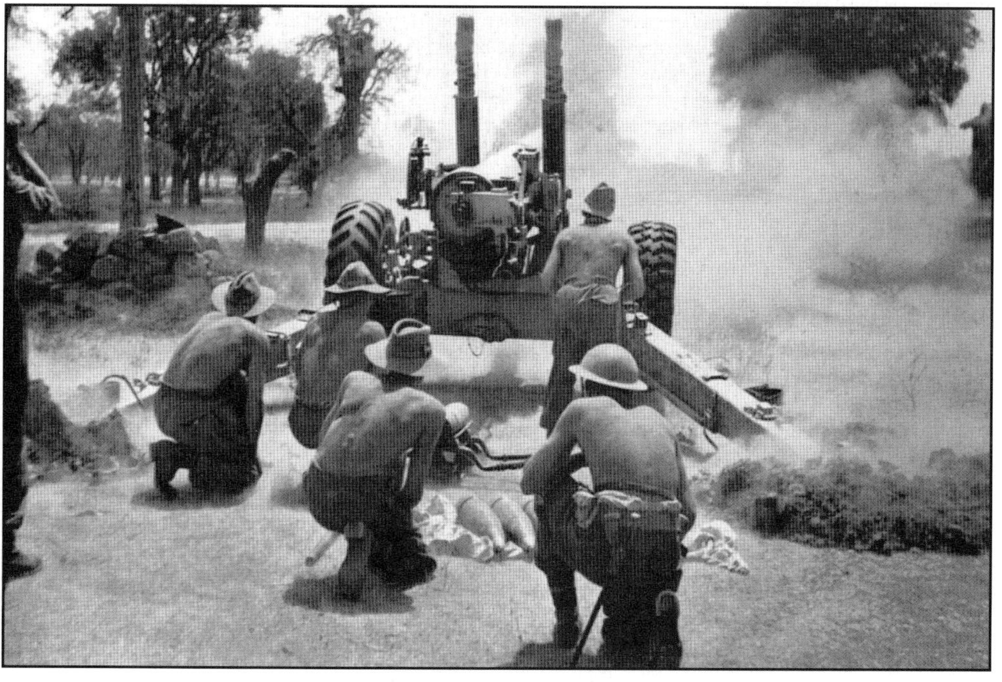

25. 5.5-inch gun of 1st Medium Regiment shelling Fort Dufferin, Mandalay, 9th March 1945.

26. A 6-inch howitzer of 134th Medium Regiment engaging Fort Dufferin, Mandalay, March 1945. (IWM)

27. Umrao Singh VC. Photographed as a subadar after the war.

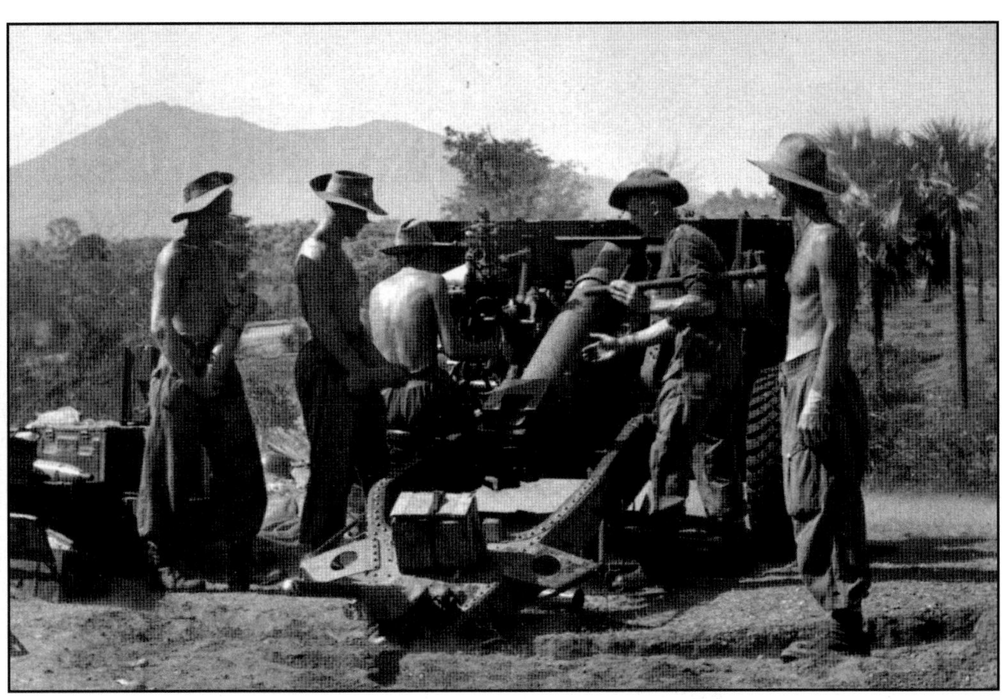

28. A 25-pounder in action near Mount Popa, April 1945. The gun has just fired and the breech is about to be opened to extract the spent cartridge and permit the loading of the next round. (IWM)

29. Manhandling a 6-inch 26 cwt howitzer of 134th Medium Regiment near Mount Popa. (IWM)

CHAPTER 14

CROSSING THE IRRAWADDY AND THE CAPTURE OF MANDALAY

FEBRUARY - MARCH 1945

(Maps 41, 46, 47 and 48)

By the Spring of 1945 the situation looked grim for Japan. In Western Europe the Allies had successfully established a second front and had driven the Germans back to their border. On the Eastern Front the Germans were reeling back from the Soviet onslaught. In the Pacific little could now save the Japanese forces in the Philippines. The Japanese fleet had been very severely mauled and the Americans controlled the seas and the air. This had isolated the Japanese *Southern Region* in the Netherlands East Indies, Malaya and Singapore. The American air attacks on Japan were increasing monthly and this was affecting civilian morale and industrial capacity. Finally there was every chance that the Soviet Union would declare war on Japan soon.

The Japanese *Imperial General Staff* reckoned that the Americans would advance on Japan by the most direct route, gaining airfields from which to bomb that country into submission (Map 41). Next they would seize Iwojima, the Ryukyu Islands, the Bonin Islands and Formosa. The *Imperial General Staff* therefore determined to build up home defence and pursue a policy of defending the outer perimeter of whatever they currently held to the last man. They reasoned that the American public would be afraid of a drawn-out period of fighting resulting in high casualties and, therefore, that was what they must ensure occurred. *Southern Army* was to hold French Indo-China, then still partly under Vichy French control, the Philippines, Siam, Malaya and Sumatra, and it was to fight for every inch of Burma. The real problem was at home. All able-bodied men had already been called up or were employed in essential war work, yet Japan needed some 40 new divisions and air defence units. Accordingly they gave priority to the expansion of fighter and anti-aircraft formations and the work necessary to create equipment for them.

Local forces were to be raised in Korea and in China. The army in China was reduced and told simply to hold where it was. *71st Division* was moved from China to Formosa and eight new divisions were to be formed in Manchuria. *10th Area Army* was formed to command the defence of Formosa and the Ryukyu Islands. Five local brigades were to be formed on Formosa. Then on 28th February, *38th Army* seized full control of Indo-China from the French.

The problem of the air defence of Japan remained. It had received little attention, as an air threat to the Home Islands had not been contemplated. There was no basic structure in place. *1st Air Army* was formed and steps were taken to produce large quantities of 120mm anti-aircraft guns. But they could do little against the new American B-29 bombers which could fly at and attack from 30,000 feet. By the end of January 1945 the Japanese had only 750 aircraft left in the Home Islands, most of which were no match for the Americans, and some 600 anti-aircraft guns of all types. The Americans were, by then, using airfields in the Mariana Islands and were attacking industrial targets at Tokyo, Nagoya and Osaka regularly. Any attempt by the Japanese to attack these American airfields failed because their aircraft were too few and many were obsolete. Accordingly air formations were brought back from *Southern Region* in spite of the adverse effect on operations there. Maximum effort was allotted to aircraft production so that by the end of March there would be some 3,100 Navy and 2,100 Army aircraft available to meet the expected increase in American air attacks.

Iwojima was a vital staging post for the Japanese and had three good airfields. It was also close to mainland Japan and must not fall into enemy hands. It was obviously the next US objective. *109th Division* and other forces had been preparing powerful defences on the island since mid-1944. Realising that he could not hold the beaches against US firepower, the commander, Lieutenant General T Kuribayashi, decided to create fortresses which could dominate the island and the beaches. 7th USAAF began regular air raids which increased in intensity.

The Japanese were proved right when, at 0600 hours on 19th February 1945, the heaviest naval and aerial bombardment of the war in the Far East began against all known Japanese defences on Iwojima. Seven battleships, seven cruisers and a fleet of destroyers blasted the island for 25 minutes, then stopped to allow a massive attack by carrier-borne aircraft operating from some 17 carriers of the fast carrier force under Vice-Admiral MA Mitscher. Another 25 minutes of naval bombardment followed as the assaulting waves of US Marines raced for the shore. As had already happened on other islands the defences, in spite of the bombardment, came to life and the fighting was again extremely severe. By last light a major beachhead had been won. However, it was not until 26th March, over a month later, that all resistance ceased. The Japanese garrison of 21,000 died almost to a man, only 200 prisoners were taken. The Americans suffered 26,000 casualties of which some 6,800 were killed. The fleet carrier *Saratoga* was put out of action by a *Kamikaze* attack and had to return home for repair and the escort carrier *Bismarck Sea* was sunk. But the airfields were soon in use by B-29 bombers and other aircraft. By the end of the war some 2,400 sorties by these great aircraft had mounted attacks on Japan from Iwojima.

In ALFSEA much planning had been taking place to ensure the destruction of the Japanese in Burma (Map 49). Many alternatives were discussed but everything depended on logistics. 14th Army's advance towards the Irrawaddy was moving fast and had momentum. This had to be maintained. The construction of all-weather airfields at Akyab and Ramree was a top priority, but it was clear that there were not enough resources to support both 14th Army and 15th Indian Corps on major operations at the same time. Accordingly Mountbatten met his commanders on 23rd February and said that the battle for Mandalay/Meiktila must have priority and must be won by the end of March. His aim then was to isolate and destroy the Japanese armies by striking towards Loilem with one corps while, at the same time, another corps raced for Rangoon. Leese gave orders based on this strategy and on 25th February he told Slim that some 15 transport squadrons would be available from 1st March, and six more from Akyab and Ramree. These would, he said, provide the air supply he needed. The road Tamu - Kalewa and the IWT service on the Chindwin from Kalewa to Myingyan was also available. These resources would provide support for his plans.

Leese told Sultan to destroy all enemy forces in the area of Kyaukme - Lashio and then turn south-west and assist in the destruction of the enemy around Mandalay. Slim was to destroy all enemy in the Mandalay area and capture Rangoon before the monsoon. In the Arakan (Map 46), Christison was to reduce his forces as planned, move onto a sea supply system, destroy all enemy in the An valley and operate from the Taungup bridgehead towards Prome as resources permitted, but without air supply. The Arakan and Ramree airfields would support 14th Army. Mountbatten then turned his attention to the next phase of the conflict. He told the Chiefs of Staff that, subject to the fall of Rangoon, his next objective would be Singapore. He planned to land on Phuket Island in June and at Port Swettenham and Port Dickson in Malaya in October, reaching Singapore between December 1945 and January 1946. To prepare for this General

Auchinleck, Commander-in-Chief India, was told to form 34th Indian Corps at Poona with 25th Indian and 81st West African Divisions. Lieutenant General OL Roberts was to be in command and was to present his plans by 1st April.

Activity was reaching a crescendo, however, along the banks of the Irrawaddy in the early days of February 1945 (Map 48). Slim aimed to deceive the Japanese into thinking that his main crossing would be in the north against Mandalay and that the force in the Myittha valley was a diversion. If this could be done, 4th Indian Corps was to seize rapidly a bridgehead at Nyaungu with 7th Indian Division and then 17th Indian Division was to pass through and race for Meiktila before the Japanese realised what was happening. The enemy would then be cut off around Mandalay. To achieve this, 19th Indian Division would be the first to cross at Kyaukmyaung. It would capture Singu from where a good all weather road ran direct to Mandalay. Next 20th Indian Division would cross at Myinmu, making as great a show of force as possible and conduct the aggressive build-up of a large bridgehead then swing east as ordered.

By this time the mountain artillery had been redistributed as follows:

Regiment	Indian Mountain Batteries	Divisions
20th Mtn	24th, 25th, 26th	19th Indian
21st Mtn	1st (Kohat), 6th (Jacob's), 37th	17th Indian
23rd Mtn	3rd (Peshawar), 8th (Lahore), 31st (Jammu)	20th Indian
24th Mtn	2nd (Derajat), 11th (Dehra Dun), 20th	5th Indian
25th Mtn	13th (Dardoni), 23rd Bikaner Bijay	7th Indian
30th Mtn	27th, 32nd, 33rd	26th Indian
32nd Mtn	12th (Poonch), 17th (Nowshera), 28th	36th British

The batteries of 1st Indian Survey Regiment, Lieutenant Colonel SA Brighty, were in action by early 1944. 1st Indian Survey Battery, under Major BC Slater, joined 2nd British Division and 2nd Indian Survey Battery, under Major FA von Goldstein, joined first 11th East African Division and then 19th Indian Division. Both batteries were heavily involved in the fireplans for the crossing of the Irrawaddy and later around Mandalay, but they could not keep pace with the advance later on and returned to India in May 1945.

Provision of air defence for the advance was, as always, far from easy. Once again the threat was not high but it could not be ignored. However, the anti-aircraft batteries were playing an increasing part in ground operations so their inclusion had a double value. The CCRA of 33rd Indian Corps, Brigadier DJ Steevens, decentralised 101st HAA Regiment and 44th LAA Regiment to divisions and kept control of 52nd HAA and 2nd Indian LAA Regiments. 2nd British Division was given 226th HAA and 75th LAA Batteries, while 20th Indian Division had 227th HAA and 239th LAA Batteries. For the actual crossings he concentrated 101st HAA and 44th LAA Regiments. He ordered 52nd HAA and 2nd Indian LAA Regiments to protect the lines of communication back to India. 101st Regiment had two batteries in the air defence role and 297th HAA Battery manning a troop of two 7.2-inch howitzers. Meanwhile 4th Indian Corps had 67th HAA and 28th LAA Regiments. The going was not easy; the guns and instruments, including the cumbersome GL Radars, had covered 350 miles, often having to be 'double tractored' and winched up gradients of 1 in 5. 187th HAA Battery was deployed to defend Sinthe airfield as soon as it was captured, 188th HAA Battery covered the crossings at Myitche and 189th HAA Battery passed through the bridgehead with 17th Indian Division. 28th LAA Regiment drove off a number of low level air attacks during the crossing operations and then sent a battery with 17th Indian Division. 189th HAA and 250th LAA Batteries accompanied 17th Indian Division to Meiktila and came into action to deal with repeated air and ground attacks and were frequently mortared and shelled. Later, 271st LAA Battery and 52nd HAA Regiment arrived to assist in the defence of Meiktila.

'A' Flight 656 AOP Squadron was allotted to the crossing operation and pilots were allocated with Captain Ted Maslen-Jones to 20th Indian Division, Captain Pip Harrison to 2nd British Division, Captain Frank McMath to 19th Indian Division and Lieutenant Ian Walton was kept in reserve at 33rd Corps Headquarters. To begin with all sections operated from a flight location on 2nd British Division's axis. Pip Harrison, with 2nd British Division, had some splendid shoots as it closed on the Kabo Weir which it had captured intact. Once Shwebo fell McMath set off by road to join 19th Indian Division at Onbauk. General Rees and the CRA Brigadier Macdonald understood and liked the AOP and made full use of them, frequently being flown to visit brigades or carrying out a reconnaissance by air. McMath was constantly in the air and carrying out a great variety of missions which Rees relied on, engaging opportunity targets while doing so. The most difficult task was still that of locating enemy guns, since Japanese concealment remained excellent, but the division knew that as long as there was an Auster in the air the Japanese guns were unlikely to fire - a sort of negative deterrence. Soon, however, McMath had to send for a second aircraft to meet the demands of 19th Indian Division as it maintained its positions across the Irrawaddy. On 19th February McMath took over 'A' Flight from Captain George Deacon, who was returning to the UK, and so left 19th Indian Division with which he had been flying for 14 months.

At 'A' Flight Headquarters McMath found some astonishing figures. The Flight had six Auster IVs with a pilot each. In six weeks it had flown 600 hours in just over 600 sorties or an average 100 sorties and hours per pilot. This was an outstanding record by the pilots and perhaps even more so for the mixed RAF/RA ground crews who kept the aircraft in trim in such very difficult conditions, for ever on the move, under enemy threat, in high temperatures and in very dry dusty conditions. All flights were linked by radio to squadron headquarters and these were manned by four Gunner signallers who did an outstanding job. They linked the outlying sections to flight headquarters and then flight headquarters to squadron headquarters. At the time 'A' Flight was at Shwebo, 'B' Flight at Gangaw and 'C' Flight at Akyab, with squadron headquarters at Kalemyo. These involved huge distances over jungle-clad mountains and it says much for the standard of the operators that voice conversation was possible between them almost all the time. Two additional pilots arrived, Captains Mike Gregg and FSB Mehta, the first Indian pilot to serve with AOP and who had trained at Deolali in 1587 Flight which had been set up by the commanding officer of 656th Squadron. Being from Bombay Captain Mehta was quickly, if unoriginally, christened 'Duck'. He went to 19th Indian Division.

Slim anticipated that his plan would draw all Japanese reserves to the north as they recognised a threat to Mandalay which was, in any case, real. One day after the crossings in the north, 7th Indian Division, using as much deception as it could, would cross as quietly as possible around Nyaungu. Then, as soon as possible, the Meiktila Strike Force would drive hard for Meiktila out of the bridgehead established by 7th Indian Division. This Force consisted of

17th Indian Division	less 99th Indian Infantry Brigade,
255th Tank Brigade	less 116th Tank Regiment but with the addition of 16th Indian Light Cavalry
59th (SP) Field Battery of 18th (SP) Field Regiment	

The whole of this force, including the infantry, was motorised. It was to move fast by way of Taungtha. It was not to try to keep the road behind it open as it advanced. 7th Indian Division would do this later. As soon as the airfield at Meiktila had been secured, 99th Indian Infantry Brigade and 21st Mountain Regiment, without its animals, would be flown in. Finally 2nd British

Division was to mop up around Sagaing and cross near the Ava bridges as soon as landing craft became available, and then attack Mandalay from the south. That was the plan for crossing the Irrawaddy. As we saw, 2nd British Division carried out a major operation to deal with the village of Ywathigyi when Captain Pip Harrison of 656 AOP Squadron set up the astonishing record of registering 27 targets from the air in one sortie for the fireplan. The subsequent bombardment showed the accuracy of his shooting because it enabled the attacking infantry to walk unmolested through the ruins of the village.

Lieutenant General Messervy, 4th Indian Corps, gave Major General Evans, 7th Indian Division, his orders to capture Pakokku and then to cross the river on or about 15th February (exact date to follow). Evans too worked out a deception plan to conceal his real crossing. 28th (EA) Infantry Brigade Group's move to Seikpyu, already mentioned, was part of this deception. It was here, on 9th February, that Lieutenant GW Gorman of 136th Field Regiment won a Military Cross for providing continuous and accurate fire for 'D' Company 46th Battalion KAR as it advanced through the hills around Seikpyu, and then, when they were counter-attacked, he destroyed the enemy by the deadly fire of his guns. That was not all. As the Japanese prepared to renew their attacks this splendid young officer crept forward alone with a telephone line to within 50 yards of the enemy. He then brought down gunfire onto them while he was under aimed rifle fire himself. The whole battalion spoke of his great courage, devotion to duty and disregard for his own safety. His part in the whole operation was of the highest importance.

An OP with another company of 46th Battalion KAR on 15th February was heavily mortared and grenaded by Japanese who were all round it. The OP Officer continued to bring down fire while Gunner F Carr, his signaller, manned a Bren gun in the platoon area they were occupying. He defended single handed one flank of the position and drove off attack after attack. For this he was awarded an immediate Military Medal. BSM H Raistrick, also of 347th Battery, 136th Field Regiment, was also awarded the Military Medal for manning his OP long after the infantry had left and for holding off several enemy attacks. 114th Indian Infantry Brigade was given the Pakokku task, 89th Indian Infantry Brigade was to cross at Pagan as a diversion and the main crossing was to be further north by 33rd Indian Infantry Brigade with an assault force consisting of 2nd South Lancashires, who had made the sea assault in Madagascar, 4/15th Punjab, 4/1st Gurkhas, 1st Burma Regiment, one company of 13th Frontier Force (FF) Rifles Machine Gun Battalion, one troop of 24th Anti-Tank Regiment, one battery of 3-inch mortars, observation and reconnaissance parties from the corps and divisional artilleries, one VCP and nine tanks of 116th Regiment RAC.

On 7th February 114th Indian Infantry Brigade attacked Pakokku and found the enemy strongly dug in at Kanhla and in spite of hand-to-hand fighting was unable to clear them out until the 10th. Slim then ordered the general advance across the Irrawaddy. In the north 19th Indian Division had crossed and reached Singu on 13th February. 20th Indian Mountain Regiment reported crossing the Irrawaddy on 12th February at Shwedaik and moved south with 64th Indian Infantry Brigade towards Singu. Both Major Kelly and Major Dowson of the regiment were awarded the Military Cross for gallantry in the bridgehead and for several preceding operations. Gracey ordered his 20th Indian Division to cross on the night 12/13th. It was here that Captain McMath did much splendid work continuously providing information and controlling fire. He was in the air for some 120 hours in 30 days of fighting.

Further south, 2nd British Division had cleared Ondaw and Saye and its 5th British Infantry Brigade was ready to cross when ordered. Rees of 19th Indian Division, ordered his 62nd Indian Infantry Brigade and 20th Indian Mountain Regiment to advance on Mandalay by way of Maymyo on an all pack basis. The route was over some terrible country and the regiment had great difficulty in keeping up but 24th Mountain Battery was present when Maymyo fell on 17th March.

64th Indian Infantry Brigade was to move south down the track to Nyaungwun with the armour while 98th Indian Infantry Brigade remained in reserve at Singu. Progress was good and Nyaungwun was secure by 2nd March. Rees then ordered 98th Indian Infantry Brigade to pass through and take the lead and seize the Chaungmagyi Chaung. Soon 62nd Indian Infantry Brigade had cleared the mouth of this chaung and Sambo Island. By 19th March, Rees had formed 'Stiletto Force' to strike at Madaya and cut off the Japanese holding Chaungmagyi Chaung.

In 20th Indian Division, Major General Gracey planned that 100th Indian Infantry Brigade would cross and seize a bridgehead near Myinmu, which it achieved after bitter hand-to-hand fighting. Magnificent air support was a feature of these operations and 23rd Mountain Regiment report being in action as a regiment for the first and only time. 80th Indian Infantry Brigade was to wait to pass through and race for Kyaukse, the divisional objective.

Up to the time 2nd British and 20th Indian Divisions reached the Irrawaddy, all fighting had been on a divisional basis. It was then decided that the crossing operations should be conducted as a corps plan. Thus the fireplan was laid down by the CCRA, Brigadier DG Steevens, whose HQRA divorced itself from Corps Headquarters and deployed into the gun areas just east of Myinmu, to control the fire. Next to it was a landing strip for the AOP Squadron. The idea was to position the Corps Artillery Group so that all batteries could cover the crossings of both divisions in great depth from the home bank. 1st Medium Regiment, 12 x 5.5-inch guns, one battery of 134th Medium Regiment, 6 x 6-inch howitzers, 101st HAA Regiment, 16 x 3.7-inch HAA guns and 4 x 7.2-inch howitzers, 18th (SP) Regiment, less 59th Battery, 16 x 105mm and 9th, 10th and 114th Field Regiments, each with 24 x 25-pounders, were deployed in a corps gun area surveyed to 'theatre' grid. 44th LAA Regiment provided air and ground defence of the gun areas. 1st Indian Survey Regiment, as well as completing the survey, established sound ranging and flash spotting cover of the whole front and soon established that most of the Japanese artillery was located in a small area four to five miles south of the Irrawaddy. The crossing of the whole division was expected to take some ten days.

The AOP Squadron had a major role to play. Captains George Deacon, Mike Gregg and Arthur Rogers spent much time registering every potential 'Victor' target to be fired from the great assortment of guns assembled. Because all were surveyed on to 'theatre' grid it was enough to see one gun on each target, leaving the Gun Position Officers of each battery to calculate their own fire orders from that data. But some targets demanded more precision, especially those allotted to the 7.2-inch howitzers, the 3.7-inch HAA guns and the 6-inch howitzers. While this was in progress, Captain Ted Maslen-Jones and Lieutenant Pip Harrison were flying missions for 20th Indian and 2nd British Divisions, which were to carry out the crossings. By this time Maslen-Jones had been awarded a 'Certificate of Gallantry in Action' signed personally by Lord Louis Mountbatten, which brought much credit to the squadron. It was on 19th February, as this battle raged, that Deacon handed over 'A' Flight to Frank McMath.

100th Indian Infantry Brigade crossed the Irrawaddy during the night of 12/13th February, as planned, at Allagappa and by last light on the 13th the brigade secured a bridgehead 2,500 yards wide and 1,000 yards deep. Once across an intense bombardment of enemy artillery took place. This fire was then directed at enemy counter-attacks as they woke up to what was happening. Lieutenant Colonel AP Curzon-Howe, the commanding officer of 18th Field Regiment, was 'CCRA's Representative' on the corps artillery net with authority to call for 'Victor' targets. The crossings continued and went well, although 32nd Indian Infantry Brigade had bad luck. Many boats were swept away by rough water, enemy artillery was very accurate and on landing the men who did get across met strong enemy positions. For the next few days there was more bitter hand-to-hand fighting as the enemy did all they could to prevent 32nd and 100th Indian Infantry Brigades from linking up, trying hard to mount counter-attacks. Major AHG Barton of 10th Field

Regiment controlled the fire of the corps artillery during the crossing and it was largely due to his skill that repeated enemy counter-attacks were all defeated by devastating concentrated firepower. His personal contribution to the success of the crossing was immense, especially as for much of the time he was under fire and involved with the fighting. Both he and Captain Hamilton of 10th Field Regiment, who led a counter-attack himself, were awarded the Military Cross for their gallantry together with Sergeant Wynn and Bombardier Gunns who received the Military Medal.

On the night of 16/17th February, near Mingyan 8th and 31st Mountain Batteries of 23rd Mountain Regiment with a troop of artillery mortars were supporting 1st Northamptons on the river bank. Captain, Temporary Major, CJS Burne, commanding 31st (Jammu) Mountain Battery, was FOO with the leading company when the enemy launched a violent attack with accurate artillery fire at 0300 hours. Burne had with him Second Lieutenant John Cameron-Hayes. He reports, 'There was a good moon until about 0200 hours when it set. The Jap started shelling at 2330 hours . . . His shelling was quite accurate. . . When the battle started I put down my DF but it can't have been very effective as he came in with great speed and was . . . quickly into the position. I had call on, and had previously registered, 31 and 8 Btys and a troop of arty mortars. [The leading infantry section immediately withdrew when the Japanese attacked and this let the enemy into the position and led Burne to assume command of those Northamptons who remained and a few Jats from an adjoining battalion] From the beginning all of the inf Bren guns were out of action - jammed with sand . . . grenades were unprimed and we had to do this in the middle of the fight - my OP party did a lot of it. (I had John (2/Lt John Cameron-Hayes), my Signal NK [Wali Mohd], a telephonist, a wireless operator and two orderlies in the comd post' (Burne).

This gallant officer and his handful of men, together with some 9th Jat machine gunners, continued to defend the position. Eventually the infantry returned and the position held. It was the fire of Burne's guns and the example he set that saved the day and he was later awarded a well-earned Distinguished Service Order, the citation for which concluded, 'It was entirely due to his magnificent bravery and resolute devotion to duty over the six hours of fighting which resulted in the position being held . . . his quick assumption of command of the infantry was beyond all praise . . .' In the same battle a posthumous Victoria Cross was won by Jemadar Parkash Singh of 14/13th FF Rifles near Myinmu on 18th February. Some of the fiercest fighting took place around the village of Talingon. The Japanese increased their attacks with more tanks and artillery. Hurricanes of No. 20 Squadron RAF destroyed many tanks and the bridgehead held.

656 AOP Squadron continued to do excellent work. During the first few days of the battle it kept one aircraft airborne for all the hours of daylight. This aircraft was able to engage enemy concentrations of tanks and infantry as they formed up with the 3.7-inch HAA and 5.5-inch guns. Again, as soon as an AOP was airborne, enemy guns remained silent because they knew they would be located if they opened fire. These pilots covered every move of the crossing of 20th Indian Division and then turned their attention to that of 2nd British Division on 24th February. It was at this time that Frank McMath reported how the flying rose to a maximum with two aircraft permanently on call as well as the sections flying with 19th and 20th Indian Divisions and corps headquarters. Captain Eric Southern arrived from 'B' Flight to help. McMath reported, 'The rest of us kept the heavier artillery busy with tremendous concentrations on every well-defended locality, as well as plastering the enemy's gun areas and possible forming-up points. After a few days' heavy fighting the bridgehead expanded to the edge of quite a large riverside village called Ngazun, where we had some of the best shooting of the whole campaign. The Japs had fortified a number of solid buildings which we had the intense pleasure of destroying, using just one 6-inch howitzer and taking them one after the other until we had reduced the village to a smoking shambles.' Ted Maslen-Jones reported engaging a Japanese battery of three 75mm guns

three miles south west of Kalewa with a section of 7.2-inch howitzers at a range of 12,000 yards, one enemy gun was certainly destroyed by a 200 lb shell. During these actions, a visit by the CCRA, Brigadier DJ Steevens, to 'A' flight was the occasion for the presentation of the Military Cross to Frank McMath mainly for his work with 19th Indian Division.

2nd British Division began to cross near Ngazun on 24th February. 32nd Indian Infantry Brigade linked up with 100th Indian Infantry Brigade at Kanlan and on 5th March 20th Divisional Artillery crossed the river. Enemy artillery fire, however, remained heavy and accurate throughout this period. Also, by this time, 13 Japanese battalions had been identified from *2nd, 31st, 33rd* and *53rd Divisions* facing the Myinmu bridgehead. Slim feared a major counter-attack and ordered 5th Indian Division, less 9th Indian Infantry Brigade, to concentrate forward at Monywa and be ready to support either 4th or 33rd Indian Corps. 9th Indian Infantry Brigade was to wait at Palel to be flown in to Meiktila when the time came. 2nd British Division crossed the Irrawaddy with 5th British Brigade leading between Tadaing and Myittha during the night of 24/25th February. As dawn broke on the 25th the crossing continued covered by a heavy artillery attack and smoke screen and by last light 1st Camerons and 2nd Dorsets had established a bridgehead around Ngazun. Captain JO Moreton of 393rd Field Battery of 99th Field Regiment was up with 'A' Company of 1st Camerons and engaged enemy forming up to counter-attack. Captains Sebag-Montefiore and PM Weatherby of 394th Field Battery were across and heavily engaged. 472nd Field Battery was at this time involved in clearing up enemy around Saye and did not cross the river until 22nd March. It was at Saye that Gunner P Vine of 472nd Field Battery earned the Military Medal for setting, 'a very fine example on his troop gun position of cheerfulness and determination under fire and complete disregard for his own personal safety which has been an inspiration to the men around him.' (From his citation). Saye was taken in the early afternoon of 20th February.

On 27th February, 6th British Infantry Brigade crossed the river and passed through 5th Brigade deepening the bridgehead. Next came 4th British Infantry Brigade which crossed and exploited west to link up with 20th Indian Division. Lieutenant Colonel RJ Uniacke, commanding 16th Field Regiment, reported crossing with 4th British Infantry Brigade Headquarters. He related how his Signal Officer, Captain Charles Barker, Royal Signals, was awarded the Military Cross for laying and then maintaining the line to the guns across the river under fire and from a leaking boat which eventually sank. Without his action the link to the guns would have been lost at a critical moment in the battle. He said that 16th Field Regiment crossed during the night 2/3rd March while he played poker with the commander of 5th British Infantry Brigade, Brigadier MM Alston-Roberts-West. The regiment came into action just south of Ngazun. By 2nd March, when the Divisional Artillery completed its concentration across the river, the 2nd British Division bridgehead was four and a half miles wide and two miles deep. 393rd Field Battery of 99th Field Regiment reported crossing the Irrawaddy on 4th March and moving into Ngalun where it exchanged its 3.7-inch howitzers for 25-pounders with their longer range. 394th Field Battery was with 6th British Infantry Brigade, with Major Bonsor, Captain Sebag-Montefiore and Captain Thom as FOOs. The Japanese made fanatical attacks with grenades, sub-machine guns and even their swords, knocked out several tanks moving with their turrets open, and attacked the gun positions but by 5th March the whole of 2nd British Division was across and ready to break out towards Ava. It had been a superbly organised crossing and a model of its kind.

'Soon after the crossing [of the Irrawaddy] a battery of 99th Field Regiment tapped a telephone line and heard a Jap RTO in a village a mile or two ahead detailing his departure programme for that night and describing a train loaded in the station. The battery shot up the station and were disappointed to hear the RTO announce that the rounds were falling near a pagoda 200 yards away.

The pagoda was marked on the map and the battery commander corrected his fire. The train was found burning next morning. Perhaps it was the only occasion on which a Jap, and an RTO at that, ranged a British battery.' (Lieutenant Colonel RLT Burges in Duncan).

After a spell with 4th British Infantry Brigade helping with their attack on Thagon, Uniacke reported moving to Headquarters 6th British Infantry Brigade to cover the general advance towards Mandalay on a two brigade front starting on 9th March. By this time the strain was beginning to tell on the pilots of the AOP Squadron. The seven pilots with 2nd British and 20th Indian Divisions flew 140 hours in the last week of February with a record on the 26th of 30 hours. All this kept squadron headquarters working very hard indeed to keep up the flow of combat supplies, repairs and, where possible, reinforcements. There was, after all, no AOP organisation above 'Squadron' in the Theatre. This meant that Major Denis Coyle and his team simply had to work wonders to keep the aircraft in the air and to ensure that the huge contribution this single squadron was making to the success of operations was maintained.

Slim had achieved his deception perfectly. The whole Japanese effort was directed on the northern bridgehead, so much so that they hardly noticed the silent dispersed crossings of 7th Indian Division at Nyaungu. This was an ambitious undertaking, the largest opposed river crossing attempted in any theatre in the Second World War. The river was over 2,000 yards wide in 7th Indian Division's area. Led by Special Boat Sections, 33rd Indian Infantry Brigade with nine tanks was first to go. The river had risen, the wind was strong and the current making 3 knots. It was decidedly 'lumpy.' They were soon discovered and heavily engaged and casualties began to mount, one company of 2nd South Lancashires got across but by 0800hours it was isolated. Enemy artillery fire increased. Then 4/15th Punjab was sent across under a massive artillery attack with air support at 0945 hours. Messervy was faced with a decision - should he continue, since the crossing was clearly going wrong?

He decided to try once more, the enemy gave ground under the concentrated firepower of the corps artillery and aircraft, which were followed up with the greatest courage by the infantry. An observer reported, 'More and more boats followed, heavily laden with troops, until boats were going in both ways in an almost continuous stream while the air and artillery curtain of fire moved gradually downstream and then back again behind the cliffs and beaches.' (Kirby). This showed a remarkably high standard of all arms training. By last light the brigade was across, a splendid effort by all arms working well together. Covering the crossings on the night of 14th and during 15th February were 136th Field Regiment, less 347th Battery, 139th Field Regiment, 24th Anti-Tank Regiment, equipped mainly with mortars, less 284th Anti-Tank Battery, 23rd Mountain Battery, 2nd Indian Field Regiment, 8th Medium Regiment and 59th (SP) Field Battery of 18th Field Regiment. Several targets had been registered in case of need. Now that 4th Indian Corps was taking a bigger part in the battle, it was the turn of 'B' flight 656th AOP Squadron to start work in earnest after their battles in the Chindwin area and it did so for the crossings at Nyaungu.

The subsidiary crossing at Pagan had also met trouble. An infantry patrol lying up in Pagan reported enemy entering the village just as the first wave in local boats left the departure bank. The local boatmen refused to proceed and the boats began to drift downstream. As the officers struggled to regain control, a single boat flying a white flag then approached from the enemy bank; in it were two INA officers who said the enemy had gone on to Nyaungu and had left their INA company to defend Pagan, but they wanted to surrender. By nightfall 1/11th Sikhs were all across. Their FOO was Captain ME Brown, of 'D' Troop 348th Field Battery, 136th Field Regiment, who established an OP on top of a pagoda. On 18th February he handed over to Captain Pat Griffin of 500th Field Battery of the same regiment. Throughout the 15th the rest of the division crossed. Major FR Clark and Captain JF Daykin of 348th Field Battery crossed with 4/8th Gurkhas and more OP parties of 500th Field Battery crossed with the KOSB.

The movement control of the crossing operation was brilliantly carried out by 5th (Mahratta) Anti-Tank Regiment. A large party of Japanese was resisting strongly from the catacombs in Nyaungu and these were blown in with high explosives by the Sappers, killing and burying an unknown number of enemy. By the 16th a link was made with the Sikhs at Pagan and the bridgehead was some 6,000 yards wide and 4,000 yards deep, with 89th Indian Infantry Brigade holding the west end and 33rd Indian Infantry Brigade holding the east. 114th Indian Infantry Brigade was still mopping up at Pakokku, with 28th (EA) Infantry Brigade withdrawing to Letse pursued by a strong Japanese column.

Slim, anxious to keep up the momentum, then ordered 17th Indian Division to cross the river. 48th Indian Infantry Brigade began on 17th February, closely followed by 63rd Indian Infantry Brigade on the 18th. By this time the 4th Indian Corps ferry was working to capacity and in the next five weeks it was to ferry some 10,000 vehicles, including tanks and guns, across one of the world's greatest rivers without any accidents, even though some rafts were sunk by enemy air attack. It was a magnificent effort by the Sappers. 348th Field Battery crossed on the 18th February and came straight into action, as Captain Pat Griffin was already calling for fire. 500th Field Battery crossed on 20th February and came into action alongside 348th Field Battery. A force went out to reconnoitre the tracks to Taungtha and a counter-attack was beaten off by 89th Indian Infantry Brigade and the guns. What had in fact happened was that 7th Indian Division's crossing had hit the junction of *15th* and *28th Armies* and both were obsessed with the northern crossings. Credit must, however, go to Messervy for pressing on when both his initial crossings looked like failures. 7th Indian Division's next job was to extend the bridgehead south to Chauk, capture Myingyan, which was to become the Forward Base for 14th Army and its main river port, and Taungtha so as to open the road to Meiktila once 17th Indian Division had passed through.

The enemy's position was serious but he still had a considerable force in the area. *15th* and *53rd Divisions* were pulling back to new positions south of Mandalay, *31st Division* less *58th Regiment* was opposite the Myinimu Bridgehead while *33rd Division* had *214th Regiment* at Pakokku, *213th* at Myingyan and *215th* at Taungtha. Chauk and the Yenanggyaung oilfields were held by *28th Army* which had *158th Regiment (Matsu Force)* of *49th Division* and *61st Regiment* of *4th Division* in that area.

Cowan's plan for 17th Indian Division was for 48th Indian Infantry Brigade, with a squadron of tanks, 59th (SP) Field Battery, and air support, to secure the Pyinbin road junction. He was then to seal off Taungtha while 255th Tank Brigade by-passed it and went on to capture Mahlaing. On 19th February Pyinbin was reported clear so 48th Indian Infantry Brigade moved at once; there was a brief fight at Oyin and another at Kamye while 255th Tank Brigade overran Welaung. 48th Indian Infantry Brigade took Taungha on 24th February, leaving Divisional Headquarters, 255th Tank and 63rd Indian Infantry Brigades to sweep past and move on towards Meiktila. The advance was led by one of the tank regiments supported by a battalion, 'Whichever regiment led made little difference to 59 Field Battery, who were always in the vanguard. Taungtha was taken with relatively light opposition by 24th February.' (Preston). Thabutkon airfield was occupied on the 26th and, after rapid repairs had been made, 99th Indian Infantry Brigade flew in on the 27th even though the airfield was still under fire.

It was during these battles that Lance Bombardier GC Huntley of 129th Field Regiment was at his OP when his OP officer was killed. Huntley then made his own fire plan to neutralise the enemy but when the fighting became too confused he organised a stretcher party, saved a wounded officer, recovered the body of his FOO and displayed the greatest gallantry throughout and was a magnificent example to all around him. For his outstanding gallantry in action he was awarded the Distinguished Conduct Medal. Sadly this gallant young NCO was killed in action by an enemy shell at Meiktila in April. By last light on 27th February, 9th Border was within six miles of Meiktila. On the following day 48th Indian Infantry Brigade cleaned up Taungtha, re-joined the division and took the lead. By last light it was some two miles north of the town, while 255th Tank Brigade, with 59th (SP) Field Battery in support, had made a wide sweep to seize the airfield on the east of the town. 'B' Troop, 59th Field Battery's tank OP and a troop of 9th Royal Deccan Horse met opposition at Thazi. All was now set for an assault on 1st March 1945.

But the Japanese had reoccupied Taungtha behind them and this cut the road putting 17th Indian Division back onto air supply. 7th Indian Division immediately began to clear the rear areas around Nyaungu, Myingyan, Taungtha and Welaung. The division had 116th Regiment RAC (6th Gordons), with medium tanks, a section of medium guns and a section of 7.2-inch howitzers so placed that they could cover all brigades. 89th Indian Infantry Brigade was also pushing south towards Chauk to prevent a counter-attack from that direction. 'Puffcol' was formed under Lieutenant Colonel LHO Pugh, commanding officer of 25th Indian Mountain Regiment. It consisted of one squadron 16th Cavalry less a troop, two companies 2nd South Lancashires in lorries, a platoon of medium machine-guns and the mechanised Bikanir Bijay Mountain Battery. It was to clear up the Kyaukpadaung - Mount Poppa - Seiktein area. For three weeks this little force dominated a wide stretch of country, destroying and harassing the enemy, inflicting many casualties and gaining much useful information. Lieutenant Colonel Lewis Pugh showed great energy, leadership and gallantry and was later promoted to command 33rd Indian Infantry Brigade, handing over 'Puffcol' to Lieutenant Colonel Mainprise-King when it became 'Kingcol.' Major GA Rowley-Conwy assumed command of 25th Indian Mountain Regiment. To the north of the bridgehead 33rd Indian Infantry Brigade had some tough fighting as it advanced to capture Myingyan and Taungtha and a posthumous Victoria Cross was won, this time by an infantry officer, Lieutenant WB Weston of The Green Howards, then attached to 1st West Yorkshires.

At Meiktila 17th Indian Divisional Artillery, 1st Indian and 129th Field Regiments and 21st Indian Mountain Regiment under the CRA, Brigadier HK Dimolene, was coming into action around Antu with 63rd Indian Infantry Brigade. 21st Indian Mountain Regiment, commanded by Lieutenant Colonel JB Chaplin, and 88th Anti-Tank Battery had arrived by air at Thabutkon on 1st and 2nd March. 99th Indian Infantry Brigade was already at Thabutkon. Cowan was ready to strike. At dawn on 2nd March 63rd Indian Infantry Brigade cleared the western outskirts of the town, while 48th Indian Infantry Brigade attacked from the north and met stubborn resistance especially from mortars, mines and artillery. 255th Tank Brigade reached the east shore of the southern lake and took the eastern airfield. The fighting in the town resumed in earnest on 3rd March and was still tough but by last light the town was clear and patrols had reached Thazi and Pyawbwe, both of which were taken and held. Also on 3rd March 'A' Troop Tank OP of 59th Field Battery with a squadron of tanks and a company of infantry set off to destroy an enemy position on the Mandalay road, capturing 2 x 37mm and 4 x 75mm guns.

The capture of Meiktila meant that the trap was closed around the Japanese *15th* and *33rd Divisions*. To complete this process 19th Indian and 36th British Divisions were advancing from the north and north east. 2nd British, which had by then crossed the Irrawaddy, and 20th Indian Divisions were advancing from the south and west, but the Japanese were not finished yet.

By 1st March 'B' Flight 656th AOP Squadron was established at Meiktila where the strip was under observed fire and two aircraft suffered damage. The flight moved to a lakeside strip which was safer and all aircraft were soon serviceable again. 'A' Flight crossed the Irrawaddy on 6th March. At this time 'C' Flight was at Ramree Island and Squadron Headquarters at Monywa, with Major Denis Coyle still in command. The part played by the squadron in these critical operations was of the greatest possible value. This was recognised by the end of March by the awards of the Military Cross, later changed to the Distinguished Flying Cross, to Captains W Boyd, EW Maslen-Jones and FJ McMath. Maslen-Jones's citation referred to his great contribution to successful operations by so many tree-top reconnaissances over enemy positions and by compiling sketches and controlling fire, especially in operations around Monywa. A similar award of the DFC was made to Captain Gregg, and his citation also refers to his accurate dropping of up-to-date maps to forward troops and FOOs and to his accuracy in control of the fire of the guns. During this time No. 1587 Flight at Deolali in India, under Captain Trevor Jones and later Captain RD Henshaw, was busy training pilots for the squadron.

We must next see what was happening on the northern front (Map 48). By 1st March the Chinese Yunnan divisions were returning to China. General Sultan's 30th Chinese Division had reached Hsenwi and 50th was at Namtu. 36th British Division was still forging down the eastern bank of the Irrawaddy and the Shweli valley towards Kyaukme via Mongmit and Mogok. It was however still held up at Myitson. There was hard fighting here for both 26th and 72nd British Infantry Brigades as they crossed the Shweli, while 29th British Infantry Brigade pressed on westwards from Twingge via Nabu towards Mongmit. Then, once across, the Japanese counter-attacked in force but this was driven off with heavy casualties to both sides. The Japanese then pulled back and Mongmit fell on 7th March while, on the 8th, 38th Chinese Division at last captured Lashio.

About this time General Wedemeyer began to put pressure on Mountbatten to release all Chinese and US forces for operations in China in May and June 1945 but Mountbatten explained to the Combined Chiefs of Staff that he needed this force to protect the Burma Road and to operate on his left flank as he advanced towards Rangoon. Thus their departure would have serious effects on his strategy. Leese reported to Mountbatten that, without the Chinese/US Forces of NCAC, his chances of reaching Rangoon before the monsoon were 'negligible.' Mountbatten met Chiang Kai-shek at Chungking on 6th March to discuss these issues. He got agreement to phase out the Chinese divisions according to the progress of the advance on Rangoon but that 475th US Regiment could go on 11th March to begin the training of the newly-formed divisions in China.

Now back to the situation developing south and east of the Irrawaddy. With four secure crossings, 5th Indian Division in reserve at Monywa, Meiktila in his hands and his southern flank held, Slim felt he was in a strong position and ready to strike for Mandalay. His task was to destroy the Japanese armies around that town while ensuring that his garrison at Meiktila kept them cut off. But the enemy still had the remains of *15th, 31st, 33rd,* and *53rd Divisions* and smaller forces equivalent to about two more divisions. All had sustained crippling losses and were badly under strength, though their morale remained high. But Slim had the initiative and the morale of 14th Army had never been higher. At this stage he put 5th Indian Division under command of Messervy's 4th Indian Corps; its 9th Indian Infantry Brigade had already been flown forward from Palel to Meiktila. 7th Indian Division still held the Nyaungu bridgehead although Japanese pressure against it was increasing. On 14th March 4/1st Gurkhas with 116th Regiment RAC and 139th Field Regiment attacked Taungtha, where the fighting was again very hard. Messervy then allocated 161st Indian Infantry Brigade of 5th Indian Division to Evans and at the same time received intelligence that Major General Yamamoto was planning a major attack from the south to capture Nyaungu, Sinthe and Myitche.

By this time 17th Indian Division was secure in Meiktila but was itself surrounded by superior numbers. Cowan, however, decided to retain the initiative by a policy of aggressive defence. 99th Indian Infantry Brigade was responsible for the defence of the town while 48th and 63rd Indian Infantry Brigades patrolled well outwards from a series of strong points in the town, having the guns of 21st Mountain Regiment in their support. These operations began on 5th March against Mahlaing, Zayetkon, Pyawbwe, Thazi and Wundwin. 1st Royal (Kohat) Mountain Battery moved with an armoured column in a sweep of the Wundin Road and came under fire from an enemy

75mm gun at Ywadan. After a tough all arms fight the village was captured, the Japanese leaving 250 dead, eight prisoners, one 105mm and four 75mm guns, two MMGs, two LMGs and 20 swords behind. (War Diary 21st Indian Mountain Regiment).

Another column, moving up towards Wundwin and consisting of a squadron of 5th Probyn's Horse, a company of 6/15th Punjab and a battery of 21st Indian Mountain Regiment, met an enemy strong point at Thedaw. The guns came into action and, with infantry riding on the tanks, a right flank attack was mounted. The enemy's guns, however, were too strong so an air strike was called and the guns marked the targets with coloured smoke. The tanks and infantry again attacked and the Japanese withdrew, leaving six guns and 110 dead behind them. A second series of raids was mounted against Pyawbwe and Mahlaing which involved some ferocious fighting and more were carried out locally but, although these kept the enemy at bay, he was in fact closing in relentlessly. At Pyawbwe on 8th March 6th (Jacob's) Mountain Battery, with a mixed patrol under Lieutenant Colonel JB Chaplin, destroyed a force of some 15 enemy vehicles. On the 11th the 1st Royal (Kohat) Mountain Battery, under Major JOS Janson, was supporting 9th Border at Yindaw when the gun position was rushed and overrun. The enemy was quickly turned out with the bayonet, suffering many casualties. The attack went on all night and 27 enemy dead were counted at dawn. 37th Mountain Battery, commanded by Major N Rawlins, operated with a motley selection of vehicles with great success around Thedaw.

Further north 33rd Indian Corps was preparing to capture Mandalay. Rees, with 19th Indian Division, had his orders and was about to cross the Chaungmagyi Chaung with 98th Indian Infantry Brigade. He had formed 'Stiletto Force' on 5th March, under the command of Lieutenant Colonel S Gardiner which consisted of 1/15th Punjab, carried in lorries, C Squadron 7th Light Cavalry, 240th Field Battery of 115th Field Regiment, a troop of 82nd Anti-Tank Regiment, a machine gun company and a troop of Indian Engineers. 'Stiletto Force' began its advance at 0800 hours 5th March, by-passed Madaya and made straight for Mandalay where it drove into the outskirts, scattering surprised Japanese, and by 0615 hours on 8th March 240th Field Battery opened fire on Mandalay Hill, '. . . and Captain IA Wallace smashed a Jap counter-attack which threatened Divisional Tactical HQ at the foot of the hill, where General Rees in his familiar red dust scarf was as usual inspiring his men to victory. The rest of the regiment fought a spirited infantry battle in the process of coming into action near Kabaing, 4000 yards from the city. While the second-in-command, Major AD Foxon, and recce parties, under the eyes and support of our CRA, Brigadier McDonald, (armed with a carbine), attacked a Jap rearguard in the village, RHQ on the outskirts engaged the Japs as they fled over the fields. Disappointed by his failure to compete with the marksmanship of his adjutant, the CO somewhat unsportingly increased his 'bag' by using a handy 25-pdr and directing airburst HE from the top of the 'quad'.' During this action Lieutenant DJ Currall was killed and Lieutenant HG Hampshire severely wounded. (RAG Nicholson in Duncan). Soon 'Stiletto Force' had seized the pagoda-crowned northern slopes of Mandalay Hill. While this was happening, 98th Indian Infantry Brigade with 480th Field Battery attacked Madaya, which it soon cleared. It then moved fast to join 'Stiletto Force,' its 8/12th FF Regiment attacking the northern wall of Fort Dufferin which was intact in spite of heavy bombing. The fort was very strong and was going to be difficult to take.

64th Indian Infantry Brigade, following Rees's orders, isolated the town from the east. Rees also told 98th Indian Infantry Brigade to capture the fort under the heaviest artillery attack he could arrange, using a medium gun firing point-blank at the north gate of Fort Dufferin. The Berkshires began to clear the west of the town. The medium gun opened fire at 0930 hours 9th March and had opened a breach by 1300 hours. An AOP officer reported that this was useable as the rubble formed a ramp on the inside. Then, under a heavy concentration by the guns of 19th Indian Division, 4th Indian, and 115th Field Regiments, 8/12th FF Regiment and a detachment of engineers assaulted the breach. They followed close to the falling shells but, as soon as the guns lifted, they started to take casualties and by 1600 hours they had lost a third of their numbers. Rees, who was watching, called it off. By 10th March he had most of the town but he realised that Fort Dufferin was still going to be a very hard nut to crack. However, slowly in the next four days, it was surrounded. Meanwhile the Japanese on Mandalay Hill fought to the death and were not finished off until 13th March. Captain D Hine of 480th Field Battery was presented with a Japanese sword in recognition of the splendid part played in this action and because he was the first British officer to reach the summit. 64th Indian Infantry Brigade relieved 98th Indian Infantry Brigade on 15th March. 64th Indian Infantry Brigade had five battalions, a squadron of 150th Regiment RAC, 134th Medium, 115th Field and 33rd Anti-Tank/Mortar Regiments and 65th Field Company IE.

At the same time 2nd British Division was battling its way through Ava, which also contained a formidable fort, while 20th Indian Division captured Kyaukse to cut off the Mandalay garrison. By 14th March 80th Indian Infantry Brigade had occupied Dwelha and 100th Indian Infantry Brigade was up to the Panlaung river. Both were meeting heavy enemy artillery fire. By 13th March 6th British Infantry Brigade had cut the road running south from Ava and 5th British Infantry Brigade had reached Tadau. It was becoming obvious that enemy pressure everywhere north of Mandalay was slackening, while that against Meiktila was growing, clearly to relieve the pressure on Mandalay. Accordingly Stopford ordered Gracey, with 20th Division, to change direction and push south east towards Meiktila and Nicholson, with 2nd Division, to take Ava and link up with 19th Indian Division in Mandalay. Gracey acted quickly. He reinforced 100th Indian Infantry Brigade with a tank regiment, two squadrons of armoured cars and 114th Field Regiment, and ordered them to go fast and clear all enemy southwards towards Wundwin, to make physical contact with 17th Indian Division and then to strike at Kyaukse from the south.

In March 145th (Berkshire Yeomanry) Field Regiment arrived in Bombay from the UK and went to Dehra Dun for training. On 5th August, Lieutenant Colonel Rodney Burges, no stranger to the Burma scene, assumed command with Major David Campbell as his second-in-command, Major JA Palmer Tomkinson commanding 395th Field Battery, Major R Verney commanding 396th Field Battery and Major RM England commanding 509th Field Battery. The regiment was told to prepare for Operation ZIPPER, the plan for the invasion of Malaya.

We now know that the Japanese were taking desperate steps to save their armies. They had been completely wrong-footed by 17th Indian Division's rapid move to Meiktila and, although they had recognised the threat, they were too slow in moving forces to defeat it. Lieutenant General E Naka had been ordered to take his *18th Division* to Meiktila but was too late. On arrival at Kume on 4th March he was told to attack it. He was to take under command *119th Regiment, 214th Regiment* and the remnants of *14th Tank Regiment,* together with an artillery group. *49th Division* would co-operate by attacking from the south. Then Honda was told to take command of operations to re-take Meiktila with his *33rd Army.*

By 16th March 64th Indian Infantry Brigade had planned a silent attack on Fort Dufferin but, before this could take place, 221 Group RAF decided to try some 2000lb bombs on the 15th. It was to no avail, the bombs did not hit the wall and unless they did nothing happened. Meanwhile several medium guns, both 5.5- and 6-inch, had been pounding away at point blank range and a number of breaches had been created on the north and east walls. Then a silent breach was attempted at 2200 hours 17th March. By 2300 hours two companies of infantry and engineers went across the moat in rubber boats in the north-east and north-west corners of the fort, but it was not to be. They came under very heavy small arms fire and there was nothing the guns could do to help. At no point did they penetrate the fort without drawing a murderous fire from the defenders. By this time Rees had news from a prisoner that all was not well inside the fort and that resistance would stop when the defenders realised that no relief was possible. Thus he ordered all brigades to begin to encircle the fort. He then brought up some 6-inch howitzers to within 300 yards of the walls and by last light on the 18th there were 17 more breaches on the northern and eastern walls; shades of the siege of Badajoz in 1812 or of Delhi in 1857. After a heavy air attack on the 20th, six Burmans were seen emerging from the east gate carrying a white flag and a Union Jack and making their way towards the gun positions of 134th Medium Regiment. They said that there were no Japanese left in the fort, and they wanted to surrender. Accordingly a force from 62nd Indian Infantry Brigade entered the fort at last. At 1330 hours, and most appropriately, a Gunner from 134th Medium Regiment nailed a Union Jack to the fort flagstaff. It was over, Mandalay had fallen and a few days later the Gunners provided detachments for a Guard of Honour for the hoisting of the Union Jack by General Slim over the ruins of Government House. The remains of *15th Division* had gone.

5th British Infantry Brigade had captured the fort at Ava without difficulty on 18th March and had secured the north end of the great Ava bridge. Meanwhile 6th British Infantry Brigade had secured the Myitnge bridge which was damaged but could be repaired. It was here that during a highly successful attack on Sado under the fire of 16th Field Regiment, Major Wilfred Foster, Battery Commander 72/86th Battery, was killed in action by a burst of machine gun fire. A sad loss to his regiment, he had led his battery across Burma and the Irrawaddy with the greatest distinction. Then on 21st March Major Watty Scott-Plummer and Gordon Daniels, his staff captain, were killed by a mine. Everywhere small parties of Japanese fought to the end. About 500 were killed and only two taken prisoner. The remains of the Japanese forces were, however, still escaping through Kyaukse before it was captured by 20th Indian Division. 5th Indian Division was next ordered to move on Chauk, 19th Indian Division to consolidate Mandalay and then move on Meiktila and Thazi, when relieved by 36th British Division. 20th Indian Division formed 'Barcol' consisting of 7th Light Cavalry less two squadrons, 11th PAVO Cavalry less two squadrons, a squadron of 150th Regiment RAC, 18th (SP) Field Regiment less 59th (SP) Field Battery, 4/10th Gurkhas lorry-borne, a VCP and 401st Field Squadron IE. Its task was to race round through Pyinzi and Pindale and cut off the enemy at Wundwin some 70 miles away. It was there to harass enemy attacking Meiktila from the north. By the 22nd, having surprised enemy everywhere, it was established around Wundwin. It did much damage and managed to contact 17th Indian Division. It was then ordered to attack Kume from the south. At 1700 hours on the 23rd 'Barcol' burst into the town and scattered some 300 astonished Japanese who took to the hills, having received a taste of their own methods. 32nd Indian Infantry Brigade advanced southwards, making contact with 17th Indian Division on 30th March.

While all this had been going on, life had not been easy for the defenders of the bridgehead over the Irrawaddy. Heavy attacks were made from the south on Letse, west of the river and Chauk, to the east. On 18th February with tanks and the guns of 136th Field Regiment. 89th Indian Infantry Brigade had advanced down the east bank of the river towards Chauk, which it did not reach until 20th April. Right from the start the fighting was very hard. 28th (EA) Brigade, with 347th Battery of 136th Field Regiment, advanced down the west side of the Irrawaddy early in February and on the 22nd was relieved by one battery of 2nd Indian Field Regiment, then serving as 4th Indian Corps Troops. Together with RHQ of 2nd Indian Field Regiment, the battery formed the artillery for operations in the Letse area. On 25th February they again fought with outstanding gallantry to beat off a Japanese attack. 2nd Indian Field Regiment was commanded by Lieutenant Colonel PS Gyani. It had already fought in the Western Desert, at Bir Hacheim, with great distinction. Many years later the regiment was awarded the Honour Title 'Letse' in recognition of its performance. Colonel Gyani was awarded the OBE. The gun positions of 136th Field Regiment were attacked and enemy got right up to the guns themselves but were beaten off. On 4th March 'B' Company of 4/8th Gurkhas was surrounded on a small hill near Milaungbya when the commanding officer of the battalion, who was watching, ordered the guns of 136th Field Regiment to engage. The leading Japanese had closed to within grenade range when the shells of the regiment arrived amongst them; they disappeared in the smoke and flame and when it cleared there were many dead and the rest had gone. Regrettably, so close was the target that one shell fell among the Gurkhas and several were killed and wounded.

'At this time when an AOP was called for we invariably got an American L5 which would land and pick up a Gunner officer to act as OP. On one occasion Captain [ME] Brown was airborne and indicated a target with yellow smoke for a squadron of Hurri-bombers to great effect. Most officers in the regiment did at some time carry out shoots from the L5s.' (136th Field Regiment War Diary). These light aircraft, attached to 89th Indian Infantry Brigade for liaison and casualty evacuation duties, were flown by American sergeants who, like the officers of 136th Field Regiment, had received no training in AOP work. Major Robertson observed that no officers had even flown before. This unusual form of 'liaison' continued for some time and was an undoubted success before and after the clearing of Chauk and the recrossing of the Irrawaddy by 89th Indian Brigade.

By 20th March the fighting was still very tough. Then 4/8th Gurkhas and 136th Field Regiment attacked again and drove the enemy back at Milaungbya Hill where a patrol base was established. Life on this hill became a nightmare, it was under constant attack and it was near here that Major Firth, commanding 347th Field Battery, was killed. He had served with the battery since September 1942 and was sadly missed by all ranks. On 21st March, after a heavy bombardment, a violent attack was made against 28th (EA) Infantry Brigade dug in at Letse, by *153rd Regiment.* This was eventually driven off with some 250 casualties, about half lying over the wire against which they had hurled themselves. To the east of the river 4/8th Gurkhas raided Singu and destroyed three guns. They went back the second night and held the place. These two actions were in fact the final throes of Major General T Yamamoto's offensive from the south; it had failed. 161st Indian Infantry Brigade, with 139th Field Regiment and a squadron of 116th Regiment RAC, attacked Taungtha yet again. The fighting was fierce raging amongst some sheer-sided ravines throughout 18th and 19th March. Success was mainly due to the amazing courage of a young Sikh officer, Lieutenant Karamjeet Singh Judge, directing tanks onto Japanese bunkers while not taking cover himself. His great gallantry was to be posthumously rewarded by a Victoria Cross. It was here too that Gunner H Bones, of 139th Field Regiment, was acting as FOO's signaller when the OP was caught by heavy mortar and machine gun fire. His FOO was wounded but Bones remained by his radio, in a jeep in a very exposed position, to complete the smoke screen which his FOO had been laying. He then rescued his FOO and several wounded Indian soldiers under heavy fire and for these acts he was awarded the Military Medal. The town was taken.

At Meiktila the Japanese realised that they must re-take the airfield and this resulted in bitter fighting round the perimeter on 16th and 17th March. Lieutenant Colonel Chaplin, of 21st Indian Mountain Regiment, insisted on strict discipline by all ranks on the perimeter. He ordered that no man was to open fire unless he was certain of a kill. One night while going round his posts he asked a young Indian Gunner if he had seen anything and the Gunner replied in a whisper, 'Yes sir, two Japs are on the wire about 20 yards away.' Chaplin said, 'Why do you not fire?' The Gunner replied, 'I am afraid I am not a very good shot sir, and I am not certain I can kill them!' (Chaplin).

The fly-in of 9th Indian Infantry Brigade was interrupted by Japanese attacks on Meiktila airfield and from 18th March flying had to stop, but eventually the brigade got in under fire thanks to the gallantry of the American pilots of the Dakotas. A serious Japanese attack developed on the south-east corner of the town when *106th Regiment* attacked, with *49th Artillery Regiment* being boldly handled. At one stage a 75mm gun was brought into action only 15 yards from a 1/7th Gurkha Rifles position and only stopped when its whole crew had been killed. Lieutenant Spencer of 21st Indian Mountain Regiment found himself being engaged over open sights as he sped across the airfield towards his OP in a jeep. All this was due to Colonel T Uga who commanded these guns to good effect. He was to cause heavy casualties to 255th Tank Brigade during March. He died beside his guns at the end of the month, a formidable foe.

The enemy kept up his pressure from Kindo and Nyaungbintha, two small hamlets near Meiktila. 99th Indian Infantry Brigade was sent to clear the north-west sector and did so as far as Mahlaing, linking up with 5th Indian Division. On the airfield 9th Indian Infantry Brigade was under continuous attack from 21st March by *18th Division* and *18th Mountain Artillery Regiment*. An attack on 48th Indian Infantry Brigade's perimeter during the night 22nd/23rd March lasted until dawn and 195 enemy dead were counted afterwards. The guns and mortars had caused most of the casualties and 21st Indian Mountain Regiment was specially mentioned for its very accurate and effective fire which had landed within 50 yards of the perimeter wire. On the 23rd a very heavy attack was made on the gun positions on the eastern edge of Meiktila and 1/7th Gurkhas fought gallantly around the guns. Lieutenant Mallinson, of 6th (Jacob's) Mountain Battery, was responsible for some very accurate close DF which caused many casualties. The fighting reached a climax on 24th/25th and was severe in the extreme on the airfield. Finally 48th Indian Infantry Brigade, with 1st Indian Field Regiment and two squadrons of tanks, counter-attacked but it took three days of desperate fighting to drive off the Japanese. A 'cab-rank' was used to apply air power for the first time in these battles and it provided instant air support and was a great success. Napalm was used for the first time.

It was on 22nd March that Messervy gave his orders for the next stage of the battle. As soon as the Japanese had been cleared from the Meiktila area, 4th Indian Corps was to concentrate there and prepare for the advance on Rangoon. 5th Indian Division was now under the command of Major General Robert Mansergh, Major General Warren having been killed in an air crash. Mansergh had been CRA of the division, so knew it well. He was an impressive man possessed of great charm and experience. He had commanded a battery at Keren in Eritrea and was greatly respected throughout the division. After the war he too was to become Master Gunner St James's Park. On 22nd March 1945, 5th Indian Division's orders were to capture Taungtha and then relieve 17th Indian Division at Meiktila. 7th Indian Division was to pass under the command of 33rd Indian Corps for the advance. 17th Indian Division was, meanwhile, to destroy all enemy around Meiktila.

It was here, on the night of 24/25th March, that 21st Indian Mountain Regiment repeatedly engaged enemy attacking the 9th Indian Infantry Brigade Box. Captain Bill Spencer was FOO, his telephone line was the only one that remained 'through' all night. Although enemy tanks broke in, he remained at his post calling for fire. He alone was responsible for beating off the attack which would otherwise almost certainly have overrun the position. At this time 6th (Jacob's) Mountain Battery had three OPs out. Lieutenant Ernest Hadfield with 1/7th Gurkhas, Subadar Mohammed Khan with 4/12th Frontier Force Rifles and Lieutenant Percy Mallinson with 3/2nd Punjab. During the night a heavy Japanese artillery attack was followed up by tanks and infantry. Percy Mallinson moved to get better observation and brought fire down so effectively that he stopped them dead. Then their tanks came on again and one broke right into the position. Mallinson hunted it with a PIAT and knocked it out. He was awarded the Military Cross for his action that night and his citation reads 'There is no doubt that the extremely accurate fire brought down by Lieutenant Mallinson prevented this attack developing further and his own gallant individual action against an enemy tank stopped others from penetrating the position.' (quoted by Chaplin).

The fighting around Meiktila still raged. The history of 59/73rd (SP) Battery states, 'It was undoubtedly the OP parties, working with the infantry/tank columns, who bore the brunt of the action.

Each day a different sortie would be made by a column which, so far as we were concerned, generally consisted of a squadron of tanks, an infantry battalion and a tank OP. It was during one of these sorties, to the south of Meiktila that [Captain] Francis Allom, 'B' Troop Commander was severely wounded, dying in hospital in Meiktila later, before he could be evacuated. His place as 'B' Troop Commander was taken by Lt Peters. Similarly, during one of the attacks to clear the airfield, which encountered heavy artillery and mortar fire, Capt Preston was slightly wounded, and thereafter, 'A' Troop was commanded by Lt Birch . . . The two Troop Tank OP crews, although under severe strain, insisted in remaining in their teams and once again it was one of these, L/Bdr Lillis, who suffered, losing an eye whilst supporting an assault to clear the airfield.' (Preston). 59th Battery had been continuously spearhead of the attack by 255th Indian Tank Brigade, itself the spearhead formation of 14th Army from the end of January at Gangaw to the battles for Meiktila at the end of March. Some nine weeks right out in front against a powerful enemy; it was a wonderful record.

5th Indian Division had a fierce fight on its hands around Taungtha and at Kyaukse where the Japanese fought to the last man but by 25th March the first convoy got through to Meiktila. Cowan ordered 99th Indian Infantry Brigade to advance to Pyawbwe by way of Thazi. 5th Indian Division arrived in Meiktila on 1st April and the airfield was opened for use. The battle of Meiktila was at last over but the cost had been high. 4th Indian Corps lost some 4,000 killed and wounded and another 4,000 from sickness. 33rd Indian Corps, which was larger and had fought longer, had some 5,500 killed and wounded and some 3,500 sick, a total from all causes of some 17,000 casualties. The fighting in and around Meiktila is honoured in the Royal Regiment of Artillery because of the ubiquitous and gallant action of 59th (SP) Field Battery, later to become 148th (Meiktila) Commando FOU Battery, an Honour Title which was granted in 1975 and which ensures that the performance of the Regiment in this struggle is not forgotten.

In his report for April 1945 to the BRA ALFSEA, Brigadier LC Manners-Smith, Lieutenant Colonel Charles Younger, of 129th Field Regiment in 17th Indian Division, remarked on the toughness of the fighting around Meiktila. He records that the use of airburst projectiles had almost stopped enemy snipers positioning themselves high in the trees. 'Tree snipers have recently gone out of fashion and in recent attacks I have noticed that the majority of enemy snipers have been in positions on the ground such as tree roots.' He also stresses the importance of all Gunners being expert at local defence '. . . the number of times when one can sit back and say that the infantry will hold the fort for you are few and far between these days or in our experience in the past.' Gun positions were enemy priorities for attack. He then goes on to say of fire plans that 'We have seen plenty in the last two months . . . I am more sure than ever that "at call" is the answer practically every time and that with our communications and a little foresight this presents no difficulties. They require control by an FOO with the lead infantry. This is because the infantry can never be sure of their speed across the ground in the jungle against a resolute foe. Finally he comments on the Home Leave Scheme of which, he said, 'It proved a very unsettling business in the early days . . . I have 37 men away from the regiment without relief at a time when they can ill be spared.' (Younger).

The RAF had played a major part in these battles and flew some 4,360 close air support sorties and 2,300 air supply sorties. Air strikes were a daily occurrence and the machinery and procedures developed by 221 and 224 Groups RAF were by then working very effectively. Seldom had land/air co-operation worked so well for so long and the gallantry of the pilots earned the greatest respect of all soldiers at that time. There were of course extensive strategic air operations in progress as well, essentially involved with cutting the Japanese lines of communication and with attacks on Japanese forces in China.

24th AA Brigade, consisting of 5th Indian HAA and 2nd Indian LAA Regiments, took over the air defence of Meiktila. Its airfield was in constant use for flying in reinforcements and supplies. Meanwhile 52nd HAA Regiment replaced 67th HAA Regiment in 4th Indian Corps and 28th LAA Regiment was split up amongst divisions. 33rd Indian Corps retained 101st HAA and 44th LAA Regiments. (Routledge).

As the comparative cool of the month of March gave way to the fierce pre-monsoon heat of April, an even greater sense of urgency gripped the men of 14th Army. From its commander downwards every man sensed victory and was determined to capture Rangoon before the elements were added to their enemies.

Before we turn to that next phase of the war in the next chapter it is necessary to look at developments in NCAC. After protracted discussion Leese eventually accepted that, since he was going to lose all Chinese forces before long anyway, he could no longer rely on them in his plans to capture Rangoon. Therefore he would not stand in the way of their departure to China if this would help the overall war effort. He asked that 36th British Division should pass to him once it reached Kyaukme in order that he could release 19th Indian Division from Mandalay. Mountbatten supported this view but said that he must keep at least one Chinese division until he was satisfied that there was no longer a threat to the Burma Road and that he could not spare aircraft to move the Chinese. Eventually it was agreed that all US/Chinese forces would leave SEAC by 1st June when it was expected Rangoon would have fallen.

Having established an airfield at Mongmit, 36th British Division began its advance on Mogok on 14th March which was occupied on the 19th. Monglong fell on the 22nd and the division set off for Kyaukme where it linked up with 50th Chinese Division. It then moved to Mandalay to come, once again, under British command.

By 1st April 1945, exactly as planned by General Slim, 14th Army stood poised for its final test in Burma, the race for Rangoon. The country was more open and favoured the use of tanks and artillery and it was his superiority in these two combat arms that he intended to exploit. The part played by the Royal Regiment in getting the army across the mighty Irrawaddy was fundamental to success. Wherever possible, guns were used concentrated to great effect but only when controlled by a team of highly competent and very courageous observers either on the ground or in the air. On the ground the artillery commander had to be alongside his infantry or tank commander at every level.

Great was the ingenuity shown by Gunners everywhere. The measures taken to maintain an outstanding record in keeping communications 'through' in appalling conditions, in finding gun areas and in carrying out some kind of survey, tested everyone to the limit. Seldom did the guns make a mistake, although in such conditions it was inevitable that from time to time a round did fall in the wrong place and occasionally hit our own troops, but it was very rare. The use of the 3.7-inch HAA guns against ground targets, the 5.5-inch guns and the 6-inch howitzers against the walls of Fort Dufferin and the deadly ultra-close defensive fire used by all regiments, none more so than the mountain units, had great effect on the outcome of battle. It had been a great period in the history of the Regiment.

CHAPTER 15

THE RACE FOR RANGOON

APRIL - MAY 1945

(Maps 48 and 49)

The plan for the offensive to capture Rangoon depended once again on logistics and the availability of land and air transport. The effective radius of action of supply aircraft was 250 miles from their airfields at Imphal, Agartala, Chittagong, Akyab and Ramree. Delivery from forward bases and dropping zones would be by road and river boat. Myingyan was to be the advanced base but it had not yet been captured. From Map 50 it will be seen that the first three airfields listed above could stock and maintain a base at Myingyan. In addition Slim ordered that aircraft at Akyab and Ramree would provide air supply to the forces on the move south from Mandalay. But this and the maximum possible use of river transport would not be enough. The lines of communication transport would have to be continuous from Dimapur through Kalewa to Myingyan and then this would need to be supplemented by railways as they were brought back into operation. But even so, the force itself would have to be cut in size in order to reduce the demand. It was a risky plan as it could not stand much delay due to bad weather or enemy action.

Slim decided that 4th Indian Corps would spearhead the advance and would be supplied by air. The corps was first to clear up the enemy around Taungtha and hold the line Seikpyu - Chauk - Kyaukpadaung. It was then to capture Pyawbwe by 1st April and concentrate around Meiktila and Thazi ready for the advance on Rangoon. Meanwhile 33rd Indian Corps was to clear up all enemy around Mandalay, Maymyo, Kyaukse and Wundwin. 20th Indian Division was to prepare for the advance down the Irrawaddy, 2nd British Division was to go to the Myingyan - Nyaungu area and 19th Indian Division to the Meiktila - Thazi area. There would then be a major re-grouping for the advance south. 7th Indian Division would pass from 4th to 33rd Indian Corps, 19th Indian Division would pass from 33rd Indian Corps to come under the direct command of 14th Army while the Indian 7th Light Cavalry and 18th (SP) Field Regiments would pass from 33rd to 4th Indian Corps. 4th Indian Corps would then advance down the Sittang to Toungoo while 14th Army, using 19th Indian Division and the 8th Light Cavalry, would be responsible for the protection of its left flank. 33rd Indian Corps was to advance down the Irrawaddy capturing Seikpyu, Chauk, Yenangyaung, Magwe and Prome on the way. Some formations, probably 2nd and 36th British Divisions, would then be flown out to India to reduce the logistic load at the appropriate time.

The Main Headquarters of 14th Army and HQ No 221 Group RAF would move to Meiktila as soon as possible with a view to proceeding on to Toungoo and Rangoon as the advance continued. Meiktila would also be the main medical centre, with subsidiaries at Toungoo and Magwe as they were cleared. Then, in order to help his administrative problems, Mountbatten ordered a modified Plan DRACULA to land at Rangoon and advance north to meet 14th Army opening up the port in doing so. He ordered 15th Indian Corps to plan this operation with 26th

Indian Division, reinforced by armour, artillery and a parachute battalion from 44th Indian Parachute Division; 2nd British Division was to be the follow-up force. Mountbatten accepted that this operation could delay subsequent operations against Malaya. Accordingly 2nd British Division would be flown out to Calcutta by 15th April to begin training for amphibious landings. The aim of all these operations was still to capture Rangoon before the monsoon in May/June and to prepare the port and airfields around it for subsequent operations to capture Malaya and Singapore as soon as possible thereafter. While this work was proceeding Slim was planning clandestine operations for Force 136 throughout southern Burma and there was also the imminent possibility of a rising of local forces in Burma. This was going to need careful control because its leaders were still under suspicion of collaborating with the Japanese. This rising did indeed begin on 27th March, despite 14th Army's efforts to delay it.

Although the enemy air threat was not serious it did exist and from time to time the Japanese could still mount effective air attacks. In 4th Indian Corps batteries of 28th LAA and 52nd HAA Regiments were allotted to divisions as follows:

5th Indian Division:
106th LAA Battery
155th and 271st HAA Batteries.

17th Indian Division:
250th LAA Battery
159th HAA Battery.

4th Indian Corps:
112th LAA Battery (To protect forward airstrips for the AOP Flights).

The most serious air attacks suffered by the corps were onto airstrips and moving columns but the RAF quickly dealt with them, although the LAA Gunners shot down two low-flying enemy fighters. The HAA batteries were used mainly in the ground role but the defence of the airfields at Payagyi and Pegu and the Sittang Bridge would need all the guns of 271st HAA Battery and eventually all three batteries of 28th LAA Regiment.

In 33rd Indian Corps the CCRA kept 101st HAA Regiment under his command and used it mainly in the ground role. However he used 297th and 379th HAA Batteries and all 44th LAA Regiment for the defence of Magwe airfield when it fell to 20th Indian Division on 19th April. During the advance on Prome both 44th and 101st Regiments fought for a while as infantry, guarding the gap between the two advancing corps. They sent out fighting patrols and fought several actions with Japanese trying to escape eastwards. At one stage a fighting patrol of 75th LAA Battery was attacked and surrounded and in the battle that followed it lost some 15 men killed or wounded. Both regiments were concentrated at Allanmyo for a rest before continuing with a similar list of ground and air defence tasks. As the advance continued, the guns of 24th AA Brigade followed up until eventually they took over the air defence of Rangoon.

15th Indian Corps was free to operate southwards and eastwards in the Arakan in the knowledge that the Royal Navy dominated the Bay of Bengal. It was clear that *121st Regiment* of *54th Division* was holding the coast from Dalat to Taungup, and *55th Division* was thought to be around Taungup. On 18th February Christison reckoned that the other two regiments of *54th Division* were in the An valley. He therefore decided to clear this valley as soon as he could. He wanted to prevent all Japanese forces in the Arakan from reinforcing enemy forces on the Irrawaddy front. His plan was for Stockwell's 82nd West African Division, less 2nd (WA) Infantry

Brigade at Kangaw, to advance via Kyweguseik and Dalat and attack An from the north. 2nd (WA) Infantry Brigade was to pass through 25th Indian Division's beachhead at Ruywa and attack from the west while 22nd (EA) Infantry Brigade, passing through a beachhead to be established by 26th Indian Division at Letpan, would attack An from the south. 25th Indian Division was also to capture Tamandu and establish a maintenance centre. Then 26th Indian Division was to take Taungup.

We now know that Lieutenant General S Miyazaki, commanding *54th Division*, had ordered *111th* and *154th Regiments* together with *14th Anti-Tank Battalion* and *54th Artillery Regiment* to hold Letmauk and the line of the Dalet Chaung and also cover the defence of An. *121st Regiment* was to cover the Taungup - Prome road. Miyazaki was then ordered to send most of *154th Regiment* to assist in the defence of the Irrawaddy, which meant that in effect he had only four infantry battalions, his artillery regiment and a reconnaissance battalion left.

By 27th February these operations down the Akyab coast were under way. 2nd (WA) Infantry Brigade was held up at Sabagyi about five miles west of An. It was then told to head north towards Letmauk. 25th Indian Division with 53rd and 74th Indian Infantry Brigades was secure at Ruywa. At this point Christison was told to destroy all enemy around An and operate from Taungup towards Prome but without air supply as from 7th March. This meant a change of plan. He told Major General GN Wood, commanding 25th Indian Division, to capture Tamandu by 4th March and set up a Forward Maintenance Area (FMA). He told Stockwell to leave 1st (WA) Infantry Brigade at Dalet and then to move on Letmauk from the north. He was then to take his division, less 1st and 2nd (WA) Infantry Brigades, down the coast and move into Tamandu. Once this was cleared he was to attack Letmauk from the west. Meanwhile 2nd (WA) Infantry Brigade was already directed at Letmauk from the south. All was ready by 3rd March.

On the 4th, 74th Indian Infantry Brigade entered Tamandu after some hard fighting. On 6th March 2nd (WA) Infantry Brigade had cut the road south of Letmauk but had been driven into the hills. On the 7th, 82nd West African Division arrived in Tamandu as planned and on the 8th Stockwell attacked Letmauk. But air supply had by then stopped apart from a special effort for 2nd (WA) Infantry Brigade south of Letmauk. Operations against An made little progress during the next week. 4th (WA) Infantry Brigade with 8th Field Regiment and a squadron of 19th Lancers advanced from Tamandu on 12th March but did not occupy Letmauk until the 17th. By this time 1st (WA) Infantry Brigade had swung round behind 4th (WA) Infantry Brigade, reaching Letmauk on the 20th. Also on 20th March 22nd (EA) Infantry Brigade arrived at Tamandu. Stockwell next decided to advance on An. By this time 4th Indian Infantry Brigade of 26th Indian Division had landed at Letpan unopposed and was exploiting inland. By 19th March it was held up along the Tanlwe Chaung. It had with it 146th Regiment RAC, 160th Field Regiment, one battery, less one troop, of 6th Medium Regiment, 1st Indian Anti-Tank Regiment, less two batteries, and some engineers. All was going well until Christison received reports that the Japanese were moving east from An towards the Irrawaddy and it was this he was trying to stop. Accordingly he ordered Stockwell to press on to An as fast as possible. 22nd (EA) Infantry Brigade was to move south to Letpan. Near Taungup 4th Indian Infantry Brigade had secured a bridgehead over the Tanlwe Chaung by 22nd March and had established an FMA at Kindaunggyi.

In the An area 1st (WA) Infantry Brigade, with 8th Field Regiment and a troop of 6th Medium Regiment, made contact with 2nd (WA) Infantry Brigade south of Letmauk on 24th March. By the end of the month 25th Indian Division had concentrated at Akyab for its return to India. By then too 71st Indian Infantry Brigade of 26th Indian Division had arrived in Madras. It was in this situation that Christison received his orders to plan the airborne and amphibious landings to capture Rangoon. Thus 26th Indian Division was ordered to concentrate on Ramree Island to prepare and 71st Indian Infantry Brigade had to return to Ramree from Madras. Stockwell was told to release 4th Indian Infantry Brigade around Taungup and then to capture the place with his own resources. He had 1st (WA) Infantry Brigade at Letmauk protecting Tamandu but patrolling towards An, which did not fall until 23rd April. By then the Japanese had pulled out.

Around Taungup Stockwell had his 4th (WA) and 22nd (EA) Infantry Brigades. He established a firm base at Palawa and cut the Taungup - Prome road. 2nd (WA) Infantry Brigade then rejoined him. Before it left, however, 4th Indian Infantry Brigade got patrols into Taungup and on 29th April the place was occupied by 4th (WA) Infantry Brigade. Then, on 1st May, 82nd West African Division came under direct command of ALFSEA, leaving 15th Indian Corps in order to plan and then conduct Operation DRACULA.

On 1st April Major General HM Chambers succeeded Major General CEN Lomax in command of 26th Indian Division. Lomax had commanded the division with great distinction since the first Arakan battles in 1943 and was off to another appointment in India. Chambers was appointed as Army member of the Assault Force Headquarters with Rear-Admiral BCS Martin and Group Captain H Pleasance. The plan was for 26th Indian Division to make the assault with 2nd British Division following up. In addition there was available 19th Lancers, the Gurkha Parachute Battalion, of 50th Indian Parachute Brigade, and 41st Beach Group. The plan was in four phases, with D-Day being on 2nd May.

Phase 1: One battalion landing by parachute on D minus 1 to secure Elephant Point. A brigade landing from the sea on the west bank and a battalion landing from the sea on the east bank of the Rangoon River estuary.

Phase 2: The landing of the rest of 26th Indian Division, the establishment of an FMA at Kyauktan and the exploitation northwards.

Phase 3: The landing of a brigade of 2nd British Division to hold the FMA while 26th Indian Division captured Syriam.

Phase 4: The assault on Rangoon by 2nd British Division.

It was thought that the garrison of Rangoon could be as high as 10,000 and that much of *28th Army* might lie between Rangoon and Pegu. Accordingly a massive naval force of the whole East Indies Fleet, plus 21st Assault Carrier Squadron and a large number of landing craft, minesweepers and escorts, was assembled. Some 38 squadrons of fighters and bombers were also gathered to cover the landings. One of the vital tasks was the destruction of the enemy batteries at Elephant Point and the seizing of the banks of the Rangoon River, so that the minesweepers could clear the harbour and get logistic ships in as soon as possible for the advancing 14th Army before the monsoons started in earnest. By 26th April, Chambers, of 26th Indian Division, issued his orders for the landings. The mission was that '26th Indian Division, with naval and air support, will assault land in the Rangoon River and capture the general area Syriam - Kyauktan with a view to establishing a firm base there from which subsequent operations can be conducted against Rangoon.' (Kirby). The stage was set.

On the Central Front 14th Army was preparing to advance southwards. By 1st April Japanese attempts to re-capture the Meiktila - Nyaungu area had failed. *15th* and *33rd Armies* were withdrawing towards Pyawbwe and Mount Popa. Slim ordered a regrouping for the advance. Like all his plans this was one of great simplicity. No one had to move to regroup. In the end 4th Indian

Corps was to advance down the east route along the Sittang valley with 5th and 17th Indian Divisions and 254th Tank Brigade. 33rd Indian Corps, with 2nd British and 7th and 20th Indian Divisions and 255th Tank Brigade, was to advance down the Irrawaddy valley. The scene was vividly captured by John Masters when he described the Indian divisions moving on Rangoon from Mandalay. 'This was the old Indian Army going down to the attack, for the last time in history, exactly two hundred and fifty years after the Honourable East India Company had enlisted its first ten sepoys on the Coromandel Coast. . .' (Masters).

In 4th Indian Corps's sector, Cowan's 17th Indian Division was advancing on a two brigade front, with 48th Indian Brigade making for Pyawbwe by the direct route and 99th Indian Infantry Brigade moving by way of Thazi. Both were in contact by 1st April. On 2nd April 1/3rd Gurkhas attacked Okpo near Thazi with Captain Bill Spencer of 1st Royal (Kohat) Mountain Battery as FOO. They were held up by a 75mm gun at the north-west corner of the village. Bill Spencer, who was bringing down heavy and accurate fire close to his infantry, moved to an exposed flank to engage the gun. With a direct hit he knocked it out, killing the whole detachment. Okpo was cleared and the advance continued. Spencer was awarded the Military Cross for this and several other actions during the Meiktila battles.

Meanwhile Captain Ernest Hadfield, who was attached to 21st Indian Mountain Regiment, was with 'C' Company 6/15th Punjab Regiment in the same area. By constantly exposing himself to enemy fire, by constantly bringing down the fire of his battery and of 129th Field Regiment and by his personal acts of gallantry, he kept up the momentum of the advance. He too was awarded the Military Cross and his citation concludes, 'The gallantry, coolness and devotion to duty of this officer was an inspiration to all ranks.' (Chaplin).

63rd Indian Infantry Brigade had been relieved by 5th Indian Division, under Major General Mansergh, which was concentrating as reserve for 4th Indian Corps's advance. 33rd Indian Corps was gearing itself up for the advance down the Irrawaddy with 7th Indian Division, under Major General Evans, now under command, which had 114th Indian Infantry Brigade in the Letse area having taken over from 28th (EA) Infantry Brigade. To the east of the river 89th Indian Infantry Brigade was in contact at Singu. 33rd Indian Infantry Brigade was moving into the Nyaungu area. 2nd British Division under Major General Nicholson, less 5th British Infantry Brigade advancing on Mount Popa, was concentrating around Myingyan prior to being flown out to India. 268th Indian Infantry Brigade was also at Myingyan, while 20th Indian Infantry Division, under Major General Gracey, was mopping up in the Kyaukse - Myittha - Kume area. 19th Indian Division, under Major General Rees, was in the Mandalay area waiting to hand over to 36th British Division commanded by Major General Festing.

The first step was to be the capture of Pyawbwe which covered the entrance to the Sittang valley. Cowan planned an enveloping operation using 48th and 99th Indian Infantry Brigades from the north and 63rd Indian Infantry Brigade and 'Claudcol,' which included armour and 59th (SP) Field Battery of 18th Field Regiment, from the west at Yanaung. 'Claudcol' captured Point 900 and handed it over to 63rd Indian Infantry Brigade while it raced on through Ywadan to cut the road south of Pyawbwe at Sedwin. Lieutenant Colonel Chaplin, of 21st Indian Mountain Regiment, stated that he had control of 129th Field Regiment, his own 21st Mountain Regiment and a medium battery for 99th Indian Infantry Brigade's operations. By 9th April 48th Indian Infantry Brigade was at Nyaungnwe and 63rd Indian Infantry Brigade was at Kyauktaing. Then 99th Indian Infantry Brigade, with the aid of air strikes and the concentrated fire of the divisional artillery, overran the airstrip just north of Pyawbwe while a battalion group of 48th Indian Infantry Brigade was sent round to cut off the town from the east. It was during this fighting that the guns of 21st Indian Mountain Regiment distinguished themselves to such an extent that 1/3rd Gurkha Rifles later presented them with a captured Japanese sword. In clearing up the area, Lieutenant

Mallinson conducted patrols consisting of Gunners from 6th (Jacob's) and 37th Mountain Batteries. The War Diary of 6th (Jacob's) Battery states, 'A party of Japs were reported at a copse 100 yards from the position. A patrol under Captain Hadfield and Lieutenant Mallinson went after them and, after a short skirmish, flushed them out. The score was three killed and the rest left five rifles, a machine gun, a mortar and other odds and ends behind. While searching a dead officer, Lieutenant Mallinson found a leather case containing several marked maps which showed details of all *49th Division's* positions and headquarters.' As a result of this find 17th Divisional Artillery attacked *49th Division's Headquarters* at Yindaw and many other targets with great effect.

Pyawbwe was thus surrounded by last light on 9th April. The fighting that followed was bitter as the Japanese fought to the last. 1,110 dead were counted in the town afterwards, only 29 were captured, the rest got out in ones and twos and 13 guns were captured. It was near Pyawbwe that 1st Sikh Light Infantry attacked Point 825. Jemadar Raza Mohammed of 6th (Jacob's) Mountain Battery was FOO. A fireplan of field and mountain guns to last 15 minutes was arranged. 'The fire plan was absolutely grand - it made a hell of a mess of the position and broke the Japs up completely. The Sikhs went in with their usual dash and within twenty five minutes of the pimples being taken, the provisional fire plan was put into operation. The attack was a complete success and what few Japs remained on Point 825 were killed. This gave us a very good vantage point overlooking Pyawbwe.' (Chaplin). Frequently in the lead was Jemadar Raza Mohammed, constantly adjusting the fire with great skill and bravery so that the Japanese were never able to influence the battle. His was the last Military Cross awarded to 21st Indian Mountain Regiment in the war for this and several other actions. His citation concluded, 'This officer has shown himself fearless in action throughout the operations and his accurate fire has proved invaluable to the infantry on many occasions.' (quoted by Chaplin). Pyawbwe was to be the only major action in the advance to Rangoon and it shattered the remains of *33rd Army.* On 11th April, 5th Indian Division less 9th Indian Infantry Brigade passed through to take over the lead while 17th Indian Division cleared up around the town. Allied air cover at this stage was highly effective but enemy air attacks did occur and the guns of 28th LAA Regiment shot down two enemy aircraft attacking Pyawbwe airstrip.

In the meantime Stopford had given orders to 7th Indian Division to capture Seikpyu and Chauk with one brigade moving down the river on boats and rafts. 2nd British Division was to send 5th British Infantry Brigade by way of Welaung and Kyaukpadaung to help with the capture of Chauk. 6th British Infantry Brigade was clearing up at Myingyan and 4th British Infantry Brigade was mopping up around Pyinzi and Mahlaing. All were to be flown out to India on 10th April. After clearing up around Kyaukse, 20th Indian Division was to concentrate in the Myittha - Wundwin area and then advance on Magwe by way of Meiktila, Zayetkon and Natmauk. 19th Indian Division was to assemble in the Kyaukse area while 268th Indian Infantry Brigade was to clear up the Taungtha area. Because of the wide frontage, Stopford allotted most of his artillery to his divisions. 2nd Indian Field Regiment went to 7th Indian Division and 8th (Mahratta) Anti-Tank Regiment less one battery went to 2nd British Division while one battery of 99th Field Regiment, one battery of 1st Medium Regiment and one troop of 44th LAA Regiment went to 268th Indian Infantry Brigade. In addition to the divisional artillery, Evans was allotted 1st Medium Regiment, less one battery, 12 x 5.5-inch medium guns, and one battery of 134th Medium Regiment, 6 x 6-inch howitzers. In 7th Indian Division Brigadier Tim Hely placed most of his artillery under brigade command for movement but retained control of fire himself to ensure maximum flexibility.

114th and 89th Indian Infantry Brigades began their attacks on Seikpyu and Chauk respectively on 11th April and found them strongly defended. 114th Indian Infantry Brigade had an artillery group consisting of 2nd Indian Field Regiment, less one battery, and 25th Indian Mountain

Regiment, also less one battery, while 89th Indian Infantry Brigade had 136th Field Regiment, one battery of 1st Medium Regiment and one battery of 3-inch mortars from 8th (Mahratta) Anti-Tank Regiment. The advance of 5th British Infantry Brigade with tanks and 10th Field Regiment began on 1st April. The first objective was Legyi just north of Mount Popa which was held in force by a very determined enemy. It then took four days to capture. Meanwhile 33rd and 268th Indian Infantry Brigades attacked Kyaukpadaung on 11th April. During this battle a company of 4/15th Punjab with an FOO made a wide detour to the west of the town and at dawn arrived on a high feature to the south. This gave a magnificent view of the whole battle and the FOO was able to direct fire with great accuracy throughout 12th and 13th April.

The Japanese were holding the Mount Popa area with *154th Regiment* and part of *112th Regiment*. By the morning of 12th April 268th Indian Infantry Brigade with one battery of 2nd Indian Field Regiment and 5th (Bombay) Mountain Battery, of 25th Indian Mountain Regiment, had cut the Taungtha - Kyaukpadaung road south west of Mount Popa. Kyaukpadaung fell after a stiff fight on 12th April. Further west 20th Indian Division was beginning its push southwards with 32nd Indian Infantry Brigade leading. It reached Natmauk by the 12th, an advance of 60 miles in three days. It then pressed on towards Magwe. Thus, with five divisions on the move by 12th April, the pursuit had begun. The RAF provided advanced mobile groups to ensure constant air cover. The whole operation was controlled from the joint headquarters of 14th Army and 221 Group RAF at Meiktila.

The advancing forces were moving from the dry plains into the wetlands and the monsoon was approaching. The heavy storms of the pre-monsoon period soon made all unmetalled roads impassable to wheeled traffic, while streams turned into roaring torrents. The climate became very humid and heat exhaustion, prickly heat and jungle sores became a problem. But the tempo of operations was kept up in the race for Rangoon. General Shozo Sakurai, *28th Army* , had major problems. His forces in the Arakan would be cut off if he did not act quickly. He decided that he must hold Yenangyaung and Mount Popa on the east of the Irrawaddy and Salin and Sidoktaya to the west in order to extract his Arakan forces to Allanmyo, but he was already too late. His forces simply had no time to react, such was the speed of the British advance. How the tables had turned since 1942! Meanwhile General Heitaro Kimura, commanding *Burma Area Army* since the previous September, resolved to defend Rangoon to the last and began to assemble several *ad hoc* forces with which to do so.

33rd Indian Corps began to close on the Yenangyaung oilfields on 13th April. At the same time 33rd Indian Infantry Brigade, commanded by Brigadier LHO Pugh, with 139th Field Regiment, one battery of 134th Medium Regiment and a mortar battery from 24th Anti-Tank Regiment, began its attack on Chauk from the south east. 89th Indian Infantry Brigade co-operated from the north. During this battle a Japanese 155mm gun with a quantity of ammunition was captured and taken into use by 139th Field Regiment to great effect until its ammunition ran out, when it was destroyed. 114th Indian Infantry Brigade, west of the river, was still held up at Letse. The enemy at Chauk did not fight but slipped across the river to Seikpyu under British artillery and air attack. The guns with both 33rd and 89th Indian Infantry Brigades, some 48 x 25-pounders, 8 x 5.5inch guns and the captured Japanese 155mm gun, attacked Seikpyu which resulted in many buildings being set on fire and many casualties being inflicted on the retreating enemy. By this time the 7th Indian Divisional Administrative Area had been established at Yenangyaung and was protected by 7/2nd Punjab and the Bikanir Battery of 25th Indian Mountain Regiment.

Evans decided to press on to Salim with 114th Indian Infantry Brigade and to Yenangyaung with 33rd Indian Infantry Brigade. 268th Indian Infantry Brigade continued to attack Mount Popa where Japanese artillery was particularly strong and effective. By the 19th, in conjunction with 5th British Infantry Brigade, 268th Indian Infantry Brigade captured Mount Popa along with several guns and much transport. Gracey then ordered 32nd Indian Infantry Brigade to advance on Taungdwingyi, which it occupied without opposition on 15th April. He then told 80th Indian Infantry Brigade to attack Magwe which it did on the 19th. Stopford told his divisional commanders to press on with maximum speed to seize Prome and Toungoo as soon as possible. Evans still had to capture the Yenangyaung oilfields which he planned to do under maximum artillery fire by 1st May. In the early morning of 20th April patrols reached the Pin Chaung and one battery of 139th Field Regiment, supporting 1st Queens, fought a successful duel with some Japanese 75mm guns which were holding up the crossing. As this attack went in, dense clouds of smoke rose from the oilfields indicating wholesale demolitions. Evans seized his chance and swung all his artillery to cover the approach of 33rd Indian Infantry Brigade. Events then moved with great speed. The artillery was ordered to concentrate forward as quickly as possible, so much so that Stopford, on his way to watch the battle, was overtaken by a medium battery rushing into action to cover the attack. Then the rains came and many of the Japanese escaped. 'Brigadier Lewis Pugh was awarded a bar to his DSO for his skilful handling of 33rd Indian Infantry Brigade in these actions, the success of which were due to his energy, personal example under fire and brilliant planning.' (Graham).

Evans next ordered 89th Indian Infantry Brigade, with 136th Field Regiment, to cross the river to the west and move south from Salin. By 25th April 114th Indian Infantry Brigade advancing south linked up with 89th Indian Infantry Brigade, and 33rd Indian Infantry Brigade was on the move towards Magwe to link up with 20th Indian Division. Stopford ordered 20th Indian Division to advance to Allanmyo and then move on Prome and Tharrawaddy, leaving all mopping up to 268th Indian Infantry Brigade which followed and was to come under its command in order to do so. Meanwhile 7th Indian Division operating on the west bank was to capture the Ngape - Minbu road, thus blocking the route from An, and then the Mindon - Thayetmyo road to block the next escape route from the Arakan. It had 254th Indian Tank Brigade in reserve. By this time the whole of 2nd British Division had left for India to begin training for the amphibious landings and the capture of Rangoon from the south.

100th Indian Infantry Brigade reached Allanmyo on 28th April. There was little opposition although 89th Indian Infantry Brigade, by then across the river, met strong enemy positions along the Man Chaung just north of Minbu. The advance was going better than had been hoped, the limiting factor as always being supplies, much of which were dropped by aircraft based at Akyab and Ramree. The problem of maintaining supplies became so severe that 33rd Corps's advance could, from then on, only be continued on a one brigade front and could, therefore, only be a diversion for the 4th Indian Corps advance and for the DRACULA landings. Thus Gracey ordered 100th Indian Infantry Brigade to seize Prome, then 33rd Indian Infantry Brigade would pass through and race for Rangoon. 80th Indian Infantry Brigade would secure the Allanmyo - Prome road and 268th Indian Infantry Brigade would cross the river and assist 7th Indian Division in destroying all Japanese to the west of the Irrawaddy and those trying to escape eastwards from the Arakan.

To the south of Minbu the enemy fought hard with single guns being used at point blank range to stop tanks. Evans ordered 89th and 114th Indian Infantry Brigades to destroy an enemy strong point at Padan by an encircling movement, while 33rd Indian Infantry Brigade followed along the east bank of the river to prevent any enemy from escaping in that direction. Torrential rain fell but it cleared on 5th May as the 4/5th Gurkhas closed on Padan. The fighting was very hard. The lead company was ambushed and two tanks were destroyed by point-blank artillery fire. Four officers were killed in this action, one being Captain Conway, the FOO, and another Janardhan Singh of 8th (Mahratta) Anti-Tank Regiment, but the attack went in and was successful. Further south 1/11th Sikhs, leading 89th Indian Infantry Brigade, hit strong opposition at Yenanma which it crushed after a stiff fight.

By this time *54th Division* had been ordered to move from the An valley to Allanmyo, but Sakurai realised that, if he was to save anything of his force, he must get it all back to the Pegu area as fast as he could. He therefore diverted *54th Division* further south to cross the Irrawaddy near Pyalo south of Allanmyo. The Japanese were in real trouble and they would be lucky to get out at all.

As a result of these moves 100th Indian Infantry Brigade had a grim fight near Pyalo on 1st May. The Japanese fought desperately, several threw themselves in front of tanks with explosives strapped to their bodies. But in spite of this the brigade entered Prome on 3rd May with no opposition in the town itself. Accordingly, as planned, 32nd Indian Infantry Brigade passed through on the Shwedaung - Rangoon road. By 6th May the last Japanese troops had left the Arakan but they had delayed too long and much of *54th Division* was by then trapped west of the river. The situation was desperate for *28th Army* .

We must next look at the fortunes of 4th Indian Corps advancing against *33rd Army* down the Sittang valley. After the fall of Pyawbwe the pace of the advance increased. Every time the Japanese stopped to fight, 17th Indian Division was onto them before they could prepare positions, once again so very different from the battles in the same area in 1942. Messervy had ordered Mansergh's 5th Indian Division to take the lead and seize Toungoo and its all-weather airfield by 25th April at all costs. On 7th April 123rd Indian Infantry Brigade of 5th Indian Division, with 116th RAC, less a squadron, 7th Light Cavalry, less two squadrons, and 16th Light Cavalry, 18th (SP) Field Regiment, less two batteries, one battery of 5th (Mahratta) Anti-Tank Regiment and a VCP, moved forward to take the lead. It met strong opposition at Yamethin on 11th April and an attack had to be mounted on the 12th under heavy air and artillery bombardment. Even so it did not fall until 14th April and this put the programme well behind schedule. Accordingly 161st Indian Infantry Brigade took over the lead with the same armour and artillery.

While this was happening 19th Indian Division, under Rees, was mopping up around Wundwin and Thazi. Later it moved eastwards to protect the left flank in May and June. Here 246th Medium Battery of 8th Medium Regiment distinguished itself in some very difficult country. 36th British Division took over the rear areas and 19th Indian Division was ordered to follow the 5th. Meanwhile Honda decided to withdraw to Pyinmana and to make a stand there with *18th* and *53rd Divisions.*

By 1600 hours on 14th April the advance guard of 161st Indian Infantry Brigade made contact with the Japanese on the Sinthe Chaung, 22 miles further south. They were soon across and next day met the enemy again at Shwemyo. Mansergh decided that 161st Indian Infantry Brigade would by-pass this position and head for Pyinmana while 123rd Indian Infantry Brigade seized Shwemyo. The former hit trouble trying to by-pass the Japanese but the latter soon captured the town and a very successful operation resulted in the capture of Shwemyo airstrip. Then 123rd Indian Infantry Brigade handed over to 99th Indian Brigade, which had come forward with 21st Indian Mountain Regiment, to take the lead. 24th Indian Mountain Regiment had gone ahead, less its 11th Mountain Battery, on a jeep basis. It suddenly looked as if the advance would be held and that Toungoo airfield might not be in British hands by the 25th in time to support the DRACULA landings. But the enemy were in a poor state. Mansergh's plan to thrust with two brigades had unnerved them and during the night 18/19th April the shattered, worn out remains of *18th* and *53rd Divisions* fell back. 161st Indian Brigade surged forward and captured the bridge north of Pyinmana intact, even though it was fully prepared for demolition, by 0730 hours on 19th April with 20th Mountain Battery well up in front. Racing on, they came upon Headquarters *33rd Army* trying to escape and after a grim fight Honda and his staff got out only on foot, fleeing over the hills. By that evening Pyinmana was in British hands. The advance was only four days behind schedule and was moving fast. Lewe fell on 20th April and 123rd Indian Infantry Brigade, once again, took the lead reaching Yedashe on the 21st, only 16 miles from Toungoo.

On 22nd April Mansergh took Toungoo airfield three days ahead of schedule without opposition. After a march of 215 miles on foot in 17 days in blazing hot weather, 20th Indian Mountain Regiment reached Toungoo to join 98th Indian Infantry Brigade. The monsoon began to break and heavy rain fell flooding all low lying areas. But there were still pockets of enemy to be dealt with and the regiment was kept very busy answering calls from the AOP. Toungoo airfield was open for operations on the 24th, a great triumph. It was pretty clear that *HQ Burma Area Army* had by then lost control. By this time the pursuers were outstripping the pursued. On 23rd April 161st Indian Infantry Brigade handed Pyinmana over to 9th Indian Infantry Brigade in readiness to take the lead and seize 5th Indian Division's last objective at Pyu. As it drove forward it captured many members of the INA but the Japanese they met died fighting or committed suicide rather than surrender. There was much abandoned equipment everywhere. As 161st Indian Infantry Brigade moved into the lead once more it was attacked by eight Japanese fighter aircraft and suffered some 30 casualties, so the enemy was not dead yet. It was the splendid 4th Royal West Kents of Kohima fame who were the spearhead of the advance. It reached Oktwin and the armour, with one battery of 18th (SP) Field Regiment, raced ahead. The only contact was when one Japanese gun destroyed a tank just south of Pyu Chaung but the job was done and Toungoo had fallen.

17th Indian Division hurried forward to Toungoo to continue the advance to Pegu, while 19th Indian Division set off to meet growing enemy resistance around Mawchi on the left flank. It soon met up with the disorganised remains of *18th, 49th* and *53rd Divisions* of *33rd Army,* shattered by the speed and power of 4th Indian Corps's southward drive. Honda gradually established some control and began organising the withdrawal to the Sittang estuary by way of the east bank of the river beginning on 29th April. Throughout these moves the Japanese were attacked by 19th Indian Division's artillery from positions on the west bank of the river. But the *15th Division* had been moved up to strong positions around Mawchi and 98th Indian Infantry Brigade of 19th Indian Division could not move it.

During the battles for Mawchi, Brigadier JH Beattie, CRA of 19th Indian Division, organised an extra AOP to work alongside 'B' Flight 656 AOP Squadron. He managed to borrow an L5 aircraft and Captain David Hine, of 'E' Troop 480th Field Battery of 115th Field Regiment, was chosen as observer. Pilot Officer JS Williams RAF was the pilot. The observer sat in the rear seat with his own radio and trailing aerial. There was a simple 'inter-com' but it could not be used when either pilot or observer were speaking on their own radios. The pair soon developed AOP techniques. A prompt report of 'Shot' from the guns was essential to enable the pilot to position the aircraft so that the observer could see the fall of shot, never easy in the jungle. They made several sorties each day and had considerable impact on operations. For these and many other actions as FOO, Captain Hine was awarded the Military Cross.

At dawn on 28th April 1945, 17th Indian Division moved into the lead. It passed through the forward positions of 5th Indian Division at Penwegon. It was at last to get its revenge for the defeats of 1942. It had with it a powerful armoured and artillery force including 255th Indian Tank Brigade and the tireless 18th (SP) Field Regiment. By 0900 hours it was at MS100 north of Rangoon. There were small running fights all day until, on 29th April, it met an enemy position at Pyinbongyi. This was attacked and overrun before the main position, which was protected by mines, was met at Payagyi. The mines included Japanese soldiers with hand detonated charges sitting in holes waiting to explode them as tanks passed over them. An attack went in with a heavy bombardment on 30th April and caused many casualties. Payagyi was taken by 1700 hours that evening. This attack and the subsequent capture of Waw cut the final escape route from Pegu and Rangoon and much traffic was destroyed along that road as it desperately tried to get away. Then

Messervy ordered 9th Indian Infantry Brigade to be air-lifted from Lewe to the Waw - Shwegyin area and advance south to Mokpalin to dominate the Sittang estuary. 1st Burma Regiment, with a battery of 24th Indian Mountain Regiment, flew into Pyuntaza airstrip and immediately deployed to Shwegyin. Contact was soon made with the enemy. The arrival of 9th Indian Infantry Brigade in the Waw area had secured the left flank of 17th Indian Division in its attack on Pegu which began on 29th April. Then a British officer, who had been captured in Singapore in 1942, appeared at Headquarters 48th Indian Infantry Brigade at Kadok to say that 437 British prisoners of war were in a village near Pegu; they had been turned loose by the Japanese, a sure sign that the enemy were cracking.

Cowan gave orders for the attack on Pegu on 30th April and it went in later that day. To begin with, the Japanese fought hard and held the initial assault. By nightfall the town was surrounded and after dark patrols from 63rd Indian Infantry Brigade entered and found the enemy pulling out. At day-break the tanks of 255th Indian Tank Brigade broke in and by last light Pegu had fallen. Rangoon was only 50 miles away. Then torrential rain began to fall, stopping all flying and making road movement hazardous in the extreme. It was the splendid 17th Indian Division, still commanded by Cowan, which had been driven out of Pegu three years previously and which was now leading the triumphant advance. The town was re-captured by the same five battalions who had been present in 1942; 7/10th Baluch, 4/12th Frontier Force Regiment and the 1/3rd, 1/7th and 1/10th Gurkhas. Revenge was sweet.

Now changes were beginning to occur within 5th Indian Division. It was at Pegu that 56th Anti-Tank Regiment said farewell to the division and gave a farewell parade for Major General Bob Mansergh, the divisional commander. Next 4th and 28th Field Regiments departed. They had fought with the division in all its battles since those in East Africa, with the greatest distinction. Their places were taken by 4th and 5th Indian Field and 5th Indian Anti-Tank Regiments. It was at Waw nearby that the division handed over to 7th Indian Division in order to go and prepare for Operation ZIPPER, the attack on the Japanese in Malaya.

Meanwhile Operation DRACULA was under way. The Fleet had attacked targets in the Nicobar Islands and Port Blair in the Andamans, and the RAF attacked Victoria Point, Port Blair and the Nicobars to keep the enemy guessing. 'C' Flight, 656th AOP Squadron, went aboard the carrier HMS *Khedive* ready for DRACULA.

The allocation of artillery for the landings south of Rangoon was:

36th Indian Infantry Brigade, landing on the west shore:
27th Field Regiment, less two batteries.
One troop (2 x 7.2-inch howitzers), 6th Medium Regiment.
One troop (6 x SP 40 mm Bofors guns), 36th LAA Regiment.

71st Indian Infantry Brigade, landing on the eastern shore:
One battery, 27th Field Regiment.
Three OP and reconnaissance parties, 8th Field Regiment.
One battery, less one troop, 6th Medium Regiment (4 x 5.5inch guns).
One troop 36th LAA Regiment, (6 x SP 40mm Bofors guns).
43rd Survey Battery, less its Flash Spotting Troop.

4th Indian Infantry Brigade, passing through on eastern shore:
8th Field Regiment.

Follow-up, also on the eastern shore:
7th Indian Field Regiment.
One battery, 27th Field Regiment.
6th Medium Regiment, less one battery (2 x 7.2-inch and 4 x 5.5inch guns).
1st Indian Anti-Tank Regiment.
36th LAA Regiment, less one battery and two troops.
Flash Spotting Troop, 43rd Survey Battery.
One Tentacle with HQRA and 'C' Flight 656th Squadron, initially operating from the carrier HMS *Khedive* and then ashore as soon as possible.

At 0545 hours on 1st May a Gurkha parachute battalion, of 50th Indian Parachute Brigade, was dropped near Elephant Point. It was to be the only occasion that parachute units were used in a parachute role in operations in South East Asia. Regrettably, a supporting air raid on Elephant Point saw a stick of bombs fall short causing 32 Gurkha casualties. Again the rains came and the paratroops had to struggle across flooded ground to make contact with an enemy strong point which fell after a short and fierce fight. Of 37 Japanese defending it, only one was taken alive but the Gurkhas lost 21 killed and 57 wounded including those bombed by mistake. During the afternoon aircraft reported seeing the words 'Japs Gone. Extract Digit' painted on the roof of Rangoon gaol. The use of this RAF slang convinced the Allies that this was no trap. Meanwhile the follow-up landings went as planned, covered by air and artillery attack from landing craft. The landings were unopposed and 71st Indian Infantry Brigade soon had Kyauktan and Syrian. Then Wing Commander AE Saunders RAF landed his Mosquito at Mingaladon (Rangoon) airfield and, with his navigator, made his way to Rangoon gaol where he was told the Japanese had gone. Saunders found a boat and sailed down the river to meet the invaders and give them the news and 36th Indian Infantry Brigade entered the city on 3rd May 1945. With it were the OP Parties of 24th Field Battery, of 27th Field Regiment. They claimed to be the first Gunners into Rangoon. The guns arrived on 4th May and harboured on the Golf Course near the Shwedagon Pagoda. 'C' Flight 656 AOP Squadron landed at Mingaladon airfield on 4th May and on the 9th made contact with 'B' Flight at Prome. By 12th May both flights were together at Rangoon. Soon after this they went back to Madras to prepare for operations in Malaya.

Rangoon had fallen without a shot being fired and the population turned out in force to welcome the British back but the destruction everywhere was very great and nothing was working. On 5th May Headquarters 26th Indian Division hoisted the Union Flag on Government House. The next day the division came under the command of 14th Army and the Lincolns linked up with the Gurkhas at Hlegu. Operation CAPITAL was complete just two days before the news of Victory in Europe reached the weary men of 14th Army. When this news reached 14th Army they were of course delighted even though they could not yet see the end in the Far East. In 19th Indian Division the divisional artillery decided to mark the occasion with a '*feu de joie*' at one round troop fire at one second intervals. This was followed by a one round salvo by all 78 guns in range, with live ammunition of course.

There was still much to be done. On 4th May General Leese gave orders that 2nd British Division was to remain in India. Operation DRACULA had enabled the Port of Rangoon to be opened by 14th May some three weeks earlier than would otherwise have been possible. Thus the operation was justified because the monsoon had started with a vengeance. The great gamble had just succeeded and good planning and determined, well trained and highly motivated men of high morale had made it possible. The dominating factor had been the constant close support provided by the RAF and the USAAF and the aggressive use of tanks and fast moving artillery. The Japanese had no answer to the Shermans, Grants and Priests except by using their field and anti-aircraft guns as anti-tank guns at point blank range. British tanks and SP guns were also used to ferry infantry, thus keeping up the momentum of the advance. Guns were used concentrated at every enemy strong point and they enabled the tanks and infantry to close, frequently before the enemy had had any chance of preparing his positions. Finally, the fact that the Allies could be supplied by air, often entirely, enabled them to press on when otherwise they would have had to stop and wait for combat supplies to catch up.

There was still much to do. Mingaladon airfield had to be made operational and required protection. 52nd HAA Regiment, 2nd Indian LAA Regiment and a battery of 1st Indian LAA Regiment were deployed, with 24 x 3.7-inch and 78 x 40mm guns, to protect the airfield, the docks and the oil installations at Syriam. At the end of May another battery arrived from 5th Indian HAA Regiment and yet another from 1st Indian LAA Regiment. At Rangoon they found 4 x 3.7-inch HAA and 2 x 4-inch naval guns and several 40mm Bofors which had been disabled in 1942 but restored to working order by the Japanese. (Routledge).

By 11th May it was clear that the enemy would try to break through the Taungdaw valley. They did and encircled two companies of 4/8th Gurkhas. They then attacked each in turn and in the attack on one a Victoria Cross was won by Rifleman Lachiman Gurung. 1/11th Sikhs came to the rescue and all available artillery and air strikes were used. 136th Field Regiment had one FOO with each of the Gurkha companies. Although one, Lieutenant KET Bark, was seriously wounded by a sniper, there was never a moment when fire was not brought down quickly and accurately during three days and nights of intense fighting. 'As observation from the two forward OPs was considerably restricted, an L5 was made available and on 12th Lieutenant FD Thomas of 348 [Field Battery] made several sorties. . . [13th May] Support from the RAF was now made available and just after midday a force of Hurricanes attacked the small village of Kakkalu just north of Taungdaw, where the Japs were suspected of having their local HQ. To indicate the target to the aircraft was difficult. It was too near our own troops for the guns to mark it with yellow smoke and the VCP was back at Battalion HQ. The procedure adopted was for the VCP to brief the pilots circling above of the approximate position and description of the target and instruct one aircraft to dive as if to bomb it but neither to release a bomb nor fire its cannon. The OP on the valley floor, then in charge of Bombardier W Woods, would observe the dive and comment on its accuracy and pass any corrections necessary. These instructions were radioed back to Lieutenant Colonel Armstrong's set who had the VCP at his elbow, and they in turn relayed them to the pilot. This improvised system worked very well and the Hurricanes destroyed the village very effectively. . . 14th May was . . . the day on which the RAF paid attention to the village of Taungdaw. The VCP officer first went up in our own tame L5 to see the layout of the target in relation to our own positions and spot useful landmarks. When the Hurricanes arrived overhead he was able to explain in their own technical terms exactly what was required. . . [they] came down in a power dive to release their bombs . . . The nearest Gurkhas were only 50 yards away according to some accounts and 348's OP party claim they were 150 yards distant. . . It was a remarkable demonstration of precision bombing which flattened the small village and with no casualties inflicted on our own troops. (Robertson).

The Gunner grouping for the advance on Rangoon was as follows:

4th Indian Corps:
18th (SP) Field Regiment RA
8th Medium Regiment RA
52nd HAA Regiment RA (including 2 x 7.2-inch howitzers)
28th LAA Regiment RA
5th (Mahratta) Anti-Tank Regiment IA

1st Survey Regiment RA, less one battery
'B' Flight, 656th AOP Squadron

33rd Indian Corps:
2nd Indian Field Regiment IA
5th Indian Field Regiment IA
1st Medium Regiment RA
134th Medium Regiment RA
101st HAA Regiment RA (including 4 x 7.2-inch howitzers)
44th LAA Regiment RA
8th (Mahratta) Anti-Tank Regiment IA
1st Indian Survey Regiment IE
'A' Flight, 656th AOP Squadron

It had been a great triumph, morale was sky high, all arms were working together like a well-oiled machine. Nothing could stop them. But the rest of Burma still had to be taken, the Salween had to be crossed and longer term plans had to made for the re-capture of Malaya, Singapore, the Netherlands East Indies, the rest of South East Asia and, as all then thought, Japan itself.

The Gunners could congratulate themselves on their contribution to victory in Burma. Their rapid movement and concentrated fire had enabled the tanks and infantry to keep up their momentum. Along with air attacks, AOP observation and the battle-winning system of having artillery commanders at every level, integrating firepower with manoeuvre forces, they overwhelmed the enemy before he could react. The provision of air defence, covering the whole operation with guns which could also be used in the ground role, showed the great flexibility of the Regiment. Command of artillery was particularly good by this time. Commanding officers played a major part in the planning for, and the execution of, operations at brigade level, tying these together through CRAs at division and they in their turn through CCRAs at corps. Command downwards, always good, was even better. Battery commanders played a major part in the lives of battalions and they moved from one battalion to another with ease, but by then most commanders of all arms knew each other. As ever the troop commanders, the OPs and FOOs displayed the courage and sheer professional skill which ensured that firepower was applied to the battle where it was wanted, and when it was wanted and it was often they who said when this should be.

As always, the Gunners who fought in Burma speak to this day of the great respect they had for their comrades in the infantry. Their gallantry, frequently displayed in appalling conditions, actually won the battles, but they could not do it unless all the combat arms worked together as one team, tanks, gunners, engineers, signallers, airmen and infantrymen backed by the outstandingly capable services, RASC, RIASC, RAOC, REME, and so many others, which kept the fighting soldiers supplied and supported by air, road, track and river, very often in particularly dreadful circumstances.

30. A 25-pounder in action at night near Mount Popa, May 1945. (IWM)

31. A battery of 'Priest' 105mm self propelled guns in action on the road to Rangoon. The concussion caused by their firing has shaken the camera. (IWM)

32. A 25-pounder leaving a landing craft at Rangoon beach head. (IWM)

33. Manhandling a 25-pounder, Rangoon, 2nd May 1945. (IWM)

34. A 3.7-inch HAA gun of 66th HAA Regiment, at a Ledo Road airfield. (IWM)

35. A survey regiment's flash-spotting tower. (IWM)

36. Austers in splinter-proof pens, Imphal seige. (Douglas Cross via EW Maslen-Jones)

37. Auster Air OP in flight. (IWM)

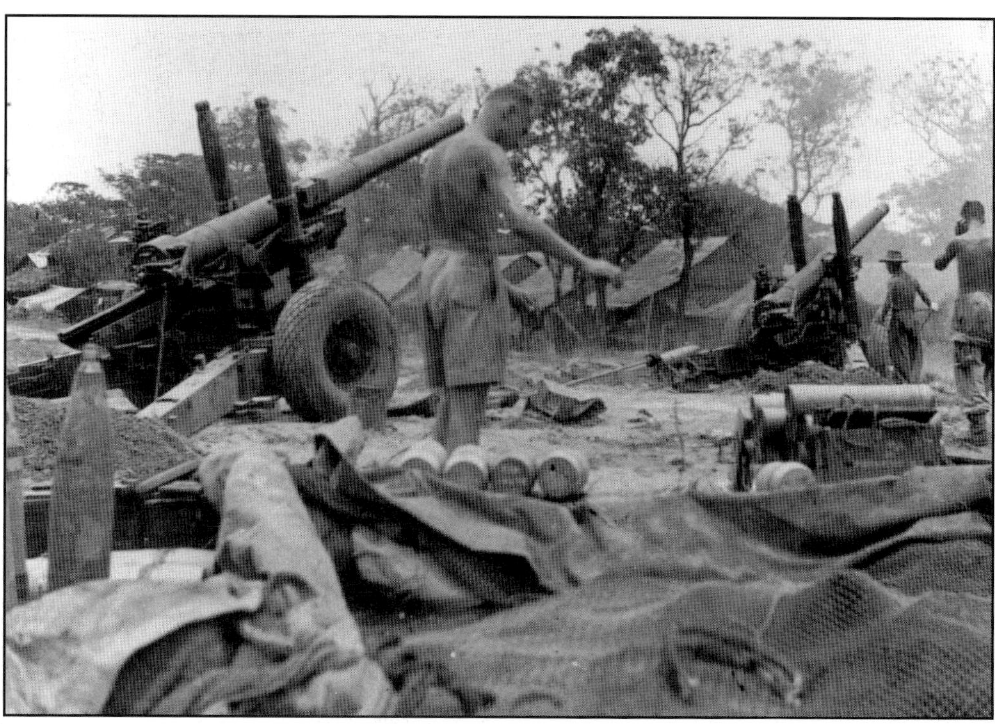

38. 5.5-inch guns of 63rd Medium Battery, 1st August 1945. (IWM)

39. An Auster Mark V of 'A' Flight, No 656 Air OP Squadron over Java, 1946, (EW Maslen-Jones)

CHAPTER 16

VICTORY IN THE FAR EAST

MAY 1945 - NOVEMBER 1946

The End in Burma, the Re-occupation of Malaya and Singapore, the Surrender of Japan and Operations in Sumatra and Java

(Maps 50, 51, 52, 53 and 54)

While the final battles for the conquest of Burma were being fought out by 14th Army, planning was in progress for the re-capture of Singapore. The planners recommended that the best course of action was to seize Phuket Island, Operation ROGER, an advance down the Tenasserim - Kra - Malaya peninsula, together with amphibious landings, Operation ZIPPER, in the Port Swettenham - Port Dickson area. These would be followed by an advance on Singapore, Operation MAILFIST. Mountbatten wanted to launch the attack on Phuket on 1st June 1945 and Operation ZIPPER, with four divisions, in October. He was convinced that he had enough landing craft, naval support vessels and air power to do so. Speed and maintenance of momentum were of the essence. The Combined Chiefs of Staff approved these plans but wanted Mountbatten to omit the attack on Phuket and launch ZIPPER in August. For this they made extra shipping and aircraft available. Mountbatten agreed.

On 6th May 1945 Slim assumed command of all Allied Forces in Burma. 15th Indian Corps Headquarters was withdrawn to India. Slim was told to complete the destruction of the remaining Japanese in Burma and release forces for Operation ZIPPER. Meanwhile the Japanese were in disarray. There was still a considerable force cut off west of the Irrawaddy under Lieutenant General Shigesaburo Miyazaki. It was trying to assemble around Kama (Map 49). Lieutenant General Shozo Sakurai was in the Pegu Yomas with elements of *54th* and *55th Divisions* and many logistic units. Lieutenant General Masaki Honda, with the remnants of *33rd Army*, was in the Sittang valley around Waw and Mokpalin, trying to keep an escape route open for those forces still to the west. The remains of *15th Division* was in the hills east of Toungoo.

Stopford, with 33rd Indian Corps, made plans to isolate the Japanese west of the Irrawaddy while Messervy, with 4th Indian Corps, moved to stop those in the Pegu Yomas from crossing the Sittang and joining Honda. 7th Indian Division, under Major General Evans, had 114th Indian Infantry Brigade in contact around Minbu, 89th Indian Infantry Brigade at Yenanma advancing on Shandatkyi, with 33rd Indian Infantry Brigade in reserve at Magwe. He also had under command

268th Independent Indian Infantry Brigade at Thayetmyo. 20th Indian Division, under Major General Gracey, was further south with 80th Indian Infantry Brigade just north of Prome, 100th Indian Infantry Brigade just south of Prome and 32nd Indian Infantry Brigade moving towards Tharrawaddy. With the division was 3rd (Peshawar) Mountain Battery, in mule pack, moving down the east bank of the Irrawaddy and 8th (Lahore) Mountain Battery, as part of the divisional rearguard, moving down the road to Prome. This road was infested by small enemy parties each of which had to be winkled out using guns and infantry operating very closely together. The Japanese were still fighting hard, as we saw in the previous chapter.

In these battles Gunners and Infantrymen worked closely together. As batteries moved forward they had a company for close protection and Gunner vehicles ferried infantry wherever they could. The local inhabitants here were very helpful. Captain Michael Brown, of 349th Field Battery of 136th Field Regiment, was asked by a headman, 'How is the King Emperor?' and was delighted to know His Majesty was well! Apparently the Japanese had told them he had been killed in London. On 9th May in the Pani Chaung valley, Captain GW Gorman and his OP party, with a company of 1/11th Sikhs, were surrounded on three sides. It was here that Bombardier J Black, the radio operator, continued to transmit Gorman's fire orders, under heavy machine gun fire. These brought down 180 rounds from 'B' Troop, 348th Field Battery, very close to the position and this saved them all. No friendly troops were hit but 17 of the enemy were killed. Close air support by Hurricanes was also most effective during these operations, using the procedures developed earlier in the Arakan and in the advance on Rangoon.

After these battles the Commanding Officer of 1/11th Sikhs wrote to Lieutenant Colonel Armstrong of 136th Regiment on 12th May 'I would like to bring to your notice the outstanding work of Captain AW Bell and Captain G Gorman during the period that 347 Battery has been in support of my Battalion. Often in unpleasant situations, with forward platoons, they have shown a complete disregard for their own safety in their eagerness to get right forward so that they could personally see and direct the supporting fire. They have at all times been an inspiration to the men of my Battalion and I consider them more than worthy for a Periodical Mention in Despatches. Captain Bell was particularly outstanding at Tetma and Captain Gorman during the present operation at Shandatgyi.

I would also like to thank you on behalf of all ranks for the help, co-operation and support which your Regiment and particularly 347 Battery have always been eager to give.

I also enclose herewith a citation for the Immediate Award of the Military Medal to Bombardier Black.' (Robertson) By then 114th Indian Infantry Brigade's area was clear of enemy so it crossed to the east bank at Magwe.

Further south 32nd Indian Infantry Brigade reached Tharrawaddy with 71st Indian Infantry Brigade, of 26th Indian Division, advancing northwards to meet it from Rangoon. Everywhere there were minor clashes as the enemy filtered eastwards. 7th Indian Division's plan was to destroy the enemy west of the river, with 89th Indian Infantry Brigade attacking from the north west on Kama, and 268th Indian Infantry Brigade, with 1st KOSB and 500th Field Battery, of 136th Field Regiment, leading, from the north-east, both on the west bank. 33rd Indian Infantry Brigade waited on the east bank to deal with any who got across. On 20th May 1/11th Sikhs dealt with a party of enemy at Kabaing before the whole force closed on Kama. But on 27th and 28th May the Japanese fought their way through the cordon which surrounded them but at a heavy price. Everywhere the fighting was fierce and the casualties to both sides were severe. By 30th May, however, the remains of *54th Division* had been destroyed, much to the credit of the way in which Evans manoeuvred 7th Indian Division.

By 20th May Main Headquarters 7th Indian Division was at Allanmyo, Rear Headquarters was at Yenangyaung, 114th Indian Infantry Brigade was concentrating at Magwe while 33rd Indian

Infantry Brigade was moving towards Prome. 268th Indian Infantry Brigade, with 4th Indian Field Battery, 44th LAA and 101st HAA Regiments, was moving down the east bank of the Irrawaddy and 89th Indian Infantry brigade was moving on Kama. At this stage the weather broke and heavy rain storms made all movement extremely difficult. Opposition was relatively light and a cordon was established along the river astride Zalon by 21st May. Two batteries of 44th LAA Regiment, operating as infantry, were covered by the guns of 139th Field Regiment. They were waiting for the enemy to hit this cordon.

The battle for Kama went on for several days and absorbed much effort. Using them as a distraction the enemy attacked 1st Queens in the cordon on 26th May, killing two officers and an FOO of 139th Field Regiment. For the rest of the month the enemy made repeated and determined attacks to break out over the river and into the Pegu Yomas to the east. The cordon was strengthened but the enemy pressed on. Typical was the action at Wettigau involving a major ambush by the men of 1st Indian Field Regiment on 28th May, but it was all over by the 30th, by which time a further 2,000 Japanese had been killed or wounded.

Next were operations around Prome. On 30th May at MS 20 on the Prome - Pakkaung road a two battalion attack was mounted by 114th Indian Infantry Brigade. It was during this fighting that 362nd Field Battery of 129th Field Regiment was hit by heavy counter-battery fire and Lieutenant CG Johnstone was killed along with several others. Operations remained continuous and strenuous until mid-June when the pressure slackened. 7th Indian Division was ordered to move to the Sittang river where it was to fight 'The Battle of the Bend', the last major battle for Burma. During this battle the divisional commander was Brigadier, acting Major-General, 'Tim' Hely, the CRA. At the same time the division was sad to say farewell to 24th Anti-Tank Regiment which had fought with it for so long and with such distinction. The division took under command 9th Indian Infantry Brigade at Hlegu. 136th Field Regiment was also there, while 25th Indian Mountain Regiment was further south at Taukkyau and 247th Medium Battery at Payagyi.

On 7th May 4th Indian Corps was spread along the Rangoon - Meiktila road from Hlegu in the south to Pyawbwe in the north. 17th Indian Division less 99th Indian Infantry Brigade was around Hlegu. 5th Indian Division was between Payagyi and Pegu with its 9th Indian Infantry Brigade operating eastwards in the Waw area. 19th Indian Division less 64th Indian Infantry Brigade was in the Toungoo area operating eastwards along the Mawchi road. 64th Indian Infantry Brigade was taking over Kalaw from 36th British Division, which was about to be withdrawn to India. 255th Indian Tank Brigade was around Pegu. Messervy decided to destroy the remaining enemy in two areas, first, between the Pegu Yomas and the Sittang river and second, on the coastal strip between the Sittang and Salween rivers. 17th Indian Division was to re-deploy forthwith along the road between Pyinbongyi and Pyu to the north of 5th Indian Division. This was to prevent enemy escaping eastwards and the division was to capture Kyaikto and Bilin east of the Sittang. 19th Indian Division was to remain responsible for the northern sector.

The 'Battle of the Sittang Bend' started on 10th May when 9th Indian Infantry Brigade of 5th Indian Division attacked Nyaungkashe three miles East of the Sittang Bridge which was further damaged and the whole western bank area was flooded. Severe fighting developed with a strong Japanese force west of the river and two field batteries were forced to withdraw to Abya as flood waters rose again. Then the fighting died down. Further north 64th Indian Infantry Brigade was locked in battle to capture the road known as the Staircase where it zigzagged up a precipitous 1,200 foot escarpment on the Mawchi road. This was finally completed, thanks to the fire of 5th Indian Field Regiment, on 30th May.

The fighting for Mawchi was tough and every yard had to be fought for. It took seven days to capture a mile and a half of road. 98th Indian Infantry Brigade had taken over on 24th May and on the 25th the regiment's mules got a severe attack of 'surra' and many died. The rest had to be evacuated. Thereafter the regiment was jeep-borne. 115th Field Regiment also reported its action in the battles for Mawchi. It came into action alongside 62nd Indian Infantry Brigade in a very open position with the guns wheel to wheel. The regiment came under heavy enemy fire and an ammunition lorry was hit. 'BSM NM Brummel most gallantly led a party to clear the ammunition, which he succeeded in doing though surrounded with bursting charges. As the last round was moved to safety, the Sergt Major and others were hit by a Jap shell and killed. He received a posthumous MM for his gallantry.' (The March of 115th Field Regiment). Another Military Medal was won later by BSM Hayes for great gallantry in dragging away a blazing limber full of ammunition, again saving many lives on the tightly-packed gun position of 480th Field Battery. The final attack was made on 30th May when 5th Indian Field Regiment arrived and 20th Indian Mountain Regiment joined it for the attack. Further south the Japanese west of the Sittang were also defeated.

Lieutenant Arthur Adamson of 500th Field Battery was employed as an AOP in an American L5, or Stinson Sentinel, flown by both US and RAF pilots during the 'Battle of the Sittang Bend.' He was mainly in support of 89th Indian Infantry Brigade, especially 4/8th Gurkhas at Nyaungkashe, using 'E' Troop, 500th Field Battery. He also used two 5.5-inch guns of 247th Medium Battery and the 4.2-inch mortars, which had just arrived, of 8th Mahratta Anti-Tank Regiment.

On 1st June 1945 a newly-formed 12th Army, under General Stopford, assumed command of all operations in Burma and 14th Army Headquarters was withdrawn to Delhi under General Christison. 12th Army consisted of 4th Indian Corps, 5th, 17th and 19th Indian Divisions and 255th Indian Tank Brigade, in the Sittang valley, and 7th Indian Division, with 268th Indian Infantry Brigade under command, and 20th Indian Division in the Irrawaddy valley, and 22nd (EA) Infantry Brigade at Prome. 26th Indian Division and 254th Indian Tank Brigade left for India later in the month. General Slim was also back in India. Two major lines of communications were established from India, the first via Dimapur to Ledo and the second via Chittagong and Akyab, to Ramree Island. These were poised to support operations eastwards. No. 221 Group RAF deployed to Rangoon to support 12th Army. It had four squadrons of Thunderbolt fighters, one fighter reconnaissance squadron, four Spitfire squadrons, a Beaufighter squadron and two squadrons of Mosquito light bombers. In Madras 656th AOP Squadron was giving all aircraft a much needed base overhaul. Most had to have their mainplanes re-covered as the fabric had deteriorated so much in the intense jungle operations of 1944/45. The Squadron then flew to Ceylon to board a carrier for Operation ZIPPER, while the ground parties sailed in LSTs.

June was spent mopping up in the Irrawaddy valley. Pockets of resistance held out at Kalaw, Mawchi, Paukkaung and in the Sittang Bend, where conditions were appalling during the monsoon, especially for the Japanese. Drenching rain, sweltering oppressive heat and swarms of insects caused terrible jungle sores and these, coupled with bitter fighting, made life extremely hard for everyone. The Japanese were trying to concentrate in order to break out eastwards into Siam and the British were determined to stop them. By the middle of the month the Japanese had assembled over 9,000 men at Paukkaung and 114th Indian Infantry Brigade was trying to destroy them, while 33rd Indian Infantry Brigade held Prome and 89th Indian Infantry Brigade was at Thayetmyo. 20th Indian Division was further south with brigades at Paungde, Tharrawaddy and Hmawbi. Then on 19th June 7th Indian Division was ordered to move to the Pegu area to take over from 5th Indian Division which was to move to India to prepare for ZIPPER.

3rd Indian AA Brigade arrived and took over all air defence tasks in Burma with 5th and 52nd HAA and 2nd and 5th Indian LAA Regiments. 9th HAA Brigade, by then renamed 60th AGRA/AA, began training for Operation ZIPPER. However, by September 1945 all AA tasks in Burma were terminated and 13th and 24th AA Brigades were disbanded, 14th AA Brigade returning to West Africa. By the end of October all British AA regiments were on their way home their job done. There is no doubt that the anti-aircraft regiments had so often achieved very high standards getting their guns into near impossible places in near impossible conditions. Throughout they had taken a heavy toll of enemy aircraft, frequently forcing them to fly only at night or so high that their attacks were inaccurate. The men of the anti-aircraft regiments of 14th Army could be well proud of their achievement.

The Japanese, meanwhile, were struggling eastwards through the Pegu Yomas and there was tough fighting on the Mawchi road, first by 99th Indian Infantry Brigade, until it was relieved by 62nd Indian Infantry Brigade, who fought on. General Sakurai was still planning a major breakout with what was left of *28th Army*, some 30,000 men. He planned to move across Sittang on four axes, starting on 20th July. The northern route would be used by *54th Division*, some 9,300 men, on four routes between Yetho, crossing just south of Toungoo, and Pyu. The next would be *28th Army Headquarters Group* of some 7,300 men which would cross at Kanyutkwin, south of this would be the *Shimbu Group* (*55th Division*), now consisting of some 6,800 men, and the southernmost crossing would be at Nyaunglebin by the *Kan-I Group* of 4,350 men. A patrol of 1/7th Gurkhas captured a map containing the plan for the *Shimbu Group* in great detail albeit without a date. Messervy regrouped rapidly to cover the area of the crossings more strongly in the light of this information. Meanwhile *33rd Army* was doing all it could to hold the east bank and provide artillery to cover the break-out. The pressure on the British was greatest at Nyaungkashe where the flooding was so bad that digging was impossible. Casualties mounted from enemy artillery. On 7th July Brigadier AF Hely, acting divisional commander, ordered it to be evacuated to avoid further casualties and three 25-pounders which could not be moved were destroyed. The Japanese also had their problems and began to withdraw.

It was then that the new Labour Government in London decreed, without reference to the army, that men with long war service in the Far East were to have home leave and very large numbers were entitled, which played havoc with establishments. Nevertheless, many officers and men who had fought with great distinction were ordered home, among them Lieutenant Colonel Geoffrey Armstrong who had served as commanding officer of 136th Field Regiment with such great distinction and before that as a battery commander in the HAC in the desert. For his outstanding achievements he was awarded the Distinguished Service Order.

The battles, however, went on. 136th Field Regiment now commanded by Lieutenant Colonel GHF Chaldecott, fought alongside 1st Queens to capture the village of Letpauthonbin in the Sittang Bend, 348th Field Battery being heavily involved. At this battle they were joined by more and more guns, among them 3.7-inch HAA guns and a 7.2-inch howitzer. Several thousand rounds were fired. Then suddenly came the news of the atomic bombs and the surrender on 14th August 1945. Accordingly at 0700 hours on 15th August all guns in range fired a Victory Salute and then silence! It was over. To the men on the spot it was that sudden. True, later that morning at 1000 hours, a patrol of the 6/15th Punjab called for a concentration which was fired by 'D' Troop of 348th Field Battery. These 20 rounds 'proved to be the last . . . fired in anger by the Regiment and indeed by any Regiment in Burma. It is probable that they were the last fired anywhere in World War 2.' (Robertson). In fact, more would be fired in Java and Sumatra.

At the same time 129th Field Regiment reported many actions in the 'Battle of the Sittang Bend.' In May they learned that Lieutenant Colonel Charles Younger their outstanding commanding officer, had been awarded the Distinguished Service Order, Majors PM Brown and WA Liston the Military Cross and Gunner Nichol the Military Medal, a most satisfactory finale to a great performance in battle.

It is now necessary to go back in time and get up to date with the final stages of the war elsewhere.

33rd Indian Infantry Brigade took over the Sittang Bend area and the Japanese slowly fell back over the river after their spirited rear-guard actions. Preparations were made for the occupation of Tenasserim. 7th Indian Division was concentrated at Hlegu, still in training for the second phase of ZIPPER, and 17th and 19th Indian Divisions were to continue southwards. At the same time steps were taken to create a staging post, airfield and base on the Cocos Islands for the forthcoming operations against the Japanese in Malaya and Singapore (Map 51). The plan for ZIPPER was to be carried out by 34th Indian Corps using 5th, 23rd, 25th and 26th Indian Divisions, 3rd Commando Brigade and 50th Indian Tank Brigade. The main assault was to made by 5th and 25th Indian Divisions and this would go in at 0645 hours on 9th September 1945 at Morib, with a subsidiary attack by 37th Indian Infantry Brigade of 23rd Indian Division at Kluang Bagan Lalang. The first objectives would be the Kelanang and Port Swettenham airfields, while 37th Indian Infantry Brigade would make for Sepang and then turn south for Port Dickson. Naval fire support would be provided by one battleship, one cruiser, four destroyers, two sloops and 13 landing craft. 21st Aircraft Carrier Squadron of nine escort carriers would provide air cover. 224 Group RAF would land to conduct air operations and would build up to 12 squadrons ashore by D-plus 12. We now know that the Japanese estimate of the British attack was reasonably accurate. The defence was planned by *Headquarters 7th Area Army* in Singapore and *29th Army* in Taiping. North-western Malaya was to be held, together with the Nicobar and Andaman Islands and Malaya as far south as Johore; but for this only *37th, 46th* and *94th Divisions* were available. *16th Army* remained in Java and *37th Army* in Borneo. It was known that there were some nine battalions and a number of field, medium and mountain batteries in Singapore.

ZIPPER was to be mounted from India. Auchinleck was to increase the Indian base so that it could support 18 divisions, ten of which were to be moved from Europe shortly after the defeat of Germany. The Indian Army would be increased to 2.67 million men. Then the effect of the political decision to reduce the qualifying period for men going on leave to UK to three years and four months, known as 'Python', began to have real effect. Some 20,000 men suddenly qualified to go home on leave and there was not enough shipping to get them home and mount ZIPPER on time. 36th British Division ceased to be operational and had to be broken up. 34th Indian Corps would have to reduce its medium artillery by two regiments to find enough men for the other two and Engineers and Signals suffered similarly. At the end of July Mountbatten told London that he could either mount ZIPPER on time and postpone the start of 'Python' leave or start 'Python' as promised and postpone ZIPPER, giving the Japanese more time to prepare defences. In the end it was agreed that ZIPPER should go ahead as planned with six divisions and delays in starting 'Python' be accepted but not beyond the end of the year. There was also the problem that the Indian Army saw the British going on 'Python' leave and asked, not unnaturally, 'What about us?' A plan had to be made for them too. The situation was getting out of hand and it was clear that politicians had no idea of the practical effect of their scheme. Sir James Grigg, Secretary of State for War, refused to recant and the compromise went on. In the end, of course, it was never tested.

The Gunner Order of Battle for Operation ZIPPER was to have been:

34th Corps Artillery:
18th (SP) Field Regiment
208th (SP) Field Regiment
6th Medium Regiment
86th Medium Regiment
1st Indian Medium Regiment
1st HAA Regiment Hong Kong-Singapore Artillery
8th Sikh LAA Regiment
9th Rajput LAA Regiment
Flight 656th AOP Squadron

5th Indian Division:
4th Indian Field Regiment
5th Indian Field Regiment
24th Indian Mountain Regiment
5th Mahratta Anti-Tank Regiment

23rd Indian Division:
158th Field Regiment
178th Field Regiment
28th Indian Mountain Regiment
2nd Indian Anti-Tank Regiment

25th Indian Division:
8th Field Regiment
27th Field Regiment
33rd Indian Mountain Regiment
7th Indian Anti-Tank Regiment

26th Indian Division:
160th Field Regiment
7th Indian Field Regiment
30th Indian Mountain Regiment
1st Indian Anti-Tank Regiment

Meanwhile the situation in Japan was deteriorating fast. There was, as always, the continuing rivalry between the Imperial Navy and the Imperial Army. Servicemen demanded priority everywhere and this caused friction with the civil population. Air attacks were increasing in numbers and intensity; food, clothing and accommodation became scarce. Japanese fighter aircraft were ineffective and air defence artillery little better. In 1,595 sorties, 9,000 tons of bombs were dropped on Japan and only 20 US aircraft were lost, 16 to the guns and four to the fighters. By July Japan lay helpless. The Americans had attacked Okinawa on 1st April 1945 with two corps consisting of three US Marine and four Army divisions. The British Pacific Fleet, consisting of HM Ships *King George V* and *Howe*, four carriers, six cruisers and eleven destroyers, took part in preliminary fleet operations and in support of the landings. It was here that the Japanese employed mass *Kamikaze* attacks with considerable effect and several British ships were hit. The fighting on Okinawa was vicious. The battle raged for three months and some 80,000 Japanese perished. The Americans lost almost 50,000 men killed and wounded. Over 400 ships were hit, most by *Kamikaze* attacks.

General MacArthur was poised to invade the Philippines by July 1944. In New Guinea the Australians had their 3rd, 5th, 6th, 7th, 9th and 11th Divisions still in action based on Lae and Madang. By March 1945 MacArthur had taken Manila, but the fighting in Luzon went on until the end of hostilities. Landings took place on Mindanao on 17th April 1945, while 1st Australian Army attacked New Britain and Bougainville and fighting there also went on until the surrender in August. In March 1st Australian Corps's 7th and 9th Divisions attacked Borneo but it took until the end of July before all resistance there ceased.

Operations in China proceeded apace. The Japanese offensive, ICHI-GO, had come to an end in December 1944. Lieutenant General AC Wedemeyer, commanding all American Forces in China and Chief of Staff to Chiang Kai-shek, started to build up a force of 36 divisions to go onto the offensive and recapture Kweilin, Liuchow and possibly Hong Kong. Unbelievably the Japanese reinforced China and went onto the offensive themselves under General Y Okamura's *China Expeditionary Force*. But they were held in the mountains some 50 miles short of the American airfield at Laohokow. At this stage it became clear that Russia might declare war on Japan at any moment and Okamura was ordered to reinforce Manchuria. This forced him to withdraw, leaving only *23rd Army*, of three divisions, to hold the Liuchow Peninsula, the Hong Kong - Canton area and Swatow. At this time the situation inside China was becoming very unstable and Wedemeyer warned the US that anything could happen on the Japanese surrender, even civil war.

It is not necessary to detail the plans that were being developed for the invasion of Japan, but by April 1945 these were well advanced. The British Pacific Fleet and the Far East Air Force were to play their part. Meanwhile the bombing campaign grew in intensity, especially after the fall of Okinawa. Japan was cut off from all sources of oil so the American bombers concentrated on oil storage and refinery plants. The Japanese fought back. On 26th July they attacked and sank the American cruiser *Indianapolis* and continued to make more *Kamikaze* attacks. By early August the Japanese economy was in dire straits and morale was failing everywhere. Efforts were made through Sweden to negotiate a peace settlement but the Allies would not hear of it. Unconditional surrender was all they would accept.

An American Joint Chiefs of Staff assessment in June 1945 concluded that the Japanese Army was still two million strong and, though an attempt to force a surrender by bombing and blockade might produce results, it would not do so before November 1946. The best plan therefore was to continue with plans to invade Kyushu in November 1945 and Honshu in March 1946, but they also recognised that an invasion of Japan would result in desperate fighting for every inch of ground and millions would be killed, both American and Japanese. Nevertheless the President, on 18th June, confirmed the plan but stated that every means of forcing a surrender before 1st November 1945 must be tried.

It was at the Potsdam Conference that the first international discussions about the possible use of the new atomic bomb took place. All options were considered. Would the Soviet Union's entry into the Far East War result in a Japanese surrender? It was thought not, only massive casualties would achieve it. Would bombing and blockade end the war? Again all were convinced that this could only result in massive civilian casualties. All their reasoning showed that the use of the atomic bomb would end the war and that, although there would be heavy casualties at 'Ground Zero', a new term introduced to warfare, this could be controlled and heavy, as they would be, they would be less than in the other options.

At Potsdam the Prime Minister, by then Clement Attlee and the President, by then Harry Truman, persuaded Stalin that the Soviet Union must enter the Far East war. While the conference was in session Japan sought Russian intervention to negotiate peace. Moscow simply declined to answer. Accordingly, when the final sentence of the Potsdam Declaration contained the words 'the alternative to surrender for Japan is prompt and utter destruction', the Japanese mis-read the message, which was to give a clue that something terrible was to happen, to mean that there was an alternative to surrender. The text was received in Tokyo at 0600 hours 27th July and was passed to Shigenori Togo, the new Foreign Minister who was an advocate of friendship with the Soviet Union, who noted that Stalin's signature was not on it. In fact this was simply because the Soviet Union was not then at war with Japan. He read into it that the Russians must be trying to do something for him, and that after all, there was an alternative to unconditional surrender and that Stalin must have included this phrase to say so. The Japanese thus decided to await Russia's reply to their request to intervene. At this stage the Japanese Overseas Broadcasting Organisation had announced that the Japanese Government was ignoring the ultimatum. This was confirmed at a press conference on 30th July.

On hearing this the Americans deduced that the Japanese had rejected the declaration; this caused Truman to confirm his order to General Spaatz to prepare to drop the first atomic bomb on Hiroshima, the *Headquarters of Second General Army* and a major military logistic base. Accordingly, at 0815 hours on 6th August 1945, the bomb was dropped. It caused complete devastation, set the whole city on fire, caused 78,150 killed and 51,048 injured, most from horrifying burns. On 7th August the President sent another ultimatum which said that, unless Japan surrendered immediately, similar bombs would be dropped elsewhere in Japan. The news of the destruction at Hiroshima did not reach Tokyo until 1800 hours and the first assessment stated that very little military damage had been done, *Headquarters 2nd General Army* was intact and other damage, though severe, was no worse than a major B29 air raid. The *Supreme War Council* agreed that it was urgent to seek peace but only on acceptable terms. Then, early on 9th August, the Soviet Union declared war on Japan. The Supreme War Council met the same day. Togo said that the military situation was by then quite hopeless and he advocated peace terms which would avoid the occupation of Japan. The military leaders, however, were against unconditional surrender. It was while they were deliberating that the second atomic bomb was dropped, this time on Nagasaki, causing a further 23,750 killed and 43,000 injured. It is important to keep these figures in perspective and to note that in the big bombing raid on Tokyo on 9/10th March, 84,000 were killed and 40,000 injured. Of course the long-term effect on the injured was the major difference.

When the news reached the *Supreme War Council*, their deliberations went on, but on the same lines and they could still not reach agreement. At 2300 hours Togo and the Prime Minister, Kantaro Suzuki, went to the Emperor who agreed to call an *Imperial Conference* immediately. It met shortly before midnight. After assessing the whole situation the Emperor gave his agreement to the acceptance of the Potsdam Declaration, subject to the one condition that the Imperial House should not be deposed. By 0400 hours on 10th August 1945 this was unanimously approved and was transmitted to Washington and London via Sweden at 0700 hours that day. This was accepted by the Allies and their response reached Tokyo on the 12th. A final meeting of the *Imperial Conference* accepted the terms and a cable was sent to the Allies to say so. The war was over. The first American occupation troops landed on the 28th August, and the main force on the 30th. At 1405 hours that day General MacArthur landed at Atsugi airport in Tokyo and the instrument of surrender was signed on board the battleship USS *Missouri* at 0900 hours on 2nd September, with Admiral Sir Bruce Fraser representing Great Britain.

On 5th August Mountbatten was ordered to start planning for an emergency occupation of Singapore in the event of a Japanese surrender. Clearly his most readily available formations were those preparing for ZIPPER. It was agreed that the landings at Port Swettenham and Port Dickson should be carried out on 9th September as planned. It was, however, decided that Sabang near the north tip of Sumatra and Penang should be occupied by 3rd Commando Brigade on 26th August to act as a staging post to Singapore. 5th Indian Division would move to Rangoon, ready to occupy Singapore. At this point Slim returned to Rangoon and gave orders that the priority for re-occupation would be Burma, Malaya/Singapore, Saigon, Bangkok, Batavia and Sourabaya, Hong Kong and then all remaining areas.

From these orders it was decided that Headquarters 15th Indian Corps under Christison with 5th Indian Division would re-occupy Singapore. 12th Army under Stopford would re-occupy Burma, sending 7th Indian Division to Bangkok and 20th Indian Division to Saigon. 14th Army, now commanded by Lieutenant General Sir Miles Dempsey, was to send 26th Indian Division for operations in Siam if required and he was to submit a new plan for ZIPPER. Headquarters 12th Army would move to Bangkok to command all operations in Siam and French Indo-China while Messervy's 4th Indian Corps was to command all operations in Burma. Finally Fourteenth Army was to occupy the Netherlands East Indies. Then all events were postponed, on MacArthur's order, until the surrender had been signed on 2nd September.

On 26th August a Japanese delegation arrived in Rangoon and met General Browning of Mountbatten's staff. The Japanese were told to order a ceasefire throughout the whole of SEAC, to assist immediately with the release of prisoners of war and to start the removal of all impediments to movement, notably mines. Browning was to make it clear that Mountbatten would accept the full surrender of all Japanese forces in Singapore from Field Marshal Count Terauchi, Commander-in-Chief *Southern Army*, at a later date. On 30th August 15th Indian Corps and one brigade of 5th Indian Division sailed for Singapore. The Royal Navy began the clearance of the Straits of Malacca. 114th Indian Infantry Brigade, of 7th Indian Division, flew to Bangkok on 3rd September, while 20th Indian Division began its flight to Saigon on the 9th. There were of course huge logistic problems involved which do not concern us here, but the urgent need to bring succour of all types to the occupied areas was supreme. Transport, fuel, medical stores, food, even currency had to be provided and new systems to manage them. For this an Allied Control Commission was set up.

The most urgent problem was the repatriation of prisoners of war and internees. Again it is not our business to set out the elaborate organisation which was put in place for this purpose. Suffice it to say that by May 1946 some 96,500 prisoners of war had been evacuated to India, Australia and Great Britain.

In Burma 4th Indian Corps began its clearance of the south-east. The first signs that the Japanese on the ground had got the news of the surrender came on 22nd August when a patrol of 6/15th Punjab at Nyaungkashe met a Japanese patrol, who immediately surrenderd. They linked them to the local Japanese commander who met representatives from 4th Indian Corps at Abya and agreed to a cease-fire. They said they could not surrender as they were yet to be told to do so. They agreed to withdraw all Japanese troops behind the Sittang and not to destroy anything. On 20th September 17th Indian Division was ordered to re-occupy Tenasserim as far as Victoria Point. By 15th October this was done with Headquarters 17th Indian Division at Moulmein. Revenge, yet again, was sweet; by then over 50,000 Japanese had surrendered. 12th Army had become Headquarters Burma Command and on 16th September Civil Government was restored in Burma and the arrest of war criminals had begun. By January 1946 Burma Command had 82nd West African Division in the Irrawaddy valley, 19th Indian Division in the Sittang valley, 17th Indian Division in Tenasserim, the Lushai Brigade in the Karen Hills and 22nd (EA) Brigade in Rangoon.

There were some internal security problems in Burma but these were contained while the new Burma Army was being established and trained. On 16th January it was agreed that 82nd West African Division, 22nd (EA) Brigade, 1st Indian Armoured Brigade, formerly 255th Indian Tank Brigade, and the Lushai Brigade should return to India. Meanwhile 17th and 19th Indian Divisions would amalgamate and form one division of four brigades to be known as 17th Indian Division. This left 2nd Indian Field Regiment, three infantry battalions and support troops un-brigaded and they too were to return to India. Stopford left at the end of January to take command in the Netherlands East Indies and Briggs took command in Burma. Trouble flared up around Myitkyina and Briggs sent two battalions and a field battery there to subdue it. With the departure of so many units, Headquarters 17th Indian Division was moved to Maymyo. A Burma Artillery Headquarters and School of Artillery was established at Meiktila.

On the morning of 27th August 1945 a convoy sailed for the Straits of Malacca. The sea was calm and very blue and the voyage uneventful. For a week the fleet steamed on until dawn on 3rd September, the sixth anniversary of the outbreak of war, when the men on board saw in the distance the hills of Penang. The veterans present recalled the Sudan, Ruweisat Ridge, Alam Halfa, the Tiddim Road, the Arakan and finally the race for Rangoon. What an adventure it had been and now at last the final stage, as they then thought, the re-occupation of Singapore. (Brett-James). On the morning of 4th September, aboard HMS *Sussex*, Lieutenant General Sir Philip Christison, with Major General Robert Mansergh at his side, accepted the Japanese surrender of Penang.

At 1100 hours on 5th September 1945 the first men of Major General Mansergh's 5th Indian Division disembarked in Singapore. On 6th September the assault divisions of Operation ZIPPER, covered by the battleship HMS *Nelson* and the French battleship *Richelieu*, sailed towards their disembarkation beaches. Two Spitfire squadrons had arrived on the 6th. The whole island of Singapore was occupied by the 8th. Headquarters 15th Indian Corps landed on the 9th and established itself in the old Headquarters at Fort Canning. 161st Indian Infantry Brigade moved over the causeway into Johore Bahru. It was an emotional time, as so many old scores were being settled. Also on 9th September, 25th Indian Division landed on the beaches at Morib in Malaya but without covering fire. 37th Indian Infantry Brigade landed further south and 23rd Indian Division landed some eight miles north west of Port Dickson. The landings were in fact more difficult than expected. An account of 145th Field Regiment's experience reported, '. . . intelligence about the beach gradient was faulty. Although the tide was approaching high water, the ships grounded on a sandbank three hundred yards from the shore. The shore proved to be mud and loose sand, instead of the hard shingle anticipated. A scene of much disorder followed, while vehicles and troops tried to struggle, fully laden, through four or five feet of water. . . Two of our guns and quads were not hauled out for three days. Had the landing been opposed by even a moderate enemy, nothing could have prevented a shambles.' (Skrine). With no opposition, the infantry were soon well inland and by 1630 hours Port Swettenham, Klang, Telok Datuk and Kelanang airfield were secure. 15 Spitfires, Headquarters 224 Group RAF and 656 AOP Squadron were ashore by last light.

Now it really was all over. On 12th September back in the Municipal Buildings in Singapore, beneath a picture of King George VI and the flags of the Allies, the stage was set for the formal surrender. Mountbatten was driven along the streets lined by sailors, soldiers and airmen in an open car driven by a recently-released prisoner of war, to be greeted on the steps by his Commanders-in-Chief. While he inspected the Guards of Honour, the bands played 'Rule Britannia' and the Gunners fired a 17 gun salute. Once in the hall the Japanese arrived; Itagaki, Kimura, Nakamura, Kinoshita and others led by Terauchi. Mountbatten read the instrument of surrender. Before he left he stood on the steps as the Union Flag, which had been flown in Singapore up to February 1941 and which had been kept concealed in Changi gaol throughout the war, was hoisted once again and the National Anthem was played. Great was the joy at the release of the prisoners of war at last and many of them were Gunners. There were 32,000 prisoners released in Singapore alone including 16,000 Indians, 6,000 British and 5,000 Australians, Dutch and civilians. Lieutenant Colonel JF Carrol, GSO 1 of 5th Indian Division wrote at the time, 'the bearing and morale of our prisoners of war was a sight I shall never forget; it has made one proud of one's fellow men. They were magnificent, despite the appalling times they had been through and endured.' (quoted by Brett-James).

On 13th September the Japanese surrendered to General Roberts of 34th Indian Corps in Kuala Lumpur. Seremban was retaken by 23rd Indian Division and by 25th September Christison reported the whole of Malaya re-occupied. 656 AOP Squadron established itself on Kuala Lumpur Golf Course with billets in the Bukit Bintang Road. 'C' Flight went to Ipoh with 25th Indian Division where it was located on the race course. 'B' Flight was at Trengannu on the east coast with 23rd Indian Division, while 'A' Flight was with 5th Indian Division at Johore Bahru. In its three years of life this splendid squadron had earned two MBEs, two MCs and nine DFCs. It was then to begin a long period of post-war operations in the Far East.

Slim ordered the disbandment of 34th Indian Corps and ordered 15th Indian Corps to move to Java. 14th Army was to become Malaya Command at Kuala Lumpur. At the end of October 5th Indian Division was ordered to Java and 2nd British Division, less 6th British Infantry Brigade which was to go to Japan, was ordered to take over from it in Malaya. It was at this time that the first unrest, including some bitter fighting between Chinese and Malays, broke out in north Malaya; this was to become the forerunner of many problems. Civil government was re-established on 1st April 1946. The military forces now consisted of Singapore District, 2nd British Division less one brigade, 7th Indian Division, 5th Parachute Brigade and logistic troops. The total strength, including coast defence units and the Malay Regiment in Malaya and Singapore was about 103,000, including some 25,000 British.

On 29th August 1945 Rear Admiral CHJ Harcourt, Flag Officer 11th Aircraft Carrier Squadron, British Pacific Fleet, arrived off Hong Kong with a task force of two carriers, cruisers and other vessels. He was soon joined by the battleship HMS *Anson*. He was greeted by Mr FC Gimson, who had been the colony's Colonial Secretary before the war and had been taken prisoner. He had now been released. A Japanese officer was flown to HMS *Indomitable* for orders. On the 30th the first Royal Marines landed and the surrender of the Japanese was complete by 1st September. The formal surrender took place aboard HMS *Duke of York* on 14th September and all Japanese, about 21,000 all told, were rounded up on the mainland. It was not until 1st May 1946 that Sir Mark Young, after a period of rest following his captivity, returned to be installed as governor and civil government was re-established.

On 3rd September Headquarters 7th Indian Division arrived in Bangkok, secured the surrender of all Japanese and began the release of prisoners of war. On the 6th 114th Indian Infantry Brigade arrived to undertake guard duties. 33rd and 89th Indian Infantry Brigades arrived on 10th October and the divisional artillery was allotted the area Ubon, Lampang and Chienmai to administer. It was at this stage that the old division began to break up as units and men left for demobilisation. The divisional history records, 'Never was a division better served by its artillery. They never failed to "deliver the goods" at the right time and place if it were within the bounds of human ability to do so. In the happy band of warriors that wore the Golden Arrow there was no happier combination than that of Brigadier 'Tim' Hely, his four regimental commanders, Lieutenant Colonels Hall, Armstrong, Pugh and Cole, and those that served with them. Things were never quite the same after they began to drop out.' (Roberts).

136th Field Regiment reported their arrival at Don Muang airfield near Bangkok, not knowing what to expect. The regiment enjoyed its brief stay in Siam but left Bangkok for Singapore on 15th January. From there it went to Malacca where it remained until its return to Liverpool in March and April 1946. At the end of January 7th Indian Division left for Malaya and was complete there by the end of April.

General Gracey led his 20th Indian Division into Saigon on 13th September to find law and order breaking down and much anti-French feeling. He took drastic action and imposed a form of martial law, closing newspapers and controlling the radio. There was much talk of the establishment of a Vietnamese Republic. At this stage he had only his 80th Indian Infantry Brigade to keep order. Mountbatten gave Gracey full support but the unrest remained a problem. Gracey was forced to use Japanese troops to help his own force. On 5th October the French General PFM Leclerc, who had commanded the French 2nd Armoured Division with such distinction in the west, arrived. 5th French Colonial Regiment disembarked the same day. Two days later 32nd and 100th Indian Infantry Brigades of 20th Indian Division began to arrive and 114th (Sussex) Field Regiment began to land. 9th French Colonial Division was on its way from France. General Leclerc was the French Commander in Chief Far East and further units were sent to him. Cambodia was occupied without trouble. Meanwhile 20th Indian Division deployed its brigades around the country and began to disarm Japanese troops, apart from those who were employed in guarding important places, and there was some fighting with Vietnamese (Annamite) guerrillas, leading to some casualties. Captain Stanley Crooks recorded that he was the first to land in 114th Field Regiment at Saigon '. . . and had the queer experience of being handed a Jap truck with a Jap driver . . .' to enable him to set up accommodation for his regiment. Operationally he was later '. . . given a single-engined two-seater as a flying OP, with a Jap warrant officer as pilot . . . I flew quite a number of sorties with the same pilot and in spite of the obvious language difficulty, as neither of us spoke the other's language, got to know him quite well and, in fact, like him.' (Crooks).

At the end of the year the French assumed full responsibility for Indo China and 20th Indian Division began to leave; 32nd Indian Infantry Brigade to Borneo and 80th Indian Infantry Brigade to Celebes. On 28th January command passed to the French and 20th Indian Division less two brigades returned to India. Some British remained under Brigadier MSK Maunsell, a Gunner who had fought with 2nd British Division. Peace did not last for long. When a French force tried to land at Haiphong it came under fire, an omen of what was to follow.

Of all the territories which were re-occupied after the war, the one which presented the greatest problem and the only one in which there was heavy fighting, was Java (Map 53). The Japanese had gone out of their way to stir up anti-Dutch feeling during their occupation. They also promoted the idea of Indonesian independence. Further, on 5th September Field Marshal Terauchi had declared a Republic of Indonesia under Dr A Soekarno, and this caused much trouble. A small parachute group from Force 136 was dropped near Batavia on 8th September to make contact with the Japanese and this was followed up by a naval force on the 15th. They discovered a disturbing situation. Soon political tension began to rise and acts of violence occurred. On 19th September General Slim ordered 23rd Indian Division, with two brigades, to move to Java and put one brigade at Batavia and the other at Sourabaya. The situation continued to deteriorate sharply and 1st Seaforth was sent to Batavia in advance of this move and was soon involved in dealing with looting and with dispersing rioters. Christison was himself dispatched to take command and arrived on the 29th to find that an Indonesian Republic, under Dr Soekarno, had gained a large measure of control in Java.

On 6th October the Deputy Governor of the Netherlands East Indies, Dr CO van der Plas, broadcast to say that the Dutch were there to outline advances in self government. Soekarno said that he would do all he could to help. Christison stressed that British troops were only there to take the Japanese surrender and to co-ordinate the return of prisoners of war. The situation improved until the Dutch Government foolishly repudiated the content of the Deputy Governor's broadcast and all co-operation ceased. Soekarno said he would not try to control the extremists and would fight the British if they showed any sign of helping the Dutch. Mountbatten protested about the Dutch action to the Chiefs of Staff. He said that he only had two options; first to disarm the Japanese, recover the prisoners and withdraw, or to assume full responsibility for law and order. For the latter he would need a full Corps plus Dutch troops. Meanwhile he ordered 23rd Indian Division to move speedily and to occupy Batavia, Buitenzorg, Bandoeng, Sourabaya, Semerang and Magelang all of which contained prisoners and internees.

On 13th October Mountbatten reported that aggressive action by the few Dutch forces in Java had seriously worsened the situation. Christison had therefore withdrawn them and urgently needed political direction on the nature of his task. He said the country was close to civil war and that British and Indian troops were liable to be drawn into it. The Dutch agreed to negotiate but not with Soekarno. Mountbatten decided to send 1st Indian Infantry Brigade Group, under Brigadier RCM King, consisting of 178th Assault Field Regiment, 1/16th Punjab and 1st Patiala Infantry to join up with 1st Seaforths. Main Headquarters 23rd Indian Division, commanded by Major General DC Hawthorn, reached Batavia on 23rd October, closely followed by No. 904

Wing RAF, with Nos. 60 and 81 Squadrons, equipped with Thunderbolts, and 31 Squadron, with its Dakotas. Meanwhile 26th Indian Infantry Division began to land in Sumatra on 10th October and came under Christison's command.

On 4th October 1st Indian Infantry Brigade was made responsible for law and order in Batavia. 178th Assault Field Regiment took over the guarding of internment camps, the airfield and the docks. The Indonesians began to put up road blocks, clashes soon started and casualties occurred. On 15th October 37th Indian Infantry Brigade, under Brigadier N Macdonald, disembarked at Batavia. It consisted of 3/3rd, 3/5th and 3/10th Gurkhas. They occupied Buitenzorg and Bandoeng and saved the lives of many Dutch and local Christians. 3/10th Gurkhas went to Semarang where fighting between extremists and the Japanese had broken out. Thanks to the work of Major Kido, a Japanese officer who was placed in command of the Kido Battalion, formed from fellow prisoners of war, and who did all he could to help, peace was restored and prisoners released. But trouble broke out in the surrounding area. On 20th October Brigadier RWB Bethell, the CRA of 23rd Indian Division, who commanded an *ad hoc* brigade composed of 6/8th Punjab and two companies of 5/8th Punjab, was sent to Semerang to take command of 3/10th Gurkhas and restore order. The 3/10th was attacked by large numbers of well-armed Indonesians at Magelang and Ambarawa. The situation in Batavia was also worsening and several Europeans and Japanese were murdered.

On 25th October, 49th Indian Infantry Brigade, commanded by Brigadier AWS Mallaby, with 6/5th Mahrattas and 5/6th Rajputs, landed at Sourabaya and moved to occupy key points; again the Indonesians put up road blocks. It was at this stage that General Mansergh's 5th Indian Division, less 161st Indian Infantry Brigade, was ordered to Sourabaya. Two Indian cavalry units, 11th Cavalry (PAVO), with Stuart tanks, from Port Dickson and 13th (DCO) Lancers, with Sherman tanks, from India, were to join the division.

At Sourabaya the Indonesians refused to allow Mallaby to start landing so he sent his brigade second-in-command, Colonel LHO Pugh to the Oranje Hotel to negotiate. Pugh wrote, 'Every quarter of a mile the car was halted at a barricade covered by machine guns. From the shadows emerged excited Indonesians, some in uniform and others in civilian clothes, armed with rifles, swords and spears. These bore down upon the car from all sides demanding the business of the occupants, thrusting rifle muzzles in through the open windows, all talking at once, all with fingers on the triggers . . . There appeared to be no end to this nerve-wracking performance.' (quoted in Kirby). But 49th Indian Infantry Brigade started to land, although it could not get at the Ferwerda Drawbridge, the Power Station or the airfield, which the Indonesians held in strength. Nevertheless an agreement was reached leaving the Indonesians with their arms and prisoners were released. Then, unknown to Mallaby, an RAF Dakota flew over dropping leaflets issued by Headquarters 23rd Indian Division which said that British Military Administration was taking over and that all weapons must be handed in and anyone who did not do so would be shot. The Indonesians said they had been tricked but Mallaby told them he had no option but to obey orders, even though the leaflets had appeared without his knowledge.

Firing broke out all over the town at 1630 hours 29th October. All 49th Indian Infantry Brigade posts were attacked. Many officers and men had to run the gauntlet to safety and women and children were murdered. A small escort of Mahrattas guarding a convoy of internees was attacked and, although they resisted gallantly, all were killed and the internees massacred. Sourabaya was soon in flames, everywhere the crackle of small arms fire could be heard along with the thump of mortars. Soekarno arrived with Hawthorn and Mallaby on the 30th and met the local leaders who agreed to stop the fighting; but they were not in control and the fighting went on. Mallaby's Brigade Major tried to make contact with the local leaders, but was captured and killed. Mallaby himself went to meet Indonesian leaders but was intercepted and murdered. The situation was critical.

Colonel Lewis Pugh, on hearing of the murder of Mallaby took command of 49th Brigade. This involved him driving five miles across the town under fire, but he got through. He found on arrival, that as well as Mallaby, 18 officers and 374 men were casualties mostly killed. He re-organised the brigade and held the airfield while extricating some 6,000 Dutch women and children to Singapore. For this outstanding work he was awarded a second bar to his Distinguished Service Order where the citation stated, 'Throughout the whole operation Colonel Pugh showed the highest qualities of leadership; his complete disregard of personal danger and his unruffled and cheerful efficiency at all times were an example and inspiration to all ranks.' He had certainly brought great credit to the Regiment by his services in Burma and Java.

The news flashed round Java that the Indonesians were in control. It was then that 3/10th Gurkhas at Magelang was surrounded by a large Indonesian force with guns and mortars. Tension rose in Batavia and terrorists increased their activities against Europeans everywhere and made determined efforts to seize Japanese weapons. 5th Indian Division with tanks and artillery was ordered to Sourabaya with all speed; it would arrive in the nick of time. Slim told Mansergh, before his departure, that on arrival he was to take command of the Sourabaya area. He would be supported by warships and supplied by air. On 31st October Christison issued a warning to all Indonesians that, unless attacks on British forces stopped immediately, he would bring in the full might of his land, sea and air forces and use it until they were crushed. HQ 656 AOP Squadron, now under command of Major Frank McMath, arrived in Sourabaya with 'A' Flight.

Meanwhile, in Sourabaya Pugh had concentrated his force in the dock area with his infantry and he put 3rd Indian Field Regiment, 71st Indian Field Company IE and two companies 5/6th Rajput in the Darmo area to guard the hospital and the internment camps. 9th Indian Infantry Brigade, under Brigadier Brain, with 2nd West Yorks, 3/2nd Punjab and 1st Burma Regiment landed on 1st November and took over from 49th Indian Infantry Brigade in the docks. 5th Indian Divisional Headquarters arrived on 3rd November with 123rd Indian Infantry Brigade, commanded by Brigadier HJ Denholm-Young. Mansergh arrived and was met by Pugh who briefed him. Also that day 2nd (Derajat) Mountain Battery, led by Major J Nettelfield, landed but as yet without its guns. These followed on 4th November and soon the battery was in action covering the perimeter. The rest of 3rd and 5th Indian Field Regiments were on their way. For his work in Sourabaya at this time Major Nettelfield was awarded the Military Cross.

Mansergh's orders were to hold the airfield and the docks and keep the port in operation, while calling for the surrender and disarmament of the extremists. Meanwhile Anglo-Dutch relations were becoming strained, since The Hague refused to talk to Soekarno. Mountbatten's assessment had changed. Even if a reasonable settlement was reached between the Dutch and Indonesians, he would still need a corps of three divisions with armour and artillery in Java to complete the removal of the Japanese and all prisoners. This meant an extra division and the only one available was 2nd British Division just arriving in Malaya, less its 5th Brigade which was on its way to Japan as part of the occupation forces. If, however, the talks broke down he would need two corps, each of three divisions with full naval and air support. The Chiefs of Staff replied to say that he must restrict his operations purely to the disarming and evacuation of the Japanese, to ensuring the safety of allied prisoners and internees and to the establishment of secure bases for their evacuation, through which Dutch forces could be passed if required. Meanwhile every effort would be made to persuade the Dutch to come to a reasonable settlement. Mountbatten stressed the difficulty of even this task with 129,000 people to evacuate from all over the country and there was no sign yet of adequate Dutch forces. The Chiefs of Staff still had not confirmed whether British and Indian forces would remain after all Japanese and internees had been accounted for.

The situation became even more complex as it was realised that there were many thousands more European, Chinese and Indian people in Sumatra and Java, who would be at risk if the British left and the Dutch could not cope. Mountbatten agreed that the area Batavia - Bandoeng - Buitenzorg was best suited as a concentration area for all prisoners, internees and now refugees. 36th Indian Infantry Brigade, of 26th Indian Division, had arrived on 10th December, together with 5th Parachute Brigade from Malaya and 49th Indian Infantry Brigade from Semarang; these three formations were told off for this task while 161st Indian Infantry Brigade, of 5th Indian Division, was to go to Batavia. Meanwhile, on 3rd and 4th November, evacuation of dependants and internees continued with difficulty from Sourabaya. Mansergh called a meeting in Sourabaya on 9th November with an Indonesian leader, Mr Soerio, who regarded himself as governor of East Java, and told him to control his men, stop looting and murder, return all allied personnel and equipment and remove his men from the airfield which he was going to secure that afternoon. He then left the meeting leaving Pugh to discuss the detail.

Nothing happened and an ultimatum was given to the population by leaflet. This gave the Indonesians until 1800 hours 10th November to hand over hostages and illegal arms and for their leader to meet Mansergh at his headquarters at the same hour. Thereafter Allied forces would search the town and any unauthorised person carrying arms would be sentenced to death. Mansergh gave orders for the full occupation of Sourabaya starting at 1800 hours 10th November, if the ultimatum was ignored. Artillery firepower was provided by 5th Indian Field Regiment, Lieutenant Colonel RFD Legh, supplemented by the destroyers *Caesar*, *Carron* and *Cavalier*. 12 Mosquitoes and two squadrons ofThunderbolts were standing by and a Visual Control Post was also ready.

It was on 10th November 1945 that tragedy struck 5th Indian Division. Brigadier Robert Loder-Symons, the CRA, asked General Mansergh if he could fly over Sourabaya to see what was happening. Then, when taking off, for some reason the aircraft failed to rise and crashed, killing him and the pilot. Loder-Symons had been one of those distinguished and gallant Horse Artillery battery commanders who did so outstandingly well in the early days in the Western Desert and Tobruk. In Burma he was soon loved and respected by Indian and British alike. His death deprived the Army and the Regiment of one of its greatest sons. Loder-Symons was one of the outstanding young officers of the war. He was 32.

By 1800 hours no reply had been received from Soerio. Accordingly 123rd Indian Infantry Brigade began its advance against sniping and automatic fire. 9th Indian Infantry Brigade moved into the area east of Kali Mas, two concrete pillboxes were destroyed by 6-pounder anti-tank guns and 40 extremists were killed. Sourabaya Radio poured out appeals to resist, to kill prisoners and to poison food and water.

Sourabaya was occupied by 5th Indian Division advancing slowly and methodically, using both artillery and tanks, sometimes against fanatical opposition. Each locality was consolidated and cleared of all extremists, so that the normal life of the town could continue. Indonesian casualties were heavy as they made suicidal attacks against trained experienced troops. It was a model of restoring order and peace in a highly serious stuation. Air support was used against main centres of resistance. By 28th November the task was completed. Forward defended areas were established along the line of the canal from the Darmo Barracks to the sea, with 123rd Indian Infantry Brigade on the right and 9th Indian Infantry Brigade on the left. 161st Indian Infantry Brigade had by then arrived and it took up positions in the Grand Hotel - Courts of Justice area. Indonesian casualties were about 4,700. 15 tanks, 36 AA guns, seven anti-tank guns, 11 mortars, 75 MMGs, 44 LMGs, 794 rifles, 580 miscellaneous weapons and 400 tons of ammunition were taken. Allied casualties in Java, nearly all in Sourabaya by 22nd November, were 11 officers and 87 other ranks killed and 14 officers and 183 other ranks missing.

Throughout December the search for arms went on; there were more casualties and more weapons were found but the situation was under control and improving. On 4th December 145th Field Regiment, commanded by Lieutenant Colonel RLT Burges, arrived and its 509th Field Battery was soon in action along the south edge of the town. Then on 5th December 161st Indian Infantry Brigade was sent to Batavia where the situation was worsening. By the end of the month peace had returned to Sourabaya and 5th Indian Division had extended its control out to some ten miles beyond the town in all directions. 145th Field Regiment reported working with 9th and 23rd Indian Infantry Brigades as it extended the controlled area out to Sidoarjo, Menganti and Domas. It reported excellent support from 656th AOP Squadron during this period. On one occasion the regiment hit a 20mm AA gun which had been engaging an Auster.

We left 3/10th Gurkhas surrounded by some 5,000 Indonesians with mortars and guns at Magelang at the end of October. Christison sent in a very successful air strike which enabled the Gurkhas to concentrate and improve their position. On 2nd November Soekarno went to Magelang with Brigadier Bethell and a cease fire was arranged. The evacuation of Japanese prisoners and internees went on, but there was still much treachery and murder. At Ambarawa 29 women and children were murdered when extremists threw grenades among them. Then on 9th November the messages from Radio Sourabaya about the Indonesian seizure of control were picked up at Semarang and tension mounted. On the 17th two British officers were murdered and another wounded. Bethell ordered action and the occupation of the town. Heavy fighting broke out; 1500 Indonesians attacked from the east but were almost all destroyed by naval gunfire. New attacks came in on the 25th supported by artillery; after losing 800 killed, the remainder fled, but their artillery continued to fire and killed 47, including 20 soldiers, before the guns were silenced by the Royal Air Force.

On the 27th 49th Indian Infantry Brigade came to the rescue. The brigade was now under the command of Brigadier A de B Morris, Pugh having returned to the United Kingdom. There has always been some mystery about Pugh's return to the UK, for he blamed Mansergh for sacking him for his outspoken criticism of operations. This is almost certainly not true. It is almost certainly true that he was removed by his own GOC, Hawthorn and later, in India, General Dempsey decided that it would be in everyone's interest if Pugh returned home, which he was due to do anyway. Whatever the reason, nothing reduces his great ability, bravery and leadership epitomised by his three DSOs. He also brought the greatest credit to the Regiment in the Far East.

By 10th December some 11,000 internees and some 200 Chinese were safely in Semarang, guarded by 49th Indian Infantry Brigade, of three battalions, 11th Indian Cavalry, 6th Indian Field Battery, one troop of 2nd Indian Anti-Tank Regiment, the Kido Battalion and support troops. The CRA's *ad hoc* brigade was then disbanded. On 11th January 1946 5th Parachute Brigade, under Brigadier JNH Poett, took over the area and 49th Indian Infantry Brigade moved to Batavia. Peace returned to Semarang. 145th Field Regiment was broken up and 395th Field Battery went to join 178th Field Regiment at Batavia.

We must next look at the effect of the terrorist actions at Sourabaya and Magelang which began to be felt in Batavia early in November. Here 23rd Indian Division had Brigadier King's 1st and Brigadier Macdonald's 37th Indian Infantry Brigades; the former in Batavia and the latter in Bandoeng with a detachment at Buitenzorg guarding the road between the two. Clashes began and casualties occurred. Dutch troops were very trigger-happy and had to be replaced. Then on 24th November the 23 survivors of a Dakota which crashed in the jungle were massacred. Torrential rain and floods hindered both sides but a convoy near Buitenzorg was attacked and in a fierce battle some 50 Indonesians were killed for the loss of 13 Gurkhas; Mosquito bombers were also used. The road was kept open only by the use of tanks and armoured cars. 23rd Indian Division was moved there in February and 50th Indian Tank Brigade arrived to reinforce 36th and 161st Indian Infantry Brigades in Batavia.

By 12th January 1946 Lieutenant General Sir Miles Dempsey, GOC Malaya and formerly the C-in-C 2nd British Army in north-west Europe, pressed for Dutch/Indonesian talks to begin and for plans to be made to evacuate all British and Indian troops. On 1st February Stopford succeeded Christison, who returned to the United Kingdom to become Commander-in-Chief Northern Command. Stopford began to plan with the Dutch authorities, notably Dr JH Van Mook, who had been head of the Netherlands East Indies Provisional Government in Australia, and Dr Van de Plas. There were still some 73,000 Japanese troops in Java, Bali and Lombok and some 160,000 displaced persons of all categories to evacuate and protect. There was an uneasy peace throughout February and evacuations continued. During this period a plan was made to hand over to the Dutch when they arrived. They had already taken over in Bali and Lombok. Then, on 10th March, a convoy for Bandoeng ran into an ambush some 20 miles south of Buitenzorg. A column consisting of a squadron of 13th Lancers, with Shermans, and a company of Bombay Grenadiers set out to help but hit mines at Soekaboemi. A column from Bandoeng, consisting of 5/6th Rajputana Rifles, a troop of tanks and a troop of 25-pounders, was ambushed at Tjitaroem suspension bridge and suffered 22 casualties. Efforts were made all day on 12th November to reach the stricken convoy when a third column left Bandoeng under Brigadier Wingrove, who was now commanding 1st Indian Infantry Brigade. It too hit road blocks and enemy resistance. It was here that 'B' Troop of 395th Field Battery, which had recently joined 178th Field Regiment from 145th Field Regiment, fired over 400 rounds under its FOO Captain RAJ Middleton. A link-up was eventually made on the 14th, but at the cost of 17 killed and 88 wounded.

The Dutch Army began to arrive on 9th March and to take over. Brigadier Bethell again formed his *ad hoc* brigade and relieved 37th Indian Infantry Brigade so that it could return to India. The hand over went on throughout May and June, but it was not until 29th November that Rear Headquarters 15th Indian Corps left Batavia and the British task was complete. Negotiations went ahead to produce a political settlement which resulted in the creation of the Republic of Indonesia. In all, operations in Java cost 2,136 British and Indian casualties of whom 622 were killed. In his final message Dr Van Mook said, 'You came to save and you stayed to protect; your departure coinciding with the dawn of peace in this country leaves us with feelings of gratitude and regret and with the memory of an arduous task well done.' Dr S Shahrir, who became Prime Minister of the republican government in 1945, said 'Under all circumstances, even in unfriendly contact or in conflict with us we learnt to appreciate and admire you, your politeness, your kindness and your dignified self-restraint. Long after you have left, when the wounds caused by war and revolution have been healed, I think this final impression of your Army will be the lasting memory for our people of your stay in our country.' It was a fine epitaph.

During April the various units of 5th Indian Division sailed back to India and the relief of Sourabaya was completed by 8th May. The hand-over went smoothly but it was not without a tinge of regret that the division had to leave behind 20 x 25-pounders which had served it so well for so long. These had been sold to the Dutch. On 23rd April 1946 General Mansergh left the division to become GOC-in-C Allied Forces Dutch East Indies at Batavia. The square in front of Divisional Headquarters in Sourabaya, the former Town Hall, was re-named 'General Mansergh Plein.' The new CRA, Brigadier GK Bourne, took command of the division and took it back to India. (Brett-James).

After the war there was some high level criticism levelled at Mansergh for his conduct of this part of the Java campaign in 1946, something which is easy to do with hindsight. He was criticised for siding with the Dutch and for not being even-handed. However, evidence from those who were there, gathered together by John Tucker who served at Headquarters 5th Indian Division, shows otherwise. The evidence shows how, even under the greatest provocation,

Mansergh remained firm and balanced, saving both Dutch and Indonesian when threatened in his own quest to save prisoners of war and others. It was clear that the Indonesians were terrorising their own citizens and were incapable of maintaining law and order. The only hope was to hand over to the Dutch Army in order that the British could withdraw from a situation which was neither of their making nor their concern. Even so, many Indonesians criticised him and many Dutch thought that he deliberately handed over Java too easily.

Much was happening elsewhere. The Japanese had conquered Borneo, Celebes, part of New Guinea and hundreds of small islands. All had been occupied by the Australian 7th and 9th Divisions after the Japanese surrender. The Indonesian nationalist movement had not affected British Borneo and was weak enough in Dutch Borneo and the outer Islands to enable the Australians to hand them over direct to the Dutch. Consequently only two British/Indian brigades went to this area. 32nd Indian Infantry Brigade, under Brigadier ECJ Woodford, left Saigon on Christmas Day 1945 and landed at Labuan on the 29th, sending 4/2nd Gurkhas to Jesselton and 9/14th Punjab to Kuching. There were no problems and by 28th May the civil administration had been established and 32nd Brigade left for Madras. 80th Indian Infantry Brigade, commanded by Brigadier DE Taunton, moved to Makassar in Celebes on 1st February. Here the brigade acted as a mobile reserve in case it was needed in any of the hundreds of small islands in the area. Law and order was maintained by the Dutch who had been put in place by the Australians. Some 180,000 Japanese surrendered in the outer islands, including some 20,500 in British Borneo. Allied prisoners were quickly evacuated. Lieutenant General Robert Mansergh who had assumed command of Allied Forces Netherlands East Indias, authorised 80th Indian Infantry Brigade to hand over all responsibilities to the Dutch on 14th July 1946, after which it left for India.

Finally there was Sumatra (Map 54) where there were 71,500 Japanese of Lieutenant General M Tanabe's *25th Army* to be dealt with, some 2,200 prisoners of war and over 14,550 internees to be rescued. The first lift of 26th Indian Division, under Major General HM Chambers, sailed from Madras on 4th October 1945 and comprised divisional headquarters and 71st Indian Infantry Brigade commanded by Brigadier HPL Hutchinson. On 11th October simultaneous landings were made at Padang, by divisional headquarters and 71st Brigade less one battalion, and at Medan, by HQRA under Brigadier TED Kelly with 6th South Wales Borderers. 7th Indian Field Regiment, less 16th Field Battery which had left the regiment to go to Japan in September to join the British Commonwealth Division, arrived at Medan on 22nd December 1945. On 29th, 2nd Patiala Infantry, ISF, and 1st Indian Anti-Tank Regiment arrived to operate as infantry. They then began a long period of eleven months on counter-insurgency operations. Throughout this period the main problem was collecting, organising and administering released allied prisoners of war and internees, known as RAPWI. By January 1946 over 10,000 had been assembled at Medan. Soon an Indonesian Army, the TRI, began to emerge. It was well-armed and determined to achieve independence from the Dutch. 17th and 18th Field Batteries of 7th Indian Field Regiment were soon firing their guns in support of infantry battalions operating in the Medan area.

On 21st October 1945 Chambers received the formal surrender of the Japanese and work started to round up and disarm them and to locate the prisoners of war. The local inhabitants were at first indifferent to the British and Indian troops but when they found the Dutch working with them they became very hostile. Some Japanese, whose behaviour was perfectly correct throughout, were used to help police Palembang. On 29th October 4th Indian Infantry Brigade, Brigadier JFR Forman, arrived and also went to Padang. The Rajputana Rifles went to Medan under the command of the CRA, with 12th Frontier Force Regiment, a machine gun battalion, and 7th Indian Field Regiment.

Trouble soon broke out and there were several murders and kidnappings aimed at both the Dutch, other Europeans and Eurasians, Chinese and Ambonese, but not against the British. In early December the Brigade Major of 71st Indian Infantry Brigade and a female Red Cross worker were kidnapped and murdered. Drastic action was taken and several armed Indonesians were rounded up and shot. Headquarters 26th Indian Division then moved to Medan, now under Major General RCO Hedley. When the Dutch landed on Banka Island, the Indonesians reacted violently and tension increased in Palembang. Then, on 25th February, three British naval officers were captured and two were murdered. By mid-March Headquarters 71st Indian Infantry Brigade had moved to Palembang with 1st Lincolns. There were several clashes and some casualties until they were relieved by the Dutch in November.

The first clash in Medan came on 8th March when a patrol was ambushed and a few days later 2/7th Rajputs had to call for artillery to clear some road blocks. The situation became tense in both Medan and Padang. There were several clashes while the evacuation of Japanese went on. By the end of May 48,000 had gone. By mid-June there were six battalions (including 8th Mahratta Anti-Tank Regiment in the infantry role), a squadron of armoured cars, 7th Indian Field Regiment less one battery, an RAF Squadron and 10,900 Japanese troops at Medan. There were two battalions at Padang and two at Palembang. The Japanese were employed to guard the oilfields. July and August were relatively quiet. In the latter month, 5th Indian Field Battery from 3rd Indian Field Regiment in Java joined 7th Indian Field Regiment and moved to Padang.

Tension rose in September when it became known that the Dutch were coming back in October; clashes again occurred and road blocks had to be removed by force. There were daily clashes when the first Dutch arrived on 26th October. Sweeps were carried out by the Padang Brigade, commanded by Brigadier NG Thompson, CRA 26th Indian Division, with 1st Garhwal Rifles, 8/8th Punjab and 2nd Kumaon Regiments together with one battery of 7th Indian Field Regiment. There was no further trouble. The last British troops left Palembang on 9th November and Medan on 21st November 1946. 7th Indian Field Regiment left for Ranchi on the 18th, where it remained until the great upheavals of partition. The last troops left Padang on 28th November 1946, just one day before the Rear Headquarters 15th Indian Corps, (AFNEI), left Batavia.

During the occupation of Sumatra 68,402 Japanese were evacuated and about 13,550 Dutch Civilians were evacuated to Holland. 26th Indian Infantry Division suffered 303 casualties, including five officers and 55 men killed. It had been another testing task for the men to face when the war was over and they longed to get home. That they completed some of the most thankless tasks and complex duties with great success is greatly to their credit. They were of course witnessing a pattern of operations which were to persist for the British Army until, and beyond, the end of the 20th Century.

So the war was over and the immediate peace restored. There was still much going on to bring help and succour to the countries that had suffered and endured so much. Civilian rule had to be re-instated after a period of conquest and the military slowly had to back out of the administration of the territories whose freedom had been restored. Supreme Headquarters moved from Ceylon to Singapore. A Governor General was to be appointed in Malaya in May 1946, with a Special Commissioner to deal with economic problems. The run-down of the armed forces went ahead while consideration was given to the post-war military structure to be adopted in the Far East. The Right Honourable Malcolm Macdonald arrived in Singapore on 21st May 1946 as the first Governor General and Lord Killearn became Special Commissioner. Mountbatten left on the 31st May after two and a half momentous years as Supreme Allied Commander. Stopford assumed command on 1st June. Before he left Mountbatten recommended the appointment of a Supreme Commander for the new Far East Command with three Commanders-in-Chief under him. Malcolm Macdonald and Lord Killearn agreed, but the Chiefs of Staff did not and Attlee supported them so it was not done until 1963 when Mountbatten himself became Chief of Defence Staff.

The officers and men of the Royal Regiment of Artillery, together with their comrades from India and what is now Pakistan, Australia and East and West Africa, fought with the greatest distinction in the Far East. They produced the vital firepower for battle wherever it was fought and in the most testing and appalling conditions. They suffered greatly from wounds, sickness, climate, terrain and terror. Many fell in the defence of the guns, many were captured and suffered extra hardship, terror and cruelty. Many were wounded and returned, maimed for life, but by their gallantry and devotion to duty the guns were used to the greatest effect. On 31st March 1945 the strength of the Royal Artillery in India Command alone was 67,284 officers and men, to say nothing of the growing strength of what was at that time the Royal Indian Artillery, the Royal Regiment of Australian Artillery, the Royal Regiment of New Zealand Artillery or the Gunners of East and West Africa. When the fighting stopped there were 45 British, Indian and African field regiments, eight medium regiments, 29 light anti-aircraft/anti-tank regiments, 13 mountain regiments, one heavy regiment, two survey regiments, 16 heavy anti-aircraft regiments, seven coast regiments, one maritime regiment, one searchlight regiment, one defence regiment, seven counter-mortar batteries and one air observation squadron. In addition there were artillery headquarters at every level of higher command.

Great gallantry was shown throughout these battles and although no attempt has been made to include all who received awards, a number have been mentioned in the context of the fighting at the time. The Gunner casualty figures in the Far East theatre were not light, as much of the fighting was at very close quarters, with gun positions themselves frequently under direct attack. The struggle of the Gunners on the guns has few equals. Movement was a nightmare over the trackless jungles and mountainous tracks in extremes of climate. To have to fight the guns when under attack themselves, firing very large quantities of ammunition, all of which had to be carried to the guns, put huge pressures on the men and supply services. It did not matter whether this was the field guns, the mountain guns, the anti-tank, anti-aircraft or coast guns, the pressure was the same. The work of the signallers in keeping open the vital communications, without which the guns were useless, was the greatest triumph. Only on the rarest occasions do we read of radio failure; indeed, more often than not entire battles were fought on Gunner communications. The work of command post staffs, surveyors and instrument operators who worked out the firing data in extreme conditions, and of the drivers and the fitters in keeping the guns up with the battles that raged across half a continent and kept them in action, were outstanding.

As always it was the OP parties, in company with the infantry, which had the very worst time. They had to be very close to the enemy in order to control the fire at all, as often as not within listening range of Japanese voices. They suffered heavy casualties and on a fair number of occasions an FOO took command of an infantry company when it lost its own officers. But also, time and time again, it was the deadly accurate fall of shot often only 25 yards, or even less, in front of the infantry that saved the day. The FOOs were seldom relieved until they were re-grouped. Battalions came and went but the FOOs stayed put. Their survival rate was not high but their contribution to victory was very great indeed. Amongst them must be included the outstanding performance of 656th Air Observation Post Squadron whose Gunner pilots did more than most to achieve victory.

The artillery commanders at all levels were very professional. They knew their job and Gunner regiments were always well-handled as indeed were divisional and on occasions corps artilleries. Many Gunners filled positions of high command and had great influence on the outcome of the war and in doing so brought great credit to the Regiment. They are listed at Annex V.

As for the equipments, the guns themselves, the vehicles, instruments, radios, radars and the animals, the mules and horses, were all crucial to success and stood up to the test extremely well.

At Annex X is an extract from the REME War Report on Artillery Equipments which shows that they came through remarkably well, a great tribute to their design and the care lavished on them by the men in the batteries.

The Far East War had a very special dimension in the vicious and often cruel nature of combat brought about because of the clash between two very different cultures. It produced greater suffering than in most theatres. It meant those who were wounded or became sick were at much greater risk, a situation made worse because of the long distance from medical facilties, alleviated so often by the pilots, very often American, who flew their light aircraft with skill and gallantry in evacuating the wounded and sick. It also meant that those who were captured suffered untold agony as they awaited the day of deliverance. They too served by their dignity in adversity.

Finally, because so much was about to happen in the great Indian sub-continent as it became independent after the war, at Annex J is included details of the expansion of The Indian Regiment of Artillery. This shows the enormous expansion it achieved and the magnificent service of its regiments in the face of the enemy. Few regiments have ever expanded at such a rate during a fight for their existence and that they did so and achieved such incredibly high standards, deserves the highest accolade. Those links forged in battle during those dramatic years will be maintained for ever between the officers and men of the artillery regiments of that part of the Commonwealth who fought in the Far East. Those from Africa, Australia, Britain, Ceylon, Hong Kong, Burma, India, Malaya, New Zealand, the future Pakistan and Singapore who fought alongside each other during those eventful years are bound together by something very special indeed.

Of Burma, Slim wrote at the end of the war, 'We regained Burma because we were a team, a team of many races, services and arms, in which each worked not only for his own show but for the whole side. In this team the Gunners, British, Indian and African, played an outstanding part. They were in on everything. For artillery it was the most difficult theatre of all. The immense effort in moving the guns through jungle, the problems of clearance, often of a meagre ammunition supply, the lack of visibility and the constant threat of Japanese infiltration, might have reduced the guns to comparative impotence. Yet all of these, and a dozen other handicaps, were overcome by brains, brawn and determination. Gunners developed new techniques of co-operation with infantry, tanks and air. They became adept at close defence. They took on any job - road making, lorry columns, air supply. They acted as infantry, and more than once artillery officers took command of infantry units which had lost all their own officers. They packed themselves and their equipment into aircraft as readily as they undertook a move by road. They mounted their guns in ships and manned them. Nor did three years in the jungle make them slow-moving or static-minded. When we broke out into the plains of Central Burma, they without hesitation adapted themselves to almost desert tactics and mobility.

They earned the admiration and gratitude of our own troops and of our allies for gallantry, efficiency and unselfish devotion in their support.

I saw them come out of Burma in 1942, grimly covering the rearguard; I saw them go back with the foremost troops in 1944 and 1945. For me their spirit is typified by the gunner on the Toungoo road, stripped to the waist, glistening with sweat, slapping shells into the breech of a 25-pdr, who, when I said to him, 'I'm sorry you've got to do all this on half rations,' replied, 'Never mind about that, sir! Put us on quarter rations, give us the ammo, and we'll get you into Rangoon!' No wonder we got there.' (Duncan).

EPILOGUE

Great Britain, her Empire and the Commonwealth were critically over-extended by late December 1941. They were locked in mortal combat with Germany, Italy and Japan. They had lost most of their allies, who had been overrun by the Axis Powers, and the war had extended right round the Globe. There was, however, one advantage; Japan's attack on Pearl Harbour on 7th December 1941 had brought the Americans into the war with their huge potential manufacturing ability and armed forces. Early discussions between Churchill and Roosevelt determined that the strategic priorities should be first, the defeat of Germany and Italy and second, the defeat of Japan.

The first 30 months of war had brought many defeats for Britain. First in Norway and France, then in Greece and Crete. But there had been victories too, in East Africa, in the Western Desert and in the Battle of Britain. Then disaster had struck in the Far East with the loss of Hong Kong, Malaya, Singapore, the Netherlands East Indies and Burma. Hitler was in danger of over-extending himself with his attack on the USSR in June 1941. Nevertheless the situation at end of that year did not look at all good for the British and their allies, facing the enemy alone in North Africa and with the Battle of the Atlantic at its height, when the Japanese struck at Pearl Harbour.

The Gunners had played their part in all these battles including the Battle of Britain and the Battle of the Atlantic. They provided the vital firepower of battle, the first component in the formula 'Fire and Movement,' the basis of all combat. Field, medium and heavy guns fought alongside the other combat arms, while anti-tank and anti-aircraft artillery engaged enemy armour and aircraft with direct fire wherever they met them. Coast guns surrounded the shores of the Empire and fought with vigour in the battles for Hong Kong, Singapore and across the Straits of Dover. Survey regiments, searchlight regiments, observation regiments appeared in the order of battle to ensure the accuracy of fire at all times and in all conditions. Soon Air Observation Post squadrons and parachute and air-landing artillery took the Gunners into the air as well. Everywhere and in every battle there were Gunners until, by 31st December 1941, their total strength world-wide was 678,736. This amounted to a massive expansion and its achievement was a very great tribute to those who organised and trained the new men and the new regiments. To them must be added the men of the Empire and Commonwealth, who were organised and equipped in much the same way as their comrades from the United Kingdom.

So many early failures were caused by the huge shortages and years of neglect of the armed forces. When this happens in peace time and for a long period the armed forces cannot rectify their shortcomings quickly. Dependence on warning time is highly dangerous, first, because politicians seem unable to believe the warning signals they get until it is too late, and second, for fear that to react will be to provoke. The problem then is not only one of mobilisation of manpower and creation of a defence industrial capability, but the training of officers and men in the tactical, operational and strategic conduct of war and the ability of the three services to work together and, within the Army, all arms to work together and at speed. All this takes much time and cannot be rushed or disaster will always strike, as it did in the Second World War. Things have not changed with modern technology in this respect and it could happen again.

In the Far East, once the equipment began to arrive, once the great expansion of the Indian Army had occurred and once the officers and men had learned how to fight in the jungle and against one of the most ruthless enemies the World has ever seen, things began to change, but all this took three years. It was only in 1944, first in the Arakan, then at Kohima and later at the crossing of the Irrawaddy, that victory became possible. By the end of the war in the Far East a great price had been paid. Including prisoners of war, some 72,503 British casualties had occurred. Of these the total Gunner battle casualties was 8,720 from all causes. It had been a mighty test and they did not fail.

We must pay tribute to the dedicated loyal service of the Gunners of the Empire who rallied to the cause and in particular to the massive expansion and devoted service of the Gunners of India. Without them, victory in South East Asia simply would not have been possible, their magnificent contribution to the defeat of the enemy was second to none. It must go down in the annals of our history as service to the guns of the very highest order epitomised in the award of the Victoria Cross to Umrao Singh in the defence of his gun, our Colours.

Much has been written about the Forgotten Armies of Burma, Malaya, Singapore, Hong Kong and the East Indies. There can be no doubt that theirs was a very different campaign. Wilson Stephens, then a troop commander in 86th LAA Battery of the famous 24th LAA/Anti-Tank Regiment, which fought so gallantly in the Battle of the Box in the Arakan, and who was later to become editor of *The Field*, wrote:

'. . . Everything we had left at home seemed fictional. The thought of returning filled us with apprehension. Separation and isolation had made us of the 14th Army a race apart, in a world peopled only by ourselves and the enemy, totally dependent on each other, the road back consequently longer and more fraught. . . The enemy, a ferocious, disciplined, dedicated, valorous, implacable, physically fit, brutal and efficient force . . . at first outnumbered and outfought us in the retreat and First Arakan respectively. But with numerical parity, better training and better generals we defeated them in the decisive battles of the Second Arakan and Imphal/Kohima. Finally on the Irrawaddy shore, at Meiktila and Mandalay, we destroyed them. It was by any standards a momentous feat of arms. . . Here on the other side of the world, people still talk of the 14th Army as the Forgotten Army. Forgotten by whom? For those who served in it, it is the Unforgettable Army - not just because it resurrected victory from defeat, but because of the spirit that infused it.'

The Gunners who served in the battles of the Far East, who survived the horrors of prison camp and the privations of one of the World's most hostile environments, deserve our greatest admiration and it is vital that their story is fully recorded for posterity. It is also vital that the memory of those who did not return is never forgotten. This book aims to ensure that their story is recorded. In this respect I can only repeat the immortal words on the great Memorial put up by the Second Division at Kohima;

'When You Go Home,
Tell Them of Us and say,
For Your Tomorrow,
We Gave Our Today.'

Annex A

ARTILLERY ORDER OF BATTLE HONG KONG, SINGAPORE, MALAYA AND JAVA DECEMBER 1941

Commanding Officers' names given are of those in command at the start of the campaign. There were many changes.

HONG KONG - DECEMBER 1941

CRA: Brigadier T McLeod.

Unit	Batteries	Remarks
1st Hong Kong Regt HK-S RA Lt Col JCL Yale	1st & 2nd Mtn Btys; 3rd, 4th & 25th Med Btys	Each Mtn Bty 4: x 3.7-in and 4 x 4.5-in hows. Each Med Bty 4: x 6-in hows.
5th AA Regt RA Lt Col FD Field	7th RA and 17th HK-S RA HAA Btys & 18th LAA Bty HK-S RA	5th AA Bty: Saiwan Redoubt (HKVDC). 7th AA Bty: West Bay, Wong Nei Cheong, Saiwan Redoubt.17th HAA Bty: Pinewood, Mount Davis, Brick Hill, Waterfall Bay. 18th LAA Bty: Stanley, D'Aguilar, Albany Road.
8th Coast Regt RA Lt Col S Shaw	12th, 30th & 36th Btys	Eastern Fire Command: 12th Bty: Stanley, 3 x 9.2-inch guns. 30th Bty: Bokhara, 2 x 6-inch guns. 36th Bty: Collinson, 2 x 6-inch guns & Chung am Kok, 2 x 6-inch guns.
12th Coast Regt RA Lt Col RJL Penfold	24th Bty RA & 26th HK-S RA Bty.	Western Fire Command: 24th Bty: Mount Davis 3 x 9.2-inch guns. 26th Bty*: Stonecutters, 3 x 6-inch guns & 2 x 60-pounders, Jubilee: 3 x 6-inch guns.
	965th Defence Bty Maj BTC Forrester	Belcher's Upper, 1 x 6-inch Belcher's Lower, 2 x 4.7-inch Repulse Bay, 2 x 18-pounders Tytam Bay, 2 x 18-pounders Stanley Bay, 2 x 18-pounders Promontory Bay, 1 x 2-pounder Island Bay, 1 x 2-pounder Deepwater Bay, 1 x 2-pounder Tai Ho Wan, 1 x 2-pounder
The Hong Kong Volunteer Defence Corps	Headquarters 1st Bty - Capt FG Rees 2nd Bty - Lt DJS Crozier 3rd Bty - Capt GWL Cole 4th Bty - Lt KMA Barnett 5th AA Bty - Lt L Goldman	The HKVDC manned the following batteries: In Eastern Fire Command: D'Aguilar Battery: 2 x 4-inch guns, Bluff Head Battery: 2 x 6-inch guns & Aberdeen Battery: 2 x 4-inch guns. In Western Fire Command: Pakshawan Battery: 2 x 6-inch guns. Saiwan AA Bty: 2 x 3-inch guns

* This Battery had been 20 Coast Battery RA but, because of the shortage of British coast artillery personnel, orders had been given for the battery to be converted to a battery of the HK-S RA with the number 26 since there already was a 20 Battery HK-S RA. The date for this reorganisation and redesignation was 8th December 1941.

COAST DEFENCES, SINGAPORE, PENANG AND BORNEO - FEBRUARY 1942

Commander Fixed Defences, Singapore: Brigadier AD Curtis

Unit	Batteries	Remarks
7th Coast Regt RA Lt Col HD St G Cardew	11th & 31st Btys RA & 5th & 7th Btys HK-S RA	Faber Fire Command: 11th Bty: Connaught Bty 3 x 9.2-in guns, Serapong Bty 2 x 6-inch guns, Siloso Point 1 x 12-pounder, Pulau Hantu 2 x 12-pounders, Berhala Reping 2 x 6-pounders. 31st Bty: Buona Vista Bty 2 x 15-in guns, Tanjong Tereh 1 x 12-pdr, Batu Berlayer 2 x 12-pounders, 5th Bty: Silingsing Bty 2 x 6-in guns, Siloso Bty 2 x 6-in guns. 7th Bty: Labrador Bty 2 x 6-in guns, Pasir Laba Bty 2 x 6-in guns.
9th Coast Regt RA Lt Col CP Heath	7th, 22nd & 32nd Btys RA	Changi Fire Command: 7th Bty: Johore Bty 3 x 15-in guns, Betang Kusar 2 x 6-in guns. 22nd Bty: Tekong Bty 3 x 9.2-in guns, Sphinx Bty 2 x 6-in guns, Ladang 1 x 12-pounder, Pulau Sajahat 2 x 12-pounders, Calder Harbour 2 x 12-pounders, 32nd Bty: Pengerang Bty 2 x 6-in guns, Changi Bty 2 x 6-in guns, Changi Outer 2 x 6-prs, Changi Inner 2 x 6-prs.
11th Coast Regt RA Lt Col ML More	8th Coast & 20th HAA Btys HK-S RA	Penang Garrison: 8th Bty: Cornwallis Bty 2 x 6-in guns. 20th Bty: Batu Maung Bty 2 x 6-in guns. Evacuated Penang 18.12.41 and the personnel were dispersed to coast units in Singapore.
16th Defence Regt RA Lt Col MSH Maxwell-Gumbleton	966th RA and 967th & 968th Batteries HK-S RA	Formerly 10 Mobile Coast Regt RA. 966th & 968th Btys had 18-pounders. 967th Bty had 2-pounders All were used for beach defence.
	Detachment HK-S RA, Christmas Island	5 British & 26 HK-S RA Gunners manned 2 x 6-in guns
	Detachment HK-S RA, Lutong, Sarawak	10 British & 41 HK-S RA Gunners manned 2 x 6-in guns.

ANTI-AIRCRAFT DEFENCES MALAYA, SINGAPORE, JAVA AND SUMATRA

Commander Air Defences, Singapore: Brigadier AWG Wildey
Commander Malayan AA Brigade: Brigadier HV Allpress
Commander 16th AA Brigade, Java: Brigadier HDW Sitwell, later SR Pearson.

Unit	Batteries	Remarks
1st HAA Regt HK-S RA Lt Col AE Tawney	6th, 9th & 10th HAA Btys HK-S RA	6th Bty at Johore & Sungei Buloh with 8 x 3.7-in guns. 9th Bty at Johore & the Naval Base with 2 x 3-in & 8 x 40mm guns.

Unit	Batteries	Remarks
2nd HAA Regt HK-S RA Lt Col R McL More	11th, 12th & 13th HAA Btys HK-S RA	12th Bty at Nee Soon & Singapore City with 8 x 3.7-in guns. 13th Bty at Singapore City with 4 x 3.7-in & 4 x 3-in guns.
3rd LAA Regt HK-S RA Lt Col DV Hill	14th &16th LAA Btys HK-S RA	14th Bty at Johore with 7 x 40mm guns. 16th Bty at Johore with 8 x 40mm guns.
3rd HAA Regt RA Lt Col FE Hugonin	11th, 29th & 30th HAA Btys RA	11th Bty at Ayer Hitam with 6 x 3.7-in guns. 29th Bty at Singapore City with 8 x 3.7-in guns. 30th Bty at Singapore City with 8 x 3.7-in guns.
1st Indian HAA Regt IA Lt Col JR Williamson	2nd, 3rd & 4th Btys IA	2nd Bty at Blakang Mati with 4 x 3-in & 8 x 40mm guns. 3rd Bty at Kallang airport with 8 x 3-in guns. 4th Bty at Bukit Ayer & Tengah with 4 x 3-in & 8 x 40mm guns.
	1st Indian LAA Bty IA	1st Bty at Sembawang & Singapore City with 10 x 40mm guns
	5th Indian LAA Bty IA	
35th LAA Regt RA Lt Col HJ Bassett	78th, 89th & 144th Btys RA	78th Bty to Java with 8 x 40mm guns. 89th Bty at Kallang 4 x 40mm less two troops 8 x 40mm which went to Java. 144th Bty at Johore with 12 x 40mm guns.
6th HAA Regt RA Lt Col GWG Baass	3rd, 12th & 15th Btys RA	HQ 6th HAA Regt RA went to Java. 3rd Bty remained in Singapore City with 8 x 3.7-in guns. 12th Bty to Java with 8 x 3.7-in guns. 15th Bty to Java with 8 x 3.7-in guns.
5th Searchlight Regt RA Lt Col RAO Clarke	13th, 14th, 315th & 316th Btys RA	All in Singapore. 315th SL Bty reformed in Ceylon.

SUMATRA

Unit	Batteries	Remarks
6th HAA Regt RA, less 3rd Bty Lt Col GWG Baass	12th & 15th Btys RA	Regt was at P1 & P2 Airfields in Sumatra then served as infantry in Java.
35th LAA Regt RA (Part)	78th LAA Bty RA Two Troops, 89th LAA Bty RA	Bty was at P1 & P2 Airfields in Sumatra then as infantry in Java without guns. Tps were at P1 & P2 Airfields in Sumatra then elements as infantry in Java without guns.

JAVA

Unit	Batteries	Remarks
6th HAA Regt RA Lt Col GWG Baass	12th & 15th HAA Btys RA	In Java. No guns arrived. Served as infantry.
21st LAA Regt RA Lt Col MDS Saunders	48th, 69th & 79th LAA Btys RA	48th Bty in Java with 40mm guns. Captured. 69th Bty in Java with 40mm guns. Captured. 79th Bty in Bali with 8 x 40mm guns. Captured.
35th LAA Regt RA (Part)	78th LAA Bty RA Two Troops, 89th LAA Bty RA	Served as infantry in Java without guns.
48th LAA Regt RA Lt Col SR Pearson	49th, 95th & 242nd LAA Btys RA	Regt in Java with 40mm guns. Captured.
77th HAA Regt RA Lt Col JR Stanton	239th, 240th & 241st HAA Btys RA	Regt in Java with 24 x 3.7-in guns. Captured.

FIELD AND ANTI-TANK ARTILLERY, MALAYA AND SINGAPORE

CRA 8th Australian Division: Brigadier CA Callaghan, Lt Col CA McEachern RAA
CRA 11th Indian Division: Brigadier AE Rusher (later BRA Malaya)
CRA 18th British Division: Brigadier HC Servaes

Unit	Batteries	Remarks
8th Australian Division		
5th Field Regt RA Lt Col EWF Jephson	63/81st and 73rd Field Btys RA	16 x 4.5-inch howitzers.
2/10th Field Regt RAA Lt Col AW Walsh RAA	19th, 20th & 60th Field Btys RAA	12 x 18-pounders and 6 x 4.5-inch howitzers.
2/15th Field Regt RAA Lt Col JW Wright RAA	29th, 30th & 65th Field Btys RAA	3-in mortars; to 25-pounders in Dec 1941.
2/4th Anti-Tank Regt RAA Lt Col CA McEachern RAA	13th, 15th &16th A/Tk Btys RAA	36 x 2-pounders.
11th Indian Division		
135th Field Regt RA (Hertfordshire Yeo) Lt Col PJD Toosey RA	336th, 344th & 499th Field Btys RA	344th Bty had 8 x 4.5-in hows. 336th & 499th Btys each had 8 x 25-pounders.
155th Field Regt RA (Lanarkshire Yeo) Lt Col A Murdoch	B and C Field Btys RA	A Bty had remained in India to form 160th Fd Regt. B & C Btys each had 8 x 4.5-in hows initially. C Bty re-equipped with 8 x 25-pounders in Jan 1941.

Unit	Batteries	Remarks
22nd Mountain Regt IA Lt Col GL Hughes	4th (Hazara), 7th (Bengal), 10th (Abbottabad) and 21st Mountain Btys	Each bty started with 4 x 3.7-inch howitzers.
80th Anti-Tank Regt RA Lt Col WES Napier	2nd (Minden), 215th, 272nd and 273rd A/Tk Btys RA	36 x 2-pounders.
85th Anti-Tank Regt RA Lt Col AJ Lardner-Clarke	45th, 251st, 270th & 281st A/Tk Btys RA	36 x 2-pounders.
18th British Division **88th Field Regt RA** Lt Col SC D'Aubuz	351st, 352nd and 464th Field Btys RA	24 x 25-pounders.
118th Field Regt RA Lt Col CE Mackellar	259th, 260th and 483rd Field Btys RA	24 x 25-pounders.
137th Field Regt RA Lt Col GD Holme	349th, 350th and 501st Field Btys RA	24 x 25-pounders but by 30 Jan it had only 8 x 75mm howitzers.
148th Field Regt RA Lt Col SW Harris	419th, 420th and 512th Field Btys RA	24 x 25-pounders.
Corps Troops **122nd Field Regt RA** Lt Col G St JA Dyson	278th and 280th Btys RA	24 x 25-pounders.
125th A/Tk Regt RA Lt Col J Dean	A, B, C and D A/Tk Btys RA	This Regiment was on the *Empress of India* when she was sunk near Singapore on 5th February 1942 and lost all but 4 x 2-pounders. The men who survived fought as infantry.
	The Federated Malay States Volunteer Battery	On 30 Jan 1942 had 4 x 18-pounders.
	Singapore (Volunteer) Beach Defence Battery RA	8 x 18-pounders in single beach defence positions.

LOCATION, MOVEMENT AND FATE OF THE GUNS IN HONG KONG

8th - 25th December 1941

Taken from The Guns and Gunners of Hong Kong by Denis Rollo

FIXED DEFENCES

Eastern Fire Command

Unit	Location	Guns	Fate
12 Coast Bty	Stanley Fort	3 x 9.2-in Mk VII	Captured 25 Dec
30 Coast Bty	Bokhara Fort	2 x 9.2-in Mk V	Blown up 19 Dec
36 Coast Bty	Collinson Fort	2 x 6-in CP II	Blown up 19 Dec
	Chung Hom Hok	2 x 6-in CP II	Blown up 19 Dec
1 Bty HKVDC	D'Aguilar Fort	2 x 4-in naval	Blown up 19 Dec
2 Bty HKVDC	Bluff Head Fort	2 x 6-in naval	Captured 25 Dec
4 Bty HKVDC	Pak Sha Wan Fort	2 x 6-in CP II	Captured 18 Dec

Western Fire Command

Unit	Location	Guns	Fate
24 Coast Bty	Mount Davis	3 x 9.2-in Mk V	Blown up 25 Dec
26 Coast Bty	Stonecutters	3 x 6-in CP II	Blown up 10 Dec
	Jubilee	3 x 6-in CP II	Blown up 25 Dec
3 Bty HKVDC	Aberdeen	2 x 4-in naval	Blown up 25 Dec
Parade Bty	Stonecutters	2 x 60-pdr	Blown up 10 Dec

965th Defence Battery

Position	Armament	Date destroyed
Belchers Upper	1 x 6-in	25 Dec
Belchers Position	2 x 4.7-in	25 Dec
Repulse Bay	2 x 18-pdrs	23-25 Dec
Tytam Bay	2 x 18-pdrs	24 Dec
Stanley Bay	2 x 18-pdrs	18 Dec
Promontory	1 x 2-pdr	24 Dec
Island Bay	1 x 2-pdr	24 Dec
Deepwater Bay	1 x 2-pdr	24 Dec
Tai Ho Wan	1 x 2-pdr	18 Dec

AIR DEFENCES

5th Anti-Aircraft Regiment RA

Battery	Section Positions	Fate
7th AA	West Bay	Captured 25 Dec
	Wong Nei Chong	Captured 18 Dec
	Saiwan Redoubt	Captured 18 Dec

5th AA (V)	Saiwan Redoubt	Captured 18 Dec
17th AA	Pinewood	Destroyed 15 Dec
	Mount Davis	Blown up 25 Dec
	Brick Hill	Captured 25 Dec
	Waterfall Bay	Blown up 25 Dec
18th AA	Stanley	Captured 25 Dec
	D'Aguilar	Blown up 10 Dec
	Albany Road	Captured 25 Dec

MOBILE ARTILLERY HEADQUARTERS

HQRA Mainland:	7 Dec Waterloo Road, North End
	11 Dec Wong Nei Chong Gap.
RHQ 1st Hong Kong Regiment:	11 Dec Wong Nei Chong Gap
	14 Dec absorbed by HQRA West Group
HQRA East Group:	7 Dec Tytam Gap
	19 Dec Stanley Fort
HQRA West Group:	7 Dec Wanchai Gap
	14 Dec Wong Nei Chong Gap
	19 Dec Wiped out
	20 Dec Reformed Wanchai Gap
	22 Dec Victoria Gap
	25 Dec Capitulated
HQ Counter Bombardment Group:	14 Dec Wong Nei Chong Gap
	19 Dec Wiped out

Movement of 1st Mountain Battery:

Troop 4 x 3.7-inch howitzers:	7 Dec Customs Pass. 11 Dec Two guns to Tates Cairn and two to forward positions; all four guns to Devil`s Peak. 14 Dec Two guns to Gauge Basin, destroyed by enemy action. 18 Dec One gun to Saiwan Redoubt, lost to enemy action. One gun to Stanley, captured 25 Dec.
Troop 4 x 4.5-inch howitzers:	7 Dec Two guns to Red Hill. Destroyed by enemy action 19 Dec. Two guns to Sanatorium handed over to 2nd Mountain Battery 17 Dec and took over Tytam Hill from them. Destroyed 25 Dec.

Movement of 2nd Mountain Battery:

Troop 4 x 3.7-inch howitzers:	7 Dec Two guns forward at Tai Wai, two guns at Main Filters. 11 Dec One gun lost during withdrawal, one gun to Victoria, two guns to Stanley Gap. 13 Dec One gun from Victoria to Stanley Gap. 19 Dec Three guns lost at Stanley Gap to enemy action.
Troop 4 x 4.5-inch howitzers:	7 Dec Two guns forward, two guns at Main Filters. 11 Dec Two guns at Coombe Road, two guns at Tytam Hill. 13 Dec Two guns at Coombe Road moved to Kellett.

19 Dec Two guns at Tytam Hill lost to enemy action.

25 Dec Two guns at Kellett lost to enemy action.

Movement of 25th medium Battery:

7 Dec Two guns forward, two guns at Main Polo.

11 Dec Two guns at Caroline Hill, two guns at Tiger Balm.

16 Dec Two guns at Tiger Balm to Stanley Gap and lost on 19 Dec.

17 Dec Two guns at Caroline to Jockey Club Stables, destroyed 20 Dec.

Movement of 3rd Medium Battery:

7 Dec Two guns at Mount Parker destroyed by enemy action 19 Dec.

Two guns at Saiwan destroyed by enemy action 19 Dec.

Movement of 4th Medium Battery:

7 Dec Two guns at Gough put out of action 25 Dec.

Two guns at Mount Austin put out of action 25 Dec.

Annex C

PERFORMANCE OF THE FIXED DEFENCES AT SINGAPORE February 1942

Based on a report written by Lieutenant Colonel HD St G Cardew RA while in Changi Gaol as a Prisoner of War.

1. Early in January it became apparent that the guns of the fixed defences of Singapore might be called upon in the not far distant future, to fire upon land targets in the State of Johore, in the areas opposite the north and east coasts of Singapore Island directed by FCs to register likely targets in the areas mentioned. This raised certain difficulties viz;

a. The areas that could be covered by coast artillery were very limited either by inadequate range or insufficient arc of fire or both, eg, the only bty that could reach the town of Johore Bahru and the causeway connecting that town with Singapore Island was the 15 inch bty at Johore Fort. Of this bty only the two Mark II equipments could bear. The 15 inch bty at Buona Vista was useless for this purpose as the dead arc prevented any firing northwards.

b. In order to diminish the threatened danger from low flying aircraft 6 inch batteries had been fitted with overhead concrete cover. This considerably diminished the landward arcs of these btys.

c. Ammunition suitable for landwards firing was scanty, only 50 rds of HE being allowed for the 6 inch guns, 25 for the 9.2 inch batteries and none at all for the 15 inch guns.

d. OPs from which the effect of long range fire could be reported were hard to find and communications were non existent. The whole solution of these problems obviously depended on the probable dispositions of the troops of the Field Army.

2. Largely in view of the difficulties mentioned above, the coast artillery had been directed only to register certain land targets selected by the General Staff on and near the east and south coasts of Singapore Island and on the north coast of the Pengerang Promontory.

3. a. In view of the situation everything possible that could be done was at once put in hand to increase the arcs of fire of the 6 inch batteries by demolishing parts of the concrete overhead cover (at the expense of protection) and all the batteries by cutting down trees obstructing lines to the north and west.

b. The naval authorities were asked if they could supply any 15 inch HE ammunition but were able to find only one which was transferred to Johore Fort. In reply to a cable from the Supreme Commander SW Pacific application was made for a considerable increase in the stocks of HE ammunition for the 6 inch and 9.2 inch guns and of an initial supply for the 15 inch guns. This ammunition however never arrived.

c. CO 9 Coast Regt (Fire Command Changi) whose guns were the most likely to be useful in the circumstances, organised a layout for observation of fire and of enemy flashes with a central plotting room at Changi. He established an OP on the north coast of P Tekong and he had made arrangements for another in Johore, north of Pengerang on the Bukit Bulungor but occupation of the latter was not permitted by higher authority. Other OPs were established at Kitchener Barracks, Changi and Loyang.

4. Meanwhile, it is now understood, a reconnaissance entirely independent of the CFD [Commander Fixed Defences] was being carried out dealing with the possible disposition of troops of the Field Army if and when they were withdrawn to Singapore Island. This included reconnaissance by 122nd Fd Regt RA of OPs and gun positions for the Divisional Artilleries.

5. Eventually about the end of January the BRA III Corps reached Singapore Island and was appointed BRA Malaya Command. At a conference with him CFD stated what had hitherto been done and offered the services of Maj Madden, 9 Coast Regt (who was in charge of the landwards firing organisation, Changi FC) as Corps Counter Bombardment Officer with the subsidiary role of liaison with FD. This arrangement was confirmed at a larger conference attended by all CRAs, but AIF remained outside the organisation making their own arrangements for CB work and for observation.

6. HQ Malaya Command eventually endorsed a recommendation by the CRAs Conference that Corps CBO should have the right to call upon fire commanders direct for landwards firing except in respect of the 15 inch equipments. In view of the possibility of attack from the sea and of the relatively short life of the 15 inch guns, demands for landwards firing for them had to be referred to CFD.

7. Arrangements were made to lay the necessary telephone cables from CBOs office to FCs and to link up the OP system organised by FC Changi with that of III Corps.

8. Detailed reports of the effect of landwards firing of coast guns were unfortunately not available, though general reports on the effects of concentrations were sometimes received.

Anti Aircraft Defence

9. As most of the FD works were outside the protection afforded by the main AA Defences of Singapore, their safety in the face of determined attack from the air had always been a constant anxiety to CFD. During January 5 Bofors 40mm guns were however allotted for the special purpose of protecting the 15 inch guns. Emplacements with alternative positions were prepared for these at Johore and Buona Vista Forts.

10. These weapons were at first manned by naval detachments (survivors of HM Ships Prince of Wales and Repulse) and, when these were withdrawn, by spare personnel of the Fixed Defences. The guns themselves remained at the disposal of CAAD and were constantly changed as the operations proceeded.

11. No special AA defences other than light automatic weapons were ever afforded to the exposed forts at Pengerang and on Tekong Island.

Recovery of Weapons from the Naval Base.

12. The Naval base was evacuated without any notice being given to CFD, leaving there a 4 inch equipment previously allotted for the defence of the Detached Mole, Singapore Roads.

13. On or about 2, 3 or 4 February a party under Lt Cherry, 7 Coast Regt, recovered the equipment from the Naval Base together with other equipments and ammunition which under the circumstances might have proved very valuable.

Reports and Signals

14. a. In the early stages of the operations round Singapore Island, ie when British aircraft were operating freely, trouble was caused by such aircraft making signals, afterwards said to be recognition signals, which were incorrect. This applied to some extent to pyrotechnics sent up from both naval patrols and posts on land.

b. Later when troops were coming in by sea from the west in small parties, generally in native craft, the absence of any recognition signals and indeed the apparent lack of knowledge that any such signals were necessary must have resulted in considerable loss of life.

c. Throughout the entire period of the operations, false reports of enemy landings were frequent. It seems probable that such reports in general were based on landing of our own stragglers without proper investigation before the report was transmitted. The whole effect was confusing.

ANNEX D

COLONEL PJD TOOSEY AND THE PRISONERS OF WAR (Later Brigadier Sir Philip Toosey Kt, CBE, DSO, TD, DL.)

Condensed from, The Man Behind the Bridge. by Peter N Davies.

Philip John Denton Toosey was born in Birkenhead on 12th August 1904. On leaving school at the age of 18 he was apprenticed to some cotton merchants in Liverpool. In 1927 he decided to follow the example of many of his friends and he applied to join the Territorial Army. His education at Gresham's School, Holt, and connections were sufficient to ensure the necessary introductions and on 1st November 1927 he was commissioned Second Lieutenant in 59th (4th West Lancashire) Medium Brigade. He had joined Baring Brothers, the merchant bankers, in their Liverpool office in 1927 and remained with them for 40 years.

He was promoted Captain in 1931 and, in 1933, became battery commander of 236th Battery equipped with 6-inch howitzers. His battery won the King's Cup in 1937. 59th Medium Regiment was ordered to mobilise on 26th August 1939 at the Drill Hall, Edge Hill, Liverpool. They became the first TA Gunners to land in France, on 3rd October, and came under command of 2nd Corps. The regiment was evacuated from Dunkirk on 2nd June and reformed at Larkhill on 5th July. It then moved to East Anglia and Toosey became Second-in-Command. He was promoted Lieutenant Colonel in September and took command of 135th (Hertfordshire Yeomanry) Field Regiment in 18th Infantry Division. The Regiment sailed from Gourock at the end of October 1941 for Halifax, Nova Scotia. There it was transferred to the SS Mount Vernon and left for Capetown. Next it headed for Madagascar before being diverted to Singapore, arriving there during an air raid on 13th January 1942.

The regiment was issued with 25-pounders from the Singapore Ordnance Depot and moved north to join 11th Indian Division on the west coast of Johore. On 30th January it was back in Singapore. The GSO1 of the division then records, 'On 5th February the mass of the Japanese artillery came into action. The Japanese said afterwards that it was the greatest concentration of fire ever laid down. Our guns replied with vigour. Outstanding in courage was Lieutenant Colonel Philip Toosey, the Commanding Officer of 135th Field Regiment. Wherever things were hottest he would be found, whether it was at an observation post, a section emplacement or somewhere where communications had been broken. He took no rest and his example was an inspiration to all ranks.' Toosey was awarded the DSO for his conspicuously gallant leadership. Wavell asked that his congratulations be sent to 135th Field Regiment. The regiment's part in the Malayan Campaign and in the defence of Singapore is told in the text. At 1500 hours on 15th February it was told to destroy all equipment and surrender. Though offered the chance, Toosey had refused to be evacuated saying that his place was with his men at their time of need. He was marched into Changi gaol with them by the Japanese. Later the regiment was moved to Bukit Timah where he became first the deputy commandant and later Camp Commandant.

On 22nd October 1942, Toosey was ordered by the Japanese to take a force of men to Malaya. He took 500 from his own 135th Regiment and about 150 from the Norfolks, Suffolks and RASC and marched them to Singapore Railway Station. They then had a terrible train journey of four days and nights up the length of Malaya to Banpong in Thailand. After an awful night they were moved on 50 miles to Tamarkan where a series of atap-covered bamboo huts were in the course of erection by a party from 80th Anti-Tank Regiment. It was agreed by all concerned that Toosey should be the Senior British Officer. He was told by the Japanese on 27th October that his task was to provide labour to build two bridges over the Kwai Mekong, later referred to as the River Kwai ('kwai' being the Siamese for 'river'). The first was to be a temporary wooden structure and the second an eleven-truss steel bridge, both were to carry a single track railway over the river.

During the terrible months that followed Toosey did all he could to alleviate the sufferings of his men and took a stand against the Japanese on many issues for which he was severely punished himself and suffered both physically and mentally, but he never wavered in his work. By April 1943 the two bridges were complete and the majority of the fit men were deployed to other camps further up the line. Many owed him their lives because of what he did for them and for the order he managed to achieve where chaos would have otherwise reigned. Toosey was ordered to organise Tamarkan as a base hospital and he was separated from his regiment. His success in dealing with appalling problems in the monsoon and lack of medical supplies was quite outstanding. Many independent sources stress the beneficial impact which Toosey exerted on the lives of all who came to Tamarkan. This began with their arrival for, irrespective of the time or state of the weather, he always made it his business to meet every party. He welcomed every individual personally, encouraging and assuring them. He always helped to carry stretcher cases and ensured that everyone was given a cup of tea before being allocated to a hut. Then before an hour was out, a hot meal of some kind was invariably provided. The net effect of these activities was that each person felt that he had entered a new world, far superior to the one he had just left and that for the first time there was someone who was really interested in his welfare.

Toosey also managed to make contacts with the local Thai people and got money and extra rations from them. Then on 3rd December 1943 he was moved to a camp at Nong Pladuk which had been established in June 1942 and was under the command of Major WE Gill of 137th Field Regiment. Toosey took command and was there for a year doing the same thing. The prisoners were working in some adjacent goods yards. Allied bombers had raided the yards on three occasions between September and December 1944. 104 prisoners were killed and some 400 wounded and this proved an extra test of his leadership qualities. In December he was moved again, this time to an 'officers only' camp at Kanchanaburi (known to many prisoners as 'Kanburi') where there were 3,000 Australian, British and Dutch officers in one of the smallest and dirtiest fixed camps in Thailand. The Japanese ordered Toosey to be the Senior British Officer, even though he was by no means the most senior. However he was soon accepted by everyone, but it was not easy. Nevertheless by his efforts conditions improved.

In the camp were two Captains, brothers, in the Malay Regiment who were operating a secret radio. The prisoners ordered it to be destroyed in case the Japanese discovered it and carried out harsh reprisals. Toosey said that he, and he alone, would take responsibility for its existence and that it should continue. The Webber brothers were filled with admiration and the radio stayed in operation several more months, keeping a vital link to the outside world until its batteries finally gave up.

As the victorious Fourteenth Army advanced into Burma the Japanese moved all POWs to eastern Siam from May 1945 onwards. In June Toosey was told that the Kanchanaburi camp was to be closed and that the officers were to move in small parties of 400 to a new location at Nakhom Nayak in virgin jungle north of Bangkok. Toosey was to take the first party and build the camp from whatever they could find.

On 15th August, the camp staff told them of the Japanese surrender. Toosey called a parade and made a brief announcement that the war was over and that they must wait in the camp. Extra rations arrived and conditions improved. Toosey commandeered a Japanese truck to take him and a number of officers into Bangkok. There he made arrangements for the repatriation of the camp and he found out that his beloved 135th Regiment had been moved to Ubon on the Indo-Chinese border. He then made a 300 mile rail journey and 'Received the most wonderful welcome you could believe possible.' The regiment eventually returned to the UK together on the SS *Orbita* from Rangoon.

Toosey reformed 368th Medium Regiment in 1947. He became commander of 87th AGRA and retired in 1954. He remained Honorary Colonel of 368th Regiment until 1970. He was awarded the CBE in 1955 to mark his long and outstanding service to the TA, but his main concern remained the welfare of those who had suffered with him as prisoners in the Far East. When the Far East Prisoners Of War Association (FEPOW) was formed in 1947, Toosey became Vice-President to General Percival and he became President when Percival died in 1967. Toosey arranged with the Liverpool School of Tropical Medicine for all FEPOWs to be medically examined and treated as necessary. This system was extended throughout the country. He achieved a special disability pension for many of the FEPOWs and worked fearlessly in their interests. He was elected President of the Liverpool School of Tropical Medicine in 1965 and in the same year he became High Sheriff of Lancashire. He was awarded a knighthood in 1974. He died on 22nd December 1975.

He was a great man and did more than most to look after Gunners at a time of their greatest need and in doing so he brought huge credit to the Royal Regiment of Artillery.

ANNEX E

THE LOST SOULS OF RABAUL

(This material is supported by research notes and letters held by the RAI. Whilst perhaps not proven history it is a record of courage that should not be forgotten.)

From the pages of 'What Price Bushido' by the Reverend Alfred Baker I discovered that in February 1942 when Singapore was surrendered to the Japanese forces and many thousands of British and Commonwealth forces were incarcerated in prison camps. In many cases they were starved almost to the point of death and treated with brutality by their captors.

Eight months later, already emaciated and suffering from every tropical disease possible, six hundred men of the Royal Artillery were forced at bayonet point into the foul smelling hold of a sea going transport. Lieutenant Colonel John Basset, his officers and men of the 144th Battery of 35th LAA Regiment, the 7th, 9th and 11th Coast Regiments and the 2nd and 3rd HAA Regiments and the 5th Searchlight Regiment were packed like sardines. There was no sanitation arrangements and little sympathy from their guards.

After eighteen days of horror, on the 5th of November 1942 they arrived at the port of Rabaul in New Britain, one of their number died en route. The main body comprising 517, were transshipped to the Solomon Islands and landed at Ballali to be employed as slave labour, building Japanese fortifications. After the war the remains of 432 soldiers were found in a mass grave on the island. There is no firm information on how they died. After the War, their remains were re-interred in a Military Cemetery in Port Moresby, New Guinea.

Back in Rabaul, the remaining 82 prisoners were sent inland to Kokopo, where once again they were to be subjected to the horrors of the slave camps. Under the most terrible conditions, the morale of the troops was upheld as much as was possible by a few stalwarts. Two of these Lance Bombardier Joe Blythe and Gunner Alf (Blacky) Baker were themselves caught and severely tortured for daring to steal scraps of food for their companions. In spite of their efforts the prisoners died one by one and were given the nearest thing to a Christian burial by the two unofficial camp padres. As they carried out their sad duties, they kept what records they could and it was from this meagre Roll of Honour that I discovered that far from having no grave my brother is buried in Death Valley Kokopo, New Britain and was given a Christian burial by his comrades and friends, in a corner of the prison camp.

Out of the initial six hundred Gunners who left Singapore on that fateful day in 1942, there were only eighteen survivors who managed to return to their homeland via various hospitals in Australia. There were many requests from the survivors that the two stalwarts be recognised for their efforts in the prison camp, but, because there were no officers amongst the survivors, their requests were refused.

Joe Blythe settled down, once again serving those around him to the best of his ability as a lay preacher. He died in 1987 in his early eighties. His friend and fellow prisoner Alfred (Blacky) Baker, also returned to religion and is now (1993), the Reverend Alfred Baker, author of his own true story, 'What Price Bushido' and having read it, I am convinced that even now it is not too late to say, 'Thank You, Blacky Baker, Ex-Gunner, Royal Artillery for upholding the highest tradition of your Regiment.'

Bernard Hallas. Ex Royal Marines

ANNEX F

THE GUNS 1941-46.

Note: It should be understood that figures given for maximum range should be treated with great caution. There are many influences on range including, among other things, the condition of the gun, the type of mounting, the type of projectile, meteorological conditions and the characteristics of the sighting and predicting instruments controlling fire.

Where anti-aircraft guns are concerned, the maximum height achievable was of little relevance, so the effective ceiling is given instead. This was the maximum height at which an effective engagement, lasting 20 or more seconds, could be achieved.

It is also important to realise that there were many marks of gun and carriage, for mobile guns, or mounting, for fixed guns. These affected the performance of the gun, so figures quoted here are in the nature of indications only.

Sources employed for these tables are publications by Ian V Hogg and LF Thurston and by Peter Chamberlain and Terry Gander, mentioned in the list of References. Major Denis Rollo also made an important contribution.

The following abbreviations are used: HE, high explosive; AP, armour piercing; APC armour piercing, capped; S, shrapnel.

Field guns and howitzers

Gun	**Calibre, inches/mm**	**Projectile, lbs**	**Maximum range, yards**	**Weight, lbs**
18-pounder	3.3/83.8	18.5 HE	11,100	3,228
25-pounder	3.45/87.6	25 HE	13,400	3,968
Baby 25-pdr*	3.45/87.6	25 HE	10,800	3,015
Jury axle 25-pdr*	3.45/87.6	25 HE	13,400	
3.7-in How**	3.7/93.98	20 HE	4,500***	1,856
3.7-in How	3.7/93.98	20 S	6,000	1,856
105mm SP Priest****	4.134/105	33 HE	12,500	
4.5-in How	4.5/114.3	34.5 HE	6,600	3,291

* *see* Annex L.
** The 3.7-inch howitzer was originally intended for movement in mule pack and was, therefore, capable of being dismantled, the barrel itself being in two parts. Later, a single-piece monobloc barrel was also produced but the figures given here relate to the first version.
*** A supercharge was developed giving a range of 7,150 yards.
**** An American 105mm howitzer M2 mounted on a greatly modified M3 (Lee/Grant) tank chassis.

An addition to the above is the Skoda gun used by 15th (Jhelum) Mountain Battery for a brief period in Burma. It is described by Graham as a 77mm piece. Skoda produced a number of 76.5mm guns of which the Model 1928 was both a field and mountain gun; it could be dismantled into three loads. It fired a 17.64 pound HE shell to a maximum range of 14,330 yards. There was also a M.17 in the same calibre (3-inch) which could also be broken down for movement, which had similar characteristics to the M.1928 with a maximum range of some 12,500 yards. This may be the gun taken over by 15th Mountain Battery as it remained in production until 1938. What either of these weapons were doing in Burma has not yet been discovered but the Colonial Office may have obtained them after Burma ceased to be governed from India.

Medium and heavy guns and howitzers

Gun	Calibre, inches/mm	Projectile, lbs	Maximum range, yards	Weight, lbs
60-pdr	5/127	60 HE	16,400	12,048
5.5-in	5.5/139.7	100 HE	16,200	13,646
		80 HE	18,100	
6-in 26 cwt	6/152	86 HE	11,400	9,262
		100 HE		
155mm M1917	6.1/155	94.71 HE	20,100	20,100
7.2-in How*	7.2/182.9	202 HE	16,900	22,760

*Mark 1, 2, 3 or 4, a conversion from a British or American 8-inch howitzer on a two-wheel British 8-inch howitzer carriage.

Mortars

Mortar	Calibre, inches/mm	Bomb, lbs	Maximum range, yards	Weight, lbs
3-in	3/76.2	10 HE	2,750	126
4.2-in	4.2/106.7	20 HE	4,100	1,320

Anti-Tank guns

Gun	Calibre, inches/mm	AP shot, lbs	Penetration, 1000 yds, 30 degs, mm	Weight, lbs
2-pdr	1.575/40	2	42	1,757
6-pdr	2.24/57	6	74	2,521
57mm*	2.24/57	6.28	73 at 20 degrees	755 plus carriage

* The American version of the 6-pounder, the 57mm Gun M1.

Anti-Aircraft guns

Gun	Calibre, ins/mm	Projectile, lbs	Rate of fire, (rpm) practical	Maximum effective ceiling, feet	Weight, lbs
20mm Oerlikon*	0.787/20	0.2621 HE	465-480 cyclic	3,600	147 plus mtg
40mm Bofors*	1.575/40	1.96 HE	60-90, 120 cyclic	5,000	4,368
3-in 20 cwt*	3/76.2	16.5 HE	20-25	15,700**	6,000
3.7-in*	3.7/94	28.56 HE	10-20	32,000***	20,541
4.5-in	4.45/113	54.43 HE	8	34,500****	29,505

* Mobile
** Maximum horizontal range 10,800 yards

*** Maximum horizontal range 20,600 yards
**** This is a 1944 figure, the guns in Singapore would have had a lower effective ceiling. Maximum horizontal range 22,800 yards

Coast guns

Gun	Calibre, ins/mm	Projectile, lbs	Rate of fire (rpm)	Range, yards
Twin 6-pdr	2.44/62	6.25 HE	75-80*	5,500
12-pdr QF	3/76.2	12.5 HE	15	10,100
4.7-in	4.7/120	45 semi-AP	8	11,800-16,500
6-in Mk VII	6/152	102 AP & HE	7.5	14,000
6-in Mk V	6/152	102 AP & HE	7.5	19,000
9.2-in Mk X	9.2/233	380 AP & HE	3	21,000
9.2-in Mk X/Mk VII mtg	9.2/233	380 AP & HE	3	36,700
9.2-in MksVII & IX	9.2/233	380 AP & HE	3	29,200
15-in	15/380	1,938 APC	2	36,900-42,000

* This twin mounting within a turret could, with a well trained detachment, attain up to 120 rpm

Japanese guns, howitzers and mortars

Gun/mortar	Calibre, ins,mm	Projectile, lbs	Range, yards	Weight in action, lbs
37mm Type 94*	1.46/37	1.07 HE	5,000	714
70mm Type 97**	2.76/70	8.36 HE	3,000	770
75mm Type 41***	2.95/75	13.27 HE	7,675	1,195.5
75mm Type 94****	2.95/75	13.62 HE	8,938	1,181.3
150mm mortar Type 97	5.9/150	57 HE bomb	2,187	770
150mm How Type 96	5.9/149.2	68 HE	12,970	9,100

* A former anti-tank gun
** Battalion gun
*** Regimental gun
**** Mountain gun

See Brigadier AL Pemberton's The Development of Artillery Tactics and Equipment War Office, 1950.

ANNEX G

ARTILLERY ORDER OF BATTLE
BURMA - MAY 1942

BURMA ARMY

Brigadier Royal Artillery: Brigadier JHB Birbeck

BURCORPS

Commander Corps Royal Artillery: Brigadier G de V Welchman

Corps Troops:

8th HAA Bty, 4 x 3-in 20 cwt guns, Major GH Eden
8th Indian HAA Bty, 4 x 3-in 20 cwt guns, Major RA Roberts
3rd Indian LAA Bty, 12 x 40mm Bofors, Major CHT MacFetridge

7th Armoured Brigade Group

414th Bty RHA*, 8 x 25-pounders, Major B deH Periera
A Battery, 95th A/Tk Regt RA, 12 x 2-pounders, Major RA Hemelryk

1st Burma Division:

27th Indian Mountain Regt, Lt Col G Constable
2nd (Derajat) Mountain Bty, 4 x 3.7-in howitzers
5th (Bombay) Mountain Bty, 4 x 3.7-in howitzers
23rd Mountain Bty, 4 x 3.7-in howitzers

8th Indian Anti-Tank Bty (2nd Indian Anti-Tank Regiment), 4 x 2-pounders

17th Indian Division:

1st Indian Field Regt
1st Indian Field Bty
2nd Indian Field Bty
12 x 25-pounders

12th(Poonch) Mountain Bty (27th Mountain Regt, 4 x 3.7-inch howitzers

5th Indian Anti-Tank Bty (2nd Indian Anti-Tank Regt), 4 x 2-pounders

Lines of Communication:

2nd Indian Anti-Tank Regt
3rd Anti-Tank Bty

28th Mountain Regt, Lt Col AH Peskett , Lt Col JW Kaye
15th (Jhelum) Mountain Bty
28th Mountain Bty
8 x 3.7-inch howitzers

5th Field Bty BAF
6 x 18-pounders

1st HAA Regt BAF
One battery 8 x 3.7-inch guns
One battery 8 x 40mm guns

*Expanded to become 14 Regt RHA on 1 September, with 414 and 525 Btys RHA.

ANNEX H

ARTILLERY ORDERS OF BATTLE
CEYLON - 1942 - 1944

Including Ceylon, East African and Indian units

JANUARY 1942

HQRA Ceylon

6th Coast Regiment RA, 15th and 18th Coast Batteries, 2 x 9.2-in & 3 x 6-in Trincomalee
1st Coast Regiment CGA, 1st, 2nd and 3rd Coast Batteries, 2 x 9.2-in & 4 x 6-in Colombo

1st AA Brigade RM, MNBDO
1st HAA Regiment RM, 1st, 2nd and 3rd Batteries
22nd LAA Battery RM
14th HAA Battery RA
2nd HAA Regiment CGA, 5th and 6th Batteries

NOVEMBER 1942

HQRA Ceylon

51st Field Regiment RA, 24 x 25-pdrs, arrived Feb 1942 to 34 Ind Div, to 70 Brit Div India Feb 1943
114th Field Regiment RA, 24 x 25-pdrs, arrived Jul 1942, to 20 Ind Div, to India Jul 1943
115th Field Regiment RA, 24 x 25-pdrs, arrived Jul 1942, to 20 Ind Div, to India Nov 1943
162nd Field Regiment RA. Became 303 (East African) Field Regiment EAA in May 1943.
'Z' Field Battery RA
3rd Indian Anti-Tank Regiment IA, 9th, 10th, 11th and 12th Batteries
12th Field Battery CGA
6th Coast Regiment RA, 15th and 18th Batteries
1st Coast Regiment CGA, 1st, 2nd and 3rd Batteries

Air Defence Command Ceylon

23rd AA Brigade

52nd HAA Regiment RA, 155th, 159th and 271st Batteries, 24 x 3.7-in, arrived May 1942 with 154, 155 & 271 Btys, 154 to 53 HAA Regt in exchange for 159 Jan 1943
65th HAA Regiment RA, 181st, 183rd and 196th Batteries, 24 x 3.7-in, to Middle East May 1943
2nd HAA Regiment CGA, 5th, 6th and 8th Batteries
23rd LAA Regiment RA, 73rd, 74th and 130th Batteries, 24 x 40mm (54 x 40mm May 1943), arrived Jul 1942
43rd LAA Regiment RA, 147th, 148th and 264th Batteries
315th SL Battery RA

1st AA Brigade RM*

54th HAA Regiment RA, 159th, 160th and 161st Batteries, 24 x 3.7-in, arrived Sep 1942, to Suez May 1943
63rd HAA Regiment RA, 177th, 178th and 269th Batteries, 24 x 3.7-in, arrived Jul 1942, to India Apr 1944, disbanded Oct 1944
1st HAA Regiment RM, 'B', 'C' and 'D' Batteries
55th LAA Regiment RA, 163rd, 164th and 165th Batteries
76th LAA Regiment RA, 226th, 227th and 228th Batteries, 36 x 40mm, arrived May 1942, disbanded Jan 1945
22nd LAA Battery RM
7 LAA Bty CGA
405th SL Battery RA

* Brigade went to India in June 1943

OCTOBER 1943

HQRA Ceylon

HQ CEAA 11th East African Division

115th Field Regiment RA, 239th, 240th and 480th Batteries
303rd EA Field Regiment EAA, 53rd, 54th and 55th Batteries
587th Field Battery RA
Trincomalee Field Battery CGA
3rd Indian Anti-Tank Regiment IA, 10th and 12th Batteries (17th & 34th Indian Divs)
6th Coast Regiment RA, 15th and 18th Batteries
1st Coast Regiment CGA, 1st, 2nd, 3rd and 4th Batteries
1st Coast Regiment RM, Devon and Chatham and Z Batteries
3rd Coast Regiment RM, Kent, Portsmouth and 'X' Batteries

23rd AA Brigade

52nd HAA Regiment RA, 155th 159th and 271st Batteries
9th Punjab HAA Regiment IA, 10th, 24th and 26th Batteries
2nd HAA Regiment CGA, 5th, 6th and 8th Batteries
23rd LAA Regiment RA, 73rd, 74th and 130th Batteries
43rd LAA Regiment RA, 147th, 148th and 264th Batteries
Devon LAA Battery RM
7th LAA Battery CGA
315th SL Battery RA
9 SL Bty CGA

24th AA Brigade

63rd HAA Regiment RA, 177th, 178th and 269th Batteries
2nd HAA Regiment RM, 'A' and 'B' Batteries

76th LAA Regiment RA, 226th, 227th and 228th Batteries
23rd LAA Battery RM
10th SL Battery CGA

JUNE 1944

HQRA Ceylon

HQCEAA, 11th East African Division

302nd EA Field Regiment EAA, 55th, 59th and 60th Batteries
303rd EA Field Regiment EAA, 53rd, 54th and 58th Batteries
304(EA) ATk & LAA Regiment EAA, 101st & 102nd ATk Batteries & 203rd and 204th LAA Batteries.
601st Field Battery RA
12th Field Battery CGA
101 ATk Battery EAA
102 ATk Battery EAA
6th Coast Regiment RA, 15th, 18th, 462nd, 463rd and 464th Batteries
1st Coast Regiment CGA, 1st, 2nd, 3rd, 4th, 13th and 14th Batteries
53rd Coast Observation Detachment CGA, formed June 1944
54th Coast Observation Detachment CGA, formed June 1944

23rd AA Brigade

52nd HAA Regiment RA, 155th, 159th and 271st Batteries
13th Indian HAA Regiment IA, 36th, 37th and 38th Batteries, arrived Ceylon Oct 1944
76th LAA Regiment RA, 226th, 227th and 228th Batteries
HQ 3rd SL/LAA Regiment CGA
502nd Indian Composite AA Battery IA
315th SL Battery RA
9th SL Battery, CGA

24th AA Brigade**

9th Punjab HAA Regiment IA, 10th, 24th and 26th Batteries
2nd HAA Regiment CGA, 5th, 6th and 8th Batteries
43rd LAA Regiment RA, 147th, 148th and 264th Batteries
74th LAA Battery (of 23rd LAA Regiment RA)
7th LAA Battery CGA
405th SL Battery RA
10th SL Battery CGA

** Brigade went to India March 1945

The following officers were among those who commanded formations and units in Ceylon during the Second World War:

1st RM AA Bde. Brigadier WFB Lukis
23rd AA Bde. Brigadier Hunt
24th AA Bde. Brigadiers AJR Leslie; JD Edge; GD Holmes

51st (Westmorland & Cumberland Yeo) Field Regt. Lieutenant Colonels HSJ Bourke; JDC Thomson
114th (Sussex) Field Regt. Lieutenant Colonels PS Whitehead; MHF Waring; SF Herbert
115th (North Midland) Field Regt. Lieutenant Colonel MR Simpson
3rd Indian A/Tk Regt. Lieutenant Colonel IP Clarke

52nd HAA Regt. Lieutenant Colonel F Hevey
54th (City of London) HAA Regt. Lieutenant Colonel JA Morton
63rd (Northumbrian) HAA Regt. Lieutenant Colonel CH Wright
65th HAA Regt. Lieutenant Colonel WA MacLellan
23rd LAA Regt. Lieutenant Colonels CD Holmes; TWR Hill; Hon VHO Herbert
43rd LAA Regt. Lieutenant Colonels WB Fletcher; FHB Jenkins
55th LAA Regt. Lieutenant Colonels AG Hunt; JM Kerr; SCC Sewell
76th LAA Regt. Lieutenant Colonels DE Jones; RJ Cockwell; Major EV Proffitt

302 (EA) Fd Regt. Lieutenant Colonel S Southey
303 (EA) Fd Regt. Lieutenant Colonel HM Ingeldew

ANNEX J

THE REBIRTH AND EXPANSION OF THE REGIMENT OF INDIAN REGIMENT OF ARTILLERY (ROYAL INDIAN ARTILLERY from October 1945) 1935 - 1946

FIELD ARTILLERY

Unit/CO	Batteries	Remarks
1st Indian Fd Regt GA Rickards RVM Garry ME Dennis LA Harris HGG Digges (1942) DWD Nicholl LS Gallagher	1st (Madras), 2nd and Scindia* (from 1943) Field Btys.	Raised as A Fd Bde I. Arty on 15 Jan 35. Moved to School of Artillery Deolali by 1941, reorganised and mechanised. With 1 and 2 Btys to 17th Indian Div, Burma, in Mar 42 (16 x 25 prs). Returned to India May 42 with 4 guns saved. Refitted, given Scindia Bty by Gwalior State, retrained and returned to 17th Indian Div, Assam late in 1944. After the war, on return to India converted to SP.
2nd Indian Fd Regt G Horsfield JHH Willans (Oct 42) PS Gyani I Arty (Nov 44) WT Sedgewick (early 46)	3rd, 4th and 7th Field Btys.	Raised 15 May 40 with 3 and 4 Fd Btys. To Iraq with 6th Indian Div Nov 41. Acquired 7 Fd Bty, and moved to Western Desert Feb 42 under 3rd Indian Motor Bde Gp. Bir Hacheim 27 May 42. 46 tanks destroyed, 11 guns saved. Returned to 6th Indian Div Aug 42 and back to India in Feb 44. Retrained for jungle warfare. To 14th Army, Assam, Oct 44. Returned to India Feb 46. Converted to SP.
3rd Indian Fd Regt HGG Digges JFS Rendall	5th, 6th and Hyderabad Fd Btys.	Raised 1 Apr 41 with 5 Bty at Deolali and 6 Bty on the NWF. Then concentrated at Deolali and given Hyderabad State Forces Bty, and moved to Calcutta 43. To 23rd Indian Div, Imphal Oct 44, and then Java in 45.
4th Indian Fd Regt JF Adye GH Inglis JA Ackroyd-Hunt	8th, 9th and 10th Field Btys.	Raised 1 Dec 41. To 19th Indian Div, Assam Oct 44. To 5th Indian Div, Singapore Oct 45.
5th Indian Fd Regt RA Cock FRD Leigh	11th, 12th and 13th Field Btys.	Raised 1 Dec 41. To 25th Indian Div. Arakan Mar 44. To 14th Army Arakan/Assam Apr 45. To 5th Indian Div, Singapore, Oct 45 and then Java.
6th Indian Fd Regt WJ Cooper PHL Findlay AV Brooke-Webb	14th and 15th Field Btys.	Raised 15 Jun 42. Established as a British-Madras Regt 13 May 43 (as for 7 Fd Regt earlier). In 1946 at Latipur near Jhansi. Refurbished Sep 46 and moved for 6 months to S. Iraq with an Independent Infantry Bde. Returned to India and disbanded but revived after Partition, 15 Aug 47.
7th Indian Fd Regt FR Wetherfield WRB Sample JH Gregson OStJ Skeen GMT Morphew JHL Parker	16th, 17th and 18th Field Btys.	Raised 1 Dec 42 as a British/Madrassi Regt (Overlay of British senior Ranks, progressively dispersed after a year or so.) To 15th Indian Corps, Arakan Mar 44. To 26th Indian Div, Arakan Mar 44, then to Sumatra sec 45. (16 Bty to British Commonwealth Occupation Force, Japan Sep 45. Replaced by 5 Bty from 3rd Indian Fd Regt, Java Aug 46.)

Unit/CO	Batteries	Remarks
8th Indian Fd Regt WMC Wall	19th, 20th and 21st Field Btys.	Raised 1 Jan 43. While undergoing final training at Ranchi, chosen for conversion to 1st Indian Medium Regt Oct44 (Two btys only retained).
9th Indian Fd Regt	22nd, 23rd and 24th Field Btys.	Raised 1 Apr 43. Became Para Field.
10th Indian (Reserve) Fd Regt Lt Col TWM Johnson	25th, 26th and 27th Field Btys.	Raised 15 Jul 43. A Training Regt at Chindwara, part of 14th (Infantry) Training Div. Post -War disbanded.
11th Indian Fd Regt	30th, 31st and 32nd Field Btys.	Converted from 18th Indian LAA Regt 2 Oct 45. (Similar conversions AA to Field followed; also AA to Medium Artillery Regiments)

Note: The allocation of btys to 9, 10 and 11 Fd Regts are taken from Orders of Battle published at the time.

MEDIUM ARTILLERY

Unit/CO	Batteries	Remarks
1st Indian Med Regt	1st and 2nd Med Btys.	Converted from 8th Indian Field Regt 30 Sep 44.
2nd Indian Med Regt	3rd and 4th Med Btys.	Converted from 3rd Indian HAA 29 May 45.
3rd Indian Med Regt	5th and 6th Med Btys.	In ORBAT of Southern Command, India, in Jan 1946.

ANTI-TANK ARTILLERY

Unit/CO	Batteries	Remarks
1st Indian A/Tk Regt Lt Col RG Lascelles	1st, 2nd and 30th A/Tk Btys.	Raised 1 Aug 40 as K A/Tk Regt. Two btys to Iraq in 40, balance of regt to Iraq 22 Nov 41. 10th Indian Div in Iraq Mar 42. 26th Indian Div Ramree Island Mar 45.
2nd Indian A/Tk Regt Lt Col WR Kaye Lt Col DR Corner	5th, 6th, 7th and 8th A/Tk Btys.	Raised 1 Apr 41. Rangoon 9 Feb 42 with 20x2 prs. 23rd Indian Div Oct 43-44. Reorganised in 43 as 2nd LAA/A/Tk Regt with 205th and 208th LAA Btys, 6th and 7th A/Tk Btys.
3rd Indian A/Tk Regt Lt Col JHH Willans Lt Col IP Carter	9th, 10th, 11th and 12th A/Tk Btys.	Raised 1 Nov 41. 34th Indian Div, Ceylon Jul 42.
4th (Mahratta) A/Tk Regt		Converted from 8/5 Mahratta LI 1 Jan 42. To Iraq with 18-pounders Aug 42. 8th Indian Div.
5th (Mahratta) A/Tk Regt	17th, 18th and 19th A/Tk Btys.	Converted from 9/5 Mahratta LI 1 Jan 42. 5th Indian Div in ME Aug 42. India Mar 43 36x6-pdrs. 14th Army at Imphal Mar 45. With 5th Indian Div in Singapore Oct 45.
6th Indian A/Tk Regt	21st, 22nd, 23rd and 24th A/Tk Btys.	Raised 1 Feb 42. 7th Indian Div Jun 42. Converted to light mountain btys with 3-in mortars in Jul 43. Btys renumbered as 37th, 38th, 39th and 40th Light Mountain Btys.

Unit/CO	Batteries	Remarks
7th Indian A/Tk Regt Lt Col PGP Bradshaw	25th, 26th, 27th and 39th A/Tk Btys.	Raised 1 May 42. 25th Indian Div Oct 43. Late 44 Reorganised into 9th, 25th and 26th A/Tk Btys. Was also LAA/A/Tk for a while in 1944 with 33 Corps Troops. 25th Indian Div Mar 45 and in Malaya in 46.
8th (Mahratta) A/Tk Regt Lt Col GFA Barff Lt Col Collingwood	35th, 36th, 37th and 38th A/Tk Btys.	Converted from 7/5 Mahratta LI 1 Oct 42. 44th Indian Armoured Div Oct 43. 14th Army at Indainggyi Mar 45. 7th Indian Div May 45 with 35th, 36th and 37th Btys only, 36x6-pdrs.
15th (Punjab) A/Tk Regt	28th, 29th, 30th and 31st A/Tk Btys in Mar 43.	Converted from MG Bn 15 Punjab Regt 1 Aug 42. Disbanded 7 Nov 44.
16th (Punjab) A/Tk Regt	32nd, 33rd, 34th and 40th A/TK Btys in Mar 43	Converted from MG Bn 16 Punjab Regt 1 Aug 42. This was a Reserve A/Tk Regt.

MOUNTAIN ARTILLERY

The older Indian Mountain Batteries were named as well as having numbers. These were 1 Royal (Kohat), 2 (Derajat), 3 (Peshawar), 4 (Hazara), 5 (Bombay), 6 (Jacob's), 7 (Bengal), 8 (Lahore), 9 (Murree), 10 (Abbotabad), 11 (Dehra Dun), 12 (Poonch), 13 (Dardoni), 14 (Rajputana), 15 (Jhelum), 16 (Zhob), 17 (Nowshera), 18 (Sohan) and 19 (Maymyo). 20 to 25 Mountain regiments were old-established units, each of one British and three Indian Mountain Batteries. On losing their British batteries in 1936/37 a newly raised Indian battery was added.

Unit/CO	Batteries	Remarks
20th Indian Mountain Regt Lt Col HH Mackenzie Lt Col JH Birbeck Lt Col CEC Burton Lt Col CCM MacLeod-Carey Maj MF Kemmis-Betty	23rd 24th, 25th, 26th. In 1941 23 Bty went to 27 Regt and was replaced by 1st Gwalior Mtn Bty* (ISF). The latter was replaced by the Bahawalpur Bty ISF*. This bty went to 29 Regt in 1944.	Raised before 1935. NW Frontier until 44. 19th Indian Div Nov 44, 12x3.7-in hows. Returned to India Mar 46 and disbanded.
21st Indian Mountain Regt Lt Col A Paton Lt Col JW Cooper Lt Col PER Dawson Lt Col JB Chaplin	1st, 6th, 9th and 14th Mtn Btys. Later 1, 6 and 37 Btys.	Raised before 1935. 17th Indian Div, Burma. Became 21st Light Mtn Regt with 1st, 6th Btys.17th Indian Div at Imphal Jan 43, at Shillong May 43. 37th Bty joined with 16x3-in mortars May 43. Imphal Nov 43, Tiddim Dec 43-44. Sep 44 to Ranchi. Fly to Meiktila Mar 45. May 45 Pegu. Feb 46 at Maymyo.
22nd Indian Mountain Regt Lt Col GL Hughes Lt Col DGC Cowie	4th, 7th, 10th and 21st Mtn Btys.	Raised before 1935. 11th Indian Div in Malaya from 7 Dec 41. Lost Singapore Feb 42.

Unit/CO	Batteries	Remarks
23rd Indian Mountain Regt Lt Col BC Barford Lt Col DL Betts Lt Col JMW Titley	3rd, 8th, 12th and 17th Mtn Btys. In 1941 12 Bty went to 27 Regt and was replaced by 2nd (Jammu and Kashmir) Mtn Bty (ISF)* which was later redesignated 31 Bty. 17 Bty left for 32 Regt in early 45.	Raised before 1935. 14th Indian Div in the Arakan Dec 42. 20th Indian Div Aug 43. 20th Indian Div Jan 45. 12x3.7-in hows. To Malaya and Indo-China in 46.
24th Indian Mountain Regt Lt Col SF Fiskin Lt Col RHM Hill Lt Col WBP Milne	11th, 16th and 20th Mtn Btys. In 1943 16 Bty went to 28 Regt and in Dec 1943 2 and 12 Btys joined from 27 Regt when it disbanded. In 1944 12 Bty went to 32 Regt.	Raised before 1935. 23rd Indian Div in Burma 42. 5th Indian Div, Burma 44-45.
25th Indian Mountain Regt Lt Col JH Birbeck Lt Col HH Mackenzie Lt Col EV Booth Lt Col LHO Pugh Lt Col GA Rowley-Conwy Lt Col ED Garnett	5th, 13th, 15th and 19th Mtn Btys. In 1942 5 Bty went to 27 Regt, 15 Bty to 28 Regt and Bikaner Bijay Bty* and 23 Bty joined from 27 Regt. In 1943 13 Bty went to 28 Regt. In early 1945 19 Bty went to 33 Regt.	Raised before 1935. 7th Indian Div May 43-45, Burma, 12x3.7-in hows.
26th Indian Mountain Regt Lt Col JC Allardyce Lt Col PHL Findlay	18th, 22nd, 27th and 1st (Jammu and Kashmir)* Mtn Btys. 1st (Jammu & Kashmir) Bty redesignated 30th Bty in 42.1st (Gwalior) Bty* joined regt Aug 43.	Raised 1941 in Palestine while the four batteries were fighting in East Africa and Abyssinia. In early 42 the batteries joined the regt in Palestine. Regt, less 27th Bty, returned India and the regt was on the NW Frontier 42-45.
27th Indian Mountain Regt Lt Col WG Constable	2nd, 12th and 23rd Mtn Btys. 5th joined in 42. In 43 23 Bty joined 25 Regt. 2 and 12 Btys to 24 Regt when regt disbanded.	Raised 1 Nov 41. Landed Rangoon 28 Nov 41. 2nd & 23rd Btys to 1st Burma Div Dec 41. 5th and 12th Btys with 17th Indian Div. Arrived India with guns: 2nd Bty 4x3.7s, 12th Bty 2x3.7s, 23rd Bty 4x3.7s and 5th Bty no guns. 26th Indian Div 43. Disbanded 21 Aug 43.
28th Indian Mountain Regt Lt Col AH Peskett Lt Col FBB Knight Lt Col LH Landon Lt Col WMC Wall	15th and 28th Mtn Btys. 16 from 24 Regt and 13 from 25 Regt joined in 43. In 44 28 Bty went to 32	Regt. Raised 1 Jan 42. Landed Rangoon 14 Feb 42, to 17th Indian Div. Arrived India May 42 with 4x3.7s. Reformed in India in 43 with 13th, 15th, 16th and 28th Mtn Btys, then to 23rd Indian Div. Regt on Op ZIPPER in 45.
29th Indian Mountain Regt Lt Col G Horsfield Lt Col JM Hepper Lt Col JSW Tremenheere	9th and 14th Mtn Btys. 38th Mtn Bty joined in Jun 43.	Raised Oct 42 from 21st Mtn Regt. 17th Indian Light Div Dec 42. Jun 43 38th Bty joined regt with 16x3-inch mortars. To Peshawar 44.
30th Indian Mountain Regt Lt Col TWR Hill	32nd, 33rd and 34th Mtn Btys. In Feb 44 34 Bty left for 33 Regt and 27 Bty joined from 31 Regt.	Raised 15 Feb 43. 26th Indian Div Feb 44. 7th Indian Div in Siam Dec 45. 25th Indian Div in Malaya 46.

Unit/CO	Batteries	Remarks
31st Indian Mountain Regt Lt Col GP Cunningham	27th, 29th, 35th, 2nd (Gwalior) (ISF)* and Patiala (ISF)* Mtn Btys. 27 Bty went to 30 Regt in Feb 44. 35 Bty to 33 Regt in Oct 44.	Raised 15 Apr 43. Remained at Kohat.
32nd Indian Mountain Regt Lt Col RC Yeo	12th, 17th and 28th Mtn Btys.	Raised 15 Sep 44. 36th British Div in Burma 45.
33rd Indian Mountain Regt Lt Col RS Ellis	19th, 34th and 35th Mtn Btys, 19 Bty from 25 Regt and 35 from 31 Regt.	Raised 1 Oct 44. 25th Indian Div in Burma and Malaya Nov 44-46.

SURVEY ARTILLERY

Unit/CO	Batteries	Remarks
1st Indian Survey Regt Lt Col Hunter Lt Col SA Brighty	1st and 2nd Survey Btys.	Raised in Aug 42 from 1 Survey Bty (raised 22 Jan 41). To 33rd Corps.

HEAVY ANTI-AIRCRAFT ARTILLERY

Unit/CO	Batteries	Remarks
1st Indian HAA Regt Lt Col JR Williamson	1st, 2nd, 3rd and 4th HAA and 1st LAA Btys. 1st HAA Bty went to Digboi, Upper Assam, in Jun 42. 5 LAA Bty joined in Singapore.	Raised 1 Oct 40 as R HAA Regt. To Malaya less 1st Bty 19 Jul 41. 1st Bty had 5x18-pounders on high-angle mounts. Regt lost at Singapore in Feb 42.
2nd Indian HAA Regt Lt Col EA Barlow	1st, 7th and 8th HAA Btys.	Raised 1 Apr 41 as S HAA Regt. Calcutta Oct 41. Dec 41 8th HAA Bty to Rangoon. Destroyed their 4x3 in guns at Ye-U on 1 Apr 42. Under command 9th AA Bde in Assam and Poona Dec 41-44. 3rd AA Bde in Assam Oct 44.
3rd Indian HAA Regt	5th, 6th and 11th HAA Btys. 4 LAA Bty was intended to join but remained independent.	Raised 1 Jun 41. Bihar and Bengal early 42. Converted to 2nd Indian Medium Regiment 29 May 45.
4th Indian HAA Regt, later 4 Indian AA Regt. Lt Col RLO Carew	Originally 9th, 10th and 11th HAA Btys. Later 10 HAA Bty went to 9 HAA Regt and 1 HAA Bty went to 3 HAA Regt and 10th and 11th LAA Btys joined.	Raised 1 Nov 41. End 42 moved to Vizagapatam. RHQ disbanded in 43 and btys dispersed to other regts.
5th Indian HAA Regt Lt Col RC Elliott Lt Col OCD Berry	12th, 13th and 14th HAA Btys.	Raised 1 Mar 42. 9th British AA Bde Assam 43. 3rd Indian AA Bde in Assam Oct 44. 61st AGRA Jun 45.
6th Indian HAA Regt	15th, 16th 17th and 35th HAA Btys.	Raised 1 Sep 42. 13th British AA Bde in Arakan Oct 43. Chittagong Mar 45. 61st AGRA Jun 45.

Unit/CO	Batteries	Remarks
7th (Rajput) HAA Regt	18th, 19th and 20th HAA Btys.	Converted from 8/7 Rajput Regt 1 Feb 42. 9th British AA Bde Assam Jun 43. 13th British AA Bde Arakan Oct 44. Dohazari Mar 45.
8th (Rajput) HAA Regt	21st, 22nd and 23rd HAA Btys.	Converted from 7/7 Rajput Regt 1 Apr 42. Jan 45 to Madras. Disbanded 4 Jun 45.
9th (Punjab) HAA Regt	10th, 24th, 25th and 26th HAA Btys.	Converted from 14/8 Punjab Regt 1 Jun 42. 24th AA Bde Trincomalee Oct 44. Disbanded 4 Jun 45.
10th Indian HAA Regt	27th, 28th and 29th HAA Btys.	Raised 15 Nov 42. Jan 45 in Bengal.
11th Indian HAA Regt	30th, 31st and 32nd HAA Btys.	Raised 1 Apr 43. Jan 45 in Bengal. Disbanded 4 Jun 45.
12th Indian HAA Regt	33rd. 34th and 35th HAA Btys.	Raised 1 May 43. Jan 45 in Bombay.
13th Indian HAA Regt	36th, 37th and 38th HAA Btys.	Raised 1 Jun 43. 23rd AA Bde Ceylon Oct 44-45.
14th Indian HAA Regt	39th, 40th, 41st HAA Btys.	Raised 1 Jul 43. Jan 45 in Bengal. Converted to 3 Indian Medium Regt 1946
15th Indian HAA Regt	42nd, 43rd and 44th HAA Btys.	Raised 1 Oct 43. Converted to 15th Indian LAA Regt 1 Jun 44.
16th Indian HAA Regt	None allocated	Raised 7 Jul 44. Converted to 16th Indian LAA Regt 15 Oct 44.
20th Indian HAA Regt	501st, 502nd and 503rd HAA Btys.	Raised 1 Apr 43. Jan 45 in Bengal.
21st Indian HAA Regt	504th, 505th and 506th HAA Btys.	Raised 1 Jun 43. Jan 45 in Bengal.
25th Indian HAA Regt	72nd, 73rd and 74th HAA Btys.	Raised 1 Mar 43. 13th British AA Bde, Cox's Bazaar Mar 45.

LIGHT ANTI-AIRCRAFT ARTILLERY

Unit/CO	Batteries	Remarks
1st Indian LAA Regt Lt Col GC Fawns Lt Col R Philip Lt Col Woodruff Lt Col BLE Herbert	1st, 2nd and 3rd LAA Btys. 1 Bty went to Singapore with 1 HAA Regt and was replaced by 6 LAA Bty.	Raised 1 Mar 41. Dec 41 moved to Calcutta. 3rd Bty served in Burma 41-42. Feb 42 joined 9th AA Bde in Assam. 3rd Indian AA Bde 43. Late 44 retrained with SP Bofors. 24 AA Bde Burma in 45 and 61 AGRA (AA) in late 45.
2nd Indian LAA Regt Lt Col EC Kensington Lt Col RGB Reed	7th, 8th and 9th LAA Btys.	Raised 1 Oct 41. To Bengal, 14th (WA) AA Bde. In 42. In Assam Feb 43. End 44 retrained with SP Bofors. 14th Army Mar 45. 61st AGRA Jun 45.

Unit/CO	Batteries	Remarks
3rd Indian LAA Regt Lt Col Glover (killed in air crash late 42. Lt Col HT Hogan	10th and 11th LAA Btys. Later, 12th, 13th and 14th LAA Btys.	Raised 1 Feb 42. 13th British AA Bde Arakan Oct 44, Chittagong Mar 45.
4th Indian LAA Regt Lt Col CHW Taylor	13th, 14th and 15th LAA Btys, 13 and 14 Btys to 3 LAA Regt and 16th and 17th Btys joined.	Raised 1 Sep 42. Under command 14th (WA) AA Bde, Surma Valley Mar 45.
5th Indian LAA Regt Lt Col JHR Edleman I Arty Lt Col CESP Gaussen	16th, 17th and 18th LAA Btys. Later, 18th, 31st and 32nd LAA Btys.	Raised 15 Dec 42. 9th British AA Bde in Assam 43. 3rd Indian AA Bde in Assam Oct 44-45. 61st AGRA Aug 45.
6th (Punjab) LAA Regt Lt Col AG Tribe Lt Col JM Wood	19th, 20th and 21st LAA Btys.	Converted from 8/1 Punjab Regt 1 Feb 42. 13th British AA Bde in Arakan Oct 44. 24th Indian AA Bde Jorhat Mar 45.
7th (Sikh) LAA Regt	23rd and 24th LAA Btys.	Converted from 8/11 Sikh Regt 1 Apr 42. Disbanded 15 Aug 43.
8th (Sikh) LAA Regt	25th, 26th and 27th LAA Btys.	Converted from 9/11 Sikh Regt 1 Apr 42. 13th British AA Bde in Arakan Oct 44. Chittagong Mar 45.
9th (Rajput) LAA Regt	10th, 22nd, 28th and 30th LAA Btys. 11th LAA Bty joined later.	Converted from 9/6 Rajputana Rifles 1 May 42. 28 Bty disbanded Aug 43 and 22nd Bty Feb 44.
10th Indian LAA Regt	33rd, 34th and 35th LAA Btys.	Raised 1 Feb 43. Jan 45 in Bengal.
11th Indian LAA Regt	36th, 37th and 38th LAA Btys.	Raised 1 Apr 43. 13th British AA Bde in Arakan 44-45.
12th Indian LAA Regt	39th, 40th and 41st LAA Btys.	Raised 1 May 43. Jan 45 In Bengal.
13th Indian LAA Regt	43rd LAA Bty. Others not known.	Raised 1 Jul 43. Regiment disbanded 1 Mar 44 but 43rd LAA Bty independent under 13th British AA Bde in the Arakan.
14th Indian LAA Regt	Not known.	Raised 1 Oct 43. Jan 45 in Bengal.
15th Indian LAA Regt Lt Col CH Wright	43rd, 48th and 49th LAA Btys.	Raised 1 Jun 44 from 15th HAA Regt. 13th British AA Bde at Feni Mar 45.
16th Indian LAA Regt	106th, 107th and 108th LAA Btys.	Raised 15 Oct 44 from 16th HAA Regt. Jan 45 in Bengal.
17th Indian LAA Regt	11th, 101st and 103rd LAA Btys. Later 11th LAA Bty to 9th LAA Regt.	Raised 1 Apr 43. Mar 43 in Ceylon. Disbanded 4 Jun 45.
18th Indian LAA Regt Lt Col WA Fearnley-Whittingstall	42/13th, 104th and 105th LAA Btys. Later, 42nd, 104th and 105th LAA Btys.	Raised 1 Jun 43. 14th (WA) AA Bde at Sylhet Oct 44. Surma Valley Mar 45. Converted to 11th Indian Field Regt 2 Aug 45.

COAST ARTILLERY

Unit/CO	Batteries	Remarks
1st Indian Coast Regt	7th, 8th and 9th Coast Btys.	Raised 41. Addu Atoll 27 Nov 41. Disbanded 31 Jul 44.
2nd Indian Coast Regt	1st, 10th and 11th Coast Btys.	Raised 15 Dec 41. Karachi. Disbanded 1 Aug 42.
3rd Indian Coast Regt	2nd, 6th and 14th Coast Btys.	Raised 1 Feb 42. Bombay with detachment of 14th Bty at Madras in anti-MTB role.
4th Indian Coast Regt	3rd, 4th, 5th and 17th Coast Btys.	Raised 1 Sep 42. 3rd Battery to Addu Atoll 27 Nov 42. 4th Bty to Addu Atoll 1 Feb 44. 5th Bty to Vizagapatam 1 Feb 44. 17th Bty Anti-MTB role.
	12th, 13th, 15th, 16th and 18th Independent Coast Btys.	12th Coast Bty at Diego Garcia on 12 Sep 42. 13th Coast Bty at Cocos Islands on 7 Dec 42. 15th Coast Bty at Bombay.16th Coast Bty at Diamond Harbour. 18th Coast Bty at Vizagapatam.

ANTI-AIRCRAFT BRIGADES

Brigade	Units	Stations
1st Indian AA Bde Brigadier GP Thomas	95th HAA Regt RA joined Apr 42 53rd HAA Regt RA joined May 42 24th LAA Regt RA joined May 42 66th HAA Regt RA joined Jun 42 8th HAA Regt RA joined Aug 42	India.
2nd Indian AA Bde Brigadier HHM Oliver	3rd Indian HAA Regt 2nd Indian LAA Regt 9th (Rajput) LAA Regt 14th Indep Indian LAA Bty	At Jamshedpur, India.
3rd Indian AA Bde Brigadier K Hargreaves Brigadier NG Thompson	7th (Sikh) LAA Regt 8th (Rajput) HAA Regt 4th Indian LAA Regt As at 12 Oct 44: 66th HAA Regt RA at Digboi 2nd Indian HAA Regt at Jorhat 5th Indian HAA Regt at Panitola 1st Indian LAA Regt at Tinsukia 5th Indian LAA Regt at Jorhat	Raised at Bombay Aug 42. Madras Nov 42. Panitola, Assam Jun 44.

* INDIAN STATES FORCES ARTILLERY

Nine batteries of Indian States Forces artillery were offered to, and accepted by, the Indian Army. Bahawalpur provided a mountain battery which went to 20th Mountain Regiment. Bikaner provided a mountain battery which went to 25th Mountain Regiment. Gwalior provided Scindia Field Battery which went to 1st Indian Field Regiment and two mountain batteries, 1st to 20th Mountain Regiment and later to 26th Mountain Regiment, and 2nd to 31st Mountain Regiment. Hyderabad provided a field battery which went to 3rd (Indian) Field Regiment. Jammu and Kashmir provided two mountain batteries, 1st and 2nd (later 30th and 31st) which went to 26th and 23rd Indian Mountain Regiments, respectively. Patiala provided a Mtn Bty which went to 31st Indian Mountain Regiment.

GENERAL NOTES

1. The Indian Regiment of Artillery was redesignated The Regiment of Indian Artillery on 1 November 1940 and became the Royal Indian Artillery in October 1945.

2. All the commanding officers shown were RA except for Gyani, and JHR Edleman. It is possible that some of the COs of converted infantry battalions were Indian Army officers.

3. There were eight AA brigades in the theatre. One was a West African Brigade. The others were designated "British" or "Indian" according to the place where the HQ was raised. Thus 1, 2 and 3 were Indian and 9, 13, 23 and 24 were British. Towards the end of the campaign 9 and 24 AA Brigades became 60 and 61 AGRAs (AA). 11 AGRA (AA) was later formed to administer the Indian AA units remaining in SEAC.

4. It is sad that there is not enough available information to make this Annex a complete record of the Indian Artillery in the period which it covers. Several attempts have been made to ascertain what there is in India but all have ended in failure. Major Herbert Sawyer, who provided much of the information on which the Annex is based, was in contact with the Director of Artillery, Indian Army, some years ago, and was told that there appeared to be no records of the Madrassi units. Lieutenant Colonel Dick McCaig provided much information on the Indian field regiments. For those units which never left India there seems to be no record in the United Kingdom although the Orders of Battle for India and South East Asia, held by the Public Record Office, have been used to confirm the existence of some units and to determine the batteries in some of the regiments.

Annex K

REGIMENTS & BATTERIES OF THE ROYAL ARTILLERY WHICH SERVED IN INDIA, CEYLON, BURMA, HONG KONG & SINGAPORE December 1981- August 1945

This Annex does not include those units which arrived in India from UK but were simply staging there on the way to Iraq, or those which were stationed in India but left before December 1941. It does include that part of the Hong Kong - Singapore RA which was stationed in the area, because it was RA.

Unit/CO	Batteries	Remarks
14th Regt RHA Lt Col B de H Pereira	414th and 525th Btys RHA	414th Bty landed Rangoon 21 Feb 42 and fought through Burma reaching India in May with 6x25-pdrs. The bty came from 104th Regt RHA (The Essex Yeomanry). 14th Regt RHA formed at Dhond on 1 Sep 42 from 414th By. Sailed Bombay for ME 9 Oct 42.
4th Fd Regt Lt Col GER Bastin Lt Col HM Ingledew Lt Col DW Neilson Lt Col JH Branford Lt Col JA Stevens	4th, 7th, 14th and 66th Fd Btys, later 7th, 14/66th and 522nd Fd Btys	Jul 39 stationed Hyderabad. 1 Aug 39 sailed for Egypt. May 43 returned India and moved to Ranchi with 5th Indian Div. Oct 43 moved to Arakan. 21 Mar 44 flown to Palel with 7th, 14/66th and 522nd Btys. April/May 45 Meiktila with 5th Indian Div, 24x25 Drs. 10 Jun 45 with 19th Indian Div. Aug 45 with 12th Army.
5 Fd Regt Lt Col GdeV Welchman Lt Col EWF Jephson	63/81st and 73rd Fd Btys	3 Sep 39 stationed Rawalpindi. 6 Nov 41 moved Singapore with 16x4.5-inch hows. 15 Feb 42 lost at Singapore with 11th Indian Div.
8th Fd Regt Lt Col WE Walton Lt Col JCM Mead Lt Col DBJ Darley	V, W and X Fd Btys, later 578th, 579th and 580th Fd Btys	3 Sep 39 stationed Lucknow. 25 Aug 40 sailed for Egypt. 23 Mar 42 arrived Bombay joined 70th British Div. 11 Mar 43 reorganised as 8th Jungle Field Regt, joined 25th Indian Div. 21 Mar 44 arrived in Arakan. Apr 45 Ramree Island. May 45 landed Rangoon. Jul 45 joined 36th British Div Poona.
9th Fd Regt Lt Col JR Lupton Lt Col RW Sorsbie	19th, 20th and 28/76th Fd Btys	Jan 43 arrived at Bombay. 12 Mar 43 joined 39th Indian Light Div at Hazaribagh. 22 Aug 43 joined 20th Indian Div at Ranchi. 27 Nov 43 at Tamu. 24x25-pdrs. 18 Jun 45 left Rangoon for Dehra Dun under Central India Command.
10th Fd Regt Lt Col CE Barrington Lt Col EA Howard Lt Col DG Cannell Lt Col JG Wolfe-Barry Lt Col BNL Ditmus	30th, 46th and 51/54th Fd Btys	2 Jun 42 arrived Bombay with 2nd British Div, moved to Kirkee, then Trigmulgherry then Ahmednagar. 5 Apr 43 from 2nd Div to 36th Indian Div. 30th Bty 6x3.7-in hows and 46th Bty to LAA. Sep 43 to 2nd Div with 30th Bty 3.7s, 46th and 51/54th Btys 25-pdrs. Oct 43 46th Bty becomes SP with 105mm Priests but by Mar 44 is back to 24x25-prs. 5 Apr 44 with 2nd Div at Dimapur and Kohima. Apr 45 flies to Myingyang and then to Chittagong. Jun 45 at Secunderabad with 2nd British Div.

Unit/CO	Batteries	Remarks
16th Fd Regt Lt Col NC Lang Lt Col JA MacDonald Lt Col RJ Uniacke	27th, 34th and 72/86th Fd Btys	7 Jun 42 arrived Bombay with 2nd British Div, moved to Ahmednagar. May 43, 27th Bty given 3.7-in hows and in Sep, 34th Bty given 105mm SP Priests, but reverted to 25 Drs in May 44. Apr 44 flown to Manipur Road. 27th Bty still 3.7s. 17 Apr 44 2x5.5-in guns joined 72/86th Bty as G Troop. Guns wheel to wheel at Kohima. 11 Feb 45, 3.7-in HAA gun in regt fired first shell into Mandalay. 2 Mar 45 regt crosses Irrawaddy 24x2 prs. 10 Nov 45 regt flown from Myingan to Chittagong. 7 Jun 45 by rail and road to Secunderabad.
18th Fd Regt Lt Col AP Curzon-Howe Lt Col WG Lyon	59th, 93rd and 94/95th Fd Btys	24 Nov 42 arrived Bombay from UK, joined 43rd Indian Armoured Div at Secunderabad. Dec 43 converts to 24x105mm SP Priests plus 10 Sherman Tank OPs. Sep 44 at Imphal. Dec moved into Burma. Part 14th Army Artillery. 12 Feb 45 joined 16th AGRA. 11 Jun 45 left Rangoon for Madras. 1 Sep 45 sailed for Malacca, Malaya. 1 Feb 46 arrived Calcutta and moved to Secunderabad then Bangalore.
25th Fd Regt Lt Col PS Myburgh	12th, 25th, 31st and 58th Fd Btys	3 Sep 39 stationed at Jhansi. 10 Sep 40 sailed for Egypt, East Africa and then Western Desert. Oct 42 Iraq. Jun 43 India thence Burma.
27th Fd Regt Lt Col J Longden Lt Col CL Corsar Lt Col WB Wilson	21/24th and 37/47th Fd Btys	21 Jul 42 arrived Bombay, to Bangalore, to Trichinopoly. Jan 43 became Jungle Field Regt in 25th Indian Div. Nov 43 21/24th Bty given mortars and 37/47th Bty given 3.7-in hows. Sep 44 converted to 25-pdrs. Jan 45 at Akyab, moved to Ramree to 26th Indian Div. May 45 near Rangoon with additional 1x7.2 in gun.
28th Fd Regt Lt Col RA Collins Lt Col MB Lamacraft	1st, 3rd (Martinique) and 5/57th (Croix de Guerre) Fd Btys	3 Sep 39 stationed Mhow with 1/5th and 3/57th Btys. 24 Aug 40 sailed for Sudan with 5th Indian Div. 18 May 43 returned India. Became Jungle Field Regt. Moved to Arakan with 5th Indian Div. 19-24 Mar 44 flew to Imphal. Converted to 24x25-pdrs. 31 Mar 45 crossed Irrawaddy at Myaungu. 2 Apr 45 at Meiktila joined 19th Indian Div.
51st Fd Regt (Westmorland and Cumberland) Lt Col HSJ Bourke Lt Col JDC Thompson Lt Col RC Sutcliffe	203rd and 370th Fd Btys	Regiment fought in France, Norway (203 Bty onlt) and Western Desert. 26 Feb 42. Arrived Ceylon from Egypt, joined 34th Indian Div. Feb 43. Moved to Ranchi and joined 70th British Div. Sep 43 converted to L R P role, guns handed in. 587th Bty (Lanarkshire Yeo) joined regt. 24 Oct regt, with 69th A/Tk Regt, becomes 9th and 10th Columns of Wingate's second Chindit operation. 1 Mar 44. Crossed the Chindwin, 10 Apr reached 'Aberdeen.' May 44 moved to Comilla. 17 May 44. At Bangalore. 25% of regt repatriated to UK, remainder transferred to Essex Regt.
60th Fd Regt Lt Col AF Hely Lt Col GG Peel Lt Col HG de J du Vallon Lt Col P Cox	237th and 239th Fd Btys	Regt fought with distinction at Sidi Rezegh. Apr 42. Arrived India from Palestine, moved to Ranchi. Nov 42. 442nd Fd Bty joined the regt. To Bangalore, joined 70th British Div. Oct 43 converted to L R P role. Apr 44 marched into Burma, Wingate's second Chindit operation, with 23rd Bde. Jul 44 arrived Imphal, moved to Bangalore. 29 Oct 44 regt placed in SA. Personnel posted to 2nd Queens.

Unit/CO	Batteries	Remarks
88 Fd Regt Lt Col SC D'Aubuz	351st, 352nd and 464th Field Btys	7 Dec 41 arrived Singapore joining 9th Indian Div. 15 Feb 42 lost at Singapore.
91 Fd Regt Lt Col W Buffey	361st, 363rd and 466th Field Btys	May 42. Madagascar. 1 Jun 42 arrived Bombay. 20 Aug 42 sailed for Iraq.
96th (Royal Devon Yeomanry) Fd Regt Lt Col FF Maude Lt Col WG Barr Maj MI Gregson	381st, 382nd and 469th Field Btys	22 Feb 45. Arrived Bombay. Moved to Bangalore. 7 Apr 45. To 81st (WA) Div. 7 May 45. To 25th Indian Div. 3 Sep 45. Arrived in Malaya.
99th (Royal Bucks Yeomanry) Fd Regt Lt Col JP Whiteley Lt Col MSK Maunsell Lt Col JWH James Lt Col L Tetley Lt Col AL Awdrey Lt Col BC Bonsor Major E Butler-Henderson Lt Col EAH Jackson	393rd, 394th and 472nd Fd Btys	Jun 42 arrived Bombay with 2nd British Div. 27 Dec 42 regt less 394th Bty and E Troop 472nd Bty arrive Chittagong with 3.7-in hows and 25-pdrs. 1 Feb 43 First Arakan. Battle of Donbaik. 21 Apr 43 with 26th Indian Div at Buthidaung. Aug 43 rejoins 2nd British Div at Ahmednagar. Oct 43 393rd and 472nd Btys with 3.7-in hows, 394th Bty with 105mm SP Priests, 472nd Bty with 25-pdrs. Mar 44. 394th Bty with 8x25-pdrs. Regt to Dimapur. Apr-Jun 44 Kohima and Imphal. Mar 45 regt crossed Irrawaddy with 24x25-pdrs. 8 Apr 45 flown Myingyan to Dohazari. Jun 45 at Secunderabad. 30 Sep 45 placed in SA.
114th Fd Regt (Sussex) Lt Col PS Whitehead Lt Col MHF Waring Lt Col SF Herbert Lt Col R Elliott Lt Col MR MacKenzie	231st, 232nd and 479th Fd Btys	11 May 42 arrived Bombay. To Ceylon with 20th Indian Div. 19 Jul 43 to India with 20th Indian Div, converted to jungle field regiment at Ranchi. 231st Bty had mortars. 10 Nov 43 moved to Imphal. By 25 Mar 43, 232nd and 479th Btys have 4x3.7-in hows, 231st By have 3-in mortars. 4 Dec 44. Regt at Kalemyo. 24x25-pdrs plus troop of 7.2-in hows. 21 Feb 45 regt crosses Irrawaddy. 29 Sep 45 Rangoon. 6 Oct 45 Saigon, 321st Bty ambushed at Bien Hoy. 14 Jan 46 at Singapore. Moved to Kangar Kahang in Malaya.
115th Fd Regt (North Midland) Lt Col MR Simpson Lt Col RAG Nicholson Lt Col AD Foxon	239th, 240th and 480th Fd Btys	19 May 42 arrived Bombay to join 19th Indian Div at Bangalore. 4 Jul 43 to 20th Indian Div in Ceylon. 31 Oct 44 to Manipur Road with 19th Indian Div, 24x25-pdrs. Dec 44 crossed Chindwin. 11 Feb 45 crossed Irrawaddy. 30 Apr 45 at Toungoo. By Jul reached R Sittang. Sep 45 moved to Rangoon. 4 Oct 45 boarded *Jan de Witt* for UK.
118th Fd Regt Lt Col CE MacKellar	259th, 260th and 483rd Fd Btys	By Feb 42 with 18th British Div in Singapore. 15 Feb 42 lost at Singapore.
122nd Fd Regt (West Riding) Lt Col G St J A Dyson	278th and 280th Field Btys	By Dec 41. With 12th Indian Inf Bde in Malaya. 15 Feb 42 lost at Singapore.
123rd Fd Regt (West Riding) Lt Col RH Fielding-Mould Lt Col JMA Chestnutt Lt Col LP Cocks Lt Col A Cameron	283rd, 284th and 488th Fd Btys	10 Oct 42 arrived Bombay, joined 32nd Indian Armd Div at Poona. 18 Jan 45 redesignated as 123rd Parachute Field Regt, 44th Indian Airborne Div. 28 Jun 45 under command 16th AGRA, reverts to 123rd Fd Regt. 1 Dec 45 amalgamated with 3rd Mtn Regt. RA.

Unit/CO	Batteries	Remarks
129th Fd Regt (Lowland) Lt Col JHE de Robeck Lt Col CFJ Younger Lt Col JA Stevens	311th, 312th and 493rd Fd Btys	10 Aug 42 arrived Bombay, moved to Ranchi to join 70th British Div, 24x25-pdrs. 21 Nov 42 moved Chittagong to join 14th Indian Div for First Arakan. 10 Jan 43 to Imphal joined 17th Indian Div. 8 Dec 43 to Tiddim and Kennedy Peak operations. 4 Apr 44 with 5th Indian Div at Kohima and Imphal. Fired 52,091 rounds in Apr-Jun 44. 26 Oct 44 311th Bty carried out firing trials from landing craft. 31 Jan 45 in the Imphal-Palel area with 17th Indian Div. 18 Feb 45 crossed Irrawaddy. Fired 11, 721 rounds in March 45. 3 May 45 at Pegu.
130th Fd Regt (Lowland) Lt Col RG Price Lt Col RC Laughton Lt Col RAG Nicholson Lt Col JS Wilkins Lt Col GG Peel Lt Col JDC Thompson Lt Col DCB MacQueen Lt Col W Hanwell	315th, 316th and 494th Fd Btys	31 May 42 arrived India, to Comilla to join 55th Indian Inf Bde at Chittagong. Jan 43 Battle of Donbaik with 14th Indian Div. Oct 43 315th and 316th Btys had 25-pdrs, 494th and 455th (Indep) Btys had 3.7-in hows. Nov 44 455th Bty left regt, which moved to join 36th Indian Div. May 45 flew to Poona. Moved to Secunderabad, all guns were 25 prs.
134th Fd Regt (East Anglian) Lt Col RW Andrews Lt Col CJG Dalton Lt Col DW Neilson Lt Col TED Kelly	213th, 340th and 498th Fd Btys	8 Apr 42 arrived Bombay. Moved to join 19th Indian Div at Bangalore. 15 Jul 43 as jungle field regiment, moved to Deolali. 1 Oct 44 became 134th Medium Regt.
135th Fd Regt (East Anglian) (Herts Yeomanry) Lt Col PJD Toosey	336th, 344th and 499th Fd Btys	2 Feb 42 arrived Singapore with 18th British Div, joining 11th Indian Div. 15 Feb 42 lost at Singapore.
136th Fd Regt (1st West Lancashire) Lt Col OP Wagstaff Lt Col GP Armstrong Lt Col GMH Chaldecot Lt Col JC Rowlandson Maj JF Daykin	347th, 348th and 500th Fd Btys	18 Mar 43 arrived Bombay, moved Ahmednagar. May 43 joined 7th Indian Div. Oct 43-May 44 Second Arakan 24x25-pdrs. Jun-Oct 44 Ranchi. Oct-Dec 44 Kohima. Jan-Mar 45 advance to Allanmyo. Jun-Oct 45 Sittang River operations. 18 Oct 45-15 Jan 46 Siam. 18 Jan 46. Malaya. Disbanded 17 Apr 46.
137th Fd Regt (2nd West Lancashire) Lt Col GD Holme	349th, 350 and 501st Fd Btys	Arrived Singapore 28 Nov 41. 15 Feb 42 lost at Singapore.
139th Fd Regt (4th London) Lt Col HCB Hall Lt Col BC Wells	362nd, 364th and 503rd Fd Btys	17 Oct 42 arrived Bombay. Moved Nowshera and joined 17th Indian Div. 15 Jul 43 Reorganised as jungle field regt, mortars and 3.7 hows. 6 May 44 flew from Sylhet to Ranchi. 5 Oct 44 Kohima 24x25-pdrs.

Unit/CO	Batteries	Remarks
145th Fd Regt (Berkshire Yeomanry) Lt Col ML Wroughton Lt Col RLT Burges	395th, 396th and 509th Fd Btys	24 Feb 45 arrived Bombay. To Dehra Dun to join 39th Indian Div. 22 Jun 45 to Poona to join 36th Indian Div. 17 Jul 45 to Bangalore to join 26th Indian Div. 10 Aug 45 to Cocanada to join 25th Indian Div. Sep 45 to Malaya. 3 Dec 45 to Java.
148th Field Regiment (Bedfordshire Yeomanry) Lt Col SW Harris	419th, 420th and 512th Field Batteries	28 Dec 41 arrived Bombay. 8 Feb 42 arrived Singapore with 18th British Div. 15 Feb lost at Singapore.
155th (Lanarkshire Yeomanry) Fd Regt Lt Col A Murdoch	A, B and C Fd Btys	5 May 41 arrived Bombay. Moved to Kirkee. 3 Sep 41 moved to Malaya, leaving 'A' Bty behind to form 160th Fd Regt. Joined 11th Indian Div. Had 16x4.5-in hows. Fought throughout Malaya in particular at Slim River and Singapore. 15 Feb 42 lost at Singapore.
158th Fd Regt Lt Col DJ Steevens Lt Col LS Gallager Lt Col AJ Daniell Lt Col JFG Gurney Lt Col CT Hackett Lt Col JCH Mead Lt Col DEB Watson	A and B Fd Btys later became 581st, 582nd and 583rd Fd Btys	10 Jan 41 formed at Nowshera with 18x3.7-in hows and 8x18-pdrs. Nov 41 re-equipped with 25-pdrs. Mar 42 moved to Ranchi. 29 May 42 moved to Manipur Road with 23rd Indian Div. 11 Oct 42 'R' Bty formed as third battery. New bty numbers adopted. Reorganised as jungle field regt. 29 Feb 44 moved to Kabaw Valley with 1st Indian Inf Bde. Mar 44 Battle Sangshak. 26 casualties. Mortars destroyed. Oct 44 moved to Shillong then Bombay with 23rd Indian Div. 8 Jul 45 Moved to Poona with 36th British Div. 15 Feb 46 regt disbanded.
159th Fd Regt Lt Col Lamb Lt Col Ripley Lt Col Archdale Lt Col Powell-Brett	A and B Fd Btys, later became 553rd, 554th and 555th Fd Btys	1 Apr 41 Formed in India. 29 Oct 41 To Iraq. 11 Jul 44 Returned Bombay. Moved to Bangalore to 26th Indian Div. 20 Jan 45 became 159th Parachute Light Regt with 44th Indian Airborne Div. 9 Jun 45 At Bilaspur with US 75mm Pack Hows.
160th Fd Regt Lt Col AFJ Sugden Lt Col JF Williams-Wynne Lt Col DD Angus Lt Col IA Neish	A, B and C Fd Btys, later became 584th, 585th and 586th Fd Btys	Jun 41 formed from 'A' Bty 155th Fd Regt at Jhansi. Mar 42 absorbed 161st Fd Regt and moved to Ranchi joined 14th Indian Div. 5 Apr 43 moved to Calcutta then to 1st Arakan. Sep 43 Converted to jungle field regt. 5 Feb 44 formed 4x25-pr troops for Chindit operations. 11 Feb 44 moved to Bawli Bazar with 585th and 586th Btys. 'DD' Special Duties Field Battery landed with Chindits. 1 Jan 45 at Chittagong. Moved to Ramree Island. 21 May 45 At Ranchi.
178th Fd Regt Lt Col KM Wright Lt Col RJ Shaw-Hamilton Lt Col FG Wintle	122nd, 366th and 516th Fd Btys	13 Jun 43 arrived Bombay. To 33rd Indian Corps. 1 Aug 43 redesignated 178th Assault Fd Regt, 122nd Bty given 8x105mm SP Priests, 366th Bty given 6x3.7-in hows. 9 Apr 44 with 25th Indian Div, moved to 36th Indian Div at Shillong. 6 May 45 flew to Imphal. 15 May 45 arrived Poona. Joined 23rd Indian Div at Nasik. 3 Oct 45 arrived Java. Sep 46 disbanded at Batavia.

Unit/CO	Batteries	Remarks
208th (SP) Fd Regt Lt Col DDC Tulloch Lt Col PGN T-C-Worsley	607th and 608th Fd Btys	1 Apr 45 formed from 88th Medium Regt at Ranchi. 24 Jul 45 moved to Bombay with 23rd Indian Div. 1 Feb 46 moved to Meerut.
	455th (Independent) Light Bty RA	Oct 43 Under command 130th Field Regt in 36th Indian Div. Jan 45 redesignated 24th Med Bty at Ranchi and joined 88th Med Regt RA.
	601st Fd Bty	Oct 44 In Ceylon with 22nd (EA) Inf Bde. Mar 45 Ceylon Army Command.

MEDIUM ARTILLERY

Unit/CO	Batteries	Remarks
1st Med Regt Lt Col WC Grant Lt Col TAH Coltman Lt Col DG Lean Lt Col RAH Soames	1/3rd and 5/22nd Med Btys	27 Jul 42 arrived Bombay thence Bangalore with 5.5s. 4 Mar 44 in action at Waybin with 36th Indian Div. 12 May 44 1/3rdBty to 25 Indian Div. 20 May 44 regiment less 1/3rd Battery to Dimapur. 12 Jun 44. 1/3rd Bty returned. To 20th Indian Div. at Imphal. Nov 44 with 11th (EA) Division, 16x5.5-inch guns. 22 Dec 44 Crossed Chindwin. Regt less 1/3rd Battery with 19th Indian Div, 1/3rd Battery, less 'A' Troop with 20th Indian Div. 'A' Troop with 2nd British Div. 28 Jun 45 regt arrived in Rangoon.
6th Med Regt Lt Col WG Fox Lt Col PJW Wells	18th (Quebec), 19th (Niagara) and 245th Med Btys	3 Sep 39 stationed at Delhi. Apr 41. 19th Bty left for Iraq. 12 Mar 42 moved to Ranchi with 23rd Indian Div. 2 Oct 43 arrived Chittagong with 26th Indian Div. 23 Feb 44 245th Bty renamed 19th Bty. 20 Oct 44 to Arakan under 15th Indian Corps.15 Dec 44 received 2x7.2-in hows 'Uncle' and 'Auntie'. 3 May 45 arrived Rangoon. 8 Jun 45 at Secunderabad with 59th AGRA.
8th Med Regt Lt Col S Simmons Lt Col HB Jolly Lt Col TAH Coltman Lt Col GM Mackinlay	245th, 246th and 247th Med Btys. 245th Bty transferred to 6th Medium Regt in early 42.	Oct 41. Formed at Quetta in Sept 41 with 6-inch hows, in Ranchi by Mar 42. 29 May 43 Bangalore with 5.5-in guns. Dec 43 at Imphal under 4th Indian Corps. 4 Feb 44 at Tamu, 246th Bty reached Kennedy Peak. Apr 44 246th Bty with 23rd and 5th Indian Divs. 247th Bty with 20th Indian Div. 18 Sep 44 at Tiddim. 21 Feb 45 regt crosses Irrawaddy. To Meiktila. 16x5.5-inch guns and 247th Bty also had 2x7.2-inch hows manned by 67th HAA Regt. 31 Oct 45 personnel posted to 1 Med Regt and 8 Med Regt was formally disbanded at Rangoon on 1 Feb 46.
85th Med Regt Lt Col HL Lister Lt Col FWJ Robinson	157th and 158th Med Btys	1 Aug 44 Formed from 53rd (City of London) HAA Regt at Poona. 2 Sep 44 arrived Secunderabad under 9th AA Bde. 23 Dec 44 arrived Ranchi. 25 May 45 with 59th AGRA.
86th Med Regt Lt Col RH Fielding-Mould Lt Col WD Tarr	165th and 201st Med Btys	1 Jul 44 formed from 56th (Cornwall) HAA Regt at Poona with 9th AA Bde. 23 Dec 44 at Ranchi. 25 May 45 To 59th AGRA. Oct 45 Regt moved to Malaya. 1 Jun 46 Regt disbanded.

Unit/CO	Batteries	Remarks
87th Med Regt Lt Col RJ Kirton Lt Col JR Stanton Lt Col DS Thomson Maj LI King	63rd and 70th Med Btys	1 Aug 44 Formed from 63rd and 70th HAA Regts at Poona. To 9th AA Bde. 28 Dec 44 arrived Ranchi. 30 Mar 45 arrived Kohima. 63rd Bty to 19th then 17th then 7th Indian Div. 25 Jan 46 Regt moved to Ranchi. All men posted to 160th Fd Regt.
88th Med Regt	23rd and 24th Med Btys	15 Nov 44 formed at Ranchi. 455th Indep Light Bty joined and became 24th Medium Battery. 1 Apr 45 converted to 208th (SP) Fd Regt.
134th (East Anglian) Med Regt Lt Col TED Kelly Lt Col C Collingwood Lt Col KM Wright	340th and 498th Med Btys	1 Oct 44 formed Deolali from 134th Fd Regt. Dec 44 received 6-in hows and 4x25-pdrs. 6 Feb 45 at Palel under 33rd Indian Corps. 8 Feb 45 at Shwebo under 19th Indian Div, 340th Bty at Singu, then Kindaw crossing Irrawaddy at Wetto with 16x6-inch hows. 15-20 Mar 45 498th Bty breaches walls of Fort Dufferin at Mandalay at 400 yards range. 11 Apr 45 regt less 340th Bty under command 2nd British Div. 4 May 45 regt had 226th HAA Bty, one tp 3.7-in hows and one section 7.2-in hows. 9 May 45 regt complete at Magwe. Flown to Chittagong. 2 Jul 45 At Ranchi. Hands over 5.5s to 14th Indian HAA Regt and receives 3x6-inch hows from 85th Med Regt.

LAA AND ANTI-TANK ARTILLERY

Unit/CO	Batteries	Remarks
21st LAA Regt Lt Col MDS Saunders	48th, 69th and 79th LAA Btys	4 Feb 42 arrived Batavia, Java. 10 Mar 42 guns destroyed, regt captured.
23rd LAA Regt Lt Col GD Holmes Lt Col TWR Hill Lt Col The Hon VHO Herbert Lt Col VE Le Marchant	73rd, 74th and 130th LAA Btys	1 Jul 42 arrived Colombo under 24th AA Bde. 31 Mar 44 at Secunderabad. To 44th Indian Airborne Div as 23rd Parachute LAA Regt. 10 Jun 45 moved to Bilaspur.
24th LAA/A/Tk Regt Lt Col RJ Kirton Lt Col RB Cole	205th and 284th A/Tk Btys (From 82nd A/Tk Regt) and 86th and 491st LAA Btys (From 24th LAA Regt). Later had 86th, 205th & 284th A/Tk Btys only	Jan 42 arrived India. Moved to Calcutta. 26 Sep 43 arrived Chittagong with 7th Indian Div. 11 Nov 43 arrived Ranchi. 1 Sep 44 Reorganised as A/Tk regt with 86th, 205th and 284th A/Tk Btys with 36x6-pdrs & 36x3-in mortars. 10 Oct 44 Kohima with 7th Indian Div. 6 May 45 Moved Magwe to Chittagong and then to Quetta. Oct 45 sailed for UK.
28th LAA Regt Lt Col DW Bannister Lt Col JSC Coates Lt Col AG Brown Lt Col AW Hall Maj GW Jago	106th, 112th and 250th LAA Btys	10 Mar 42 arrived Bombay. 17 May 42 Moved to Calcutta-Manipur Road-Imphal, under 4th Indian Corps. 31 Dec 43 received SP Bofors. 17 Sep 44 to Ranchi. 25 Jan 45 at Imphal with 17th Indian Div. 31 May 45 at Pegu. Jun at Rangoon.

Unit/CO	Batteries	Remarks
33rd LAA Regt, later became 33rd A/Tk Regt Lt Col EA Howard Lt Col AW Woodrooffe Lt Col CL Overton Lt Col JW Wilson Lt Col DR Ledward	67th, 68th and 132nd LAA Btys with 78th, 274th and 275th A/Tk Btys	20 May 42 arrived Bombay. Moved to Madras to 13th AA Brigade. 6 Aug 43 reorganised into LAA/A/Tk Regt with 67th and 68th LAA and 274th and 525th A/Tk Btys. (The latter from 69th A/Tk Regt). 1 Sep 44 reorganised into A/Tk Regt with 78th, 274th and 275th A/Tk Btys. Moved to Imphal to join 19th Indian Div with 36x6-pdrs & 36x3-in mortars. 5 Oct 45 returned to UK and disbanded.
35th LAA Regt Lt Col HJ Bassett	78th, 89th and 144th LAA Btys	13 Jan 42 landed at Singapore. Jan 42 78th Bty and two troops 89th Bty to Java where captured in Mar 42. 15 Feb regiment less 78th Bty and two troops 89th Bty were lost at Singapore.
36th LAA Regt Lt Col PA Brooke Lt Col JC Lawrence Lt Col JS Pearsall	97th, 128th and 266th LAA Btys	12 Aug 42 arrived Bombay from UK. Moved to Ranchi. 4 May 43 moved to Arakan with 26th Indian Div. Jun 43 Chittagong under 13th AA Bde. Dec 43 under 15th Indian Corps with SP Bofors. 31 Jan 45 at Akyab. To Kyaukpyu. Jun 45 at Madras. Aug. Sailed for UK.
43rd LAA Regt Lt Col W Baldwin-Fletcher Lt Col FHB Jenkin	147th, 148th and 264th LAA Btys	4 Mar 42 arrived Colombo to 23rd AA Bde. Sep 43 to 24th AA Bde. 264th Bty to 13th AA Bde at Chittagong. Jan 45 Regiment disbands in Ceylon.
44th LAA Regt Lt Col FW Bancroft Lt Col RM Byers Lt Col RM Gibb	75th, 91st and 239th LAA Btys	24 Jul 42 arrived Bombay, to Delhi then Calcutta with 239th Bty to Chittagong. Jun 43 at Ranchi. 54x40mm Bofors. Sep 44 Imphal then Tamu and Kaleywa. Jan 45 at Yeu, crossed Irrawaddy Mar 45. 36x40mm Bofors. Jun 45 at Meiktila then Pegu.
48th LAA Regt Lt Col SR Pearson	95th and 202nd LAA Btys	Jan 42 landed Batavia. Mar 42 lost in Java.
55th LAA Regt Lt Col AE Hunt Lt Col JM Kerr Lt Col SCC Sewell Lt Col GF Wicks Lt Col WJ Landells	163rd, 164th and 165th LAA Btys. Later 165th, 203rd and 290th A/Tk Btys	4 Mar 42 arrived Colombo joined 1st RM AA Bde. 29 Jul 43 Calcutta, reorganised as LAA/A/Tk regt. 165th and 524th LAA and 203rd and 290th A/Tk Btys, the latter from 56th A/Tk Regt. 16 Dec 43 arrived Tamu, destroyed 4 Jap tanks. 29 May 44 in the Artillery Box at Bishenpur. Destroyed 12 enemy aircraft, 4 possibles. 17 Jul 44 reorganised as A/Tk regt with 165th, 203rd and 290th A/Tk Btys. Sep 44. Renamed 111th A/Tk Regt. With 20th Indian Div.
56th A/Tk Regt Lt Col BH Palmer Lt Col KP Hardinge-Carter Lt Col The Hon DA Balfour Lt Col PJF Parsons Lt Col DBJ McTurk Lt Col H Pullen	203rd, 221st, 222nd and 290th A/Tk Btys. Later 163rd, 221st & 222nd Btys	9 Mar 42 arrived Bombay, to Ahmednagar to join 70th British Div. Apr 43 had mixture of 2-pdrs, 6-pdrs and 57mm guns. Aug 43 reorganised as LAA/A/Tk regt with 55th LAA Regt with 163rd and 164th LAA and 221st and 222nd A/Tk Btys. Oct 43 arrived Chittagong. Apr 44 to Dimapur. Aug 44 reorganised as A/Tk regt with 163rd, renamed 351st and 221st and 222nd A/Tk Btys. Each battery had mortar troop. 36x6-pdrs & 36x3-in mortars. In 7th Indian Div. 17 May 45 at Rangoon. 30 Jun 45 at Ranchi. Reorganised as SP A/Tk regt. Dec 45 disbanded at Ranchi.

Unit/CO	Batteries	Remarks
59th LAA Regt Lt Col S Atkinson Lt Col BLE Hebert Lt Col MB Jennings Lt Col RM Byers Lt Col E Vaughan-Jones	179th, 183rd and 184th LAA Btys	9 Apr 42 arrived Bombay. Moved to Calcutta. 23 May 43 at Bandra with 36th Indian Div. 17 Jul 43 at Ahmednagar under 2nd British Div. 4 Dec 43 To Nira under 1st RM AA Bde. 16 Jun 44 Poona. 24 Oct 44 disbanded.
60th LAA Regt Lt Col SA Yorke Lt Col FHB Jenkin Lt Col D Terry	180th, 181st and 187th LAA Btys	8 Apr 42 arrived Bombay, to 13th AA Bde. 14 Jan 43 180th Bty to Arakan, regt less 180th Bty to Ahmednagar to join 2nd British Div. 17 Jul 43 regt complete at Bombay. Remained India. 27 Sep 44 disbanded Poona.
69th Anti-Tank Regt (Duke of Connaught's - Hampshire) Lt Col JS Wilkins Lt Col BD Anderson	274th, 275th, 285th and 292nd Anti-Tank Batteries	19 May 42 arrived Bombay, moved to Bangalore with 32x2-pr Portees, with 19th Indian Div. 6 Aug 43. Reorganised as LAA/A/Tk regiment with 285th and 292nd LAA and 132nd and 523rd A/Tk Btys. 6 Aug 43joined 70th British Div, converted to Long Range Penetration role, combined with 51st Fd Regt to form 9th and 10th Columns. 31 Jan 44 to Burma with 16th Bde. 17 May 44 at Bangalore. Disbanded Oct 44.
69th LAA Regt Lt Col TH Du Boulay Lt Col HW Hunter Lt Col P Cox	206th, 207th and 267th LAA Btys	10 May 42 arrived Bombay. Moved to Delhi. Received 36x40mm, joined 9th AA Bde. Oct 42 trials with Bofors on an elephant! Sep 43 new establishment of 54x40mm. 2 Feb 44 reorganised to 4x6-gun troops for Chindit operations. 31 Jul 44 regt at Imphal with 4th Indian Corps. 206th Bty had 18x40mm SP Bofors and 207th & 267th Btys had 18xMk1 Bofors each. 27 Apr 45 At Monywa. Flown to Ranchi. Under 59th AGRA. 21 Aug 45 embarked at Madras for UK.
76th LAA Regt Lt Col DE Jones Lt Col RJ Cockwell Major EV Proffitt	226th, 227th and 228th LAA Btys	28 May 42 arrived Colombo. Jan 45 regt disbanded.
77th LAA Regt Lt Col JC Lawrence Lt Col FJC Rybot	269th, 270th and 286th LAA Btys	7 Jul 42 arrived Bombay, moved to Barrackpore. 14 Oct 42 moved to Comilla. 1 Jan 43 To Chittagong under 13th AA Bde. 12 Nov 44 regt disbanded.
78th LAA Regt Lt Col The Hon DA Balfour Lt Col AL Murphy	143rd, 236th and 241st LAA Btys	9 Aug 42 arrived Bombay, moved to Secunderabad. 28 Mar 43 to Imphal to 33rd Indian Corps. 14 Nov 44 regt disbanded.
79th A/Tk Regt Lt Col HW Clarke	103rd, 104th and 105th A/Tk Btys	15 Oct 41 formed in India. 23 Mar 42 to Iraq.
80th A/Tk Regt Lt Col WES Napier	2nd (Minden), 215th, 272nd and 273rd A/Tk Btys	7 Dec 41 in 11th Indian Division in Malaya. 15 Feb 42 lost at Singapore.

Unit/CO	Batteries	Remarks
82nd A/Tk Regt Lt Col GP Chapman Lt Col JRS Thompson	205th, 228th, 276th and 284th A/Tk Btys. Later 87th, 228th and 276th Btys.	9 Jan 42 arrived Bombay, moved to Jhansi with 48x2 prs. 30 Mar 42 at Ranchi. Jun moved to Imphal and 17th Indian Div. 26 Nov 42 converted to LAA/A/Tk, with 87th & 88th LAA Btys from 24th LAA Regt and 205th & 284th A/Tk Btys. 25 May 43 at Shillong. 13 Nov 43 at Imphal and Tiddim. Much action. 26 Sep 44 at Ranchi. Reorganised as A/Tk Regt. 16 Jan 45 at Imphal. 21 Feb 45 crossed Irrawaddy, moved to Meiktila. 1 Apr 45 reorganised with three troops of 3-inch mortars; 36x6-pdrs & 36x3-in mortars. Moved to Pyawbwe, then Pegu. 28 Jun 45 regt disbanded.
85th A/Tk Regt Lt Col AJ Lardner-Clarke	45th, 251st, 270th and 281st A/Tk Btys	8 Feb 42 with 11th Indian Division in Singapore. 15 Feb 42 lost at Singapore.
100th A/Tk Regt (Gordon Highlanders) Lt Col RFW Johnston Lt Col SF Evans Lt Col DB Anderson Lt Col IA Campbell Lt Col Cumberledge Lt Col AM Milne	168th, 169th, 170th & 321st A/Tk Btys, later 169th, 170th & 401st Btys	17 Mar 43 arrived Bombay, joined 2nd British Div. 30 Nov 43 reorganised as LAA/A/Tk regt with 169th & 170th A/Tk and 401st & 525th LAA Btys. May 44. 169th & 170th had 3-in Mortars. 8 Apr 45 flew from Myingyan to Chittagong and then Calcutta with 36x6-pdrs & 36x3-in mortars. Jun 45 at Ranchi, converting to SP 57mm in half-tracks.
111th A/Tk Regt (previously 55th A/Tk Regt) Lt Col WJ Landells Lt Col LWG Jenkins	165th, 203rd and 290th A/Tk Btys	1 Sep 44 redesignated from 55th A/Tk Regt. With 20th Indian Div. Apr 45 165th Bty appears to have been re-numbered 524th. 36x6-pdrs & 36x3-in mortars. Apr-May 45 sank Jap boats on the Irrawaddy. Jul 45 disbanded.
118th LAA Regt Lt Col T Haighton	387th 388th and 389th LAA Btys	11 Apr 43 arrived Bombay, to Bangalore. 54x40mm. To Tezpur, under 9th AA Bde. 31 Aug 44 disbanded.
122nd LAA Regt (The Royal Warwickshire Regiment) Lt Col CD Oliver Lt Col JW Calver	400th, 401st and 402nd LAA Btys Later 168th and 321st A/Tk Btys	10 Jun 43 arrived in India. Reorganised as 400th & 402nd LAA and 168th & 321st A/Tk Btys, latter from 100th A/Tk Regt. Mar 44 168th Bty to Arakan with 130th Fd Regt. 19 May 44 to Shillong, reorganised as A/Tk/Mortar regt. 30 Dec 44 at Katha. 10 Apr 45 at Maymo, then Meiktila, then Imphal. 15 May 45 at Poona. Aug 45 with 36th Indian Div in 15th Indian Corps.
125th A/Tk Regt Lt Col J Dean	A, B, C & D A/Tk Btys	8 Feb 42 in Singapore. 15 Feb 42 lost at Singapore.
	'A' Battery 95th A/Tk Regt RA Major RA Hemelryk	Had 3 troops each of 4x2-pounders. 21 Feb 42 arrived Rangoon with 7th Armoured Bde from ME. 10 May 42 All equipment destroyed at Shwegyin. 23 Sep 43. Sailed to rejoin its regt in Basra.

MOUNTAIN ARTILLERY

Unit/CO	Batteries	Remarks
3rd Mountain Regt Lt Col JSW Tremenheere	453rd, 454th and 475th Mtn Btys	28 Jun 45 arrived Bombay. 1 Dec 45 personnel posted to 123rd Fd Regt RA and regt disbanded 1 Jan 46.

HEAVY ARTILLERY

Unit/CO	Batteries	Remarks
55th Heavy Regt Lt Col CG Richards	26th, 27th, 29th and 30th Hy Btys	29 Jun 45 arrived at Bombay with 7.2-inch hows. 25 Jul 45 arrived Akanapet, Hyderabad State. Jul 46 disbanded.

SURVEY ARTILLERY

Unit/CO	Batteries	Remarks
1st Survey Regt Lt Col CT Beckett Lt Col AK Matthews Lt Col RWC Cawthorne Lt Col L Kellett Lt Col EJ Ramus	41st and 42nd Survey Btys	21 Sep 44 arrived Bombay, moved to Ranchi. 19 Jan 45 41st Bty to 4th Indian Corps and 42nd Bty to 7th Indian Div. 5 Aug 45 At Pegu, then Toungoo. 29 Sep 45 to 12th Army.
2nd Survey Regt Lt Col DN Morgan Lt Col G Kellett Lt Col SHA Pilkington Lt Col GP Pirie-Gordon	'A' Survey Bty & 'B' Flash Spotting Bty (43rd and 44th Survey Btys)	10 Jun 43 arrived Bombay and went to Deolali. 5 Aug 43 at Ranchi, to 15th Indian Corps. 4 Feb 44 now 43rd and 44th Svy Btys. 6 Nov 44 moved to Arakan. 21 Jan 45 43rd Bty to Akyab and 44th Bty to Ramree Island to join 26th Indian Div. 2 May 45 43rd Bty in Rangoon, 44th Bty at Ranchi. 29 Jul 45 regt in South India with 34th Indian Corps.

HEAVY ANTI-AIRCRAFT ARTILLERY

Unit/CO	Batteries	Remarks
3rd HAA Regt Lt Col FE Hugonin	11th, 29th and 30th HAA Btys	3 Sep 39 stationed at Singapore. 7 Dec 41 part of Changi Fire Command. 15 Feb 42 lost at Singapore.
5th HAA Regt Lt Col FD Field	7th HAA Bty RA and 17th and 18th HAA Btys HK-S RA	3 Sep 39 stationed at Hong Kong and on 25 Dec 41 lost there.
6th HAA Regt Lt Col GWG Baass	3rd, 12th and 15th HAA Btys	13 Jan 42 arrived Singapore. 30 Jan 42 to Java, less 3rd Bty. 14 Feb 42 3rd Bty lost at Singapore. 25 Mar 42 regt, less 3rd Bty, lost in Java.
8th (Belfast) HAA Regt Lt Col F Dearden Lt Col JWP Saunders Lt Col JG Cunningham	21st, 22nd and 23rd HAA Btys	28 Jul 42 arrived Bombay with 24x3.7-in Mk III AA guns. Aug 42 in Calcutta with 1st Indian AA Bde. 1 Jan 43 with 14th Indian Div at First Arakan. 13 Nov 43 to 15th Indian Corps. 5 Feb 44 'B' Troop in 7th Indian Div Box. 9 May 44 At Ranchi, then to Second Arakan. 23 Dec 44 supplied two 7.2-in how detachments to 6th Med Regt. 31 Jan 45 at Akyab. Apr 45 left for Calcutta then Madras, under 34th Indian Div. Aug 45 sailed for UK.

Unit/CO	Batteries	Remarks
52nd HAA Regt Lt Col F Hevey Lt Col JH Gale Lt Col LA Hope	155th, 159th and 271st HAA Btys	28 May 42 arrived Colombo. 154th Bty transferred to 56th HAA Regt and 159th HAA Bty transferred from 53rd HAA Regt. 3 Dec 44t at Chittagong. Moved to Kalemyo to join 14th Army. 24x3.7-inch HAA guns. 31 Jan 45 At Shwebo, took over 2x7.2-in hows from 67th HAA Regt. Passed to 4th Indian Corps. 17 Aug 45 at Rangoon.
53rd (City of London) HAA Regt Lt Col HL Lister	157th, 158th and 159th HAA Btys	1 May 42 arrived Bombay with 24 Static 3.7-in guns. Less 159th Bty moved to Calcutta to join 1st Indian AA Bde. 159th Bty joined 52nd HAA Regt in Ceylon and 202nd HAA Bty from 56th HAA Regt joined. Converted to mobile 3.7-inch guns. Moved to Nira under 9th AA Bde. 18 Jun 44 at Poona. Became 85th Med Regt and 202nd HAA Bty rejoined 56th HAA Regt.
54th (City of London) HAA Regt Lt Col JA Morton	160th, 161st and 312th HAA Btys	9 Jul 42 arrived Colombo with 24x3.7-in static AA guns. At Trincomalee. 4 May 43 sailed to Suez.
56th (Cornwall) HAA Regt Lt Col J Daniel	165th, 201st and 202nd HAA Btys	4 Mar 42 arrived Bombay, moved to Madras. 4 Apr 42 202nd Bty to join 53rd HAA Regt. 1 Jul 44 reorganised and redesignated 86 Med Regt.
63rd (Northumbrian) HAA Regt Lt Col CH Wright Major PS Mackey	177th, 178th and 269th HAA Btys	29 Jul 42 arrived Colombo. To 1st RM AA Brigade. 24 Apr 44. Jubbulpore. 1 Aug 44 placed in SA and the remaining personnel reorganised into 63 Med Bty which went to 87 Med Regt.
65th HAA Regt Lt Col WA MacLellan	181st, 183rd and 196th HAA Btys	15Mar 42 arrived Colombo. 4 May 43 sailed for Middle East.
66th (Leeds Rifles) HAA Regt Lt Col JH Gale	184th, 185th and 296th HAA Btys	11 May 42 arrived Bombay, 24x 3.7-inch static AA guns. To Calcutta under 1st Indian AA Bde. Jan 43 Manipur Road area. By Jul at Digboi. 1 Apr 45 placed in SA.
67th (York and Lancaster) HAA Regt Lt Col HHM Oliver Lt Col JR Stanton Lt Col LA Hope	187th, 188th and 189th HAA Btys	1 Jan 42 arrived Bombay, moved to Manipur Road less 189th Bty which went to Imphal. All under 9th AA Bde. 26 Jan 44 under 4th Indian Corps at Seijang. Sep 44 all equipment handed over to 1st (WA) HAA Regt. Became infantry under 4th Corps. 24 Nov 44 received 2x7.2-inch hows. Later received 16x3.7-inch AA mobile guns. 1 Jan 45 resumed AA role. Moved to Kaw. 2 Feb 45 189th Bty to 17th Indian Div at Pauk. Bty crossed Irrawaddy and went to Meiktila. 17 May 45 flew to India.
70th (3rd West Lancs) HAA Regt Lt Col EF Carne Lt Col RP Napper Lt Col HW Hawkins Lt Col RJ Kirton	211th, 212th and 216th HAA Btys	11 May 42 arrived Bombay, moved to Madras. 27 Mar 43 to Calcutta under 1st Indian AA Bde. 10 Nov 43 to Chittagong under 13th AA Bde. 14 May 44 to Piska. Jun 44 disbanded at Piska, the remaining personnel being reorganised into 70 Med Bty which went to 87 Med Regt.
77th HAA Regt Lt Col JR Stanton	155th, 240th and 241st HAA Btys	Jan 42 arrived at Batavia. Mar 42 lost in Java.

Unit/CO	Batteries	Remarks
95th (Birmingham) HAA Regt Lt Col K Hargreaves Lt Col AG Godefroy	204th, 293rd and 340th HAA Btys	11 Apr 42 arrived Bombay, moved to Calcutta under 1st Indian AA Brigade. 1 Apr 43 disbanded.
101st HAA Regt Lt Col HV Kerr Lt Col J Green Major HE Ruddock	226th, 297th and 379th HAA Bty	1 Jul 43 arrived Bombay, moved to Avadi under 3rd Indian AA Brigade. 226th and 297th Btys were mobile, 379th was static. 27 Sep 44 at Imphal under 33rd Indian Corps. 'A' Troop 226th Bty took over 4x7.2-in hows. 31 Dec 44 at Kalewa in ground role. Jan-Jul 45 Fired 15,550 rounds 3.7-in and 2,000 rounds 7.2-in. 1 Sep 45 disbanded at Rangoon.
	313rd HAA Bty	Oct 44 with 13th British AA Bde at Feni.

COAST ARTILLERY

Unit/CO	Batteries	Remarks
6th Coast Regt Lt Col AJ Godfrey	15th, 18th Coast and 14th AA Btys	3 Sep 39 stationed in Ceylon. Nov 43 462nd and 463rd Coast Btys formed. Jun 44 464th AA Bty formed with 5.25-inch AA/Coast guns. Oct 44 at Colombo.
7th Coast Regt Lt Col HD StG Cardew	11th and 31st Coast Btys	3 Sep 39 stationed Singapore in Faber Fire Command. 15 Feb 42 lost at Singapore.
8th Coast Regt Lt Col S Shaw	12th, 30th and 36th Coast Btys	3 Sep 39 stationed at Hong Kong. 25 Dec 41 lost there.
9th Coast Regt Lt Col CP Heath	7th, 22nd and 32nd Coast Btys	3 Sep 39 stationed Singapore in Changi Fire Command. 15 Feb 42 lost at Singapore.
10th Mobile Coast Regt, later 16th Defence Regt Lt Col MSH Maxwell-Gumbleton	10th RA and 21 and 22 HK-S RA Mobile Coast Btys, later 966th RA and 967th and 968th HK-S RA Defence Btys	15 Oct 1939 formed as 10 Mobile Coast Regt. 24 Feb 41 became 16 Defence Regt. Manned 18-pr guns for beach defence of Singapore Island. 15 Feb 42 lost at Singapore.
11th Coast Regt Lt Col ML More	8th Coast and 20th HAA (HK-S RA) Btys	3 Sep 39 stationed Penang. 18 Dec 41 Penang evacuated and personnel moved to Singapore and posted to coast btys.
12th Coast Regt Lt Col RJL Penfold	20th and 24th Coast Btys	3 Sep 39 stationed at Hong Kong. 25 Dec 41 lost there.

AIR OBSERVATION POST

Unit/CO	Batteries	Remarks
	No. 656 Squadron RAF Major DW Coyle	Jan 44 joined SEAC. Operational under HQ 14th Army. Malaya.

MARITIME ARTILLERY

Unit/CO	Batteries	Remarks
2nd Regt Maritime Arty Lt Col RJ Longfield	10th Bty. Absorbed into 2nd Regt in Mar 45.	Sep 43 10th Bty MRA established Bombay. Mar 45 HQ 2nd Regt MRA established at Bombay and absorbed 8 officers and 480 men of 10th Bty. Then absorbed Maritime RA Detachments throughout the area. 31 Dec 45 disbanded at Shoeburyness.

DEFENCE REGIMENT

Unit/CO	Batteries	Remarks
16th Defence Regt. See 10 Mobile Coast Regt above.	965th Bty in Hong Kong Maj BCT Forrester	3 Sep 39 stationed at Hong Kong with 18-pounders for beach defence. 25 Dec 41 Bty lost at Hong Kong.

SEARCHLIGHT REGIMENT

Unit/CO	Batteries	Remarks
5th Searchlight Regt Lt Col RAO Clarke	13th and 14th Searchlight Btys	13 May 41 formed in Malaya. 7 Dec 41 In Changi Fire Command, Singapore. 15 Feb 42 lost at Singapore.
	315th Searchlight Bty	Oct 44 Under command of 23rd AA Bde Ceylon.
	405th Searchlight Bty	Oct 44 Under command of 23rd AA Bde Ceylon.

COUNTER-MORTAR BATTERIES

Unit/CO	Batteries	Remarks
	31st Counter-Mortar Bty	Jun 45 In India
	32nd Counter-Mortar Bty	Jun 45 In India.
	33rd Counter-Mortar Bty	Jun 45 In India.
	34th Counter-Mortar Bty	Jun 45 In India.
	45th Counter-Mortar Bty	Jun 45 In India.

HONG KONG-SINGAPORE ROYAL ARTILLERY

Unit/CO	Batteries	Remarks
1st Hong Kong Regt HK-S RA Lt Col JCL Yale	1st & 2nd Mtn Btys; 3rd, 4th & 25th Med Btys	Each Mtn Bty 4 x 3.7-in and 4 x 4.5-in hows. Each Med Bty 4 x 6-in hows. 15 Feb 42 lost at Singapore.
1st HAA Regt HK-S RA Lt Col AE Tawney	6th, 9th & 10th HAA Btys HK-S RA	6th Bty at Johore & Sungei Buloh with 8 x 3.7-in guns. 9th Bty at Johore & the Naval Base with 2 x 3-in & 8 x 40mm guns. 15 Feb 42 lost at Singapore.

Unit/CO	Batteries	Remarks
2nd HAA Regt HK-S RA Lt Col R McL More	11th, 12th & 13th HAA Btys HK-S RA	12th Bty at Nee Soon & Singapore City with 8 x 3.7-in guns. 13th Bty at Singapore City with 4 x 3.7-in & 4 x 3-in guns. 15 Feb 42 lost at Singapore.
3rd LAA Regt HK-S RA Lt Col DV Hill	14th &16th LAA Btys HK-S RA	14th Bty at Johore with 7 x 40mm guns. 16th Bty at Johore with 8 x 40mm guns. 15 Feb 42 lost at Singapore.

Other HK-S RA Batteries served with British artillery units and are shown with those units in this table.

Annex L

THE 'JURY AXLE' AND THE 'BABY 25-POUNDER'
THE 'JURY AXLE' 25-POUNDER

1. The 25-pounder with limber and 'Quad' gun tractor soon proved too cumbersome for jungle operations. This caused the conversion of certain field regiments into 'Jungle' field regiments in 1942/43 with jeep-towed 3.7-inch howitzers and 3-inch mortars. The first to convert was 129th Field Regiment which built up experience as a result. The big problem was that neither the 3.7-inch howitzer, with its range of 6,000 yards and 20lb shell, nor the 3-inch mortar with its improved range of 3,500 yards (with base plate) were effective enough. The regiment therefore began to work on the 25-pounder which had both range, 13,400 yards, and lethality with its 25lb shell. It also had the versatility of being a gun-howitzer for which there was a wide variety of projectiles. The problem was that the equipment was too heavy to be towed by a jeep and too wide for both jungle tracks and airmobility.

2. The regimental fitters of 129th Jungle Field Regiment, under Sergeant Farrell and Bombardier Clifford Jones worked out that they could fit a jeep axle and wheels to the gun and yet it still performed well. This was tried out in action by the regiment on the Tiddim Road in early 1944 and it was found that with a few very minor modifications to the trail and other parts of the carriage the gun remained stable when firing even the highest charges. The commanding officer, Lieutenant Colonel CFJ Younger sent details to the MGRA India in his monthly letter of October 1943. A design was eventually approved by the War Office which entailed modifying the existing gun axle and fitting slightly modified jeep-sized wheels.

3. Lieutenant Colonel Younger reports that such a modified gun arrived for trial in November 1943 and this was probably the first 'Jury Axle' 25-pounder to come into service. Further trials were conducted and in his January 1944 letter to the MGRA India, Colonel Younger reported that 'Jury axles have now had sufficient trials to prove their worth, not only as a means of movement, but also as a stable gun carriage, provided they are given a reasonably flat platform. Guns on Jury Axles have fired many hundreds of rounds alongside other guns in the line and have proved satisfactory. A complete troop on a jeep axis [Jury Axle] is at present being handled without difficulty in a mobile role on the right flank of the Division. A traverse of 3 degs has been put on during firing, without incident, and trials in this connection are proceeding. We still only have 6 Jubblepore (converted gun) axles and one MT pattern. The other 2 Jubblepore axles have disappeared on the L-of-C.'

4. The War Diary of 9th Field Regiment in 20th Indian Division records the results of tests with a 'Jury Axle' 25-pounder, in January 1944 as follows, 'Behaviour of both gun and jeep was found to be satisfactory, particularly when the weight of the shield and one or two of the detachment was added to the front of the jeep to give additional purchase. Various experimental brakes were tried and a shortened cam-rod is now awaited. It took 1.5 hours to convert a 25-pounder to a Jury Axle 25-pounder. On dry ground the jeep would pull the gun up a slope of 1:4.'

5. It seems that there was a plan to issue reduced size gun-platforms in early 1945. In March 1945 Colonel Younger reported, 'We look forward to the arrival of the conversion sets for our jury axle guns, so far only platforms without tie-bars have been received.'

6. 136th Field Regiment report receiving eight Jury Axle 25-pounders while still in action in the Arakan in April 1944. The 25-pounder with Jury Axle, no platform and no shield was much

lighter and was airportable in a Dakota (C 47) or Commando (C 46) aircraft. Thus the plan was to issue each field regiment with enough Jury Axles for one battery so that each had at least one battery that could be made airportable at short notice. It was, however, never easy to load and unload such a gun into or out of an aircraft. A letter from Colonel JF Dixon-Nuttall, late RA but then Adjutant of 5/1st Punjab Regiment, recalls that 'On 7 Oct 1944 a 'Jury Axle' 25pr was taken over the Goppe Pass - no mean feat in the prevailing conditions on a winding, muddy and narrow track over this pass - to Goppe Bazaar on the R. Kalapanzin. There it was broken down, loaded into a sampan, and floated down to Taung Bazaar where the 'Post Troop' of 585 Bty 160 Fd Regt were with 5/1st Punjab. . . once reassembled it quickly dealt with the Jap gun that was out of range of the 3.7in hows of the 'Post Troop'.

7. It is not known whether the 16 x 25-pounders used in the Second Chindit operation had Jury Axles or not. There were some available.

8. RA Notes No 25 of February 1945, paragraph 1436 lays down the drills for the movement of Jury Axle 25-pounders in very rough country at the height of the monsoon as follows:

Method 1, Movement by Jeep loads (only in dry weather)

Jeep 1, Barrel and Jacket.
Jeep 2, Sight bracket and breech ring.
Jeep 3, Saddle and breech block.
Jeep 4, Buffer, recuperator and cradle.
Jeep 5, Towing carriage.
Jeep 6, Gun stores.

Method 2, Tow by a D4 Bulldozer (any conditions).

Method 3, Manhandling. This is described as the best and safest method but the effort is very great. It takes 30 men per gun, three drag ropes with 10 men on each. When moving down a steep slope, one drag rope should be on the 'curb-side' wheel, one on the central forward towing hook and one on the trail to act as a brake. When pulling up slopes, one drag rope should be on the central forward towing hook and one on each of the wheel drag washers.

THE 'BABY 25-POUNDER'

9. In the SW Pacific area the Australians had the same problems with their 25-pounders but their solution was different. They reduced the length of the barrel and fitted a muzzle cap to protect the buffer-recuperator from blast when the gun fired. Shortening the barrel and the carriage tended to upset the balance of the gun, making it somewhat unstable when firing. It was also a little easier to tow. However, it was much easier to dismantle, into 13 loads, and re-assemble. It could be transported by small vehicles, boats and aircraft. In draught the gun was designed to be towed by jeep. The carriage was much altered and shortened to form the Carriage 25 pdr Light Mark I (Aust) which was followed by a Mark II version, with a reduced axle, which was preferred. Australian Gunners put one battery per field regiment onto a 'Baby 25-pounder' basis for the same reasons as the British followed with the Jury Axle gun in jungle field regiments. The British stuck to the Jury Axle and the Australians to the 'Baby 25-pounder' and both played

a useful part in subsequent operations. The ‘Baby 25-pounder’ came into its own in New Guinea during the rapid advance to Lae when these guns were moved so quickly that they kept in range of a fast advance where the infantry used parachute drops. Some examples were employed by US troops in New Guinea as well.

ANNEX M

No 656 AIR OBSERVATION POST SQUADRON RAF

FORMATION

1. No 656 AOP Squadron was formed on 31st December 1942 at RAF Westley, a small grass airfield just outside Bury St Edmunds .

ESTABLISHMENT

2. The Establishment when the Squadron arrived in the Far East was:

Officers Royal Artillery (All Pilots) 23
Officers RAF (Not Pilots) 3
Other Ranks Royal Artillery 90
Other Ranks RAF 80
Giving a total strength of 196 all ranks.

3. Squadron Headquarters:

Officers:
Commanding Officer Major Royal Artillery
Second-in-Command Captain Royal Artillery
Pilots 5 x Captains Royal Artillery
Adjutant Flying Officer RAF*
Equipment Officer Flying Officer RAF*
Administrative Officer Flying Officer RAF*
*Could be a Warrant Officer

Other Ranks**:
Royal Artillery 42
Royal Air Force 38
**These were Drivers, Engineers, Signallers, Medical Orderlies.

Radios: two No. 22 Sets: One netted to Army HQ being supported.
One netted to the three Flights.

4. Flights

Three (A, B & C). Each comprising Flight HQ and Four Sections:

Flight Commander, a Captain Royal Artillery
Section Commanders Four Captains Royal Artillery

Other Ranks:
Royal Artillery 8
Royal Air Force 6

Radios: three No. 22 Sets. One netted to the Local Army HQ.
One netted to Sections.
One netted to Squadron HQ.

5. Sections

Section Commander Captain Royal Artillery
Fitters Airframe RAF 2
Signaller RA 1
Driver/Batman 1

Aircraft Auster Mark III or IV
Truck 15cwt
Jeep and Trailer
Radios No 22. (one to Flight HQ and one to supported HQ/Regiment)

Such a Section could be detached to work independently.

THE AUSTER AIRCRAFT

5. All Austers flown by the AOP Squadrons were built at Rearsby, near Leicester, by a firm originally known as Taylorcraft Aeroplanes (England) Ltd at Thurmaston, Leicestershire formed by the Taylorcraft Aviation Company of the United States. Over 1500 of this type, Marks III, IV and V, flew with Second Tactical Air Force in north west Europe, in north west Africa, with the Desert Air Force and in Italy. 656 Squadron was the only British user in the Far East.

6. By the time 656 Squadron went into action it was flying the Auster Mark III converting to Auster Mark IVs some nine months later. The Mark V, the major production version, fitted with blind-flying instrumentation, arrived right at the end of the Burma campaign. The Auster was a braced high-wing monoplane with a wingspan of 36 feet and a length of 22 feet 10 inches. It was fabric covered, very light and very robust. The Mark III differed from the Mark I in that it had a Gipsy Major I 130 hp engine and hand operated flaps which reduced take off from 130 to 100 yards and gave it a stalling speed of 40 mph. The Mark IV had much improved vision both forwards and backwards and was fitted with a shorter nosed Lycoming O 290 engine. All Austers were started by hand, that is by swinging the propeller.

7. A landing strip could be about 250 to 300 yards long depending on obstacles at either end. Strips were normally located as far forward as practicable and wherever possible close to artillery gun positions or to the headquarters giving the Squadron, Flight or Section its tasks.

8. The aircraft had a good radio in the No 22 set and was often used to act as a relay station for radios on the ground which could not get through.

Annex N

AMATEUR AIR OP

Major GW Robertson recalls:

The arrival of 656th Air OP Squadron in India in September 1943 and its very successful use in the 1944 campaigns meant that its services were in great demand in 1945. Two flights were allocated to 4th and 33rd Corps to cover the assault crossing of the Irrawaddy and the third flight to 15th Corps on the Arakan coast.

After 7th Indian Division had secured the crossing at Nyaungu and 17th and 5th Indian Divisions had passed through Meiktila the aircraft covering the crossing moved east to the Meiktila battleground. 89th Indian Brigade of 7th Indian Division pushed south from the bridgehead into the flat open country to the east of the river. Strong Japanese defences were soon encountered and because of the absence of any high ground, except some hills occupied by the Japanese, observation proved very difficult and it was a situation in which the Air OP would have been invaluable.

However, a section or flight of L.5 aircraft of a USAAF liaison squadron had been allocated to 89th Indian Brigade for casualty evacuation and general ‘taxi’ work. The aircraft, somewhat similar to the Austers of 656th AOP Squadron, were piloted by Sergeant Pilots. Whether permission was given officially can not be ascertained but the pilots agreed to fly officers from 136th Field Regiment to try their hand at Air OP work. As far as we know the pilots had not had any training for this task but they entered into it with great enthusiasm - a change from being taxi or ambulance drivers - and rapidly became proficient at placing the aircraft at the right spot at the right time for the observer to see the fall of shot.

All the Troop Commanders of 136th Regiment and several OPOs took their turn and some proved particularly efficient. Captain JF Daykin of 348th Field Battery proved to be the ‘ace’ observer. No doubt his mathematical brain - he was an actuary by profession - could more easily solve the problems of converting corrections of line from yards into degrees and minutes.

This amateur Air OP organisation continued until 89th Indian Brigade had cleared Chauk and then recrossed the Irrawaddy to the west bank. Progressing south down the river the brigade soon made contact with the Japanese and the amateur OP organisation started very satisfactory operations again.

While 656th Squadron would undoubtedly have been much more proficient at the work it should be borne in mind that the amateurs were self-taught on the job and almost all the officers concerned had never flown before! (Robertson)

A similar story is told of Brigadier JH Beattie, who became CRA of 19th Indian Division in late May 1945. Ground observation from OPs proved extremely limited so one of his first actions was to organise an Air OP for his division. This move was achieved by an L 5 aircraft flown by Pilot Officer JS Williams RAF. Captain David Hine of ‘E’ Troop, 480th Battery, 115th Field Regiment was chosen to be the observer. ‘In the L.5 the observer had to sit behind the pilot so that his forward field of view was severely restricted. The pilot had his own radio for communication with his base and Hine used an additional set with a trailing aerial for contact with the gun position. There was also a simple intercom, between the pilot and observer, but this could not be used at the same time as either radio set. Neither pilot nor observer could speak on, or receive, messages from the other person’s set. This led on one occasion to a message from Hine instructing the guns to “circle round for a bit” after which the pilot received a very loud “Mike Target”.

Hine received the Military Cross for his achievements as an Air OP among other acts. (Anon, ‘The Dagger Division’s Private Air OP’)

Annex O

ARTILLERY ORDER OF BATTLE
SECOND ARAKAN
JANUARY - MAY 1944

15th INDIAN CORPS

CORPS TROOPS

CCRA: Brigadier L Harris

Regiment	Batteries	Guns	CO
1 Med	1/2 & 5/22	16 x 5.5-in	Lt Col DG Lea
6 Med	18 & 19	16 x 5.5-in	Lt Col WG Fox
8 HAA	21, 22 & 23	24 x 3.7-in	Lt Col JC Cunningham
36 LAA	97, 128 & 266	30 x 40mm	Lt Col JC Lawrence
5 Indian LAA/A/Tk	17, 18 & 19	24 x 40mm	
		24 x 6-pdr	
7th Indian Fd*	16, 17 & 18	24 x 25-pdr	Lt Col FR Wetherfield

*and see 26th Indian Division below.

5th INDIAN DIVISION

CRA: Brigadier ECR Mansergh

Regiment	Batteries	Guns	CO
4 Fd	7, 14/66, & 522	24 x 25-pdr	Lt Col GER Bastin
28 Jungle Fd	1, 3 Mortar & 5/57	16 x 3.7-in hows	Lt Col RA Collins
		16 x 3-in mortars	
56 LAA/A/Tk	163 & 164 LAA	24 x 40mm	Lt Col PJF Parsons
	221 & 222 A/Tk	24 x 6-pdr	
24 Indian Mtn	2, 11, 12 & 20	16 x 3.7-in hows	Lt Col RHM Hill

7th INDIAN DIVISION

CRA: Brigadier AF Hely

Regiment	Batteries	Guns	CO
136 Fd	347, 348 & 500	24 x 25-pdr	Lt Col GR Armstrong
139 Jungle Fd	362, 364 & 503	16 x 3.7-in hows	Lt Col HCB Hall
		16 x 3-in mortars	
24 LAA/A/Tk	86 & 491 LAA	24 x 40mm	Lt Col RB Cole
	205 & 284 A/Tk	24 x 6-pdr	
25 Indian Mtn	5, 19, 23 and Bikaner Bijay	16 x 3.7-in hows	Lt Col LHO Pugh

25th INDIAN DIVISION

CRA: Brigadier AG O'Carroll-Scott

Regiment	Batteries	Guns	CO
8 Jungle Fd **	V, W & X(M)	16 x 25-pdr	Lt Col JCH Mead
		16 x 3-in mortar	
27 Jungle Fd	21(M), 24 & 37/47	16 x 3.7-in hows	Lt Col J Longden
		16 x 3-in mortars	
5 Indian Fd	11, 12 & 13	24 x 25-pdr	Lt Col RA Cook
7 Indian LAA/A/Tk	25 & 26 LAA	24 x 40mm	Lt Col PGP Bradshaw
	27 & 39 A/Tk	24 x 6-pdr	

** 8th Field Regiment was a special kind of jungle regiment and had 25-pounders.

26th INDIAN DIVISION

CRA: Brigadier CJG Dalton

Regiment	Batteries	Guns	CO
160 Jungle Fd***	585, 586 & 584(M),	16 x 3.7-in hows	Lt Col JF Williams-Wynne
		16 x 3-in mortars	
7 Indian Fd	16, 17 & 18	24 x 25-prs	Lt Col FR Wetherfield
1 Indian LAA/A/Tk	25 & 26 LAA	24 x 40mm	
	27 & 39 A/Tk	24 x 6-pdr	
30 Indian Mtn	27, 32, 33 & 34	16 x 3.7 hows	Lt Col TWR Hill

*** 160th Field Regiment sent four troops, each of four guns, four officers and 57 men to join the Chindits in February 1944. They were called 'R', 'S', 'T' and 'U' Troops. 584th (Mortar) Battery was disbanded and did not accompany the regiment to Arakan. It was not reformed until March 1944 after the arrival of 105 reinforcements.

36th INDIAN DIVISION

CRA: Brigadier GE Barrington

Regiment	Batteries	Guns	CO
130 Assault Fd****	315, 316 & 494	16 x 25-pdr	Lt Col GE Barrington
		8 x 3.7-in hows	
178 Assault Fd	122, 366 & 516	8 x SP 105mm	Lt Col KM Wright
		8 x 3.7-in hows	
		8 x 25-pdr	
122 LAA/A/Tk	168 & 321 A/Tk	24 x 6-pdr	Lt Col CD Oliver
	400 & 402 LAA	24 x 40mm	

**** Assault field regiments were specially created and trained for assault landings from the sea.

ANNEX P

EAST AND WEST AFRICAN ARTILLERY FAR EAST 1942-45

FIELD ARTILLERY

Unit Title & CO	Batteries	Remarks
101st Light Regt West African Artillery Lt Col CCF Anderson	3rd, 5th and 6th Light Btys WAA	In 81st WA Div. Each bty had one troop of 'head carried' 8 x 3-inch mortars and one troop of jeep-towed 3.7-inch howitzers. Late 44 reorganised into 3 btys of 3.7-in hows. With 81st WA Division at Chiringa Mar 45.
102nd Light Regt West African Artillery Lt Col MC Munro	1st, 2nd and 4th Light Btys WAA	Arrived India with 82nd WA Div in 44. Equipped 24 x 3.7-inch howitzers. Owing to shortage of jeeps reduced to 3 x 6-gun btys leaving six guns at Dohazari. Dec 44 began march to Kaladan River. Mar 45 landed at Ruywa for the Third Arakan Campaign. Apr 45 converted to 24 x 25-pounders. Regt fired 12,110 HE and 574 smoke in Third Arakan Campaign.
302nd (East African) Field Regt East African Artillery* Lt Col RN Syme	55th, 59th and 60th (EA) Field Btys	44- 45 with 11th EA Div. In 1945 amalgamated with 303rd Field Regt.
303rd (East African) Field Regt East African Artillery* Lt Col RFJ Anderson	53rd, 54th and 58th (EA) Field Btys	Aug 44 converted to 3.7-inch hows from 25-pounders and became 303rd EA Light Regt. 44-45 with 11th EA Div. Amalgamated with 302 Field Regt in 1945.
306th (East African) Field Regt East African Artillery Lt Col JEF Meadmore	63rd, 64th and 65th (EA) Field Btys	44-45 with 11th EA Div.
	56 (Uganda) Field Bty** Major JB Loveluck	Madagascar then to 301st (EA) Field Regt.

* 302nd and 303rd Regiments amalgamated in 1945 to become 303rd (EA) Field Regiment under Lt Col RJF Anderson

** Also referred to as the Independent East African Field Battery which served in Madagascar.

*** There was to have been a third field regiment in the Division, 301 Fd Regt, which was formed from the Independent East Africa Field Battery and 57th and 62nd (EA) Field Batteries. It was commanded by Lt Col John Stevens. The regiment was sailing to Ceylon, to join 11th East African Division, in HMT *Khedive Ismail* when the ship was torpedoed by the Japanese Submarine *I 27*. The CO was one of very few survivors.

ANTI-TANK ARTILLERY

Unit Title & CO	Batteries	Remarks
21st Anti Tank Regiment West African Artillery Lt Col O Holleyman	61st, 62nd and 63rd Anti-Tank Btys WAA	With 81st WA Div. Arrived in India as 1st LAA/Anti-Tank Regt WAA. Reorganised as Anti-Tank Regt Dec 44. With 81st WA Div at Chiringa Mar 45.

Unit Title & CO	Batteries	Remarks
22nd Anti-Tank Regt West African Artillery Lt Col HREC Fraser Lt Col TA Haighton Lt Col AL Jervis	64th, 65th and 66th Anti-Tank Btys WAA	With 82nd WA Div. Arrived in India as 2nd LAA/Anti-Tank Regt WAA Summer 1944 and converted to Anti-Tank only. All guns and transport handed in: regt served as Infantry recce Regt. Sep 45 became 22nd Light Regt with 16x3.7 inch hows.
304th (East Africa) LAA/Anti-Tank Regt East African Artillery Lt Col GG Mears	101st and 102nd Anti-Tank and 203rd and 204th LAA (EA)Btys On reorg had 101st, 102nd and 103rd (EA) Anti-Tank Btys.	Oct 44-45 with 11th EA Div. Late 44 reorganised as A/Tk Regiment.

HEAVY ANTI-AIRCRAFT ARTILLERY

Unit Title & CO	Batteries	Remarks
1st HAA Regt West African Artillery Lt Col T Nettleton Lt Col WL Abel-Smith Lt Col WS Crane	1st and 2nd (WA) HAA Btys and 197 HAA Bty RA	Aug 43 with 14th (WA) AA Bde. Oct 44 - Mar 45 with same bde at Imphal
2nd HAA Regt West African Artillery Lt Col JS Wilson	5th and 6th (WA) HAA Btys and 308th HAA Bty RA	Aug 43 - Mar 45 with 14th (WA) AA Bde Manipur Road.
3rd HAA Regt West African Artillery Lt Col JO Horne Lt Col RA O'Conor	4th, and 251st (WA), and 405th (RA) HAA Btys	Aug 43 - Mar 45 with 14th (WA) AA Brigade at Silchar and Surma Valley.
4th HAA Regt West African Artillery Lt Col RA O'Conor	7th, 8th and 313th (WA) HAA Btys	Oct 43 - Mar 45 with 14th (WA) AA Bde at Comilla. Disbanded Mar 45.
15th (East Africa) HAA Regt East African Artillery	153rd, 154th and 155th (EA) HAA Btys	

MORTAR ARTILLERY

Unit Title & CO	Batteries	Remarks
41st Mortar Regt West African Artillery Lt Col JA Macnabb Lt Col PHG Stallard	101st, 102nd and 103rd Mortar Btys WAA	Aug 44 Formed from mortar troops of 101st Light Regt WAA. Each bty 8 x 3-inch mortars, head-borne. Mar 45 with 81st WA Div at Chiringa.
42nd Mortar Regt West African Artillery Lt Col LA Liddell Lt Col VF Northcott	104th, 105th and 106th Mortar Btys WAA	Aug 44 Formed from mortar troops of 102nd Light Regt WAA. Each bty 8 x 3-inch mortars, head-borne. Mar 45 with 82nd WA Div at Ruywa. In the 3rd Arakan Campaign this regt fired 8,589 HE and 2,324 smoke rounds.

Nomenclature: Although the Royal West African Frontier Force and the Kings African Rifles may be regarded respectively as the parents of West and East African Gunners the units themselves were usually referred to as West or East African Artillery, WAA and EAA. The initials RWAFF and KAR might well be appropriate to an officer serving with those units but they do not seem to have been applied to the regiments and batteries with the exception of the Coast Defence Unit, later the Coast Defence Battery, KAR, at Mombasa. Colonel Stanford has pointed out that it was more common to use the title 'East Africa Artillery' and to use the term 'East African Artillery' adjectively.

Frank Cole, who served with 42nd Mortar Regiment WAA, records that 'Many of the 90,000 or so East and West African soldiers serving in Burma were recruited from remote agrarian communities. Training brought them into contact with the products and aspects of modern industrial society - weapons, motor transport, regular meals and medical care. A great number had never seen the sea, let alone the ocean going transports which carried them in most unpleasant conditions to a distant theatre of war. Outwardly these new experiences were accepted as a fact of army life - only occasionally were they greeted with wide-eyed wonder.'

ORDER OF BATTLE IN THE SECOND CHINDIT CAMPAIGN MARCH- JUNE 1944

SPECIAL FORCE also known as **3rd INDIAN INFANTRY DIVISION:**

Major General OC Wingate
Major General WDA Lentaigne from 27 Mar 1944

The division comprised: 3rd West African, 14th, 16th, 77th and 111th Brigades, Morrisforce, Dahforce and Bladet.

16th BRIGADE:

Brigadier BE Fergusson

2nd Field Coy RE
51st/69th Field Regt RA, Columns 51 and 69
1st Bn The Queen's Regt, Columns 21 and 22
2nd Bn The Leicestershire Regt, Columns 17 and 71
45th Reconnaissance Regt, Columns 45 and 54
Medical Detachment

Columns 51 and 69: These Columns were formed from 51st Field and 69th Anti-Tank Regiments of 70th British Division. At first they were designated 9 and 10 Columns but were later allowed to use their own regimental numbers. Both were highly experienced as they had fought for several months in the Western Desert.
Commander: Lieutenant Colonel RC Sutcliffe RA.

Field Artillery - Special Force (3rd Indian Infantry Division)

CRA Special Force: Major RGA Duxbury*.

R Fd Troop, 160th Field Regiment, 4 x 25pdrs, Captain G Hepburn RA.
S Fd Troop, 160th Field Regiment, 4 x 25pdrs, Captain SR Nicholls RA.
T Fd Troop, 160th Field Regiment, 4 x 25pdrs, Captain A Mondus RA*
U Fd Troop, 160th Field Regiment, 4 x 25pdrs, Captain P Young RA*.

A total of 12 officers and 228 men.

Anti-Aircraft Artillery - Special Forces

W LAA Troop, 69th LAA Regiment, 6 x 40mm, Captain P Cox RA.
X LAA Troop, 69th LAA Regiment, 10 x 0.5-inch AAMG then 6 x 40mm, Captain TH Braid, Captain R Moody RA.
Y LAA Troop, 69th LAA Regiment, 6 x 40mm, Captain GJ Smith RA.
Z LAA Troop, 69th LAA Regiment, 6 x 40mm, Captain AE Meager, Captain TH Braid*.

A total of 12 officers and 296 men.

* Killed in action or died of wounds.

23rd Infantry Brigade: Brigadier LECM Perowne

This formation was taken from the Chindit order of battle and employed against Japanese communications west of the Chindwin.

12th Field Coy RE
60th Field Regt RA, Columns 60 and 88
2nd Bn Duke of Wellington's Regt, Columns 33 and 76
4th Bn Border Regt, Columns 34 and 55
1st Bn Essex Regt, Columns 44 and 56

Columns 60 and 88: These columns were formed from 60th Field Regiment which was also experienced from the Western Desert having fought with great distinction at Sidi Rezegh.

Commander 60 Column: Lieutenant Colonel HG de Jacobi du Vallon RA
Commander 88 Column: Lieutenant Colonel NS Hotchkin RA

ANNEX R

ASPECTS OF DAILY LIFE

NOTES by Major GW Robertson, late 136th Field Regiment RA.

1. For the vast majority of Gunners, officers and men, who were sent to the Far East Theatre it was their first journey abroad. Up until then a 'long journey' was a three or four hour train ride to a seaside resort for their annual holiday. So a two month voyage round the Cape, without a glimpse of land for most of the time, meant we were travelling distances beyond our comprehension.

I remember that on a day in October 1943 when, after 48 hours of continuous very hard labour in the tropical heat, we completed my troop's first 'in action' position in the Arakan my GPOA told the inhabitants of the Command Post "I estimate we have now travelled over 12,000 miles." After a pause one of the signallers spoke up "Jim, you mean we are 12,000 miles from home."

In the months that followed the occasional quiet spell gave us the opportunity to review our situation - not only were we a very long way from home but until early 1945 we could see no prospect of starting that return journey.

2. Gunners in action lead a very isolated life. A 25-pdr gun pit would never have more then three men in it unless a heavy programme were to be fired. The other numbers of the detachment would be engaged in fatigues of various sorts, or humping ammunition or manning defence posts.

Since the gun pits would be in the open in order to obtain a good field of fire movement about the gun position would be kept to the minimum for purposes of concealment. At dusk all movement ceased and remained so throughout the hours of darkness. From October to April the nights were very long.

3. Most of the campaigning took place in the dry season - October to May - when the shade temperature was always in the 90s. Camouflage nets would normally be in use but they afforded little shade from the sun in a cloudless sky. New arrivals in the Theatre required several weeks of gradually increasing exposure of the skin to the sun before it was safe to adopt the daytime dress of hat, shorts and stockinged boots. This was gun position dress but for OP parties or others in a forward area shirt and trousers had to be worn. Before dusk, in the gun areas too, shirt and trousers well tucked into socks were necessary to thwart the attacks of insect hordes.

4. The most important item in the Gunner's life was tea. It was necessary to drink considerable quantities of liquid to replace the sweat that even the slightest activity would produce. Failure to keep the level of body fluids to the required level would result in Heat Exhaustion which could be fatal. Supplies of drinking water were usually of doubtful quality and had to be chlorinated before it was safe to drink, but this treatment gave the water a very unpleasant taste so the only satisfactory solution was to use it for making tea. Well laced with sugar and tinned milk it was the Fourteenth Army's life blood. To replace the essential salt that the human body needs and which it loses with the sweat it was necessary in the hotter parts of the year to add salt to the drinking water - this did not improve the taste! Tea, sugar and tinned milk were always the Army's most important supplies.

5. Once into action there appeared to be no arrangement for supplying razor blades, soap, toothpaste or even the occasional bottle of beer. The issue cigarettes which did come regularly

with the rations were of very poor quality. This was the situation for the 1943 and 1944 campaigns. But in 1945 supplies improved when mobile shops, run by the WASBs (Womens Auxiliary Services Burma) were operating near the combat zones. In this year too tinned Canadian beer was made available to the forward divisions but it rarely seemed to exceed one can per man per month. These shortages added to the feeling of being in 'The Forgotten Army'.

6. But one remarkable good feature of life in the East was the efficiency of the Postal Services. Once North Africa had been cleared in early 1943 and regular air services between the UK and India had been re-established transit time dropped from 3 months by the Cape route to 7 or 10 days. Provided that one did not move from one's unit delivery was remarkably efficient.

Annex S

THE ARMY AIR SUPPORT ORGANISATION, ARAKAN 1944-45

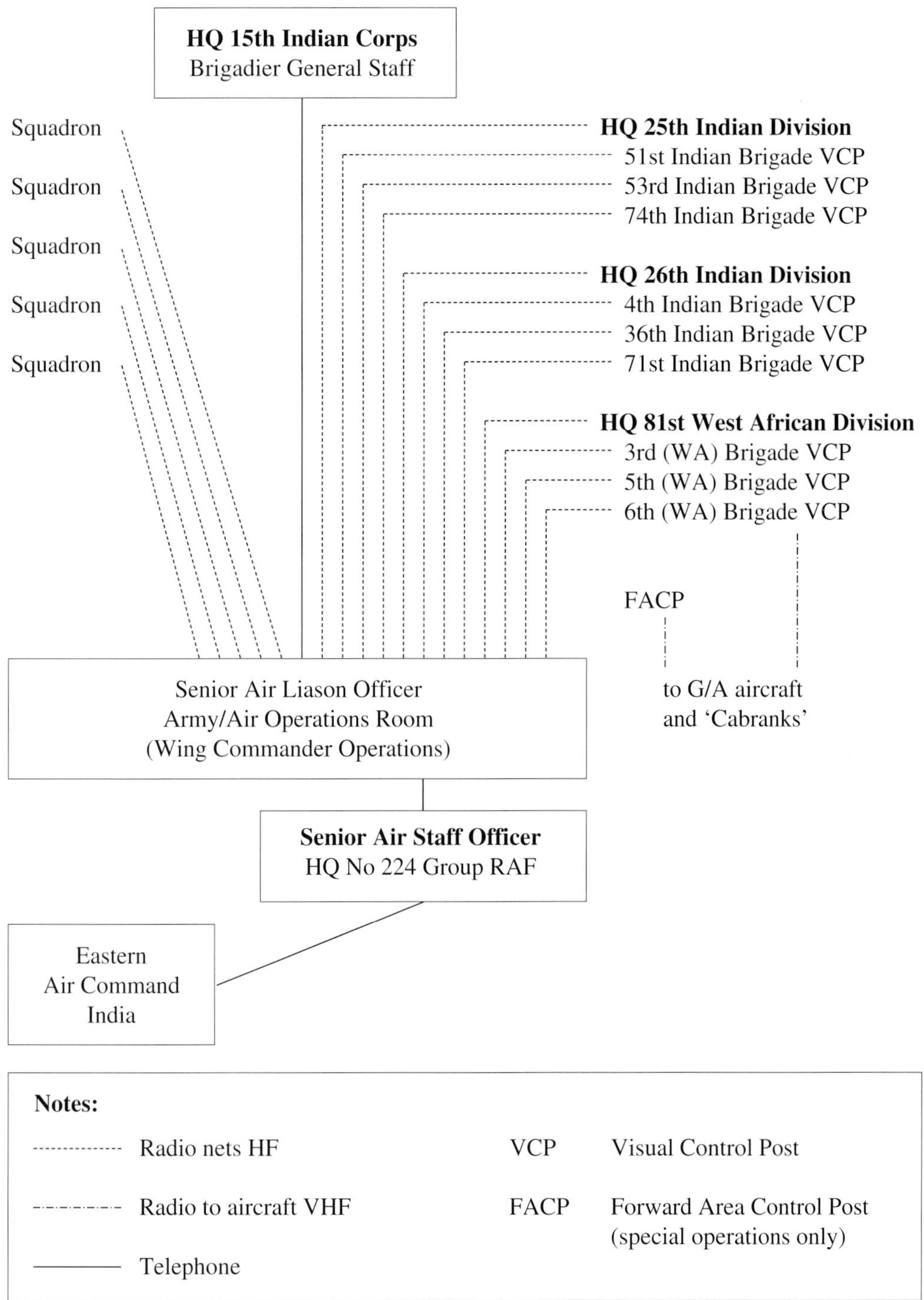

Notes:

------------	Radio nets HF	VCP	Visual Control Post
-·-·-·-·-	Radio to aircraft VHF	FACP	Forward Area Control Post (special operations only)
————	Telephone		

ANNEX T

FIELD ARTILLERY ORGANISATION AND GUNNERY PROCEDURES

(Based on an account by Lieutenant Colonel BAT Hammond who served as a subaltern in C Troop 34th Field Battery, 16th Field Regiment in the Burma Campaign)

Establishment

1. The War Establishment was II/187/1 dated 23 June 1943 for an RHQ with two 25 pr Batteries and one light battery. The total personnel allowed, less attached Royal Signals and REME, was;

Officers	37
Other Ranks including ACC Cooks	641
Total	678

2. Vehicles authorised were;

25 pr Guns	16
3.7 inch howitzers	8
Trailers Artillery (25 pr only)	32
Motor Cycles	44
Armoured OP Vehicles (Carriers)	9
'B' Vehicles	114

3. Allocation of posts in RHQ;

Appointment	Rank	Number
Commanding Officer	Lt Col	1
Second-in-Command	Maj	1
Adjutant	Capt	1
Assistant Adjutant	Lt	1
Regimental Survey Officer	Lt	1
Quartermaster	Lt	1
Medical Officer	Capt	1
Other Ranks RA		50
Other Ranks ACC		3
REME Armourer		1

Signals Section R Sigs

Light Aid Detachment REME

Chaplain

4. a. Establishment - 25 pr Battery HQ

Battery HQ	**Appt**	**Rank**	**Number**
Battery Commander	BC	Maj	1
Battery Captain	BK	Capt	1
Command Post Officer	CPO	Lt	1
Assistant CPO	ACPO	Subaltern	1
Battery Sergeant Major	BSM	WO2	1
Battery Quartermaster Sergeant	BQMS	Staff Sgt	1
Signal Sergeant		Sgt	1
Tradesmen - Clerks, Driver Mechs, Equipment Repairer, Fitter, Motor Mechanics, Technical Storeman			15
Non-Tradesmen - Batmen, Drivers, OP Assistants, Signallers, Command Post Assistants, Despatch Riders, Sanitary Man, Storemen, Water Dutyman.			40

b. Vehicle allocation to BC/OP Parties

Type of Vehicle	**Role Code**	**Passengers**	**Qty**
Armoured OP	X	BC. Dvr/Mech, 2 x Dvr/Ops	1
Jeep and Trailer	X2	BC's OPA, Dvr, Sig, Batman	1
Motor Cycle	M/C	BC's DR	1
Armoured OP	RC	Tp Comd, Dvr Mech, 2 x Dvr/Ops	1
	RD	ditto	1
Jeep and Trailer	RC2	OPA and Sig	1
	RD2	ditto	1
Motor Cycle	M/C2, M/C3	Tp i/c Sigs	2

c. Vehicle allocation to 'A' Echelon

Type of Vehicle	**Role Code**	**Passengers**	**Qty**
Battery HQ			
Quad FFW Bty CP	H	CPO, 2 x CPAs, 2 x Dvr /Ops	1
Quad FFW	Y	ACPO, Dvr, Dvr/Op	1
15 cwt Line Truck	M1	Sig Sgt, Dvr, 3 x Sigs	1
Motor Cycle	M/C4	BSM	1
Motor Cycle	M/C5	CPOA/Bty TARA Sgt	1
Motor Cycle	MC/6	CPO's DR	1
	RD2	ditto	1
Motor Cycle	M/C2, M/C3	Tp i/c Sigs	1
Troop			
Quad FFW Tp CP	GC, GD	CPO, 2 x Dvr/Ops, Batman	2
Quad FFW	TLC2, TLD2	Tp Leader, CPOA, Dvr, Batman	2
15 cwt Line Truck	M2, M3	Dvr, 4 x Sigs, 2 x LMG Nos	2
15 cwt Line Truck	M4, M5	Dvr, 4 x Sigs, Fitter	2
Motor Cycle	M/C 7 & 8	TSM	2
Motor Cycle	M/C 9 & 10	Gun Fitter	2
Quad, Limber and Gun	A Sub to H Sub	Sgt, 3 x Gnrs, Dvr, Dvr Mech	8

d. Allocation of vehicles to 'B" Echelon

Type of Vehicle	Role Code	Passengers	Qty
Jeep & Trailer	K	BK, Dvr/Op, Batman	1
Quad FFW Bty Office	K2	2 x Clerks, Sig, Dvr/Op	1
Motor Cycle	M/C 11	BK's DR	1
Motor Cycle	M/C12	Fitter	1
3 ton Truck	Q1	BQMS, Storeman, Dvr	1
3 ton Truck	Q2	Tech Storeman, Eqpt Repairer, Dvr	1
3 ton Truck Cookhouse	Q3	Dvr, 6 x Cooks	1
3 ton Truck POL	Q4	Dvr Mech	1
Water Truck	Q5	Dvr, Water Dutyman	1
3 ton Truck Ammo	AMN 1	Dvr, 5 x Ammo Nos	1
3 ton Truck Ammo	AMN 2	Dvr, 2 x Batmen	1
3 ton Truck Ammo	AMN 3	Dvr Mech, 2 x LNG Nos	1

The letters shown in the Role Code column are the vehicle tactical signs which were painted on the front and rear of every vehicle. The Battery Sign was painted on the sides.

5. Summary of Battery Vehicles.

Vehicle	BtyHQ	Each Tp	Total
Armoured OP	1	1	3
Jeeps & Trailers	2	1	4
Quads FFW	3	2	7
15 cwt Line Trucks	1	2	5
15 cwt Water Truck	1		1
3 ton Trucks	7		7
Motor Cycles	7	3	13
Quad Gun Tractors		6	12
Limbers		8	8
25 pr Guns		8	8

Deployment procedures

6. The CPO and the two GPOs first go forward to reconnoitre the new position, often co-ordinated by the Second in Command. Having been given an area the GPO must find a layout which,

Permits him to cover his arc, and the line to shoot down to. This will involve some crest clearance calculations.

Gives him a frontage of at least 10 yards in the jungle with about 35 yards between guns.

Provides cover and concealment and a good track plan which will not give the position away to enemy aircraft.

Provides good all round defence against enemy infantry and tank attack.

Provides a position for wagon lines and administration with cover and protection.

7. He then sites his director and gets his Ack to set it up in the zero line, sets up his Command Post and works out an accurate eight figure map reference of the pivot, or right hand gun.

8. He then goes to meet the guns, normally at a rendezvous agreed beforehand. The guns are led by the Troop Leader. He calls the Numbers 1 together and briefs them on the method of occupation, the track plan and the zero line. He gives the Troop Leader the map reference and he goes to the director.

9. The guns occupy the position and then come into action. As soon as they are ready he passes them an angle to bring them all accurately on to the zero line and parallel. He closes his round of angles and, if within tolerance, he orders an independent "Check Zero Line". The director is moved and set up again and this time each gun passes him an angle and if each is within tolerance he knows he is accurately deployed.

10. The Numbers 1 record the angle to two aiming posts, one as far away as possible and one close in. As soon as one gun reports "Ready" and the artillery board is set up in the command post, he can accept targets. The whole process can be completed by a well-trained troop within five minutes. The GPO then goes to the command post and checks the artillery board, initialling it to say that he has done so.

11. The GPO then sets up his "Sands Graph" data which measures the bearing and distance of each gun from the pivot gun so that displacement can be added or subtracted from the ranging guns firing data when a target is being engaged.

12. The GPO then checks all communications including the fire orders to the Battery Command Post and the radio to his FOO/OP.

13. He must then prepare his slide rule, range tables, stop watch, angle of sight graph, gun programmes, barrage key lines forms, target records book and correction of the moment data which will arrive from the Battery Command Post. He is then ready for any kind of target. The Troop is then "Ready on Troop Grid".

14. Meanwhile at the guns the Numbers 1 will have started digging gun pits and slit trenches, preparing ammunition and all gun stores and tools. The fitter will visit each gun and carry out checks that all alignments and sights are in order after the journey from the last position.

15. The CPO will have checked one Troop's line and fix and either accepted it or adjusted it. Once he is happy he will announce that the Troop is now "Ready on Battery Grid". He will then do a bearing and distance exercise to the pivot gun of the other Troop, perhaps a mile away. Once this has been completed and his bearing and distance exercise closes within tolerance, he will give that Troop a new map reference and zero line bearing. The GPO of that troop will have to pass new angles to his guns and re-set his artillery board. When this is done and his two artillery boards, one for each Troop, have been set up at the battery Command Post, and checked, he can report "Ready on Battery Grid". If, by then, a target has been fired on Troop Grid its data will have to be amended on to Battery Grid before it is recorded.

16. Meanwhile, the Regimental Survey Officer is repeating this process between the pivot guns in each battery. When this has been done, the Adjutant can report, "Ready on Regimental Grid".

Eventually the Corps Survey regiment will arrive with "Theatre Grid" and then all guns of the Division and Corps are surveyed in sympathy and can be fired together on a target.

17. All this pre-supposes that all guns are calibrated to a divisional standard gun and that meteor data has arrived on all gun positions.

18. In Burma it was seldom possible to achieve the ideal layout as described above, but everyone was trying his best to do so.

Ammunition

19. The 25 pounder gun Mark II was used in Burma with no muzzle break. The range, with Charge Super, was 13,400 yards, but it was more normal to fire Charge I, II or III.

20. The 25 pounder could fire HE, AP, Smoke, Container (e.g. propaganda leaflets) or coloured smoke. The fuzes were clockwork and each had to be calculated at the Command Post and then set by hand at the gun before firing.

21. The 1st Line ammunition holdings on the gun position were;

Vehicle	No of Vehicles	No of Rounds	Total Rounds
Gun Tractor	8	32	256
Gun Limber	8	32	256
Spare Limbers	8	32	256
Section Tractors	4	32	128
3 ton Amn	2	184	368
3 ton Amn	1	112	112
Total			1,376

1,376 amounts to 172 rounds per gun of which 144 were HE, 16 were Smoke and 12 were AP.

22. It was the main duty of the Battery Captain, the BK, to maintain these levels as they were shot off. He did this by dumping the rounds held in the 3 tonners and going back to the brigade or divisional Ammunition Point and collecting it, or more often by arranging for a loaded RASC ammunition vehicle to deliver to the gun position. The RASC then fed the ammunition points from the Forward Maintenance Areas (FMA). In Burma ammunition was sometimes air dropped, as in the Arakan battles. For a major battle a dumping programme would be organised to dump several hundred rounds per gun at each gun. All had to be dug in and then each ammunition steel box broken open and the rounds assembled and prepared for action. Handling ammunition was heavy work and caused fatigue at times.

Communications

23. Radio was the main communications but wherever possible it was duplicated by line because there was heavy interference at night and it was often noisy when operating close to the enemy. Laying miles of cable and then maintaining it was tiring, and often-dangerous work, but at all costs the line had to be kept "through". Many acts of great bravery were performed in achieving this and casualties were heavy.

24. There were three types of radio used in Burma;

The No 48 Set. This was the US version of the British No 18 set. It was a man-pack set using a dry battery. It was quite heavy but would operate on the move. The range was about 4 miles.

The No 19 Set. Mounted in armoured OP vehicles. It was large, HF and had a range of about 20 miles but given proper aerials, and using Morse, it could achieve many hundred miles range. It was powered by the vehicle batteries. This Set had a remote control unit, to which a handset was connected, enabling the set to be used by an operator up to about half a mile away from the set, the connection being by line.

The No 22 Set. This was the standard all arms radio of World War 2. It was powered by separate lead/acid batteries which had to be charged using a small petrol engine generator called a "chore horse". It was normally vehicle mounted but could be dismounted and put into a trench or building. Like the No 19 Set it had a remote control unit.

25. Each BC and FOO had one of each of these sets. The No 22 Set was normally on the tank/infantry net, the No 19 Set on the regimental/battery net and the BC/FOO moved forward with the No 48 Set, relaying through either the No 19 or the No 22 Set. The CPO controlled the battery net and each battery operated on its own frequency. The Adjutant controlled the regimental net and he also had another No 19 Set on the HQRA net.

26. The biggest problems were the constant netting and re-netting of the radios on to their frequencies, interference from other military, civilian and even enemy frequencies, and the constant charging of batteries.

27. Batteries were also equipped with Lamps Signalling, Heliographs and Telescopes Signalling, all of which were used from time to time.

Dress and Equipment

28. The basic uniform was the Green Denim Battle Dress (GDBD) worn with boots and gaiters, or puttees, and a bush hat. The GDBD blouse was seldom worn. Normal wear was a shirt with a thick pullover when it was cold and a "monsoon cape" when it was wet. The shirt was thick flannel and was comfortable in hot or cold weather. The divisional sign was worn on the right arm and the unit flash on the left. For the Gunners the latter was a red and blue square.

29. Webbing was the 1937 Pattern. For normal wear it was the belt with two cross straps and a water bottle. Officers also carried binoculars, often in a case, a compass pouch and pistol holster on the belt. Badges of rank were worn but were small and were mounted on material the same colour as the denim.

30. On the gun position it was normal for only boots and trousers to be worn but steel helmets and all other kit was always close by and was taken everywhere.

31. Also carried were Very Pistols and Tactical Haversacks. The latter were slung over the shoulder and were used to carry kit which was needed all the time. The items carried were protractors, codes, sketch pads for panoramas, chinagraph pencils, standing orders for engagements, fire plans, barrages etc., mepacrine, salt tablets and morphine.

Maps

32. Quarter of an Inch to the Mile maps were available for the entire Burma campaign area. For most of the combat areas the One Inch to the Mile and 1/25,000 maps were available when needed. The accuracy of these was surprisingly good even in jungle clad hilly areas, such as the Maya Range in the Arakan. However these were not issued to 2nd Division on arrival in the Kohima area since these places were not, then, anticipated to be in a combat area.

ARTILLERY ORDER OF BATTLE
BURMA 1944 - 1945

Allied Land Forces South East Asia (ALFSEA):
BRA: Brigadier LC Manners-Smith

14th Army:
BRA: Brigadier G de V Welchman

18th (SP) Field Regiment RA
13th Medium Regiment RA
52nd HAA Regiment RA
69th LAA Regiment RA
2nd Indian Field Regiment IA
5th (Mahratta) Indian Anti-Tank Regiment IA
656th AOP Squadron, less C Flight

4th Indian Corps:
CCRA: Brigadier C Goulder

8th Medium Regiment RA
67th HAA Regiment RA
1st Survey Regiment RA
1st Indian LAA Regiment IA

5th Indian Division:
CRA: Brigadier GBJ Kellie

4th Field Regiment RA
28th Field Regiment RA
56th Anti-Tank Regiment RA
24th Indian Mountain Regiment IA

7th Indian Division:
CRA: Brigadier AF Hely

136th Field Regiment RA
139th Field Regiment RA
24th Anti-Tank Regiment RA
25th Indian Mountain Regiment IA

17th Indian Division:
CRA: Brigadier HK Dimoline

129th Field Regiment RA
82nd Anti-Tank Regiment RA
1st Indian Field Regiment IA
21st Indian Mountain Regiment IA

33rd Indian Corps:
CCRA: Brigadier DJ Steevens

1st Medium Regiment RA
44th LAA Regiment RA
101st HAA Regiment RA
8th (Mahratta) Anti-Tank Regiment IA
1st Indian Survey Regiment IA

2nd British Division:
CRA: Brigadier HSJ Bourke

10th Field Regiment RA
16th Field Regiment RA
99th Field Regiment RA
100th Anti-Tank Regiment RA

19th Indian Division:
CRA: Brigadier JA MacDonald

115th Field Regiment RA
33rd Anti-Tank Regiment RA
4th Indian Field Regiment IA
20th Indian Mountain Regiment IA

20th Indian Division:
CRA: Brigadier JAE Hirst

9th Field Regiment RA
114th Field Regiment RA
111th Anti-Tank Regiment RA
23rd Indian Mountain Regiment IA

11th East African Division:
CRA: Brigadier JVD Radford; I Whyte

302nd (EA) Field Regiment EAA
303rd (EA) Field Regiment EAA
304th (EA) Anti-Tank Regiment EAA

15th Indian Corps:
CCRA: Brigadier LA Harris

6th Medium Regiment RA
8th (Belfast) HAA Regiment RA
36th LAA Regiment RA
2nd Survey Regiment RA
C Flight, 656th AOP Squadron

25th Indian Division:
CRA: Brigadier AJ Daniell; NPH Tapp

8th Field Regiment RA
27th Field Regiment RA
33rd Indian Mountain Regiment IA
7th Indian Anti-Tank Regiment IA

26th Indian Division:
CRA: Brigadier CJG Dalton; BL de Robeck; TED Kelly

160th Field Regiment RA
7th Indian Field Regiment IA
30th Indian Mountain Regiment IA
1st Indian Anti-Tank Regiment IA

81st West African Division:
CRA: Brigadier JAE Hirst; TAH Coltman; HB Jolly

21st (WA) Anti Tank Regiment WAA
41st (WA) Mortar Regiment WAA
101st (WA) Light Regiment WAA

82nd West African Division:
CRA: Brigadier MC Munro; RHM Hill; JHH Willans

22nd (WA) Anti-Tank Regiment WAA
42nd (WA) Mortar Regiment WAA
102nd (WA) Light Regiment WAA

Northern Combat Area Command (NCAC)

612th Field Artillery Battalion, US Artillery, (Pack)

36th British Division:
CRA: Brigadier GH Inglis

122nd Field Regiment RA
130th Field Regiment
178th Field Regiment RA
3rd Meteorological Detachment
32nd Indian Mountain Regiment IA

SENIOR OFFICERS OF THE ARTILLERY OF THE COMMONWEALTH WHO SERVED IN THE FAR EAST 1939-46

Only Gunner Officers generally of and above the rank of Brigadier are shown

CHIEF OF STAFF

SEAC: Lieutenant General Sir Henry Pownall

MAJOR GENERAL ROYAL ARTILLERY INDIA:

Major General WPJ Ackerman; Major General WHB Mirrlees

DEPUTY DIRECTOR OF ARTILLERY INDIA

Brigadier AL Pemberton

BRIGADIER GENERAL STAFF COMBINED OPERATIONS

Brig M W M Macleod

GENERAL OFFICERS COMMANDING

Burma: Lieutenant General TJ Hutton

Western Army, India: General Sir John Brind

Southern Army, India General Sir John Brind; General Sir Noel Beresford-Pierse

Western Command, India: Lieutenant General TJ Hutton; Lieutenant General EF Norton

British Troops Java: Major General HDW Sitwell

GENERAL OFFICERS COMMANDING (GOC)

2nd British Division: Major General CGG Nicholson

3rd Indian Division: Major General OC Wingate

4th Indian Division: Major General NM de la P Beresford-Peirse

5th Indian Division: Major General ECR Mansergh

7th Indian Division: Acting Major General AF Hely

44th Indian Armoured Division: Major General CGG Nicholson

BRIGADIERS ROYAL ARTILLERY, (BRA)

Eastern Army, India (became 14th Army): Brigadier AD MacPherson; Brigadier AL Pemberton; Brigadier GEW Franklyn; Brigadier DW Bannister; Brigadier BC Trappes-Lomax

North Western Army: Brigadier JN Thomson; Brigadier AJT Farfan;
Brigadier G Horsfield

Southern Army, India: Brigadier AB van Straubenzee; Brigadier ME Dennis; Brigadier DJ Steevens; Brigadier G de V Welchman; Brigadier JH Frowen; Brigadier JM MacNicoll

Central Command, India: Brigadier JW English; Brigadier H Greene

Western Command, India: Brigadier EW Goodman; Brigadier DJ Steevens; Brigadier GH Johnstone

Burma Army: Brigadier JHB Birbeck

Malaya: Brigadier AE Rusher

11th Army Group, India: Brigadier W Swinton

12th Army, India: Brigadier DJ Steevens; Brigadier JD Shapland

14th Army, India: Brigadier GEW Franklyn; Brigadier G de V Welchman; Brigadier AJD Ronald; Brigadier HJ Parham

Allied Land Forces, South East Asia: Brigadier W Swinton; Brigadier LC Manners-Smith; Brigadier G de V Welchman; Brigadier GG Mears

BRIGADIERS ANTI-AIRCRAFT ARTILLERY INDIA AND CEYLON

Ceylon: Brigadier CT Brown; Brigadier W Swinton; Brigadier AJRM Leslie

Eastern Army: Brigadier JD Edge; Brigadier DW Bannister

Southern Army: Brigadier AJD Ronald

COMMANDERS CORPS ROYAL ARTILLERY (CCRA)

1st Burma Corps: Brigadier G de V Welchman

4th Indian Corps: Brigadier HRS Massy; Brigadier CW Allfrey; Brigadier RH Studdert; Brigadier PS Myburgh; Brigadier FP Hallifax; Brigadier C Goulder; Brigadier LA Harris

15th Indian Corps: Brigadier GEW Franklyn; Brigadier G de V Welchman; Brigadier LA Harris; Brigadier FP Hallifax

21st Indian Corps: Brigadier BC Trappes-Lomax

33rd Indian Corps: Brigadier W Swinton; Brigadier DJ Steevens

34th Indian Corps: Brigadier RH Studdert; Brigadier PS Myburgh; Brigadier C Goulder

COMMANDERS ROYAL ARTILLERY (CRA)

2nd British Division: Brigadier CB Findlay; Brigadier GI Thomas; Brigadier JD Shapland; Brigadier HSJ Bourke; Brigadier REH Hudson

3rd Indian Division: Brigadier CM Vallentin

4th Indian Division: Brigadier A Maxwell; Brigadier WHB Mirrlees; Brigadier JF Adye; Brigadier HK Dimoline; Brigadier HCW Eastman; Brigadier RG Loder-Symonds

5th Indian Division: Brigadier ECR Mansergh; Brigadier A van Straubenzee; Brigadier BJ Fowler; Brigadier GBJ Kellie; Brigadier RG Loder-Symonds; Brigadier GK Bourne

6th Indian Division: Brigadier RH Studdert; Brigadier JN Thomson; Brigadier ME Dennis; Brigadier TS Dobree; Brigadier GR Mockler; Brigadier BL de Robeck

7th Indian Division: Brigadier AF Hely; Brigadier JR Lupton

8th Indian Division: Brigadier RVM Garry; Brigadier MB Jennings; Brigadier MN Dewing; Brigadier FC Bull; Brigadier TS Dobree; Brigadier R Morley

9th Indian Division: Brigadier AH Peskett

10th Indian Division: Brigadier CM Vallentin

11th Indian Division: Brigadier AE Rusher

12th Indian Division: No Artillery

14th Indian Division: Brigadier EH Blaker; Brigadier NC Lang; Brigadier CJG Dalton; Brigadier GE Barrington; Brigadier JFG Gurney

17th Indian Division: Brigadier G de V Welchman; Brigadier JC Allardyce; Brigadier JHE de Robeck; Brigadier HK Dimoline; Brigadier F StD B Lejeune; Brigadier JH Gregson

18th British Division: Brigadier HC Servaes

19th Indian Division: Brigadier JHB Birbeck; Brigadier C Goulder; Brigadier JA Macdonald; Brigadier WPA Robinson; Brigadier JH Beattie

20th Indian Division: Brigadier LA Harris; Brigadier JEA Hirst

23rd Indian Division: Brigadier C Goulder; Brigadier RW Andrews; Brigadier RBW Bethell

25th Indian Division: Brigadier GH Johnstone; Brigadier AG O'Carroll-Scott; Brigadier AJ Daniell; Brigadier NPH Tapp

26th Indian Division: Brigadier WC Grant; Brigadier CJG Dalton; Brigadier BL de Robeck; Brigadier TED Kelly

34th Indian Division: Brigadier RG Price

36th Indian Division (36th British Division from 1 Sep 44): Brigadier JP Whiteley; Brigadier MB Jennings; Brigadier CE Barrington; Brigadier GH Inglis

39th Indian Light Division: Brigadier FC Picton

31st Indian Armoured Division: Brigadier CPB Wilson; Brigadier R Morley

44th Indian Armoured Division: Brigadier AW Hervey

70th British Division: Brigadier PS Myburgh; Brigadier HSJ Bourke

11th East African Division: Brigadier JVD Radford

81st West African Division: Brigadier TAH Coleman; Brigadier HB Jolly; Brigadier JAE Hirst

82nd West African Division: Brigadier MC Munro; Brigadier RHM Hill; Brigadier JHH Willans

COMMANDERS ANTI-AIRCRAFT BRIGADES

1st Indian AA Brigade: Brigadier GP Thomas

2nd Indian AA Brigade: Brigadier HHM Oliver

3rd Indian AA Brigade: Brigadier K Hargreaves; Brigadier NG Thompson

9th British AA Brigade: Brigadier DW Bannister; Brigadier F Dearden; Brigadier GD Holmes

13th British AA Brigade: Brigadier HN Leveson-Gower

14th (West African) AA Brigade: Brigadier DHM Carberry

16th British AA Brigade (Java): Brigadier HDW Sitwell

23rd British AA Brigade: Brigadier GV Hunt

24th British AA Brigade: Brigadier AJRM Leslie; Brigadier GH Dallas; Brigadier GD Holmes; Brigadier VRW Crawford

Malayan AA Brigade: Brigadier HV Allpress

1st Royal Marine AA Brigade: Brigadier WFB Lukis; Brigadier JH Wills

COMMANDERS ARMY GROUPS ROYAL ARTILLERY (CAGRA)

16th AGRA: Brigadier P Mews

59th AGRA: Brigadier WGH Pike

60th AGRA: Brigadier EJC Chaytor

61st AGRA: Brigadier JM Kerr

COMMANDERS ROYAL ARTILLERY in AFRICA

HQ West Africa: Brigadier HW Deacon; Brigadier RG Gill; Brigadier J Barron

HQ East Africa: Brigadier JY Ormsby; Brigadier SK Thorburn

COMMANDER ROYAL ARTILLERY HONG KONG

Brigadier T McLeod

COMMANDER COAST ARTILLERY SINGAPORE

Brigadier AD Curtis

COMMANDER AIR DEFENCE SINGAPORE

Brigadier AWG Wildey

AUSTRALIAN FORCES SOUTH EAST ASIA AND THE PACIFIC

LAND HEADQUARTERS PACIFIC

MGRA: Major General JS Whitelaw

BRA: Brigadier LES Barker

NEW GUINEA FORCE

GOCs: Lieutenant General CA Clowes; Lieutenant General Sir Edmund Herring

BRA: Brigadier HB Sewell; Brigadier LES Barker; Brigadier EM Neylan

1ST AUSTRALIAN CORPS

GOCs: Lieutenant General Sir John Lavarack; Lieutenant General Sir Edmund Herring; Lieutenant General FW Berryman

CCRAs: Brigadier CA Clowes: Brigadier HB Sewell; Brigadier LES Barker; Brigadier WE Cremor; Brigadier LGH Dyle

6th AUSTRALIAN DIVISION

GOCs: Major General Sir Edmund Herring; Major General GA Vasey

CRAs: Brigadier Edmund Herring; Brigadier HW Strutt; Brigadier R Daley; Brigadier WE Cremor; Brigadier J Reddish

7th AUSTRALIAN DIVISION

GOCs: Major General Sir John Lavarack; Major General GA Vasey

CRAs: Brigadier EJ Milford; Brigadier FH Berryman; Brigadier HG Rourke; Brigadier GRL Adams; Brigadier TC Eastick; Brigadier GH O'Brien

8th AUSTRALIAN DIVISION

CRAs: Brigadier CA Callaghan; Lt Col CA McEachern

9th AUSTRALIAN DIVISION

CRAs: Brigadier AH Ramsey; Brigadier STW Goodwin; Brigadier WN Tinsley; Brigadier TC Eastick

NEW ZEALAND FORCES IN THE PACIFIC

3rd NEW ZEALAND DIVISION

CRA: Brigadier CJS Duff

ARTILLERY ORDER OF BATTLE
BRITISH, INDIAN AND AFRICAN REGIMENTS
AUGUST 1945

ALLIED LAND FORCES SOUTH EAST ASIA
BRA: Brigadier LC Manners-Smith

12th Army
BRA: Brigadier JD Shapland

Army Troops
4th Field Regiment RA
27th Field Regiment RA
1st Medium Regiment RA
87th Medium Regiment RA

61st AGRA AA - Brigadier JM Kerr

1st Indian LAA Regiment RIA
2nd Indian LAA Regiment RIA
5th Indian LAA Regiment RIA
2nd Indian HAA Regiment RIA

14th Army
BRA: Brigadier G de V Welchman

Army Troops
2nd Indian Field Regiment RIA
18th (SP) Indian Field Regiment RIA
13th Medium Regiment RA
5th (Mahratta) Anti-Tank Regiment RIA
2nd Indian LAA Regiment RIA
69th LAA Regiment RA
52nd HAA Regiment RA
656th AOP Squadron RAF less 'C' Flight

4th Indian Corps
CCRA: Brigadier C Goulder

Corps Troops
8th Medium Regiment RA
1st Indian LAA Regiment RIA
44th LAA Regiment RA
52nd HAA Regiment RA
67th HAA Regiment RA
1st Survey Regiment RA

5th Indian Division (GOC: Major General ECR Mansergh)
CRAs: Brigadiers GBJ Kellie, RG Loder-Symonds, GK Bourne

3rd Indian Field Regiment RIA
5th Indian Field Regiment RIA
5th Mahratta Anti-Tank Regiment RIA
24th Indian Mountain Regiment RIA

7th Indian Division
CRAs: Brigadiers AF Hely and JR Lupton

136th Field Regiment RA
139th Field Regiment RA
8th (Mahratta) Anti-Tank Regiment RIA
25th Indian Mountain Regiment RIA

17th Indian Division
CRAs: Brigadiers HK Dimoline, JH Gregson

1st Indian Field Regiment RIA
129th Field Regiment RA
82nd Anti-Tank Regiment RA
21st Indian Mountain Regiment RIA

33rd Indian Corps
CCRA: Brigadier DJ Steevens

Corps Troops
8th (Mahratta) Anti-Tank Regiment RIA
1st Medium Regiment RA
44th LAA Regiment RA
101st HAA Regiment RA
1st Indian Survey Regiment RIA

2nd British Division
CRAs: Brigadiers HSJ Bourke, REH Hudson

10th Field Regiment RA
16th Field Regiment RA
99th Field Regiment RA
100th Anti-Tank Regiment RA

19th Indian Division
CRAs: Brigadiers WPA Robinson, JH Beattie

4th Indian Field Regiment RIA
115th Field Regiment RA
33rd Anti-Tank Regiment RA
20th Indian Mountain Regiment RIA

20th Indian Division
CRA: Brigadier JAE Hirst

9th Field Regiment RA
114th Field Regiment RA
111th Anti-Tank Regiment RA
23rd Indian Mountain Regiment RIA

11th East African Division
CRA: Brigadier JDV Radford

302nd (East African) Field Regiment EAA
303rd (East African) Field Regiment EAA
304th (East African) Field Regiment EAA

15th Indian Corps
CCRAs: Brigadiers LA Harris, FP Hallifax

Corps Troops
6th Medium Regiment RA
8th (Belfast) HAA Regiment RA
36th LAA regiment RA
2nd Survey Regiment RA
'C' Flight, 656th AOP Squadron RAF

25th Indian Division
CRAs: Brigadiers AJ Daniell, NPH Tapp

8th Field Regiment RA
27th Field Regiment RA
33rd Indian Mountain Regiment RIA
7th Indian Anti-Tank Regiment RIA

26th Indian Division
CRAs: Brigadiers CJG Dalton, BL de Robeck, TED Kelly

7th Indian Field Regiment RIA
160th Field Regiment RA
30th Indian Mountain Regiment RIA
1st Indian Anti-Tank Regiment RIA

81st West African Division
CRA: Brigadier HB Jolly

21st West African Anti-Tank Regiment WAA
41st West African Mortar Regiment WAA
101st West African Light Regiment WAA

82nd West African Division
CRA: Brigadiers RHM Hill, JHH Willans

22nd West African Anti-Tank Regiment WAA
42nd West African Mortar Regiment WAA
102nd West African Light Regiment WAA

NORTHERN COMBAT AREA COMMAND

612th US Field Artillery Battalion (Pack)

36th British Division
CRA: Brigadier GH Inglis

122nd Field Regiment RA
130th Field Regiment RA
178th Field Regiment RA
32nd Indian Mountain Regiment RIA
3rd Meteorological Detachment RAF

Note: Units are mentioned twice where they move from army command to corps or divisional employment.

Annex X

EXTRACTS FROM THE REME WAR REPORT ARTILLERY EQUIPMENTS

Numbers of guns

1. In the Far East there were the following artillery equipments, the figures are approximate:

Equipment	Number
6-pounder 7 cwt anti-tank gun	102
57mm anti-tank gun	307
25-pounder field gun/howitzer	509
5.5-inch medium gun	66
3.7-inch mountain howitzer	249
6-inch 26 cwt howitzer	16
7.2-inch howitzer*	8
40mm Bofors Light AA gun	602
3.7-inch mobile Heavy AA gun	183

* The report does not list any 7.2-inch howitzers but they are mentioned in the report of serviceability.

Serviceability Reports

2. a. 6-pounder and 57mm anti-tank guns. These weapons proved to be most reliable requiring very little repair. They were principally used in this theatre for bunker-busting.

b. 25-Pounder. This gun proved to be reliable, giving little maintenance trouble. There were a number of cases of the breech block flying open at high angles of Quadrant Elevation when firing Super-Charge.

c. 5.5-inch Gun. This gun has been generally reliable. Many cases have occurred of prematures taking place in the barrel with stripping and flattening of the lands. The great majority of prematures took place whilst firing Charge IV even with Fuse 106E. One case did occur when Charge II was used with Fuse 106E. Reports indicate that the ammunition is at fault. It is the considered opinion of this theatre that the damage to the barrels is as a result of the break up of the shell, the stripping of the lands occurring when the shell is burst by an explosion not amounting to a detonation and the bursting of the barrel when a full detonation occurs. In all cases no defects of the barrel have occurred prior to the damage, and both new and old barrels have been affected.

d. 3.7-inch Howitzer. This gun has been very reliable giving little maintenance trouble.

e. 6-inch Howitzer. An extremely reliable gun, practically trouble free.

f. 7.2-inch Howitzer. This gun has been most satisfactory from a maintenance point of view. It is considered that in future, when a new piece is designed, the carriage should be designed simultaneously to go with it, instead of adapting an obsolete carriage from another equipment.

g. 40mm Bofors LAA Gun. The gun has proved a very reliable weapon. There have been no maintenance problems.

h. 3.7-inch HAA Gun. This gun has proved generally reliable and regimental workshops have been capable of carrying out the majority of repairs. It was mainly used in the ground role due to lack of suitable AA targets and its excellent range.

3. **Other Items**

a. Brake Fluid. This was so short that hundreds of vehicles were running with water in their braking systems.

b. Waterproofing. Buoyancy tanks had to be fitted to the universal (Bren) carriers for the crossing of the Irrawaddy. This was done with iron bars stripped from Shwebo gaol and 40 gallon petrol drums. The vehicles, being very old and strained, leaked badly, but it worked.

c. Shortage of Spares. The desperate situation was only saved by cannibalisation. This was difficult to control and in many formations was in the hands of the senior E.M.E.

d. Tropicalisation. Virtually no tropic-proofing was carried out since no facilities were available.

The above is taken from an extract from 'R.E.M.E. WAR REPORT' promulgated by the Directorate of Mechanical Engineering, Allied Land Forces South East Asia, and was prepared by the Royal Electrical and Mechanical Engineers and by the Indian Electrical and Mechanical Engineers. The RAHT holds a typescript copy of part of the Report. Additionally Major GW Robertson provided a manuscript copy of entries covering the various artillery equipments.

GLOSSARY AND ABBREVIATIONS

The definitions given below relate to meanings contemporary with the events they describe in this book and may not be accurate or even relevant today. The titles of units are those employed at the time; some have short titles found in war diaries which are not the official short titles.

Numbering. The prefix '2' before the number of an Australian Imperial Force unit is employed to distinguish that unit from one with the same number which fought in the First World War. In British use a prefixed figure before the name of an infantry regiment indicates the number of the battalion. '2/Norfolks or 2nd Norfolks' for example, refers to the Second Battalion, The Royal Norfolk Regiment. The same applies to Japanese battalions but Roman numerals are used instead: II/218th Regiment represents the second battalion of the 218th Regiment. In the Indian Army each infantry regiment had a serial number which was preceded by the appropriate number of the battalion. Thus '1/11th Sikhs' refers to the first battalion of the 11th Sikh Regiment. Gurkha regiments were separately numbered, outside the serial numbering of the Indian Army but following the same rule, so '3/10th Gurkhas' refers to the third battalion of the 10th Gurkha Rifles.

AA	Anti-Aircraft (of formations, units, sub-units and guns).
ABDA	American, British, Dutch, Australian (Command), a short lived international command, the first such, under General Wavell, formed to meet the rapid Japanese multi-branched advances in 1942; it existed only briefly.
ACPO	Assistant Command Post Officer (of a battery), a subaltern.
ACC	Army Catering Corps.
ADS	Advanced Dressing Station, the first point at which a wounded soldier could receive treatment before being moved to the MDS.
AFNEI	Allied Forces Netherlands East Indies.
AFV	Armoured Fighting Vehicle; tanks, armoured cars and 'Bren' or Universal carriers.
AGRA	Army Group Royal Artillery, a formation consisting of a number of artillery regiments, usually four, commanded by a brigadier and usually under corps command. AA AGRAs were also created.
AGRE	Army Group Royal Engineers. A formation similar to an AGRA and like it usually employed under corps command.
AIF	Australian Imperial Force. The same term had been used during the First World War; so units having the same number or designation in the second conflict were given the prefix '2'.
AI Sigs	Assistant Instructor Signals. A senior NCO responsible for the radio and telephonic communications of a battery.
ALFSEA	Allied Land Forces South East Asia, under Lieutenant General Sir Oliver Leese, succeeded 11th Army Group on 12th November 1944.
Angle of Sight (A/S)	The angle formed between an imaginary line drawn between gun and target and the horizontal; taking into account the difference in height above sea level of the gun and of the target.
AOC (in C)	Air Officer Commanding (in Chief).
AOP	Air Observation Post, a unit or sub unit equipped usually with Auster aircraft; Armoured Observation Post equipped with universal (Bren) carriers or, occasionally, light tanks.

AP	Armour piercing (of a projectile).
APC	Armour piercing capped (of a projectile).
A/S	Angle of Sight (qv).
Assam Rifles	A force of five military police battalions maintained by the Assam Government, and composed of Gurkhas commanded by British officers seconded from the Indian Army.' (Thompson).
A/Tk	Anti-tank, of a gun, battery and regiment, usually equipped with the 2-pounder, 6-pounder or 57mm anti-tank gun (the last being an American version of the 6-pounder).
AVG	American Volunteer Group, American airmen and aircraft who served against the Japanese in China and Burma. Part of the Chinese Air Force. Commanded by Major General CL Chennault.
BAF	Burma Auxiliary Force.
BC	Battery Commander, usually a major. In Indian Mountain Artillery the commander of a battery was known as the Commandant.
BCHQ	Bombardment Control Headquarters (RN)
Bde	Brigade.
Bdr	Bombardier, the artillery equivalent of Corporal
BFF	Burma Frontier Force.
BK	Battery Captain, the second in command of a battery, responsible for its logistics.
BLO	Bombardment Liaison Officer.
BMRA	Brigade Major Royal Artillery, the staff officer to a CRA (qv).
Bn	Battalion.
BNA	Burma National Army, commanded by Aung San.
BOR	British Other Rank(s) in a mixed British/Indian unit.
BQMS	Battery Quartermaster Sergeant, usually a staff sergeant.
BRA	Brigadier Royal Artillery, the brigadier who commands the artillery of an army, or similar large formation, and advises the army commander on its employment.
BSM	Battery Sergeant Major, a Warrant Officer Class II who is the senior non-commissioned soldier in a battery.
Bty	Battery, a sub unit of an artillery regiment, commanded usually by a Major.
Carabineers	3rd Carabineers (Prince of Wales's Dragoon Guards) *and see* 25th Dragoons.
CB	Counter Battery or Counter Bombardment, fire primarily used to suppress or destroy enemy guns or ships.
CBI	China Burma India, American designation for one of the US theatres of operations.
CBO	Counter-Bombardment Officer
CCRA	Commander Corps Royal Artillery, the brigadier who commands the artillery of a corps and advises the corps commander on its employment.
CGA	Ceylon Garrison Artillery.
Chaung	a stream or river (Burma)
Coy	Company, of an infantry battalion.
CP	Command Post.
CPBC	Capped Piercing Ballistic Capped (of a projectile for attacking armour and concrete etc.)
CPO	Command Post Officer, the lieutenant who commands the guns of a battery.

CPOA	Command Post Officer's Assistant.
CRA	Commander Royal Artillery, the brigadier who commands the artillery of a division and advises the divisional commander on its employment.
CRASC	Commander Royal Army Service Corps, the senior officer of this corps in the division having, in supply matters, functions comparable to those of a CRA, CRE etc.
CRE	Commander Royal Engineers, in a division, the officer who has duties of command and advice in military engineering matters similar to those of a CRA in artillery matters.
CREME	Commander Royal Electrical and Mechanical Engineers, the senior officer of this corps, in a division, having the same duties of command and advice in mechanical and electrical engineering matters similar to those of the CRA in artillery matters.
DCM	Distinguished Conduct Medal.
DF	Defensive Fire.
DIS	Daily Issue Store. Also the name given to a feature fought over during the Battle of Kohima.
Div	Division
DLI	Durham Light Infantry.
DSM	Distinguished Service Medal, an American award for 'exceptionally meritorious service . . . in a duty of great responsibility' usually awarded to senior officers (Boatner).
DSO	Distinguished Service Order.
DUKW	Manufacturer's (General Motors Corporation's) designation, DUKW 353, a truck, 2½ ton, 6 x 6 wheeled amphibious vehicle. Popularly known as a 'duck'.
Dvr IC	Driver Internal Combustion (engine), the basic driver grade.
Dvr Mech	Driver Mechanic; a title higher than Dvr IC.
Dvr Op	Driver (wireless) Operator.
DWR	The Duke of Wellington's Regiment
EAA	East African Artillery, employed by 11th East African Division.
ESS	Eastern Shuttle Service (Maritime RA).
FC	Fire Command, controlling one or more coast batteries.
Fd	Field, of a gun, battery and regiment, usually equipped with 25- pounders but also with the 3.7-inch (mountain) howitzers and even mortars.
FD	Fixed Defences, non-mobile coast defence batteries.
FF	Frontier Force.
FFW	Fitted for Wireless (of a vehicle)
FMA	Forward Maintenance Area.
FMSVF	Federated Malay States Volunteer Force.
FOB	Forward Observer Bombardment, directing the fire of naval guns onto land targets.
FOO	Forward Observation Officer, accompanying infantry or armour to direct fire on to the targets as the battle progresses.
FOU	Forward Observation Unit.
FSD	Field Supply Depot.
GOC	(in C) General Officer Commanding (in Chief)
GPO	Gun Position Officer, a lieutenant or second lieutenant who commands the

	gun position of a troop of usually four guns.
GPOA	Gun Position Officer's Assistant, a Gunner or junior NCO who works in the troop command post. Also known as a GPO Ack.
GPT	General Purpose Transport.
GS	General Staff; General Service.
GSO 1, 2, 3	General Staff Officer, Grade 1 (Lieutenant Colonel), 2 (Major) or 3 (Captain).
HAA	Heavy Anti-Aircraft, of guns, batteries, and regiments equipped usually with the 3.7-inch HAA gun but also with the up-rated form of the 3-inch 20 cwt gun and the 4.5-inch gun.
Havildar	*see* Indian Army Ranks
HE	High Explosive.
HF	Harassing Fire.
HK-S RA	Hong Kong - Singapore Royal Artillery, a regular force too rapidly expanded in 1941 by the hurried recruitment of soldiers who received very little training; raised in India to defend Hong Kong and Singapore, though frequently served elsewhere, part of the Royal Artillery.
HKVDC	Hong Kong Volunteer Defence Corps.
HMAS	His Majesty's Australian Ship.
HMIS	His Majesty's Indian Ship.
HMNZS	His Majesty's New Zealand Ship.
HNMS	Her Netherlands Majesty's Ship (a British designation).
HQCEAA	Headquarters Commander East African Artillery
HQRA	Headquarters Royal Artillery, of a formation, ie, at divisional level and above.
Hy	Heavy, of guns, batteries and regiments.
IA	Indian Army; Indian Artillery.
IAC	Indian Armoured Corps.
IDSM	Indian Distinguished Service Medal.
IE	Indian Engineers *qv.*
INA	Indian National Army, in Burma fighting alongside the Japanese, commanded by Subhas Chandra Bose.
Ind	Indian; Independent
Indian Army ranks	Viceroy's Commissioned Officer (VCO), Indian junior officers promoted from the ranks holding the ranks of Jemadar, Subadar and Subadar Major roughly equating to the second lieutenant, lieutenant and captain in their duties but all were junior to a British Second Lieutenant. They could hold honorary rank as Lieutenant or Captain. Indian other ranks, though with different titles, equated with British other ranks; Sepoy (Private, Gunner), Lance Naik (Lance Corporal/Lance Bombardier), Havildar (Sergeant) and Havildar Major (senior Sergeant/Sergeant Major), these being, *inter alia*, infantry and artillery terms, cavalry junior officers (VCOs) and NCOs were differently titled. A private soldier in the Indian Artillery was known as a Gunner.
Indian Artillery	See Chapter 7 and Annex J.
Indian Engineers	Were nominally in three groups, as part of the Indian Army, taking their titles from the former Presidency armies: Queen Victoria's Own Madras Sappers and Miners, King George V's Own Bengal Sappers and Miners and

	the Royal Bombay Sappers and Miners. All became part of the Indian Engineers (IE). Officers were both British (RE) and Indian (IE).
IOM	Indian Order of Merit.
IOR	Indian Other Rank(s) in a mixed British/Indian unit.
ISF	Indian State Forces; those units raised by Indian States, some of which were placed at His Majesty's disposal by the rulers of those states; organised and equipped on much the same lines as British and Indian units.
IWT	Inland Water Transport. At first based on the pre-war Irrawaddy Flotilla Company and later extended to the Chindwin and to many other rivers and chaungs and to Arakan coastal waters. This organisation played a vital part, in the hands of the Royal and Indian Engineers, the Royal Army Service Corps, the Royal Indian Army Service Corps and the Royal and Royal Indian Navies, in the supply of 14th Army and 15th Corps operating a large variety of vessels from small native craft, launches and purpose-built barges to river steamers. Two very successful vessels, Pamela and Una were designed and built by the Royal Engineers at Kalewa on the Chindwin and manned by the Royal Navy.
KAR	King's African Rifles, forming 11th East African Division including its artillery, though this was usually known as EAA, East Africa(n) Artillery.
KNIL	Koninklijk Nederlands Indische Leger (Royal Netherlands Indies Army).
KOSB	The King's Own Scottish Borderers.
KOYLI	The King's Own Yorkshire Light Infantry.
LAA	Light Anti-Aircraft, of regiments, batteries and guns; employing the 40mm Bofors gun or machine guns on high-angle mountings.
LAD	Light Aid Detachment of the REME. Each artillery regiment had one for first line repair of guns, vehicles and equipment.
LF	The Lancashire Fusiliers.
Light	When used in relation to artillery units, indicates that the equipment employed is the 3.7-inch howitzer or 3-inch mortar.
LMG	Light machine gun.
L of C	Lines of Communication, the routes employed and staffed for the supply of a force and for its contact with its rear area and for the evacuation of casualties.
Loyals	The Loyal Regiment (North Lancashire).
Lushai Brigade	An independent brigade formed in March 1944 by Brigadier PC Marinden and operating under the direct command of 14th Army to hold the Lushai Hills and harass the enemy in the Chin Hills. The brigade consisted of 1st Battalion 9th Jat Regiment, 7th Battalion 14th Punjab Regiment, 1st Bihari Battalion (ISF), two groups from V-Force (qv), 1st Battalion the Assam Rifles (qv), the Western Chin Levies and the Lushai Scouts. (Thompson).
MC	Military Cross.
M/C	Motor cycle.
MDS	Main Dressing Station, a stage of the route to a Base Hospital after the ADS.
Med	Medium, of guns, batteries and regiments, usually equipped with the 5.5-inch or 6-inch 26 cwt. howitzer.
Meteor	Meteorological Telegram, a weather forecast provided by the RAF containing information which would affect the flight of a projectile, eg wind speed and direction, barometric height etc.

MG	Machine gun
MGRA	Major General Royal Artillery, the senior Gunner officer at Command or Army Group level who advises the commander on artillery matters and commands that artillery.
'Mike' Target	A target engaged by all the guns of a regiment of artillery; see 'Uncle' and 'Victor'.
MLI	(5th) Mahratta Light Infantry.
MM	Military Medal.
MNBDO	Mobile Naval Base Defence Organisation, a Royal Marines formation which included an important air defence element.
MRA	Maritime Royal Artillery, the regiments and the men who served AA guns mounted in merchant ships.
MS	Milestone, a geographical reference employing the colonial government-installed milestones especially in generally unfrequented country and on the few roads there.
MT	Mechanical Transport, all types of wheeled motor vehicle together with some tracked vehicles.
MV	Muzzle Velocity (of a gun); Motor Vehicle.
Naik	*see* Indian Army Ranks.
NCAC	Northern Combat Area Command, a mixed Chinese and American Force commanded first by General Stilwell and then by General Sultan.
Nepalese troops	Infantry battalions of the Nepalese Royal Army which served in British - Indian formations, similar in some ways to Indian State Forces (qv).
OC Troops	Officer Commanding Troops, eg. aboard a troopship.
OP	Observation Post and the officer occupying it who was also known as the OPO (qv).
OPA	Observation Post Assistant, an NCO, sometimes a senior NCO, who assists the OP officer in practically every way as his second-in-command. Also known as an OP Ack.
OPO	Observation Post Officer.
PAVO	Prince Albert Victor's Own, 11th Cavalry, Indian Army
PIAT	Projectile Infantry Anti-Tank, a hand-held anti-tank weapon firing an armour-piercing hollow charge projectile.
Pivot gun/mortar	"In order to measure a switch [change of direction] and to get correct distribution [of fire] over a target, it is necessary to utilise the zero line (qv) of a particular gun. This gun is called the "*pivot gun*" and any one may be selected as such, but in practice it is almost invariably a flank gun. If there is no choice between the flanks, the right hand (No. 1) gun is taken.' *Artillery Training*, Volume II, Gunnery, HMSO, London, 1934.
POL	Petrol, Oil and Lubricants.
Portee	The carrying of a small, usually anti-tank, gun on the back of a truck.
PR	Photographic Reconnaissance, used of air units and their aircraft.
pr	Pounder as in 25-pr or 25-pounder gun, the abbreviation 'pdr' was also used.
QOGY	Queen's Own Glasgow Yeomanry
QORWK	Queen's Own Royal West Kent Regiment
Queen's	The Queen's Royal Regiment (West Surrey).
RAA	Royal Australian Artillery
RAE	Royal Australian Engineers

RAAF	Royal Australian Air Force.
RAC	Royal Armoured Corps.
RAF	Royal Air Force.
RAOC	Royal Army Ordnance Corps.
Rajputs	7th Rajputana Regiment.
Raj Rifs	6th Rajputana Rifles.
RAP	Regimental Aid Post.
RAMC	Royal Army Medical Corps.
RCAF	Royal Canadian Air Force.
RE	The Corps of Royal Engineers.
Regt	Regiment.
REME	The Corps of Royal Electrical and Mechanical Engineers.
RHA	Royal Horse Artillery.
RIA	Royal Indian Artillery, a title bestowed shortly after the war.
RIATC	Royal Indian Artillery Training Centre.
RIAF	Royal Indian Air Force.
RIASC	Royal Indian Army Service Corps.
RIN	Royal Indian Navy
RMAA	Royal Marines Anti-Aircraft (units).
RNR	Royal Naval Reserve.
RNVR	Royal Naval Volunteer Reserve.
R Neth AF and RNEIAC	British forms of initials for the Royal Netherlands Air Force and the Royal Netherlands East Indies Army Air Corps, *and see* KNIL.
R Neth N	British form of initials for the Royal Netherlands Navy.
RNZAF	Royal New Zealand Air Force.
Round	of ammunition, the parts of which are the projectile, its fuze, the propellant charge and the initiating explosion which fires that charge; informally the term tended to be used to mean the projectile and its fuze only.
rpg	Rounds per gun, an allotment or expenditure of ammunition.
RS	The Royal Scots.
R Sigs	The Royal Corps of Signals. An element of this corps, commanded by an officer, was attached to each artillery regimental headquarters and handled signals activities upwards to divisional level.
RTO	Railway Transport Officer.
RWAFF	Royal West African Frontier Force, forming the infantry and artillery element of 81st and 82nd West African Divisions. The artillery was usually known as WAA, West Africa(n) Artillery.
RWF	The Royal Welch Fusiliers.
SA	South Africa
SA	Suspended Animation
SAAF	South African Air Force.
S & M	Sappers and Miners, a term which came to be replaced by IE, for Indian Engineers (qv) and later by RIE for Royal Indian Engineers.
SEAC	South East Asia Command.
Section	Two guns, their vehicles, stores and detachments, commanded by a subaltern, two sections usually making up a troop.
Sig	Signals, signallers
Sitrep	Situation Report, a tactical report rendered to a (usually) higher authority to

	keep all those who need to know apprised of a local situation of which otherwise they might be unaware.
SL	Searchlight, of regiments and batteries so equipped.
SLI	The Somerset Light Infantry (Prince Albert's).
South Lancs	The South Lancashire Regiment.
SP	Self Propelled, a field gun or howitzer mounted on a tracked chassis which was derived from a tank from which the turret and upper deck had been removed. In this work the reference is to the American 105mm howitzer mounted on the chassis of a Lee/Grant tank, known as the Priest. Not the same as *portee* where an anti-tank or small field gun was mounted on and fired from the back of a lorry.
SS	Special Service, brigades and units made up of Army and Royal Marines commandos. Low numbers (1, 2, 3 etc) indicate army units and numbers running from 40 upwards indicate units of the Royal Marines
SSVC	Straits Settlements Volunteer Corps
Subadar	*see* Indian Army Ranks.
Sub-section	a gun, its vehicle (or mules) and detachment, usually commanded by a sergeant.
TOT	Time on Target; the time at which the projectile is to arrive on the target.
TRI	Tentera Repoeblik Indonesia (Indonesian Republican Army).
Troop (Tp)	the sub-division of a field, medium, anti-aircraft battery, commanded by a captain. Anti-tank troops were usually commanded by Subalterns. Mountain regiments, having four guns in a battery, did not employ the term.
Twenty-fifth Dragoons	an offshoot of the 3rd Dragoon Guards and partly manned by that regiment.
'Uncle' Target	a target to be engaged by all the guns of a division, see 'Mike' and 'Victor'.
USA	United States of America; United States Army.
USAAC	United States Army Air Corps.
USAAF	United States Army Air Force replaced the USAAC from 2nd March 1942 on the major reorganisation of the United States Army
V-Force	A guerrilla organisation established on General Wavell's orders to attack Japanese lines of communication should an attack be launched against Assam. It was made up of platoons lent by the Assam Rifles [qv] which were supported by about a thousand hill tribesmen. The duties of the force were altered to that of gaining intelligence and maintaining outposts in front of regular British and Indian units along the Chindwin to Kalewa and then across the northern Arakan. (Thompson).
VCP	Visual Control Post, the position from which an officer of the RAF could control air strikes close to the troops he was supporting.
'Victor' Target	a target to be engaged by all the guns of a corps; see 'Mike' and 'Uniform'.
VP	Vulnerable Point, a particularly important objective for an bomber pilot which thus requires its own anti-aircraft defence, eg a bridge or an airfield. Defence usually provided by LAA guns.
WAA	West Africa(n) Artillery.
WE	War Establishment, the number of officers and men, their specialisations (trades), the number and types of vehicles, wireless sets, guns, trailers etc laid down by the War Office. (see Annex T).
Y & L	York and Lancaster Regiment

Z Craft	Indian built barges mounting four 25-pounders (see Chapter 13).
Zero Line	On occupying a position guns were laid initially on a bearing chosen as the anticipated centre (ie zero) line of an arc of fire. 'In order to have some means of directing the fire of the guns quickly and accurately on to any target, a line of reference called the "zero line" is established. From this the angle or switch to a target can be determined. It is essential that all guns are parallel on this zero line.' *Artillery Training* Volume II, Gunnery, HMSO, London, 1934. *and see* Pivot Gun.

INDEX

Notes: Where an individual appears in the index he is accorded the rank or title he held when first mentioned in the text.

Units raised in any country, or colony are indexed under that country, or colony.

Certain organisations, formations and units changed their nationality in the course of the war. Every attempt has been made to index them correctly but it may be necessary to seek them in more than one place. The Indian Army has been separated from the British but, again, the nationality of some formations and units can vary during the course of the war.

Place names and their spellings are those generally used by the British Army at the time but in some cases the spelling in the contemporary documents has been used.

British forms of initials are used for foreign allied organisations.

Japanese names are indexed in their western rather than in their Japanese order.

Where a battery changes its role or is re-raised it is mentioned more than once.